The **Rough Guide** to

Colorado

written and researched by

Christian Williams

ROUGH
GUIDES

NEW YORK · LONDON · DELHI

www.roughguides.com

Contents

Skiing and snow-boarding insert following p.176

Colorado's protected lands insert following p.368

◄◄ Downtown Telluride ◄ Silverton, Southwest Colorado

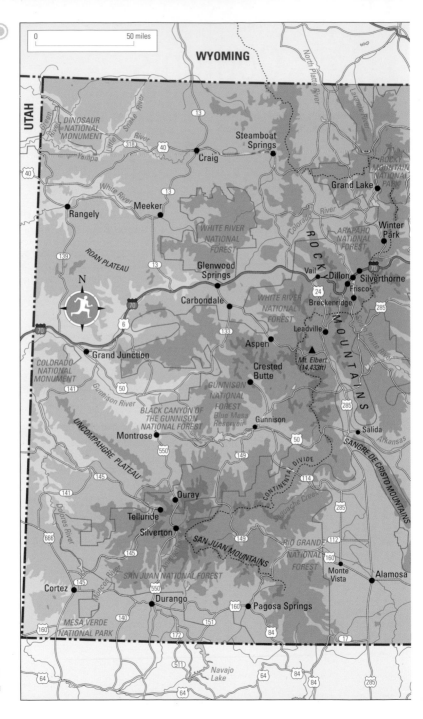

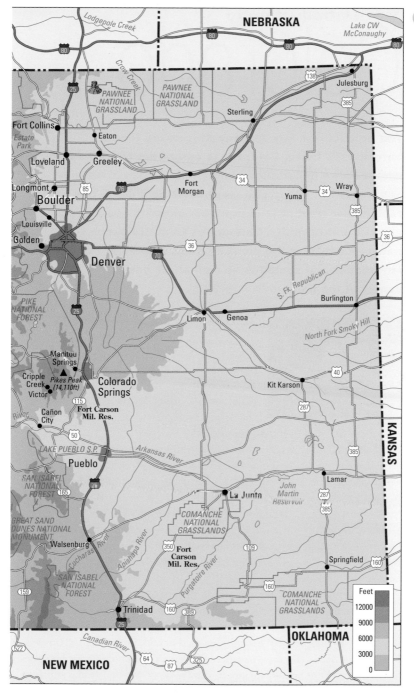

NEBRASKA

Lodgepole Creek

Lake CW
McConaughy

Crow Creek

PAWNEE
NATIONAL
GRASSLAND

PAWNEE
NATIONAL
GRASSLAND

Julesburg

Sterling

Fort Collins

Estate
Park

Eaton

Loveland

Greeley

Longmont

Fort
Morgan

Wray

Boulder

Yuma

Louisville

Golden

Denver

Limon

Genoa

PIKE
NATIONAL
FOREST

S. Fk. Republican

Burlington

North Fork Smoky Hill

Manitou
Springs

Cripple
Creek

Pikes Peak
(14,110ft)

Colorado
Springs

Victor

Cañon
City

Fort Carson
Mil. Res.

Kit Karson

River

LAKE PUEBLO S.P.

Arkansas River

Pueblo

SAN ISABEL
NATIONAL
FOREST

La Junta

John
Martin
Reservoir

Lamar

COMANCHE
NATIONAL
GRASSLANDS

GREAT SAND
DUNES NATIONAL
MONUMENT

Walsenburg

Fort
Carson
Mil. Res.

Springfield

Cucharas River

Apishapa River

SAN ISABEL
NATIONAL
FOREST

Purgatoire River

COMANCHE
NATIONAL
GRASSLANDS

KANSAS

Feet
12000
9000
6000
3000
0

Trinidad

OKLAHOMA

Canadian River

NEW MEXICO

5

Introduction to

Colorado

The product of a late-nineteenth-century federal bureaucrat's fancy, Colorado is one of the few US states whose entire boundaries simply follow lines of latitude and longitude. But unlike most of its neighbors, this vast rectangular tract of land contains amazing geographic and cultural diversity. This arises from Colorado's unique location at the meeting point of several distinct landscapes and societies as well as its position in the center of the US.

Though sandwiched between the vast prairies of the Great Plains and the dry, windswept deserts of the Southwest – and containing both landscapes in abundance – Colorado is defined by its mountains. The **Rocky Mountains** form a great north–south belt through the state, covering an area three times the size of the Swiss Alps. Unlike the Alps, the Rockies are bulky and broad-shouldered, building steadily from high-altitude basins and grassy plains to their highest reaches at around 14,000 feet. Which is not to say the scenery isn't stunning; it is. Breathing the thin air on the summit of a "fourteener" like Mt Evans, you can look west across the craggy peaks that pierce thick aspen and conifer forest and wildflower meadows, while to the east the wide expanse of the plains mirrors the skies above. Suddenly the declaration by 26th US president Theodore Roosevelt – that Colorado "bankrupts the English language" – will seem altogether reasonable.

Culturally, Colorado is an integral part of the remote and landlocked **American West**. During the nineteenth-century mining booms, Colorado's mountain wilderness – peopled until then only by resilient, nomadic Native Americans and hardy mountain men – was quickly transformed by the ramshackle towns that provided bases for grizzled miners, prostitutes, and outlaws like Butch Cassidy and the Sundance Kid. When the booms went bust the settlements did not entirely disappear: dozens of rickety and fading **mining**

towns still stand, many of which have been given a cheerful makeover, and in many cases much of the enigmatic but undeniable Wild West feel has been preserved.

There's a very different vibe outside the mountainous heartlands. The **farming**, **ranching**, and **cowboy** cultures of Kansas and Wyoming spill over, as do Hispanic and Native American traditions, particularly strong in the south, an area that once belonged to Mexico and where remarkable evidence of past **Native American** civilizations still exists. Meanwhile, the cities that form a north–south band along Colorado's Front Range – the point where the mountains meet the plains – are of a similar piece: one part hard-working industrial base and one part chic New Economy. Denver, unofficial capital of the American West, is by far the biggest in the string.

These cities have been the focus for the state's **transformation** over the last fifty years, as Colorado has become one of the nation's favorite **playgrounds**, attracting over twenty million annual visitors. At the same time a steady flow of migrants from

Fact file

- Colorado, which joined the Union in 1876, covers 104,100 square miles, making it the eighth-largest state – yet with a total population of 4,417,714, it only has around 1.5 percent of the nation's people. The US federal government owns almost forty percent of the land in Colorado.

- Colorado's population is 83 percent white (of which around 17 percent are Hispanic), 4 percent black, 2 percent Asian, and 1 percent Native American.

- With a mean elevation of 6800ft, Colorado is the highest state in the US, containing 75 percent of American land with an altitude of over 10,000ft. There are 50 mountainous peaks over 14,000ft, or "fourteeners," as they are affectionately known by climbers.

- Despite average rainfall of less than 17in per year, irrigation enables agriculture on the western and eastern sides of the state, with peaches and melons particularly renowned.

- Colorado has more microbreweries per capita than any other state, yet its citizens remain America's thinnest: only 16 percent of the population is classified as obese.

across the country has more than tripled the state's population, to 4.4 million. It's still very easy to get away from it all – the warm, dry summers here open up thousands of miles of spectacular, lonely trails for **hiking** and **mountain biking**. You'll have a good chance to spot some of the healthy **wildlife** population, too, including black bears, mountain lions, bighorn sheep, elk, moose, mule deer, and pronghorn antelope. Spring run-offs keep the myriad rivers and lakes busy with fly-fishermen and whitewater rafters. And in winter, huge piles of powdery **snow** are dumped onto some of the most incredible ski terrain on the planet – with no shortage of world-class resorts at which to enjoy it.

▼ Backcountry skiing

Where to go

Friendly and sophisticated **Denver** is the state's most obvious gateway, but is often overlooked as a destination in its own right. While it's no cultural powerhouse, it does have some good museums and plenty of top-notch restaurants and brewpubs; along with the nearby liberal college towns of **Boulder** and **Fort Collins**, it offers an ideal balance of outdoor pursuits and urban frivolity. Additionally, all three are within easy distance of **Rocky Mountain National Park**, one of Colorado's premier scenic jewels.

Along the main east-west highway I-70, you'll find the clutch of the incredible ski areas for which the state is famous: glitzy **Vail** and **Aspen**, egalitarian **Winter Park**, and the resorts of Summit County, including **Breckenridge** and **Copper Mountain**. A detour north along I-40 brings you to **Steamboat Springs**, widely acknowledged as one of the country's best all-around winter sports destinations. A detour south takes you deep into the Sawatch and Elk Mountains, where the former gold and silver mining towns of **Leadville** and **Crested Butte** are fun bases both in summer and winter.

Southern Colorado is generally far more remote and less developed. To tackle it by road, strike out on a clockwise loop from Denver, heading past

Rocky Mountain high

High altitude comes with the territory when you're in the Rockies. Even in Colorado's capital, the "mile-high" city of Denver, its effects are felt – as evidenced by the greater number of home runs that whistle through the thin air of Coors Field. That said, it's not until you head higher up into the mountains,

past the 10,000ft mark (Colorado has 50 peaks over 14,000ft, let alone 10,000ft), that you'll really notice the scarcity of oxygen in the air. At its worst, this deprivation can lead to altitude sickness, but if you're relatively fit and let your system adjust by taking it easy the first few days, you should be fine.

Pikes Peak, the magnificent mountain below which the sprawling city of **Colorado Springs** continually grows. Many touristy attractions beckon in the vicinity, but none is more impressive than the **Arkansas River**, perhaps best explored on a whitewater rafting trip from a series of modest attendant towns including **Salida** and **Cañon City**.

Colorado's strong Hispanic heritage asserts itself in the **San Luis Valley**, location of the oddly beautiful **Sand Dunes National Park**. West from here are the San Juan Mountains, where the quest for gold and silver gave rise to scores of Victorian mining camps, some of which are now quaint bases for exploring vast networks of trails and backroads. The energetic college town of **Durango** is the main center in the San Juans and also the best jumping-off point for **Mesa Verde National Park**, created to protect Ancestral Puebloan ruins.

▼ Cowboy, Northern Mountains

North from Durango, the winding San Juan Skyway takes in small mountain gems like **Silverton** and **Ouray**, leading ultimately to the trendy ski-town of **Telluride**. To complete the loop, follow the Gunnison and the Arkansas river valleys, pausing to gaze into the depths of the **Black Canyon of the Gunnison**. Head up from here to **Grand Junction** for the surrounding desert scenery or **Dinosaur National Monument**, where a giant gnarled canyon offers grand vistas and the chance to track down some ancient Native American rock art.

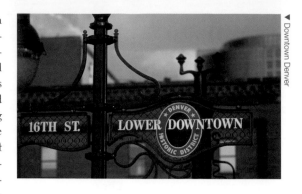

▼ Downtown Denver

When to go

The overriding assumption made by many is that visiting Colorado requires a hard-and-fast choice between a **summer** hiking vacation or a **winter** ski-trip. There is some basic sense to this seasonal split, and certainly the three months of summer (June–Aug) and of winter (Dec–Feb) do draw the bulk of visitors. But crowds at the premier attractions like Rocky Mountain National Park thin out nicely in the **fall**, which

Mining times

Though go-it-alone fur-trappers were the first whites to begin fruitful exploration of Colorado, the first big wave of permanent settlers came only after major gold strikes here in the 1850s. Upon arriving, the pioneers quickly carved up the territory, chiseling into hillsides and leaving the landscape pockmarked with tailings and mine workings. This legacy adds an atmospheric twist to the state today – some old mines are open for tours and plenty of preserved Gold Rush-era towns exist – but the real contribution of mining to visitors is the way in which its infrastructure opens up the mountains. The network of old railroads, dirt roads, and pack trails provide unusual platforms to view the surrounding wilderness by less conventional means, including steam trains, 4WD vehicles, and mountain bikes.

is also when many animals become more active as daytime temperatures begin to drop. While **spring** is rather unglamorously known as the "mud season," it can still deliver fine ski conditions to go with warm mountain sunshine. At lower elevations, the spring run-off is manna from heaven for whitewater

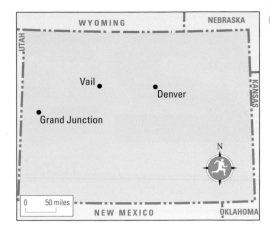

enthusiasts, with rivers at their highest and fastest. In broad terms, those wanting to **hike** and **climb** in comfortable, non-hazardous conditions will want to avoid any place still snowbound; this varies according to altitude and local climate, but the majority of mountain trails below 10,000ft are usually passable between mid-May and late September.

Average temperatures and rainfall

	Jan	Feb	Mar	Apr	May	Jun	July	Aug	Sep	Oct	Nov	Dec
Denver												
max °F	42	46	52	60	71	80	88	84	76	65	52	42
max °C	6	8	11	17	22	27	31	30	25	19	12	7
min °F	15	20	25	34	44	51	58	56	47	35	25	16
min °C	-9	-7	-3	2	7	11	15	14	9	2	-4	-8
in	0.5	0.7	1.2	1.6	2.4	1.9	1.9	1.5	1.1	1	0.8	0.6
mm	13	18	31	41	61	48	48	38	28	25	20	15
Grand Junction												
max °F	36	45	56	66	76	88	94	91	81	68	51	66
max °C	2	7	13	19	24	31	34	33	27	20	11	19
min °F	15	24	32	38	48	57	64	62	54	42	39	40
min °C	-9	-4	0	3	9	14	18	17	12	6	4	4
in	0.6	0.5	0.9	0.8	0.9	0.5	0.7	0.8	0.8	1	0.7	0.6
mm	15	13	23	20	23	13	18	20	20	25	18	15
Vail												
max °F	28	31	37	43	54	66	74	72	64	55	38	31
max °C	-2	-1	3	6	12	19	23	22	18	13	3	-1
min °F	0	1	7	17	25	32	38	37	30	22	11	1
min °C	-18	-17	-14	-8	-4	0	3	3	-1	-6	-12	-17
in	0.9	1	1.1	1.2	1.3	1.2	1.7	1.8	1.3	0.8	0.7	1
mm	23	25	28	31	33	31	43	46	33	20	18	25

23

things not to miss

It's not possible to see everything that Colorado offers in one trip – and we don't suggest you try. What follows is a selective taste of the state's highlights: scenic national parks, colorful festivals, and thrilling outdoor pursuits. They're arranged in five color-coded categories, which you can browse through to find the very best things to see and experience. All entries have a page reference to take you straight into the guide, where you can find out more.

02 Bishop Castle Page **312** • A tribute to eccentricity in southern Colorado's Wet Mountains, Bishop Castle is one man's wild (and rather rickety-looking) creation.

01 Wildflowers Pages **132** & **422** • A highlight of the hiking season, few sights in the Rockies are as photogenic as a field covered in a bright blanket of wildflowers.

03 Tattered Cover Bookstore
Page **74** • Arguably the best bookshop in Colorado, and a great place to stock up on travel literature and books of local interest.

05 Denver Pow-Wow
Page **71** • One of the country's largest annual gatherings of Native Americans features the Grand Entry, a dance with 1000 participants.

07 Strawberry Hot Springs
Page **214** • There are many hot springs in the state, but none are finer than at this remote spot, with several different soaking pools.

04 Skiing Steamboat
Page **208** • Shadows and Closet are the resort's classic aspen tree runs, where you'll find generous stashes of Steamboat's famous "Champagne powder."

06 Mt Elbert
Page **244** • Colorado's highest mountain is surprisingly accessible to the fit, requiring no real technical expertise or special equipment.

08 Backcountry boarding and skiing
Page **165** & *Skiing and snowboarding* **color section** • Though not without its dangers, heading out into the backcountry in search of virgin snow via helicopter, snowcat, or on foot is a must for experienced big mountain riders.

09 Whitewater rafting Pages 37 & 295

Churning rivers throughout Colorado provide ample whitewater adventure, for everyone from first-timers to hardcore daredevils.

10 Swetsville Zoo Page 103

See how one man's imagination – and welding skills – have run wild in this offbeat zoo.

11 Brown Palace Hotel Page 60

A perfect foil to the Rockies' rugged mountain-scapes, Denver's landmark hotel – a plush Italian Renaissance-style edifice opened in 1892 – is home to a breathtaking eight-story atrium lobby.

12 Rodeo Pages 48 & 214

Miss going to a rodeo and you'll miss a cornerstone of contemporary Western culture – not to mention one rootin' tootin' good time.

13 Devil's Causeway Page 217

Narrowing to four feet wide as it drops away 1500 feet on either side, this Flat Tops Wilderness trail is not for the faint of heart.

14 Rocky Mountain oysters Page 117 • Local delicacy that separates the men from the bulls, and is not for the squeamish.

15 Leadville Page 240 • Come as close as you can to experiencing the state during its mining days, in this ramshackle, unpretentious old mining town.

17 Fly-fishing Page 257 • Once in the mountains it's hard to find a bad river for a spot of fly-fishing; the Frying Pan near Aspen, however, is one of the best.

16 Mesa Verde National Park Page 354 • The country's only National Park devoted exclusively to archeological remains, Mesa Verde is laced with scores of cliff dwellings, once home to the Ancestral Puebloans.

18 Great Sand Dunes National Park Page 323 • Tucked up against the contrasting Sangre de Cristo Mountains, these 50 square miles of constantly shifting sand, rising up to 700ft, are the tallest dunes in the country.

19 **Ice-climbing in Ouray** Page **369** • If your idea of a winter wonderland is one accessed with crampons and an ice axe, then Ouray's where you need to head.

21 **Pearl Street Mall** Page **92** • Leafy pedestrian mall that gently sucks you into an afternoon of strolling, browsing, window-shopping, and people-watching.

22 **Rocky Mountain National Park** Page **131** • The best hiking in Colorado, along with the chance to spot plenty of wildlife, including moose, elk, and bighorn sheep.

20 **The Maroon Bells** Page **258** • Fifteen miles from Aspen's core stand these towering purple-grey peaks, two of the most attractive "fourteeners" in Colorado.

23 **Mountain biking** Pages **36** & **268** • Colorado bursts with every kind of trail for every kind of rider, from smooth, rolling single-track through backcountry groves to lift-serviced downhill courses.

Basics

Basics

Getting there

BASICS | Getting there

Colorado's main hub is Denver, which is serviced by a number of domestic and international airlines; the city also serves as a regional center for bus travel and sits at the confluence of a number of major interstates, making it easy to reach by car. There are convenient air links to a number of other cities and resorts in the state.

Airfares typically depend on the **season**. In Colorado, there are two high seasons – summer and the snowy winter months – with cheaper flights available in the spring and fall.

Some tour operators run **all-inclusive packages** that combine plane tickets and hotel accommodation with (for example) skiing, sightseeing, wining and dining, or excursions to tourist sights. It's a convenient if somewhat inflexible way of seeing the state.

From North America

Getting to Colorado from anywhere in **North America** is rarely a problem. Flying is the quickest but most expensive way to get there, and most major airlines operate daily scheduled flights to Denver from across the country. The least expensive method is traveling by bus, though the great distances and frequent stops make for slow going. Trains are almost as slow, though more comfortable and expensive. Since you'll need a car to explore much of the state anyway, the most cost-effective option may be driving.

By air

Denver International Airport (DIA) is Colorado's main **air** hub and has excellent links to the rest of the US and Canada, with daily flights to most major towns and cities on the continent.

Outside of the peak holiday periods – such as Christmas and New Year's – round-trip ticket prices to Denver start at around $250 from New York (5hr) or Los Angeles (3hr) and around Can$500 from Vancouver (6hr) and Toronto (5hr 45min).

By train

Colorado is linked to the rest of the country by **Amtrak**'s (☏1-800/872-7245, ⓦwww .amtrak.com) *California Zephyr*, which runs from Chicago to San Francisco (53 hours), calling in at Denver, Fraser/Winter Park, Glenwood Springs, and Grand Junction. In southern Colorado, the *Southwest Chief* from Los Angeles cuts through the towns of Trinidad, La Junta, and Lamar before heading on to Kansas City and Chicago.

Amtrak **fares** are often more expensive than flying, though off-peak discounts and special deals can make the train an economical choice. One-way cross-country fares are around $300, though if you're traveling round-trip you can take advantage of **Explore America** fares, which are zone-based and allow three stopovers – within 45 days – between your origin and eventual return. These fares may cut the cost by $50 or so. **Sleeping compartments**, which include meals, small toilets, and showers, cost at least an extra $150 per night for one or two people. If you are a non-US resident engaged in broader travels within the US you might consider buying an **Amtrak Rail Pass**; they're valid for either fifteen or thirty days and include unlimited stops. A fifteen-day pass starts at around $200.

By bus

Bus travel is the most tedious and time-consuming way to get to the Rockies, and bearing the discomfort won't even save you much money. **Greyhound** (☏1-800/231-2222, ⓦwww.greyhound.com), the sole long-distance operator, has an extensive network of destinations throughout the area. A one-way ticket from New York to Denver costs $120, with cheaper deals if you buy in advance.

The only reason to go Greyhound is if you're planning to visit a number of other places en route; Greyhound's **Discovery Pass** is good for unlimited travel within a certain amount of time; a US-wide pass costs $229 for seven days, $329 for fifteen, and $439 for thirty.

From the UK and Ireland

Although you can fly to Colorado from many of Britain's regional airports, the only **non-stop** flight leaves from London Heathrow, landing at Denver. The flight, a daily service with British Airways, takes around ten hours. For **one-stop** flights travelers can choose between Continental and United Airlines, who offer two daily flights to Denver from London. A basic round-trip economy-class ticket will cost around £500 in high season and about £100–200 less at other times.

The best choices for those who don't live near London are a bit different. The fastest involve taking a flight to the US from a regional airport like Manchester, Glasgow, or Edinburgh (all offered by Continental), then a connecting flight from a US airport. The cheapest, meanwhile, are usually offered by European carriers, who will fly you to a hub like Paris, Amsterdam, or Frankfurt for a connecting flight to the US, then another on to Denver. These trips can become eighteen- to twenty-hour odysseys.

There are no direct flights to Colorado from **Ireland**, so your best bet is either to take Aer Lingus to New York or fly to London, continuing on from either city. The **cheapest flights** – if you're under 26 or a student – are available from usit. Student-only return fares to Denver range from €570–800. Ordinary fares are only marginally higher.

Airlines and tour operators can be found beginning on p.21.

From Australia and New Zealand

There are no direct flights from **Australia** or **New Zealand** to Colorado. Whether you go by way of the Pacific or the more roundabout route through Asia, you'll have to touch down on the US West Coast – in Los Angeles or San Francisco – before going on to

Denver. Via the Pacific most flights are non-stop, with traveling time between Auckland/Sydney and San Francisco or Los Angeles twelve to fourteen hours. If you go via Asia, you'll usually have to spend a night, or the best part of a day, in the airline's home city.

Prices for daily flights from **Sydney** to Denver via Los Angeles or San Francisco on United and Qantas/American are from Aus$2000 (low season). By way of Asia, the best deal is often on JAL (Aus$1900–2300), which includes a night in Tokyo. If you don't want to spend the night, Cathay Pacific and Singapore Airlines can get you there by transferring, repsectively, in their home cities of Hong Kong and Singapore, for Aus$2200–2400. Prices are about the same from other Australian east coast cities, while from Perth figure about Aus$350–450 more.

From **New Zealand**, most flights are out of **Auckland** (add NZ$250–300 for Christchurch and Wellington departures), with the best deals on Air New Zealand (either non-stop or via Honolulu, Fiji, or Tonga) and Qantas (direct or via Sydney) to Los Angeles, where you would join with American for the onward flight to Denver (NZ$2300–2700). United Airlines have regular deals on fares all the way to Denver that may undercut their competition. By way of Asia, Singapore Airlines has connecting services to LA and San Francisco from NZ$2400, while the best value for the money (NZ$2000–2400) is on JAL via Tokyo.

From South Africa

The choices for getting to Colorado from **South Africa** are between flying straight from South Africa to a large international US airport like Atlanta and then taking a regional flight to Denver; or flying to Europe first before hopping on a direct flight from London, Frankfurt, or Paris to Denver. Traveling via Europe is the cheaper of the two, with flights typically coming in at around 12,500SAR. Pay another 1000SAR and you get the convenience of a shorter flight direct to the US with South African Airways. You can start your journey with an international flight from Johannesburg, Durban, and Cape Town, although Jo'burg has the best choice of connections.

Fly less – stay longer! Travel and climate change

Climate change is a serious threat to the ecosystems that humans rely upon, and air travel is among the fastest-growing contributors to the problem. Rough Guides regard travel, overall, as a global benefit, and feel strongly that the advantages to developing economies are important, as is the opportunity of greater contact and awareness among peoples. But we all have a responsibility to limit our personal impact on global warming, and that means giving thought to how often we fly, and what we can do to redress the harm that our trips create.

Flying and climate change

Pretty much every form of motorized travel generates CO_2 – the main cause of human-induced climate change – but planes also generate climate-warming contrails and cirrus clouds and emit oxides of nitrogen, which create ozone (another greenhouse gas) at flight levels. Furthermore, flying simply allows us to travel much further than we otherwise would do. The figures are frightening: one person taking a return flight between Europe and California produces the equivalent impact of 2.5 tonnes of CO_2 – similar to the yearly output of the average UK car.

Fuel-cell and other less harmful types of plane may emerge eventually. But until then, there are really just two options for concerned travellers: to **reduce** the amount we travel by air (take fewer trips – stay for longer!), and to make the trips we do take "climate neutral" via a carbon offset scheme.

Carbon offset schemes

Offset schemes run by Ⓦclimatecare.org, Ⓦcarbonneutral.com and others allow you to make up for some or all of the greenhouse gases that you are responsible for releasing. To do this, they provide "carbon calculators" for working out the global-warming contribution of a specific flight (or even your entire existence), and then let you contribute an appropriate amount of money to fund offsetting measures. These include rainforest reforestation and initiatives to reduce future energy demand – often run in conjunction with sustainable development schemes.

Rough Guides, together with Lonely Planet and other concerned partners in the travel industry, are supporting a **carbon offset scheme** run by Ⓦclimatecare.org. Please take the time to view our website and see how you can help to make your trip climate neutral.

Ⓦ**www.roughguides.com/climatechange**

Airlines, agents, and tour operators

Airlines in the US and Canada

Air Canada ☏1-888/247-2262, Ⓦwww.aircanada.com.
America West ☏1-800/235-9292, Ⓦwww.americawest.com.
American ☏1-800/433-7300, Ⓦwww.aa.com.
ATA ☏1-800/435-9282, Ⓦwww.ata.com.
Continental ☏1-800/523-3273, Ⓦwww.continental.com.
Delta ☏1-800/221-1212, Ⓦwww.delta.com.
Frontier ☏1-800/432-1359, Ⓦwww.flyfrontier.com.
JetBlue ☏1-800/538-2583, Ⓦwww.jetblue.com.
Northwest/KLM ☏1-800/225-2525, Ⓦwww.nwa.com.
Southwest ☏1-800/435-9792, Ⓦwww.southwest.com.
TWA ☏1-800/221-2000, Ⓦwww.twa.com.
United ☏1-800/241-6522, Ⓦwww.united.com.
US Airways ☏1-800/428-4322, Ⓦwww.usairways.com.

Travel agents and tour operators in the US

Abercrombie & Kent ☏630/954-2944 or 1-800/323-7308, Ⓦwww.abercrombiekent.com. Easy adventure travel for the well-heeled in Colorado, but expect to pay up to $2000 for a week's rafting, biking, hiking, etc.
Backroads ☏510/527-1555 or 1-800/462-2848, Ⓦwww.backroads.com. Well-run cycling, hiking, and multisport tours. A biking, hiking, and rafting tour from

Telluride to Silverton runs around $2000, including some very fine lodging.

Delta Vacations ☎1-800/654-6559, ⓦwww .deltavacations.com. Full ski packages, including car rental and accommodation.

Moguls ☎1-800/666-4857, ⓦwww.moguls .com.Boulder tour operator run by skiing and snowboarding enthusiasts, with packages for all budgets offered at resorts across North America. Heli-skiing trips with several of the top outfits also booked.

REI Adventures ☎1-800/622-2236, ⓦwww.rei .com. Offers fifteen itineraries on nine different rivers from half-day floats to weekend and longer trips.

Rocky Mountain Tours ☎1-800/525-7547, ⓦwww.skithewest.com. Extensive packages, including car rental and lift tickets, available for most major Colorado ski resorts.

Ski-Can ☎1-888/475-4226, ⓦwww.skican .com. Large and knowledgeable operator with ski packages to Steamboat, Aspen, and Vail.

Snow Ventures ☎1-800/845-7157, ⓦwww .snowventures.com. Experienced outfit offering budget to deluxe ski packages, including, if you so choose, equipment rental.

Airlines in the UK and Ireland

Air France ☎0845/084 5111, Republic of Ireland ☎01/605 0383, ⓦwww.airfrance.co.uk.

British Airways ☎0845/773 3377, Republic of Ireland ☎0141/222 2345, ⓦwww.britishairways .com.

Continental ☎0800/776 464, Republic of Ireland ☎01/814 5311, ⓦwww.flycontinental.com.

Delta ☎0800/414 767, Northern Ireland ☎028/9048 0526, Republic of Ireland ☎1800/414 767, ⓦwww.delta.com.

KLM ☎0870/507 4074, Northern Ireland ☎0990/074 074, Republic of Ireland ☎0345/445 588, ⓦwww.klmuk.com.

Lufthansa ☎0845/773 7747, Republic of Ireland ☎01/844 5544, ⓦwww.lufthansa.com.

United Airlines ☎0845/844 4777, Republic of Ireland ☎1800/535 300, ⓦwww.ual.com.

Travel agents and tour operators in the UK and Ireland

Alpine Answers ☎0208/871 4656, ⓦwww .alpineanswers.co.uk. London-based operator with a knowledgeable staff of skiers, specializing in condo and home rental holidays and hotel packages. Good last-minute deals often available on their website.

Inghams ☎0208/780 4433, ⓦwww.inghams .co.uk. Large and respected tour operator with ski packages to Vail and Breckenridge.

North South Travel ☎01245/608 291, ⓦwww .northsouthtravel.co.uk. Friendly, competitive travel agency offering discounted fares, the profits from which are used to support projects in the developing world, especially the promotion of sustainable tourism.

Rocky Mountain Holidays ☎0870/366 5442, ⓦwww.rockymountain.co.uk. Student and budget-minded operator with trips to ski resorts in Colorado, also a useful source for information and visas for working at a North American resort.

Ski Independence ☎0870/555 0555, ⓦwww .ski-independence.co.uk. Reputable agency with ski trips taking in a few days at a stopover city like Boston or Denver.

Ski Safari ☎01273/223 680, ⓦwww.skisafari .com. Operator with package deals available for several Colorado resorts.

STA Travel ☎0870/160 6070, ⓦwww.statravel .co.uk. Worldwide specialists in low-cost flights and tours for students and under-26s, though other customers welcome.

Trailfinders ☎020/7937 5400, Republic of Ireland ☎01/677 7888, ⓦwww.trailfinders .com. One of the best-informed and most efficient agents for independent travelers; they produce a very useful quarterly magazine worth scrutinizing for round-the-world routes. Branches nationwide.

usit CAMPUS/usit NOW ☎0870/240 1010, ⓦwww.usitcampus.co.uk, Republic of Ireland ☎01/602 1904, ⓦwww.usitnow.ie. Student/youth travel specialists, offering discount flights throughout North America.

Airlines in Australia and NZ

Air New Zealand NZ ☎09/357 3000, ⓦwww .airnz.co.nz.

American Airlines Australia ☎1300/650 747, NZ ☎09/309 0735 or 0800/887 997, ⓦwww.aa.com.

Cathay Pacific Australia ☎13 17 47 or 02/9931 5500, NZ ☎09/379 0861, ⓦwww.cathaypacific .com.

JAL Australia ☎02/9272 1111, NZ☎09/379 3202.

Qantas Australia ☎13 13 13, NZ ☎09/357 8900 or 0800/808 767, ⓦwww.qantas.com.au.

Singapore Airlines Australia ☎13 10 11 or 02/9350 0262, NZ ☎09/303 2129 or 0800/808 909, ⓦwww.singaporeair.com.

United Airlines Australia ☎13 1777, NZ ☎09/379 3800, ⓦwww.ual.com.

Travel agents in Australia and New Zealand

STA Travel Australia ☎13 17 76, ⓦwww .statravel.com.au, NZ ☎09/309 0458 or 366 6673, ⓦwww.statravel.co.nz.

Trailfinders Australia ☏ 02/9247 7666, ⓦwww
.trailfinders.com.au.

Travelplan Australia ☏ 02/9958 1888 or 1300/130
754, ⓦwww.travelplan.com.au. Specializing in mid-
range to deluxe ski packages to most major Western
resorts in North America. Particularly good for families
or groups.

usit BEYOND NZ ☏ 09/379 4224 or 0800/788
336, ⓦwww.usitbeyond.co.nz.

Airlines in South Africa

Air France ☏ 0861/340 340 ⓦwww.airfrance
.com/za.

British Airways ☏ 011/441 8600 ⓦwww
.britishairways.com.

South African Airways ☏ 0861/359 722,
ⓦwww.flysaa.com.

Online agents

ⓦ**www.cheapflights.com** Flight deals and travel
agents, plus links to other travel sites.

ⓦ**www.cheaptickets.com** Discount flight
specialists.

ⓦ**www.expedia.com** Discount airfares, all-airline
search engine, and daily deals.

ⓦ**www.hotwire.com** Bookings from the US only,
with last-minute savings of up to 40 percent on
regular published fares.

ⓦ**www.lastminute.com** Offers good last-minute
holiday package and flight-only deals. UK only.

ⓦ**www.travelocity.com** Cheap web fares and the
best deals for car rental and accommodation.

ⓦ**www.travelshop.com.au** Australian website
offering discounted flights, packages, and insurance.

ⓦ**www.zuji.co.nz** New Zealand-based company
offering hot fares and great deals for car rental and
lodging.

Getting around

Having your own vehicle is definitely the preferred option for getting around
Colorado, and absolutely essential if your trip is focused on national parks and
other backcountry destinations. Many smaller towns, national and state parks,
and ski areas are only served by infrequent public transportation or private
shuttle buses – if at all; there are many places you simply can't reach without
a car.

Driving

Driving is by far the most convenient way
to get around the state. Although distances
can be great, driving through the state is
such a fantastically scenic experience that
hours behind the wheel won't seem much
of a bother at all. And if you are planning to
camp, renting a car can save you money by
allowing access to less expensive, out-of-
the-way campgrounds.

One thing to bear in mind when driving in
the Rockies is that conditions can often be
extreme. Snow and subzero temperatures
in winter, highs of over 100°F in summer,
the altitude, and some pretty gnarly roads
once you get off the beaten track mean

you really need a reliable vehicle for major
journeys, and in many cases a 4WD is
preferable.

If you don't have one, **renting a car** is the
usual story of phoning the central reservations number of one of the majors agencies
(listed on p.24). Most have airport offices and
addresses and phone numbers are compre-
hensively documented in the Yellow Pages.

Also worth considering are **fly-drive deals**,
which give cut-rate (and sometimes free) car
rental when buying an air ticket.

Car rental

Drivers wishing to **rent** a vehicle must have
held a license for at least one year (though

Winter driving

If you're unaccustomed to driving in icy conditions, it's best to be very conservative and avoid driving during snowstorms if possible. Keep yourself informed on road and weather conditions using the Colorado Department of Transportation information services (☎303/639-1111 or 1-877/315-7623, ⊛www.cotrip.org). Basic equipment for **winter driving** in the mountains includes snow tires and/or chains, an ice-scraper for clearing your windshield, and a shovel for clearing away built-up snow. It also pays to have warm clothes, blankets, a cell phone, and extra food and water in case you do get stuck.

If your car has snow tires (you should definitely double-check this when booking a rental car for a winter trip into the mountains) you'll be in good shape for general highway and town driving in winter. Major roads are regularly cleared throughout the winter, as are town and city streets, though you should not rely on smaller county roads and such being cleared daily. At times you may see road signs indicating that drivers are required to carry chains in a certain area. If in doubt about the conditions on a certain route, check with a tourist or USFS office or at a gas station.

Even with the best of precautions, you may find yourself on a stretch of road covered in an unbroken sheet of **ice**; try to get a car with anti-lock brakes (ABS), which will help if you happen to skid. During a skid it can also be helpful (though counterintuitive) to turn the steering wheel in the *same* direction – not the other way around – as your vehicle's front end is drifting.

Finally, if you are stuck in deep snow, don't leave the engine running to keep warm, as you risk carbon monoxide poisoning.

this is rarely checked); those under 25 pay a higher insurance premium, usually levied via an extra $10–25 tacked on the daily rate. A credit card is essential, as rental agencies will rarely accept a cash deposit.

A regular sedan will be fine for major towns, national parks, and so on, but for backcountry roads or winter driving, a **4WD** is a better choice; those run at least $10 per day more. Note also that **ski/bike racks** can often be requested as well.

RVs (camper vans) can be rented for around $500 a week. On top of the rental fees, take into account the cost of gas (some RVs do twelve miles to the gallon or less) and any drop-off charges, if you plan to do a one-way trip across the state. Also, it is rarely legal simply to pull up in an RV and spend the night at the roadside – you are expected to stay in designated parks that cost $20–30 per night.

It's almost always the case that weekly **rates** provide a saving; for example, a car rented at $45 per day can often be had for $200 a week. This is a good benchmark figure for Colorado, though costs vary across the state, with prices typically increasing by half in smaller towns where there is little competition. When you rent a car, read the small print carefully for details on the **Collision Damage Waiver (CDW)** – sometimes called a Liability Damage Waiver (LDW) or a Physical Damage Waiver (PDW) – a form of insurance that usually isn't included in the rental charge but is well worth considering, especially for foreign drivers (Americans may already be covered by their own vehicle insurance or credit card). It specifically covers the car that you are driving, as you are in any case insured for damage to other vehicles. At $10–30 a day, it does add considerably to the daily rental fee, but without it you're liable for every scratch to the car – even those that aren't your fault.

Car rental agencies

Advantage ☎1-800/777-5500, ⊛www.arac.com
Alamo ☎1-800/522-9696, ⊛www.alamo.com
Avis ☎1-800/331-1084, ⊛www.avis.com
Budget ☎1-800/527-0700, ⊛www.budget.com
Cruise America ☎1-800/327-7799, ⊛www.cruiseamerica.com. RV specialist.
Dollar ☎1-800/800-6000, ⊛www.dollar.com
Enterprise ☎1-800/325-8007, ⊛www.enterprise.com
Hertz ☎1-800/654-3001, ⊛www.hertz.com

Moturis ☎ 303/295-6837 or 1-888/295-6837, ⓦ www.moturis.com. Rents out motorcycles, including Harley Davidsons, and RVs, as well.
National ☎ 1-800/227-7368, ⓦ www.nationalcar.com
Thrifty ☎ 1-800/367-2277, ⓦ www.thrifty.com

Roads and rules

In Colorado, as in the rest of the US, you drive on the **right**. You will encounter several types of road in Colorado. The best for covering long distances are the wide, straight, and fast **interstate** highways (eg I-70), usually six-lane motorways where the speed limit is 75mph, unless posted otherwise. A grade down are the state and US **highways**, which may be two or four lanes wide. Some major roads in cities are technically state highways but are better known by their local name. You'll also come across much smaller County Roads; their number is preceded by a letter denoting their county.

Once you get to built-up areas, where speed limits are typically 25 or 30mph, navigation is almost always made easier by a **grid** and **numbering system** that creates "blocks" of buildings. Addresses of buildings refer to the block, which will be numbered in sequence from a central point, usually downtown; for example, 620 S Cedar will be six blocks south of downtown. It is crucial, therefore, to take note of components such as "N" or "S" in addresses; 3620 S King St will be a long way indeed from 3620 N King St. In small towns, and parts of larger cities, "streets" and "avenues" often run

Foreign drivers

Though technically an International Driving Permit is required by all foreign nationals to confirm that they hold a **driving license** issued in their home country, in practice those with a British, Canadian, Australian, New Zealand, Irish, or South African license can use this to rent vehicles and drive in the US. If in any doubt about your driving status, check with your local **motoring organization**, such as AAA in the US.

north–south and east–west respectively; streets are usually named (sometimes alphabetically) and avenues generally numbered. In these cases addresses will usually include these numbers as in their first two digits: 3620 S King St will most likely be just south of 36th Avenue.

Bus

If you're traveling on your own and making frequent stops, **buses** are a pretty cheap way to get around, though the network around the state is far from complete. The main carrier is **Greyhound** (☎ 1-800/229-9424, ⓦ www.greyhound.com), which, together with its local partner TMN&O, links major cities and some smaller towns. If you are going to use buses extensively consider buying a **Greyhound Discovery Pass** (see p.20). All kids under twelve go half-price, and there are discounts for US students and seniors.

It used to be that any sizeable community would have a Greyhound station, though now in many places a gas station or the like doubles as the bus stop and ticket office. Reservations on the toll-free number are not essential but are recommended – if a bus is full you may be forced to wait until the next one, sometimes overnight or longer.

Rail

The **Amtrak rail service** (☎ 1-800/USA-RAIL, ⓦ www.amtrak.com) is generally very good, with reliable trains that are clean and well staffed. Unfortunately, coverage in Colorado is quite limited, and in any case there are few stations that give immediate access to the mountain towns and national parks that are most people's intended destinations. The only service of much use in getting around Colorado, connecting around half a dozen mountain towns (namely Winter Park, Granby, Glenwood Springs, and Grand Junction), is the daily *California Zephyr* on its way between Chicago and San Francisco. Even though services are only daily, at least the times and costs are reasonable: expect to pay $16 for Grand Junction to Glenwood Springs, or just $33 for the five-hour journey to Winter Park.

Mileage Chart

From \ To	Aspen	Cañon City	Colorado Springs	Cortez	Craig	Denver	Durango	Estes Park	Fort Collins	Glenwood Springs	Grand Junction	Greeley	Gunnison	Leadville	Limon	Ouray	Pagosa Springs	Salida	Silverton	Steamboat Springs	Telluride
Aspen																					
Cañon City	145																				
Colorado Springs	157	45																			
Cortez	277	302	347																		
Craig	157	242	251	377																	
Denver	162	115	70	208	196																
Durango	249	257	302	45	332	332															
Estes Park	204	183	138	445	394	71	399														
Fort Collins	223	177	132	439	169	65	394	42													
Glenwood Springs	41	198	198	259	152	159	231	196	220												
Grand Junction	130	248	287	197	248	248	169	285	308	89											
Greeley	212	166	122	428	54	54	384	50	30	258	298										
Gunnison	146	121	166	201	278	196	173	265	164	162	126	247									
Leadville	59	117	129	299	162	103	254	145	147	89	178	153	118								
Limon	230	118	73	421	296	86	375	153	147	335	134	189	239	190							
Ouray	177	222	267	118	249	297	72	355	359	97	246	194	101	219	340						
Pagosa Springs	222	197	42	105	272	60	60	341	334	229	159	60	165	66	316	132					
Salida	88	57	102	248	138	202	49	207	200	323	264	124	66	242	176	167	143				
Silverton	200	245	290	94	345	320	49	378	382	193	130	238	124	120	364	23	109	198			
Steamboat Springs	155	200	209	373	166	166	345	140	160	190	182	190	238	249	254	272	314	178	296		
Telluride	207	252	297	77	327	279	118	385	389	127	114	127	131	131	372	50	178	198	74	303	
Vail	102	133	142	320	98	131	292	292	159	61	189	150	156	156	185	220	232	98	243	250	

Mileage based on summertime travel

Shuttle buses

Numerous direct **shuttle bus** services run from the Denver airport to many of the most popular resorts, making it unnecessary to rent a car if you plan on being based in only one place. For services to Aspen, see p.247; Boulder p.89; Colorado Springs p.277; Estes Park (for Rocky Mountain National Park) p.144; Steamboat Springs p.210; Summit County p.166; Vail p.229; and Winter Park p.197. Note that seats should be booked as far in advance as possible during peak season. Otherwise you can just go to the desks of many of these companies in the airport itself and organize things on the spot.

Air

Colorado's network of regional airports means that in most instances you can **fly** to within a short drive of most major towns and to within a couple hours' drive of almost all areas of the state. Prices for this convenience are, however, quite steep and only really worthwhile if your time is at a premium and if you are visiting only a single destination such as a ski resort. The major airports are at Haden, near Steamboat Springs in the Northern Mountains; Eagle, near Vail, Aspen, and Grand Junction in central Colorado; and at Gunnison, Montrose, Durango, and Telluride in the South. Most will have several daily flights to Denver, with fares varying wildly with demand, but expect to pay about $300–400 for a round-trip flight.

Cycling

If you have the time and fitness, **cycle touring** around Colorado is a magical way to see the state. The elevation and terrain generally put off all but the hardiest, but at least summer weather conditions are good, with wind and rain rarely a problem. Most Colorado towns have bike stores that will **rent** out bikes – commonly front-suspension mountain bikes – for around $30 a day or $150 a week. Many are listed throughout this guide. Most serious bikers, though, will want to bring their own bikes; check out your **airline's policy** on bike handling *before* booking. Generally you will be charged around $80 to carry your bike on a domestic flight, while regulations for those flying in from abroad vary wildly. Often bringing a bike is free – so long as it's part of your luggage allowance – but charges of up to $160 can be levied.

Accommodation

Lodging standards in Colorado – as in the rest of the US – are high, and costs inevitably form a significant proportion of the expenses for any trip to the state. It is possible to haggle, however, especially in the chain motels, and if you're on your own, costs can be pared down by sleeping in dormitory-style hostels, where a bed will cost $15–20 a night. Groups of two or more, however, will find it barely more expensive to stay in the plentiful motels and hotels, where basic rooms away from the major cities typically cost around $50 per night. Some hotels will set up a third single bed for around $5 to $10 on top of the regular price, reducing costs for three people sharing. By contrast, the lone traveler will have a hard time of it beyond hostels: "singles" are usually double rooms at an only slightly reduced rate.

Motels are plentiful on the main approach roads to cities, around mountain resorts, and by the main road junctions in some country areas. High-rise **hotels** are common in the downtowns of larger cities and also around some of the region's largest resorts. In major cities, **campgrounds** tend to be on the outskirts, if they exist at all. Outside of cities, however, they're just about everywhere.

Wherever you stay, you'll be expected to **pay in advance**, at least for the first night and perhaps for further nights, too, particularly if it's high season and the hotel's expecting to be busy. Payment can be in cash or dollar travelers' checks, though it's more common to leave an imprint of your credit card and sign for everything when you leave. **Reservations** are only held until 5 or 6pm unless you've told them you'll be arriving late. Since cheap accommodation in the cities, mountain resorts, and close to the major national parks is snapped up fast, **book ahead** whenever possible.

Bed-and-breakfasts

Colorado **B&Bs** are typically a luxury – the bed-and-breakfast inns, as they're usually known, are often small, restored Victorian buildings filled with antiques and/or local folk art. Even the larger establishments tend to have no more than ten rooms, often without TV and phone but with plentiful flowers, stuffed cushions, and a homey atmosphere; others may just be a couple of furnished rooms in someone's home, or an entire apartment where you won't even see your host. Victorian and rustic are the dominant themes.

While always including a huge and wholesome breakfast, **prices** vary greatly: anything from $80 to $250 depending on the location and season. Most fall between $90 and $125 per night for a double, a little more for a whole apartment. Bear in mind that these are frequently booked well in advance, and even if they're not full, the cheaper rooms, which determine our price code, may be already taken.

Useful **websites** covering B&Bs in Colorado include the eponymous Ⓦwww.bedandbreakfast.com and the Inn Site, Ⓦwww.innsite.com.

Hostels

With dorm beds priced from around $15 per night per person, **hostels** are the cheapest accommodation option in Colorado besides camping. Most are independently run and not part of the Hostelling International (HI) network (Ⓦwww.hiayh.com), though this shouldn't put visitors off – unaffiliated hostels are much more common in the States than they are abroad. That said, the quality of the state's hostels is far from consistent, ranging from dilapidated and unsafe-feeling establishments to some very well-run and plush accommodations, with free breakfasts and Internet. The vast majority have no curfew.

Accommodation price codes

Throughout this book, accommodation has been price-coded according to the cost, including tax, of the least expensive double room in high season; we have given individual prices for hostels and campgrounds.

Expect prices in most places to jump into the next highest category on Friday and Saturday nights and also when a major event is going on in town.

❶ up to $30 Basic double room either sharing a bathroom in an old hotel or en-suite in a motel that's well off the beaten track.

❷ $30–45 No-frills motel room – double room with bathroom, TV, and phone – but with no amenities and probably in an unpopular location.

❸ $45–60 Standard rate for the most basic highway chain motel; rooms should be adequately comfortable and there's typically access to a pool.

❹ $60–80 Mid-priced motels in reasonable locations with more than just the very basic facilities. The room and its fittings will be bigger and more luxurious than in the highway chains – there's probably access to a hot tub, laundromat, and maybe even a coffee and doughnut for breakfast.

❺ $80–100 Well-located motels, or those with good fitness facilities and other amenities, will charge in this

bracket. Rooms in many of the least expensive bed-and-breakfasts begin at this price.

❻ $100–130 Exceptionally well-located motels and some basic hotels fall into this bracket. Most B&Bs will charge around these prices, too.

❼ $130–180 At this price you can expect to be staying in a good-quality hotel with nice facilities in a convenient location or one of the fancier antique-decorated B&Bs, where you start the day with gourmet breakfasts. Bathrooms at both may well contain an en-suite hot tub.

❽ $180–240 High standard hotels with concierge services and great facilities.

❾ $240+ Extraordinary accommodations, with outstanding service, exceptional location, and facilities, but also a little extra – like being a local historic landmark – that drives up the price.

Dude ranches

Colorado is dotted with **dude ranches**, where you can experience everything from the full-on cowboy lifestyle of rising at dawn, mucking out the stables, and tending to the cattle to a luxury lifestyle involving horseback riding, fly-fishing, hiking, and so on that just happens to be centered on a ranch.

Prices vary enormously depending on the level of luxury – cheaper options in basic, rustic cabins with no-frills communal meals start at around $100 per day, while ranches providing more opulent accommodation and gourmet meals will set you back considerably more.

A good dude ranch will provide you with the nearest you're likely to get to cowboy-style living short of signing on for a job. To find a ranch contact the Dude Ranchers' Association (☎970/223-8440, ⓦwww .duderanch.org).

Camping

Colorado **campgrounds** range from the primitive (a flat piece of ground that may or may not have a water tap) to those that are more like open-air hotels, with markets, restaurants, washing facilities, game rooms, and so on. When camping in national and state parks, as well as national forests, you can typically expect a large site designed to accommodate up to two vehicles, six people, and all the paraphernalia that Americans like to take with them. There'll be a picnic table and fire pit on the site, with a short walk to an outhouse and a drinking water tap.

Naturally enough, **prices** vary accordingly, ranging from nothing for the most basic plots up to $30 a night for something comparatively luxurious. There are plenty of campgrounds, but often plenty of people wanting to use them: take care over plotting your route if you're intending to camp in the big national parks, or anywhere at all during national holidays or the summer, when many grounds will be either full or very crowded. Vacancies often exist in the grounds outside the parks – where the facilities are likely to be marginally better – and at more isolated **backcountry campgrounds** within them. Payment for the latter is often a simple box into which you slide the $3 or so in the envelope provided.

Lastly, since much of Colorado's mountain regions are in the public domain, it is also possible to **camp wild** in many areas – particularly Bureau of Land Management lands and in National Forests, although in designated wilderness areas you will usually need a permit. You can obtain these at the nearest USFS office or agent.

Campground reservations

Campgrounds in popular national and state parks and national forests fill up quickly in summer, especially during the July and August school vacation, so it pays to **reserve** as far in advance as you can. When making reservations, be sure to have dates, locations, number of people, a mailing address, and alternative sites picked out.

Kampgrounds of America ☎406/248-7444, ⓦ www.koa.com. Oversees a multitude of family-style campgrounds throughout Colorado, most of them with a wide range of facilities, and usually close to urban areas.

National Recreation Reservation Service ☎518/885-3639 or 1-877/444-6777, ⓦ www.reserveusa.com. One-stop reservation service for many forms of public land including the Forest Service, the National Park Service, and the Bureau of Land Management.

Reserve America ☎303/470-1144 or 1-800/678-2267, ⓦ www.reserveamerica.com. Online booking system for many public and private bodies, including Colorado's state parks.

Food and drink

Outside the major towns and tourist centers, old-fashioned American food predominates. Particularly in the cattle ranching regions, red meat is almost synonymous with the term food. Preparation techniques are also of the pre-health-conscious era, with frying the main method in greasy spoon diners and truck stops – chicken-fried steak, a hunk of breaded and fried steak, is many menus' cornerstone.

Thankfully, ethnic foods have helped expand the range of choices, and you'll find pockets of good Mexican dishes throughout the region, and some respectable Asian meals as well. In college towns, the health-conscious vibe of the region comes through strongest and you'll have a wide range of decent veggie places to choose from. The last decade has also seen an increase of restaurants at the gourmet end of the scale, many of which successfully blend local ingredients like beef, trout, lamb, buffalo, or elk with international cooking styles.

Breakfast and lunch

Breakfast is likely to be the best-value and most filling meal of the day. Go to a diner, café, or coffeeshop, all of which serve breakfast until at least 11am, with some diners serving it all day. The breakfasts themselves are pretty much what you'd find all over the country: various egg and omelette combos with ham or bacon, pancakes, French toast, and waffles appear on nearly every menu. Wherever you eat, a dollar or so will entitle you to wash the meal down with as much coffee or tea as you can stomach.

Most restaurants that open for **lunch** will serve a range of smaller meals that include sandwiches, burger, salads, and even pizza by the slice. Many Mexican restaurants are good options for cheap quick lunches, selling fresh tacos and burritos for around $3–5. And of course the fast food chains are as ubiquitous here as anywhere in the US.

Dinner and dining out

In spite of the presence of fashionable regional and ethnic cuisines, **traditional American cooking** – burgers, steaks, fries, salads, and baked potatoes – is found all over Colorado. Vegetarians will usually be able to find something on the menu – the best standby in many traditional burger and steak joints being the humble baked potato.

Some upscale restaurants flout a new line in "**Rocky Mountain cuisine**," with an emphasis on dishing up local produce, and if it is native to the region then all the better: hence the interest in serving salmon, trout, elk, venison, and buffalo (bison). One eye-catching item on some menus are **Rocky Mountain oysters**, which you may or may not want to try once you find out that a bull was castrated to provide the food.

Although technically ethnic, **Mexican** food is so common that it often seems like (and, historically, often is) an indigenous cuisine, especially in southern Colorado. What's more, day or night, it's the cheapest type of food to eat: even a full dinner with a few drinks will rarely be over $12 anywhere except the most upmarket establishments. In the main, Mexican food here is different from what you'll find in Mexico, making more use of fresh vegetables and fruit, but the essentials are the same: lots of rice and pinto beans, often served refried, with variations on the versatile **tortilla**.

Other ethnic cuisines are common too, particularly budget **Chinese** and **Italian** places, though the latter can become expensive once you leave the simple pizzas and pastas to explore more specialist regional cooking. Japanese and French restaurants are also reasonably common, at least in the larger cities and resorts, though both are usually fairly pricey. **Thai**, **Korean**, **Vietnamese**, and **Indonesian** food is similarly city-based, though generally cheaper; **Indian** restaurants, on the other hand, are thin on the ground just about everywhere and often very expensive.

Drinking

Even though the gold rush is now long gone, Colorado's mountain towns still hold a strong contingent of old-fashioned **bars** that are fun to spend an evening in even if you don't plan to get legless. Many of the longer-standing and more remote bars in particular are filled with trophy heads and jukeboxes playing nothing but country music – likely venues for some of the most evocatively Western experiences.

The alternative to light, fizzy **beers** such as Budweiser, Coors (a state product), Miller, and Michelob is a fabulous range of **microbrews**. Nowhere is the growing popularity of brewpubs better represented than in Colorado. Many such operations pump out over 150,000 barrels a year and are classed as "regional breweries." Head for one of these brewpubs and you'll find handcrafted beers such as crisp pilsners, wheat beers, and stouts on tap, at prices only marginally above those of the national brews. Along the same lines, a wide range of bottled microbrews are available throughout Colorado. Many of the most highly regarded come from Fort Collins, where a disproportionate number of minor breweries have set up shop. One of the most successful of these is the **New Belgium Brewery**, whose tangy Fat Tire Ale is one of the state's most popular brews. The **Breckenridge Brewery**, a much smaller set-up than New Belgium, does the zesty Avalanche Ale, which is also widely known and acclaimed and can be had throughout the state.

Don't forget that in all but the most pretentious bars, several people can save money by buying a half-gallon **pitcher** of beer for $6–8. If bar prices are a problem, you can stock up with **six-packs** from a supermarket

Tipping

Foreign visitors should note to top up the bill in restaurants by fifteen–twenty percent; a little less perhaps if you're dining at the bar.

($3–7 for domestic, $5–9 for imported and microbrews).

Cocktails are extremely popular, especially during **happy hours** (usually between 5 and 7pm) when drinks are often half-price and there may be a free or very cheap buffet thrown in as well.

To purchase and consume alcohol in Colorado you must be 21 and you can expect to be asked for ID even if you look much older. **Licensing laws** and **drinking hours** are among the most liberal in the country, and alcohol can be bought and drunk any time between 10am (in some counties as early as 6am) up until 2am, seven days a week (except in Colorado's liquor stores, where sales aren't permitted on Sundays). As well as bars and clubs, restaurants are nearly always fully licensed too.

The media

Every major urban center in Colorado has its own newspaper, though most are parochial in the extreme, with the majority of stories covering areas well within the local horizon. Don't be surprised by a story about local bears breaking into an RV emblazoned all over the front page and an international section that's only two paragraphs long. The situation in Denver is rather better with a couple of half-decent broadsheet newspapers. Otherwise you'll find it easy to pick up a copy of the bland *USA Today* and East Coast stalwarts such as the *New York Times*, *Washington Post*, and *Wall Street Journal*, though at a slight price premium.

Foreign newspapers are almost impossible to get outside of Denver, where you might find day-or-two-old editions at downtown bookstores and newsagents. TV in the state is as everywhere else in the US, as is radio coverage, though deep in the mountains you may only be able to get a couple of stations, inevitably playing country music or classic rock.

Newspapers

The *Rocky Mountain News* (@www.rockymountainnews.com) and the *Denver Post* (@www.denverpost.com), who collaborate on weekend editions, compete as the state's most influential **newspapers**. Both are provincial affairs, slim on news, not to mention quality journalism for events outside the region. Nearly every community has at least a few free newspapers, found in street distribution bins, cafés and bars, or just lying around in piles. It's a good idea to pick up a full assortment: some simply cover local goings-on, others provide specialist coverage of interests ranging from cycling to getting ahead in business, and the classified and personal ads can provide hours of entertainment. Many of them are also excellent sources for bar, restaurant, and nightlife information; the most useful titles are mentioned throughout the guide. A prime example of a fine local newspaper is **Denver's** free weekly *Westword* (@www.westword.com), with considered and witty features along with an indispensable guide to local events.

TV

TV in Colorado is pretty much the standard network barrage of sitcoms, newscasts, sports, and talk shows. **PBS**, the national public television station, broadcasts a steady stream of interesting documentaries, informative (if slightly dry) news programs, and educational children's television. Most motel and hotel rooms in the region are hooked up to **cable**. The number of channels available to guests varies from place to place, but fifty is common and eighty isn't unheard of. Most cable stations are no better than the major networks (ABC, CBS, NBC, and FOX), though some of the more specialized channels are consistently interesting.

Radio

As with TV, the majority of **radio** stations stick to a bland commercial format. Except for news and chat, stations on the **AM** band are best avoided in favor of **FM**, in particular the nationally funded public (NPR) and college stations, typically found between 88 and 92 FM. These provide diverse and listenable programming, and they're also good sources for information on local nightlife.

Festivals

Someone somewhere always seems to be celebrating something in Colorado, although apart from the handful of national holidays, few spread between cities or valleys. Denver is particularly rich with festivals, with almost every well-represented ethnic group rolling out the barrel at some stage and the multitude of local events including art and craft shows, music festivals, and rodeos. A similar mix can be found throughout the state and it's certainly worth looking out for happenings in advance at ⓦwww.colorado.com and as you travel round. A selection of the most outstanding major events are listed below, while more localized festivities are in the relevant destination accounts.

January

National Western Stock Show and Rodeo mid-Jan, ⓦwww.nationalwestern.com. Denver's largest livestock show and rodeo runs for two weeks (see p.71).
International Snow Sculpting Championships late Jan. Offbeat Breckenridge competition where huge mythical creatures vie with man-sized abstract structures for prizes.
Colorado Mahler Fest mid-Jan, ⓦwww .mahlerfest.org. Celebrates the work of Gustav Mahler in Boulder.

February

Buffalo Bill's Birthday Celebration late Feb, ⓦwww.buffalobill.org. Ceremonies and live entertainment celebrate the life of this quintessential Western character.

March

Pow Wow mid-March, ⓦwww .denvermarchpowwow.org. Vast Native American cultural and arts and crafts festival held in Denver (see p.71).
Saint Patrick's Day March 17. Big Irish-themed festival, with parades and heavy drinking on the Saturday prior to the 17th in Denver.

April

Fruita Fat Tire Festival late May to early March, ⓦwww.fruitamountainbike.com. The biggest mountain bike festival in the state. Lasts a week near Grand Junction.

May

Cinco de Mayo May 5. Large Hispanic fiesta, particularly in Denver, Colorado Springs, and southern Colorado.

Memorial Day last Mon. Signals the beginning of the summer season. Many towns will have a small festival to celebrate, such as the Boulder's Boulder Creek Festival.

Mesa Verde Country Indian Arts and Western Culture Festival late May to early June, ⊛www .mesaverdecountry.com. Native American art market and cultural celebrations in Cortez.

June

Colorado Music Festival June and Aug, ⊛www .coloradomusicfest.org. Internationally acclaimed festival showcases classical artists in Boulder.
Rocky Mountain Stampede late June to early July, ⊛www.rockymountainstampede.com. One of the biggest rodeos in the West, held in Greeley.
Telluride Bluegrass Festival late June, ⊛www .planetbluegrass.com. Bluegrass, folk, and country music festival.

July

Independence Day July 4. Street fair and fireworks in just about every town in the state.
Pikes Peak Auto Hill Climb Sat nearest July 4, ⊛www.ppihc.com. Motor race up Pikes Peak, held annually since 1916.
Crested Butte Wild Flower Festival mid-July, ⊛www.crestedbuttewildflowerfestival.com.

Workshops, photography classes, and hikes all focus on the beauty of the thousands of local wild flowers.

August

Boom Days first weekend in Aug, ⊛www .leadvilleboomdays.com. Everyone in Leadville gets into the spirit of things, dressing up in period garb to celebrate the town's Victorian origins.
Colorado State Fair late Aug to early Sept, ⊛www.coloradostatefair.com. Big state fair in Pueblo with major rodeo, concerts, and fairground.

September

Labor Day first Mon. Signals the end of the summer season.
Telluride Film Festival early Sept, ⊛www .telluridefilmfestival.com. Indie film fest with a nationwide reputation.

October

Great American Beer Festival early Oct, ⊛www.beertown.org. Huge and prestigious sampling event in Denver.
Cowboy Gathering early Oct, ⊛www .durangocowboygathering.org. Cowboy poetry, Western art, and historical lectures convene in Durango.
Halloween Oct 31. Not a public holiday, despite being one of the most popular yearly flings.

Summer activities

Though hiking and biking have the highest profile in Colorado, several other outdoor pursuits are followed just as avidly by locals and visitors alike. Many of these are possible at equally fine locations in different parts of the state, but most have centered on a few places where they can be best exploited by local outfitters. Most "summer" activities are possible year-round somewhere in the state – even in the middle of winter the trails on the western slope and around Denver are likely to be clear of snow – while others have definite seasons: after April and May the whitewater season is effectively over and you can only hunt in the autumn. The best online resource for getting an impression of what outdoor activities are worth doing when are the Great Outdoor Recreation Pages at ⓦwww.gorp.com.

Hiking

Even in the planning stage of a trip to Colorado, you're very likely thinking about **hikes** on high mountain trails, taking in the peerless beauty of the state first-hand. Between the National Parks, National Forests, and wilderness areas, there are enough superb hiking opportunities to keep you busy for decades.

If you only hike in one area, make it **Rocky Mountain National Park**, where forested trails pass abundant wildlife to climb to seemingly endless stretches of wild alpine tundra. The Sawatch Mountains around Leadville are also great to explore: a morning is all that's needed to hike up Colorado's highest mountain, Mt Elbert. To see another type of scenery entirely – a red sandstone semi-desert – head out to the Colorado National Monument, where the huge rock arches of Rattlesnake Canyon are tailor-made to be explored on foot.

Details of specific hiking destinations, including local conditions and descriptions of some of the best trails, are included throughout this guide. If you're planning extensive exploration of one or two areas, you might consider investing in one of the comprehensive hiking guides reviewed in Contexts at the back of this book (see p.426).

Equipment

It's worth investing some thought and financial resources to insure that you have the basic hiking equipment, and that it's comfortable. First and foremost in order of importance are sturdy hiking **boots**. The main considerations when purchasing them are whether to get heavy-duty ones or something lightweight, and whether they need to be waterproof or just water-resistant. If you don't plan on spending days on end scrambling about in the backcountry, it may be best to go for a fairly light, flexible boot. There are several varieties available that mimic the comfort and flexibility of a running shoe, but also have grip and support appropriate for light to moderate hiking. If you're heading on a longer expedition and plan on carrying a heavy pack, you will certainly need a high-cut waterproof boot with a good quality sole. In either case, it's well worth being choosy and trying plenty of different styles before making a decision; indeed, you should only purchase boots from a reputable store with a knowledgeable staff that will run a series of tests to make sure the boot is right for you. Most importantly, you need to break in your boots by walking about in them for a few weeks before beginning your trip.

On most day-hikes, it's fine to wear just a T-shirt and shorts, although you should always have a **waterproof jacket** and a **fleece top** on hand in case the weather turns nasty, some **sunscreen**, and a **hat** with a wide brim to protect your face and the back of your neck from the sun. You will be most comfortable in a shirt made from polypropylene or a similar synthetic, as these don't absorb water and stay dry even as you sweat, unlike cotton. For the same reason, avoid cotton **socks** and splurge on a couple pairs of wool or synthetic wool-like socks instead.

A final note: if you're in the backcountry in the main **hunting season** insure you make yourself very visible, ideally by wearing some orange – some greenhorn hunters can get jumpy and may mistake you for their prey if it's not entirely obvious that you're a human and not an elk.

Cycling and mountain biking

Though all wilderness areas and National Park trails are out of bounds to **mountain bikes**, fat tires are welcome on almost all National Forest and BLM trails. These include thousands of miles of single track and many more miles of old logging and mining roads. Whether you are a skilled mountain biker after technical challenges or a more leisurely cyclist looking to explore the countryside on traffic-free trails, it's hard to think of a place better suited than Colorado to exploration by bicycle. The mountainous topography and high altitude of course means that it pays to be fit. For those looking for the thrills without the climbing, many resorts open their ski lifts to bikes in the summer.

The ultimate adventure in the state is the **Colorado Trail** (see *Colorado's protected lands* colour section), which crosses Colorado from Durango to Denver – a journey just short of 500 miles – and is open to bikes along its entire length. Crested Butte is one of the birthplaces of mountain biking, with several world-class trails to choose from (see box on p.268). The best ski resorts to hit up for lift-serviced trails are Winter Park, Keystone, Vail, and Breckenridge. Winter Park in particular has a huge network, while all the trails in Keystone are fairly hard – a couple of sections are the most technical lift-serviced sections in the state – while at Vail you can ride the remnants of past years' World Cup cross-country and downhill courses.

Almost every good-sized town in Colorado will have a bike shop which is always the

Hiking gear checklist

Just what constitutes essential **hiking gear** is entirely dependent upon the duration and difficulty of the hike you're undertaking. However, you should always carry at least a basic trail map, and if you're delving into backcountry areas, a compass and (waterproof) detailed topographic map become standard equipment. The most important general items to carry on any hike are plenty of **water** (you'll easily get through three liters a day in the mountains), sunscreen, energy snacks like chocolate bars and such, and some warm and waterproof gear. Use the checklist below to review your own requirements for both day-hikes and overnight backcountry trips. For an overnight, you'll need at least the "Essential" items listed below; you may want to pack a few from the "Additional" selection too.

Essential

- waterproof tent
- sleeping bag
- boots
- wool socks
- long underwear
- fleece
- waterproof gear

- first aid kit
- stove and fuel
- pots, pans, and utensils
- food (including emergency supply)
- sturdy water bottle

- matches
- thirty feet of nylon cord
- pocket knife
- flashlight, lantern, or candles
- sunscreen

Additional

- sleeping pad
- bear spray
- water purifier
- hat and gloves

- toilet paper
- bug spray
- binoculars
- camera

- tarp/ground cover
- journal
- entertainment; books, playing cards, etc

best source of advice and **information** about nearby trails and which will usually offer rent**als**. The quality of the bikes is reliably good – almost all have good front suspension and if you want to hire a full-suspension rig, it's usually easy to find one. Prices hover around $30 per day for front-suspension, $45 for full-suspension. Bike shops are usually happy to change pedals for those who wish to use their own clip-in system with a rental bike – the best option to creating a comfortable bike without bringing your own.

Wherever you bike the accepted **trail etiquette** is that bikers yield to hikers and horseback riders and if encountering another cyclist, the biker descending should give way to the biker climbing. **Helmets** are not required by law in Colorado, but clearly make good sense, particularly when riding off-road.

Climbing and mountaineering

With an abundance of peaks in the 12,000–14,000ft range, plus hundreds of precipitous walls of granite, limestone, and ice and clusters of huge boulders, Colorado has abundant **climbing** and **mountaineering** opportunities. Whether your own preference is for bagging a mighty peak, employing technical equipment and skills to scale a granite wall or a sheer sheet of ice, or undertaking some unfettered free-climbing or bouldering, you'll find plenty of routes to choose from all across the state.

Colorado's standout climbing center is **Boulder,** where the local scene is particularly vibrant thanks to the vast number of local spots. Mountaineers are spoilt for choice but certainly the peaks of **Rocky Mountain National Park**, particularly Longs Peak, should be high on the agenda. In winter ice climbers flock to Ouray.

In the US, the system used to classify the levels of technical difficulty in mountaineering is the **Yosemite Decimal System**; climbs that require technical expertise and equipment will come under the system's category 5, which breaks down further into classifications from 5.2 to 5.14. An approximate comparison with the UIAA system would be: 5.2–5.9 equals I–VI; 5.10–5.14 equals VI+–X.

Whitewater rafting, kayaking, and canoeing

You'd be hard pressed to find many other regions in the world with as many accessible **whitewater** opportunities as Colorado. There are several fast-moving rivers throughout the state fit for everyone from first-timers to experienced pros. If you fall into the former group, you'll be in need of a river guide; contacts for the best are listed throughout this book.

Colorado's top river for rafting and kayaking is the Arkansas River, the busiest stretch of whitewater in the States thanks to long runs of continuous Class III water as well as the unremitting "Numbers section" or the chunky waves at the base of the Royal Gorge, both Class IV–V. Other rivers worth exploring include the Cache la Poudre, a designated "wild and scenic river" with Class III–V rapids, and the Gunnison.

The whitewater **season** runs from late April through to September, though the early part of this season is for hardened paddlers only as the waters tend to be very fast and very cold. The months of May and June typically see rivers at their highest as a result of spring runoff, making for a faster ride and bigger rapids. Though the water flow decreases in the second half of the season, trips can be just as enjoyable as the warmer waters make for more pleasant swimming and splashing about.

Whether you are on a **raft**, **kayak**, or **canoe**, just getting out onto the water is a thrill, and one that allows you to take in a great deal of natural beauty, spy on wildlife, and often cast a line or two.

Rafting

A major reason behind the popularity of **rafting** is that anyone, including those who have never floated a river before, can participate. It's not unusual for even novice rafters, after a short riverside safety course, to bash through Class III or even occasionally Class IV rapids (see box on p.38 for classifications breakdown) in the hands of a good river guide.

The majority of rafters book their trip through a **commercial outfitter**, who will take care of any necessary **permits** and supply the necessary **safety gear** (life jackets, helmets, and, in cold water conditions, wet suits). Costs for commercial trips vary from $50 for a half-day to around $1500 for a week-long journey, including transport to and from put-in and take-out points and all meals while on the river. It's highly advisable to use a well-established company as their guides will know the river well and are trained in first aid skills.

Various types of craft are used for rafting. **Paddle rafts** are up to 14ft long, hold six to eight paddlers and a guide, and are a heap of fun in rapids. One or two-person inflatable kayaks, known as "rubber duckies," may also be available for more adventurous paddlers who want to take on the rapids alone. **Oar rafts** are up to 22ft long, controlled and paddled with a rear oar and used to transport camping gear and equipment downriver, and are often manned only by a guide and partner.

Kayaking

Many of the rivers used by rafters are also popular with **kayakers**, although on all but the gentlest of rivers kayaking requires a certain amount of experience and the ability to roll the craft. Since kayakers are more likely to ride the river independently, a good knowledge of the river and/or the ability to read river maps are vital. If you're in any

doubt about your ability, go for a rafting trip instead.

Canoeing

Canoeing is a relaxing way to discover calmer waterways and lakes, and most major lakes in Colorado have outfitters who will rent canoes by the hour, half-day, or longer. This quiet and traditional Native American method of water transport allows you to get close to waterfowl, pull up and enjoy picnics on secluded lakeside or riverside beaches, or just get in a nice, low-key workout.

Fishing and hunting

Colorado is a natural draw for **hunters** and **anglers**, with some of the finest stocks of fish and game in the Lower 48. It's impossible to list the best fishing rivers in the state simply because there are so many, but details are given in individual destination accounts throughout this guide. Suffice it to say there are enough "Blue Ribbon" or "Gold Medal" rivers throughout the region to make such terms nearly meaningless. In many places it's possible to fly-fish virtually from the roadside or even within some city centers, and if you're looking for solitude the lakes and rivers of the backcountry will provide infinite variety. Good access sites are often signposted, but don't necessarily assume you can fish anywhere you choose

River classifications

Class I Very easy Small regular waves and riffles. Few or no obstructions and little maneuvering is required.

Class II Easy Waves up to three feet. Wide, clear channels that are obvious without scouting. Low ledges and small rock gardens. Some maneuvering required.

Class III Medium Rapids with numerous high irregular waves capable of swamping an open canoe. Strong eddies. Narrow passages that often require complex maneuvering. May require scouting from shore.

Class IV Difficult Long, difficult rapids with irregular waves, dangerous rocks, boiling eddies, and constricted passages that require precise maneuvering. Scouting from shore is necessary and conditions make rescue difficult. Generally not possible for open canoes.

Class V Very difficult Long, violent rapids with wild turbulence and highly congested routes that must be scouted from shore. Rescue conditions are difficult and there is significant hazard to life in the event of a mishap.

Class VI Limit of navigation and a definite hazard to life.

– some rivers run through private land and permission must be given by the landowner before you cast a line. It's often best to stop in to discuss spots and possible guided tours with a local outfitter; again, these are listed throughout this guide. A seasonal state fishing license costs $56, a one-day license $9, five days $21. The main fishing season is June to October, although it's quite possible to fish year-round in many areas, with certain exceptions on some waters. Ice-fishing is also a popular lake option in winter.

Hunters will find a huge variety of **game**, from waterfowl and game birds to big beasts such as elk, bear, and moose. The main season is from late September to early December, when deer and elk are the big draw, especially on BLM and national forest land. Contact the Colorado Division of Wildlife (☎303/297 1192, ⊛wildlife.state.co.us) for full details of the animal you're interested in tracking down. Note that hunting and fishing licenses are nearly always also available from ranger stations, sporting goods stores, and local outfitters.

Horseback riding, golf, and hot-air ballooning

The pursuit with the longest pedigree in the region is, of course, **horseback riding**. Though some stables will hire horses to experienced riders, more common is a guided trail ride for anything between an hour (costing around $15) to multi-day forays of up to $150 per day. Such guided backcountry trips usually require a party of at least two. For a full immersion into Western life, you might like to spend time at a dude ranch; see p.29.

Golf has also taken off as a popular summertime pursuit. The region has always had its share of good smaller nine- or eighteen-hole public courses, but these have been joined by more expensive world-championship standard courses run by resorts as a summer alternative to skiing. At the height of summer tee times at these courses are booked up to a couple of weeks in advance. A good regionwide publication is *The Guide to Golf in the Rockies* by Breckenridge Publishing Company, which includes full course descriptions, fees, and contact information.

Of all the high-end sports offered in the mountains, the most thrilling, memorable, and expensive is **hot-air ballooning**. Short half-hour flights are the cheapest way to go and will cost from around $100. Most companies, though, aim for a more leisurely experience, with at least an hour of airtime. Flights are offered by Fair Winds in Boulder (☎303/939-9323 ⊛www.fairwindsinc.com), Wild West in Steamboat Springs (☎970/879-7219 or 1-800/748-2487, ⊛www.wildwestballooning.com), Camelot in Vail (☎1-800/785-4743, ⊛www.camelotballoons.com), and the Unicorn Balloon Company in Aspen and Colorado Springs (☎1-800/755-0935 ⊛www.unicornballoon.com). The greatest annual spectacles are the Grand Junction and Crested Butte hot-air balloon festivals.

Winter activities

For many Americans Colorado is a byword for winter sports and certainly its mountains attract more people in winter than in summer. Skiing and snowboarding are of course the most popular activities, but outside Colorado's 25 ski resorts lie a myriad of other opportunities. Here you can strike out alone or in guided groups to explore the backcountry on skis, snowshoes, a snowboard, or a snowmobile, while back in the resort towns you can go ice-skating and outfitters will take on sleigh and dogsled rides. Contacts for many of these activities are listed in the relevant sections of this guide, but the information desks at ski resorts and the local visitor centers can provide many more. More offbeat activities you might go out of your way to seek out include ice-climbing in Ouray and attempting stunts at a winter driving school in Steamboat Springs. A good place to whet your appetite for off-slope winter activities are the Great Outdoor Recreation Pages (GORP; ⓦwww.gorp.com).

Skiing and snowboarding

Choosing between Colorado's 25 **ski resorts** is tricky business, so the *Skiing and snowboarding* color section near the middle of the book has been designed to provide some guidance. Even once you've decided roughly where to head a few further things are worth bearing in mind, since a little advance preparation can save a lot of money, hassle, and even discomfort later on.

Costs

The **cost of skiing** in Colorado, compared to Europe or the US Northeast, is high. The most expensive place is Aspen, where tickets are getting close to the $80 mark for a one-day adult ticket. The typical price of a ticket at the larger resorts is around $65 per day, with kids skiing at around half-price.

There are of course ways you can **save money** on lift tickets. Strategies include scanning the websites of resorts for ticket offers or, once there, checking adverts in local newspapers and supermarkets for deals. The purchase of multi-day tickets will also cut the cost of a day's skiing as will visiting later in the season – killer deals are often offered in April when the snows are excellent but many have lost interest for the year in skiing. Ski packages that bundle lodging and tickets together are also a good way to cut costs, typically offering an overall discount of ten to twenty percent.

Equipment and safety

In contrast to the price of lift tickets, **equipment rental** is much better value and there is keen competition around resorts. Packages for basic skis, poles, and boots start at around $20 per day, though if you are more advanced you'd do well to spend a little more on equipment or even try out a demo package of the latest gear – usually around $40 per day. Rates for renting a board and boots start at around $30. If you plan on taking **lessons**, note that most resorts offer rental gear, a lesson, and lift-ticket packages at a fraction of the cost of the sum of their parts.

Make sure that whatever equipment you end up using **fits properly**. Incorrectly sized ski boots can quickly ruin a day on the slopes: your toes should touch the end of the boot when standing, but not when leaning forward; the buckles around your leg should be cinched as tightly as comfortably possible, while the ones over your foot should just be tightened enough to hold the shape of the boot.

You'll likely need a **credit card** and a **driver's license** or **passport** when renting; a hefty deposit is usually required. Advance online rentals are increasingly encouraged by resorts and larger stores, allowing them to guarantee gear will be available and saving you up to twenty percent per day; book as early as possible for maximum savings. The largest booking engine is at ⓦwww.rentskis .com, used by many of Colorado's larger stores.

In addition to rental equipment you'll also need to buy one or two pieces of gear. The need for **warm clothing** – including gloves, hat, and neck gaiter – is perhaps obvious, but having some form of shaded **eyewear** and **sunscreen** are also priorities. Something else to consider is buying a **helmet**, since it may save your life and will certainly make the crack on the head that you get falling from time to time much more palatable. Even more important than a helmet is having adequate **insurance** in case things do go wrong (see p.45).

Should an **accident** happen, the on-mountain procedure is to cross your skis or place a snowboard above the injured person, post another person higher up the slope to prevent collisions, and ask a passing rider to call for the **ski patrol**. Usually dressed in red jackets with white crosses, these expert skiers, avalanche specialists, and medical technicians deal with hundreds of injuries annually.

Cross-country skiing and snowshoeing

The opportunities for **cross-country (Nordic) skiing** in Colorado are vast, with thousands of miles of trails in national forests and national parks being joined by scores of cross-country ski areas with groomed terrain. These cross-country areas are commonly run alongside downhill-skiing facilities and support the activity with lessons, rentals, and a couple of warming cabins. But despite the attractions of a well-managed and supported network, it's often also worth exploring beyond the environs of busy ski resorts, to accessible locations with more scenic splendor – particularly national park areas like Rocky Mountain or Mesa Verde. Recently there has also been a surge of interest in **hut-to-hut skiing**, exploring a network of trails between backcountry cabins, furnished with enough comforts for a pleasant overnight stay and designed to be stepping stones on a multi-day skiing trip. The popularity of the sport means that reservations for huts such as those in the 10th

Mountain Division hut system (see p.245) must be made at least a month in advance.

A much tamer and less strenuous way to enjoy the backcountry is strapped to a pair of **snowshoes**. Thanks to today's high-tech models, gone are days when walking on these cumbersome items required much skill and practice. Now it's easy and worthwhile to hire a pair from a local ski shop and strike out, exploring empty local forest trails.

Backcountry skiing and boarding

Backcountry skiing takes downhill skiing and cross-country skiing one stage further, the adoption of telemark skiing equipment allowing skiers to both travel cross-country and drop down steep slopes along the way. A difficult skill, telemarking is best learnt in the confines of a resort before it becomes a skill you'd want to depend on in the wilderness. Exploring the backcountry is also understandably popular with snowboarders and downhill skiers. However, making your own way into the backcountry carries with it some grave dangers, particularly from human-triggered avalanches – steep, treeless slopes always pose a serious risk. Under no circumstances should you head into the backcountry without prior instruction, and in most cases a snow shovel and receiver should be taken as well. Colorado is known for **fickle weather**; what starts out as a bright day can turn nasty within minutes; wear sunglasses or goggles and sunscreen and drink plenty of water to guard against sunburn, windburn, and altitude sickness. Those confident of their abilities and backcountry expertise will find conditions to be optimum later in the season when your skills are at their sharpest and snows have firmed up a little, making them easier to walk on as well as diminishing avalanche dangers.

At some resorts, you can access the backcountry from gates on the ski area boundary. Here skiers and riders may exit the area legally to exercise their right to travel on National Forest land. These are usually tucked away, well out of sight of the casual skier, and are often not marked on the trail map. Backcountry riders and skiers are not the responsibility of the ski area, and if there's an accident or one becomes lost, local law enforcement will typically conduct the search-and-rescue at substantial financial expense to the victim.

Should the worst happen and you do get caught in an **avalanche**, attempt to stay on top of the snow by "swimming." Once it slows down, cup your hands in front of your face to create an airpocket. Try not to panic; dribble, and observe the path of your saliva to ascertain which way is up before attempting to dig yourself out.

Whatever your level of backcountry experience you should consult local guides, US Forest Service rangers, ski patrol, or specialist backcountry stores for insider **information** before you head out. If it's your first time off-piste use a professional guide or join a snowcat or helitrip, and then be sure to take an avalanche course. Courses are available throughout North America, offered by local colleges, resort ski patrols, backcountry guide schools, and outdoor sporting goods stores. For listings of these consult the Colorado Avalanche Information Center (ⓦwww .geosurvey.state.co.us/avalanche).

National Parks and other protected lands

The various protected backcountry areas that you'll encounter in Colorado fall into a number of potentially confusing categories, and include several different types of federally administered lands as well as state parks. The three main federal bodies entrusted with overseeing public lands and their use are the National Parks Service (NPS), the Department of Agriculture (USDA), which manages the National Forests via its US Forest Service (USFS), and the Bureau of Land Management (BLM). For an overview of the state's highlights see the color insert in the middle of this book.

National Parks and Monuments

National Parks (ⓦwww.nps.gov) are large, federally controlled and preserved areas of great natural beauty, and most comprise several different features or ecosystems. These are rightly considered to be the country's flagship public lands, showcasing the most spectacular scenery, flora, and fauna in the US. **National Monuments** are also run by the National Parks Service, but the designation is reserved for points of historical interest rather than whole landscapes so they usually include lesser or smaller sites.

Entry fees range from $5–20; if you have plans for repeat visits within a year or you have a few parks on your itinerary, pick up an annual **National Parks Pass** ($50). The pass is good for entry to all national parks and monuments for the pass-holder, spouse, and children, and can be purchased at any National Park entrance station or in advance online at ⓦwww.nationalparks.org. For an additional $15, you can upgrade your pass with a **Golden Eagle Hologram** – this adds free entry to all federal areas, such as National Forest and BLM lands, where an entry fee is charged.

National Forests

Large swathes of Colorado are designated **National Forests** (ⓦwww.fs.fed.us), which enjoy less protection than National Parks: more roads run through them, and limited commercial activities including logging and mining are allowed, subject to government approval. Ski areas also often operate on land leased from the United States Forest Service (USFS). National Forests are managed to be as multipurpose as possible, allowing for the pursuit of a wide array of interests in an attractive environment.

However, these areas tend to be categorized to some extent, with mountain biking only allowed on certain trails, snowmobiles restricted to particular areas, and so forth. Some areas of National Forest, designated **Wilderness Areas**, are however almost as tightly protected as National Parks, with all motorized and mechanized forms of transport banned and many additional local restrictions on camping in force.

Bureau of Land Management

The **Bureau of Land Management** (BLM; ⓦwww.blm.gov) administers some 264 million acres of public land, much of it in the western US. There are fewer restrictions on BLM lands than for National Forests, with most areas open for unrestricted hiking, biking, and even motor sports.

State Parks

As the name suggests, **State Parks** (in Colorado ☎303/866-3437, ⓦwww.parks.state .co.us) are administered by the state rather than the federal government, and tend to be fairly small areas focused on specific features such as lakes and dams used for recreation, or sites of geological or historical importance. **Daily usage fees** for these range from $3 to $5, usually in addition to any overnight camping fee.

 # Travel essentials

Cigarettes and smoking

Smoking is a much-frowned-upon activity in the US and it's really only in a few old-style cowboy saloons that you're likely to come across many smokers at all. However, cigarettes are sold in virtually every grocery store, drugstore, or bar, and also from vending machines. Expect to pay $4–5 for a pack.

Costs

Accommodation is likely to be your biggest single expense while visiting Colorado. It's normal to pay between $45 (£25, €36) and $80 (£44, €64) for anything halfway decent in a city or town, while rates in ski resorts can go much higher. Although some of the larger towns and some resorts have hostels offering dorm beds – usually around $15 (£8.50, €12) – they are by no means everywhere, besides which they save little money for two or more people traveling together. Camping, of course, is cheap, ranging from free to about $20 (£11, €16) a night per site.

As for **food**, $20 (£11, €16) a day is enough for an adequate life-support diet; on a daily total of around $40 (£22, €32) you can dine pretty well. Beyond this, everything hinges on how much sightseeing, drinking, and socializing you do. Much of any of these, and you're likely to go through upwards of $50 (£28, €40) a day.

The rates for **traveling around**, especially on buses, may look inexpensive on paper, but the distances involved mean that costs soon mount up. For a group of two or more, **renting a car** is a very good investment, not least because it enables you to camp or stay in the ubiquitous budget motels along the interstate highways.

Crime, safety, and emergencies

Crime in Colorado is remarkably low: residents of smaller towns boast of being able to leave their doors open day and night, although in downtown Denver the doors are often double-locked and the usual precautions advisable. Wherever you are in the state, by simply being careful, planning ahead, and taking care of your possessions, you should have few real problems.

If you must keep **valuable equipment** in your car, keep it out of sight and locked away in the trunk if at all possible. If toting a bike or ski equipment along, do not leave it unattended for even short periods of time. And in the evenings, bring all your gear into wherever you are staying – both for peace of mind and also to avoid giving burglars any specific targets.

In the event of an **emergency**, dial ☏911 from any telephone to be put in touch with the emergency services – the police, the fire department, and medical.

Disabled travelers

Travelers with mobility problems or other physical **disabilities** are likely to find Colorado to be in tune with their needs. All public buildings must be wheelchair-accessible and have suitable toilets; most city street corners have dropped curbs; and most city buses are able to kneel to make access easier and are built with space and handgrips for wheelchair users. Most hotels, restaurants, and theaters (certainly any built in the last decade or so) have excellent wheelchair access. Public attitudes towards people with disabilities are also in general very positive and helpful.

Citizens or permanent residents of the US who have been "medically determined to be blind or permanently disabled" can obtain the **Golden Access Passport**, a free lifetime entrance pass to those federally operated parks, monuments, historic sites, recreation areas, and wildlife refuges that charge entrance fees (the pass must be picked up in person from the areas described). It also provides a fifty percent discount on fees charged for camping, boat launching, and parking, and the like. The **Golden Bear Pass** (free to the disabled) offers similar concessions to state-run parks, beaches, and historic sites.

The biggest effort to offer the disabled the same opportunities as the fully able has been made by the **National Sports Center for the Disabled** (☏970/726-1540, ⓦwww.nscd.org), based in Winter Park. This accomplished center is best known for its program of instruction for disabled skiers, which has taught more than 45,000 students with either mental or physical disabilities. The resort has also created a program of summertime activities that include rafting, horseback riding, hand crank and tandem biking, rock climbing, and sailing.

Electricity

US **Electricity** is 110V AC, and most plugs are two-pronged. Most foreign-bought equipment won't work properly unless it has a voltage switching provision, common to most power supplies for electrical devices like cameras, laptops, and cell phones – though you'll still need a plug adapter to plug these in.

Entry requirements

Under the **Visa Waiver Scheme**, citizens of Australia, Ireland, New Zealand, South Africa, and the UK visiting the United States for a period of less than ninety days only need a passport and a visa waiver form. The latter will be provided either by your travel agent or by the airline during check-in or on the plane, and must be presented to immigration on arrival. Canadians can travel within the US for an unlimited amount of time without a visa. For customs information, visit ⓦwww .customs.treas.gov.

Gay Colorado

In contrast to the **gay** scene on either US coast, Colorado is a bit under-developed, occasionally even hostile to same-sex liaisons. Particularly in rural areas, gay couples may well attract unwanted attention and will find it in their interest to postpone displays of affection. In the bigger cities, things are far more liberal and almost the entire Colorado gay scene, such as it is, is based in Denver and Boulder, though Aspen, too, has a small scene and is the preferred gay mountain destination. Leading gay publications in Colorado include the biweekly *Out Front* (www.outfrontcolorado.com) and the monthly *Quest*.

Health

Health issues specific to Colorado include **altitude sickness**, although this is unlikely to bring on serious problems. Other common health issues related to the mountain environment include **dehydration/heat stroke** in summer, and **hypothermia** in winter, both of which are easily avoided by drinking plenty of fluids and by wearing a layered system of clothing in the case of the latter.

Encounters with "dangerous" animals are rare and generally easy to avoid. Although **bears** get the bulk of the publicity, moose and snakes kill more people on average each year, and all of these are invariably acting in self-defense. In all cases, by using common sense, making the animal aware of your presence, and avoiding a surprise encounter, you should easily survive your encounter with the wild.

Water quality is excellent throughout the US and it's quite safe to drink from taps. However, while mountain streams may look clean and inviting, water should be chemically treated, boiled, or filtered before you drink it to avoid the risk of *giardia* contamination.

Another small nuisance are **ticks**, which can pass on Colorado Tick Fever and Rocky Mountain Spotted Fever. If you find a tick burrowing into your skin, grab it by the head with a pair of tweezers and gently pull it out. If you experience head and muscle aches, nausea, vomiting, skin rash, or abdominal pain within two weeks, contact a doctor. It's also worth carrying insect repellent for **mosquitoes**, which can get amazingly annoying in the woods in summer.

Foreign visitors should bear in mind that many pills available over the counter at home require a **prescription** in the US – most codeine-based painkillers, for example – and that local brand names can be confusing; ask for advice at the **pharmacy** in any **drugstore**.

ID

Identification should be carried at all times. Two pieces will suffice, one of which should have a photo: a passport and credit card(s)

are your best bets. Not having your license with you while driving may be cause for arrest.

Insurance

Though the worst that befalls most travelers in Colorado is a sunburn or common cold, you will still want the security of health **insurance**. A typical policy usually provides cover for the loss of baggage, tickets, and – up to a certain limit – cash or checks, as well as cancellation or curtailment of your journey. Most exclude so-called **high-risk activities** unless an extra premium is paid: in Colorado, this can mean off-piste skiing and snowboarding, rock climbing, hiking, downhill mountain biking, whitewater rafting, and snowmobiling, though probably not kayaking or regular skiing and snowboarding.

Internet

Internet cafés are found in most towns of any size, though many travelers just use the free access provided by public libraries. A third alternative is to find a commercial photocopying shop such as Kinko's, with locations scattered throughout Colorado. Wireless Internet (WiFi) is fairly widespread; many cafés like *Starbucks* have free "hotspots," as do increasing numbers of motels and hotels.

Kids' Colorado

Children are generally well received all over Colorado, and most attractions go out of their way to entertain kids, and offer discounts on admission. Many restaurants will have a **children's menu**, and it's worth looking out for "family" restaurants where this is a certainty. In any case all but the snootiest gourmet places will be happy to serve children.

Rough Guides travel insurance

Rough Guides, with Columbus Direct, offers its own **travel insurance**, which can be tailored to suit your needs. Readers can choose from many different travel insurance products, and different sports and activities (hiking, skiing, etc) can be covered if required on most policies. Visit our website – ⓦ www.roughguidesinsurance .com – for more information or to purchase. Alternatively, UK residents should call ☏0800/083 9507; US citizens ☏1-800/749-4922; and Australians ☏1-300/669 999. All other nationalities should call ☏+44 870/890 2843.

All **ski areas** are very child-friendly with a considerable amount of thought generally having gone into the provision of day care, lessons, and adventure parks at most of the resorts. That said, although top-notch, many of these facilities are pricey, with ski area day care usually around $80 per day – also the starting price of most lesson and ticket packages.

The **mountain environment** is also on the whole welcoming to children, although a few preventive measures are recommended. To protect from the dehydration of being at altitude give kids water bottles and encourage frequent use. Children also burn more easily than adults, so insure they are slathered in sunscreen and wearing hats and even sunglasses when it's sunny. In cold weather dress the kids in layers of synthetic fabrics – wicking tops and fleeces (which draw water away from the body) – rather than cotton, which provides no insulation when wet.

Laundry

Some of the smartest hotels will provide a **laundry** service, otherwise you'll need to use a self-service laundry. Many motels have these laundries and public are usually easy to find in most towns and cities. Packets of detergent are usually available from dispensers; all told the price of washing and drying a load is around $4.

Living and working in Colorado

Ski resorts and all the attendant businesses surrounding them rely heavily on **temporary workers** – Vail, for example, hires as many as 15,000 people between its four Colorado ski areas (Vail, Beaver Creek, Breckenridge, and Keystone). Recruitment starts in late October, and legal residents or those with work authorization who show up in town during that period should have no problems finding menial work in shops, hotels, or restaurants, although if you have special skills relevant to the service industry or a sport you might find a position in your field. Don't expect to make much more than the minimum wage ($5.15/hr) doing casual work – but at least you'll get a free or heavily discounted ski pass.

Other places to look are equally seasonal. If you have experience you should be able to find a job in the **spring** guiding whitewater rafts, particularly down the Arkansas. In the **summer**, potential employers include the Forest Service, the National Park Service, and Colorado State Parks, where work, particularly looking after campgrounds, can sometimes be picked up. Ski resorts also hire during the summer, though obviously at a lower rate than in the winter. During the **fall** harvest season you may be able to help with the peach and grape harvests in orchards and vineyards around Grand Junction, though it's hot, hard work that's not to be taken lightly.

Mail

Post offices are usually open Monday to Friday from about 9am until 5pm (though some open earlier), and in some cases on Saturday from 9am to noon or later; there are blue **mail boxes** on street corners in cities and the larger towns. **Ordinary mail** within the US costs 39¢ for letters weighing up to an ounce and 24¢ for a postcard; addresses must include the **zip code** (postal code), and a return address should be written in the upper left corner of the envelope. **Air mail** letters from the western US to Europe generally take about a week and cost 84¢; postcards cost 75¢.

Measurements

In the US, distances are in inches, feet, yards, and miles, and weights in ounces, pounds, and tons. American pints and gallons are about four-fifths of imperial ones. A few important conversions to know: 1 mile = 1.609 kilometers; 1 foot = 0.3048 meters.

Money

Regular upheaval in the world **money** markets causes the relative value of the US dollar against other currencies to vary considerably. At press time, one dollar was worth 0.57 British pounds (£); 0.83 Euros (€); 1.54 Canadian dollars (Can$); 1.35 Australian dollars (Aus$); 1.55 New Zealand dollars (NZ$); and 6.19 South African rand.

Most people on vacation simply draw **cash** as needed from automatic teller machines (**ATMs**), which are pretty easy to find, even in far-flung corners of Colorado. A **credit card** is essential; Visa, American Express, and others are accepted all over, and often are necessary for deposits on cars, rental equipment, and the like. If you take **travelers' checks** it's best to have them in **US dollars** as these can be changed in all banks and used as cash in many stores.

Opening hours and public holidays

Shops and services are generally **open** Mon–Sat 8am/9am–5pm/6pm. Many stores are also open on Sundays, and larger towns and cities will invariably have 24hr supermarkets and drugstores. Some places will vary their opening hours according to season: summer is usually considered to run from Memorial Day to Labor Day (late May to early Sept). On the national **public holidays** listed in the box below, banks and offices are liable to be closed all day, as may shops which will otherwise often reduce their hours.

Phones

Public telephones can be found everywhere – on street corners, in train and bus stations, hotels, bars, and restaurants. They take 5¢, 10¢, and 25¢ coins, and the cost of a **local call** from a public phone is usually 35¢. Long-distance calls are pricier, and require plenty of change; you're much better off using a calling card from home.

There are only three **area codes** in use in Colorado (☎303, ☎970, and ☎719), and it is always necessary to include the area code when dialing beyond the local area, even though you may be in the same area code. For directory information call ☎411.

New Year's Day Jan 1
Martin Luther King Jr's Birthday
   Jan 16
Presidents' Day 3rd Mon in Feb
Memorial Day Last Mon in May
Independence Day July 4
Labor Day 1st Mon in Sept
Columbus Day 2nd Mon in Oct
Veterans' Day Nov 11
Thanksgiving Day Last Thurs in Nov
Christmas Day Dec 25

If you're coming from abroad and want to use your **mobile phone**, you'll need to check with your service provider whether this is possible, what it will cost, and how the call charges will work. Unless you have a tri-band phone, it is unlikely that a mobile bought for use outside the US will work inside the States.

Senior travelers

For many **senior citizens**, retirement brings the opportunity to explore the world in a style and at a pace that is the envy of younger travelers. Both Amtrak and Greyhound, as well as many US airlines, offer small reductions on fares to older passengers. Any US citizen or permanent resident aged 62 or over is entitled to free admission to all National Parks, Monuments, and historic sites using a **Golden Age Passport**, for which a once-only $10 fee is charged; it can be issued at any such site, and also gives a 50 percent reduction on fees for camping, parking, and boat launching.

The annual **Golden Bear Pass** ($5 to those 62 and over) offers a fifty percent discount on admission to state-run parks, beaches, and historic sites, subject to a means test. There is also a Senior Citizen Discount (based on proof of age only) giving $1 off parking and $2 off family camping, except where the fee is less than $3.

Before heading out to the mountains, though, it's worth doing your homework on **health** matters. The high altitude of the state in general can aggravate certain conditions: those with heart problems and respiratory conditions should tread carefully above 10,000ft – getting advice from a physician before your trip is best if you are in doubt.

Shopping

DVDs sold in the US have a North American region coding, meaning that they will not work on players designed for other regions.

Clothing sizes are four figures less what they would be in the UK – a British women's size 12 is a US size 8 – while British shoe sizes are 1/2 below American ones for women, and one size below for men.

Remember that a **sales tax** is added to virtually everything you buy in stores except for groceries; see also "Taxes," p.48.

Seniors on the slopes

The **70+ Ski Club** ($10/yr; ☎518/346-5505) organizes trips, prints newsletters biannually, and produces a yearly updated list of ski areas that give discounts or free tickets to over-70s. The **Over The Hill Gang** ($75/yr; ☎719/389-0022, ⓦwww .skiersover50.com) is open to skiers and snowboarders over 50, and organizes group ski days throughout Colorado. Members also receive discounts of up to 35 percent at nearly 100 resorts across North America.

Spectator sports

Colorado has professional **sports teams** playing baseball, basketball, football, and soccer; all are based in **Denver** (see p.75 for more on these teams). A number of towns throughout the state, however, boast collegiate equivalents and the chance to see rival schools going head-to-head in, say, **college football** is not to be missed. The best such example would be a game between Colorado State from Fort Collins (☎970/491-7262 or 1-800/491-7262, ⓦwww.csurams.com) and the University of Colorado from Boulder (☎303/830-8497, ⓦwww.cubuffs.com). Games are typically played on Saturday, and feature cheerleaders, marching bands, and lots of rowdy student fans.

During summer, the quintessential spectator event in the Rockies is the **rodeo** – a unique celebration of cowboy culture, with bad-tempered bulls and bucking broncos ridden by lean, laconic, tobacco-spitting types clad in tight blue Wrangler jeans and plaid shirts. This, happily, is one sporting spectacle that has changed very little over the years, and it remains a true cultural bastion in the Rocky Mountains.

The main events are the spectacular **bullriding** and **bronc-riding** competitions. Each ride is scored according to how hard the animal bucks and how well the cowboy rides – while keeping one hand swinging free in the air at all times. A minimum eight seconds is the time required to earn a score. **Calf-roping** is another crowd favorite, for its combination of daring, skill, and speed. A cowboy pursues the calf on horseback, hurls a lasso around its neck, dismounts at a full run then tackles the animal to the ground before trussing three of its legs together, thus rendering it immobile. Sounds like an afternoon's work, but in fact under ten seconds is considered a good effort.

Cowgirls often feature in the **barrel-riding**, which demands great riding skills as competitors turn tight figure-eights around barrels at a full gallop. Among other events are races and such for kids, the grand tradition of the rodeo being that everyone can be involved. Details of specific rodeos are included in the individual city and town accounts throughout this guide: the **biggest** are at Denver's Western Stock Show, the Greeley Stampede, and at the Colorado State Fair in Pueblo (see p.312). Small but frequently held rodeos can be found at Steamboat Springs (see p.208), while real fans of the sport should visit the Pro Rodeo Hall of Fame in Colorado Springs (see p.281).

Taxes

All airport, customs, and security **taxes** are included in the price of your plane ticket. The state sales tax rate is 2.9%, but additional city and county taxes may be levied upon this.

Temperatures

See "When to go" in the color introduction for a rundown on Colorado's climate. Given in Fahrenheit in the US, **temperatures** can be converted to and from Celsius using the formulas: Celsius = (Fahrenheit-32)x5/9; Fahrenheit = Celsius x9/5+32.

Time

Colorado is on **Mountain Time**, which is an hour ahead of California, two hours behind the US East Coast and seven hours behind Greenwich Mean Time (GMT).

Tipping

Tipping is expected for all bar and restaurant service at a rate between fifteen to twenty percent or so on the bill (unless the service is utterly abominable). About

Travel Talk

Post any of your pre-trip questions – or post-trip suggestions – in *Travel Talk*, our online forum for travelers at ⓦwww.roughguides.com.

B

BASICS | Travel essentials

the same amount should be added to taxi fares. A hotel porter should get roughly $1 for each bag carried to your room. When paying by credit card you're expected to add the tip to the total bill before filling in the amount and signing.

Tourist information

Advance information on Colorado can be obtained from **Colorado Tourism** via ⓦwww.colorado.com, which has lots of information to give a good overview and is also the place to order a free copy of the useful *Colorado Vacation Guide*.

Once you've arrived, you'll find most towns in the region have visitor centers of some description – often the chamber of commerce – as well as a United States Forest Service (USFS) office nearby: all are listed in the Guide. These will give out detailed information on the local area and can often help with finding accommodation. Free newspapers in most areas carry listings of events and entertainment.

Most of the tourist offices mentioned in the Guide can supply you with good **maps**, either free or for a small charge, and, supplemented with our own, these should be enough for general sightseeing and touring. For driving or cycling through rural areas, the *Colorado Atlas & Gazetteer* published by DeLorme ($20) is an invaluable companion, with detailed city plans,

marked campsites, and reams of National Park and Forest information. The American Automobile Association (☎1-866-625-3601, ⓦwww.aaa.com) has offices in most large cities and provides excellent free maps and travel assistance to its members, and to members of affiliate organizations, including the British AA and RAC.

For detailed **hiking maps**, ranger stations in parks and wilderness areas all sell good-quality local maps for $1–3, and camping stores generally have a good selection too. Most bookstores will have a range of local trail guides, the best of which are reviewed in Contexts (see p.426).

Women travelers

Practically speaking, though a **woman traveling** alone is certainly not the attention-grabbing spectacle in Colorado that she might be elsewhere in the world, the odds that you'll come across some sort of harassment are pretty high. In most cases, it won't be any more serious than the odd offensive comment, but it doesn't hurt to take some simple precautions: never hitchhike, especially not alone; avoid public transportation that puts you on buses or at deserted stations at night; and take taxis in cities if you feel uncomfortable in a neighborhood, especially at night.

Guide

Guide

1

Denver

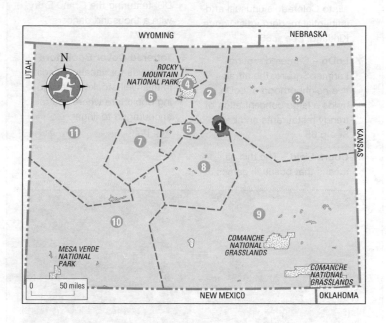

CHAPTER 1 # Highlights

* **Brown Palace Hotel** – This landmark triangular Italian Renaissance-style hotel boasts a magnificent eight-story atrium lobby. See p.60

* **Kirkland Museum** – A treasure trove of twentieth-century decorative arts, this museum is devoted, above all, to Colorado's unusual and influential modern artist Vance Kirkland. See p.65

* **LoDo** – Centered around Larimer Square, the attractive neighborhood of LoDo holds a large concentration of trendy restaurants and bars. See p.65

* **Coors Field** – The thin air means that baseball games are rarely up to much, but the setting – with the Rocky Mountains as the backdrop – and the atmosphere in this wonderful ballpark are spot on. See p.66

* **Denver Pow-Wow** – One of the largest annual Native American gatherings in the US, featuring the Grand Entry, with a thousand dancers. See p.71

* **Tattered Cover Bookstore** – Browse for vacation reading in this well-stocked, easygoing bookstore where you're encouraged to linger. See p.74

△ Denver's downtown skyline

1

Denver

A good six hundred miles from any city of even vaguely similar size, **DENVER** functions as much as a regional hub as it does as Colorado's capital – its area of influence extends well beyond state boundaries. For vacationers it forms the vital gateway to the Rocky Mountains, whose grand peaks lie tantalizingly close to even Denver's downtown. Yet despite nuzzling against mountain foothills and being dubbed the "Mile-High City" for its high elevation, Denver itself is uniformly flat, the majority of its land-hungry urban sprawl subdividing vast tracts of arid plains. In sharp contrast, the compact **downtown** buzzes with an invigorating blend of the last vestiges of a hardworking cattle center and the bustle, energy, and optimism of a town in the grip of the New Economy, where cable, communications, and space industries all play a major part in the money-making process. Here slick skyscrapers rub shoulders with gentrified warehouse districts while surrounding Victorian neighborhoods remain beautifully preserved, their many easy-going tree-lined boulevards linking some of the finest of the two hundred colorful parks that speckle the city.

All this forms a premium urban arena for the overwhelmingly youthful and active **population** of 2.5 million. The fact that a third of Denver's population is under 25 and well over two-thirds under 44 becomes tellingly obvious in the energy that drives the city. Many of these Denverites have moved here from America's East and West coasts, bringing with them urbane tastes as well as an open-minded and tongue-in-cheek appreciation of many of Denver's traditional redneck pleasures. Consequently the city's traditional preoccupations with a proliferation of sports bars, steakhouses, fanatically supported sports teams, and fondness for trucks are counterbalanced by the wildfire spread of sushi bars, gourmet restaurants, jazzy late-night clubs, top-flight arts venues, funky street fairs, and the city's commitment to mass transit. And as Denver redefines itself, a distinctive fusion culture has begun to emerge – as the popularity of the city's **Gay Rodeo** attests.

Some history

Mineral wealth has traditionally been at the heart of Denver's prosperity, with all the fluctuations of fortune that this entails. The town's original founding, in 1858, was pure chance: this was the first spot where small quantities of **gold** were discovered in Colorado. There was no significant river, let alone a road, but prospectors came streaming in anyway, indifferent to prior claims on the land, including those of the **Arapaho**, who had been guaranteed ownership of the area by the Fort Laramie Treaty of 1851. Various local communities had their own names for the settlement, but, with the judicious distribution of whiskey as bribes, one faction persuaded the rest to agree to "Denver" in 1859. Their hope was to ingratiate themselves with territorial governor **James Denver** – who unfortunately had already resigned by the time the name was chosen.

It turned out that there was actually very little gold in Denver itself, and the infant town was swarmed only briefly with disgruntled fortune-seekers, who soon decamped west to Central City after receiving news of a massive gold strike there. Despite this drain on the population, and the various 1860s fires and floods that all but destroyed the place, Denver survived tenaciously as a **supply town**, prospering further with the discovery of **silver** in the nearby Rocky Mountains. The lure of wealth led all sorts of shady characters to make Denver their home, including Jefferson "Soapy" Smith, who acquired his nickname by selling bars of soap at extortionate prices under the pretense that some contained $100 bills.

Once strengthened in its role as supply center for the mountains and market for the prairies of Colorado and Wyoming, Denver outflanked Central City and Golden to become the **state capital** in 1867. When the first railroads bypassed Denver in the late 1860s – the death knell for so many other communities – the citizens banded together and built their own connecting spur. This in turn drew ranchers, who used the rail lines to get their product off to market. By the 1880s, **cattle** had become as important, if not more, than mining, and within fifty years gigantic stockyards would dominate much of the cityscape.

In the first half of the twentieth century Denver consolidated its image of the quintessential cow-town, replete with the pool halls, saloons, and flophouses that Jack Kerouac enthusiastically championed in *On the Road*. Over the next few decades the city polished itself up somewhat, thanks to the attentions of the **oil** and **gas industry**, whose drilling operations in the region were profitable until the oil recession hit in the mid-1980s. Nonetheless, Denver residents continued to improve their city, electing the charismatic Federico Peña as the city's first Hispanic mayor in 1983. After taking office, Peña embarked upon an adventurous investment program, persuading citizens to pay more taxes and developing some extravagant infrastructure, including the foundation for the ultramodern **Denver International Airport**.

An era of great growth followed. As prices and congestion on the coasts began to encourage industry and people to **relocate**, Denver began to be perceived as a real alternative, at once modern and cosmopolitan while also offering an outdoor lifestyle that had become fashionable among college graduates. Consequently, the 1990s saw up to two thousand (overwhelmingly young) people per week migrate into the area, doubling the population to well over two million. This decade's **tech boom** also brought a cash injection, much of which was used to regenerate downtown: warehouses became galleries, chic bars, bookshops, and restaurants, while further construction produced an atmospheric **ballpark** for the Colorado Rockies and a new **stadium** for football's hugely popular Denver Broncos. But success came at a cost – namely soaring real estate prices, suburban sprawl, and heavy traffic.

Yet most consider it a reasonable price to pay for the brisk **transformation** of a flagging cow-town and declining oil-center into one of America's most attractive and well-put-together cities. Certainly the populace is unwilling to rest on its laurels, with a dynamic interest in courting progress and change typifying the attitudes of most citizens. This positive energy has backed a good number of civic initiatives, not least the city's deep commitment to creating a first-rate mass transit system. Denver has also been at the forefront of a nationwide attempt to deal with the problems of homelessness, with the current mayor, **John Wright Hickenlooper**, a tireless campaigner for the cause.

Arrival and information

The colossal, high-tech **Denver International Airport** (☎303/342-2000 or 1-800/247-2336, ☺www.flydenver.com) lies on the plains 24 miles northeast of downtown, its dramatic tented roof of Teflon-coated fiberglass fashioned into peaks resembling the Rocky Mountains. Shuttle trains connect its three vast concourses with the main terminal and baggage-claim areas, which are sensibly located alongside the numerous transport options into the city.

The cheapest way into town is on one of Skyride's **buses**, which run to downtown's Market Street Station (daily 7am–1am; 55min; $8 one-way/$14 round-trip); they depart from just outside exit 506 at the eastern end of the Central Concourse and from exit 511 at its western end. A bit more expensive are **shuttle** buses, which head to a number of downtown locations (45min); one is Super Shuttle (☎303/370-1300 or 1-800/525-3177, ☺www.supershuttle .com), which runs around $18 per person. This is about half of what you'll pay for one of the **taxis** that leave from in front of the arrivals area.

All the major **car rental** companies have kiosks within the terminals near baggage claim. It's worth noting, however, that car rental can be considerably less expensive if you rent in town and not at the airport, where various supplemental "facility usage fees" are added to prices. Some cheaper local firms without terminal outposts will pick you up if you phone ahead. The only road into the airport connects with Hwy-C470, which heads south to I-70, the main interstate that runs downtown before continuing west into the mountains. When driving into downtown, stick to I-70 until it intersects with I-25 and take the latter south into the city. There's plenty of paid **parking** downtown (typically around $14 a day) in both open lots and garages.

Amtrak **trains** arrive at the grand nineteenth-century **Union Station**, 1701 Wynkoop St (☎303/825-2583), within easy walking distance of downtown, while Greyhound buses pull into the **Denver Bus Terminal**, 1055 19th St, at Arapaho (☎303/293-6555). Both are in safe areas.

For **information**, stop by the Official Visitor Information Center, conveniently located downtown at 1600 California St (Mon–Fri 9am–6pm, Sat 9am–5pm, Sun 11am–3pm; ☎303/892-1505 or 1-800/233-6837, ☺www .denver.org), with its main entrance on pedestrian-only 16th Street. Besides running an accommodation reservation service, the center offers some useful magazine-style visitor guides as well as *The Mile High Trail*, good for a self-guided **tour** of Denver's historic downtown; they also run free guided walking tours from June through August (Mon–Sat, call number above for times; 2hr).

Getting around

Negotiating downtown Denver **on foot** is pretty straightforward, though the free **buses** (daily 6am–1am) that run for a mile up and down the 16th Street Mall at the heart of the city's grid-like street pattern are hard to pass up. RTD, Denver's excellent public transportation network (☎303/229-6000, ☺www .rtd-denver.com), also runs pay-to-ride buses ($1.25); frequent services to the various sports stadia and airport leave from the underground **Market Street Station** at Market and 16th. The bus network is supplemented by a **light railway** (same local fares as buses), whose **green D Line** runs from Littleton in the southwest across the 16th Street Mall and up to Five Points in the northeast; while the **orange C Line** begins behind Union Station, then loops around

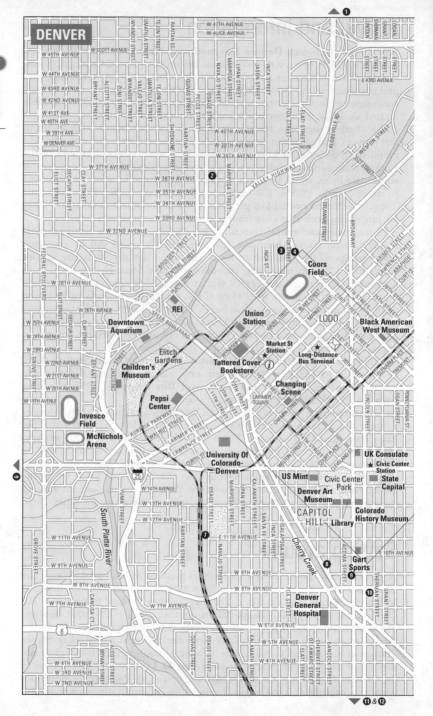

DENVER

W 47TH AVENUE
W ALICE AVENUE
W 45TH AVENUE
W SCOTT AVENUE
E 43RD AVENUE
W 44TH AVENUE
W 43RD AVENUE
W 42ND AVENUE
W 41ST AVE
W 40TH AVE
W 39TH AVE
W DENVER AVE
W 40TH AVENUE
W 39TH AVENUE
W 38TH AVENUE
W 37TH AVENUE
W 36TH AVENUE
W 35TH AVENUE
W 34TH AVENUE
W 33RD AVENUE
W 32ND AVENUE

Coors Field

REI

Union Station

LODO

Downtown Aquarium

Black American West Museum

W 28TH AVENUE
W 26TH AVENUE
W 25TH AVENUE
W 24TH AVENUE
W 23RD AVENUE
W 22ND AVENUE
W 21ST AVENUE
W 20TH AVENUE
W 19TH AVENUE

Market St Station

Elitch Gardens

Children's Museum

Tattered Cover Bookstore

Long-Distance Bus Terminal

Pepsi Center

Larimer Square

Changing Scene

Invesco Field

McNichols Arena

University Of Colorado-Denver

UK Consulate

Civic Center Station

W 14TH AVENUE
W 13TH AVENUE
W 12TH AVENUE
W 11TH AVENUE
W 9TH AVENUE
W 8TH AVENUE
W 7TH AVENUE
W 4TH AVENUE
W 3RD AVENUE
W 2ND AVENUE

US Mint

Denver Art Museum

Civic Center Park

State Capital

CAPITOL HILL

Colorado History Museum

Library

South Platte River

Cherry Creek

Gart Sports

Denver General Hospital

58

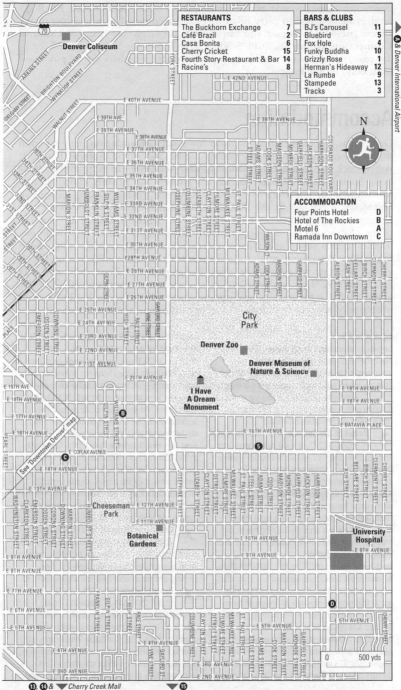

RESTAURANTS

The Buckhorn Exchange	7
Café Brazil	2
Casa Bonita	6
Cherry Cricket	15
Fourth Story Restaurant & Bar	14
Racine's	8

BARS & CLUBS

BJ's Carousel	11
Bluebird	5
Fox Hole	4
Funky Buddha	10
Grizzly Rose	1
Herman's Hideaway	12
La Rumba	9
Stampede	13
Tracks	3

ACCOMMODATION

Four Points Hotel	D
Hotel of The Rockies	B
Motel 6	A
Ramada Inn Downtown	C

Denver Coliseum

& Denver International Airport

N

City Park

Denver Zoo

Denver Museum of Nature & Science

I Have A Dream Monument

See "Downtown Denver map"

Cheeseman Park

Botanical Gardens

University Hospital

0   500 yds

13, 14 & ▼ Cherry Creek Mall   ▼ 15

downtown's western side before joining the D Line to Littleton. All RTD services are designed to carry bikes (free) and accommodate wheelchair users.

From late-May to August, you can also ride the Grey Line-operated **Cultural Connection Trolley** (8.30am–5.30pm; hourly; $16 for 1-day pass; $25 for 2-day pass), which links Denver's main points of interest; passes can be purchased (cash only) on the trolleys.

Accommodation

Denver has a good selection of downtown **accommodation**, ranging from simple hostels and motels to homey B&Bs and grand historic hotels. If you're stuck, the Visitor Information Center (see p.57) can help with reservations. Some cheaper options, particularly **motels** and **hostels**, cluster around somewhat seedy but relatively safe Colfax Avenue, within walking distance of downtown. More motels, mostly chains, are located further out on Colfax and alongside many of Denver's major cross-town highways, as well as northeast of the city, around the defunct Stapleton Airport. Many of these provide free shuttles to downtown and Denver International. Highway 6, the most direct route from downtown to the mountains, has also attracted a few motels. If you're desperate to **camp**, the drab *Camping Denver North*, I-70 exit 229 (☎303/622-9274 or 1-800/562-6538, ⊛www.campdenver.com; RVs $29–36, tents $20–22), is the most central option – but you'd do better heading twenty miles out of town to Boulder, Golden, or further into the mountains.

Hostels

Denver International Youth Hostel 630 E 16th Ave ☎303/832-9996, ⊛www.youthhostels .com/denver. Located in a dodgy area four blocks from the capitol building, this is Denver's cheapest option. You certainly get what you pay for, as the $9 dorm beds are cramped, grotty, and worn-out. Office hours daily 8–10am & 6–9pm.

Hostel of the Rockies 1717 Race St ☎303/861-7777, ⊛www.innkeeperrockies .com. Friendly and well-run 50-bed hostel – easily Denver's best – a 20min walk east of the capitol down seedy Colfax Ave to a far better part of town, with free and safe street parking. The hostel has all the usual facilities, like laundry, kitchen, and TV room, and dorm beds go for $17 a night. Private rooms ($35) are in a separate building five blocks from the hostel. On Fridays sociable cookouts take place in the back garden.

Melbourne Hostel 607 22nd St ☎303/292-6386, ⊛www.denverhostel.com. Located in a stylish but run-down former hotel, this hostel is an easy – if not all that safe – 5-min walk northeast of downtown. Beds in clean dorm rooms (sleeping up to six) cost $16 ($13 members and students), with a three-night maximum stay in summer, when reservations are advised. Many of the rooms are private singles ($27/$23 members and students) and doubles ($35/$32), some with their own bathroom.

Hotels, motels, and B&Bs

Adam's Mark Hotel 1550 Court Place ☎303/893-3333, ⊛www.adamsmark.com. This giant, 1200-room luxury hotel has somewhat pokey rooms – but they're a small price to pay for the stellar location fronting the 16th St Mall. The facilities are first-rate and include complimentary broadband Internet, a fitness center, steam room, outdoor heated pool, and a sundeck. **❼**

Best Western Stapleton Hotel 3535 Quebec St ☎303/333-7711 or 1-800/328-2268 ⊛www .bestwestern.com. Standard chain hotel off I-70 and convenient for the airport (shuttle costs $8). Facilities include an indoor swimming pool, hot tub, and exercise area that opens onto a courtyard with gazebo and picnic tables. **❹**

Broadway Plaza Motel 111 Broadway ☎303/893-0303. Within walking distance of downtown, this plain but friendly motel has large, clean rooms (with phones and cable TV), free parking, and reasonable daily and weekly rates. **❹**

Brown Palace Hotel 321 17th St ☎303/297-3111 or 1-800/321-2599, ⊛www.brownpalace.com. Beautifully maintained downtown landmark that's been in continuous operation since 1892. The Italian Renaissance-style structure has elegant dining rooms and a common area based around a sunlit, eight-story atrium lobby with tiers of iron railings. It's worth popping in even if not staying to marvel at the crafts-manship and to relax in the comfortable leather armchairs strewn about. This luxurious and solid feel finds continuity in the generously sized and well-maintained rooms. ❽

Capitol Hill Mansion 1207 Pennsylvania St ☏303/839-5221 or 1-800-839-9329, ⓦwww.capitolhillmansion.com. This luxurious B&B, housed in a turreted Victorian sandstone mansion built shortly before the 1890s silver crash, is located on a leafy street near the state capitol. Each of its eight antique-furnished rooms are delightful, and several include large whirlpool tubs. ❻

Comfort Inn Downtown 401 17th St ☏303/296-0400 or 1-800/237-1431, ⓦwww.comfortinn.com. The central location, along with a skywalk connecting it to the *Brown Palace Hotel*'s elegant restaurants and lounges, arguably makes this the best downtown bargain. Continental breakfast included. ❺

Four Points Hotel Denver Cherry Creek 600 S Colorado Blvd ☏303/757-3341, ⓦwww.fourpoints.com/denvercherrycreek. Inexpensive Sheraton hotel located five miles out of the city center. Amenities include a heated outdoor pool, restaurant, lounge, and courtesy shuttle to several downtown locations; also the Cherry Creek Mall (see p.74) is within walking distance. ❹

Hampton Inn DIA 6290 Tower Rd ☏303/371-0200 or 1-800/426-7866, ⓦwww.hamptoninn.com. One of several functional hotels a short ride from the Denver International, and fine for a one-night stay before moving on to the mountains; the airport shuttle is free, as are the cereal, pastries, and terrible coffee that make up the continental breakfast. ❺

Hotel Teatro 1100 14th St ☏303/228-1100 or 1-888/727-1200, ⓦwww.hotelteatro.com. Housed in the renovated 1911 Tramway Tower, this sophisticated downtown business hotel is stylishly themed around the theater, with performance photos and props scattered among chic Art Deco furnishings. High-ceilinged and furnished with cherrywood and cream linens, the rooms include

high-speed Internet, fax, copiers, and scanners, and grant access to a small fitness center. ❼

Luna Hotel 1612 Wazee St ☏303/572-3300, ⓦwww.thelunahotel.com. Small and sleek luxury LoDo hotel where a personal feel is combined with modern minimalist decor and swish high-tech conveniences such as in-room DVD players and WiFi throughout. Some rooms have balconies, others whirlpool tubs, all are non-smoking and share access to an exercise room. ❻

Motel 6 12020 E 39th Ave, at Peoria ☏303/371-1980. Located off I-70's exit 281, this plain and cheap motel is well outside of the downtown core, but a free shuttle service is available. A second branch of the *Motel 6*'s spartan chain (☏303/232-4924) is located west of downtown alongside Hwy-6. ❸

Oxford Hotel 1600 17th St ☏303/628-5400 or 1-800/228-5838 ⓦwww.theoxfordhotel.com. This stately abode is, along with the *Brown Palace*, one of the few nineteenth-century hotels to have survived in Denver. Its simple red sandstone exterior conceals generous marble interiors replete with stained-glass, stylish frescoes, and silver chandeliers. Rooms are either Art Deco or Victorian and furnished with European antiques. Rates include free access to nearby health club with spa and sauna. ❽

🏃 **Queen Anne Inn** 2147 Tremont Place ☏303/296-6666 or 1-800/432-4667, ⓦwww.queenannebnb.com. Central and hospitable nineteenth-century B&B overlooking a small park and pretty back garden (where breakfast can be eaten). A few of the fourteen individually decorated rooms contain extravagant murals, while others are themed after a particular artist (Calder, Remington, Rockwell). The "Rooftop Room" has the most decadent feature – an outdoor hot tub overlooking Denver's skyline. ❻

Ramada Inn Downtown 1150 E Colfax Ave ☏303/831-7700 ⓦwww.ramada.com. Good-value, straightforward motel on seedy East Colfax. The location is handy for both downtown and City Park, and facilities include a heated outdoor pool and hot tub. ❺

The City

Though a hectic spate of high-rise construction a few decades ago means that **downtown Denver** is barely recognizable as the Gold Rush town of old, it's still easy – on a map at least – to pick out its oldest section. It's the area which, in a city that stretches for miles in a regimental grid, stands at a sharp angle to the rest. Cutting diagonally through downtown's tightly packed streets is **16th Street**, where much of Denver's day-to-day activity is centered. Except for the free buses that run its length, 16th is a pedestrian zone and a fine place to wander, window-shop, or have a bite to eat. Since the mall is given over largely to dining and

DOWNTOWN DENVER

DENVER | The City

ACCOMMODATION		RESTAURANTS, BARS & CLUBS			
Adam's Mark Hotel	**H**	Bayou Bob's	**14**	Jr's La Rumba	**20**
Broadway Plaza		Breckenridge Brewery	**6**	Kevin Taylor's Restaurant	**C**
Motel	**J**	Brendan's	**9**	Mercury Cafe	**12**
Brown Palace Hotel	**G**	Bump and Grind	**17**	Ogden	**25**
Capitol Hill Mansion	**K**	Charlie's	**24**	The Palace Arms	**G**
Comfort Inn		The Church	**23**	Polly Esther's	**7**
Downtown	**E**	Colorado Triangle, Inc.	**13**	Rocky Mountain Diner	**11**
Denver International		Cruise Room Bar	**A**	Sancho's Broken Arrow	**22**
Youth Hostel	**I**	Delhi Darbar	**4**	The Soiled Dove	**8**
Hotel Teatro	**C**	Denver Chophouse	**1**	Taki's	**19**
Luna Hotel	**B**	Duffy's Shamrock	**16**	Tom's Diner	**21**
Melbourne Hostel	**D**	El Azteca	**15**	Vesta Dipping Grill	**5**
Oxford Hotel	**A**	El Chapultepec	**10**	Wazee Supper Club	**3**
Queen Anne Inn	**F**	The Grand	**18**	Wynkoop Brewing Co.	**2**

shopping, you'll need to head southeast to the **Capitol Hill District** or west to the refurbished warehouses of **LoDo** to see anything of note. On Denver's western fringes, beyond the dignified Union Station, an old area of railroad sidings has been transformed into trendy lofts, many of which overlook the **South Platte River**. A pleasant riverside path links some of the larger downtown attractions, including an aquarium, a children's museum, and two stadiums.

Capitol Hill District

Beginning at a gathering of mighty municipal buildings around Civic Center Park, the diverse square-mile-sized **Capitol Hill District**, one of Denver's oldest and best-preserved neighborhoods, stretches out from the southeast corner of downtown. Its name comes from the presence of the State Capitol, one of a group of buildings gathered around the park that include the Denver **history** and **art museums** and the **US Mint**. The area's northern fringe is defined by bedraggled Colfax Avenue, a busy stretch where some of the city that Kerouac wrote of still persists: woebegone transients stagger between bars and pawn shops, yet the road is generally safe and always entertaining. South of here is the heart of Capitol Hill, a leafy and well-preserved Victorian quarter, home to the **Molly Brown House** and **Vance Kirkland**'s old art studio, now a museum.

Civic Center Park and the State Capitol

Lassoed by several hectic roads, **Civic Center Park** is a bit too noisy to be relaxing, even though its Neoclassical follies and small grassy areas try to lure hurrying passers-by to take a break. Though the park serves as a useful venue for many Denver celebrations, its over-
whelming purpose
seems to be to
provide a fitting
frontispiece for, at
its eastern edge,
the dignified **State
Capitol** (Mon–Fri
7am–5.30pm). For
a quick apprecia-
tion of Denver's
geographical posi-
tion, climb to the
capitol's thirteenth
step on the way
up to the entrance
– exactly one mile
above sea level
– then turn back
and look west for
a commanding
view of the Rock-
ies. The capitol is
a rather predict-
able copy of the
national one in
Washington, DC,

△ State Capitol

but with the novelty that almost all the building's materials are indigenous to the state, including the pretty red onyx, of which the world's entire supply is located in Colorado. Free, pleasantly informal **tours** begin on the half-hour and hour from 9.30am to 3.30pm, and include an ascent into the dome for an even better view of the city and mountains.

Colorado History Museum

One block southwest of the capitol, the most interesting features of the **Colorado History Museum**, 1300 Broadway (Mon–Sat 10am–5pm, Sun noon–5pm; $5; Ⓦ www.coloradohistory.org), are found in its lower galleries. Here, several intricate dioramas, made under the auspices of the Works Project Administration (WPA) in the 1930s, show state historical scenes in fascinating detail, starting with the Anasazi of Mesa Verde and continuing with trappers meeting with Indians at an early 1800s "fair in the wilderness." An exhaustive photographic archive of the early West showcases the work of W.H. Jackson, and there's a model of Denver as it appeared in 1860, before it was leveled by fires and floods a few years later.

Denver Art Museum

Just west of the History Museum and the impressively modern and well-equipped Public Library lies the glass-tiled **Denver Art Museum**, 100 W 14th Ave (Tues & Thurs–Sat 10am–5pm, Wed 10am–9pm, Sun noon–5pm; tours Tues–Fri & Sun 1.30pm, Sat 11am & 1.30pm; $8; Ⓦ www.denverart museum.org). It has a solid collection of paintings from around the world, but is most noteworthy for its superb examples of Native American arts and crafts. Items includes pieces from over a hundred different tribes, include marvelous beadwork by Plains tribes and some finely detailed Navajo weavings. The pre-Columbian Central American art – particularly the extraordinary Olmec miniatures – is also spectacular.

Vastly more of the museum's holdings will soon be on show in the monumental **New Hamilton Wing**, opening in October of 2006 and increasing the museum's available space by half. Three years in the making, the new wing was designed by Daniel Liebeskind, original architect (before plans were sent back to the drawing board due to security concerns) of the Freedom Tower, which was to be built where New York's World Trade Center once stood. Liebeskind's first building in the US, the shape of the wing – a jagged pile of vast shattered slabs – was partly inspired by the craggy Rockies cliffs which greeted the architect as he flew into town, but more so, as he put it, by "the wide-open faces of the people of Denver."

US Mint

A block north of the Art Museum is the **US Mint**, 320 Colfax Ave (Mon 9am–3pm, Tue–Fri 8am–3pm; free; Ⓣ 303/405-4761, Ⓦ www.usmint.gov), one of four mints around the US – the others are in Philadelphia, San Francisco, and West Point, New York – that, taken together, produce all of the US coins in circulation. On one of the free tours given on the hour every hour, you'll get to see millions of fresh coins gushing from presses in a flurry of flashing metal. Greedy fantasies are checked, however, once you notice the machine-gun turrets on the exterior, mounted here in the depth of the money-hungry Depression.

Molly Brown House

A sight of a less governmental stripe is the proud Victorian **Molly Brown House**, two blocks southeast of the capitol building at 1340 Pennsylvania Ave

(Tues–Sat 10am–3.30pm, Sun noon–3.30pm; $6.50; ⓦwww.mollybrown.org). The "unsinkable" Molly Brown was famous for surviving the capsizing of the *Titanic* (she'd already lived through a typhoon in the Pacific) and lauded for her money-raising efforts on behalf of the shipwreck's poor immigrant survivors and their families. A penniless Irish girl who went West to marry a millionaire, she ended up mixing with high society in Denver, became a suffragette, and eventually ran (though unsuccessfully) for the US Senate in 1914. Unfortunately, the 45min **tours** (on the hour and half hour) of the 1880s house concentrate more on what the Browns owned and what the preservationists have managed to authenticate rather than on illuminating the woman's extraordinary life.

Kirkland Museum of Fine & Decorative Art

On the same block as the Molly Brown House lies the low-slung red-brick **Kirkland Museum of Fine & Decorative Art**, 1311 Pearl St (Tues–Sun 1pm–5pm; tours Thurs, Fri & Sat 1.30pm; $6; ☎303/832-8576, ⓦwww .kirklandmuseum.org). Denver's oldest commercial gallery and one of its best small museums, the building was constructed in 1910, serving in its first year as painter Vance Kirkland's **studio**. Parts of the studio have been preserved and reconstructed to show how the artist worked, including the harness that he used to dangle over his gigantic canvases. Naturally the museum is an excellent place to see originals from the artist's different and highly distinctive periods, but it's also a great place to browse a lively medley of **decorative art** chaotically packed into half a dozen different rooms. The two thousand or so objects here cover a range of twentieth-century styles, from Bauhaus sofas to Art Deco ceramics, with Art Nouveau, Wiener Werkstätte, and De Stijl also well represented.

Botanic Gardens

On the very eastern edge of the Capitol Hill District, adjacent to Cheeseman Park and a twenty-minute walk from the Kirkland Museum, lie Denver's tranquil **Botanic Gardens**, 1005 York St (May to mid-Sept Tues–Sat 9am–8pm, Sun & Mon 9am–5pm, mid-Sept to April daily 9am–5pm; $8.50; ☎720/865-3500, ⓦwww.botanicgardens.org). Spreading over 23 immaculately tended acres, the gardens celebrate horticultural diversity via small themed areas which include a Japanese garden, herb, water, and fragrance areas, and one garden inspired by the paintings of Monet. One of the main highlights is the Tropical Conservatory, where a riot of verdant undergrowth thrives within the confines of a concrete and plexiglass dome. Of greater local interest, however, is the alpine rock garden, where the explanations of Rocky Mountain flora are useful to help the mountain-bound bone up on nature.

LoDo and around

Immediately northwest of Denver's soaring downtown, the stocky brick buildings of the Lower Downtown neighborhood, universally known as **LoDo**, present a far more cheerfully human scale. Here, on the lower lands that slope toward the adjacent Cherry Creek and South Platte River – in between Wynkoop, Larimer, 14th, and 20th streets – is where Denver began and where much of what made it into a regional hub took place.

One of LoDo's main focal points is **Larimer Square**. It was here, where the intersections of Market and 14th and 15th streets now lie, that William Larimer built Denver's original four log cabins in 1858, with doors made out of coffin lids. Many of the buildings in this area were the first in town to be built with bricks, and also the first to be restored in the late 1980s when the warehouses

Vance Kirkland

Beneath the thick-set glasses and unassuming appearance of **Vance Kirkland** (1904–1981) lay a uniquely sparkling and visionary mind. His Directorship of Denver University's School of Art lent him a freedom from financial pressure, enabling him to paint as he pleased. This found him exploring and pioneering several **surreal** and **expressionist** styles, which despite his artistic isolation in Denver, took his work to exhibitions across the USA and Europe.

Kirkland moved from Cleveland, Ohio – where he had failed his first year watercolor class – to Denver, where he stayed and painted until his death 53 years later. During this time his work divides into five distinctive painting **periods**, all of which share a distinctive energy: Designed Realism (1926–1944), Surrealism (1939–1954); Abstractions From Nature (1947–1957); Abstract Expressionism (1950–1964); and The Dot Paintings (1963–1981).

His experiences in the Rockies particularly inspired his **Surrealist** period. While mountain climbing, Kirkland became particularly fascinated with the cycle of life as vividly displayed by plants growing out of rotting deadwood. He played with these eerie shapes often bringing the dead vegetation back to life – giving a root or tree eyes, legs or claws, wings to fly or perform a ghostly dance. The sad carnage of World War II inspired Kirkland to bring humans into his art as naked cavemen to underscore society's lack of progression beyond our savage, pre-historic ancestors.

Even more lively and inspiring are Kirkland's **cosmic paintings**. Painting in an era well before proper space exploration he portrayed far away galaxies and nebulae as brilliant abstractions – incorporating ideas of energy, vast distances, long durations of time, and mysteries of outer space. Kirkland explained his fascination with time and space in inquisitive and abstract ways: "I think a great deal about what could have happened and how little we know about the universe in which we live, and the fragment of time that can be called known history of this earth. ... I am trying to paint something I do not know exists in a tangible way... If I am looking at space, who is going to say it never existed? It has existed in my mind."

Just as Kirkland invented his own cosmos, the challenge of depicting these extra-terrestrial surfaces and colliding, kinetic worlds in the grip of nuclear fission drove him to invent his own **techniques** and **media**. Working as a master watercolor painter he found a mix of oil and water gave a textured, cratered, alien appearance to his paintings and mixing his watercolors with denatured alcohol produced strange resist patterns. Finally Kirkland began to use dots of oil paint on wooden dowels to further break up the surface and to interact with the oil and water forms underneath. These techniques produced work quite unlike that of any other abstract expressionist.

and goods yards here began to be revitalized. Artists began the process by using these warehouses as studios and galleries, so that by the early 1990s gentrification was spreading rapidly.

Today, with much of the late-Victorian appearance restored and enhanced with plenty of colorful awnings and hanging flower baskets, there are few studios and galleries left, as the area has become a high-rent district dotted with specialty shops, restaurants, and bars. This has made it the city's premier district for after-hours carousing – and for celebrating the victories of Major League Baseball's Colorado Rockies (see p.75), who play in the lovely **Coors Field**, which combines state of the art facilities with a relaxing vibe and fine views of the mountains. Informative 75min **tours** of the ballpark, on the district's northeast side (Mon–Sat 10am–2pm every half-hour, 10am & 2pm on game days; $6; ✆ 303/762-5437), include a peep into the press boxes, clubhouses, and dugouts. The tours are interesting enough, though a distant second to actually seeing a game.

Black American West Museum

A five-minute walk northeast of LoDo is Denver's most prominent African-American neighborhood, the old Five Points District, created in the 1870s to house black railroad workers. Here, the **Black American West Museum**, 3091 California St (May–Sept daily 10am–5pm; Oct–April Wed–Sun 10am–2pm; $6; ☎303/292-2566, Ⓦwww.blackamericanwest.org), tells the story of black pioneers and outlaws in the Old West, including the myth-debunking fact that one-third of all cowboys were black, many of them slaves who had been freed after the Civil War.

Along the South Platte River

Along the **South Platte River** on the west side of town are a number of Denver's larger, and particularly child-orientated, attractions, as well as two of the town's stadiums. All these are connected to each other and downtown via either light rail (C Line) from Union Station or the **Platte River Trolley** (April–May & Sept–Oct Fri–Sun noon–3.30pm, June–Aug Thurs–Sun noon–3.30pm; $3; Ⓦwww.denvertrolley.org). The latter runs parallel to the Platte River Greenway, a 30-mile riverside **bike path** that cuts north-south through town and forms the backbone of Denver's 400-mile-long cycle trail network. Linked to the path beside the REI outdoors store is the Cherry Creek bike path, which heads four miles southeast to the eponymous mall. See the listings on p.76 for bike rental information.

Downtown Aquarium

As commercial and tacky as it is slick, the **Downtown Aquarium**, 700 Water St (Sun–Thurs 10am–10pm, Fri & Sat 10am–11pm; before 6pm $13, after 6pm $10, parking $5; ☎303/561-4450, Ⓦwww.downtownaquariumdenver.com), explores several different aquatic ecosystems with mixed results. Thanks to tunnels and glass ceilings you'll get to view the fish from all angles, and then wander through theatrical-style sets that portray more exotic locales: a seaside,

△ Downtown Aquarium

a wharf, a coral reef, and – with the help of a robotic orangutan and some real tigers – a rainforest. Despite these unconvincing (and somewhat incongruous) sideshows, the aquarium is worthwhile for its extravagant and imaginative tanks, containing a multitude of sea life from tiny seahorses to brooding sharks. Kids might love hanging around with the aquarium's cuddly and upbeat mascot Sharkey and touching manta rays, but adults may well rather forgo the whole experience and simply escape to the quirky cocktail bar or novel restaurant, whose walls are lined by magnificent aquariums.

The Children's Museum, Elitch Gardens, and Water World

If you're in Denver with kids there are three addresses you should seriously consider visiting. The least expensive is the **Children's Museum of Denver**, 2121 Children's Museum Drive (Mon–Fri 9am–4pm, Sat & Sun 10am–5pm; $7; ☎303/433-7444, ⓦwww.mychildsmuseum.org), which successfully blends education with fun. Here, interactive "Playscapes," including a fire station and a supermarket, use an element of role play to engage young children – almost like being in a life-size Lego playset.

An even bigger hit with kids is the nearby **Six Flags Elitch Gardens** theme park, 2000 Elitch Circle (June–Sept daily 10am–10pm; Oct–May irregular hours; $38, parking $9; ☎303/595-4386, ⓦwww.sixflags.com), where around forty rides, including the white-knuckle *Mind Eraser*, which catapults you at 60mph through terrifying corkscrew loops, and a water park are included in the (admittedly high) price of admission.

If water park is going to be the main attraction, though, you'd do best to head straight out to the vast **Water World** (late May to early Sept daily 10am–6pm; $28; ☎303/658-7618, ⓦwww.waterworldcolorado.com), where an abundance of aquatic thrill rides can easily amuse the shortest of attention spans for an entire day. Water World is located eight miles north of downtown in Thornton; take buses #18x or 6 or drive fifteen minutes on I-25 and get off the freeway at exit 219.

Invesco Field and the Pepsi Center

Spend any significant amount of time in Denver and you'll hear the stadiums of **Invesco Field** and the **Pepsi Center** referred to with almost religious respect by local fans of, respectively, the Denver Broncos football and Colorado Avalanche ice hockey teams (see p.75 for more). Both venues are certainly best visited during a match, though those without an accommodating schedule or the right finances – tickets to either team's games often reach the stratosphere – along with die-hard fans, who need to see every hallowed inch, might consider a stadium **tour**. Invesco Field, 1701 Bryant St (☎720/258-3888), do 75-minute tours leaving on the hour (Thurs–Sat 10am–2pm; $6) and maintain a modest **Colorado Sports Hall of Fame** (same hours; free). Tours of the **Pepsi Center**, 1000 Chopper Place (☎303/405-8556), are 75-minute as well (Mon & Wed 10am, noon & 2pm; Sat 10.15am & 12.15pm; $5) and also take in the facilities used by Denver's much less popular and successful basketball, arena football, and lacrosse teams. Invesco Field is a short ride on light rail (C Line) from Union Station, the Pepsi Center an easy ten-minute walk west from LoDo.

City Park

Denver's largest park, the unimaginatively named **City Park**, was established in the Victorian era, as its wide lakeside paths – designed for dignified peram-bulating – and the presence of the occasional folly continue to remind. But great swathes of the 330 acres are a little dowdy and unkempt, so perhaps what saves the park is the presence of the **Denver Museum of Nature & Science**, the city's **zoo**, and, on summer Sundays, free open-air **jazz concerts** between 6 and 8pm (Ⓦwww.cityparkjazz.org). All this is at the eastern end of the park; the only thing of any real interest in the west is the noble **"I have a dream" Monument**, a tribute to Dr Martin Luther King, Jr, and other civil rights activists including Rosa Parks, Sojourner Truth, Frederick Douglass, and Mahatma Gandhi. Background information on these brave men and women is supplied by boards gathered around the monument, the work of local sculptor Ed Dwight.

To get to City Park, take **bus** #32 from Market Street Station, or spend around half an hour walking here through the pleasant and safe residential streets that lie between the 16th Street Mall and the park.

Denver Museum of Nature & Science
One highlight of the **Denver Museum of Nature & Science**, at the eastern edge of City Park at 2001 Colorado Blvd (daily 9am–5pm; museum $10, planetarium $8, IMAX $8, all three $20; Ⓣ303/322-7009 or 1-800/925-2250, Ⓦwww.dmns.org), is the "Prehistoric Journey" exhibit, showcasing wonderful dinosaur displays alongside a working fossils lab, and scores of wildlife scenes featuring animals from as far off as Australia and Africa. Even more spectacular is the "Space Odyssey" exhibit, which relies on digital multimedia to narrate the extraordinary story of space exploration. High-tech is also at the core of the **Planetarium**, which a few years ago underwent a grand overhaul that equipped it with the most advanced computer graphics and video system of any planetarium anywhere; it's certainly worth a look. The museum also has an IMAX theater, as well as a good deal of fascinating – though somewhat out-of-place – anthropological material on Native Americans.

The Denver Zoo
Roughly dead center in the park is the large, popular **Denver Zoo** (daily: April–Sept 9am–5pm, Oct–March 10am–4pm; admission April–Sept $11, Oct–March $9; Ⓣ303/376-4800, Ⓦwww.denverzoo.org), whose four thousand residents include a couple of huge lowland gorillas in a spacious, thickly wooded sanctuary. The zoo's latest ambitious project was the opening of "Predator Ridge," where ferocious carnivores, including lions and hyenas, roam a recreated African savannah.

Eating

Though Western-themed steak and barbecue places abound, many of Denver's **restaurants** have begun to embrace a more refined "Rocky Mountain cuisine," emphasizing game and other local products such as trout and lamb. Additionally, Southwestern-style food options are copious, and there's a cosmopolitan selection of international restaurants to choose from. Of the several distinct restaurant districts, **LoDo** – Larimer Square in particular – is the most easily accessible on foot; it also represents a good cross-section of the town's restaurant scene. Several of the city's brewpubs also serve good-quality meals; see "Nightlife and entertainment" on p.72 for these. For further dining **listings**, check the reviews in the free weekly *Westword*, available from bars, restaurants, and newsboxes.

Bayou Bob's 1635 Glenarm Place ☎303/573-6828. Authentic and good-value Louisiana-style Cajun lunches and dinners keep this inexpensive, no-frills bistro busy. Choose from options like jambalaya, red beans and rice, po'boy sandwiches, shrimp gumbo, or fried catfish. Closed Sunday lunch.

The Buckhorn Exchange 1000 Osage St ☎303/534-9505. Opened in 1893, the oldest restaurant in town was started by a keen hunter who covered the walls with over five hundred stuffed trophies. Nowadays, the natural history museum-like dining areas set the tone for the meaty menu, featuring various game dishes, steak, and novelty items like rattlesnake and alligator tail. Dinner entrees are expensive ($20 and up), but lunches are more reasonable at about half that price. There's live folk and cowboy music in the saloon upstairs Thurs–Sat nights. Closed Sat & Sun lunch. Reservations recommended.

Bump and Grind 439 E 17th Ave ☎303/861-4841. Cheap café/bistro just outside downtown that's the flamboyant hub for the local gay social scene, particularly during Sunday brunch when the waitstaff is almost exclusively transvestite. The food is excellent, creative, and inexpensive – the eggs Benedict on sourdough bread costs just $6.

Café Brazil 3611 Navajo St ☎303/480-1877. Unassuming tiny and cheerful Brazilian restaurant serving excellent food at moderate prices. Particularly good are national dishes like the *feijoada completa*, a black-bean stew full of sausages and accompanied by fried plantains. Dinner only, closed Sun & Mon.

Casa Bonita 6715 W Colfax Ave ☎303/232-5115. A short drive out on Colfax, this absolutely wild Mexican restaurant seats 1200 diners and features staged gunfights, cliff dives, and "abandoned mines" you can explore. The only weak link is the food itself, but it's a lot of fun (especially for kids) and won't break your bank.

Cherry Cricket 2641 E 2nd Ave ☎303/322-7666. Excellent burgers and Mexican food served up in a generally dingy sports-bar ambiance make this a great place (near Cherry Creek Mall) to nurse a hangover or work on getting one (there are 120 different beers on offer) while watching televised sports. Open 11am–2am.

Delhi Darbar 1514 Blake St ☎303/595-0680. Relaxed haunt with decent North Indian food, including a number of unusual tandoori dishes like quail, shrimp, or lamb sausage. The $6 lunch buffet is an inexpensive way to sample the menu, but otherwise it's on the expensive side with a two-course dinner running around $25.

Denver Chophouse and Brewery 1735 19th St ☎303/296-0800. Classy but casual brewpub in a former Union Pacific railroad depot that's better known for its food than beers and so makes a good alternative to some of the town's pricey steakhouses – though you'll pay over $10 for a burger here and at least double that for most dinner entrees. Local sports stars certainly seem to agree, and can often be spotted here tucking into the enormous portions. Thick cuts of beef headline the menu, from top-quality Kansas City strips to filets and rib-eyes. All are well and imaginatively prepared – grilled portobello mushrooms dipped in Worcestershire sauce and garlic make perhaps the best veggie option.

El Azteca 301 16th St. Lunchtimes, office workers arrive en masse for the authentic top-notch Mexican food served in this small eatery in the basement of a dreary food-court. Prices are low, service quick, and the food – particularly the *carne asada* – excellent.

Fourth Story Restaurant & Bar 2955 E 1st Ave ☎303/322-1824. Gracing the top floor of the Tattered Cover Bookstore (see p.74), this relaxed restaurant has a wonderful front lounge with overstuffed couches and chairs, while in the stylish dining room you'll be served snacks and meals (lunch and dinner entrees priced $12–21) from a frequently changing creative American menu. The wine list is superb. A very popular place to hang out, especially during Sunday brunch when there's live music.

Kevin Taylor's Restaurant in the *Hotel Theatro*, 1106 14th St ☎303/820-2600. This formal restaurant serves up imaginative and eclectic contemporary dinners, including seared New York State foie gras, Maine lobster ravioli with asparagus and sweetcorn, and roasted rack of Colorado lamb, charging around $25 for two courses. *Jou Jou's*, the cheaper, more casual bistro next door, has the same management and is also open for breakfast, lunch, and dinner. Both serve relatively good-value pre-theater set meals.

The Palace Arms in the *Brown Palace Hotel*, 321 17th St ☎303/297-3111. This small and classy restaurant is the ultimate splurge in town. The menu features mostly seasonal game specialties like pheasant, buffalo, and venison, all of which run over $30 and are prepared to perfection. The interior is decorated using antiques from the Napoleonic period, including a pair of the French general's own dueling pistols.

Racine's 850 Bannock St ☎303/595-0418. Just south of downtown, this large, laid-back place is a Denver institution. Housed in a former auto showroom, the inexpensive restaurant serves excellent egg-based breakfasts (try the superb Florentine Benedict) and a range of great classic salads, inventive pastas, and reliably good sandwiches along with some Mexican entrees later in the day. The in-house bakery provides superb desserts including moist carrot cake and some excellent brownies. **Rocky Mountain Diner** 800 18th St ☎303/293-8383. Diner with big booths and a Western theme

serving up standard fare like good Yankee pot roast and mashed potatoes, along with more creative dishes like roast duck enchiladas. Breakfast or lunch costs around $7, dinners about $13 for two courses.

Taki's 341 E Colfax Ave. Giant and inexpensive portions of Japanese food are served in this friendly and longstanding local family business,

Mile-High Festivals

It may sound cliche to say so, but there always seems to be some major **event** or **festival** going on in Denver; what's even more surprising, though, considering the glut, is the scale of local involvement in virtually all of these.

Denver's two largest festivals give evidence of the city's continued role as cradle of US Western culture. In mid-January, the **National Western Stock Show and Rodeo** (☎303/297-1166, ⊛www.nationalwestern.com) takes over the Denver Coliseum at 4600 Humboldt St (take the Brighton Blvd exit off I-70). This almost century-old stock show is one of the most significant in the region, yet it's the large-purse rodeo, one of the nation's largest, that attracts most of the 600,000 people here over the festival's sixteen days. Other attractions include live country music, line-dancing, and Native American food and crafts. Admission runs about $15 to get into the show and around the same again for rodeo tickets.

Also held at the Coliseum is the **Denver Pow-Wow** (☎www.tesorofoundation .org), a three-day gathering in mid-March that's attended by 60 tribes and 100,000 spectators and is focused around the swirling and rhythmic dancing of Native Americans in their sensational traditional costumes. The highlight of this pow-wow, one of the country's largest annual Native American gatherings, is the Grand Entry, a massive dance with up to one thousand participants. Native oral traditions are also kept alive by storytelling events, as are traditional arts and crafts through workshops and sales. The entry fee is $6.

Further ethnic festivals dot Denver's calendar throughout the summer months. The large Hispanic shindig is on the **Cinco de Mayo** weekend in early May (☎303/534-8342, ⊛www.newsed.org) and claims to be the largest celebration in the US. During the festival strolling mariachi bands, colorfully costumed Aztec dancers, and lots of contemporary Latin bands take over downtown. Other festivals that hit the streets include **Japanese** and **Greek** (both June), **Irish** and **pan-Asian** (both July), **Scottish** (Aug), and a **German Oktoberfest** (Sept).

The eclectic **Capitol Hill People's Fair** (⊛www.peoplesfair.com) in early June has no real theme or agenda, yet sees much more than just the local neighborhood turn up to simply hang out and enjoy live music, arts, crafts, and a food bazaar. Bigger still is July's **Cherry Creek Arts Festival** (⊛www.cherryarts.org), the nation's premier arts and crafts exhibition, which attracts crowds of a quarter million. As well as the exhibits, all sorts of hands-on events are organized, particularly with children in mind. Then, as a final summer fling on Labor Day weekend (early Sept), **A Taste of Colorado** (⊛www.atasteofcolorado.com) sees many of Denver's restaurants set up stalls for on-the-hoof samples.

Though strictly speaking not festivals, Denver also seems to be the city of the **free concert**. Among the larger series are the June **Film on the Rocks** season (⊛www .redrocksonline.com), when local bands perform in front of blockbuster movies on giant screens out at Red Rocks Amphitheatre; **Hot Sounds at the Pavilions** (⊛www .denverpavillions.com), which brings concerts to the 16th Street Mall; and the series of free jazz shows in City Park, for which many Denverites turn up with picnic meals. The Visitor Information Center (see p.57) can furnish you with a **guide** of what freebies are on in the coming days.

with cafeteria-style ordering that gets you the food fast. The miso soup is too good to miss and the salmon bowl – a sizeable piece of salmon smothered in a zesty, mustardy sauce with rice – is exceptional, and costs under $5.

Tom's Diner 601 E Colfax Ave. Wonderfully gritty and authentic 24hr diner at the seedy end of town. The menu has been made-over to include items like garden burgers, but the cheap deals on big portions of stock diner food remain.

Vesta Dipping Grill 1822 Blake St ☎303/296-1970. Attractive restaurant in a renovated LoDo warehouse serving tasty food in unusual combinations; its menu, rather pretentiously, is based

around the "art" of dipping, but it actually works. You can personalize each entree – including a range of kebab-style meat or veggies – in a spectrum of flavors (Mediterranean, Asian, Mexican...); try the tuna roll in a wasabi cream sauce to start. Two courses will set you back around $20, and there's live jazz on Thurs.

Wazee Supper Club 1600 15th St ☎303/623-9518. Well-established LoDo dining room, serving good cheap burgers, deli sandwiches, and superb pizzas, plus a full range of beers, in a retro Art Deco atmosphere. One of the few places open really late (1.30am most nights).

Nightlife and entertainment

Though business booms for Denver's numerous downtown brewpubs, an onslaught of sports bars in the LoDo district, particularly near Coors Field, have mostly taken over as the city's liveliest **nightlife** area. If sports bars don't appeal, there are plenty of other more stylish or relaxing places to drink in town as well. The majority of places close around 1am, except Saturdays when most have extensions until 2am.

While you can find some **live music** downtown, much of Denver's live music scene is headquartered elsewhere, along Colfax Avenue or at large out-of-town venues. Denver's best-known big concert venue is the remarkable **Red Rocks Amphitheatre** near Golden (see p.85), despite the fact that the larger capacity of the **Coors Amphitheatre**, 6350 Greenwood Plaza Blvd (ⓦwww.hob.com/venues/concerts/coors), means that this venue tends to attract bookings from the biggest acts. For news of musical happenings of all shapes and sizes, consult the free weekly *Westword*, or the "Weekend" section of the *Denver Post*.

The higher arts can most easily be enjoyed at the modern **Denver Performing Arts Complex** (the "PLEX") on 14th and Curtis streets (☎303/893-4100, ⓦwww.artscomplex.com), home to the Denver Center Theater Company, the Colorado Symphony Orchestra, Opera Colorado, and the Colorado Ballet. Facilities include the **Symphony Hall** (in the round, giving it superb acoustics), as well as eight individual theaters.

If you're in the mood for a bit of stand-up **comedy**, both local and big-name, head to Comedy Works, 1226 15th St (☎303/595-3637, ⓦwww.comedyworks.com), Denver's major comedy venue just off Larimer Square. Shows kick off nightly at 8pm, with several performances on weekend nights. For improv, head to the **Bovine Metropolis Theater**, 1527 Champa St (Thurs–Sun; ☎303/758-4722, ⓦwww.bovinemetropolis.com). Tickets at both normally start at around $10. In the hunt for **tickets** to all cultural and sporting events, both Ticketmaster (☎303/830-8497) and Ticketman (☎303/430-1111) can usually help. You can try the Ticket Bus, parked on 16th and Curtis, in person (daily 10am–6pm), where you'll often find last-minute **deals** on shows that have yet to sell out.

Bars and clubs

Breckenridge Brewery 2220 Blake St ☎303/297-3644. Atmospheric brewpub opposite Coors Field – making it a lively

hangout after a ballgame – with a cozy pub atmosphere, quality craft beer brewed on the premises, and a killer range of delicious barbecue grub.

The Church 1160 Lincoln St ☎303/832-3528. A dance club located inside a gutted cathedral, this significant downtown nightlife landmark combines a wine bar, sushi bar, and three invariably busy dance floors, getting down mostly to garage, hard house, and techno. Cover $5–15.

Cruise Room Bar 1600 17th St ☎303/628-5400. Inside the *Oxford Hotel*, this bar is worth a stop for the atmosphere – it's a replica of the Art Deco bar on the *Queen Mary* ocean liner – and its mean martinis.

Duffy's Shamrock 1635 Court Place. Friendly local downtown bar that also serves food, including good fried chicken. Open daily 7am–1.30am.

Funky Buddha 776 Lincoln St ☎303/832-5075. Chic and dimly-lit urban bar where a DJ provides the ambiance at weekends (no dance floor) and there's a good selection of appetizers, including stuffed mushrooms, hummus, red pepper dip, and lamb skewers. The long happy hour (4–8pm) makes it popular with the after-work crowd, who pack the lively rooftop patio.

Mercury Cafe 2199 California St ☎303/294-9281, ⓦwww.mercurycafe.com. When there's not jazz on, there's swing dancing, poetry readings, or some other form of entertainment. The club is combined with a good-value restaurant, serving lots of healthy choices, many vegetarian.

Polly Esther's 2301 Blake St ☎303/382-1976. Massive and consistently popular club with Seventies and Eighties hits playing on two floors. Cover $5–10.

Sancho's Broken Arrow 741 East Colfax Ave ☎303/832-5288. Dive bar dedicated to the Grateful Dead and all those that worship them (in Denver, that means a lot). Sociable and friendly even if you're not tie-dyed; there are pool tables in the back.

Stampede Mesquite Grill and Dance Emporium 2430 S Havanna St, at Park Rd ☎303/337-6909. The massive antique saloon bar is the centerpiece of this Country and Western pick-up joint. Located in suburban Aurora, it's only worth the drive if you're dying to do some boot-scooting.

Wynkoop Brewing Co. 1634 18th St ☎303/297-2700. Opposite Union Station, the state's first brewpub serves up good home-brewed beers and great bar food. There's an elegant pool hall upstairs, and live entertainment Thurs–Sat. Brewery tours, with free samples, are given on Saturdays (1–5pm).

Live music venues

Bluebird 3317 E Colfax Ave ☎303/333-7749. Former Art Deco film theater hailing from 1914 that now serves a good range of local microbrews and hosts a variety of live bands.

Brendan's 1624 Market St ☎303/595-0609. Small basement pub in the LoDo with regular live blues; big-name acts pop by a few times a month and cover is rarely more than $10.

El Chapultepec 1962 Market St ☎303/295-9126. Tiny, very popular LoDo jazz venue that's been hosting acts for more than fifty years. Local bands play nightly, and bigger names occasionally stop by.

Grizzly Rose 5450 N Valley Hwy ☎303/295-1330, ⓦwww.grizzlyrose.com. Celebrated Country and Western venue a 10min drive north of downtown on I-25 (take exit 215). The huge venue has bands every night, attracts famous names regularly, and has been named the Country's Best Country Music Club several years running. Cover $5–10.

Herman's Hideaway 1578 S Broadway ☎303/777-5840. Located just south of I-25, *Herman's* is one of Denver's best rock clubs, with live music from Wed to Sat. Cover $5.

Ogden 935 E Colfax Ave ☎303/830-2525. Small, gritty joint with dense crowds and mostly local rock bands.

The Soiled Dove 1949 Market St ☎303/299-0100, ⓦwww.soileddove.com. Massively popular bar with an often rowdy rooftop overlooking Market St. There's an eclectic variety of live music on almost every night, from local to national names in everything from jazz to rock.

Gay Denver

Though small and a bit subdued by national standards, Denver's **gay and lesbian** scene is certainly the liveliest in Colorado, and is centered around thirty or so low-key neighborhood bars rather than flamboyant clubs. The biggest event on Denver's gay calendar, attracting around 150,000 people, is the annual **Pride Fest** (☎303/733-7743, ⓦwww.coloradoglbt.org), a splashy show of unity – and an unabashed celebration – held in June to coincide with pride celebrations across the globe. The colorful Pride Parade begins at Cheeseman Park (incidentally Denver's prime cruising area), before dancing, singing, and marching its way through downtown to Civic Center Park, where festivities continue. A more uniquely Denver celebration is the cheerful **Colorado Gay Rodeo** ($10; ℡ 303/333-4486, 🅦 www.cgra.net), a longstanding three-day event with many of the usual rodeo competitions alongside more tongue-in-cheek categories such as "goat dressing" and a "wild drag race." For other gay events in Denver, check out local gay papers *Out Front* and *H Ink*, or websites 🅦 www.outindenver .com or 🅦 www.denvergay.com.

BJ's Carousel 1380 S Broadway ℡ 303/777-9880. A flamboyant and highly diverse crowd patronizes this chaotic dive bar where there always seems to be something going on: karaoke on Wed, beach volleyball on Thurs, regular (and infamously bawdy) drag shows, and drink specials every night.

Charlie's 900 E Colfax Ave ℡ 303/839-8890. The gay scene is fused with traditional Denver culture at this Country and Western music bar which also has a popular restaurant for lunch and dinner. The atmosphere is always upbeat, whether on dancing – dance and house music are popular on one floor, C&W on the other – or karaoke nights. Also hosts popular drag nights when as many straights as gays seem to turn up. Nightly until 2am.

Colorado Triangle, Inc. 2036 Broadway ℡ 303/293-9009. This large pick-up joint is one of America's oldest openly gay bars; it began as a leather bar in 1970 and has been a community cornerstone ever since, with a dance floor, a schedule of regular events, and charity shows. Nightly until 2am.

Fox Hole 2936 Fox St ℡ 303/298-7378. The unassuming exterior makes this unpretentious and perpetually packed lesbian watering hole tricky to find. Once you do, though, the spacious sunlit patio is a big plus, and packs out for riotous Sunday barbecues, with food and drink specials, DJs, and dancing. Closed Tues & Wed.

The Grand 538 E 17th Ave ℡ 303/839-5390. Upscale piano bar where weekend nights buzz with live music and cabaret and a balanced mix of gays and lesbians.

Jr's 777 E 17th Ave. Highly fashion-conscious two-tiered gay bar in uptown – the overwhelmingly residential area that spreads east of downtown – where it's largely men that hang out around the antique bar, play bingo, or watch drag shows. Rowdiest during "liquor bust" weekends, when $8 buys you all-you-can-drink well drinks.

La Rumba 99 W 9th Ave ℡ 303/572-8006. Catch salsa, merengue, and other theme nights in this club that always strives to offer something a little different – constant make overs perpetually keep it on the cutting edge of the local gay scene.

Shopping

The obvious place to start any Denver **shopping** expedition, particularly if you're on foot, is the **16th Street Mall**, which includes the Denver Pavilion Mall, the home of countless boutique clothing and accessory stores. That said, the best place for browsing and off-beat items is usually elsewhere in the city. It is also outside the immediate downtown area that you'll find some of the great **outfitters** that will set you up with all the gear you need for a trip to the mountains – see below for a couple of these.

If it's a generic mall and a large range of boutique shops you're after, the most expansive and central option is the **Cherry Creek Mall** (🅦 www.cherrycreekmall .com), four miles southeast of downtown. Opposite the mall's main entrance is undoubtedly Denver's best place to buy reading material, the **Tattered Cover Bookstore**, 2955 E 1st Ave (℡ 303/322-7727), which spreads over four extremely well-stocked floors. There's another branch of the bookstore close to Union Station in LoDo, from where it's a ten-minute walk northwest to **REI**, 1416 Platte St (℡ 303/756-3100), a gigantic outdoors store in a huge former railway building, replete with its own climbing wall and off-road cycle course for testing gear. A more dedicated sports retailer with a gigantic

Colorado presence is **Gart Sports**, whose 1000 Broadway branch (☎303/861–1122) is within walking distance of downtown. Broadway is better-known, however, for its concentration of **antiques dealers**, with around 200 located in the dozen blocks between 400 and 2000 S Broadway. For a cheaper rummage through second-hand goods, try the **thrift stores** that line Colfax Avenue east of town, or head up to the Mile-High Flea Market (Sat & Sun 6am–5pm; $2), held on 80 acres of land at I-76 and 88th Ave, about a twenty-minute drive from downtown.

Spectator sports

All of Colorado's top-level professional **sports** teams – playing football, baseball, basketball, and ice hockey – are based in Denver. As such, going to a game is a big deal here, and certainly something that must be done to begin to understand a city where fan devotion has taken on almost religious proportions. For **transportation** to downtown sporting events contact RTD (☎303/299-6000, ⓦ www.rtd-denver.com), which organizes shuttles to games from numerous locations throughout Denver.

The **Denver Broncos**, the city's much-loved (American) football team (☎720/258-3333, ⓦ www.denverbroncos.com), enjoy enormous state-wide support, and their eight regular season (Sept–Jan) home games are typically sold out an entire year in advance. The team plays at Invesco Field, 1701 Bryant St. If you can get tickets, expect to pay at least $70. If you can't, then a close second in terms of atmosphere are the LoDo brewpubs, with their mammoth screens and high-spirited patrons. Most games are played on Sundays, but if the Broncos are playing on a Monday night, then watching the game often is the start of a big night out.

The **Colorado Rockies** (☎303/292-0200 or 1-800/388-7625, ⓦ www.coloradorockies.com) is the sole Major League Baseball team in Colorado, and their state-of-the-art Coors Field has become one of the most popular ballparks in the country. The thin air here favors batting over pitching, traditionally making the park the setting for high-scoring affairs. Tickets for games cost $5–75 per seat, and are generally available on the day of the game; very few of the 162 games each season (April–Oct) sell out.

The only Colorado-based NBA team is the **Denver Nuggets** (☎303/405-1212, ⓦ www.nba.com/nuggets), who play in the Pepsi Center (see p.68) in a season that runs from November until the playoffs in May. Games last for an exhausting 48 minutes of playing time, though with stoppages and commercial breaks they typically take around two hours to complete. Tickets cost $30–90.

Understandably in a state known for winter sports, ice hockey enjoys considerable popularity in Colorado, and the **Colorado Avalanche** (☎303/405-1212, ⓦ www.coloradoavalanche.com) are consistently good, winning the Stanley Cup, hockey's highest prize, in 1996 and 2001. The "Avs," as they're known, are one of the league's most dominant teams, so it can be difficult to get tickets ($30–175) during the October to April regular season.

Listings

Banks There are numerous ATMs and banks with full exchange facilities downtown. For travelers' checks American Express is at 555 S 17th St (℡303/383-5050).

Consulates A British consulate is located in the World Trade Center Tower at 1675 Broadway (℡303/592-5200, ⊛www.britainusa.com); the Australian consulate is at 9200 West Cross Drive, suite 110, Littleton (℡303/321-2234).

Cycling Blazing Saddles, 1426 Market St (℡303/534-5255), rents out bikes from $25–45 per day. Colorado State Parks, 1313 Sherman St #618 (℡303/866-3437), is a good place for extensive information on the city's network of cycle paths.

Golf An information line (℡303/964-2563) has details of numerous courses in the Denver area. The public City Park course, E 25th Ave and York St, is the most central ($20–24 for eighteen holes; ℡303/295-4420). One of the most beautiful courses is the Arrowhead Golf Club near the red-rock Roxborough State Park, a 45min drive southwest of Denver at 10850 W Sundown Trail ($125 for eighteen holes; ℡303/973-9614).

Internet There are plenty of free public Internet terminals spread over the seven floors of the impressive central Denver Public Library, 10 W 14th Ave (Mon & Tues noon–8pm, Wed–Fri 10am–6pm, Sat 9am–5pm, Sun 1–5pm; ℡720/865-1351).

Laundry In the northeast, try the *Melbourne Hostel*; the best southeast side option is Cycles Laundry, 320 Broadway.

Medical Walgreen's, 2000 E Colfax Ave (℡303/331-0917), operates a 24hr pharmacy. Denver General Hospital is at 6th Ave and Bannock St (℡303/436-6000, ⊛www.denverhealth.org).

Post office The main downtown branch is at 951 20th St (Mon–Fri 8am–5pm; zip code 80201).

Taxis Yellow Cab ℡303/777-7777, Metro Taxi ℡303/333-3333, and the cheapest company in town, Zone Cab ℡303/444-8888. Charges are $2 for the first 1/8 mile, plus 25¢ for each additional 1/8 mile. The meter will also automatically charge 37.5¢ per minute when the vehicle speed is less than 15mph.

Travel details

Flights

(All services are via United Airlines unless otherwise stated.)

Denver to: Alamosa (3 daily; 1hr; Great Lakes Airlines); Aspen (11 daily; 45min); Colorado Springs (18 daily; 40min); Cortez (3 daily; 1hr 20min; Great Lakes); Durango (7 daily; 1hr 25min); Eagle (for Vail; 7 daily; 50min); Grand Junction (10 daily; 1hr 10min; United and Great Lakes); Gunnison (4 daily; 1hr); Hayden (for Steamboat; 6 daily; 50min); Pueblo (2 daily; 40min; Great Lakes); Telluride (5 daily; 1hr 10min).

Trains

(All services are Amtrak.)

Denver to: Glenwood Springs (1 daily; 6hr); Granby (1 daily; 2hr 30min); Grand Junction (1 daily; 8hr); Winter Park (1 daily; 2hr).

Buses

(All buses are Greyhound unless otherwise stated.)

Denver to: Alamosa (1daily; 5hr 25min; TNM&O); Boulder (24 daily; 50min; RTD); Colorado Springs (30 daily; 1hr 40min; TNM&O and FREX); Durango (1 daily; 10hr 20min); Fort Collins (1 daily; 1hr 15min); Frisco (2 daily; 1hr 30min) Glenwood Springs (2 daily; 3hr 25min); Grand Junction (4 daily; 4hr 20min to 5hr 20min); Limon (1 daily 1hr 20min); Montrose (1 daily; 6hr 50min); Pueblo (8 daily; 2hr 40min; TNM&O); Silverton (1 daily; 8hr 30min); Trinidad (2 daily; 4hr 30min; TNM&O); Vail (2 daily; 2hr 10min).

The Northern Front Range

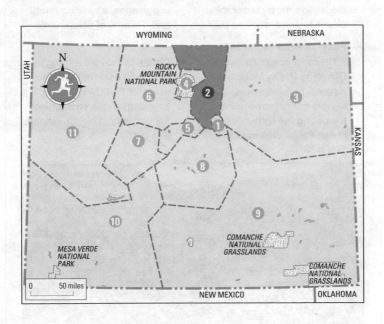

CHAPTER 2 # Highlights

* **Dakota Ridge** – Hike or mountain bike this spectacular ridge, linking fine views over Denver with dinosaur footprints and the Red Rocks Amphitheatre. See p.84

* **Red Rocks Amphitheatre** – Natural red sandstone amphitheater with excellent acoustics, undoubtedly one of the world's most memorable places to see a gig. See p.85

* **Peak-to-Peak Highway** – The most scenic route from Denver to Rocky Mountain National Park connects several quirky former mining towns and the lightly visited Indian Peaks Wilderness. See p.86

* **Boulder** – Liberal college town in the Rocky Mountain foothills, with an attractive downtown and easy access to some of the world's best climbing. See p.89

* **Swetsville Zoo** – One zoo where you can't feel sorry for the animals, since they're all the product of one man's imagination, a welding torch, and a bunch of scrap metal. See p.103

* **Cache la Poudre** – A rugged river, with excellent opportunities for fly-fishing, rafting, kayaking, and even spotting the occasional bighorn sheep. See p.106

△ Cache la Poudre

The Northern Front Range

Cast a quick eye on a map of Colorado and it's easy to see that the area north of Denver, huddled against the Rocky Mountain foothills – the **NORTHERN FRONT RANGE** – is the state's most heavily developed. It's a strip that combines the charms of liberal and artsy college towns with invigorating mountain activities on the one hand and easy access to the bright lights of Denver on the other. Understandably it has become one of the most popular spots for those relocating to Colorado, and the number of residents in the region continually grows. Yet it's still easy to get away from it all. Thanks to the efforts of a highly environmentally aware populace, great swathes of adjacent foothill lands remain protected from development as **mountain parks**, and area tourism is based largely around exploring them. Some towns have the odd sight or attraction worthy of a detour, but mostly they just make pleasant bases for a day in the mountains.

The Northern Front Range begins on the very outskirts of Denver. Here below ever-roaring I-70 sit two endearing communities: tiny **Morrison**, beside the world-famous Red Rocks Amphitheatre, and the sleepy brewery town of **Golden**. Dotted around both are half a dozen or so beautiful mountain parks ideal for quick jaunts into the countryside from Denver. The stunning **Peak-to-Peak Highway** effectively starts from Golden and offers the most scenic and interesting route to Rocky Mountain National Park, covered in Chapter 4. The highway cuts through alpine scenery, rather crassly made-over casino towns like Black Hawk and Central City, rustic Nederland and the neighboring Indian Peaks Wilderness, and the small-time ski hill Eldora.

The best way to appreciate the Front Range is to stay just beside the foothills in the likeable, progressive college towns of **Boulder** and **Fort Collins**, visiting the mountains from there. Boulder's leafy pedestrian mall and multitude of restaurants are welcome respite after a day of outdoor activities, while further north, just 40 miles shy of the Wyoming border, Fort Collins feels a bit less touristy.

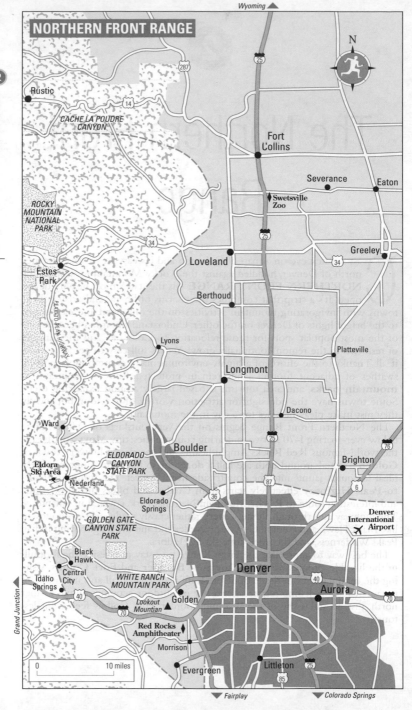

NORTHERN FRONT RANGE

Wyoming ▲

N

Rustic

CACHE LA POUDRE CANYON

ROCKY MOUNTAIN NATIONAL PARK

Estes Park

PEAK-TO-PEAK HIGHWAY

Fort Collins

Severance

Eaton

Swetsville Zoo

Greeley

Loveland

Berthoud

Lyons

Platteville

Longmont

Ward

Dacono

Eldora Ski Area

Nederland

ELDORADO CANYON STATE PARK

Boulder

Brighton

Eldorado Springs

GOLDEN GATE CANYON STATE PARK

Denver International Airport

Black Hawk

Central City

Idaho Springs

WHITE RANCH MOUNTAIN PARK

Denver

Aurora

Grand Junction ◀

Lookout Mountain

Golden

Red Rocks Amphitheater

Morrison

Evergreen

Littleton

0   10 miles

▼ Fairplay   ▼ Colorado Springs

Jefferson County

Of all the counties into which Denver sprawls, **Jefferson County** deserves special mention, as it's literally where the Great Plains meet the Rocky Mountains. Here Denver's humdrum western suburbs melt into the foothills, and between the two are a couple of interesting sights and communities: **Golden**, which retains a small-town feel despite the threat of being slowly consumed by the suburbs, and the tiny, slightly oddball burg of **Morrison**, beside the magnificent **Red Rocks Amphitheatre** and **Dakota Ridge**, where dinosaur footprints are clearly visible.

But Jefferson County's real trump card – what makes it Denver's premier after-work outdoor playground – are its **mountain parks**. These varied parks include rolling grasslands, craggy rock formations, natural foothills, rugged mountains, and tumbling streams, all of which seem all the more impressive when contrasted with the views they offer of downtown and the plains. Hikers, bikers (the non-motorized variety), and snowshoers can be found in the parks every day of the year, although outside peak periods (evenings and weekends) things are generally quiet.

The two main organizations that administer open space in the foothills are the Denver Parks and Recreation Department (☏303/964-2462, ⓦwww .denvergov.org) and Jefferson County Open Space (☏303/271-5925, ⓦwww .co.jefferson.co.us); both bodies' websites have good information about their public lands. Golden's Chamber of Commerce, with a good stock of leaflets, is also helpful (see below).

Golden

GOLDEN, just ten miles west of Denver along Hwy-6, sprung up as a mining camp that dwindled in the absence of significant amounts of ore, and rose to prominence only briefly in the mid-1860s as the seat of state legislative assemblies. As such, today Golden holds more interest for its location beside several superb mountain parks rather than for its small-town charms or couple of sights. The massive brewery is pretty impressive, though.

Since the 1860s Golden has really become synonymous with beer giant **Coors** (Mon–Sat 10am–4pm; free; ☏303/277-2337, ⓦwww.coors.com), the world's largest brewery. Located three blocks east of Washington Avenue, Golden's main thoroughfare, the brewery serves up one-and-a-half-hour-long tours full of corporate self-promotion. The tour ends in a tasting session (bring ID) of their numerous products, including their much-maligned (or –loved, depending on whom you talk to) "Silver Bullet," the light beer for which the company is most famous.

The town's other big employer, the Colorado School of Mines, runs a small **geology museum** at 16th St and Maple (Mon–Sat 9am–4pm, Sun 1–4pm; free; ☏303/273-3823). The museum has a diverting selection of pre-electricity mining lamps, as well as a good selection of rock and ores, which might help you appreciate the economic history of the state's mountains. Another modest attraction is the **Golden Pioneer Museum**, 923 10th St (Mon–Sat 10am–4.30pm; early Sept to late-May Sun 11am–5pm as well, free; ☏303/278-7151, ⓦwww.goldenpioneermuseum.com), which is largely devoted to a predictable array of pioneer artifacts; one notable, odd exception is a picture made entirely from the hair of a single family.

Practicalities

Buses from downtown Denver stop beside Golden's central **Chamber of Commerce**, 1010 Washington Ave (Mon–Fri 8.30am–5pm, Sat & Sun

10am–4pm; ☎303/279-3113, ⊛www.goldencochamber.org). For a small town, Golden has a number of decent **accommodation** options, including the modest *Golden Motel*, south of downtown at 510 24th St (☎303/279-5581; ❸), with basic units, some with kitchenettes; and the friendlier and more central *Williamsburg Inn*, 1407 Washington St (☎303/279-7673; ❹). Breakfasts are included in room rates, as at *The Dove Inn B&B*, 711 14th St (☎303/278-2209 or 1-888/278-2209, ⊛www.doveinn.com; ❺), a pleasant former 1860s pioneer home. The modern *Golden Hotel,* 11th St and Washington (☎303/279-0100 or 1-800/233-7214, ⊛www.golden-hotel.com; ❻), includes amenities like an exercise room, hot tub, and pool, along with an airy, Western-decorated lobby and rooms. If you're driving an RV, try the *Clear Creek RV Park*, a few blocks west of downtown on 10th St (☎303/278-1437; $20); it has a pool and hot tub.

Simple, cheap, and filling is the order of the day in most of Golden's downtown **restaurants**. *Kenrow's*, 718 12th St (☎303/279-5164), has a good buffet breakfast for $7, with burgers, sandwich lunches, and prime-rib dinners starting at around $6; it's also one of Golden's most popular **bars**, with pool tables and live music most weekends. If you're looking for a bit of a splurge – by Golden standards, at least – head to the *Table Mountain Inn Restaurant,* 1310 Washington Ave (☎303/271-0110), which serves mostly American specialties like prime rib of buffalo and grilled salmon, spiced and prepared Southwestern-style.

Lookout Mountain

Leave Golden by heading west along 19th Street and you'll soon find yourself climbing up to the grand vistas of **Lookout Mountain**. A little over a mile up here is the final resting place of famed frontiersman and showman William Cody – aka **Buffalo Bill** (see box opposite) – who died in Denver in 1915. A museum adjacent to his grave sheds light on the life of this Western archetype, while bordering both are two mountain parks: **Lookout Mountain** and **Apex**, which together offer a tight network of hiking and mountain biking trails, with great views at almost every bend.

The Buffalo Bill Museum and gravesite

Occasionally (and rather optimistically) billed as the "Graceland of the Rockies," the **Buffalo Bill Museum** (May–Oct daily 9am–5pm, Nov–April Tues–Sun 9am–4pm; $3; ⊛www.buffalobill.org) does a thorough job of outlining Cody's past: the man worked almost every quintessential Wild West job before going on to fortify and even create many of its myths in his globe-trotting circus. Some of the more gruesome yet intriguing elements on display include a pistol whose handle has been fashioned from human bone, and an account of Bill scalping a Native American – a race he mostly got on with and also integrated into his circus.

A short walk from the museum, and with grand vistas over the plains he knew so well, is Buffalo Bill's **grave**. Yet at the time of his death his choice of site was hotly disputed, and some citizens of Cody – the city he founded in Wyoming – remain resolute in their claim that he's buried in the wrong place. In the years following his death the threat of disinterment was such that the National Guard was, for a time, brought in to watch over the gravesite, with the aid of a tank, no less.

Lookout Mountain and Apex parks

Together, the adjacent **Lookout Mountain** and **Apex parks** spread over 771 acres of thickly wooded but extremely accessible terrain high up in the Rocky

Buffalo Bill

The much-mythologized exploits of **William Frederick "Buffalo Bill" Cody**, born in Iowa in 1846, begin when Bill was just eleven, when the murder of his father forced him to take a job as an army dispatch rider. An early escape from ambush brought Cody fame as the "Youngest Indian Slayer of the Plains"; four years later he became the youngest rider on the legendary **Pony Express**. After a stint fighting for the Union during the Civil War, Cody found work – and a lifelong nickname – supplying buffalo meat to workers laying the transcontinental railroad. He killed over 4200 of the beasts in just eighteen months, before rejoining the army in 1868 as its chief scout. In the next decade, when the **Plains Indian Wars** were at their peak, he earned a Congressional Medal of Honor and a remarkable record of never losing any troops to ambushes. Among battles in which he took part was the 1877 encounter with Sioux forces when he killed – and scalped – Chief Yellow Hand.

By the late 1870s, exaggerated accounts of Cody's adventures were appearing back East in the "dime novels" of Ned Buntline, and with the Indian Wars all but over Bill took to guiding Yankee and European gentry on buffalo hunts. He referred to the vacationers as "dudes," and called his camps "dude ranches." The theatrical productions he laid on for his rich guests developed into the world-famous **Wild West Show**. First staged in 1883, these spectacular outdoor carnivals usually consisted of a re-enactment of an Indian battle such as Custer's Last Stand, featuring Sioux who had been present at Little Bighorn, trick riders, buffalo, clowns, and a shooting and riding exhibition by the man himself. The show spent ten of its thirty years in Europe, where, dressed in the finest silks and sporting a well-groomed goatee, Cody stayed in the grandest hotels and dined with heads of state; **Queen Victoria** was so enthusiastic in her admiration that rumors circulated of an affair between them.

Later in life, a mellowing Cody played down his past activities, to the point of urging the government to respect all Native American treaties and put an end to the wanton slaughter of buffalo and game. Although the Wild West Show was reckoned to have brought in as much as one million dollars per year, many of his investments failed badly, and, in January 1915, Buffalo Bill died a penniless 69-year-old at his sister's home in Denver.

Mountain foothills on the fringes of Golden. Their combined ten miles of trails offer hikers and bikers quick escapes from Denver's urban overspill, as well as excellent views of it.

If you arrive by car, the logical place to start is Lookout Mountain's **Nature Center** (Tues–Sun 10am–4pm), which has some fairly limited displays on local natural history and useful pamphlets with maps of the two adjacent parks. Next door is the 1917 **Boettcher Mansion**, the one-time summer home and hunting lodge of millionaire Charles Boettcher, who arrived in the US in the 1870s with nothing and went on to ride high on the Leadville mining boom; he subsequently became one of Denver's leading citizens. The magnificent gray stone house borrows heavily from Tudor design, including a half-timbered, stuccoed exterior and heavy wooden doors, while inside the stone walls a colossal fireplace and wrought-iron lights help create the ancient castle atmosphere in vogue at the time. Inherited by Boettcher's granddaughter, the mansion and surrounding 110-acre estate was donated to the county in 1968 and has since been opened to the public as a unique venue for weddings and meetings. From the mansion and nature center a couple of easy **trails** loop around for a mile or so to return back to their starting point.

For a longer hike, follow Lookout Mountain Trail one mile south from the nature center and explore the network of trails inside **Apex Park**; the best views are to be had from the Grubstake Loop. Be warned that Apex is very popular with mountain bikers – the rocky trails are great fun for the experienced – so it might be worth avoiding at weekends and in the evening if you're on foot. If you do intend to explore the park by **mountain bike**, consider pedaling up Lookout Mountain Road and, having explored Apex, drop back down into Golden via the thrilling **Apex Trail** and a connecting bike path. Note that this seven-mile loop can take a couple of hours, especially if you thoroughly explore the park's other trails.

White Ranch

Despite lying only a mile or so northwest of Golden, **White Ranch**, a park home to abundant wildlife among its meadows, forests, canyon, and gnarled rocks, is rarely busy. The secluded nature of its hiking trails make it easy to forget how close you are to a city, until at regular intervals trees thin to offer arresting views over it and the surrouding plains. To get here follow Hwy-93 north from Golden, then onto 56th Street for half a mile; the main trailhead parking lot is near the junction with Pine Ridge Rd. A second trailhead is an extra ten minutes' drive along 56th St and Golden Gate Canyon Rd, and has the advantage of cutting out a large climb up into the park. Leaflet dispensers are on hand at both trailheads to provide maps. The density of the trail network makes it easy to create a route length suitable for most hikers, while only skilled mountain bikers will enjoy White Ranch's steep, rough terrain.

Red Rocks and Matthews/Winters parks

The two mountain parks you should be sure not to miss in Jefferson County are **Red Rocks** and **Matthews/Winters**. Adjacent to one another, these parks have excellent hiking and biking trails which join in a varied six-mile loop that affords some remarkable views in all directions. The presence of various attractions off this, including dinosaur footprints and the Red Rocks Amphitheatre, mean you should allow at least four hours to complete the hike, or as much as half if you're on a bike, since much of the trail is extremely challenging. If you're short of time, drive right up to the footprints and amphitheater instead and explore the parks that way; look for signs along Hwy-26.

The best place for hikers and bikers to **park** is at the lot just south of I-70 on the northern side of Matthews/Winters Park. From here you'll have to nip over the main road to begin the clockwise hiking and biking loop. Immediately the rocky trail climbs steeply and steadily to the top of the impressive **Dakota Ridge**, part of a fourteen-mile-long ridge known as "the hogback" for its arched shape. The trail clambers south along this ridge, offering exceptional views over Denver and the Red Rocks Amphitheatre on either side, before dropping back down to Hwy-26.

The Dakota Ridge Trail continues on the other side of the road, but before heading on first walk a couple of hundred yards northeast down Hwy-26 to view some fossilized **dinosaur footprints** by the roadside. The world's first large dinosaur discovery (a stegosaurus) occurred here in 1877, quickly setting off the "dinosaur gold rush," in which numerous scientists converged, eventually excavating over seventy species. A tiny **visitors' center** (Mon–Sat 9am–5pm, Sun noon–5pm; ☎303/697-3466, ⓦwww.dinoridge.org) at the base of the road on the eastern side of the ridge has a little more information on the discoveries.

Continuing on, the trail climbs steeply again to regain the ridge before descending in a series of switchbacks to a highway you cross in order to join

△ Red Rocks Amphitheatre

the **Red Rocks Trail**, which heads back to the Matthews/Winters parking lot around four miles away. But the Red Rocks Trail soon crosses the Red Rocks Trail Road, which leads after a mile to the remarkable **Red Rocks Amphitheatre** (℡303/694-1234, ⓦwww.redrocksonline.com). Open free of charge during the day, this 9000-seat amphitheater has been the venue for thousands of rock and classical concerts, though none more famous than that documented by U2's *Under a Blood Red Sky*. Squeezed between two 400ft red-sandstone rocks that glow under the late evening sun, the setting is magnificent, with commanding views over Denver.

Having explored the amphitheater, leave it by following the road from its top, West Alameda Parkway, which descends back to the Red Rocks Trail by a different and more interesting route, thanks to numerous contorted red-sandstone rocks along the way.

Morrison and Tiny Town

Despite its proximity to Denver's anodyne suburbs, one-street **MORRISON**, about five miles south of Golden, has somehow preserved its slightly oddball mountain-town feel, with independent businesses overwhelmingly inhabiting the rag-tag wooden buildings on its main street. If you've got kids in tow, and you've already shown them the dinosaur footprints at Dakota Ridge, you may want to head out to **Tiny Town**, 6249 S Turkey Creek Rd (May–Sept daily 10am–5pm, Oct Sat & Sun 10am–5pm; $3; ℡303/697-6829) – it's five miles southwest of Morrison via Hwy-8 South and Hwy-285 West – where a fun miniature steam train will shuttle you to a hundred or so engaging miniature buildings. For somewhere to eat in Morrison before or after a concert or hike, try the *Morrison Inn*, 301 Bear Creek Ave, for good Mexican food and potent margaritas.

The Peak-to-Peak Highway

The scenic **Peak-to-Peak Highway** begins in Idaho Springs and runs seventy-odd miles north through the casino towns of **Central City** and Black Hawk; past **Golden Gate Canyon State Park** and **Nederland**; and on to Estes and Rocky Mountain National parks. The route is confusingly composed of three highways: Hwy-119, Hwy-72, and Hwy-7, which together line up to form the south–north stretch. Views on much of the route are splendid, with the high peaks of the Continental Divide to the west and thousands of square miles of plains to the east. Though a popular summer weekend drive, traffic is rarely busy enough to be a problem except around Central City and Black Hawk, when the addition of casino-bound vehicles can slow things down. The road makes an excellent **cycle ride** for the committed gear-head, particularly at its northern end where the views are most exceptional and the traffic lightest.

Central City

Once crumbling Victorian mining towns, **CENTRAL CITY** and the adjoining, smaller Black Hawk each spent the last decade transforming themselves into shiny casino centers. With little else to drive the economy, it's easy to understand why the local electorate, with the proviso that casinos had to be located in historic buildings, turned to legalized gambling. That said, it's hard to cheer the fact that the once potent atmosphere of these fabled mining towns has been forever lost to the clatter of slot machines.

Central City originally began as an amalgamation of mining camps along steep-sided Gregory Gulch. Soon dubbed "the richest square mile on Earth," the place grew quickly, thanks partly to *New York Tribune* writer **Horace Greeley**. Having been shown a "salted" mine here – one into which local miners had shot gold dust – Greeley returned east to write the famous lines, "Go West young man and grow with the country." By the time of the Civil War, the city had mushroomed to 15,000 strong, making it the territory's largest settlement. It was by all accounts a rough place. City records from 1861 list 217 fistfights, 97 gunfights, eleven Bowie knife fights, and one dog fight – though amazingly no one was killed until 1896. Even Kerouac's 1950s writings found Central City to be a wild outpost:

Central City is two miles high; at first you get drunk on the altitude, then you get tired, and there's a fever in your soul. We approached the lights around the opera house down the narrow dark street; then we took a sharp right and hit some old saloons with swinging doors. Most of the tourists were in the opera. We started off with a few extra-size beers. There was a piano player. Beyond the back door was a view of mountainsides in the moonlight. I let out a yahoo. The night was on.

Jack Kerouac, *On the Road* (1957)

Today the last vestige of this rowdiness is found on the third Saturday in June, **Madame Lou Bunch Day**, named after the last (officially) operating madam in town, when locals dress up as Victorian prostitutes and patrons. The highlight is the Brass Bed Race, complete with its occupant posing as a "sporting house girl" – aka a prostitute. Central City has a softer side too, its **Central City Opera House**, in the town's center (☎303/292-6700 or 1-800/851-8175, ⓦ www .centralcityopera.org), showing off a cosmopolitan air. The opera season runs from mid-July to mid-August and includes both classical and modern pieces. The nearby **Teller House**, 120 Eureka St (10am–4pm; $3; ☎303/582-3200), is a former hotel in which mining baron Horace Tabor kept a large suite for his mistress "Baby Doe" (see box p.243). It's now curiously famous for a face painted on the barroom floor – a confusing tale best explained by the helpful staff. A good impression of what the frontier town must have been like in the mining days can be gained at both the **Gilpin County Historical Museum**, 228 E High St (May–Sept daily 11am–4pm; $3; ☎303/582-5283), and the **Thomas House**, 120 Eureka St (May–Sept Fri–Mon 11am–4pm; tours on the hour; $3). The latter, a 1894 Greek Revival residence, was boarded up in 1917, only to reopen years later to give a time-capsule-like look at 1900s-era domestic life.

Practicalities

Information can be had at the **Central City Visitors' Center**, 141 Nevada St (Mon–Fri 8am–5pm, ☎303/582-0889). Most of the **accommodation** options in both Central City and Black Hawk are in the larger casinos. In Central City, *Harvey's Wagon Wheel Hotel and Casino,* 321 Gregory St (☎303/582-0800 or 1-800/924-6646; ❻), has basic modern rooms, some with good views over town, and free breakfasts. In Black Hawk, the massive *Isle of Capri Casino,* 401 Main St (☎1-800/743-4753, ⓦwww.isleofcapricasino.com; ❻) is a resort aspiring to Las Vegas proportions, featuring restaurants as well as (predictably cheesy) live music and an on-site cabaret. More homey options include the *Shamrock Inn,* 351 Gregory St (☎303/582-5513; ❸), with four small and plain rooms, and the more upmarket *High Street Inn B&B*, 215 W High St (☎303/582-0622; ❺), housed in a beautiful Victorian. Two miles above Central City past its old cemeteries is the *USFS Columbine Campground* (late-May to mid-Oct; ☎303/567-2901), which accommodates both RVs and tents ($12). Thanks to casino deals like prime rib and French fries for $3, there are few other **places to eat** in town. One longstanding local institution, the *Black Forest Inn,* 260 Gregory St (☎303/279-3333), serves up German-style wild game and schnitzel entrees from around $9.

Golden Gate Canyon State Park

While traveling the Peak-to-Peak Highway, it's well worth stopping off to appreciate the landscape from the other side of your car windshield. One excellent place to do this is **Golden Gate Canyon State Park** ($5/vehicle; ⓦwww.parks.state.co.us), where 35 miles of trails cross through aspen forests and lush meadows, giving fantastic views over the Indian Peaks Wilderness and the Continental Divide.

From Black Hawk, the park is eleven miles along Hwy-119 and Golden Gate Canyon Road; it's just 30 miles from downtown Denver, making the park a popular day-trip for citydwellers, who come to escape the summer plains heat and hike, bike, or fish. In winter the park is popular for cross-country skiing, snowshoeing, ice-fishing, skating, and sledding.

For an overview and good introduction to the park, head to the **visitors' center** at the park's eastern fringe (daily 9am–5pm; ☎303/582-3707). The center dispenses free permits for backcountry sites and several Appalachian-style park shelters. Several serviced **campgrounds** (reservations ☎303/470-1444 or 1-800/678-2267, ⓦwww.reserveamerica.com; $7–22) are also available, including the massive *Reverend's Ridge Campground* or the much more pleasant *Aspen Meadow*, with 35 tent sites.

Nederland and Eldora Mountain

Affectionately known as "Ned," the mountain backwater of **NEDERLAND** is a laid-back old mining center that's become a hippie favorite. Sprawling across an entire valley floor eighteen miles north of Central City and seventeen miles east of Boulder, it sits in an attractive location at the head of a reservoir, surrounded by the Roosevelt National Forest and backed by the snow-capped peaks of the Indian Peaks Wilderness Area. Most activity in town centers around a shopping mall and a short street of old clapboard houses nearby, where in the evenings the wooden barroom floors vibrate with the bluegrass and acoustic acts of the surprisingly vibrant local music scene. But it's the town's mountain and forest setting along the Peak-to-Peak Highway that generally attracts visitors to hike and bike in the warmer months. Two miles beyond the Eldora turnoff is a relatively small wooded recreation area, **West Magnolia**, where there's a dense network of trails including some good single-track mountain biking.

The big draw in winter is the **Eldora Mountain Ski Area** (mid-Nov to mid-April; snow reports ☎303/440-8700, ⊛www.eldora.com), just four miles south of town. While not exactly one of Colorado's flagship resorts – the annual snowfall (311in), size (680 acres), and summit elevation (10,600ft) are rather modest by state standards – the relatively cheap lift tickets ($45/day) and convenient location keeps the place busy with beginners and intermediate skiers and boarders. Weekends are not ideal if you're not used to crowds, as even the hectic pace of the lodge can be unsettling. Rated twenty percent beginner, fifty percent intermediate, and thirty percent expert, the slopes feature some solid glade runs as well as a small rail-oriented terrain park, and a steep half-pipe much loved by boarders. Its 45 miles of cross-country tracks also make it a good venue for Nordic skiers.

Practicalities

Bus "N" from Boulder (approximately hourly 5am–10pm; $2.75) – the only way to get here by **public transport** – stops in front of the **visitor information** cabin (unreliable opening hours; ☎303/258-3936 or 1-800/221-0044) and continues, in winter, to the Eldora Mountain Ski Area (40min from Boulder; $3.75) The visitor information cabin is just beside the town's roundabout and adjacent to a small area of old wooden buildings, containing shops and a couple of bars. The *Best Western Lodge*, in the center of town at 55 Lakeview Drive (☎303/258-9463 or 1-800/279-9463, ⊛www.bestwestern.com; ❹), has fine modern **rooms** and an outdoor hot tub, which, along with the lodge's reasonable Eldora ski packages, make it particularly enticing in the winter. Further down along the main road (Hwy-119), opposite the shopping mall, is the small *Nederland Hostel* (☎303/258-7788) which has dorm beds ($15) and some newly refurbished private rooms ($35). About four miles east out of town in the village of Eldora is the cozy, antique-furnished *Goldminer Hotel*, 601 Klondike Ave (☎303/444-4705 or 1-800/422-4629, ⊛www.goldminerhotel .com; ❻), where both hiking and cross-country skiing trails begin just outside the back door. To **camp**, try the USFS *Kelly-Dahl Campground,* three miles east along Hwy-119, which has pretty lakeside sites ($12) with excellent views and a number of nearby trailheads.

Nederland has quite a few places to **eat**. In the old railway carriages in the center of town, *Cools Beans Espresso* is a popular morning hangout, serving excellent espressos, vast slabs of cardamom cake, and thick chocolate brownies. Opposite, *Once Again Books and Café* (☎303/258-3695) can provide a number of snacks along with Internet access and a fine collection of used books. Up in the historic district, the popular *Neapolitan's*, 1 W 1st St, bakes massive pizzas, served alongside vast portions of good pasta ($6) in a candlelit, cabin-style restaurant. Across the road, the all-wood *Pioneer Inn* is open all day and late into the night, serving breakfasts, burgers, and Mexican dishes like green chili burritos ($7). The *Inn*'s **bar** is busy with locals all day and really gets going with live music on Fridays. The most upmarket eating choice is the *Black Forest Restaurant*, just above the shopping mall; it has the same owners, rustic style, and German menu as the longtime favorite in Central City (see p.86).

Boulder

One of the country's liveliest college towns, **BOULDER**, just under 30 miles northwest of Denver on Hwy-36, is filled with a youthful population that divides its time between healthy daytime outdoor activities and almost equally unhealthy nighttime ones. Founded in 1858 by a prospecting party who erroneously felt that the nearby **Flatiron Mountains** – enormous sandstone monoliths that lean against the first swell of the Rockies – "looked right for gold," Boulder bloomed with the addition of a railroad and a university in the 1870s, and hasn't stopped growing since. Thanks largely to the presence of the **University of Colorado–Boulder** and its 26,000 students, the small town has fostered an offbeat, liberal vibe, making it one of the West's major centers for alternative medicine and spirituality. Additionally, Boulder's mountainous location – ideal for cycling, hiking, and climbing – has attracted scores of outdoor enthusiasts, who continue to flock here despite closely guarded city restrictions on growth. Consequently, overcrowding is a major concern, harking back to an Arapaho **curse** placed on the town when the natives were forced into the mountains. According to the hex, all those setting eyes on the area would be unable to leave, leading to overpopulation and ultimately destruction.

Arrival and information

The main point of entry for local and long-distance **buses** is the Transit Center, 14th and Walnut streets (☏303/442-1044). Regular services from Denver International ($10) and the city itself ($3.75) arrive here as well. For city information, visit the hospitable, low-key **Boulder Convention & Visitors Bureau**, 2440 Pearl St (Mon–Fri 9am–5pm; ☏303/442-2911 or 1-800/444-0447, ⓦwww.bouldercoloradousa.com). If you're planning on having a detailed look around town head first to Historic Boulder, 646 Pearl St (☏303/444-5192), a non-profit organization which sells brochures ($3) for seven self-guided walking **tours** of the city's various districts.

For information on public lands around Boulder, contact the City of Boulder Open Space & Mountain Parks department (☏303-441-3440 ⓦwww.ci.boulder.co.us/openspace), which manages large chunks of land in the neighboring foothills. The USFS (aka US Forest Service) **Boulder Ranger District Office**, 2995 Baseline Rd (☏303/444-6600, ⓦwww.fs.fed.us/r2/arnf), provides information and camping permits for the Roosevelt National Forest and the Indian Peaks Wilderness Area.

Getting around

One of Boulder's chief attractions is that it's easy and pleasant to get around, and between most of its most interesting parts – downtown, the University Hill district, Boulder Creek, and Boulder Mountain Park – you can do so **on foot**. If you tire of walking you can use the town's excellent **bus** service: HOP shuttle buses (every 15min Mon–Sat 7am–7pm, until 10pm Thurs–Sun during college

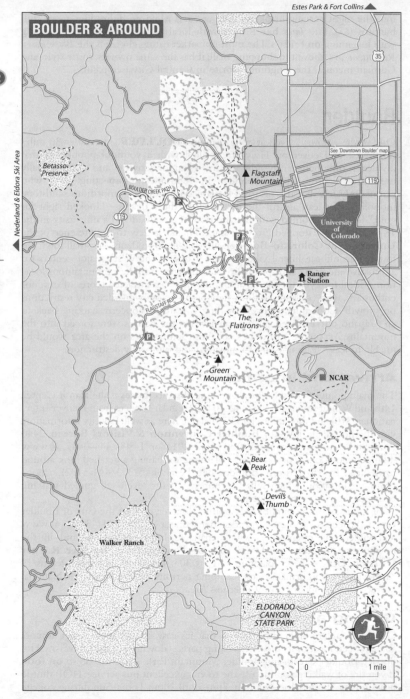

BOULDER & AROUND

Estes Park & Fort Collins ▲

Nederland & Eldora Ski Area ▲

Betasso Preserve

BOULDER CREEK PATH

119

See 'Downtown Boulder' map

▲ Flagstaff Mountain

7   119

University of Colorado

P

P

P ★ Ranger Station

FLAGSTAFF ROAD

▲ The Flatirons

P

▲ Green Mountain

■ NCAR

▲ Bear Peak

▲ Devils Thumb

Walker Ranch

ELDORADO CANYON STATE PARK

N

0   1 mile

terms; $1), link downtown, the university, and the major shopping center, Crossroads Mall. SKIP (Mon–Fri 5.30am–midnight, Sun 7.30am–10.30pm; $1) is another useful service, running back and forth along most of Broadway; it picks up every 10 minutes on the weekdays, every 30 minutes after 7pm and on the weekends. For a **taxi**, try either Boulder Yellow Cab (T303/777-7777) or Metro Taxi (T303/333-3333).

Accommodation

Due in large part to the university's busy schedule of events, Boulder **accommodation** is more or less full up all year, though the official peak season is between May and October. Most of the town's upscale **hotels** and **B&Bs** are dotted around the Pearl Street Mall, while cheaper, locally owned **motels** are mostly found a half-hour walk out of town along the attractive Boulder Creek Path towards the mountains. There's also a large, well-organized **hostel** in the student end of town. If you get stuck, or are content with a spot by a major highway, a number of large motels line 28th St, around three miles east of downtown. If you're looking to **camp** in the area, there are no options in town; the *Boulder Mountain Lodge*, four miles away (see below), is your best bet.

Best Western Boulder Inn 770 28th St T303/449-3800 or 1-800/233-8469, Wwww .boulderinn.com. A plain, hundred-room motel across from the CU-Boulder campus's southern end. Facilities include a hot tub, sauna, and outdoor pool (open seasonally); admission to the nearby fitness center is also included. Free continental breakfast daily. **⑤**

Boulder Creek Quality Inn 2020 Arapahoe Ave T303/449-7550 or 1-800/449-7550 Wwww .qualityinnboulder.com. Slick motel within walking distance of downtown and the university. Rooms have free high-speed internet and cable TV and access to an indoor pool, fitness room, hot tub, and sauna. A good buffet breakfast is included in rates. Refrigerators and microwaves available in some units. **⑥**

Boulder International Youth Hostel 1107 12th St T303/442-0522 or 1-888/442-0522, Wwww.boulderhostel.com. Businesslike but sociable hostel in the bustling University Hill district. Dorm rooms cost $20. There are also several private rooms ($49 per double) with weekly rates available.

Boulder Mountain Lodge 91 Four Mile Canyon Rd T303/444-0882 or 1-800/458-0882, Wwww .bouldermountainlodge.com. Both motel rooms and camping sites are available in and around this stone lodge, a former old narrow-gauge train depot five miles west of town along Hwy-119. There are around twenty shady spots to camp ($18), and many of the rustic motel-style units have kitchenettes or full kitchens. Hot tubs are next to the creek, and a pool is open in summer. **④**

Boulder Outlook Hotel 800 28th St T303/443-3322 or 1-800/542-0304, Wwww.boulderoutlook .com. Well-maintained motel with 165 large, clean

rooms. The on-site fitness center includes a climbing wall and rock, a large indoor pool, hot tub, and sauna. Like all the other hotels along this part of 28th St, it's very close to the university. **⑦**

Briar Rose 2151 Arapahoe Ave T303/442-3007, Wwww.briarrosebb.com. Welcoming B&B with landscaped gardens within walking distance of Crossroads Mall, CU-Boulder, and downtown. Some of the antique-furnished rooms have woodburning fireplaces, while both breakfast and afternoon tea – often served on the cheery sun porch – feature home-baked treats. **⑦**

Colorado Chautauqua 900 Baseline Rd T303/442-3282 ext 11, Wwww .chautauqua.com. In a splendid location below the Flatirons, the *Chautauqua* was envisaged as a simple retreat and has successfully remained so. Both plain rooms and cottages are available from June through August, but can only be booked for four nights or more. The one- to three-bedroom cottages have full kitchens, but no telephones, a/c, or TVs. They do, though, have one of the most beautiful locations in town and are often booked up six months in advance. **④**

Foot of the Mountain Motel 200 Arapahoe Ave T303/442-5688 or 1-866/773-5489, Wwww .footofthemountainmotel.com. Clean and friendly log-cabin-style motel, nine blocks from downtown beside Boulder Creek at the foot of Flagstaff Mountain. All rooms have refrigerators and cable TV. **④**

Hotel Boulderado 2115 13th St T303/442-4344 or 1-800/433-4344, Wwww.boulderado.com. This local landmark, opened in 1909 and only a block from Pearl St, is the town's first and still finest hotel. Each of the

160 lavishly decorated, Victorian-style rooms have wrought-iron or four-poster beds, and past guests include Robert Frost and Louis Armstrong. **7**

The Inn on Mapleton Hill 1001 Spruce St ☎303/449-6528 or 1-800/276-6528, ⓦwww .innonmapletonhill.com. Victorian residence nestling under towering cottonwoods on a quiet street two short blocks from the Pearl Street Mall. As the only Boulder B&B with resident owners, it provides unrivalled personal touches, as evidenced in the floral-decorated, antique-furnished rooms. **6**

Lazy L Motel 1000 28th St ☎303/442-7525. No-frills motel – probably as cheap and convenient as you'll find in Boulder – on the 28th Street strip, just opposite the University of Colorado campus. Units come with kitchenettes and there's a pool. **4**

Pearl Street Inn 1820 Pearl St ☎303/444-5584 or 1-888/810-1312, ⓦwww.pearlstreet.com.

Elegant B&B with antique-furnished rooms overlooking a quiet central courtyard three blocks east of the Pearl Street Mall. Thanks to a high fence around its pretty gardens, the B&B maintains a secluded feel. Afternoon refreshments are also included. **6**

Silver Saddle Motel 90 Arapahoe Ave ☎303/442-8022 or 1-800/525-9509, ⓦwww.silversaddlemotel .com. Large motel on the edge of town, around 20min walk from the center along the Boulder Creek Path. All units have refrigerators and microwaves **4**

University Inn 1632 Broadway ☎303/471-1700, ⓦwww.boulderuniversityinn.com. The most central motel in town is nothing fancy, though rooms have cable TV and there's free coffee and doughnuts for breakfast. There's also a tiny pool (alongside the busy Broadway Ave) and laundry facilities available. **5**

The Town

It's the town's students, hippies, and New Age residents who have made Boulder an offbeat and popular tourist destination. In fact, there are few attractions in the renovated Victorian **downtown** area and mostly visitors just browse up and down its pedestrian mall. To the south, the lively **University Hill District** also has only a couple of modest museums, though again just wandering around is pleasant enough. Pretty soon you'll probably find yourself heading out of town, along with the locals, to the town's real gems: the easily accessible **Mountain Parks** just west of town that have become an adventure playground for hikers, bikers, and climbers.

Downtown Boulder

Downtown centers on the leafy pedestrian mall of **Pearl Street**, lined with all sorts of lively cafés, galleries, and stores that can easily take a few hours to explore. The most notable sight is the redbrick **Hotel Boulderado**, just north of the mall at 2115 13th St. It's hard to believe that only a few decades ago this magnificently restored 1909 structure, with a cantilevered cherrywood staircase and an Italian stained-glass ceiling, was on the verge of total decay. Like the rest of downtown, the hotel was hit hard by the decline that came as businesses moved into the suburbs. Things were so bad for awhile that in the 1960s a snowstorm crashed in the glass ceiling, cooks hung bait to deter rats, and vagrants slept in empty rooms.

A few blocks south, on the opposite side of the Pearl Street Mall, runs the **Boulder Creek Path**, cutting through downtown between Canyon Boulevard and Arapahoe Avenue. The nine-mile-long path follows the creek through a canyon and out to the eastern plains, making for a great jog, skate, or bike ride. On hot summer afternoons, walking west from downtown, then **floating** back down the creek on an inner tube (on sale at local gas stations, more cheaply outside of downtown) is hard to beat.

The University District

Boulder owes much of its identity to the **University of Colorado** (☎303/492-1411, ⓦwww.colorado.edu), whose pleasant landscaped redbrick-and-tile **campus** bustles with life during term-time, as does the adjacent

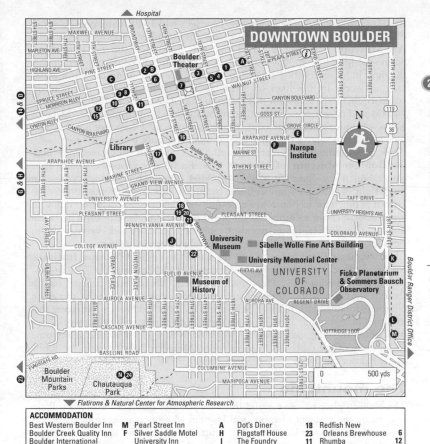

DOWNTOWN BOULDER

N

▼ Flatirons & Natural Center for Atmospheric Research

ACCOMMODATION						RESTAURANTS & BARS			
Best Western Boulder Inn	M	Pearl Street Inn	A	Dot's Diner	18	Redfish New			
Boulder Creek Quality Inn	F	Silver Saddle Motel	H	Flagstaff House	23	Orleans Brewhouse	6
Boulder International		University Inn	I	The Foundry	11	Rhumba	12
Youth Hostel	J			Illegal Pete's	22	Rocky Mountain	
Boulder Mountain Lodge	D	RESTAURANTS & BARS		K's China	19	Joe's Café	7
Boulder Outlook Hotel	L	Alfalfa	17	La Iguana	20	Round Midnight	8
Briar Rose	E	bd's Mongolian		Moshi Moshi Bowl	4	Sherpa's	15
Chautauqua Park	N	Barbecue	5	Mountain Sun		Sunflower	1
Foot of the Mountain Motel	G	Boulder Dushanbe		Pub & Brewery	3	Tra-Ling's	
Hotel Boulderado	B	Teahouse	16	Pasta Jay's	9	Oriental Café	21
The Inn on Mapleton Hill	C	Catacombs	2	Red Lion Inn	14	The Walrus	13
Lazy L Motel	K	Chautauqua Dining Hall	24			West End Tavern	10

shopping district known as "The Hill." In the 1960s, the campus environs were seen as a regional counterculture stronghold, attracting hippies and generally propagating dissent, earning the town the "People's Republic of Boulder" tag that's since stuck. Though the town of Boulder still has a very enlightened liberal attitude, today this stems much less from the activities of CU students, many of whom are far more likely to engage in the almost annual frat-house riots than dabble in politics.

Campus tours (Mon–Fri 10.30am & 2.30pm; ☎303/492-6301) and maps are available at the **Memorial Center**, Broadway and Euclid, (Mon–Thurs 7am–midnight, Fri & Sat 7am–1am, Sun 11am–midnight), though meandering through the leafy campus alone is easy enough. For a sense of the place's history have a quick wander around the **Heritage Center** (Mon–Fri 10am–4pm; free;

ⓣ303/492-6329,ⓦwww.cualum.org/heritage),which celebrates over a century of university life and alumni achievements. Of the other campus museums, the **Art Museum**, in the Sibell-Wolle Fine Arts Building (Mon–Fri 10am–5pm, Sat noon–4pm; free; ⓣ303-492-8300, ⓦwww.colorado.edu/cuartmuseum), is the most impressive, with a collection that includes around five thousand wide-ranging works by the likes of Rembrandt, Hogarth, Picasso, and more. In comparison, there's really not that much to the **CU Museum**, 15th and Broadway (Mon–Fri 9am–5pm, Sat 9am–4pm, Sun 10am–4pm; free; ⓣ303/492-6892, ⓦwww.cumuseum.colorado.edu), though it's worth a look for its dinosaur skeletons and whatever traveling exhibit that's currently being hosted.

Not associated with CU, but just southwest of campus on University Hill, is the **Boulder Museum of History**, 1206 Euclid Ave (Tues–Fri 10am–4pm, Sat & Sun noon–4pm; $5; ⓣ303/449/3464, ⓦwww.boulderhistorymuseum .org). Built in 1899 as a summer home by a New York merchant, the building is known as much for its impressive nine-foot-tall Tiffany stained-glass window as for its assortment of memorabilia on the history of Boulder County. The ragtag downstairs collection relates mainly to mining, ranching, and everyday life in Boulder, while the second floor holds a sizeable costume gallery.

Likewise unaffiliated but nearby is the Buddhist-inspired **Naropa Institute**, on the north edge of the university campus at 2130 Arapahoe Ave (ⓣ303/444-0202, ⓦww.naropa.edu). This unconventional liberal arts college blends Eastern intuition with Western logic, including writing courses at the Allen Ginsberg-founded Jack Kerouac School of Disembodied Poetics (whatever that means). The institute is also the venue for various performances and workshops throughout the year, and visitors are welcome to have a look around at any time or join one of the fairly dull campus tours (Mon–Fri 2pm; meet in the lobby of the Admin building).

The mountains

The obvious place to aim for, and the focal point of Boulder's Mountain Parks system, are the adjacent Flatirons and Flagstaff Mountain areas. Both are accessible on foot from the University Hill District and a helpful **Ranger Cottage**, just west of the Chautauqua (see opposite; Mon–Fri 8.30am–5pm, irregular weekend hours; ⓣ303/441-3408), is well stocked with hiking information. They also sell the *Boulder Mountain Parks Trail Map* ($5), an indispensable source of information on the 100 miles of hiking trails throughout the area.

If you want to do more than just hike you'll probably want to go further afield, and so require some other form of transport. Since mountain bikers are banned from Flagstaff and Flatiron area trails – with the exception of the excellent **Walker Ranch** (see opposite) – the best place to ride is west up **Boulder Canyon**, particularly the Betasso Reserve and the Switzerland Trail. Climbers too will find that although there is excellent climbing around the Flatirons, most of the really world-class stuff is down in **Eldorado Canyon**. The situation is similar for kayaking and fishing: there are good spots in and around town, but the best places are a little ways out. For detailed advice and gear head to one of Boulder's many outfitters, some of whom are detailed in the box on p.96. The other good place to bone up in advance is the City of Boulder Open Space & Mountain Parks website, ⓦwww.ci.boulder.co.us/openspace/index.htm.

The Flatirons and around

On the southwest fringe of town, the landmark **Flatirons** form the centerpiece of the Boulder Mountain Parks. This network of rocky peaks and valleys is laced with some 8000 acres of trails and copious amounts of rough climbing, taking in Bear Peak, Green and Flagstaff mountains, and Mount Sanitas. The Flatirons themselves are part of a string of formations along the Front Range that include the Garden of the Gods in Colorado Springs and Red Rocks near Denver. All are former oceanic sediments tilted in the fold-and-thrust construction of the mountain range over the last 65 million years. Hugely popular with climbers, these rock faces offer superb no-bolt **sport climbing**; the first and second flatirons are frequently free-climbed, but the third (counted north to south) definitely warrants rope. That said, the third has been climbed without using hands, wearing roller skates, naked, and in under eight minutes, all by separate climbers looking for a new challenge.

Practically at the base of the Flatirons lies the **Colorado Chautauqua**, 900 Baseline Rd (☎303/442-3282, ⓦwww.chautauqua.com), a community of wooden cabins and houses first opened in 1898 as a retreat for Texans, as part of a movement that built around 400 retreats nationwide to foster adult education and cultural entertainment. The term "chautauqua" was originally applied to a late-nineteenth-century popular educational movement which involved regular assemblies throughout rural America until the mid-1920s. When the chautauqua came to town, it brought entertainment for the whole community, with speakers, teachers, musicians, entertainers, and specialists of the day. No longer nomadic, Boulder's chautauqua is centered around the grand auditorium and dining hall; the grounds are also the venue for summer events like the **Colorado Music Festival** (☎303/449-1397, ⓦwww.coloradomusicfest.org), a well-regarded classical music event that begins in mid-June.

Of the **trails** that begin beside the Chautauqua, the best is probably the McClintock Trail, an easy and mostly shady hike that follows the contours of the mountain below the Flatirons. The trail climbs gently for two miles beyond the Ranger Cottage before joining the Mesa Trail, which heads south to Eldorado Canyon, a further five miles away. But only a mile past the intersection of the two trails is the **Natural Center for Atmospheric Research** (Mon–Fri 8am–5pm, Sat & Sun 9am–3pm; ☎303/497-1174, ⓦwww.ncar.ucar.edu), a facility that researches and monitors climate; it's a three-hour round-trip hike from the Ranger Cottage. While free tours of the center are given daily at noon, self-guided ones can be taken at any time. Unfortunately, the exhibits on climate change and weather research are disappointing, as is the uneventful sight of some of the world's beefiest computers performing billions of calculations per second.

Flagstaff Mountain

Striking out in the opposite direction to the McClintock Trail, Baseline Road passes the Chautauqua complex to ascend **Flagstaff Mountain**, also part of the Boulder Mountain Parks system. The hike or drive up this road are obvious excursions for great views over the plains and further into the Rockies; it's a particular favorite of local cyclists. For the most part, hiking routes avoid the steep road and take considerably longer than the drive up, so it's generally better to drive to one of the trailhead parking lots ($5/day) for access to scenic hikes away from the road. Mountain bikers should follow Flagstaff Road part of the way back down the mountain's west side to the **Walker Ranch Loop**, a wooded and mostly straightforward eight-mile single- and double-track loop (popularly done counterclockwise) that takes around two hours to bike. The forest trail here feels wild; there's a relatively good chance of spotting mountain lions or black bears; and the loop twice crosses a sizeable creek that has good fly-fishing holes.

Betasso Reserve and the Switzerland Trail

West along Boulder Canyon, the **Betasso Reserve** is a great place for mountain biking, offering a smooth two-mile single-track loop (2hr) with some fine views of Boulder along the way; it's the best you can do direct from the city. It's also good for hiking, but try to go on a Wednesday or Saturday when the trails are closed to bikers and so are far more relaxing. To **get here**, leave town by heading west along the Boulder Creek Path to its terminus, then use the busy Hwy-119 and quieter Sugarloaf Road to complete the six miles to the reserve. If you've ridden here, once you complete the signposted loop you should turn east out of the reserve lot to enjoy the thrilling off-road descent and taxing switchbacks on the Boulder Canyon Link Trail, which weaves its way back to Hwy-119. Further up the Boulder Canyon, the rugged and little-used 4WD **Switzerland Trail** offers the highlight of an excellent 30-mile day-trip of mostly downhill riding, courtesy of the local bus starting from either Nederland or Boulder. Be sure to pick up a **map** before you go, since many of the trails along the way are not signposted. From Boulder, take the "N" **bus** to Nederland (approximately hourly 5am–10pm; $2.75; bikes taken for free), from where you cycle south down the Peak-to-Peak Highway for eight miles to the turn-off for CR-120 (not signposted). The CR-120 leads to a number of different trails, including the Switzerland (again not signposted) alongside peaceful Fourmile Canyon, all culminating at the conical Sugarloaf Mountain. Sugarloaf Road begins here, and heads downhill back to Boulder

Outdoor outfitters

With a population that's universally keen on outdoor recreation, there's no shortage in Boulder of places to get sports equipment and advice about where to use it. The best all-around store is REI, 1789 28th St (☏303/583-997), but you will probably find better local advice and gear at the smaller specialist shops.

Climbers will find Mountain Sports, 821 Pearl St (☏303/443-6700), useful and central, but much better is the well-stocked climbing, hiking, and Nordic ski specialist Neptune Mountaineering, south of town in the Table Mesa shopping center, at 633 S Broadway (☏303/499-8866). Look for the seminal work on climbing in the area – Richard Rossiter's *Boulder Climbs South* (Chokestone Press) – in the store's excellent book department. Also of interest might be a local climbing school, the Boulder Rock School (☏303/447-2804 or 1-800/836-4008, ⓦwww.boulderrock.com), which offers courses for all ages and skill levels.

Small **biking** stores are dotted all around town and include Full Cycle, on University Hill at 1211 13th St (☏303/440-7771), and University Bicycles, at Pearl and 9th streets (☏303/444-4196). Both rent out front-suspension mountain bikes from around $25/day. The one essential item to pick up if you're interested in exploring more widely is the *Boulder County Mountain Bike Map* ($9), available from all Boulder bike shops.

Local **kayakers** head to Boulder Creek, and it's certainly worth joining in the fun, but for longer trips ask at the Paddle Shop, 1727 15th St (☏303/786-8799), or the Boulder Outdoor Center, 2510 47th St (☏303/444-8420), both of which offer kayak instruction, raft trips, and rentals. For advice on **fishing** visit the Front Range Anglers, 629-B S Broadway (☏303/494-1375) or Kinsley Outfitters, on University Hill at 1155 13th St (☏303/442-6204).

For **ski** and **snowboard** rentals contact Doc's Sports, 627 S Broadway (☏303/499-0963), who also do overnight repairs, or Boulder Ski Deals, 2525 Arapahoe Ave (☏303/938-8799), where cut-price lift tickets for some of Colorado's ski resorts are often up for grabs.

via Hwy-119 and Boulder Creek Path. If you still have energy left towards the end of the ride, make the turn into Betasso Reserve just two miles shy of the main road.

Eldorado Canyon State Park

Though there's no shortage of great climbing rock in the Boulder Mountain Parks, expert climbers in the area often head out to the sheer cliffs of **Eldorado Canyon State Park**, eight miles southwest of Boulder along CR-93 to CR-170 ($2/person or $5–6/vehicle; ☎303/494-3943, ⊛parks.state.co.us). With vertical cliffs up to 850ft high, the park is known as one of the country's premier sites for difficult (class 5.6 to 5.9) **climbing**. Perhaps the park's climbers are inspired by Ivy Baldwin, an eccentric daredevil who tightrope-walked across a 500ft cable spanning the Bastille, a rock tower on the south side of the canyon, and the Wind Tower to the north, 89 times between 1906 and 1926. If you'd rather not defy gravity, you might be tempted by the good rainbow trout **fishing** in the canyon's creek or the **hot springs** at Eldorado Springs, a small resort just east of the state park where you can have a soak (June–Aug 10am–6pm; $6; ☎303/499-1316).

Eating

From hippie-styled vegetarian cafés to all-American burger bars and elegant dining options, Boulder **restaurants** are surprisingly diverse. Most are found either downtown around Pearl Street or in the University Hill area.

Alfalfa1651 Broadway. Large wholefood supermarket with deli, serving pizza slices ($3) and grilled chicken, a huge salad bar, and juice bar. A great place to stock up for a picnic.

bd's Mongolian Barbecue 1600 Pearl St. As with other Mongolian BBQ spots, customers do a great deal of the work here. Food is a buffet DIY-style; pile your plate high with meat, veggies, oils, and seasoning, then have it fried on a massive hotplate. Healthy but not too cheap.

Boulder Dushanbe Teahouse 1770 13th St ☎303/442-4993. Easily Boulder's oddest building is this ornately handcarved and painted Persian teahouse, brought here from Boulder's twin city of Dushanbe in Tajikistan. Inside the teahouse is equally lavishly and authentically decorated, with fourteen Siberian cedar pillars surrounding a grand central fountain. The menu offers food from the world over, with emphasis on Asian dishes, naturally including several Tajik lamb specialties. Appetizers run $5–6; dinner entrees $10–18. But the real specialty is the tea – around seventy varieties are available, three of which are served, along with pastries, at the very civilized afternoon teas (daily 3–5pm; $16; reservations required).

Chautauqua Dining Hall 900 Baseline Rd ☎303/440-3776. Thoughtfully prepared selections are served on the lovely patio overlooking the park, or in a large dining hall with a slightly institutional feel. Try the berry waffles for breakfast ($8); a selection of salads, the grilled vegetable and goats' cheese sandwich, or the grilled salmon melt for lunch ($10); and grilled lamb or Rocky Mountain trout for dinner ($20). Good fruit pies make the perfect dessert.

Dot's Diner 2716 N 28th St and 1333 Broadway. Reliable, busy local diner with all the usual inexpensive favorites for breakfast or lunch, including some of the best buttermilk biscuits in town, along with good *huevos rancheros*. In two locations, one near the town's motel row (28th Street), the other just north of the University Hill District.

Flagstaff House 1138 Flagstaff Rd ☎303/442-4640. A good upmarket choice – it's the only restaurant the Emperor and Empress of Japan deigned to dine in on their 1994 visit to the States – with superb views from its 1000ft-high vantage-point above town. Good local game dishes are sprinkled among the more than 30 gourmet entrees on offer; two courses run to about $40. Jacket and tie required.

Illegal Pete's 1320 College. Bustling takeaway or eat-in Mexican restaurant, serving large portions of low-priced food into the small hours of the night. Try the massive and excellent potato burrito ($5).

Moshi Moshi Bowl 1628 Pearl St ☎720/565-9787. Cavernous and stylish Japanese fast-food joint a short walk east of the Pearl Street Mall. Perfect for a quick bowl of noodles or an inexpensive sushi fix.

Mountain Sun Pub and Brewery 1535 Pearl St ☎ 303/546-0886. Bright ethnic-style decor, hippie ambiance, and a laid-back crowd make this popular microbrewery feel very Boulder. The vast beer selection – seven are made on the premises – accompanies inexpensive sandwiches, burgers, burritos, and fish and chips. Weekend nights often see live bluegrass. Open for both lunch and dinner.

Pasta Jay's 1001 Pearl St. A warm exposed-brick trattoria with bright red-check tablecloths and large, fresh portions of pasta. Try the excellent gnocchi or tortellini ($7) with any of their tasty homemade sauces. Open for lunch and dinner.

Red Lion Inn Boulder Canyon Drive, 2.5 miles west of town on the road to Nederland ☎ 303/442-9368. This rustic restaurant has served Central European and wild game dishes, such as boar, for as long as anyone can remember – even the sides, like the red cabbage and spaetzle noodles, have a strong Austro-German influence. Cheap early dinner deals are available before 6pm; after that expect to pay around $15 for a dish.

Redfish New Orleans Brewhouse 2027 13th St. Trendy exposed-brick restaurant with excellent but pricey helpings of Cajun food. The menu changes frequently, but appetizers usually include seafood gumbo, crawfish Caesar, and fresh oysters. Entrees are also mostly based around fresh seafood, though there are some good steaks here too. Six home-brewed beers are on offer and the wine list is extensive.

Rhumba 950 Pearl St. Slightly pretentious but nonetheless popular bar and restaurant serving great rum cocktails (happy hour 4–6pm) and zingy Caribbean cuisine: snapper roasted in banana leaves, conch chowder, catfish egg rolls, and jerk chicken. Open daily for lunch (except Mon) and dinner.

Rocky Mountain Joe's Café 1410 Pearl St. Decorated with local historic photos, *Joe's* serves numerous breakfast options and wholesome quiches, soups, and sandwiches for lunch. The excellent fresh muffins and tasty banana bread are both worth stopping in for. Open daily until 2pm.

Sherpa's 825 Walnut St ☎ 303/440-7151. Run by a former native Nepali mountain guide, this restaurant is designed to be a place for climbers and adventurers to congregate, as the climbing memorabilia and good little travel library suggest. The reasonably priced food includes wonderful *momo* (nepali dumplings) and many other Himalayan takes on recognizable North Indian fare.

Sunflower 1701 Pearl St ☎ 303/440-0220. High prices, healthy lifestyles, and cosmopolitan preoccupations collide in this thoroughly Boulder fine dining establishment. The cheerfully bright place is a particularly good choice for visiting gourmet vegetarians, but also offers a large number of omnivorous choices for others. The menu is built entirely from fresh, organic, and free-range ingredients, an ethos which extends to the beer and wine list. Among the many imaginative possibilities are the pepper-seared charbroiled ahi tuna, a tempeh scaloppini, and the Chilean sea bass.

Tra-Ling's Oriental Café 1305 Broadway. Grungy canteen-style restaurant with outstanding and amazingly cheap Chinese food bought by the scoop. The sweet and sour chicken is excellent, as are the crispy spinach or crab wontons; vegetarians will love the hot and spicy tofu.

Nightlife and entertainment

For a town of only 100,000, Boulder more than does itself justice once night rolls on thanks largely to the gregarious CU crowd. Not only do the students keep the few small bars on University Hill lively, they also spill downtown onto **Pearl Street**, where the combination of revelers and evening buskers often keep it as busy as it is during the day. And while the bulk of the local **nightlife** (including the brewhouses listed above) is dotted around the pedestrian mall, the live music scene is centered up on the Hill. The **Fox Theatre**, 1135 13th St (☎303/443-3399, ⓦwww.foxtheatre.com), a converted movie theater, and the longstanding **Tulagi**, 1129 13th (☎303/938-8090), both pull in local and decently well-known national bands.

While dance and theater performances are put on by the university in various campus halls, the major non-school venue in town is the **Boulder Theater**, 2032 14th (☎303/786-7030, ⓦwww.bouldertheater.com), where the **Boulder Philharmonic** (☎303/449-1343, ⓦwww.boulderphil.com) often plays on Fridays and Saturdays. Up-to-date listings can be found in the "Friday" magazine in the *Daily Camera*, available from newsagents, and the free *Boulder*

Planet and *Boulder Weekly* papers, available in cafés and numerous downtown dispensers. A note to **smokers**: restrictions on smoking in public buildings are enforced throughout town, so to take a drag you'll have to head out onto the street or into a sealed room within a bar.

Catacombs in the *Hotel Boulderado*, 2115 13th St. Atmospheric vaults beneath the oldest hotel in town draw a mixed crowd – not just students – to its almost nightly live blues, jazz, and acoustic music.

The Foundry 1109 Walnut St ☎ 303/447-1803. The bulk of this club's huge area is devoted to a dozen or so full-size pool tables. The small bar beside offers numerous draft beers and hums on weekend nights, when jazz and blues plays alongside the tiny dance floor.

K's China ☎ 303/413-0000. Budget Chinese restaurant, whose role as late-opening (until 2am), crowded, and boisterous rooftop bar – from where there are superb views of downtown Boulder and the Flatirons – has long overshadowed its importance as an eatery.

La Iguana 1301 Broadway ☎ 303/938-8888. Large, gregarious outdoor bar, often with cheap deals on Mexican beers, at the northern end of the Hill district.

Round Midnight 1005 Pearl St ☎ 303/442-2176. The packed weekend dance floor – which vibrates to mainly hip-hop – is your best bet for getting your groove on downtown. Cover $3.

The Walrus 1911 11th St. Good atmosphere in a consistently bustling bar, with pool tables, a juke-box, plenty of neon, and shells from free peanuts scattered throughout by a self-consciously grungy college crowd that heads here to party.

West End Tavern 926 Pearl St ☎ 303/444-3535. Great venue for live jazz and comedy, with local microbrews and spectacular Flatiron views from the roof terrace.

Listings

Banks ATMs are located all along the Hill and Pearl St. Wells Fargo, just beyond the pedestrian mall on 1242 Pearl St (☎ 303/442-0351), offers most other banking services.

Books Boulder Bookstore, 1107 Pearl St (☎ 303/447-2074 or 1-800/244-4651), is the best all-round bookstore in town. There are also several special-interest bookshops along Pearl Street.

Car rental See Basics for national numbers of major chains or try cheap local company Price King (☎ 303/545-6600).

Internet The public library, 1000 Canyon Drive (☎ 303/441-3111), has numerous free public terminals and a free WiFi hotspot.

Laundry Doozy Duds, 1150 University Ave (7am–11.30pm), is one of a number of places around the University Hill area.

Medical The supermarket King Soopers, 1650 30th St (☎ 303/444-0164), has a 24hr pharmacy. Boulder Community Hospital is off N Broadway at 1100 Balsam Ave (☎ 303/440-2273).

Post office Boulder's main post office is at 1905 15th St.

Fort Collins

With a rising population of almost 120,000, **FORT COLLINS** straddles the fine line between big town and small city. In its first incarnation as an 1862 military post, it was humble Camp Collins, established to protect traders traveling through the region. When the camp was washed out by a flood in 1864, the new settlement was given grown-up status as a fort. Today, Fort Collins is largely known as the home of **Colorado State University**, somewhat secondary in status to Boulder's CU. You may even hear the town referred to as "Boulder, without the hippies"; although this description might dismay the hippies who do amble the streets of Fort Collins. In any event, it is the town's proximity to Rocky Mountain National Park – fifty miles, and just under an hour's drive from the park's eastern entrance – and neighboring **Cache la Poudre Canyon**, together with the energy which accompanies any college population, that have combined to put Fort Collins near the very top of the list of ideal "lifestyle" cities in the US.

Arrival, information, and getting around

Driving into Fort Collins from just about any direction can be a little dispiriting. There's not much mountain romance about the bland stretch of I-25 which runs from Denver via Fort Collins and on to Laramie, Wyoming, while much of I-287 – the road between Loveland and Fort Collins – is lined with car dealers and a succession of bland shopping malls and fast-food outlets. Things brighten considerably, however, as soon as you reach the CSU neighborhood around College Avenue and Laurel Street, and historic Old Town is just a few blocks further north. The **bus terminal** for Greyhound and TMN&O is at the junction of Riverside Ave and East Mulberry (office open daily 7.30am–12.30pm & 2.30–6.30pm; ℡970/221-1327).

The town has two **tourist offices**: the larger Convention and Vistors Bureau, four miles east of town, near I-25 exit 268, at 3545 Prospect Rd (Mon–Sat 8am–5pm; ℡970/491-3388 or 1-800/274-3678, ⓦwww.ftcollins.com), and the far smaller but more convenient Downtown Visitors Information Center, in the middle of Old Town Square (℡970/419-1050). There is also a **USFS office** at 2150 Centre Ave (Mon–Fri 8am–5pm; ℡970/295-6700, ⓦwww.fs.fed.us/arnf), which has useful information on recreation in nearby Cache la Poudre Canyon.

The **local bus** network, Transfort (Mon–Sat; $1.25; ℡970/221-6620 ⓦwww.fcgov.com/transfort), operates fifteen routes throughout Fort Collins; pick up a schedule including color-coded route maps from a visitor center or on board a bus. For local **taxis** and a shuttle service to Denver International Airport ($26) call Shamrock Taxis (℡970/482-0505, ⓦwww.rideshamrock.com).

Accommodation

Accommodation in Fort Collins is most scarce during the summer, when some National Park visitors use it as their base. It's otherwise hard to predict when the town will be busiest, since a college event or football game can be enough to stretch lodging resources on any weekend. Most of the more desirable places to stay are clustered around the university, while the town center, several blocks to the north of the campus, is inexplicably short on accommodation of any kind. If you've arrived by car and don't have a reservation, you may well find yourself resorting to one of the standard chain **motels** strung along E Mulberry (Hwy-14).

The Armstrong Hotel 259 S College Ave ℡970/484-3883, ⓦwww.thearmstronghotel.com. The only accommodation in downtown Fort Collins – only yards from a multitude of restaurants and bars – is this 37-room hotel. Built in 1923 in a Victorian style, a recent refurbishment has successfully preserved its historic character: the rooms are stylishly spartan and provide high-speed Internet access. The place is popular, so try to book as far in advance as possible. ⑤

Best Western Kiva Inn 1638 E Mulberry St ℡970/484-2444 or 1-888/299-5482, ⓦwww.bestwestern.com. The newest of the chain properties east of town, with scrupulously clean rooms and impressive facilities including a pool, sauna, and hot tub; a decent continental breakfast is included in the rate. ⑥

Best Western University Inn 914 S College Ave ℡970/484-1984 or 1-800/528-1234, ⓔbwuniveristyinn@aol.com. This no-frills motel, handily positioned right across from the CSU campus, is aging fairly gracefully. Facilities include an outdoor pool and hot tub, and a basic continental breakfast is included. ⑤

El Palomino Motel 1220 N College Ave ℡970/482-4555. Usually the cheapest digs in town, this basic, fairly down-at-heel motel is only a mile north of downtown. ②

Elizabeth Street Guest House 202 E Elizabeth St ℡970/493-2337. Although located right on a street corner, this 1905 B&B is in a peaceful spot and set on perfectly trimmed, leafy grounds. There are four comfortable rooms with homey touches, but only two have private bath. ④

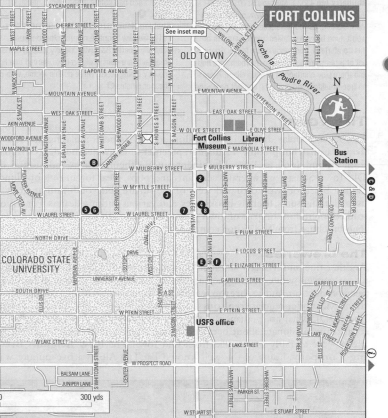

FORT COLLINS

See inset map

OLD TOWN

Poudre River

Bus Station

COLORADO STATE UNIVERSITY

USFS office

Fort Collins Museum

Library

0   300 yds

▼ **9** (2 miles)

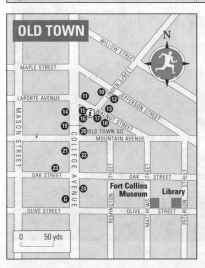

OLD TOWN

0   50 yds

Fort Collins Museum

Library

ACCOMMODATION

The Armstrong Hotel	**G**
Best Western Kiva Inn	**C**
Best Western University Inn	**E**
Elizabeth Street Guest House	**F**
El Palomino Motel	**A**
Mulberry Inn	**D**
Sheldon House	**B**

RESTAURANTS, BARS & CLUBS

Aggie Theatre	24	Pickle Barrel	7
Avogadro's Number	3	Silver Grill Cafe	11
Big City Burrito	2	Starlight	14
Cafe Bluebird	5	Starry Night Coffee	
Conor O'Neill's	13	Company	22
Coopersmith's, Pub &		Suite 152	19
Brewing	18	Surfside	15
Cozzola's Pizzas	10	Taj Mahal	23
Deja Vu Coffee House	4	Thai Pepper	8
Elliot's Martini Bar	12	Vault	16
Lucky Joe's Sidewalk		Woody's	6
Saloon	20	Young's Cafe	9
The Matrixx	1	Zydeco's	17
Nico's Catacombs	21		

Mulberry Inn 4333 E Mulberry St ☎970/493-9000 or 1-800/234-5548, ⓦwww.mulberry-inn.com. As long as you have a car you probably won't mind being four miles from downtown at this comfortable mid-range motor lodge. Space is not at a premium out here, so the rooms are huge and there's no shortage of parking either. There's no free breakfast, although you can get packaged muffins and bad coffee in the lobby until about 10am. ❹

Sheldon House 616 W Mulberry St ☎970/221-1917, ⓦwww.bbonline.com/co/sheldonhouse. Centrally located B&B with friendly, helpful owners; breakfasts are deliciously creative, served in a light and airy dining room. Three double rooms, with one cheaper single. ❻

The Town

The most popular daytime Fort Collins activity is perambulating about **Old Town**, a small but proudly maintained precinct of renovated buildings that date from around 1860 to 1900. Prominent among them, and in and around the Old Town Square, are several restaurants and pubs, ideal for an outdoor lunch. Walk a block or two north and west of the square and you'll find an array of used clothing spots, friendly bookstores, and various antique dealers. For a more studied interest in this part of town pick up the free *Fort Collins Historic Walking Tour* brochure from the visitor center.

The breweries

Another fine and leisurely summer option is to sit in the square and listen to a free concert while quaffing a microbrew. Fort Collins is a noted locale for beer production, and its **breweries** are big business, with no less than six in town. Most offer regular **free tours**, which all finish with the requisite samples (bring ID). What are perhaps the three most interesting breweries – all small local firms, passionate about beer and handcrafting a wide variety of different brews – are all fairly short walks from Old Town. The **New Belgium Brewing Company**, home of the well-known Fat Tire Ale, is a five-minute walk

△ New Belgium Brewery

north of town at 500 Linden St (self-guided tours Mon–Sat 10am–6pm, guided tours Mon–Fri 2pm & Sat hourly 11am–4pm; ☎970/221-0524), while the **Odell Brewing Company**, 800 E Lincoln Ave (tastings Mon–Fri 10am–6pm, Sat noon–5pm; tours Mon–Fri 11am, 1 & 3pm, Sat 1, 2 & 3pm; ☎970/498-9070, ⓦwww.odellbrewing.com), and the **Fort Collins Brewery**, at no. 1900 (Mon–Thurs 10am–5.30pm, Fri 10am–6pm, Sat 1pm–5pm; ☎970/472-1499, ⓦwww.fortcollinsbrewery.com), are, respectively, two and three miles east along Lincoln Ave. Odell is best known for its flagship 90 Shilling beer, a lightened-up, medium-bodied version of the traditional Scottish amber ale that's irresistibly smooth and delicious. In contrast, the most highly rated of the Fort Collins Brewery beers are some of its heaviest, with the annual batch of the malty Spring Bock – matured in cellars for four months – the drink of choice among beer fanatics.

Undoubtedly the most generic of the bunch and so perhaps the least interesting is **Anheuser-Busch**, the brewers of Budweiser; they're beside I-25 exit 271 at 2351 Busch Drive (☎970/490-4691, ⓦwww.budweisertours.com). The main attraction here is the chance to see the famous **Budweiser Clydesdale horses** (tours June–Aug daily 9.30am–4.30pm, Sept daily 10am–4pm, Oct–May Thurs–Mon 10am–4pm; phone to check that the horses are not away on tour). If you'd rather not venture that far off, grab a sample tray from microbrewers **Coopersmith's**, 5 Old Town Square (☎970/493-0483, ⓦwww.coopersmithspub.com). Brewery enthusiasts may wish to obtain a complete list of tours from visitor information. Also note that the annual **Colorado Brewers' Festival**, held in late June, provides further grist (or yeast, as the case may be) for connoisseurs of the amber liquid in the form of tastings and beer-themed celebrations.

Fort Collins Museum and the Swetsville Zoo

One attraction not beer-related is the **Fort Collins Museum**, 200 Matthews St (Tues–Sat 10am–5pm, Sun noon–5pm; free, donations appreciated; ☎970/221-6738, ⓦwww.fcgov.com/museum), which has a collection of artifacts depicting the town's professional and civic life, much of it from the early twentieth century. Among the more evocative items are a physician's kit from 1925 and an old telephone switchboard, still in pretty good condition; a room devoted to revolving photographic exhibitions takes up a third of the museum's space.

There's not much happening on the **university campus**. During the fall months, though, it's well worth getting out to see Colorado State's football team (the Rams) play a game at Hughes Stadium (tickets $30–40; ☎970/491-7267, ⓦwww.csurams.com). They've built quite a fanatical following in recent seasons on the back of several courageous wins, including a couple over their historically superior rivals down in Boulder at CU.

To see what's easily the most offbeat attraction in Fort Collins you'll need to head south to the fringes of town along I-25. Just east of exit 265, you'll find the humorous and engaging **Swetsville Zoo** (dawn–dusk; free; ☎970/484-9509), the life's work of one Bill Swets. A former fireman with no formal training in welding, he has created a zoo of 150 creatures built out of defunct car parts, farm machinery, and other metal scraps. These were all constructed without ever putting pen to paper, on the basis of nothing more than a mental picture. Yet despite the ad hoc method and the primitive and awkward materials, the aliens, insects, and dinosaurs have been given real and often perceptive characters. Swets' ingenuity has also extended to creating a ten-seater bicycle and a motorhome from the remains of two city buses. Certainly the attraction is a local hit, reeling in around 20,000 annual visitors, one of whom unwittingly burnt down Bill's house with a discarded cigarette in 1998 – which he's since rebuilt.

Eating

You won't be in town very long before someone is sure to inform you that, per capita, per square mile, and pound-for-pound, Fort Collins has more **restaurants** than any place else in Colorado. From top-notch yet affordable student places to a surprising range of ethnic restaurants, you can eat well regardless of your budget. Fort Collins is further blessed with two very good **ice-creameries**: *Kilwin's*, 114 S College Ave (Mon–Thurs 10am–9pm, Fri & Sat 10am–10pm, Sun noon–6pm), which also has homemade chocolates and fudge, and the equally excellent but slightly cheaper *Walrus Ice Cream*, 125 Mountain Ave (Mon–Thurs 11am–11pm, Fri & Sat 11am–midnight, Sun noon–11pm).

Avogadro's Number 605 S Mason St ☎970/493-5555. A college favorite for burgers, microbrews, hanging out, and sometimes even dancing. On any night of the week you could encounter anything from a bluegrass band to a poetry reading. Good selection for vegetarians. Open daily, closing time varies.

Big City Burrito 510 S College Ave. Does a great job serving students with gigantic custom-made burritos ($4–6); you get to choose the type of tortilla wrap, from spinach to jalapeno, as well as from a variety of meats, salsas, salads, and three types of beans.

Cafe Bluebird 524 W Laurel St. Plenty of vegetarian items at this campus-side diner, plus homemade breads, soups, and tasty breakfast dishes, including an excellent eggs Benedict. Open until 2pm daily.

Cozzola's Pizzas 241 Linden St ☎970/482-3557. Conveniently central, people allegedly drive down from Laramie, WY, to quell their pizza craving here. A monster sixteen-inch pie goes for $13–16. Open for lunch and dinner Tues–Sat, dinner only Sun, closed Mon.

Coopersmith's Pub & Brewing 5 Old Town Square. The biggest of the square's brewpubs, this is also the most popular for outdoor dining; there are usually some steak and seafood specials to go along with the standard list of burgers, sandwiches, appetizers, and Mexican items. Daily from 11am.

Deja Vu Coffee House 646 1/2 S College Ave. This is the university neighborhood's coffee place; there are light lunches and soups available, but most people just sit for a chat over coffee with a muffin or piece of carrot cake.

Nico's Catacombs 115 S College Ave ☎970/484-6029. The surest way to divest yourself of student dining company is to settle in at *Nico's* for an evening of continental cuisine and ambiance. The filet mignon gets doused in a rich, boozy sauce, but then so does just about

everything else, while the extensive wine list will provide you with further reason to indulge. Entrees $25–35. Closed Sun.

Pickle Barrel 122 W Laurel St. A prime college hangout, with big, tasty sandwiches and freely flowing microbrews. Open daily; closes early Sun.

Silver Grill Cafe 218 Walnut St. This bright and cheerful diner-grill is where Fort Collins goes for breakfast – enormous cinnamon rolls ($2) are what they're famous for, and you need to get in early if you want one topped with pecans. The lunch menu is popular as well, featuring a good range of inexpensive grills, sandwiches, and salads. Daily until 2pm.

Starry Night Coffee Company 112 S College Ave. Downtown coffeehouse with low-key, casual interior. There are usually some fairly exotic sweet pies to go with the range of coffees, along with light meals such as a veggie pitta pocket, soups, and focaccia. Daily 7am–10pm.

Taj Mahal 148 W Oak ☎970/493-1105. Dependable and central Indian restaurant, with plenty of vegetarian items on the menu, including a fine tandoori eggplant. The $7 lunch buffet (11am–2.30pm) makes for an inexpensive all-you-can-eat range of textures and flavors; entrees are $11–15.

Thai Pepper 109 E Laurel St ☎970/221-3260. Range of fresh and delicious Thai standards including yellow, green, and red curries with your choice of meat and vegetables, and a delicious pad Thai. Entrees $6–9, open Mon–Sat for lunch and dinner, Sun for dinner only; closes at 9pm all nights.

Woody's 518 W Laurel St. Basically a beer and pizza joint, staffed and largely patronized by college kids, but the Monday dinner special is the best deal in town – $5 for all the (surprisingly good) wood-fired pizza, soup, and salad you can eat. The system for determining what pizza combinations are dished up is impressively fair and democratic too: if you yell "chicken-pineapple-mushroom-and-barbecue-sauce" loud enough, then that's what they'll make. Open late, til 2am daily.

Young's Cafe 3307 S College Ave #114 ☎970/223-8000. An award-winning Vietnamese restaurant well worth the 5min drive from downtown – it's tucked in a mall, so look for the *Red Lobster* sign on your right as you drive

south. Bird's Nest chicken and Vietnamese-style duck are among the specialties, and everything is excellent, fresh, and well-presented. Entrees around $12. Open daily for lunch and dinner.

Drinking and nightlife

Naturally enough, you'll find plenty of **musical** goings-on in Fort Collins, although when school is out there's very little happening. For places to get down, you don't need to go much beyond Old Town Square, as this is where the **DJs** and **dancefloors** are. For full **listings**, including live bands, dance events, and happy hours, pick up a copy of the monthly *Scene Magazine* (free) from a streetstand or coffeeshop. During summer, check the schedule of shows coming up at the **Mishawaka Amphitheater**, 25 miles west of town in the Cache la Poudre Canyon; big-name artists and a fine outdoors setting make for some inspiring concerts.

Aggie Theatre 204 S College Ave ☎970/482-8300, ⓦwww.aggietheatre.com. Having undergone numerous makeovers, the Aggie otherwise remains the town's largest live-music venue, hosting the bigger touring acts that come through – the place is usually given over to bands Thurs–Sat, although special events such as the Hip-Hop Holocaust and female mud-wrestling contribute to a varied calendar.

Conor O'Neill's 214 Linden St ☎970/407-0214, ⓦwww.conoroneills.com. High-ceilinged brewpub worth checking before most of the rest for its consistent roll-call of live bands; does some decent food too, as well as a renowned, spicy Bloody Mary. Open daily from 11am, closing time and cover charge varies.

Elliot's Martini Bar 234 Linden St. This stylish, low-lit bar makes a nice change from the beery places nearby. Their specialty is, of course, martinis, with lots of different kinds, along with other exotic cocktails and cigars; the interior represents a fair stab at Art Deco, too. Nightly until 2am.

Lucky Joe's Sidewalk Saloon 25 Old Town Square ☎970/493-2213, ⓦwww.luckyjoes.com. The crowd here is pretty mixed, though at times thick with tourists. There are big-screen TVs for sporting events, a good range of microbrews, hardly ever a cover charge, and the music is non-threatening – mostly solo singer-guitarists. Open daily 11am–2am.

The Matrixx 450 Linden Center Drive ☎970/407-0738. Decked out in stark techno moderne, supposedly in keeping with the movie *The Matrix*,

this is the most genuinely dance-oriented club in town, where DJs spin a fair mix of techno, new R&B, and Top 40 hits. Mon–Sat 10pm until early in the morning. Cover $7–10.

Starlight 167 N College Ave ☎970/484-4974. Currently the down-and-dirty home of mostly college bands, which means the mood is very "rock" and the quality variable. Check the posters out front before you commit; cover charge varies, open 2pm–2am.

Suite 152 23 Old Town Square ☎970/224-0888. Upstairs is a bar-restaurant, downstairs is a cavern-like space with a DJ and dancefloor. The music or fashion theme could be anything, although one night per week is "college night" (aka cheap booze), while another, usually Weds or Sun, is set aside for under-21s (aka no booze).

Surfside 150 N College Ave. This dimly lit place is popular with students for its solid bar menu of appetizers, salads, and burgers, as well as the inevitable microbrews.

Vault 146 N College Ave ☎970/484-0995. One of the more appealing buildings among the music venues, this historic former bank occasionally hosts smaller bands and duos, but seems to be transforming into a mellow lunch-and-supper club, judging by the increased number of solo acts and the improved menu. Mon–Fri 11.30am–2am, Sat 2pm–midnight.

Zydeco's 11 Old Town Square ☎970/224-4100. Rounds out the clutch of bars in the square with a pub menu, small dancefloor, occasional DJs, and various themed happy hours. Tues–Sat 11am–2am.

Listings

Airport shuttle Airport Express (☎970/482-0505) runs a dozen services daily between Fort Collins and Denver International ($17 one-way, trip takes almost 2hr); the shuttle leaves Fort Collins from *Holiday Inn University Park*, 425 W Prospect Rd, and the *Courtyard Marriott*, 1200 Oakridge Drive; pick-up elsewhere in Fort Collins is $4–7 extra. Shamrock Airport Shuttle ☎970/686-9999 departs from the *Hampton Inn*, 1620 Oakridge Drive, will also pick up elsewhere, and is slightly cheaper.

Bike and skate rental Lee's Cyclery, 202 W Laurel St (Mon–Fri 9am–7pm, Sat 9am–6pm, Sun 11am–5pm; ☎970/482-6006), rents mountain bikes from $30 per day; The Wright Life, 200 Linden St (Mon–Wed & Sat 9.30am–7pm, Thurs & Fri 9.30am–9pm, Sun 10am–5pm; ☎970/484-6932) rents in-line skates at $7 for 4hr or $15 for 24hr.

Bookshop Old Corner Bookshop, 216 Linden St (Mon–Sat 10am–6pm, Sun noon–4pm), buys, sells, and trades a range of used books.

Car rental Inexpensive local firms include Advantage (☎970/224-2211), Midtown (☎970/484-7443), and Price King (☎970/490-1512).

Hospital Poudre Valley Hospital, 1024 S Lemay Ave (☎970/495-7000), has 24hr emergency care.

Internet access Fort Collins Public Library, 201 Peterson St (Mon–Thurs 9.30am–9pm, Fri 10am–6pm, Sat 10am–5pm, Sun 1–5pm; free; ☎970/221-6687); Kinko's Copies, 130 W Olive St (open 24hr; $12 per hour).

Laundry American Coin Laundry, 415 S Mason St (daily 7am–11pm).

Police 15 Old Town Square (Mon–Fri 9am–5pm; ☎970/221-6540).

Post office 301 S Howes S (Mon–Fri 7.30am–5pm, Sat 10am–2pm).

Sports and outdoor equipment EMS, just off College Ave about three miles south of downtown at 101 E Foothills Pkwy (Mon–Sat 9am–9.30pm, Sun 11am–6pm); Gart Sports, College Ave, at Mulberry (Mon–Sat 9am–9pm, Sun 10am–7pm); REI, 4025 S College Ave (Mon–Sat 9am–9pm, Sun 10am–5pm).

Taxi Shamrock Taxi (☎970/686-5555).

Cache la Poudre Canyon

Those fun-loving French fur-trappers of the 1800s get the credit for so many imaginative names on Rocky Mountains maps that they deserve special mention for an uncharacteristic show of pragmatism when it came to naming the picturesque **Cache la Poudre Canyon**. The story goes that a group of trappers were caught in a fierce snowstorm in the winter of 1836, and, desperate to lighten the loads they were carrying, decided to bury some barrels of gunpowder along the riverbank with the plan to return for them the following spring.

Today, the powder stashes have been recovered, but the canyon road (Hwy-14) is still well worth driving as a **scenic route**, with a stop for a picnic lunch coupled with the chance to spot bighorn sheep. The fairly narrow and rocky canyon is covered in dense and diverse vegetation, with mountain mahogany, sagebrush, and bitterbrush on the lower slopes, and ponderosa and lodgepole pine, cottonwoods, aspens, and Rocky Mountain junipers and various firs looming higher up. The valley's real pearl, the wide, flat-bottomed river itself, is officially classified as a "**National Wild and Scenic River**," which means the flow of water is uninterrupted by dams and other impediments and the banks have been left in their natural state. As such, the river offers superb opportunities for fly-fishing, whitewater rafting, and kayaking. The section which runs from the junction of Hwy-14 and I-287 just outside Fort Collins to the tiny village of Gould 66 miles further west contains the best scenery and watersports possibilities. A **bighorn sheep viewing station**, little more than a raised platform beside the road, is 41 miles west of the highway junction.

Staying in Cache la Poudre Canyon

There are eleven riverside USFS **campgrounds** dotted alongside Hwy-14, all of which have toilets but no showers or drinking water. Sites cost $12–15 and vary in size between 12 (*Stove Prairie*) and 45 sites (*Chambers Lake*). Contact the USFS office in Fort Collins for more information. In Rustic itself, you can rent attractive, fully equipped **cabins** for a minimum two-night stay at *Bighorn Cabins*, 31635 Poudre Canyon Rd (℡970/881-2142; ❹). The nearby *Glen Echo Resort*, 31503 Poudre Canyon Rd (℡970/881-2208 or 1-800/348-2208), has modern cabins with private bathrooms (❹) and rustic cabins with shared facilities (❸) as well as a small grocery store and restaurant.

Outdoor activities

A useful brochure entitled *Cache la Poudre – a Wild and Scenic River* is available at the USFS office in Fort Collins; it provides a concise overview of campsites, trailheads, and points of interest within the canyon, and details the fishing regulations that govern different stretches of the river. Around the town of **RUSTIC**, anglers go after wild trout under tightly regulated conditions, while other sections are regularly stocked with hatchery-raised rainbow and brown trout, and so are less tightly controlled. Fort Collins' Rocky Mountain Adventures (℡970/493-4005 or 1-800/858-6808, ⓦwww.shoprma.com), runs guided fly-fishing (half-day $125) on the Cache la Poudre.

The absence of river dams accounts for much of the river's **rafting** and **kayaking** appeal; though keep in mind that as waterflow is uncontrolled, conditions are not easy to predict. June is the most reliable month, though suitable conditions may persist from mid-May until early August. Rafting companies based in or near Fort Collins include Rocky Mountain Adventures (see above), A Wanderlust Adventure (℡970/484-1219, ⓦwww.awanderlust adventure.com), and A-1 Wildwater, Inc. (℡970/224-3379 or 1-800/369-4165, ⓦwww.a1wildwater.com), all of which run regular half-day (around $60–65) and day-trips ($95–100) through Class III and IV rapids; extremely demanding Class V trips are available, too, subject to private arrangement.

As for **hiking**, trailheads that lead off into the Comanche Peak Wilderness south of the highway and the Rawah Wilderness to the north are marked on the canyon brochure. The USFS Arrowhead Lodge outpost, just east of Rustic at 34484 Poudre Canyon Rd (summer only Thurs–Sun 9am–5pm), also has information on area hikes.

Travel details

Buses

Boulder to: Denver (24 daily; 50min; RTD); Fort Collins (2 daily; 2hr 15min; Greyhound).

Fort Collins to: Boulder (2 daily; 2hr 15min; Greyhound); Denver (3 daily; 1hr 15min; Greyhound).

Golden to: Boulder (11 daily; 45min; RTD); Denver (7 daily; 1hr; RTD).

3

The Northeastern Plains

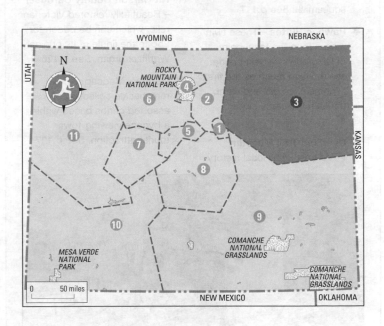

WYOMING

NEBRASKA

UTAH

N

ROCKY
MOUNTAIN
NATIONAL PARK

4

6

2

3

KANSAS

11

5

1

7

8

10

9

COMANCHE
NATIONAL
GRASSLANDS

MESA VERDE
NATIONAL
PARK

COMANCHE
NATIONAL
GRASSLANDS

0   50 miles

NEW MEXICO

OKLAHOMA

CHAPTER 3 # Highlights

✳ **Fort Vasquez** – This accurately reconstructed 1830s trading post gives a glimpse of early frontier life. See p.116

✳ **Bruce's** – Welcoming and authentically Western locals' bar famous for its Rocky Mountain oysters, a regional delicacy not for the squeamish. See p.117

✳ **Pawnee Buttes** – These twin mesas form the focal point of Colorado's wildest prairie: see the land much as the first pilgrims once did and camp beneath the starry sky. See p.119

✳ **Overland Trail Museum** – The best small local history museum on the plains is crammed with old pioneer relics that give a sense of the region's heritage. See p.121

✳ **Burlington Livestock Exchange** – Visit this regional cattle market for an entertaining insight into local life. See p.126

✳ **Kit Carson County Carousel** – Beautifully restored Victorian relic, which can be ridden for 25¢ to the jingle of its original Wurlitzer organ. See p.126

✳ **Genoa** – Madcap and ramshackle collection of assorted curios based within a bygone viewing-tower tourist attraction. See p.127

△ Overland Trail Museum

3

The Northeastern Plains

Ever since the West opened up, Colorado's **NORTHEASTERN PLAINS** have, first and foremost, been an area of transit. Trappers, traders, and homesteaders once blazed trails across the region, while now truckers and vacationers pound its two interstates. Almost uniformly flat, these prairies are a world apart from the mountains that draw most visitors to Colorado. But by making up forty percent of the state the plains are of course almost as representative of Colorado as its mountains. Despite their dull reputation, the subtle beauty of the uniform lands and distant horizons pinned down by vast moody skies is unquestionable. And these often intoxicatingly dramatic skies can be every bit as impressive as the mountain ranges, particularly at night when amazing starscapes form a backdrop for the dazzling pyrotechnics of frequent lightning storms. Major attractions may be absent, but it would be a shame not to stop, stretch your legs, and gain a sense of slow-paced, small-town USA by chatting with some of the state's friendliest and most welcoming people.

Aside from the small farming communities that dot the landscape at regular intervals (the South Platte Valley is particularly prized for its sugar beets) all the region's larger settlements flank its interstates, with the exception of the largest town, **Greeley**. In the far north **Interstate 76** runs alongside the South Platte River, once the course of one of America's major transcontinental pioneering trails. A short drive north from this artery, the **Pawnee National Grassland** offers the areas's most appealing landscape. It gives insight into what the land was like before white faces arrived, when roaming bands of Cheyenne and Arapaho followed great herds of buffalo and made the prairie their home. Further south, bisecting the state's prairie heartland on its westerly course from the Kansas border, lies the far duller **Interstate 70**.

Greeley

If you arrive in the leafy college town of **GREELEY** from the west you'll truly feel that you've left the Rockies behind; the mountains may still be on the horizon but the local focus has shifted towards the plains. The town's annual

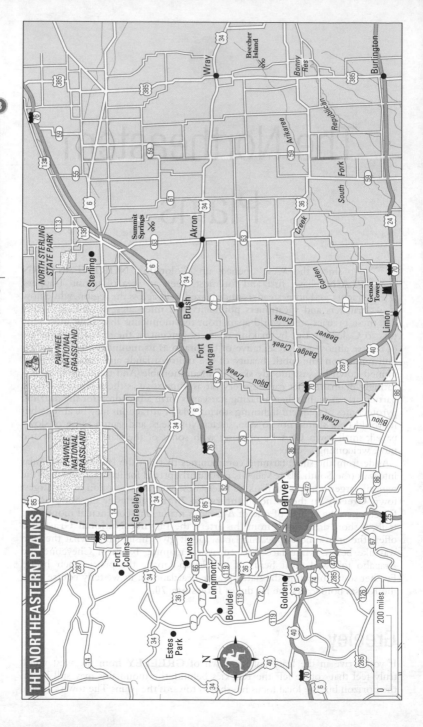

THE NORTHEASTERN PLAINS

rodeo is the big deal – and the only real reason to pay a visit – and the main roads are lined with businesses providing services, machinery, and goods to farmers and ranchers. Your arrival in an agricultural town, this one included, is often confirmed as soon as you leave your vehicle. If the wind is blowing the wrong way the air fills with the stench of cow dung and slaughterhouses. Eric Schlosser, in *Fast Food Nation* (2002), writes:

The smell is hard to forget but not easy to describe, a combination of live animals, manure, and dead animals being rendered into dog food. The smell is worst during the summer months, blanketing Greeley day and night like an invisible fog. Many people who live there no longer notice the smell; it recedes into the background, present but not present, like the sound of traffic for New Yorkers.

Greeley was named in tribute to *New York Tribune* editor **Horace Greeley** (famous for boldly exhorting "Go west young man, and grow with your country") by his idealistic agricultural editor Nathan Meeker, who spearheaded this, one of America's most successful colonization experiments, and strove to create a town that would be an exalted example to those who heeded the advice to go west.

Meeker called for ambitious individuals with high moral standards to form a colony based on principles of cooperative farming, temperance ("Thou shalt not sell liquid damnation within the lines of the Union Colony" was one commandment), religion, and education. From the three thousand responses, 59 well-to-do individuals eventually formed a joint stock company known as the **Union Colony** in 1869. The following year the colonists arrived from New England on the newly completed Denver Pacific Railroad, establishing itself close to the confluence of the South Platte and Cache la Poudre rivers around 60 miles north of Denver. Irrigation canals were quickly dug and the community church built.

△ Greeley cattle

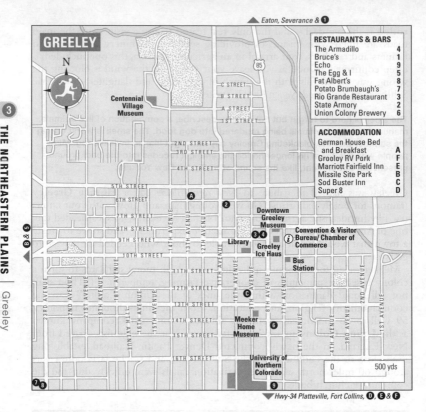

By the mid-1870s when Horace Greeley paid his only visit he found a small wealthy community with stores, homes, offices, and fields where irrigated tomatoes, melons, and fruit trees grew. In 1889 the town established a college, the **University of Northern Colorado**, which still helps shape the town's character, while at the same time the settlement developed as an important ranching center. As a result, today the **Greeley Independence Stampede** (℡970/356-2855 or 1-800/982-2855, Ⓦwww.greeleystampede .org), a grand rodeo, is the town's biggest party, attracting around half a million visitors during the two weeks before the Fourth of July, the climax of the proceedings.

Arrival, information, and getting around

Both **Greyhound** (℡970/353-5050) and **Powder River Transportation** (℡970/353-5050 or 1-800/231-2222) travel to Greeley, dropping their passengers off at 1030 7th Ave – though most people arrive **by car**, entering the city just south of downtown along Hwy-34. The hub for Greeley's **public bus** service, "the Bus" ($1; ℡970/350-9287, Ⓦwww.greeleythebus.com), is just a block north of where Greyhound and Powder River let off, at 9th Ave and 7th St. Nearby, at 902 7th Ave, is the Chamber of Commerce (℡970/352-3566 or 1-800/449-3866, Ⓦwww.greeleycvb.com), which operates a **visitors' center** in the old Union Pacific Railroad Depot, on the eastern side of downtown.

From here the tiny downtown area is easily navigable **on foot**, though to reach most of Greeley's attractions you'll need to have your own wheels or hire a local **taxi** like Shamrock Yellow Cab (☎970/352-3000).

Accommodation

Greeley's biggest clutch of **accommodations** are the chain motels on the south side of town at the junction of 29th St and Hwy-34. For **camping** try the *Greeley RV Park*, 501 E 27th St (☎970/353-6476, ⊛www.greeleyrvpark .com; tents $13, RVs $26), or the more pleasantly rural, basic sites at *Missile Site Park*, 10611 Spur 257 (☎970/381-7451; $5 per site; toilets, but no showers).

German House Bed & Breakfast 1305 6th St ☎970/356-1353, ⊛www.bbonline.com/co /germanhouse. Enjoy German hospitality just four blocks from Lincoln Park in this Victorian property, where the gorgeous grounds incorporate a croquet lawn and swimming pool. The four small guest rooms – two with private baths – have savagely mismatched decor, though personal heirlooms lend unique personality (if doubtful charm). Light continental breakfast included. ❻

Marriott Fairfield Inn 2401 W 29th St ☎970/339-5030, ⊛www.fairfieldinn.com/ftcgr. Relatively upscale motel located just a block from a major mall. The spacious and well-lit pastel-decorated rooms come with free WiFi and cable TV; there's also a hot tub and an indoor pool. A decent continental breakfast buffet is included. ❻

Sod Buster Inn 1221 9th Ave ☎970/392-1221, ⊛www.thesodbusterinn.com. Unusual octagonal B&B, located between UNC and the downtown shopping district, where the wraparound verandah is a sociable focal point. The ten unique rooms – each themed with local places or historical figures – all have a certain rustic charm and include en suite bathrooms. Free WiFi and extraordinarily good gourmet breakfasts. ❻

Super 8 2423 W 29th St ☎970/330-8880 or 1-800/800-8000, ⊛www.greeleylodging.com. Cheap, cheerful, and dependable motel. The rooms are clean and a basic continental breakfast is included. ❸

The Town

Greeley's attractions are limited to a couple of decent local history museums, one of which takes the shape of a mock "living history" village. The tidy **downtown** is uniformly dull, though its epicenter, Lincoln Park, has some shaded spots good for picnicking. Other than that there's very little to do – even the shopping is limited.

Downtown Museum

Perhaps the most interesting and certainly one of the plushest central addresses is the modern **Downtown Museum**, 714 8th St (Tues–Sat 10am–4pm; free; ☎970/350-9220, ⊛www.greeleymuseums.com), which has a relatively small but attractive exhibition hall on Greeley's staid local history. A bit of excitement is provided by a display given over to the story and rifle of the aptly named Katherine Slaughterback, who shot and killed 140 rattlesnakes in one sitting and requested her nickname "Rattlesnake Kate" be put on her gravestone. Her snakeskin dress is on display at the Centennial Village Museum (see below). The rest of the museum is a bit hit-and-miss: aside from the collection of painfully clichéd Western art, most of the rooms spreading over three floors host touring and temporary exhibitions, many of the latter of which are based on the historical documents and photographs of the **Colorado Collection**, an adjoining research center. One of the state's largest collections, this was the reason James Michener lived in Greeley during the 1980s, while he researched and wrote *Centennial*, his fictional account of the state's history.

Meeker House and Centennial Village museums

Union Colony founder Nathan Meeker is remembered at the **Meeker House Museum**, 1324 9th Ave (May–Sept Wed–Fri 1pm–4pm; free; ☎970/350-9220, same website as above), his stately 1870 adobe home, and one of the town's earliest buildings. The interior has many original furnishings, supplemented with period pieces to complete the picture. It's an illuminating dip into the era, though the free guided tours can, for those uninterested in Meeker minutia, be a bit overwhelming. The remarkable man met his end in the **Meeker Massacre**, near the eponymous western Colorado town (see p.404), and, as a result of his insensitive dealings with the Native Americans, casts a unsympathetic shadow on his life.

A fuller appreciation of Greeley's origins and history can be gained at the **Centennial Village Museum**, a mile north of downtown at 1475 A St (mid-April to mid-Oct Tues–Sat 10am–4pm; $5; ☎970/350-9220, ⓦwww .greeleymuseums.com). Made up of 30 buildings – some original, some relocated, and some reconstructed – this mock village tells, via living history demonstrations, the story of life on the Colorado plains between the 1860s and 1940s. Every type of early construction material (sod, adobe, wood, and rock) is represented, while buildings include an 1863 log courthouse, a smithy, a fire station, and several agricultural structures such as a granary and a sugar beet shanty. There's even a 1917 wagon house, supposedly the forerunner of the RV.

Fort Vasquez

Moving another step back in time, glimpse frontier life at **Fort Vasquez**, 13412 Hwy-85 in Platteville, about eighteen miles south of Greeley (late-May to early Sept Mon–Sat 9.30am–4.30pm, Sun 1pm–4.30pm; early Sept to late-May Wed–Sat 9.30am–4.30pm, Sun 1pm–4.30pm; free; ☎970/785-2832, ⓦwww .coloradohistory.org). This WPA version of the original low-slung 1835 adobe fort, built here as a trading post rather than a military garrison, reconstructs the place where plains tribes, traders, and mountain men swapped furs for weapons and tools. The visitor center and its knowledgeable staffers help shed light on the early nineteenth-century fur trade along the South Platte River that drove all this.

Eating and nightlife

You'll find all the usual fast-food chains on the major arterial roads, but also a few good **restaurants** lining a couple of short blocks downtown. The 10,000-strong UNC student body has led this formerly temperate town to develop some **nightlife**, though this remains mostly underwhelming. Greeley has philharmonic and chamber orchestras and a number of **theater** groups, some of which perform in UNC's Little Theater of the Rockies (☎970/351-2200, ⓦwww.arts.unco.edu/calender). For other events and goings-on, the Chamber of Commerce publishes a useful guide.

Echo 1702 8th Ave ☎970/351-8548. This quality Japanese restaurant is a good alternative to the filling all-American selections that overwhelm most plains menus. The long-standing family business has good sushi, but are renowned for their tempura ice cream, deep-fried and smothered in chocolate sauce.

The Egg & I 3830 W 10th St ☎970/353-7737. Breakfasts are best bought two miles west of downtown along 10th Street, where eggs are served in almost every thinkable way, including delicious frittatas and open-faced omelettes. Wonderful soups, salads, and sandwiches follow for lunch. Most dishes around $5.

Fat Albert's 1717 23rd Ave ☎970/356-1999. Diner in the Cottonwood Square Mall that's great for lunch with thick sandwiches, salads, and burgers, and a reliable dinner choice for reasonably priced, more substantial meals including trout, steak, and several chicken dishes. Leave space to sample the zany dessert selection, which usually includes chocolate zucchini cake and peanut-butter pie.

Potato Brumbaugh's 2400 17th St ☎970/356-6340. This special-occasion restaurant in a circular building in the Cottonwood Square Mall is one of the few places on the Northeastern plains where you'll find linen tablecloths and napkins. The menu is varied and changes often, but slow-roasted prime rib and steaks are the specialty. Most dinner entrees run $16–22. Closed Sun.

Rio Grande Restaurant 825 9th St ☎970/304-9292. Dependably lively downtown eatery with a large sidewalk patio and hearty Mexican entrees for $6–10.

State Armory 614 8th Ave ☎970/352-7424. Winner of local awards for "Best Bar," "Best Burger," and "Best Place to Meet People" – this is *the* place to meet the college crowd.

Union Colony Brewery 1412 8th Ave ☎970/356-4116. Greeley's cheerfully formulaic microbrewery must have the town's teetotaling founders turning in their graves, but none of the locals playing pool here seem to give that much thought.

The I-76 corridor

What is today the **I-76 corridor** was once the location of one of the great trails in American history. Variously called the Denver Road, the Overland Trail, or the South Platte River Trail, this was the principal east–west route between 1862 and 1868. These days it's all too easy to charge through the area, driving from Denver northwest to Nebraska (or the reverse) in under four hours, at the expense of exploring the many modest small towns that dot the stretch, with their old-fashioned general stores and little watering holes-cum-social centers. The main lures are the vast tracts of awesome prairie scenery in the **Pawnee National Grassland** and a couple of mildly interesting small-town attractions in **Fort Morgan** and **Sterling**.

Both the former route of the Overland Trail and I 76 follow the course of the South Platte River, once described by Mark Twain as "a melancholy stream straggling through the center of an enormous flat plain, and only saved from being impossible to find with the naked eye by its sentinel rank of scattering trees standing on either bank...." It's certainly not a proud or impressive channel, and yet it sustains a string of close-knit agricultural communities and feeds several reservoirs.

In the 1860s travelers joined the pioneer highway at departure points dotting the Missouri River before rolling along the Platte River through Nebraska

Rocky Mountain oysters

"Come to Severance and have a ball," the charismatic owner of *Bruce's* (☎970/686-2320) likes to say. And by this he means drive to the small town of **SEVERANCE** – midway between Fort Collins and Greeley – and eat a bull's testicle. His bar sells 20 tons of these so-called **Rocky Mountain oysters** every year – not as surprising as you might think, since after this local delicacy has been breaded, deep-fried, and served with garlic sauce it's easier to stomach. Friday and Saturday locals chow down at the $7 oyster buffet (6–9pm). Edible oddities aside, *Bruce's* is a great place to absorb some local color, where townspeople let their hair down and chat to anyone. The place also fairly rocks on weekend nights, with live country music until 2am. During the day it's popular for inexpensive (around $6) lunch specials of hearty American food like meatloaf. To get to Severance, eighteen miles from Greeley, head north on Hwy-85 to Eaton, where you turn west on Collins Street, which becomes 4th Avenue before arriving in Severance, six miles away.

to Colorado, where they turned to follow the river's south fork to Denver. In its heyday the road carried 20,000 people per year: a mix of fortune-seekers, merchants, and homesteaders. Much to the consternation of the native populace, some of the latter began to settle the lands around the trail, creating frictions that led to the **Indian Wars** (see pp.122–123). After these conflicts, the vast majority of the Indians were forced out to the barren lands of the South-western states. In 1869 the Union Pacific Railroad forged through Colorado, effectively making the Overland Trail obsolete.

Pawnee National Grassland

Encompassing an area almost three-quarters the size of Rocky Mountain National Park, the **Pawnee National Grassland** preserves the remnant of native short-grass prairie that once covered the entire semiarid Midwest. Despite being, in its own subtle way, quite dramatic, it's extremely lightly visited and so well worth the detour from the region's major highways not only to see what northeastern Colo-rado looked like before settlement, but also to experience some real solitude in the vast wide-open spaces. A seemingly endless and arid expanse blankets the horizon here; the few cattle and windmills that pepper it help give a sense of scale.

The prairie's complex array of grasses once provided the nutrient-rich diet for gigantic herds of **buffalo** who in turn sustained the nomadic population of Plains Indians, providing meat, clothing, shelter, and tools. This centuries-old

Grassland practicalities

Access **roads** to the grasslands are generally well-signposted, but it helps to have a map, since the 125-mile route through them that links Fort Morgan (see opposite) and Greeley is complicated and involves negotiating a confusing array of dirt roads.

To get to the Pawnee Buttes (see opposite) **from Greeley** take Hwy-85 north to Ault, then head east on CO-14 as far as Briggsdale. Here, turn onto CR-77 heading north to Grover, from where the route to the Pawnee Buttes is signposted. Once at the buttes you can continue past them on the same road, which then links to a series of roads leading to Fort Morgan. **From Fort Morgan** drive north on Hwy-52 and then 84 RD to Raymer; the route to the buttes is signposted from there. Note that dirt roads effectively close after heavy rain, otherwise everday vehicles should have no problems making the trip.

You can pick up a pamphlet with directions from the Chamber of Commerce or Library in Fort Morgan; Greeley's Visitor Center has the same thing. For detailed infor-mation head to the **USFS Pawnee National Grassland Ranger Station**, located off CO-85 just north of Greeley at 660 O St (Mon–Fri 8.30am–4.30pm; ☎970/353-5004, ⓦwww.fs.fed.us/grasslands).

The only developed **campground** is at Crow Valley, 24 miles east of Ault via Hwy-14, where ten sites ($12) are shaded by cottonwoods and elms. If you don't mind the extra bit of roughing it, take the chance to camp on the grasslands themselves. You can camp anywhere on public land that is not within 200ft of the Pawnee Butte Trail or any windmill or stock tank. If this doesn't appeal, try booking a **room** at the *Plover Inn*, 223 Chatoga St (☎970/895-2482; ❹), a B&B that's popular with birders, or have a real Western experience at the 🏇 *West Pawnee Ranch* (☎970/895-2482, ⓦwww.bbonline.com/co/pawnee; ❹), a working cattle ranch northwest of Grover at the intersection of Roads 130 and 59. They arrange horse rides over to the buttes, or you can join a cattle drive; call in advance for dates.

As far as **food** goes, bring provisions wherever you are staying. Grover has a small café and tiny grocery store, but there's little else in the area.

equilibrium began to be undermined from the mid-1800s as homesteaders moved in, replacing the buffalo with cattle and turning the prairie into agricultural land. Unsustainable dry land farming methods took their toll, and by the early 1930s had combined with drought so that topsoil blew away and families were forced off the land. Consequently the US government stepped in, purchasing the land from bankrupt farmers and replanting it with native grasses to restore the natural ecosystem. Today the grassland remains preserved as open range and is home to around 300 species of birds, including songbirds, hawks, falcons, burrowing owls, mountain plovers, and lark buntings, Colorado's state bird. **Birding** is best from February to July, after which activity dies down. You may also be able to spot pronghorn antelope, mule dear coyotes, foxes, badgers, and prairie dogs.

The Pawnee Buttes

Standing bolt upright and towering more than 250ft above the surrounding desolate, dry prairie, the twin **Pawnee Buttes** are probably the most visually impressive natural wonder of Colorado's plains and certainly the most arresting feature in the grasslands. They owe their existence to a layer of hard sandstone at their summits that has helped them resist the erosive forces that leveled surrounding areas. Throughout history, the buttes have attracted both people and animals: Pawnee Indian tools have been found around them, and skeletons of prehistoric animals unearthed. *Alticamelus*, a cross between a giraffe and camel, and *Amphicyon*, a dog-bear cross, have been found around the buttes' base.

The buttes are accessed from obvious **hiking trails** that start out from the two nearby parking lots – one on the bluff overlooks the other. Both trails join at a gate where they again branch out. To the right, the Overlook Trail (1.5 miles; closed March–July to protect nesting) leads to its impressive namesake, while the other leads to the base of the West Butte (4 miles). Be alert for **rattlesnakes** on both trails: the reptiles are common and particularly active at dawn and dusk.

Minuteman III silo

In sharp contrast to the general beauty of the surrounding plains are the grassland's **intercontinental ballistic missile** (ICBM) **sites**. During the Cold War there were around 200 scattered around the region; one can be viewed near the abandoned town of Keota, eight miles southwest of Grover along 390 RD. From Keota drive north three miles on 105 RD, then east onto 104 RD for another two miles; the active **Minuteman III silo** is to the north, its gleaming facade a deadly obelisk on the quiet plains. Keep a good distance from the perimeter fence and don't hang around too long, as these sites are subject to 24hr surveillance and guards will arrive at this deserted spot surprisingly quickly to ask what you're up to.

Fort Morgan

The agricultural shipping and distribution hub of **FORT MORGAN** first took root in 1864 as a military outpost, a result of Indian attacks along the South Platte River Trail. By 1870 the trail had fallen out of use and the native threat had passed, so the fort was dismantled; but when the present town was founded in 1884 the old name seemed the obvious choice.

Aside from appreciating the pleasant small-town feel, there's not a lot of reason to visit, although if you've arrived from the east, Fort Morgan is the best place to veer off the interstate and head up to the Grassland. For die-hard **Glenn Miller** fans the town is a point of pilgrimage as the musician's childhood home: he formed his first band here, the Mick-Miller Five, and every late-June around 500 folks gather to celebrate the big-band favorite. The town is also the final resting place of influential science fiction writer **Philip K. Dick**, whose work inspired the films *Blade Runner* and, more recently, *Minority Report*. Though buried in the town cemetery alongside his twin sister (who died an infant), Dick never lived in Fort Morgan – his parents simply took a shine to the place when they passed through during their courtship days. The cemetery is located northwest of downtown on West Riverside Ave (Hwy-144).

If you're just stopping off for a leg-stretch, be sure to take in the **Riverside Park and Canfield Recreation Area**, a pretty 240-acre greenspace and wild-life area along the South Platte just off I-76 (exit 80). Here you'll find shaded lawns, picnic areas, extensive playgrounds, tennis and basketball courts, and a swimming pool ($1.50); there's also a good chance of seeing herons, eagles, deer, and foxes.

With more time to spare you might pay a quick visit to the **Fort Morgan Museum**, which shares a building in the center of town with the public library, 414 Main St (Mon & Fri 10am–5pm, Tues–Thurs 10am–8pm, Sat 11am–5pm; free; ☎970/867-6331). This local history museum has a couple of interesting displays on the Koehler Site, a prehistoric campsite found at a nearby landfill, and information on Glenn Miller, including a few photos of him as a teenager.

Practicalities

Greyhound (☎970/867-8072) drops off at 835 E Platte Ave, half a mile east of Main Street, while those traveling **Amtrak**'s *California Zephyr* (☎1-800/872-7245, ⓦwww.amtrak.com) will disembark at the Ensign Street depot just west of Main. The Fort Morgan **Chamber of Commerce** is up the road at 100 Ensign (Mon–Fri 8am–5pm; ☎970/867-6702, ⓦwww.fortmorganchamber .org), though the info at the combined library and Fort Morgan Museum should be enough for most travelers.

Glenn Miller

Though an outstanding trombonist, **Glenn Miller** (1904–1944) was never quite in the same league as the true jazz greats. As a musical perfectionist, this was a constant source of frustration for him, until he eventually found his niche and genius in direct-ing and arranging. Yet success even here was slow to come and it wasn't until the late 1930s that Miller established a band with the unique sound it needed to become noticed. After much experimentation and hard work, he crafted a new sound based on making a clarinet play the melodic line with a tenor sax on the same note, while three saxophones harmonized. A stroke of luck then brought the Glenn Miller Band a sponsor and a gig at New York's Glen Island Casino, providing all the exposure Miller needed. Immediately his new band attracted big crowds and a series of recordings followed. Beginning in June 1938, Miller began to dominate the charts, with *In the Mood* holding the top spot for over fifteen weeks in early 1940 and *Tuxedo Junction* taking over and keeping Miller at number one into the summer. On February 11, 1942, Miller was presented with the first-ever gold record for *Chattanooga Choo Choo*. Meanwhile, the radio-based *Chesterfield Show* made Miller a household name. Sadly the Second World War brought an abrupt end to both the show, after a tearful last outing, and Miller's life. Having volunteered for the armed forces he ended up in the Army Air Corps and fell victim to friendly fire over the English Channel on an aborted mission – though his plane was never recovered, leading to speculation that he might have survived the war.

You don't have to drive far from the interstate to find **accommodation**; a number of motels line Platte Ave (aka Hwy-34) and the northern end of Main. Among these is the family-owned and very clean *Central Motel*, 201 W Platte Ave (℡970/867-2401, Ⓦwww.centralmotel.biz; ❸), where the well-priced rooms have microwaves and fridges. For a bit extra try the *Best Western Park Terrace Inn*, 725 Main (℡970/867-8256 or 1-888/593-5793; ❹) which has a swimming pool, hot tub, and the popular *Memories Restaurant* on the premises. To really experience something of the area, though, stay at the *Pioneer Trails Lodge Bed and Breakfast* in Stoneham (℡970/735-2426, Ⓦwww.pioneertrailslodge.com), 33 miles northeast of Fort Morgan. The owners of this 2000-acre elk and buffalo ranch will take you on a tour of their rolling grasslands and even bake you your favorite pie. If you're looking to **camp**, head to the Riverside Park and Canfield Recreation Area (see opposite) for free RV (with hookups) and tent sites.

One reliable place for **food** is *Best Western's* (see opposite) *Memories Restaurant*, which serves decent, reasonably priced all-day breakfasts and tasty Mexican and American food. For inexpensive but really good homecooking head to *Cable's Italian Grille*, 431 Main St (℡970/867-6144), where the minestrone with Italian sausage is excellent. Possibly the town's best restaurant, though, is the *Country Stake Out*, 19592 E 8th Ave (℡970/867-7887; closed Mon), where excellent steaks, salad bar, and lunch buffets pack the place out on Tuesdays and Sundays. If it's just a coffee or snack you're craving, head to the relaxed *In the Mood Coffeehouse*, 307 E Kiowa Ave, where you might find occasional **live music** and even theater, along with tasty soup and sandwich specials.

Sterling

Locals from the compact ranching town of **STERLING** proudly say that theirs is the largest settlement in Colorado east of Pueblo – which actually says more about the sparsely populated lands east of Pueblo than to suggest that Sterling is some kind of plains metropolis. All the same, Sterling has a small, wanderable downtown and, somewhat unexpectedly, is also a college town. However, the impact of the Northeastern Junior College on local small-town life seems remarkably understated; the place gets most of its identity from the series of agricultural and livestock shows that are the cornerstones of its calendar.

Sterling began life well after the Overland Trail had ceased to exist, with its first few sod huts built in the 1870s. What really got the place off the ground was the initiative of a local landowner who gave the Union Pacific Railroad 80 acres of land, thus encouraging them to build a depot here and include the town on the railroad network. As a result Sterling grew swiftly during the 1880s, with most of its early inhabitants pioneers from Mississippi and Tennessee.

The Town

Should you decide to stop off, a few things beg closer investigation. Close to I-76 (exit 125) and opposite the Visitor Center (see p.124) is the town's tidy and well-ordered local history museum, the **Overland Trail Museum**, situated inside a replica of an old fort (April–Oct Mon–Sat 9am–5pm, Sun 1pm–5pm; Nov–March Tues–Sat 10am–4pm; $2; ℡970/522-3895). Contrary to what you might expect, there's not all that much in the museum about the Overland Trail; rather there's no end to interesting late-nineteenth and early twentieth-century curios: Native American and pioneer clothing, tools and weapons, obscure agricultural implements, a two-headed calf (seemingly the *de rigeur* artifact for any small-town plains museum) – there's even a grand piano that was hauled from Mississippi by oxen in 1889. Sadly the absence of much explanation leaves you guessing, though the place oozes small-town appeal. Some of the buildings the museum is spread across were hauled here for preservation – a schoolhouse, a blacksmith's, church, and barber's – and these are decked out with vaguely relevant collections, including, in the smithy, an 1890s penny-farthing bicycle in

The Indian Wars 1864–1869

Though precious little visible history remains, Colorado's western plains once were the stage for one of American history's darkest moments. In the late 1860s the final chapter in the resistance of the largest Native American tribes to US encroachment on tribal lands was written. The conflicts, which have since become popularly known as the **Indian Wars**, not only put an end to Native Americans' nomadic way of life – thereafter tribes were largely confined to reservations in the Southwest – but also spawned a whole genre of cowboy-and-Indian Western fiction and film. Elements of the wars, during which brutal atrocities occurred on both sides, were used to portray Native Americans more generally than just in the context of these six years.

The first frictions began in April 1864 when ranchers along the South Platte River claimed Indians had stolen their stock. More likely was that much of the stock had simply wandered off, yet the US military snatched at this as a pretext to punish the natives. And so on May 2nd the Colorado Cavalry attacked an Indian village near the South Platte River. A string of isolated hostilities followed, escalating over the summer, particularly after the well-publicized murder of the Hungate family on a ranch 25 miles east of Denver. A reprisal was conducted by **Colonel John Chivington** in November 1864, who led the volunteer troops of Colorado's Third Regiment to attack a peaceful band of Cheyennes and Arapahos camped at Sand Creek. Over the course of a bloody and merciless seven hours – while the young men of the village hunted – the troops hit the village with artillery before butchering 163 old men, women, and children before mutilating their bodies. Many of the scalps taken by the **Bloody Thirdsters** would later be displayed in a Denver theater. Several half-hearted federal investigations were launched into the attack, yet none found anyone accountable.

The attack was essential in galvanizing the plains tribes, uniting them in an unprecedented way and making them determined to repel settlers from their territory. Retaliation came on **January 7th, 1865**, when 1500 Cheyenne, Arapaho, and Sioux warriors led coordinated attacks on all US settlement along the South Platte River Trail. Stage and telegraph stations, ranches and wagon trains were systematically pillaged and torched in raids that resulted in over 250 army and civilian deaths; the attacks effectively closed the Overland Trail and cut off Denver from the rest of the world for a month. Only two residences remained intact, one of which was Holen Godfrey's ranch near Merino; he fended off the marauders from his windows while local women and children reloaded his guns, earning his ranch the nickname **Fort Wicked**. In response 8000 Union troops were diverted from the Civil War to reopen and protect the Overland route.

After this came something of a lull. The tribes seemed to successfully maintain and protect their ways while settlers continued to arrive, seeking a greater toehold in the area. But during the impasse the Indian marauding of wagon trains and ranches steadily continued, so that in 1868 a small company of scouts was dispatched under **Colonel George Forsyth** to explore and create a plan of action. The group moved out over the Kansas plains for over a month, picking up signs that a large number of Indians were traveling ahead of them and keeping a close watch on their movements. On September 16th the scouts camped beside the Arikaree River by a small tip-top condition, and a series of bewildering telephone switchboards. There's also an interesting display on the process of "rural electrification," which transformed locals' lives after being initiated by Roosevelt under his 1930s New Deal.

Across the road by the Information Center is one of the sculptures of local artist **Brad Rhea** (Ⓦ www.thesculptor.net). By all accounts a remarkable man, he became an accomplished artist after already having a degree in nuclear

island, later known as **Beecher Island** (see p.126), with a sense that engagement was imminent. At dawn large numbers of Cheyenne, Arapaho, and Sioux appeared, surrounding the company, who dug in on the river island to defend themselves from a series of attacks and a siege that lasted nine days. Forsyth was shot in three different places and cut the bullets out of his flesh himself; while Beecher, his second-in-command, was killed during the first onslaught. On the fourth day the great Cheyenne chief **Roman Nose** led the battle's decisive charge, heading 400 men toward Forsyth and his soldiers as they crouched behind their dead horses. Yet the charge was no match for the company's deadly rifles, and a hail of bullets killed many of the attackers, including Roman Nose. The howling and grieving of squaws from the distant encampment was audible from the island where the men remained another five days, surviving on horse meat and wild plums, before the cavalry arrived and freed them. By the end of the conflict fourteen of Forsyth's men lay dead or seriously injured while over seventy Indians had perished in the Battle of Beecher's Island, now widely regarded as the event that turned the tide and balance of power in the Indian War.

But the final unpleasant chapter of the Indian Wars would be played out a day's ride to the northwest of Beecher Island at the **Battle of Summit Springs** near Sterling. The sequence of events was precipitated by the flight of a band of Cheyenne Dog Soldiers (the most elite Cheyenne military forces, who swore never to retreat in battle) from their Oklahoma reservations to rejoin their tribe in Kansas. The 250-strong Fifth Cavalry under **Major General Eugene A. Carr** was dispatched, ostensibly to send them back, but on finding them in Beaver Creek, Kansas, the cavalry launched a surprise attack, killing around 25 Indians. In retaliation the Dog Soldiers raided deep into Kansas, killing settlers and capturing two women including a **Susanna Alderdice**, a five months' pregnant mother of four, whose children they killed before raping and nearly starving her to death. The Fifth Cavalry, including 50 Pawnee Scouts, rode in pursuit, eventually catching the Cheyenne just over a month later. On July 11th, 1869, they discovered their encampment at Summit Springs and immediately went to attack. A 15-year-old boy was the first to see the approaching army, and managed to race back to the camp to raise the alarm, but even so the great Cheyenne chief **Tall Bull** and 51 other braves were killed at the camp along with an untold number of women and children. **Buffalo Bill** (see p.83) was involved in the carnage and later boasted of killing Tall Bull, but this was almost certainly untrue. The only non-Indian casualty was Susanna Alderdice, who was hurriedly tomahawked to death as the cavalry approached. After the battle all Indian possessions – beadwork, blankets, dresses, robes, and many tons of dried meat – were systematically burnt, thus effectively ending the Indian Wars and symbolically securing the fate of those nations.

Little is made of the vital sites in Colorado, although in 2000 federal permission was granted to create a **Sand Creek Massacre National Historic Site**, near the insensitively named settlement of Chivington, in recognition of one of the most potent symbols of the Native American struggle to exist on their ancestral lands. Presently the National Park Service (Ⓦ www.nps.gov/sand) is acquiring lands around which the massacre site lies with the goal of creating a commemoration and interpretation center.

medicine under his belt. His unusual gimmick was to carve his sculptures in situ out of Sterling's condemned trees. For a time, this caused the town to market itself as the **City of Living Trees**, but the reality today is a good deal less impressive. Part of the problem has been weathering. Out in the elements these wood carvings quickly began to decay, so today many are missing, awaiting conversion into durable bronze busts. Pick up a map of the sculptures' locations at the Information Center. The most impressive are the Skygrazers in **Columbine Park**, on US-6 between S 3rd and Division; the park also makes a great picnic spot.

For more picnicking, along with camping, all sorts of watersports, and good warm water fishing, it's worth heading up to **North Sterling State Park**, twelve miles north of town along 7th Ave ($5/day; ☎970/522-3657, ⓦwww .parks.state.co.us/north_sterling). Another interesting destination is the **Summit Springs Battlefield**, where the Indian Wars effectively came to an end. With the exception of a few markers commemorating the life of Susanna Alderdice (see box, p.123), the approximate site of Tall Bull's death, and the location of the Indian White Butte Creek encampment, there's not much to see – though the place is made more evocative once you know the nature of the events that took place here. To get to the battlefield leave I-76 at exit 115 (Atwood) and drive southeast on Hwy-63 for about five miles. Then head four miles east to the end of RD 60 before one last mile south on a dirt road to a windmill and the site.

Practicalities

Greyhound (☎970/522-5522) buses pull in two miles south of Sterling at the *Travel Lodge*, beside Hwy-61. Sterling's swanky **Information Center** (☎970/522-7649, ⓦwww.sterlingcolo.com) is also two miles from downtown, but close to I-76 on the east side of town and opposite the Overland Trail Museum.

Unusually, most of Sterling's **motels** don't crowd the interstate exit, but instead dot the quiet edges of downtown. One clean, basic, and inexpensive choice is the *Crest Motel*, 516 S Division St (☎970/522-3753; ❷), one of several family-owned motels that line the road. For more amenities, including a sauna and pool, try the *Ramada Inn*, 22140 E Hwy-6 (☎970/522-2625; ❺), opposite the Info Center and by I-76. **Campers** can pull in or pitch for free in **Pioneer Park** on the western edge of town beside Hwy-14; or, if you want to get out of town, try for a site at one of three popular campgrounds in North Sterling State Park (☎303/470-1144; ☎1-800/678-2267, ⓦwww.reserveamerica.com; $12–18).

Sterling offers a fair range of places to chow down on some tasty home-cooked **food**. Basic and enduringly popular is the smoky *J & L Café*, 423 N 3rd (☎970/522-3625), an eatery that's been serving filling meals on its Formica tables to local ranchers for as long as anyone can remember; breakfast here is hard to beat. *The Shake, Rattle & Roll Diner*, 1107 W Main St (☎970/526-1700), a standard wannabe 1950s joint with all-day breakfasts, burgers, malts, and cardiac-arrest desserts, is also decent enough. More interesting is the menu at the clutter-packed *T.J. Bummer's*, 203 Broadway St (☎970/522-3897), which serves excellent green chili-smothered breakfast burritos, sandwiches and burgers for lunch, steaks and prime rib for dinner, and fine homemade desserts; everything's inexpensive, too, starting at just $5 for the Hobo Dinner, a basic stew. Barely more pricey is the excellent Mexican food at ⚑ *Delgado's Dugout*, 116 Beech St (☎970/522-0175; closed Mon & Sun), hidden in the basement of a former Baptist church at the corner of 2nd and Beech. If you arrive in town late, or are just looking for a place to drink a beer or two, head to *Fergie's West Inn Pub*, 324 W Main (☎970/522-4220; closed Sun) a small bar open until 2am with good sandwiches, soups, and nachos.

The I-70 corridor

Colorado's most heavily used arterial road, **Interstate 70**, bolts west 177 miles from the Kansas state line to Denver. Along the way there's precious little to see apart from big skies looming over the oft-frantic highway, though the highway does pass two sizeable towns, **Burlington** and **Limon**. The former

△ Kit Carson County Carousel

is far more attractive and interesting, though each has a couple of attractions worthy of closer investigation – particularly the antique **Kit Carson County Carousel** in Burlington and the decidedly off-beat **Genoa Tower**, just west of Limon.

Burlington

Once the largest grain-shipping point between Omaha and Denver, **BURLINGTON** is now somewhat of a nonentity. That said, agriculture remains the town's mainstay, and if you really want to see what makes the place tick, try to arrive for a cattle auction at the **Burlington Livestock Exchange** (Thurs; 1pm), two miles west of town along Hwy-24. Otherwise, westbound travelers will find it a good place to pick up information about the state at the highwayside **Colorado Welcome Center** (daily 9am–5pm; ☎1-800/288-1334).

Behind the info center is the **Old Town Museum** (late May to early Sept daily 9am–6pm; early Sept to late May Mon–Sat 9am–5pm, Sun noon–5pm; $6; ☎719/346-7382), a sanitized living history museum with craft demonstrations and other performances – including cancan dances and gunfights – in its group of Western buildings. The mix of restoration and replica structures, done up to re-create buildings like a saloon, drugstore, smithy, and bank, are particularly worth visiting if you're with kids, and give a good picture (though without the grit) of how the West once was.

The Old Town Museum offers wagon rides ($2) seven blocks north to the town's real pride and joy, the **Kit Carson County Carousel** (late-May to early Sept 1–8pm; rides 25¢; ☎719/348-5562, ⓦwww.carousel.org/kcc), an antique fairground carousel that's an impressive relic of an era of finely handcrafted toys. Built in 1905 for Denver's Elitch Gardens (see p.68), the carousel – which is revealing of the worldview and aesthetic of the American Victorian middle-class – became the speculative investment of Kit Carson County councilors in 1928. The move caused local indignation about the investment's frivolity and councilor resignations inevitably followed. But hindsight has judged the decision kindly and the carousel is now unquestionably the town's most-loved possession. The carousel's acquisition came on the eve of the Great Depression, during which Burlington buckled down and used its assets as carefully as it could. The town elected to use the carousel as a grain store to insure against hunger, and so grain was simply poured through a hole in the roof, over animals, organs, and all. Unfortunately, mice soon got into the grain and over the course of the decade much of the carousel was ruined. Interest and finances returned in the 1970s when painstaking restoration work began to expose the original paintwork and coax the organ back to life.

If you're in town overnight, or want somewhere pretty to stretch your legs, head to the **Bonny State Recreation Area**, 22 miles north of town via Hwy-385 (ⓦwww.coloradoparks.org). Aside from being a relaxing spot to explore on foot there's also particularly good warm-water fishing (walleye especially) and good facilities for picnicking and camping (see below). If you've made it up here then you may also like to drive another 24 miles north along Hwy-385, east along 22 RD, and finally south down LL RD to the site of the **Battle of Beecher Island**. A monument marks the spot and you can wander across to the island itself and imagine the scene here in 1868 (see box p.123).

Practicalities

Only twelve miles from the Kansas border, Burlington is an obvious psychological milestone for east–west travelers and so has plenty of reasonably priced

motels and **eateries**. *Sloan's Motel*, 1901 Rose (℡719/346-5333; ❸) may be the cheapest, but the rooms are spotless; a light continental breakfast is included and there's even an indoor pool and children's play area. The town's *Super 8*, 2100 Fay St (℡719/346-5627; ❹) is similarly clean and rates also include breakfast. **Campers** can head to the RV-oriented *Campland*, east of town at 4th St and Hwy-24 (℡719/346-8763; sites $12), or, better still, drive up to the Bonny State Recreation Area (℡303/470-1144; $12–22), where campsites, spread among four campgrounds, gather beneath the shady cottonwood trees that fringe the lake.

Burlington has several good places to **eat**, and *Interstate House*, I-70 exit 437, 415 S Lincoln St (℡719/346-7041), is as popular with the locals as any. It opens at 6am for good cheap breakfasts – $2 and up – and serves all manner of inexpensive standards like burgers, tacos, and burritos until 9pm. For a classier bite, head to the solid-wood booths of the *Route Steakhouse*, 218 S Lincoln (℡719/346-8790), where huge sandwiches ($8) make good lunch options and rib-eye steak ($15) is the house specialty.

Limon

A scruffy town strung out between two highway exits, **LIMON** (pronounced *Ly*-mon), is as dull as Colorado towns get. Thankfully, though, the local weather – bitingly cold in winter, searingly hot in summer, and frequently wracked by severe thunderstorms – often provides topic for conversation. Weather brought the town into the news in 1990 as downtown was slowly and forcibly torn apart by a tornado that wreaked $20 million in damage; miraculously no one was killed.

It's hard to see the after effects of the tornado anywhere today, but for a good look at the events, including video footage, head to the **Limon Heritage Museum and Railroad Park**, on East Ave and 1st St in the original Union Pacific Railway Depot (June–Aug Mon–Sat 1pm–8pm; free; ℡719/775-2373). Other objects of interest include three boxcars and an eighteen-foot replica of a Cheyenne teepee.

Limon has long been a stopping-off point for passers-by, and nowhere can you get a better sense of this than at the **Genoa Tower**, three miles east of town along I-70 (late-May to early Sept daily 8am–8pm; ℡719/763-2309), a relic from a bygone era when roads were smaller, speeds were slower, and endearingly simple attractions stopped the traveler. Claims that you can see six states from the tower's summit, which technically sits on the highest point between Denver and New York, prompted motorists in the Twenties and Thirties on the now-defunct Hwy-24 to stop and investigate, pick up fuel, and recharge in a grotto-style diner. The buildings have long gone out of their original use, and are now employed as a museum of sorts for a collection of everything from downright junk to intriguing curios and even archeological and mammoth remains. The collection's owner and proprietor, Jerry Chubbock, even discovered the Olsen-Chubbock archeological site, to which he gave his name. This exciting site offers evidence of the cooperative way in which Paleo-Indians (9000–6000 BC) hunted bison. The beasts were encircled by hunters on foot and stampeded off of a cliff in large numbers before being stabbed to death below with spears. Around 200 were killed in a single sitting at this site, their remains no doubt providing an abundance of food, shelter, and clothing for the tribespeople.

Practicalities

Unusually, Limon is as well-endowed with family-owned **motels** as it is with the big chains, and, with both largely lining Main Street between the town's two highway exits, neither are hard to find. The *Safari Motel*, 637 Main (℡719/775-2363; ❸), is a good way from the hum of the interstate and has a heated outdoor pool; rates include a light continental breakfast. The *Midwest Country Inn*, 795 Main St (℡719/775-2373; ❹) has less amenities but rooms are a little more cheerful, thanks to the presence of some antique furnishings. The selection and quality of **eateries** in Limon is generally poor – fast-food abounds – but one central choice for decent Mexican food is the *Fireside Junction*, 888 Main St.

Travel details

Buses

(All buses below are Greyhound.)

Denver to: Fort Morgan (2 daily; 1hr 30min); Greeley (2 daily; 1hr); Limon (1 daily; 1hr 20min); Sterling (2 daily; 2hr 20min).

Rocky Mountain National Park and around

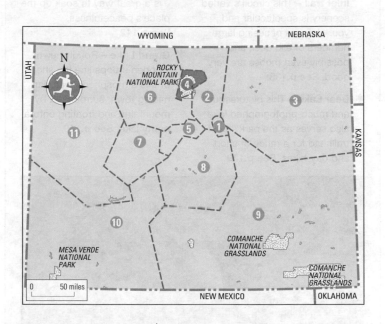

CHAPTER 4 # Highlights

* **Backcountry camping** – For a short adventure in the wilds book a night at a backcountry campsite, then hike in with all your gear. See p.135

* **Trail Ridge Road** – Take a leisurely drive on one of the state's most scenic roads, crossing stunning high alpine scenery, replete with wildflowers and grazing animals. See p.136

* **Hike the Tonahutu and North Inlet trail** – This circuit's varied scenery is spectacular and your chances of seeing large numbers of elk, deer, and possibly even moose are very good. See p.138

* **Bear Lake** – This picturesque and much-photographed lake also serves as the park's best trailhead for a range of short and day-hikes. See p.139

* **Longs Peak** – One of Colorado's quintessential mountain climbs, delivering grandiose views in every direction. See p.140

* **Learn to climb** – Get up close and personal with the park's rock on a course with the Colorado Mountain School. See p.141

* **Fishing** – A spot of fly-fishing on the park's waters – many of which have been stocked – is a great way to soak up the place's peacefulness. See p.142

* **Grand Lake** – Rough-hewn wooden stoops line the shops of this atmospheric Victorian mining town, surrounded by mountains and fronting onto a pretty lake. See p.149

△ Elk, Rocky Mountain National Park

4

Rocky Mountain National Park and around

Any foray into northern Colorado should include a visit to **Rocky Mountain National Park**, which offers arguably the best hiking in the state along with excellent wildlife-viewing opportunities. The main question when heading to the park is whether to camp within its boundaries or to establish more civilized digs in a nearby town and visit the park from there. The main, heavily touristed gateway is **Estes Park**, on the eastern border, while a more peaceful and scenic alternative, with great "doorstep" access to several trailheads – though it has less in the way of accommodation choices, shopping, fast food, and amusements – is **Grand Lake**, which straddles the park's western boundary.

Visiting the park

By far the majority of visitors approach Rocky Mountain National Park **from the east**, either from Denver, Boulder, or any number of Northern Front Range communities. You barely penetrate the foothills of the Rockies before you arrive at Estes Park, 65 miles northwest of Denver via US-36, and every weekend throughout summer a chain of cars, SUVs, and monster RVs link the capital with the park entrance here. Most arriving after 4pm without pre-booked accommodation head straight out again on US-34, towards the barely cheaper motels in Loveland, thirty miles east of Estes Park. You might find some relief from the weekend traffic by traveling along Hwy-72, which parallels US-34 to the west and becomes Hwy-7 over the last fifteen miles; this is also the more scenic road, punctuated by some dramatic rock formations.

While your point of entry will probably depend on the broader picture of your travels in the region, it's worth considering approaching the park **from the west**, via the town of Grand Lake. Although by no means untouched by mass tourism, it's still a far cry from the tacky scene at Estes Park, and its scenic lakeside location is bordered by a number of dramatic 12,000ft peaks looming just to the east. Winter visitors will fare best around Grand Lake, as a number of trails here are ideal for Nordic skiing and snowmobiling.

Rocky Mountain National Park

Based on its name alone, one might imagine that a visit to **ROCKY MOUN-TAIN NATIONAL PARK** is essential in order to appreciate the full splendor of the Rockies. In fact, the park's 415 square miles take up a relatively minuscule section of the mountain range. A tenth the size of Yellowstone, RMNP attracts almost as many visitors – around three-and-a-half million per year – and with the bulk of those coming in high summer, its lone arterial highway, **Trail Ridge Road**, can get incredibly congested. However, the park is undeniably beautiful, straddling the Continental Divide at elevations in excess of 10,000ft, while an even fairer measure of what to expect is the number of **summits over 12,000ft** – there are 76 of them. A full third of the park is above the treeline, and large areas of snow never melt; the name of the **Never Summer Mountains** speaks volumes about the long, empty expanses of **arctic-style tundra**. Lower down are patches of lush greenery which support the park's grazing animals, and you never know when you may stumble upon a sheltered mountain meadow flecked with wildflowers.

Although there's never a shortage of people making a quick foray into the park from Denver or Boulder, it would be a mistake to try to see anything much on a **day-trip**, since this realistically would allow you only to dip a few miles into the park's eastern fringes. About the furthest base that makes for a comfortable day-trip is Fort Collins; at 49 miles from the park's eastern entrance it's not a lot closer than Denver, but the drive is much easier. It's also worth noting that the west side of the park enjoys more **rainfall** – around twenty inches annually, compared with fifteen at Estes Park – so the forests and meadows here are notably more green and lush. While it's certainly possible to take in the alpine splendor of the park from your vehicle, you should ideally try to set aside three or four days to **hike** some trails, perhaps pitch a tent in the backcountry, and drive Trail Ridge Road at a leisurely pace.

Some history

For all its natural appeal, Rocky Mountain National Park is not an area that humans have ever made their permanent home. During the warmer summer months the Ute people would come here to hunt, before being driven west of the Continental Divide by the Arapaho. The Colorado Gold Rush of the 1860s and 1870s saw some hardy prospectors gravitate towards the region, but by 1879 the land had yielded little in the way of mineral wealth, and the miners' shanty towns crumbled almost as quickly as they had appeared.

The dedicating of these mountains as Rocky Mountain National Park was largely the work of one man, **Enos Mills**, a naturalist who wrote and lectured on the area for much of his life. Mills lobbied Congress to create this, the

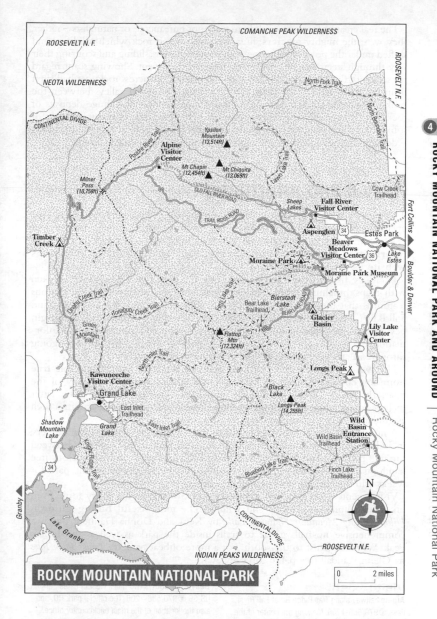

country's tenth national park, and his wish was granted on January 26, 1915. The original proposal was for it to be much bigger, extending from the Wyoming border south to Pikes Peak, but the boundaries were drawn as a compromise following negotiations with Colorado's powerful logging and mining interests. There has been just one small land acquisition since: 465 acres on the eastern edge around Lily Lake, absorbed in 1990.

The real creative forces at work here were not bureaucrats or naturalists – rather, they were the mighty **glaciers**, huge beds of ice and rock which solidified and shifted under the power of their own accumulated mass, sliding and scouring their way through steep canyons, widening them as they went. Showing scant regard for seniority, the 10,000 to 15,000-year-old glaciers slid across rock that had risen from the earth millions of years earlier, carving out broad valleys between the peaks. When the last Ice Age ended and the glaciers receded, huge deposits of rock and debris called **moraines** were left behind, effectively damming parts of some valleys and creating lakes, some of which would in turn become meadows – delicate touches added to the massively sculpted mountain terrain.

Arrival and information

The park **entrance fee** for a private automobile is $20, valid for seven days; cyclists and motorcyclists pay $5. Keep your receipt so you can leave and re-enter the park during that period. An annual pass costs $35. For general **information**, phone park headquarters (℡970/586-1206) or check the park's **website** (𝕎www.nps.gov/romo).

There are five **visitor centers** servicing the park (see below), each stocked with maps, brochures, books, exhibits, and interpretive displays. One curious feature is that three of the five visitor centers – Kawuneeche, Lily Lake, and Fall River – are located outside the park, and a number of trailheads also begin beyond park boundaries. It is thus perfectly feasible to collect maps and information at a visitor center and then do any number of hikes without ever going through an entrance station and paying for a park permit.

The two essential pieces of printed material you'll require are available **free** from any entrance station or visitor center: a park **map** and a copy of the quarterly *Rocky Mountain National Park High Country Headlines*. The latter includes comprehensive **listings** of the excellent, free ranger-led activities such as guided walks and campfire talks.

A number of detailed **topographic maps** are available at the visitor centers, including the waterproof 1:59,000 Trails Illustrated map. However, between the free park map, the well-marked and maintained trails, and the various free handouts with trail and campsite descriptions, you could explore the park for weeks without needing to purchase any additional information.

Visitor centers are also well stocked with **books**, covering every topic from hikes and climbs to geology and wildlife. The most **useful hiking guide** is *Hiking Rocky Mountain National Park*, by Kent and Donna Dannen; this is a comprehensive, no-frills guide to trails inside the park as well as the Indian Peaks Wilderness just to the south. For a more offbeat read, try *Longs Peak Tales* by Glenn Randall (see p.426 for a review).

Visitor centers

Alpine halfway along Trail Ridge Rd at Fall River Pass ℡970/586-1206. Marking the center of the park, this is really the only requisite stop for any visitor happy enough to see the alpine tundra by car. The center has exhibits relating to the tundra's flora and fauna and there are good positions for wildlife viewing a little further east along Trail Ridge Rd. Open daily May–Aug 9am–5pm, Sept 10am–4.30pm, closed Oct–April.

Beaver Meadows two miles west of Estes Park on US-36 ℡970/586-1206. The official park HQ, and also the location of the main backcountry office. There are several wildlife exhibits and regular audiovisual presentations. Daily: June–Aug 8am–9pm, Sept–May 8am–5pm.

Fall River five miles west of Estes Park on US-34 ℡970/586-1206. The newest visitor center. In the tacky tradition of Estes Park, the information desk and interpretive center here are tiny in relation to the gift shop. The cafeteria has a salad bar, burgers, cinnamon rolls, and clean restrooms. May–Sept daily 8am–8pm, winter hours variable.

Kawuneeche one mile north of Grand Lake on US-34 ☏ 970/627-3471. For those entering the park from the western side, this is the only visitor center and an essential port of call for maps, information, and backcountry camping permits. A large, 3D map of the park highlights the major peaks, including Longs. Daily: May–Sept 8am–6pm, Oct–April 8am–5pm.

Lily Lake three miles south of Estes Park on Hwy-7 ☏ 970/586-1206 This small visitor center is far less busy than the rest, though you can still collect a park map and other information; it's also a handy place to check conditions on nearby Longs Peak. May–Sept daily 9am–4.30pm, closed in winter.

Camping

The places to stay within park boundaries are five National Park Service **campgrounds**. Reservations can be made up to five months in advance (with credit card) for sites at *Moraine Park* and *Glacier Basin* (☏ 301/722-1257 or 1-800/365-2267, ⊛ reservations.nps.gov), both of which are on the eastern side of the park and fill daily in summer. *Aspenglen, Timber Creek,* and *Longs Peak* campgrounds all operate on a first-come, first-served basis; try to claim a spot before noon. There's little to separate the campsites in terms of facilities or attractiveness, so your choice should be made according to which areas of the park you're planning to explore. The **maximum length of stay** is generally seven nights, except for *Longs Peak*, which has a three-night limit. All campgrounds have toilets, water, and firewood, but no showers or electrical hookups. *Longs Peak* is the only campground without a public phone. Each campsite allows for one vehicle and one camping unit, whether tent, RV, or trailer. All sites are $20 per night (the rate drops to $15 for Oct–April at the three campgrounds that remain open year-round).

Aspenglen elevation 8230ft, just inside the Fall River entrance on the eastern edge of the park. Open May–Sept, though exact dates vary according to weather; 54 sites, no reservations.

Glacier Basin elevation 8600ft, on the east side of the park, just off Bear Lake Rd. Open May–Sept, though it tends to open a week or so later than *Aspenglen* and close a week earlier. Handy to a number of gentle, scenic trails; 150 sites, reservations required.

Longs Peak elevation 9400ft, beside the Longs Peak trailhead. Open year-round, but with running water only late May to mid-September, this campground primarily serves climbers intending to tackle the peak; 26 sites, tents only, no reservations.

Moraine Park elevation 8150ft, just west of the Moraine Park Museum, off Bear Lake Rd. Open year-round (running water mid-May to late Sept), with access to several popular trails that lead up to the Continental Divide via a series of alpine lakes; 247 sites, reservations required between May and September.

Timber Creek elevation 8900ft, the only serviced campground on the west side of the park, at the northern end of the Kawuneeche Valley. Open year-round (running water late May to mid-September), it's close to both the easy and attractive Colorado River Trail and the more challenging Timber Lake Trail, in an area that offers a good chance for viewing moose; 100 sites, no reservations.

Backcountry camping

An alternative to staying at the established campgrounds is to camp in the **backcountry**. The advantages of this are numerous: you'll leave most of the day-hikers behind; your tent won't be hemmed in by RVs and trucks; you're far more likely to see wildlife behaving naturally (ie, ignoring you); and the best way to experience the dizzying highs of the alpine tundra is to camp at sites just below the treeline, from where you can hike at your leisure across terrain with

△ Rocky Mountain National Park

the finest views and perhaps bag a 13,000-foot peak.

There are two main park offices which issue **backcountry permits**: the small building 100 yards east of the Beaver Meadows Visitor Center (☎970/586-1242 for both information and advance backcountry campsite bookings) and inside the Kawuneeche Visitor Center. From mid-May until the end of September reservations are only accepted in person or by mail; write to receive a map of backcountry sites plus a request form (Rocky Mountain National Park, Estes Park, CO 80517). From May through October, backcountry permits ($20) are also available at the Longs Peak and Wild Basin ranger stations (daily 8am–4.30pm). The permit covers one person for up to seven days; however, a new one is required for each separate trip into the backcountry. Put simply, if you do a three-day hike and then drive to another trailhead to begin hiking a different route, you need a new permit. As well as getting a backcountry permit, you also need to book the actual campsites in advance. This can be a bit tricky if you are hiking a route that you are unfamiliar with, since you won't know how far you'll comfortably get, but rangers will assist in this by suggesting realistic goals for a day's hike with a full backpack. They can also advise which are the more secluded or scenic campgrounds. Note, that an open fire, which adds greatly to the evening atmosphere, is allowed at only a small number of grounds.

The campground at **Sprague Lake**, which is accessible by car, is specifically designed to accommodate **disabled visitors**, up to twelve people plus six wheelchairs at a time, for a maximum stay of three nights. The half-mile nature trail around the lake is level and wheelchair-accessible, too. A backcountry permit is required, and reservations should be made through the backcountry office (see above).

Exploring the park

The showpiece of Rocky Mountain National Park is **Trail Ridge Road**, which connects Estes Park and Grand Lake. This 45-mile stretch of Hwy-34, the highest paved highway in the US, affords a succession of tremendous views; the definite highlight is the stretch on both sides of the Alpine Visitor Center, where high-altitude peaks and alpine tundra will literally take your breath away. The road is normally open from Memorial Day to mid-October, though as winter progresses and snow falls the road becomes progressively blocked lower down, but you can always expect to get as far as **Many Peaks Curve** from the east or the **Colorado River Trailhead** from the west (snowfall is typically heaviest during March and April). Note that there are **no gas stations** en route – rangers advise allowing three to four hours' driving time.

During summer, you can also drive along the unpaved **Old Fall River Road**; completed in 1920, this was the first road to be built in the park. Running one-way (east to west) through a valley bed carved by glaciers into a U-shape, it does not have open mountain vistas, but is much quieter than the Trail Ridge Road, and offers a good chance of spotting **wildlife**. Although the drive is only eleven miles, it's worth investing in the *Old Fall River Road* guide (available at visitor centers; $2), which takes you through the road's history, geography, geology, and variations in landscape and wildlife habitat. The speed limit is 15mph, so clearly not one for the impatient. The narrow, curved road passes through thick forests on the way to its terminus at the 11,796ft Fall River Pass. Along the way are several short trails leading off to waterfalls, streams, and lakes that are worth a look. Stop at Willow Park, just before the road enters the zone of alpine tundra, where elk are often spotted in the foliage.

Just inside the park, near the Estes Park entrance, a spur road, open year-round, leads south to two small and pristine alpine lakes: Sprague and Bear. On the way, the **Moraine Park Museum** (summer only, daily 9am–4.30pm; free) has a well laid-out set of exhibits on the park's natural history. The broad, marshy meadow of Moraine Park is a rare example of development in reverse: there were three hotels, a post office, and a golf course here until the 1950s, when the National Parks Service removed the buildings and set about restoring the landscape to its original state.

To ease traffic, frequent and free **shuttle buses** operate beyond Moraine Park Museum. The museum itself is on the Moraine Park Route (mid-June to mid-Sept daily 7.30am–7.30pm; every 30min), which connects the Fern Lake trailhead in the west with the Glacier Basin campground in the south. Here you can jump on a connecting shuttle to **Bear Lake** (mid-June to mid-Sept daily 7am–7pm every 10–15min). The classic viewpoint here is probably the park's most photographed, the mountains framed to perfection beyond the cool, still waters. Also here is the Bear Lake trailhead, by far the park's busiest (see p.139).

Hiking

Recommending any one **hiking** trail over another is not necessary as there are literally dozens of superb hikes to choose from. Instead, think about what sort of experience you want to have – photographing a particular animal, fishing an alpine lake, hiking across the Continental Divide – and then plan around that with help from one of the many rangers.

The best way to gain a sense of this extraordinary environment is to begin a hike at a relatively low elevation (around 8000ft) and head right up onto the **alpine tundra** (11,500ft). Along the way you take in the ponderosa pine, lodge-pole pine, and Douglas fir forests of the **montane** ecosystem (7000–9500ft), then feel the air start to cool and thin as you reach the stands of subalpine fir and Engelmann spruce in the **subalpine** strata (9500–11,000ft). Finally, you break out above the treeline onto the windswept tundra, where the sun is as

Hiking hazards

There are a number of special safety considerations that apply to hiking in Rocky Mountain National Park that you may not have encountered elsewhere in the Rockies. The park's lowest elevations are around 8000ft, and some of the hiking and climbing routes top 13,000ft; by way of comparison, the highest point at most Colorado ski resorts is well below 11,000ft. The **potential dangers** are all related to altitude: **dehydration** and **altitude sickness** are not uncommon, while afternoon thunderstorms regularly produce **lightning strikes** on the exposed alpine tundra. Several lives are lost in the park every year, so a healthy measure of respect for this dramatic mountain environment is essential. Plan your hikes conservatively, keep an eye on the weather, and heed the advice of rangers.

If you've recently arrived from somewhere near sea level, let your system adjust to the altitude before you try hoofing it up a five-mile trail to 12,000ft. A perfect way to start is with a scenic trail that's not very steep; you get to enjoy the surroundings as you keep an eye out for wildlife. With that under your belt, you may feel ready to hike up to the treeline at around 11,000ft. It's extremely unwise to be exposed above the trees when the lightning storms roll in, so start out early and plan to be heading down by early afternoon. The key to enjoying yourself while hiking is to stay properly hydrated and not to push too hard; plan on walking about two miles an hour, and drinking about five pints (three liters) of water a day. Note too that distances marked at trailheads are one-way; a four-mile hike is actually eight miles there and back. For general tips on hiking safety, see p.35 in Basics.

strong as the air is bracing. From this vantage, it's easy to appreciate the sheer size of the mountains and the effect of glacial shifts upon their shape, and to reflect upon the stark changes in the environment, apparent as you pass through the three distinct ecosystems.

Around Grand Lake

The trailheads for the popular Tonahutu, North Inlet, and East Inlet trails start from just outside the park in Grand Lake. The **Tonahutu** and **North Inlet** link into a challenging loop which takes you up onto the alpine tundra at just over 12,000ft; it takes two long days and at least one night camping at a backcountry site (requires advance reservation) (see p.136) to complete the circuit. Along the way you will be able to trace nature's gentle transitions as you leave the stands of aspens that encircle Grand Lake to climb alongside thundering mountain streams into a thick and dark evergreen forest. Hours of steep climbing on rocky switchback trails later, you emerge from the trees to take in unexpectedly bleak views, with craggy valley upon valley fanning out from the Continental Divide like the spokes of a wheel. Carefully picking the right spoke, you then descend back to the lush meadows of the valley bottoms. You could also start from Bear Lake on the eastern side of the park, although you'll need an early start to get over **Flattop Mountain** before the threat of lightning becomes too great.

If all this sounds like too much of an expedition, then do as many other visitors do, and simply hike three or four miles along either forested trail before retracing your steps. Around four miles along the Tonahutu trail you reach Big Meadows, where elk and moose often graze in the early evening.

The **East Inlet** trail, a fourteen-mile round-trip, is also a great place to start, as it offers views of some spectacular peaks, meadows frequented by deer, elk, and moose, and several picturesque alpine lakes as you get into the upper reaches. The first couple of miles are a gentle climb, while the stretch leading up to

Lone Pine Lake gets progressively steeper. You can carry on via three more lakes, although this requires a very early start or a night out in the backcountry.

A few miles north of the Kawuneeche Visitor Center are a couple more promising trailheads. The **Green Mountain** trail links up with Tonahutu near Big Meadows, and allows for a moderate 7.5-mile loop beginning at either the Green Mountain or **Onahu** trailhead. Having completed one of the easier day-hikes, **Timber Lake** makes a great warm-up for a more ambitious backcountry expedition; in the course of 4.9 miles you gain 2060ft in elevation – a strenuous hike to 11,000ft, with a pristine lake as your reward.

Most people planning to stay **overnight** in the backcountry have the high alpine reaches as their goal, and for many the icing on the cake is to cross the Continental Divide. The only trail that does this, however, is the **Flattop Mountain** trail, which meets the North Inlet-Tonahutu loop at around 12,000ft in the shadow of Flattop Mountain.

Around Alpine Visitor Center

Perched high on the tundra at 11,796ft, the Alpine Visitor Center is usually jammed with people admiring the breathtaking mountain vistas; however, that's typically all they do, as there are few hiking trails anywhere in this area because the flora is so fragile and lightning an ever-present danger. Nevertheless, the four-mile trail down to **Milner Pass** is a bracing way to take in this harsh but stunning environment, offering a good chance of seeing herds of bighorn sheep while crossing the Continental Divide. A more challenging, and far more peaceful, option is to pick up the **Chapin Creek** trail from Old Fall River Road below the visitor center and climb to the top of **Mt Chapin** (12,454ft); from there you can walk down the adjoining saddle and up to the peak of **Chiquita** (13,069ft), and continue on to **Ypsilon** (13,514ft). It's a tough 3.5 miles (one-way) at this altitude, but it's also a unique opportunity to get access to alpine tundra within the first mile and bag three immense peaks during a single hike – each with astounding views of multiple surrounding mountain ranges in every direction. The views on Mount Chapin are particularly spectacular, while from Ypsilon the unmatched panorama takes in the picture-perfect Ypsilon and Spectacle lakes, though you may be distracted by the many marmots and pikas that make the summit rocks their home. There is no actual trail beyond Mt Chapin, but you can see where you're headed and the park rangers don't mind a few people walking across the tundra, although they do ask you not to walk single-file so that the impact is spread somewhat. It's important to start early and watch the weather, as there's no cover if a lightning storm hits.

Around Bear Lake

The fact that there's a 250-space parking lot at the **Bear Lake** trailhead – plus more parking below near the *Glacier Basin* campground and a bus which shuttles people in between – should provide some idea of just how heavily used this area is. While the parking lots and trails can be hopelessly crowded, it's still easy enough to enjoy this area simply by visiting early or late in the day; try to arrive by 8am, or else (weather permitting) wait until after 3pm. Parking capacity isn't the real reason the area is so popular; rather its popularity lies in the sheer quality and accessibility of trails ideal for short hikes of a couple of hours, day hikes, and even as a launching area for multi-day hikes that take in Grand Lake via the North Inlet trail (see p.138).

The easiest is probably the half-mile trail around ice-cool and clear **Bear Lake**; the trail is maintained so that older or disabled visitors and young children can enjoy it. The next easiest and almost as popular is the two to three-hour round-trip to the aptly named **Emerald Lake**, via **Dream Lake** and the one-mile interpretive nature trail that circles **Nymph Lake**.

To get away from the busier areas try hiking south of Bear Lake and up **Glacier Gorge**, a narrow canyon and alpine valley of magical beauty that leads to sparkling lakes and tarns. The 8.4-mile out-and-back trip to **Black Lake** follows Glacier Creek through stands of aspen and over marshy areas. A little over half a mile into the hike the canyon's walls begin to close in and the creek makes its spectacular plunge at **Alberta Falls**. Beyond this the trail leads to tranquil Mill's Lake before winding through a landscape of dwarf fir until steep walls block the canyon. Here lies Black Lake, a splendid terminus, since it is cradled by a cirque below McHenrys Peak, its dark and looming east face reflected in the lake's tranquil waters.

If you'd rather not retrace your steps on the return leg but are looking for a great day-hike, try taking the shuttle bus up to Bear Lake and then hiking up to **Bierstadt Lake** – 2.5 miles which take around an hour and a half. From here you get grand views of Longs and other peaks along the Continental Divide, including Flattop. Depending on your energy level and the time numerous possibilities exist to return to various points on the shuttle bus route from Bierstadt Lake. You can descend directly to the road or explore more of the park by returning via trails that head to the **Mill Creek Basin** or **Fern Lake** trailheads, both of which are on the Moraine Park shuttle route.

If you have it in mind to tackle the trail to **Flattop Mountain**, pack weatherproof gear and lots of water; what looks like a reasonably short hike on the park map is in fact 4.4 miles with an elevation gain of almost 3000ft. Allow about three hours to reach the mountain's base, and if you intend to spend some time on the tundra, don't set out any later than 9am. Many people take this trail so that they can cross the Continental Divide, spend a night in the backcountry, and then hike right down to the park's western boundary. Very few have the stomach for the return trip, however, and – having left a vehicle parked at the Bear Lake trailhead – find themselves hitchhiking down to Grand Lake in search of an (expensive) shuttle ride back to their car with a company like Mountain Goat Tours (see p.154).

Longs Peak

Officially the **highest point** in Rocky Mountain National Park, 14,255ft **Longs Peak** gets all the attention it deserves from both hikers and climbers. The easiest route to the summit is known as the Keyhole, and even this approach does not guarantee a successful assault. Note too that the Keyhole route does demand technical equipment and expertise when under winter conditions; snow may persist from mid-September until early or mid-July.

Whatever the time of year, a certain degree of **planning** is required for this hike, which from the trailhead is about eight miles one-way with an elevation gain of 4855ft. Beginning at Longs Peak Campground and Ranger Station, (elevation 9400ft), the trail leads six forested and progressively steeper miles to the accurately named Boulderfield. The hop and dodge between these lasts around one mile, until you arrive at the Agnes Vaille Shelter Cabin (13,100 ft) and the beginning of the **Keyhole Route**. A series of red and yellow paint markings trace this route over a series of ledges and a broad couloir from which it's a steep six hundred feet up a combination of snow and talus to a notch where the route swings to the south side of the peak. Here it crosses **The Narrows**, the most spectacular part of the climb. Though fairly exposed, these are broad enough to be easily crossed if there is no snow. In snow – a possibility well into July – an ice axe is a necessity here and on the short, shallow couloir that leads beyond to the summit.

To have a realistic chance of reaching the top ahead of the afternoon weather, most people start out well **before sunrise**, having camped at *Longs Peak* campground (see p.135) beside the trailhead. Another option is to camp at one of the backcountry sites closer to the peak; this alleviates some of the urgency of time, so you might even consider a sunrise stop at Chasm Lake, from where it's worth trying for a photo of the **Diamond**, the (diamond-shaped) east face of the mountain favored by technical climbers. Even if you don't intend scaling the peak, the hike in to **Chasm Lake** is highly rewarding.

Climbing

There are some popular destinations nearby for **rock climbers** besides the high-profile Longs Peak, including **Lumpy Ridge**, two miles north of Estes Park via Devil's Gulch Road, which offers a good variety of mostly short climbs. Assaults on many of the alpine summits require a night spent camping close to the base or even on the rock-face itself; a special bivouac permit (free) is available to technical climbers for overnight stays in certain areas – contact the backcountry office at park HQ for details. The Colorado Mountain School, 351 Moraine Ave, Estes Park (T970/586-5758 or 1-888/267-7783, Wwww .cmschool.com), is a good point of contact for information and instructional courses, including a technical climb of Longs Peak. The school is currently the only company authorized to take people climbing in Rocky Mountain National Park; prices for its highly regarded courses – some of which include ice-climbing or even an overnight mountain bivouac – start at $175 per day. Right in town, Estes Park Mountain Shop, 358 Elkhorn Ave (T970/586-6548 or 1-800/504-6642), has an indoor climbing gym and offers indoor and outdoor instruction.

Winter in Rocky Mountain National Park

As in summer, a **winter experience** of Rocky Mountain National Park is a tale of two climate zones. The western side receives a great deal more snow than the east, so while cross-country ski enthusiasts and snowshoers are startling wildlife along trails from Grand Lake in January, hikers heading in from Estes Park and other eastern points may well find themselves on snow-free terrain.

Some excellent and fairly moderate **Nordic skiing** can be had north of Grand Lake in the Kawuneeche Valley and along trails that lead into the Arapaho National Forest. Popular routes include the East Inlet trail into the national park from Grand Lake, and the Continental Divide trail which heads west into the Arapaho National Forest from *Winding River Resort* (see p.151). Among several recommended **winter hikes** on the east side of the Continental Divide are easy walks to Cub Lake (2.3 miles one-way; park at road closure on Moraine Park Rd and walk to Cub Lake trailhead) and the Pool (2.5 miles one-way; start from the Fern Lake trailhead, a half-mile beyond the Cub Lake trailhead). Hiking can be a labored and dangerous affair in deep snow, so it's important to check current conditions before setting out during winter.

Snowmobiling has been a highly controversial winter activity in the park for several years, with packs of snowmobilers making their presence felt on trails in and around Grand Lake. The machines are banned in the national park, although Grand Lake continues to attract snowmobilers to the national forest trails just outside park boundaries.

Fishing

Many of RMNP's lakes and streams have been stocked with brown, brook, and rainbow trout, and some support small numbers of endangered native greenback cutthroat and Colorado River cutthroat trout. Seeing as **regulations** vary depending on the species and area – fishing is banned altogether in some waters – you'll need the park's *Fishing Information* leaflet to sort things out. A standard Colorado **state fishing license** is required ($9/day), available at sporting goods stores in Grand Lake and Estes Park. Generally speaking, the lakes at higher altitudes support the fewest fish. The best stretch of river for **fly-fishing** is the North Fork of the Big Thompson, in the northeast corner of the park; this is accessed via a service road off Devil's Gulch Road, which leads to the North Fork trailhead. The seven miles between the trailhead and Lost Falls offer fine fishing, and there are a dozen scenic backcountry campsites over the three miles between Lost Falls and Lost Lake, too.

Wildlife viewing

The mix of excitement and frustration experienced by people hoping to **spot particular animals** stems, of course, from the fact that the park's animals are wild; they don't show up on demand, and the more intelligent and secretive of them make a point of avoiding human contact altogether. The largest you're most likely to encounter is the **elk** (also called *wapiti*, an appropriately descriptive Native American word meaning "white rump"). There may be as many as four thousand of them inside the park during summer, the larger bulls weighing up to 900 pounds and sporting huge antlers. The most dramatic time to observe the elk is during the **fall rut**, which generally begins in September and may go on into early November. The most extraordinary part of this display is an unearthly call by the bulls to a potential mate, called **bugling**; rather than the macho bellow one might expect, it's an ear-piercing squeal which lasts several seconds.

Although not originally native to the area, a few of a group of **moose** transplanted into the adjacent Arapaho National Forest in 1978 wandered across to the Kawuneeche Valley at the park's western edge, and soon established themselves in the marshy meadows alongside the Colorado River. There are now thought to be about thirty roaming the park, and they are still seen almost exclusively along the wetter western boundary in the **Kawuneeche Valley** – notably the half-mile north of Onahu Creek trailhead. Another member of the deer family, **mule deer**, are far more common; look out for them along both the stretch of Hwy-34 between the Fall River entrance station and the Endovalley picnic area and the Bear Lake Road.

The title of Rocky Mountain National Park mascot goes, of course, to the extraordinary **Rocky Mountain bighorn sheep**. Nearly eliminated from within the park's boundaries by the early twentieth century, a reintroduction and management program has since seen sheep numbers return to over one thousand animals. Rams put on an extraordinary display during the **rutting season**, roughly mid-November through December, when from a safe distance you can sometimes see them square off and crack horns with a sickening impact. Bighorns are the archetypal high-country dwellers; look for them in the Horseshoe Park area, particularly around Sheep Lakes, or check with staff at Alpine Visitor Center for current viewing spots.

It is a source of some disappointment to many visitors that bears are very rarely seen, and indeed there aren't many of them at all residing in the park. The grizzly population was wiped out a century ago, so today the thirty or so **black bears** have scavenging rights pretty much to themselves. Though an

Mountain lions

The **mountain lion** is the most secretive predator in the Rocky Mountains. Also referred to as a puma or cougar, this sleek animal wears its Latin name best of all – *felis concolor*, the one-colored cat. Easily the largest of North America's cats, the male of the species may reach eight feet in length and weigh up to 180 pounds, while females can grow to seven feet and weigh up to 100 pounds; both male and female have a tawny-colored coat and black-tipped ears and tail.

Little is known about the mountain lion's status in the Rockies, or anywhere else for that matter. Sightings have increased in recent years – notably here in Colorado, where the lion population is thought to be 1500 to 3000 – though that's not necessarily good news. While some suggest more sightings equals an expanding population, it's more likely that their habitat is shrinking, bringing them into closer proximity with humans. The mountain lion's range covers much of the western US, including the entire length of the Rockies; specific **habitat** tends to be dictated by the presence of deer, their favorite prey.

There have been occasional attacks by mountain lions on humans, although known fatalities number less than ten over the past century. These cats prefer isolated, rough country where human contact is rare; however, **encounters with humans** do occur, and it's advisable to be aware of their possible presence, especially when hiking, jogging, or biking alone. Mountain lions silently stalk their prey or lie in ambush, and are more likely to take an interest in pets and small children than in full-grown adults. If you do come across a lion, do not approach it, but move slowly away while facing the animal and staying fully upright; running or cowering may trigger its instinct to attack. If a lion appears to be a genuine threat, appear as formidable as possible by opening your jacket and raising your arms while talking loudly but firmly. In the event of an actual attack, throw stones and sticks or arm yourself with a tree branch – lions have been driven away by prey that fights back.

opportunistic animal might forage in one of the campgrounds, contact with humans is otherwise minimal. The park's other major predator, also seldom seen, is the **mountain lion**. There are no reliable lion-watching spots, as these solitary animals keep to rugged and remote corners of the park – yet encounters with humans are not unheard of, and lone hikers in particular should be aware of their possible presence (see box, above).

Among the other interesting animals for which you'll need a fair bit of luck to see are the bobcat, badger, beaver, river otter, raccoon, muskrat, weasel, and pine marten. More common are the **pika**, a small but rotund rodent which announces its presence by squeaking loudly as it pops out from its rocky hideaway, and the **yellow-bellied marmot**, which closely resembles a groundhog.

Bird-watchers will see plenty of hummingbirds, mallards, mountain bluebirds, and red-tailed hawks, among others, while less commonly seen are the golden eagle, peregrine falcon, blue grouse, and white-tailed ptarmigan. Bald eagles are known to pass through the area, although there are most likely no nesting sites within park boundaries.

Estes Park

Named for cattleman Joel Estes, who arrived with his family in 1859 only to leave a few years later following a particularly harsh winter, **ESTES PARK** had become, by that century's end, the private hunting preserve of the Irish Earl of Dunraven. The ambitious Earl had engineered a creative scheme to take possession of virtually the entire valley: at a time when land ownership in the valley was restricted to 160 acres per person, Dunraven "sponsored" land purchases by various drifters and layabouts – and even some occupants of the local cemetery – and then transferred ownership of every parcel to himself. It's not clear how Dunraven's mini-empire unraveled, but in 1903 a far more progressive influence arrived in the person of **Freelan O. Stanley**, inventor of the "Stanley Steamer," a steam-powered automobile. Stanley came in search of relief from his respiratory ailments and ended up erecting the stunning *Stanley Hotel* in 1909 (see "Accommodation," p.146); the town soon began to take on the more democratic function it still serves, of providing Rocky Mountain National Park visitors with food and lodging. Unfortunately, as the park's **main gateway**, Estes Park now has a wide array of tacky tourist shops, mini-golf courses, and amusement arcades, along with all the traffic nightmares expected in a town whose population fluctuates seasonally between four and thirty-five thousand, with up to three million people passing through annually.

Luckily this problem is less dramatic outside the peak holiday period (June–Aug), and the scenery around Estes Park is undeniably beautiful, the green foothills of the Rockies dotted with photogenic rock formations. By mid-fall, most tourists have gone, many businesses are closing down for the winter, and herds of elk arrive, often setting up camp right in the middle of town.

Arrival and information

Arriving **by car** from the south or east, take the US-34 "Business Route," called Elkhorn Avenue as it runs through Estes Park. A shuttle service from the Denver International Airport, about two hours away, is provided by Estes Park Shuttle (three or four daily, $45 one-way, $85 round-trip; ☏970/586-5151 or 1-800/950-3274, ⊛www.estesparkshuttle.com). They will also pick you up in downtown Denver and Boulder by arrangement.

Getting **information** at the Estes Park Visitor Center, 500 Big Thompson Ave (May–Sept Mon–Sat 8am–8pm, Sun 9am–5pm; Oct–April Mon–Sat 8am–5pm, Sun 10am–4pm; ☏970/577-9900 or 1-800/443-7837, ⊛www .estesparkcvb.com), can be an ordeal; the staff is often overwhelmed, so don't expect too much warmth or interest. Indeed, if you've booked accommodations in advance, you may not need to stop in at all. There's also an under-visited **USFS office** in town, 161 2nd St (daily 9am–5pm in summer, variable at other times; ☏970/586-3440), and the staff here issue camping permits ($5) for the nearby Indian Peaks Wilderness, required from June until mid-September. The closest **National Park visitor centers** are the park headquarters at Beaver Meadows, three miles southwest on US-36, and the Fall River Visitor Center, five miles northwest on US-34.

Accommodation

Lodging can be a pretty sore topic in Estes Park, and finding **accommodation** without prior reservations is a real scramble between May and September. In summer, the visitor center will advise you take to whatever you can get, because in five minutes it will be gone. At other times you can bargain; room rates halve during winter, although some places will be closed altogether. **Cabins** represent good value when shared between four or more people, and a number of them

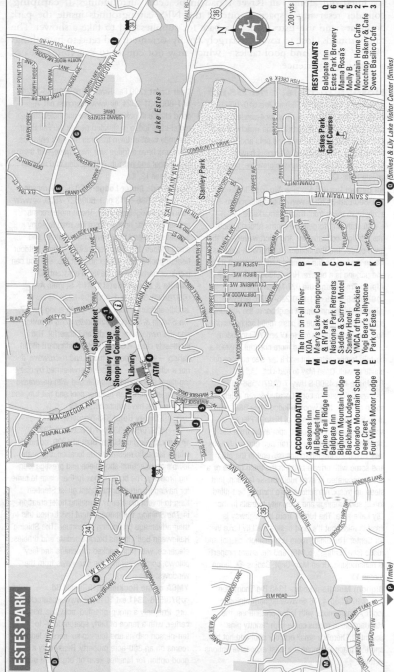

ESTES PARK

RESTAURANTS

Baldpate Inn	7
Estes Park Brewery	6
Mama Rosa's	4
Molly B	5
Mountain Home Cafe	2
Notchtop Bakery & Cafe	1
Sweet Basilico Cafe	3

ACCOMMODATION

4 Seasons Inn	B
All Budget Inn	I
Alpine Trail Ridge Inn	L
Baldpate Inn	P
Bighorn Mountain Lodge	C
Blackhawk Lodges	O
Colorado Mountain School	F
Deer Crest	N
Four Winds Motor Lodge	K
The Inn on Fall River	H
KOA	M
Mary's Lake Campground & RV Park	
National Park Retreats	G
Saddle & Surrey Motel	A
Stanley Hotel	J
YMCA of the Rockies	D
Yogi Bear's Jellystone	E
Park of Estes	

Estes Park Golf Course

Lake Estes

Stanley Park

Supermarket

Stanley Village Shopping Complex

Library

ATM

ATM

ATM

are lined out along Fall River Road in peaceful surroundings. If **camping**, consider reserving a space at one of the NPS campgrounds inside the park boundary and use Estes Park as a base for supplies and to take a shower. The campgrounds close to town are largely family-oriented, and tend to have things like TV lounges and pool tables – which may not equate to everyone's idea of a camping experience.

Hotels, motels, and B&Bs

4 Seasons Inn 1130 W Elkhorn Ave ☎970/586-5693 or 1-800/779-4616, ⓦwww.4-seasonsinn.com. Cozy, quiet, and clean are the watchwords at this motel lodge, where kids and pets and all other things noisy are prohibited. All rooms have a queen bed, fridge, coffeemaker, and microwave, plus private bath. ❻

All Budget Inn 945 Moraine Ave ☎970/586-3485 or 1-800/628-3438, ⓦwww.allbudgetinn.com. It's almost two miles from this unremarkable motel – with standard, forgettable rooms (though each has a fridge, coffeemaker, and microwave) – to the town center, but the location is otherwise ideal as it's on the way to the national park headquarters and parking is a breeze. Has outdoor hot tub. ❹

Alpine Trail Ridge Inn 927 Moraine Ave ☎970/586-4585 or 1-800/233-5023, ⓦwww.alpinetrailridgeinn.com. A neighbor to the *All Budget* and in the same league of basic motel accommodation, though its rooms (cable TV and WiFi included) are fractionally brighter and more cheerful. There's a no-frills family restaurant and a fair-size outdoor pool onsite as well. Open May to mid-Oct. ❹

Baldpate Inn 4900 S Hwy-7 ☎970/586-6151, ⓦwww.baldpateinn.com. Located seven miles south of town, this wooden lodge-style B&B, which is on the National Register of Historic Places, is secreted away in a wooded spot away from the highway. Choose between cramped and sentimentally rustic wood-clad rooms (several in the attic and some with private bath) in the main house or a cabin, decorated in even more prissy fashion, that sleep up to six. Attractions here include bird-filled forest surroundings and proximity to trails in the Lily Lake area. The turnoff from the highway is easy to miss, but it's right beside the Lily Lake Visitor Center. The dining room is pleasingly casual and rustic (see "Eating", p.148), and the entire property is nonsmoking. Open May–Sept. Cabins ❼, lodge rooms ❺

Bighorn Mountain Lodge 1340 Big Thompson Ave ☎970/586-4376 ⓦwww.bighornmtnlodge.com. A basic motel with lodge pretentions: the standard clean rooms come with "knotty pine accents". There's a small outdoor pool and hot tub, and this place is among the least expensive options in town. ❸

Deer Crest 1200 Fall River Rd ☎970/586-2324 or 1-800/331-2324, ⓦwww.deercrest.net. A good choice if looking for peace and quiet, this motel-style lodge is situated beside the Fall River one mile west of town towards the park entrance. All rooms have a fridge and microwave, and there's also a pool and hot tub. No smoking and no children under 12. ❻

Four Winds Motor Lodge 1120 Big Thompson Ave ☎970/586-3313 or 1-800/527-7509, ⓦwww.fourwindsbudgethost.com. These motel rooms are set back far enough from the road to enjoy a quiet night, and they have coffeemakers and small fridges, too. Facilities include a large outdoor heated pool, indoor sauna and hot tub, and you can picnic or barbecue on the lawn out front. ❹

Saddle & Surrey Motel 1341 S St Vrain Ave ☎970/586-3326 or 1-800/204-6226, ⓦwww.saddleandsurrey.com. A mile south along Hwy-7, the *Saddle & Surrey* is still pretty close to town, and the owners are friendly and cheerful. The spotlessly clean rooms are of the standard motel variety – with at least a fridge and microwave, if not a kitchenette – and are overwhelmed by dizzying floral bedspreads mismatched with decorative wallpaper. There's an outdoor pool and hot tub, and some rooms have kitchenettes. ❹

🏃 **Stanley Hotel** 333 Wonderview Ave ☎970/586-3371 or 1-800/976-1377, ⓦwww.stanleyhotel.com. Built in 1909, complete with a fantastic mountainside location, this is the town's architectural showpiece and prestige lodging property. The building has further claim to fame for having inspired former hotel guest Stephen King to invent his creepy, rambling hotel creation in *The Shining*; the management has turned this to their advantage by hosting an annual "The Shining" Halloween Ball. Rooms boast a sedate and timeless elegance, with high-backed armchairs and lacy pillows, complementing the fine views from the windows. ❼

YMCA of the Rockies 2515 Tunnel Rd ☎970/586-3341 ext 1010, ⓦwww.ymcarockies.org. Primarily a group-oriented, activities-based center, with a range of fairly spartan four- to ten-person cabins and four- to six-person lodge rooms on an 860-acre property. Really only a good option for families keen on organized outings such as horseback riding. Cabins $70–240, lodge rooms ④

Cabins

Blackhawk Lodges 1750 Fall River Rd ⊤970/586-6100, ⓦ www.estesparkresort.com /blackhawk. Ten cabins with wood-clad interiors and a distinct 1970s feel are gathered in a quiet spot by the river. Each has a fireplace, fully equipped kitchen, and TV; the largest can comfortably accommodate six. There's a riverside hot tub and trout fishing onsite. Summer ⑥–⑦; winter rates also available.

The Inn on Fall River 1600 Fall River Rd ⊤970/586-4118 or 1-800/255-4118, ⓦ www .innonfallriver.com. Lacy curtains adorn the windows of these otherwise simple two-bedroom riverside cabins, ideal for families with their own kitchen, fireplace, and patio or balcony. Motel-style rooms, complete with dated rustic aesthetic, are also available (⑤). Cabins ⑦.

National Park Retreats 3501 Fall River Rd ⊤970/586-4563, ⓦ www.nationalparkretreats .com. Located close to the Fall River park entrance, this resort offers a variety of simple, bright, and modern cabins that accommodate up to six people, as well as fairly pokey but clean motel rooms. The cabins have fully-equipped kitchens, bathrooms, and TV, and most have fireplaces and riverside decks. Some also have small outdoor hot tubs. Cabins (⑤) open year-round, motel rooms (④) open May–Sept. Shaded tent sites are also available for $15–28 for two people.

Hostels and camping

Colorado Mountain School 351 Moraine Ave ⊤970/586-5758, ⓦ www.cmschool.com. The closest thing to a hostel in town, but there is no communal kitchen or living area, bathroom facilities are minimal, and the building is in need of overall maintenance. On weekends, all the beds may be booked for groups on climbing courses – the real purpose of the place (see p.141). Dorm beds $20.

KOA 2051 Big Thompson Ave ⊤970/586-2888 or 1-800/KOA-1887. Along with the usual shared shower and laundry facilities there's a TV lounge and a small grocery store. Tent sites $21–28, camper cabins with bunk beds $42–63. Open late April to mid-Oct.

Mary's Lake Campground & RV Park 2120 Mary's Lake Rd ⊤970/586-4411 or 1-800/445-6279, ⓦ www.maryslakecampground.com. Although primarily an RV park, there are some shaded tent sites as well, and the location – beside the lake for which the campground is named – is a good one. There's a small heated pool plus a game room complete with pool table. Tent sites $25, sites with full hookup $39. Open May to Sept.

Yogi Bear's Jellystone Park of Estes 5495 Hwy-36 ⊤970/586-4230 or 1-800/722-2928, ⓦ www.jellystoneofestes.com. Among the family-fun attractions here are a large heated pool, basketball court, game room, TV lounge, and wagon rides for kids. As well as tent and RV sites there are three camper cabins ($66–88) and five fully-equipped cabins with kitchen and bathroom that can sleep up to eight people ($236–300). Tent sites $23, RVs $23–46. Open May–Sept

The Town

No one comes to Estes Park to visit Estes Park; there are no quaint frontier-era buildings, no Western-style boardwalks, and really no reason to be here other than its proximity to the National Park. A stroll along central Elkhorn Avenue does reveal a fair degree of commercial enthusiasm, but it's mostly of the tacky souvenir-store variety. An unavoidable landmark is the **aerial tramway**, which has little to recommend it unless you don't plan to go any further for a view of the mountains; it takes you to the top of Prospect Mountain from 420 E Riverside Drive (mid-May to mid-Sept daily 9am–6.30; $9 ⊤1–970/586-3675, ⓦ www.estestram.com).

While there's nothing much about the history of Estes Park itself that bears exploring, you can bone up on the history of Rocky Mountain National Park at **Enos Mills' Cabin**, c.1885, eight miles south of town along Hwy-7 (June–Sept Wed–Fri 10am–3pm, Oct–May call for hours; $5; ⊤1–970/586-4706). Here the work of naturalist Enos Mills, the man who lobbied Congress to create the national park, is preserved in the form of books of his writings as well as some interesting news clippings and letters. There is also a small display of Mills' photos taken at various locations in the park between 1900 and 1922 – the year he died.

Outdoor activities

While you'll probably use up your energy hiking in the National Park, there are a few diversions to consider, such as spending a day cycling about town or on the good network of trails around Glen Haven, seven miles northeast of Estes Park (no off-road cycling is permitted inside the National Park). For advice on area rides and **bike rental**, try Colorado Bicycling Adventures, 184 Elkhorn Ave (℡970/586-4241), who rent mountain bikes by the hour or for $23 per day; they also offer a variety of tours. The basic free maps available at the USFS office (see p.144) are handy if you're heading out on your own. If you'd rather let a horse do the work then head to either the National Park Gateway Stables (℡970/586-5890) or Sombrero Ranch (℡970/586-4577, ⓦwww.sombrero .com), both of which offer gentle nose-to-tail **horserides** into the national park, from one hour (around $30) to overnight pack trips ($150).

An even more relaxing alternative is to explore the small reservoir, Lake Estes, half a mile east of Estes Park on Hwy-34, where a sandy beach and wading area are beside the **Lake Estes Marina** (℡970/586-2011), which rents out canoes and fishing, pontoon, and paddle boats (from $12/hr). For a bit more excitement, join a whitewater **rafting** trip to Cache la Poudre Canyon with Rapid Transit Rafting (℡970/586-2303 or 1-800/367-8523, ⓦwww.rapidtransitrafting .com), which runs half-day trips for around $50 including transportation.

Eating and drinking

Considering the high concentration of visitors, Estes Park is a bit lacking in really notable **places to eat**. And as the town is largely the domain of climbers, hikers, and families on vacation, you'll be stretched to find any really lively **nightspots** – food and sleep are generally more pressing subjects than carousing after a day or two out in the mountains. If you do have energy to spare, try *Lonigans*, 110 W Elkhorn (℡970/586-4346), where there's often live acoustic music on weeknights and a bit of blues, rock 'n' roll, and dancing on Saturdays. The *Stanley Hotel* (see p.146) is also worth investigating, even outside the summer music festival period, particularly for its big-band night on Fridays – though it's a bit more hit-and-miss and the scene can be staid.

Baldpate Inn 4900 S Hwy-7, seven miles south of town ℡970/586-5397. A standout for its location and setting, the *Baldpate Inn* has no menu, just a $12 all-you-can-eat soup-and-salad bar, a must-visit for its hearty soups, fresh-baked gourmet breads, and good range of salads, with cheese and crackers to finish. Dinner only; reservations are essential and they stop serving at 8pm.
Estes Park Brewery 470 Prospect Village Drive. If you're just after a pizza to go with a beer and perhaps a game of pool, then this should suffice. As it's basically just a pub, and not quite in the town center, there are usually fewer "vacationers" and more hikers and climbers.
Mama Rosa's 338 Elkhorn Ave ℡970/586-3330. The Italian standards – lasagne, veal, and pizzas – on offer are decent if unspectacular; prices are also moderate and it's very central, with outdoor seating in a small plaza. Open daily for lunch and dinner.

Molly B 200 Moraine Ave ℡970/586-2766. A real stalwart, with a surprising variety of dishes and prices – some cooked breakfast combos go for diner prices. At lunch there are sandwiches, salads, seafood quesadillas, and vegetarian lasagna, while the moderately priced dinner menu stretches to trout, salmon, steaks, and even a vegetarian Indian stir-fry. May–Oct breakfast, lunch, and dinner; Nov–April breakfast and lunch only.
Mountain Home Cafe 453 E Wonderview Drive. A good spot in upper Stanley Village – the area around the *Stanley Hotel* – to fill up early in the day, with big breakfast combos at $4–5, plus huge burgers at lunchtime; veggie choices include mushroom or garden burgers. Daily 7am–2.30pm & 5–9pm.
Notchtop Bakery & Cafe 459 E Wonderview Drive ℡970/586-0272. The name doesn't quite do justice to a mix of food that stretches from fresh-baked goods, omelettes, and

pancakes for breakfast to pasta, seafood, and stir-fry specials for dinner, followed by a late-night menu of soups, desserts, specialty coffees, and microbrews. There's even occasional live entertainment, and the place is completely smoke-free; it's worth calling ahead in the evening. Daily 7am–10pm (until 11pm Fri & Sat).

Sweet Basilico Cafe 401 E Elkhorn Ave ☎970/586-3899. Popular and inexpensive place for pizzas ($10), pasta dishes, and Italian specialties, mostly chicken and veal ($8–11); the $5 focaccia with your choice of toppings includes soup or salad. Daily 11am–9 or 10pm; closed Wed in winter.

Listings

Banks First National Bank has ATMs at 334 E Elkhorn Ave in the center of town and right behind the town park at MacGregor Ave and Park Lane; a Key Bank ATM is in upper Stanley Village.
Internet access The public library is at the corner of Elkhorn and MacGregor Avenues (Mon–Thurs 9am–9pm, Fri–Sat 9am–5pm, Sun 1–5pm; free, but phone ahead in summer to reserve a computer; ☎970/586-8116); the Peace Pilgrims Shop, upstairs at 165 Virginia Drive (summer daily 10am–9pm, winter hours vary; $12/hour; ☎970/586-9301); the *Notchtop Bakery* (see opposite) has free WiFi.
Laundry Dad's Maytag Laundry, upper Stanley Village (daily 7am–9.30pm; ☎970/586-2025); public showers $3.
Medical Center Estes Park Medical Center, 555 Prospect Ave (☎970/586-2317), has 24hr emergency care; normal consultation hours are Mon–Fri 8am–5pm & Sat 8am–noon.
Pharmacy Inside Safeway, upper Stanley Village (Mon–Fri 9am–9pm, Sat 9am–6pm, Sun 10am–4pm).
Police 170 MacGregor Ave (☎970/586-4000).
Post office 215 W Riverside Drive (Mon–Fri 9am–5pm, Sat 10am–2.30pm).
Supermarket The Safeway in upper Stanley Village is open 24hr.
Tours and transport Emerald Taxi (☎970/586-1991) offers a 4hr guided tour of the National Park from $25 per person, as well as shuttle service to and from Denver (4–6 times daily) for $30 one-way; Estes Park Shuttle & Mountain Tours (☎970/586-5151) runs similar trips at slightly higher rates.

Grand Lake

Following its days in the late 1800s as a tiny lakeside supply stop for prospectors heading into neighboring mountains, **GRAND LAKE** was perhaps destined to eventually attract a fair number of summer vacation "cabin-dwellers." The lake itself is the largest natural body of water in Colorado, and back in 1901 that was reason enough to inaugurate the Grand Lake Yacht Club, which remains a prominent fixture today. Even so, the town miraculously stayed something of an unheralded hideaway for much of the twentieth century. For better or worse, a Denver travel writer in the early 1980s trumpeted Grand Lake as Colorado's last "Shangri-la," and people have since arrived en masse – a trend that cannot now be reversed.

The town's winter **population** of around four hundred nudges close to five thousand in the summer, and the presence of two mini-golf courses and a ten-pin bowling center further suggest, at least to some, the direction in which the town is headed. Others would say that to really appreciate Grand Lake, you only have to spend a day in Estes Park. In any case, the town's **lakeside setting** is superb, and the cluster of peaks that loom over the town to the east confirms that – bumper-to-bumper summer weekends notwithstanding – Grand Lake makes an excellent base for exploring Rocky Mountain National Park.

Arrival and information

It's a gentle uphill run once you leave US-40 at Granby and turn north onto US-34 to cover the fourteen-mile stretch up to Grand Lake. The tourist

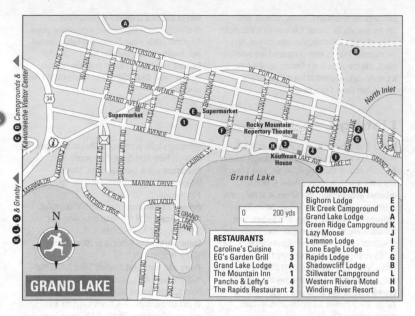

information office (Mon–Sat 9am–5pm, Sun 10am–4pm, winter hours variable; ☎970/627-3402, ⓦwww.grandlakechamber.com) is a tiny hut perched just off US-34 at the entrance to town. It's easy to drive past it as you turn off the highway, and doesn't offer much useful information anyway – the only town map available is very poor, and information on Rocky Mountain National Park is dispensed at the Kawuneeche Visitor Center (see p.135) up the road. Downtown Grand Lake is the four blocks of Grand Avenue between Vine and Hancock streets lined with an Old West-style boardwalk. Almost everything is within reasonable walking distance except for the *Grand Lake Lodge*, while *Shadowcliff Lodge* is several minutes' walk up a steep hill.

Accommodation

With trailheads leading directly from Grand Lake into the National Park, you can have the convenience of decent **accommodation** coupled with immediate access to a pristine mountain environment. You won't be able to drive much of a bargain at any of the **motels** or **lodges** between May and September, and between June and August some may insist on at least three nights' stay. **Cabins** are a great option for groups of four or more, but should be booked at least three months in advance. **Reservations** are essential during peak season, ideally several weeks ahead of time. Some places close for the winter, but although things are slower then, they're certainly not quieter, thanks to enthusiastic snowmobilers.

Excellent **hostel** accommodation is available at the *Shadowcliff Lodge*, and both private and public **campgrounds** are scattered about the town's outskirts.

Hotels, motels, and cabins

Bighorn Lodge 613 Grand Ave ☎970/627-8101 or 1-800/341-8000. Conveniently central motel with clean rooms. Open year-round; minimum stay may be required during peak times and on weekends. ⑤

Grand Lake Lodge 15500 US-34, via a signposted turnoff half a mile north of town ☎970/627-3967. The lodge itself is a National Historic Landmark, but accommodations are in the rustic cabins clustered around it – and these are often booked up a year in advance. Facilities include a restaurant and bar with unparalleled views and occasional live music, plus there's an outdoor pool and hot tub; the larger cabins have kitchens, and are good value for four to eight people. No TVs, no telephones, and no smoking. Four-person cabins from $175 per night. Minimum length of stay is usually two to three nights. Open June to mid-Sept. ⑤

Lazy Moose 1005 Lake Ave ☎970/627-1881, ⓦwww.lazymoose.com. Choose between a one-bedroom lakeside cabin with fully-equipped kitchen ($120) and a simpler studio-style cabin with queen-size bed and small bathroom. Open year-round, with some good winter deals; rates usually slightly lower for three nights or more. ④

Lemmon Lodge 1224 Lake Ave; summer ☎970/627-3314, winter 725-3511, ⓦwww.lemmonlodge.com. Twenty cabins with wildly varying rates commensurate with facilities, although all have own kitchen and bathroom but no TV or telephone. The location, beside the Grand Lake Yacht Club, is superb, quiet, and shady. The most basic four-person cabin is $110 per night. Open mid-May to Sept. ⑤

Lone Eagle Lodge 712 Grand Ave ☎970/627-3310 or 1-800/282-3311, ⓦwww.loneeaglelodge.com. Though the motel rooms are basic, friendly proprietors and a Grand Ave address make this a good choice in the middle range. ⑤

🏃 **Rapids Lodge** 209 Rapids Lane ☎970/627-3707, ⓦwww.rapidslodge.com. The original log-pine lodge is almost a century old, and there are now cabins and several condominiums at this low-key riverside location too, plus Grand Lake's finest restaurant. Rates on cabins and condos – some of which have kitchens and fireplaces – vary according to size and facilities. All rates are slightly lower for stays of two nights or more. Riverview condo ⑦, two-bedroom condo for four to six people ⑦, basic lodge room or cabin for two. ⑤

🏃 **Western Riviera Motel** 419 Garfield St ☎970/627-3580, ⓦwww.westernriv.com. A good first choice for its lakeside location, simple but comfortable rooms, and outdoor hot tub. ⑤

Hostels and camping

Elk Creek Campground a half-mile north of town and just west of Hwy-34 ☎970/627-8502, ⓦwww.elkcreekcamp.com. Tent sites for $22, sites with full hookup for $33, and bare-bones "camper cabins" for $52. There's nothing terribly attractive about the site but the bathroom facilities are well maintained and there's a small shop for necessities. Open May–Oct.

Green Ridge Campground three miles south of Grand Lake on Hwy-34, then one mile west on CR-66 ☎970/887-0056 or 1-877/444-6777. A USFS campground just below the Shadow Mountain Reservoir. Amenities include bathrooms (but no showers) and the sixty sites go for $14 a night.

🏃 **Shadowcliff Lodge** perched on the hillside just above West Portal Rd ☎970/627-9220. This gorgeous, rambling, log-built lodge offers some of the finest budget accommodation anywhere in the state. Dorm beds are six to a room, and there are clean, comfortable motel rooms with great views; big, hummingbird-visited terraces, and a serene chapel open to all. Other facilities include a small guest kitchen and a communal living area with a library and open fireplace. There are also three cabins which sleep six to eight people ($110–125 per night), but these are generally booked a year in advance. *Shadowcliff Lodge* is a nonprofit church-affiliated enterprise, and most guests cheerfully help out with a small chore during their stay. Open June–Sept. Dorms $18 ($20 for nonmembers); doubles ②.

Stillwater Campground six miles south of town, just off Hwy-34 ☎970/887-0056 or 1-877/444-6777. On the western shore of Lake Granby, this large USFS campground (130 sites) includes restrooms and showers for $17 a night.

Winding River Resort 1.5 miles north of Grand Lake along Hwy-34; the turnoff is signposted opposite the Kawuneeche Visitor Center ☎970/627-3215, ⓦwww.windingriverresort.com. Tent sites for $27 (for two people) and shaded cabins which can accommodate four people ($46). The main attraction here is proximity to the park, although it's also a pleasantly wooded spot.

△ Gift shops in Grand Lake

The Town

It doesn't take long to stroll the four boardwalk-lined blocks which mark the center of Grand Lake, but people nevertheless manage to amuse themselves by poking about in tourist knick-knack stores, watching the yachts out on the lake, or just wandering up and down the boardwalk. **Grand Lake Chocolates**, 918 Grand Ave (daily noon–10pm), is hard to ignore, for its handmade chocolates and enormous ice-cream cones in a multitude of flavors. Apart from the "family entertainments" of mini-golf and bowling, there's not much in the way of diversions – but then a little mooching about is just the thing after a day's hiking in the National Park.

The town's small **museum** is the 1892 log-built **Kauffman House**, at 407 Pitkin St (summer daily 11am–5pm; free); one of Grand Lake's original hotels, it now holds a fairly unremarkable assortment of period furniture and other bits-and-pieces.

Outdoor activities

Since **mountain bikes** are not allowed off-road inside the National Park, most bikers head for the trails in the Arapaho National Forest just west of town. A handy biking trail map, produced by the Grand Lake Metro Recreation District (℡970/627-8328), can often be picked up at Rocky Mountain Sports, 830 Grand Ave (℡970/627-8124), which also rents mountain bikes for $16 per half-day ($22/day). More trails can be explored with Sombrero Ranch (℡970/627-3514), who offer sedate **horserides** along trails in the National Park, from one hour ($30) to a half-day ($50); longer backcountry excursions can also be arranged. If looking to get out onto the lake, Boaters Choice, 1246 Lake Ave (☎970/627-9273), has a range of pontoon **boats**, **canoes**, skiffs, and motorboats for hire at various hourly and daily rates; Rocky Mountain Sports (see opposite) rents **sea kayaks** ($25 half-day, $35 full day).

Despite the National Park ban on **snowmobiling**, Grand Lake remains a popular area base from which to rev about in the neighboring National Forest. *Winding River Resort* (☎970/627-2429) and Lone Eagle, 720 Grand Ave (☎970/627-3310), have snowmobiles for $80–100 per half-day.

Eating, drinking, and nightlife

There are a number of highly satisfying **places to eat** in Grand Lake, from cheap diners to elegant restaurants with ambitious menus and prices; don't miss breakfast at the *Grand Lake Lodge* (see p.151). The **pubs** in Grand Lake are your basic barstools-and-sawdust affairs, and while they're fine for a beer, you're unlikely to get a decent meal at any of them. For occasional live rock or country music, look in at the *Lariat Saloon*, 1121 Grand Ave (☎970/627-9965). For a change of pace, check out what's playing at the highly regarded **Rocky Mountain Repertory Theater**, bang in the middle of town at 1025 Grand Ave (June–Sept; tickets $20; ☎970/627-3421, ⓦwww.rockymountainrep.com). A tiny box office on the boardwalk sells tickets for the current show; there are usually four different productions each season, mostly musicals, satire, and pantomime.

Restaurants

Caroline's Cuisine 9921 US-34 ☎970/627-9404. Although the local word is that *Caroline's* has slipped a notch in recent times, the menu is still quite a read and might just be worth the five-mile drive to peruse. Frogs legs, escargot, port-glazed venison, and linguini rock shrimp are usually featured (entrees $14–26). Open for dinner daily, lunch Wed–Sun; closed Mon in winter.

EG's Garden Grill 1000 Grand Ave ☎970/627-8404. Good-quality food served up in a cozy, color-ful dining room – the menu ranges from burgers to grilled wild boar sausages, New York steak and seafood specials like marlin and grilled salmon. You can sit indoors or in the beer garden, where happy hour runs Mon–Sat 5–7pm. Moderato prices; open daily for lunch and dinner.

🏃 **Grand Lake Lodge** 15500 US-34 ☎970/627-3185. Even if you're not staying here, a meal at the lodge should be a priority, not only for the great food, but also for the outstand-ing view over Grand Lake. Dinner entrees such as tortilla-dusted rack of lamb, elk, and other fresh game or seafood don't come especially cheap (entrees $16–26), but the all-you-can-eat breakfast buffet, which includes the lodge's famous Belgian waffles, is an exceptional value at $8. Reservations

are advised, and essential for the Champagne brunch on Sunday (9.30am–1.30pm). Open June to mid-Sept.

The Mountain Inn 612 Grand Ave ☎970/627-3385. This popular, inexpensive, and rustic restaurant serves up very good steaks ($12–17) and burgers ($7–9) but not too much else; great for carnivores but nothing doing if you're veggie. Daily for dinner.

Pancho & Lefty's 1120 Grand Ave ☎970/627-8773. This bustling Mexican bar/restaurant is popular for its inexpensive south-of-the-border standards (entrees $8–12), and the big, sunny deck overlooking the lake. Open daily for lunch and dinner, reservations for dinner advised during summer.

The Rapids Restaurant 209 Rapids Lane ☎970/627-3707. The busy but picturesque Tonahutu River runs right past the huge windows of the quiet, elegant dining room, here, the prime spot for a truly fine meal in Grand Lake. For a Northern Italian-influenced dinner of linguini with prawns, chili oil, lime, and herbs, followed by sauteed rainbow trout or veal marsala, dessert, and wine, you can expect to spend $50 per person. Daily for dinner, reservations advised.

Listings

Banks The only 24hr ATM is located at West Star Bank on Pitkin St; the ATM inside Lone Eagle Gas Station is accessible 8am–7pm.

Internet access Juniper Library, on the east side of the town park (Mon & Wed noon–6pm, Thurs, Fri & Sat 10am–3pm, closed Tues & Sun; $4 per 30min).

Post office 520 Center Drive, fifteen minutes' walk west of the town center (Mon–Fri 8.30am–5pm).

Supermarket Circle D Foods, at the corner of

Broadway and Grand Ave (daily 9am–7pm); Mountain Food Market is at the west end of town on Grand Ave (Mon–Sat 9am–7pm, Sun 9am–5pm).

Tours Mountain Goat Tours (℡970/627-1226 or 1-888/950-1226) runs charter tours of the National Park and also does shuttle runs to the Bear Lake parking lot for hikers who have left their cars at the trailhead.

The Central Mountains

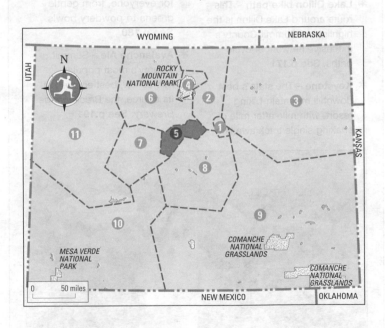

WYOMING
NEBRASKA
UTAH
N
ROCKY
MOUNTAIN
NATIONAL PARK
KANSAS
MESA VERDE
NATIONAL
PARK
COMANCHE
NATIONAL
GRASSLANDS
COMANCHE
NATIONAL
GRASSLANDS
0   50 miles
NEW MEXICO
OKLAHOMA

CHAPTER 5   # Highlights

* **The road up Mount Evans** – Arguably Colorado's most exciting road, allowing you to drive or bike to the relatively quiet summit for extraordinary views. See p.160

* **Shopping** – Silverthorne's factory outlets have great bargains, while Frisco and Dillon are both chock-a-block with outdoors outfitters. See p.167

* **Lake Dillon bike path** – This route around Lake Dillon is the highlight of Summit County's extensive network of cycle paths. See p.171

* **Keystone** – The state's best downhill mountain-biking resort, with mile after mile of snaking single track awaiting the beginner and terrifying drops and jumps on hand to tantalize experts. See p.175

* **Arapahoe Basin** – If dropping down near-vertical moguls and then barbecuing beside your truck is your idea of a good time, look no further. See p.179

* **Copper Mountain** – Under-rated ski resort with terrific terrain that has something for everyone, from gentle greens to powdery bowls. See p.180

* **Avalanche Ale** – Summit County's most popular microbrew, best enjoyed at its source, the *Breckenridge Brewery*. See p.191

△ Mountain Goats, Mount Evans

5

The Central
Mountains

J ust west beyond Denver and Golden, I-70 grinds its way into the mountains, taking with it all manner of goods and recreational traffic. Much of this goes no further than the **CENTRAL MOUNTAINS**, Colorado's most accessible and busiest outdoor playground – particularly in winter, when its five world-class ski resorts are the big draw. You won't find any of the snobbery of Vail or Aspen here, nor any really pretty and remote towns like Silverton or Crested Butte, but there is certainly plenty to do and if you are based in Denver it is all within easy range of a day-trip.

Before arriving on the other side of the Continental Divide – where most of the action is – I-70 passes through **Clear Creek Valley**. The noise and visual pollution of the highway pounding along this narrow valley does much to rob it of its attractiveness, hence the valley is all-too-often entirely passed up. Yet pulling off the road will bring you to some interesting old former mining towns as well as the road up Mount Evans, one of the state's most spectacular drives.

Leaving the Clear Creek Valley to the west, via either Loveland Pass or the Eisenhower Tunnel, you arrive on the other side of the Continental Divide, in a different county – **Summit** – and often in a new weather system. Here the interstate is forced into a steady, steep descent to Lake Dillon, where three minor, fairly workaday communities – Silverthorne, Dillon, and Frisco – are the springboards to exploring the county's maze of biking trails and cluster of stellar ski areas, the best known of which is attached to the attractive Victorian town of Breckenridge, also the area's nightlife hub. An interchangeable lift ticket system allows skiers to visit several of the resorts (and Vail – see p.229) on the same pass, greatly sweetening the deal, while moving between ski areas is further eased by the presence of an efficient, free shuttle bus service, rendering a car unnecessary.

While the area's reputation for winter sports largely speaks for itself, many of the towns and ski resorts are also promoting themselves as summer destinations, when the region is both much less crowded and far more economical to visit. Mountain biking is one of the big draws, with lots of trails on offer, including many lift-serviced by the resorts, though there's also excellent hiking and fishing.

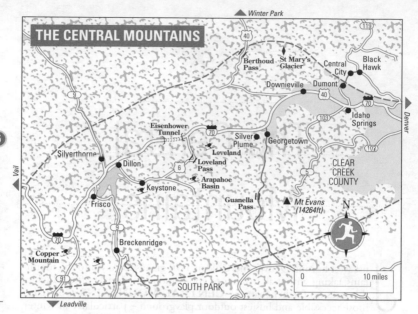

THE CENTRAL MOUNTAINS

Winter Park · Berthoud Pass · St Mary's Glacier · Central City · Black Hawk · Downieville · Dumont · Idaho Springs · Eisenhower Tunnel · Silver Plume · Georgetown · Silverthorne · Dillon · Loveland · Loveland Pass · Arapahoe Basin · Keystone · Guanella Pass · Mt Evans (14264ft) · CLEAR CREEK COUNTY · Frisco · Breckenridge · Copper Mountain · SOUTH PARK · Leadville · Vail · Denver · N · 0 10 miles

Clear Creek Valley

The **CLEAR CREEK VALLEY**, which runs fifty miles west from Denver's fringes to the Loveland Pass, sees far more through-traffic than visitors. But in fact there's plenty to detain the inquisitive along this stretch. The historic mining sites around **Idaho Springs** are a good introduction to the state's history, while the extraordinary road up **Mount Evans** and through the surrounding National Forest is a fine way to familiarize oneself with possibilities for outdoor recreation, with plenty of sparsely used hiking and biking opportunities nearby. Further west, the well-preserved Victorian settlement of **Georgetown** is a diverting place to start a steam train ride on the narrow-gauge Loop Railroad and has at its back door the scenic byway over Guanella Pass. In addition to the area's cross-country skiing and snowshoeing opportunities in winter, there's also the obvious attraction of nearby ski resorts – not only local favorite **Loveland**, but also the world-class resorts further west along the interstate. Given the relatively cheap accommodation, this is a good place to base yourself if you mean to explore several resorts on a budget.

A good trip-planning resource is the Clear Creek County Tourism Board (☎303/567-4660 or 1-800/88–BLAST, ⓦwww.colotourism.com), whose glossy leaflet *Destination Clear Creek County* is a useful source of general information and listings for the entire valley. It's available at visitor centers in both Idaho Springs and Georgetown, as well as the Forest Service's Clear Creek Ranger Station (see opposite), the best source of information on local outdoor activities.

Idaho Springs

The scruffy little town of **IDAHO SPRINGS**, just 29 miles west of downtown Denver, was in 1859 the scene of one of the first important gold finds in the Rocky Mountains. The defining moment, when Indian trader George Jackson dug his knife into frozen ground and came out with gold, is now marked by a monument a quarter-mile up Hwy-103. Within a week of his find Jackson had pulled out $2000 worth, which sparked the gold rush that founded the settlement. It was silver, however, that became Idaho Spring's really lucrative ore, with the town becoming a hub for a silver district that included Black Hawk and Central City. Once the town's mining days were over, the enterprising Jackson took advantage of the town's natural hot mineral springs and invested some of his earnings in creating the Radium Hot Springs Resort, which still exists as the *Indian Springs Resort* (see below). Today, the town attracts a smattering of visitors, either on their way into the mountains, en route up **Mount Evans**, or stopping off to learn about the town's mining history.

Information

For information head to the **visitors center** at the west end of Colorado Blvd (☏ 303/567-4382 or 1-800/685-7785, ⓦ www.clearcreekcounty.org). Here the small onsite heritage museum, half-devoted to the local Argo water treatment works, has some old mining relics on display. The best contact for recreation opportunities in the National Forest lands that surround Idaho Springs is the **Clear Creek Ranger Station**, at the base of the road up Mount Evans, on the western side of Idaho Springs, I-70 exit 240 (daily 8am–5pm; ☏ 303/567-3000).

Accommodation

Entering Idaho Springs from the east, you'll pass half a dozen **motels** that line Colorado Boulevard, making them the most obvious places to stay, though there's a grubby hostel at the heart of town and a couple of B&Bs tucked away on its fringes, too. **Campers** are best off heading to Mount Evans: there's the *Echo Lake Campground* at the base of the toll road (☏ 518/885-3639 or 1-877/444-6777; sites $12) or others north of town in the Arapaho National Forest; contact the ranger station (see above) for more detailed information.

Baxter's on the Creek 796 Hwy-103 ☏ 303/567-2164. Modern, cozy, creek-side place opposite the spooky town cemetery. The personable landlady will spoil you, plying you with huge breakfasts, spiked evening drinks, and delicious rocky road cookies. Two rooms have private baths, two share, and all can use the outdoor hot tub. ❸

H&H Motor Lodge 2445 Colorado Blvd ☏ 303/567-2838 or 1-800/445-2893, ⓦ www.hhlodge.com. Clean and simple motel where in addition to kitchenettes there's access to a hot tub and sauna. ❸

Heritage Inn 2622 Colorado Blvd ☏ 303/567-4473, ⓦ www.heritageinn.com. Dated but well-run motor lodge with kitsch touches in the decor and many different room permutations. Some include fireplaces and in-room Jacuzzi tubs; there's also a penthouse tower. Rooms on the creek have views of Argo Gold Mine. Indoor pool. ❸

Indian Springs Resort 302 Soda Creek Rd ☏ 303/989-6666, ⓦ www.indianspringsresort.com. The obvious place to stay in town if you fancy a soak in the hot springs has a range of options from standard motel rooms and "lodge" rooms with new furnishings to several small cabins with kitchen facilities. Sites at the resort's campground cost $20. All guests get a discount at spa facilities. ❹

Lodge of the Rocky Mountains 1601 Colorado Blvd ☏ 303/567-2839, ⓦ www.innkeeperrockies.com. Friendly – but extremely shabby and dirty – hostel in an old hotel once used by Doc Holiday and Wyatt Earp. Beds in four-bed dorms $20, private rooms $40.

The Town

Though the handful of nineteenth-century buildings downtown along Miner Street reflect Idaho Springs' Victorian pedigree, the real clue to its **mining past** come from the ice floes of yellow tailings spilling from holes dotting the mountainsides along I-70. A good mining intro can be had, northwest of town, by driving the evocatively named, narrow and potholed **Oh My God Road** to Central City, easily driven in a regular 2WD car and well worth it to see hillsides pockmarked by hundreds of holes and tailings, indicating how busy this area once was.

You can get a closer look into Idaho Springs' mining past at the commercialized **Argo Gold Mill Museum**, back in town at 2317 Riverside Drive (mid-April to mid-Oct daily 9am–6pm; $13; ⓦwww.historicargotours.com). Alongside the gold-panning and staged shootouts, visitors see the furnaces where ore was turned into gold ingots, and the high-security vaults in which they were stored. More enjoyable is the **Phoenix Mine** (daily 10am–6pm; $9; ⓦwww.phoenixmine.com), located a mile west of exit 239 along Frontage Road (which runs parallel to I-70) to Trail Creek Road. Mining still takes place here, but is now secondary to entertaining tours given by ex-miners, in which visitors head down 600ft to view a three-foot-long vein of gold ore, wield nineteenth-century excavating tools, and try their luck at panning for gold.

More modern is the **Edgar Experimental Mine**, 365 8th Ave (mid-June to Aug Tues–Sat 1pm, Sept to mid-June by appointment; ☎303/567-2911), an old 1870s mine now furnished with the latest technology and utilizing the newest techniques; it's used to teach students at Golden's School of Mining. For yet another perspective, visit the modest **Underhill Museum**, 1416 Miner St (June–Aug daily 9am–5pm; ☎303/567-4709), which once was an assay office and now houses information on the process of analyzing ore, together with some reconstructed living quarters from the era – an aspect of the mining life on which light is rarely shed.

Idaho Springs' natural **hot mineral springs** can be enjoyed at the *Indian Springs Resort*, 302 Soda Creek Rd (daily 7.30am–10.30pm; ☎303/989-6666, ⓦwww.indianspringsresort.com). Facilities include a covered mineral water swimming pool ($14), geothermal caves ($18.50; bathing in the nude, no under 12s), indoor and outdoor private baths (reservations required; $18.50 or $22/hr, respectively), and the unusual Club Mud ($12), a gooey total-immersion mud pool. There are discounts for combining activities and also for those staying at the resort.

Mount Evans

Together with Pikes Peak, **Mount Evans** (14,264ft) is Colorado's easiest 14,000ft peak to bag, since there's a narrow road (typically open June–Aug; $10/vehicle, $3/bicycle) that leads almost all the way to the summit. As the dominant peak in the Rocky Mountain skyline when viewed from Denver, Mount Evans is also an exceptional local vantage point; and with few other fourteeners in this part of the range, clear days promise views for 100 miles in all directions. The easy hike from the parking lot at the end of the road to the summit is only a taste of what the mountain has to offer. Protected by a wilderness area, it is crisscrossed by more than a hundred miles of hiking trails, passing through ancient stands of bristlecone pine forest, yielding great views, and sheltering ample wildlife, including yellow-bellied marmots, bighorn sheep, pikas, and mountain goats. If you fancy cycling up the mountain – which is considered one of the best road-bike routes in Colorado – expect a hard grind.

△ Mount Evans summit

Fit recreational cyclists typically take around four hours to climb from Idaho Springs fourteen miles away and then around a half-hour for the white-knuckle decent. On the route up, tranquil **Echo Lake** has not only a picnic area but also a reservable USFS campground (see "Accommodation," p.5) and a little restaurant at the *Echo Lake Lodge*.

Eating

Idaho Springs has a good selection of friendly **restaurants** serving big, inexpensive portions of American favorites. These are ideal places to grab a bite if you encounter bad traffic on the way to or from the Summit County ski resorts; taking a break may give the jam a chance to ease off.

Beau Jo's Colorado Style Pizza 1517 Miner St ☏ 303/567-4376. Opened in 1973, the first branch of what's now a state-wide chain, and a local favorite for its tasty thick-crust pizzas which come with a huge range of imaginative toppings – even the tofu pizza tastes great – and a plentiful salad bar. Mineshaft ale is among the local microbrews on offer to wash it all down.

Buffalo Bar and Restaurant 1617 Miner St ☏ 303/567-2729. Buffalo meat – a leaner version of beef – is the star here: served in black-bean chili and fajitas, on pizza, as burgers and hot dogs, and as "Buffaloaf." You can also get pizza, salads, and soups, and a selection of local microbrews in a dining room packed with old mining and pioneering artifacts. Prices are typical of upper-end bar food.

Java Mountain Roasters 1506 Miner St ☏ 303/567-0304. Popular locals' café that makes an ideal breakfast pit-stop, with live music later on. Open from 6.30am.

Mainstreet Restaurant 1518 Miner St. Start your day with good full breakfasts at this homey place, or have a sandwich or burger for lunch.

Pacos 1600 Miner St ☏ 303/567-0482. Large Mexican joint that's perhaps the pick of the bunch in Idaho Springs for an tasty inexpensive meal; there's also a lively bar upstairs.

Tommyknocker Brewery 1401 Miner St ☏ 303/567-2688. Polished sports bar with a wide selection of microbrews; apres-ski comfort food includes standard grill burgers ($8–10) plus stir-fries, "Bowl o' Lumpies" mashed potato and gravy, and chicken-fried elk steak.

Two Brothers Deli 1424 Miner St ☎303/567-2439. The best place to stop for a breakfast wrap or huge sandwich – either eat-in or to go – for around $5–8. Among the huge choice are interesting combos like the all-green veggie mix on sesame semolina bread, and the peanut butter, banana, and marshmallow fluff on sourdough.

West Winds Tavern 631 Miner St. Friendly, hard-drinking place where peanut shells scatter the floor around a couple of pool tables. There's often live music, too.

Georgetown

Nestled deep in the head of a valley beside a lake and surrounded by 12,000ft mountains, **GEORGETOWN**, 45 miles from Denver, has a marvelous setting – but for the interstate running so close to the town. Nevertheless, to drop off the highway here is to step back several decades, since the sleepy town, thanks to the hard work of its volunteer fire brigade, which spared it a major fire, is one of the best-preserved Victorian mining towns in Colorado. Georgetown made its fortunes in both gold and silver, and until the strikes at Leadville in 1878 was the major silver town in the territory. But even after Leadville took off, mining continued in this area, leading to the construction of an ambitious narrow-gauge railroad, the **Georgetown Loop**, for which the town today is most famous.

The Town

The grandeur of the mining days lives on in many of Georgetown's elegant buildings, and at weekends the local **historic society** leads ninety-minute **tours** of the downtown area (10.30am & 1.30pm; $5), leaving from the community center at 613 6th St. The tours include an informed look at two of the town's most outstanding buildings, the Gothic Revival **Hamil House**, 305 Argentine St (daily: June–Sept 10am–5pm, Oct–May noon–4pm; $5), once considered one of the most elegant Victorian homes in the Rockies, with a luxuriously furnished, polished hardwood interior containing some odd touches such as camel-hair wallpaper; and the **Hotel de Paris**, 409 6th St (same hours as above; $5; ☎303/569-2311, ⓦwww.hoteldeparismuseum .org), a far more eccentric operation run by French aristocrat Louis Du Puy. By all accounts a headstrong, maverick character, Du Puy was – apart from being a serious misogynist – a trained chef and dedicated gourmand, a background illustrated by the hotel's extravagant dining room. It's easy to imagine diners poised at tables set with fine linens, silverware, and French china, awaiting the medley of imported foodstuffs that were completely out of step with the usual Western mining camp fare. A look behind the scenes reveals an equally impressive kitchen – with antique cooking equipment and an aged stove – as well as a cellar full of old wine barrels. Elsewhere in the hotel, check out the salesmen's rooms, where salesmen could display their wares on large, elegant desks (which expanded into full-sized beds for a good night's sleep).

Georgetown is best known, however, as the starting-point of the **Georgetown Loop Railroad**, 1106 Rose St (May to early Oct daily 10am–3.45pm; $16.60; ☎1-888-456-6777, ⓦwww.georgetownlooprr.com). On the line, 1920s steam trains run a six-mile round-trip to Silver Plume, on a route which loops in big arcs – added to enable the engines to overcome the six percent climb – and includes a trip across a precarious trestle above Clear Creek. A much-vaunted engineering marvel upon its completion in 1884, the railroad was disbanded and finally sold for scrap in 1939, before being revived and entirely rebuilt by enthusiasts in 1984. Along the route to Silver Plume (where you can also pick up the train from 9.20am to 4pm), the train stops at the defunct **Lebanon Mine** ($6), now offering tours 600ft down into the cold and damp for a thorough look at the nitty-gritty of the silver-mining process – the unpleasant working conditions certainly being the most memorable part. If you stop at the mine you can catch the next train, which will make your round-trip around two and a half hours; skip the mine and the return journey takes about an hour.

Practicalities

During the summer, Georgetown runs a **visitor information** service on 6th St (☎303/569-2888 or 1-800/472-8230, ⓦwww.georgetowncolorado.com). The town doesn't have much in the way of **accommodation**, although the *Georgetown Mountain Inn*, 100 Rose St (☎303/569-3201 or 1-800/884-3201 ⓦwww .georgetownmountaininn.com; ❹) is a very pleasant motel close to the historic district. All rooms are clean and well maintained, with free WiFi and access to the heated pool; the "Colorado" rooms come with hand-hewn log furniture and ironwork. A more upscale lodging option is available five miles east in the tiny town of **Empire**, where the *Peck House*, 83 Sunny Ave (☎303/569-9870, ⓦwww.thepeckhouse.com; ❹), is the oldest B&B in Colorado, with elegant rooms that are full of antiques; the most inexpensive share a bathroom.

For **food**, head to the *Happy Cooker*, 412 6th St (☎303/569-3166), which does superb home-cooked meals, though service is on the slow side. Great breakfasts include filling egg dishes and fluffy waffles, while later in the day good soups are served with thick slabs of homemade bread. There's also quiche, creative salads, or chunky sandwiches, with delicious pies for dessert. A decent place to grab some basic bar food is the *Red Ram*, 606 6th St (☎303/569-2300), a neighborhood pub serving huge salads, burgers, ribs, homemade chili, buffalo wings, and potato skins. The place is busy on weekends, but quiet midweek, with the occasional exception of the laid-back basement, with couches and big-screen TV.

Loveland Ski Area

Spilling off the Continental Divide, with a base altitude of 10,600ft and the highest chairlift in the world, it's little wonder to see the phrase "In most states, getting this high is a felony" on T-shirts around **Loveland**. But Loveland is more than just altitude. This unpretentious resort 53 miles west of Denver – the closest of all those on the I-70 Corridor – not only averages more snowfall, has a longer season (a few runs are usually open by Halloween; the record is late September), and boasts a larger ski area (with equally extreme terrain) than many of the more celebrated Colorado resorts, but also has lower lift ticket prices and free parking.

Most visit Loveland for the day from Denver, an easy hour's drive away, so the ski area has developed little more than a basic base. Its cafeteria means you won't go hungry, and equipment stores can provide rental gear, but there's **no resort lodging** – though Loveland's Central Reservations (☎1-800/225-LOVE ⓦwww.lovelandreservations.com) offers ski-and-stay packages in various Clear Creek County towns from $125 per person per night.

Loveland divides into two interconnected areas: a gentle beginners' mountain in **Loveland Valley**, and **Loveland Basin**, a huge, mostly open bowl that funnels

5

Loveland Ski Area

Information ☎303/571-5580 or 1-800/736-3754, ⊛www.skiloveland.com; snow report ☎303/571-5580 ext 221.

Ticket prices and operating times $50; Oct–May Mon–Fri 9am–4pm, Sat & Sun 8.30am–4pm.

Mountain statistics base elevation 10,600ft, summit elevation 13,010ft, vertical drop 2410ft, acreage 1365, average snowfall 400in.

Lifts and trails nine lifts serve 77 trails: beginner 13 percent, intermediate 41 percent, expert 46 percent.

around the freeway and reaches up to the Continental Divide. Note that Loveland Basin is notorious for high winds on its often icy uppermost slopes, so be sure to have a neck warmer for the chairlift, even if it's sunny and warm at the base area.

Lift tickets, lessons, and rentals

Loveland offers several discounted **ticket options**. Buying from a local supermarket or gas station will save a few bucks off the $50/day price, while season passes are relatively inexpensive at $339. Skiing or snowboarding **lessons** (☎303/571-5580 ext 170) are available from $64 for a two and a half hour session including lift ticket and rentals, or $43 for the lesson only. The kids' skiing program is particularly good value at $69 for the day, including lunch, lessons, lift pass, and rentals. Skiing starts at age four, riding at seven. The ski area offers **daycare** (☎303/571-5580 ext 118) for kids aged between one and twelve years.

Rentals are limited, especially for boarders, but prices are reasonable: $28 per day for a snowboard package, $20 for ski. The rental hub of Clear Creek County is the truck stop in Downieville, at I-70 exit 234 between Idaho Springs and Georgetown. Here, Breeze/Max (☎303/629-0111) is one branch of a well-stocked chain. In Idaho Springs, helpful staff at the tiny, family-owned Maison De Ski, 2804 Colorado Blvd (☎303/567-2044) have been tuning skis and fitting boots for more than thirty years.

Mountain runs

Beginners have their own facilities (ski school, restaurant, bar, rentals) at Loveland Valley, where lifts access wide-open greens, curving cat tracks, and three easy blues. Almost the entire Loveland Valley area receives snowmaking, so coverage, even early in the season, is rarely a problem. At Loveland Basin, take slow Chair 2 to Ptarmigan Roost for long, flat greens back to base. Avoid the easy route from Chair 1, as it's the crowded main thoroughfare.

Loveland Basin is ideal for **intermediates**. Most groomed trails are tree-lined blues, ideal for cruising, though intermediate snowboarders may find the cat tracks back to the base area trying.

Despite the official statistics, excellent **expert** terrain is hard to come by at Loveland, and certainly almost none of it would be labelled black over at Arapahoe Basin. But there is plenty to fill a day: for bump runs try the blacks around Chair 1, while in good snow the glades off uncrowded Chair 8 are worth exploring. If you are intent on getting fresh tracks, you'll probably need to hike out to the steep couloirs (broad mountain gullies, especially ones prone to avalanche) and cornices (overhanging masses of snow or ice formed by wind) of Porcupine Ridge on the ski area boundary.

Backcountry skiing and riding in Clear Creek County

Loveland Pass is one of the most famous backcountry areas in the US, with long, powdery slopes draped east and west off the Continental Divide, offering great skiing and riding to groups prepared to take turns shuttling a vehicle up and down Hwy-6 (take the Loveland Pass exit off I-70). The eastern descents are the more popular, where lines plunge off the horseshoe ridgeline into an open bowl crested with cornices before funnelling into tight trees. Less sheltered, longer routes off the southwest side drop all the way down into the Arapahoe Basin Ski Area but require a longer initial hike and are more prone to avalanche. The usual backcountry precautions should be taken; for avalanche information check Ⓦgeosurvey.state .co.us/avalanche.

Berthoud Pass – the pass between I-70 and Winter Park – also attracts skiers and boarders for similar reasons and is again excellent for groups who can alternate as shuttle drivers. The guys that run Mount Fun (☏303/567-2996, Ⓦwww.ski -empiresports.com) operate no-frills snowcat tours here, with their extremely well-priced trips leaving from Empire Sports, exit 234 in Downieville; prices start at $150.

If that's outside your budget, head for **St Mary's Glacier**, one of Colorado's very few glaciers. It's used by both backcountry skiers and snowboarders year-round – though it's mostly a playground for the latter, who are often found on the steeper bottom portion launching off jumps. To get there, leave I-70 at exit 238 two miles west of Idaho Springs and then head twelve miles on Fall River Road to the old ghost town of **Alice**, today nothing more than an old schoolhouse and a couple of log cabins. From here it's a half-mile walk to St Mary's Lake and the eponymous glacier.

Loveland's **terrain park** is inconsistent, so many **freeriders** simply prefer to explore the mountain. Drop below Chair 9 or traverse to skier's left off the top of Chair 2 to access the gully-side dips and jumps on South Chutes and Our Bowl, or try the area between lifts 4 and 8 which is crisscrossed with cat track launches and where the Sunburst Chutes form a natural pipe. Off of Chair 1 you can look for a few small jumps and log slides tucked away on the side; some of the largest, steepest slopes are near the top of the blacks to skier's right.

Summit County

Though its snow-covered peaks, alpine meadows, and crystal lakes no doubt inspired its name, **SUMMIT COUNTY** isn't as bucolic as you might expect: in fact, it's the busiest and most developed of all the state's mountain areas. A ninety-minute drive from Denver, it harbors the greatest concentration of ski resorts in the Rocky Mountains. But the county's epicenter is the huge earth-dammed **Lake Dillon** reservoir, around which the resorts and bustling but rather dreary service towns cluster. Here plentiful accommodation and a great range of shops keep skiers happy – yet it's still easy to get away from it all with various convenient and underused trails giving quick access to the backcountry.

The workaday mall-towns of **Silverthorne** and **Dillon** sprawl along a wide corridor on the northeastern side of the lake. Though hard to separate, the former is best known for its dozens of factory outlet stores, the latter for fairly inexpensive condo accommodation. Far more sedate and attractive is the old mining town of **Frisco**, on the lake's southwestern side, which as the center of the county's transit system is also the handiest base in the area for those without a vehicle. A short drive east of Lake Dillon is the slick but unexciting resort village of **Keystone**, around the base of the eponymous ski area, and the smaller, more basic **Arapahoe Basin** ski area, a short hop beyond. Another modern, self-contained major ski resort, **Copper Mountain**, is six miles southwest of Frisco.

In addition to the good downhill skiing, Summit County is also great for **Nordic skiing**, with several ski centers and a well-organized and extensive trails network that, in the summer, is used for cycling. As one of the state's largest bodies of water, Lake Dillon itself invites **sailors** and **anglers**. By far the liveliest of the county's towns is the charismatic Victorian mining town of **Breckenridge**, eight miles south of the lake. Lying beside its own large ski resort, Breckenridge is easily the most active area town after dark.

Although winter is still the busiest time of the year, **summer activities** are becoming increasingly important to the area's economy. Several resorts, but especially Keystone and Breckenridge, have gone out of their way to create and promote summertime pursuits, in particular by building scenic hiking trails and challenging, lift-serviced **downhill mountain bike** runs. **Golf** is also becoming a major industry, with the swanky Keystone Ranch Golf Club – which occupies the meadow where the Ute pitched their teepees during the summer hunting season – a particularly popular spot.

Arrival, information, and getting around

Getting to and around Summit County is a snap, thanks to frequent shuttles and buses from Denver and an efficient and free, though fairly slow, **bus network** that connects all the communities and resorts, effectively rendering a car unnecessary. **Greyhound** buses heading west from Denver ($11 one-way) and east from Grand Junction stop in Frisco at the **transit center**, just behind the Safeway off I-70 exit 203 at 1010 Meadow Drive (T 970/668-8917). Quicker and more convenient are the various shuttle bus companies that will whisk you from Denver's airport or downtown straight to Summit County. These include Resort Express, serving Dillon, Frisco, Silverthorne, Keystone, Breckenridge, and Copper Mountain ($52; T 970/468-7600 or 1-800/334-7433, W www .resort-express.com), while Supershuttle (T 1-800/258-3826) and Colorado Mountain Express (T 1-800/222-2112) run a more expensive door-to-door service.

For advance **information** on the area visit Summit County's website (W www .summitnet.com), which has information on accommodation, restaurants, activities, and events in both the Lake Dillon communities and Breckenridge. On arrival you can stop at **visitor centers** by the factory stores in Silverthorne, 246 Rainbow Drive (daily 9am–5pm; T 970/262-0817), in Frisco at 916 N Summit (same hours; T 970/668-2051 or 1-800/424-1554, W www.townoffrisco.com), or Breckenridge (see p.183).

Summit Stage (T 970/668-0999, W www.summitstage.com) is the county's **free public transportation** operator. Its hub is the **transit center** in Frisco, from where frequent shuttle buses run throughout the Lake Dillon area and Breckenridge. There's a large free parking lot at the transit center and buses run every half-hour during the morning and afternoon ski commute, with hourly service at other times (typically 6.30am–1.30am). Shuttles have facilities for carrying several bikes, allowing cyclists to skip sections of the cycle paths or ride one-way along routes. If you're heading between Breckenridge and either Keystone or Arapahoe Basin, avoid the much slower Summit Stage in favor of the **KAB Express** (also free; ☏970/496-4200), which leaves from Breckenridge's transport terminal and drops skiers right in front of the resorts.

Silverthorne, Dillon, and Frisco

SILVERTHORNE, **DILLON**, and **FRISCO** are all towns you tend to visit out of logistical necessity rather than as an end unto themselves. Each offers ski accommodation, restaurants, and a glut of shops (see "Gearing up," p.170) that facilitate outdoor exploration. Silverthorne, centered around a series of soulless strip-malls, is probably the least attractive of the three – though you may want to make a special trip here for a dose of retail therapy at its **factory outlet stores**. Dillon, whose boundaries with Silverthorne are indistinct, is much the same, though somewhat redeemed by its tiny, modern downtown and modest marina. The most attractive of the communities is easily Frisco, where you can get a sense of its history as a Victorian mining settlement while wandering its short main street to the pretty little marina.

Accommodation

Summit County lodging covers all budgets, with prices often almost halving in summer. The centralized booking system for hotels, B&Bs, and condominium complexes in Frisco, Silverthorne, and Dillon is **Summit County Central Reservations**, 330 Fiedler Ave (☏970/468-7851 or 1-800/525-3682, ⓦwww .skierlodging.com), who offer summertime rates as low as $50.

In summer you can also **camp**. A number of large USFS campgrounds are well placed on the shores of Lake Dillon, where sites ($11–13/night) are shaded by lodgepole pines. These include the 69-site *Heaton Bay*, a mile northeast of Frisco, usually a more attractive option than the smaller *Pine Cove* – with its own boat ramp – or the 103-site *Prospector*, further along the south shore of the lake and where few sites have water views.

Silverthorne and Dillon

Alpen Hütte Lodge 471 Rainbow Drive, Silverthorne ☏970/468-6336. Clean hostel east of the main mall of factory outlet shops and conveniently opposite the rec center. The huge bunkrooms (beds $20 in summer, $40 in winter) are comfortable enough, and there are also some private, motel-quality rooms available ($42–84). Communal facilities include laundry, kitchen, and large lounge, and an early night is ensured by the strict midnight curfew. Office hours 7am–noon and 4pm–midnight. ➍

Best Western Ptarmigan Lodge 652 Lake Dillon Drive, Dillon ☏970/468-2341 or 1-800/842-5939, ⓦwww.ptarmiganlodge.com. The only hotel near Dillon's marina and lakefront public areas has fairly plain rooms, though all have balconies and some have kitchenettes and fireplaces. Included in the price is use of the hot tub and sauna, continental breakfast, and, in some rooms, high-speed Internet access. At the height of the ski season, a five-night minimum stay is usually required. ➎

Home & Hearth B&B 1518 Rainbow Drive, Silverthorne ☏970/468-5541, ⓦwww.colorado -bnb.com/hhearth. Easy-going, good-value B&B on

LAKE DILLON & AROUND

Eagle's Nest Golf Course

Silverthorne

Ⓐ

Rec Center

Ⓑ

Ⓒ

ⓘ

1 Ⓔ Ⓓ 2

5

3

4 6 Ⓕ

Dillon

Dillon Marina

Lake Dillon

6

N

MEADOW CREEK TRAIL

Heaton Bay

Pine Cave

Prospector

10

Frisco Transit Center

Frisco Marina

Frisco

9

WHITE RIVER NATIONAL FOREST

See 'Frisco' map

PEAKS TRAIL

J

COLORADO TRAIL

GOLD HILL TRAIL

9

K

TIGER ROAD

PEAKS TRAIL

Breckenridge

Vail

70

91

TENMILE RANGE

Copper Mountain (Ski Resort)

Breckenridge (Ski Area)

See 'Breckenridge' map

N M

91

0   2 miles

THE CENTRAL MOUNTAINS

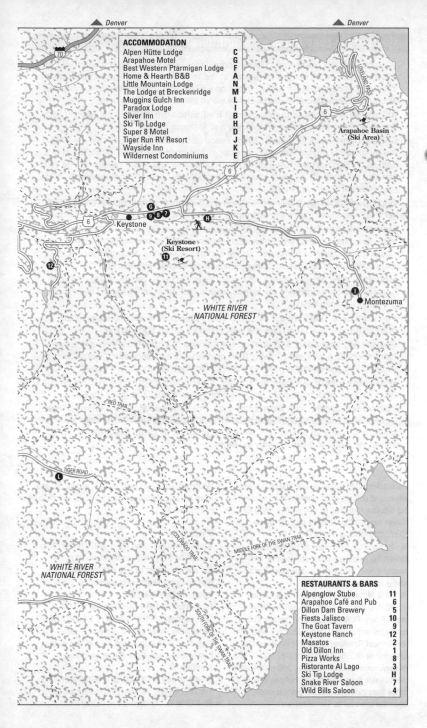

ACCOMMODATION
Alpen Hütte Lodge — C
Arapahoe Motel — G
Best Western Ptarmigan Lodge — F
Home & Hearth B&B — A
Little Mountain Lodge — N
The Lodge at Breckenridge — M
Muggins Gulch Inn — L
Paradox Lodge — I
Silver Inn — B
Ski Tip Lodge — H
Super 8 Motel — D
Tiger Run RV Resort — J
Wayside Inn — K
Wildernest Condominiums — E

RESTAURANTS & BARS
Alpenglow Stube — 11
Arapahoe Café and Pub — 6
Dillon Dam Brewery — 5
Fiesta Jalisco — 10
The Goat Tavern — 9
Keystone Ranch — 12
Masatos — 2
Old Dillon Inn — 1
Pizza Works — 8
Ristorante Al Lago — 3
Ski Tip Lodge — H
Snake River Saloon — 7
Wild Bills Saloon — 4

Winter or summer the **stores** in Silverthorne, Dillon, and Frisco are some of the least expensive and most convenient places in the mountains to get your outdoor gear. You'll almost certainly save money over slope-side outfitters and many of the retailers also offer **discounted lift tickets**. Below we've listed some of the best.

Antlers Ski and Sport Shop 900 Summit Blvd, Frisco ☎970/668-3152. Ski and bike rentals and a good selection of camping and fishing supplies.

Christy Sports 849 N Summit Blvd, Frisco ☎970/668-5417; 817 Hwy-6, Dillon ☎970/468-2329; 104 Wheeler Drive, Copper Mountain ☎970/968-2086. The area's biggest, though not necessarily cheapest, source of rentals, but convenient since you can pick up, drop off, or swap your equipment at any one of their thirty outlets in all major central Colorado resorts.

Gart Sports 306 Hwy-6 Dillon ☎970/468-1340. Branch of the popular Front Range sporting megastore chain, with extremely competitive prices.

Mountain Sports Outlet 167B Merilay Way, Silverthorne ☎970/262-2836. Rents and sells skis, snowboards, and snowshoes in the winter, in-line skates, hiking boots, sleeping bags, and camping gear in the summer. Ski rental packages start at $10, snowboards from $20, and can be prebooked on ⊛www.rentskis.com.

Mountain View Sports Hwy-6 Mountain View Plaza, Keystone ☎970/468-0396. Located beside Keystone's ski slopes, with rental skis, snowboards, snowshoes, bikes, and in-line skates.

Precision Ski & Golf Hwy-9, Frisco ☎970-668-3095. Highly experienced custom ski boot-fitting specialists, and also the best place for ski and golf tuning.

Recycle Ski and Sport 842 Summit Blvd, Frisco ☎970/668-5150. Huge second-hand sporting goods retailer with tons of used ski and snowboard equipment in winter, bikes and camping gear in summer. Also does ski and board tuning.

Wildernest Sports 171 Blue River Pkwy, Silverthorne ☎970/468-8519. Rents out bikes and skis and has a good range of hiking gear, maps, and guide books.

Wilderness Sports 400 Main St, Frisco ☎970/668-8804; 266 Summit Place, Silverthorne ☎970/468-5687. The main local backcountry store, with notice boards, great rental rates on regular skis (from $10) and boards ($20), in addition to snow-shoes, telemark, and backcountry ski rental.

the outskirts of Silverthorne, warmed by potbelly stoves and offering video games and an outdoor hot tub. One room has four bunks ($35–40). ❸

Silver Inn 691 Blue River Pkwy, Silverthorne ☎970/513-0104 or 1-888/513-0104, ℮silverinn@aol.com. Bland family-run motel, though the rooms are clean, inexpensive, and spacious, with fridges and microwaves. There's also a sauna and hot tub. ❸

Super 8 Motel 808 Little Beaver Trail, Dillon ☎970/468-8888 or 1-800/800-8000, ⊛www .super8.com. Reliable mid-priced motel with free local calls and continental breakfast included. ❺

Wildernest Condominiums 204 Wildernest Rd, Silverthorne ☎970/468-7851 or 1-877/324-7928, ⊛www.wildernest.com. Massive 200-unit development beside the interstate exit. Lodging options range from modest studios to grander multi-bedroom apartments. The complex's

clubhouse includes a pool, hot tub, and sauna, and there are free shuttle services to nearby ski areas and towns. ❻

Frisco

Alpine Inn 105 Lusher Court ☎970/668-3122 or 1-800/314-3122, ℮alpineinn@summit.net. Modern motel right by I-70 and the transit center, with an indoor heated pool and hot tub, clean rooms, and free WiFi. ❹

Best Western Lake Dillon Lodge 1202 N Summit Blvd ☎970/668-5094 or 1-800/727-0607. Dependable motel with large rooms – some with lake views – an indoor pool, hot tub, and ski shop. Family rooms with three double beds also available. ❺

Frisco Lodge 321 E Main St ☎970/668-0195 or 1-800/279-6000, ⊛www.friscolodge.com. Creaky old B&B in an old railroad inn, usually the cheapest

THE CENTRAL MOUNTAINS | Silverthorne, Dillon, and Frisco

5

deal in town. Units have kitchenettes and access to an outdoor hot tub, and cooked buffet breakfast and teatime snacks are served in the cluttered lounge. Free Internet access is included, and the friendly owners offer discounted lift tickets at Copper. Cheaper rooms share bathrooms. ❹

Galena Street Mountain Inn 106 Galena St ☎970/668-3224 or 1-800/248-9138, Ⓦwww.galenastreet.com. Bright, contemporary B&B near the bike path and a local shuttle bus stop, a half-block back from Main Street. The spacious rooms (all with private bath) refreshingly reject the Victorian lace-and-doilies look in favor of a brighter, more contemporary feel. Amenities include a sundeck, living and dining room, hot tub, and sauna. ❺

Hotel Frisco 308 Main St ☎970/668-5009 or 1-800/262-1002, Ⓦwww.hotelfrisco.com. Refurbished old townhome on Frisco's Victorian Main Street. Rooms are simply furnished, and some have their own deck and hot tub. High-speed Internet access is available in the small library, free WiFi throughout. ❹

Just Bunks 208 Teller St ☎970/668-4757, Ⓦwww.justbunks.com. Informal place, with only a tiny sign announcing it, and just two log bunk beds (linens provided) in the single bright, spotlessly clean basement bunkroom. Amenities include fireplace, TV, and use of the owner's kitchen. Bunks cost $17 in summer, $27–37 in winter, with your seventh night free. Alcohol prohibited. Free WiFi.

Sky-Vue Motel 305 2nd Ave ☎970/668-3311. Quiet and inexpensive motel two blocks from Main St. Some rooms have kitchenettes and there's an indoor pool and hot tub. ❹

Snowshoe Motel 521 Main St ☎970/668-3444 or 1-800/445-8658, Ⓦwww.snowshoemotel.com. Central budget choice with clean, no-frills rooms, though some have kitchenettes. Facilities include an indoor hot tub and sauna and continental breakfast is included. Free WiFi in all rooms. ❹

Woods Inn 205 S 2nd Ave ☎970/668-2255 or 1-877/664-3777, Ⓦwww.woodsinn.biz. Fourteen-room B&B in a pine-log building a block from Frisco's main street. Rooms – all of which have private bathrooms and phones – have their own character and theme, and are decorated with the owners' keepsakes, many of which were gathered on travels – hence the "Ancient Egypt" and "Mardi Gras" rooms. The cozy communal area has a fireplace and there's a hot tub, too. ❺

Summer activities

Though excursions to Silverthorne's factory outlet stores seem to be the most popular **summer activity**, there are plenty of opportunities for more energetic outdoor pursuits. The only real sightseeing to be had is a quick wander along Frisco's Main Street, where you'll find the town's museum, in the form of **Frisco Historic Park**, 120 Main St (May–Sept Tues–Sun 11am–4pm, Oct–April Tues–Sat 11am–4pm; free; ☎970/668-3428) where ten 1880s buildings are gathered, including the original local jail. Each is decked out with period artifacts to give you a sense of what a trapper's cabin or a Victorian schoolhouse felt like. A discreet display on one of the building's upper floors coyly alludes to the thriving trade that prostitutes once plied in town.

Otherwise, cycling, hiking, sailing, and fishing are the main forms of outdoor recreation. There's also a relatively inexpensive golf course run by the **Eagles Nest Golf Club** in Silverthorne (☎970/468-0681). At the end of the day all groups can enjoy the excellent Silverthorne Rec Center, 430 Rainbow Drive (Mon–Fri 6am–9pm, Sat 7am–9pm, Sun 8am–9pm; pool Mon–Fri 6.30am–8.30pm, Sat & Sun 9am–8.30pm; day pass including classes $8.50; ☎970/262-7372), with its pool, indoor and outdoor hot tubs, waterslide, and host of fitness amenities.

Cycling

Even before they swing a leg over, both road cyclists and mountain bikers will be delighted by the Lake Dillon area, thanks to the excellent, comprehensive, and free *Summit County Bike Trail Guide*, available from local visitor centers. It thoroughly details most road and mountain bike possibilities in the county, using careful route maps and trail descriptions.

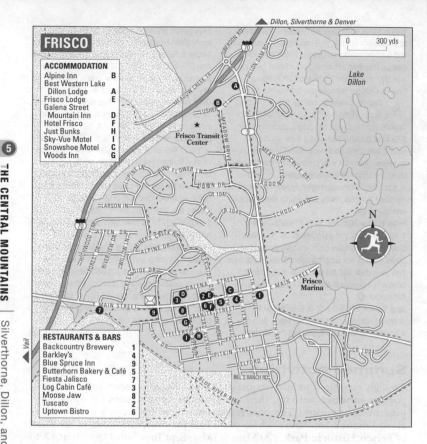

FRISCO

0   300 yds

Lake
Dillon

ACCOMMODATION
Alpine Inn   B
Best Western Lake
  Dillon Lodge   A
Frisco Lodge   E
Galena Street
  Mountain Inn   D
Hotel Frisco   F
Just Bunks   H
Sky-Vue Motel   I
Snowshoe Motel   C
Woods Inn   G

★ Frisco Transit
Center

Frisco
Marina

N

RESTAURANTS & BARS
Backcountry Brewery   1
Barkley's   4
Blue Spruce Inn   9
Butterhorn Bakery & Café   5
Fiesta Jalisco   7
Log Cabin Café   3
Moose Jaw   8
Tuscato   2
Uptown Bistro   6

Frisco, in particular, is at the heart of a superb 100-mile network of **bike paths** that include spurs to Breckenridge (10 miles), Dillon (5 miles), Keystone (12 miles), Copper (8 miles), and Vail (19 miles) – though some of the best riding, that which really gives you access to the quiet backcountry, is off-road. **Mountain bikers** of all abilities should try at least a portion of the **Colorado Trail**. This almost entirely smooth single-track trail passes through pristine stands of pine and aspen before dropping down via a series of kamikaze switchbacks to Hwy-9 at the *Tiger Run RV Resort* six miles south of Frisco. Among many of the best other local trails are those served by the lifts at Keystone resort (see p.178). Local **bike rental** costs around $30 for front suspension, $55 for full suspension; see the box on p.170 for details of rental outfits.

Hiking

A couple of the best and most easily accessible day **hikes** are around Frisco; they include the short but rewarding Gold Hill Trail and the more spectacular but far longer Meadow Creek Trail to the top of Eccles Pass. Those wanting to leave the well-developed Lake Dillon area well behind should try exploring the Ptarmigan Peaks Wilderness and Eagles Nest Wilderness, on either side of

Silverthorne. Get hold of the free *Summer Trailhead Guide*, which details hikes throughout the county, from the Frisco visitor center.

The **Gold Hill Trail** begins five miles south of Frisco, and is signposted off Hwy-9 to Breckenridge. Initially the out-and-back trail cuts through thick stands of lodgepole pine, which have been thinned in places and clear-cut in others in attempts to diversify the age of the forest and reduce wildfire risk. These clear-cuts allow for particularly grand views along the way to the rather modest summit. Push half a mile further west from here and you are on the Peaks Trail that joins Breckenridge with Frisco – ideal as part of a day hike from either one.

Another worthwhile but far longer hike is the ten-mile out-and-back **Meadow Creek Trail** to **Eccles Pass**, which starts on the northern outskirts of Frisco, just west of 1-70 exit 203. Reaching the summit of the pass amid outstanding scenery is the supremely satisfying high point of a trip that typically takes around five hours. In the last mile of the hike, the trail intersects the Gore Range Trail, which you follow north up a series of switchbacks to Eccles Pass, from where views spread out in all directions. You should be able to spot the Tenmile and Mosquito Ranges to the south and the Williams Fork Mountains rising to the east. The peaks to the north are Red Peak and Buffalo Mountain. Note that this route can experience rapidly deteriorating weather and lightning storms, even in midsummer.

Sailing and fishing

Too cold for swimming, Lake Dillon is popular with sailors, kayakers, and fishermen, though inexperienced boaters should beware of unpredictable late-afternoon heavy winds, channeled from the bowl of surrounding mountains. Between May and October various craft are available for rent from **Dillon Marina** (☎970/468-5100, ⓦ www.dillonmarina.com) and Osprey Adventures

△ Cycling around Lake Dillon

(☎970/668-5573 or 1-888/780-4970) at **Frisco Bay Marina**, both of which rent out motorboats ($90/2hr), canoes ($30/2hr), kayaks ($18/2hr), and sailboats ($50/2hr). **Anglers** will find good spots to fish along the lakeshore south of Frisco, while for fly-fishermen the 34 miles of the Blue River between Dillon Dam and the Colorado River is the main local artery. Columbine Outfitters (☎970/262-0966) offer guided trips; a half-day for two people runs around $160.

Winter activities

Cross-country skiing is incredibly popular in the Lake Dillon area thanks to an excellent network of trails along the area's bike paths, some great backcountry opportunities, and extensive facilities. Of these, the largest and most significant is the **Frisco Nordic Center**, one mile south of Frisco on Hwy-9 (winter daily 9am–4pm; $14, or beginner packages – including equipment and trail pass – from $30; ☎970/668-0866). Designed by Olympic silver-medalist Bill Koch, the center offers 43km of groomed trails, many of which overlook Lake Dillon. Free afternoon beginner lessons are available, as well as more advanced lessons and rentals (from $14) and use of a cabin for breaks. The center shares an interchangeable trail pass with the Breckenridge Nordic Center (see p.187). There are also cross-country trails at the golf course in Silverthorne, 2929 Golden Eagle Rd, and at Keystone Resort and Copper Mountain.

Other winter activities include both **snowmobiling** and **dog-sledding**; Good Times, 6061 Tiger Rd (☎970/453-7604 or 1-800/477-0144, ⓦwww.snowmobilecolorado.com), offers both, including a half-day snowmobile tour following a route that climbs up 1500ft past abandoned mines and cabins to the Continental Divide ($85). Snowmobile rental is also available for those who want to strike out on their own, exploring the company's own trail system. Another place that does both snowmobile and dog-sled is Tiger Run, 15945 Hwy-9 (☎970/453-2231 or 1-800/318-1386, ⓦwww.tigerruntours.com), who take guests up to an old mining town.

Eating, drinking, and nightlife

The Lake Dillon area is best for its range of budget and mid-range **restaurants**, with Frisco's Main Street the most appealing location for those who like to browse a selection of menus before choosing a spot. If you're looking for a big **night out**, head to Breckenridge – though Frisco does have a couple good locals' spots on Main. The local multiplex is on Hwy-6 in Dillon, with bowling and billiards up the hill in the marina district. Two notable exceptions to the prosaic local eating scene are the $75 a head **dinner cruises** arranged by Dillon Marina (☎970/468-5100; May–Oct).

Silverthorne and Dillon

Arapahoe Café and Pub 626 Lake Dillon Drive, Dillon ☎970/468-0873. Generous, healthy breakfasts and a range of entrees like trout, roast duck, and veggie pasta for lunch – most around the $6 mark. Also open for dinner, though only serving lighter meals. Open 7am–2.30pm and 5–9pm.
Dillon Dam Brewery 100 Little Dam Rd, Dillon ☎970/262-7777. Spacious brewpub where regulars of all ages prop up the giant bar and quaff good microbrews after a day in the mountains. The Dam Straight Lager is just one of the great beers that come direct from shiny vats in the corner and is ideal to wash down the inexpensive but good-quality bar food like salads, burgers, and pasta – entrees priced around $8. Open from 11am.
Fiesta Jalisco 269 Summit Place Shopping Center, Silverthorne ☎970/468-9552. Inexpensive Mexican family restaurant, serving enchiladas, burritos, and combination plates for lunch and dinner.

Masatos City Market Center, Hwy-6, Dillon
☎970/262-6600. Respectable Japanese food,
including sushi, udon soup, chicken teriyaki, and
tempura at fairly reasonable prices – particularly
the $6 lunch specials. Open daily for lunch and
dinner. Reservations recommended.
Old Dillon Inn 321 Blue River Pkwy, Silverthorne
☎970/468-2791. Impressive nineteenth-century
bar that gets packed with skiers for the inexpensive Mexican food, margaritas, and the energetic
C&W music.

Ristorante Al Lago 240 Lake Dillon Drive,
Dillon ☎970/468-6111. Extremely good, but
only moderately priced (entrees run $8–12) north-
ern Italian cuisine and seafood served in smart
surroundings; the veal dishes and sea bass are
particularly fine. Reservations recommended.
Wild Bills Saloon 119 La Bonte St, Dillon
☎970/468-2006. Low-key bar and stone oven
pizza place in Dillon Marina, with live music on
Saturdays. Daily until 11.30pm.

Frisco

Backcountry Brewery 710 Main St ☎970/668-
2337. Huge log, stucco, and stone brewpub on
the corner of Main and Hwy-6. The hand-crafted
beers are only available locally and a good bar food
selection provides something to soak up the
alcohol. Oddly, there's a lengthy salad bar, too.
Barkley's 620 Main St. Frisco's only late-night
venue, complete with live music, billiards, and an
extensive selection of margaritas to complement
the average Mexican food (entrees $10–13).
Blue Spruce Inn 120 W Main St ☎970/668-
5900. Frisco's best upscale restaurant is a worthy
splurge, though you pay at least $15 for its tasty
veal, beef, and seafood entrees. Also offers an

inexpensive but inventive bar menu. Reservations
recommended.

Butterhorn Bakery & Café 408 Old Main
St ☎970/668-3997. Superb local bakery
churning out huge delicious breads, bagels,
cookies, and cakes. It's also well known for its
succulent breakfast burrito, smoked salmon
omelet, and good range of sandwiches or soup
lunches (all $6–7). Daily 7.30am–3pm.
Fiesta Jalisco 450 W Main St ☎970/668-5043.
Frisco's best inexpensive Mexican eatery has a
good choice of all the usual items, including some
healthy/wholefood renditions, and excellent
margaritas with which to wash it all down.
Log Cabin Café 121 E Main St ☎970/668-3947.
Fiercely popular local choice for cooked breakfasts,
served until 2pm, though good burgers and salads
join them on the afternoon menu.
Moose Jaw 208 E Main St ☎970/668-3931. Dark
wooden bar serving mediocre burgers and a dreary
selection of beers until 2am – but a popular local
hangout nonetheless.
Tuscato 307 Main St ☎970/668-3644. Simple
but delicious northern Italian fare served up in
faux-rustic surroundings where pasta entrees
cost $10–15, others a few dollars more. The basic
dishes are consistently done to perfection and
highly recommended; try the crispy spinach-stuffed
baked chicken with spicy marinara sauce or the
spaghetti and tender meatballs – but leave room
for the rich and moist chocolate cake.
Uptown Bistro 304 Main St ☎970/668-4728.
Elegant, upscale restaurant with seafood and
Asian specialties including house-cured marinated
salmon and Indonesian noodle salad. Entrees
around $20.

Keystone

Squarely pitched as a family resort, **Keystone** is centered on a pleasantly
bland alpine-style village where all-inclusive vacationers can enjoy the superb
kids' facilities and conveniently mix activities like stargazing and wine-tasting
with their daily sessions on the excellent beginner and intermediate terrain.
The resort is also defined by its closeness to Denver, which means crowds on
weekends. Yet despite its popularity and typical clientele Keystone is surprising
for both its fairly reasonable prices and good expert terrain, including a couple
of quiet back bowls that lie tucked away on the resort's fringes. Keystone is
also well known for its notable snowmaking capability, which usually allows
it to open earlier than its neighbors, and for its massive **night-ski** operation
– Colorado's largest by far – with seventeen runs illuminated until 9pm.

The resort itself is not so much a village as a string of condominium complexes
strung out seven miles along the steep-sided Snake River Valley and Hwy-6.

Steamboat Springs

Ski stats

Most years the Colorado **ski season** runs from November through April, allowing for both holiday trips and late-season T-shirt skiing. Snowstorms here rarely last long and often hit at night, so while many ski areas boast annual snowfall of over 300 inches they can also advertise being blessed with more than 300 days of sunshine. The **terrain** on offer is equally remarkable and varied. In a typical day's skiing you can flit between rugged ridges, steep drops, dense glades, and lonely bowls – or just carve turns on the perfectly groomed cruising runs that snake down every mountain. The abundance of fantastic **tree-skiing** is another highlight, as is the high quality of terrain **parks** and **pipes**.

Surprisingly, on a continent specializing in gigantic proportions, even Colorado's largest resorts – though sizeable by North American standards – feel **small** compared to their sprawling European counterparts. This is compensated for by the proximity of resorts to one another and the ease of transport between them – often making multiple resorts an easy day-trip from one another. If you're feeling adventurous and have at least a couple of weeks to spare it's well worth cobbling together your own itinerary by **touring** the state's ski areas, allowing you to follow premium conditions and see a portion of the state.

However you choose to explore, the choice of ski areas in Colorado will at first seem intimidatingly large. Compare the statistics they publish about themselves (we include these as companion boxes throughout the guide) but beware that this data can paint an incomplete picture, as snow quality varies between regions and acreage size doesn't tell you how a resort's terrain is utilized. An overriding factor in your choice of resort should be your own **abilities** – but, again, be skeptical when viewing the resort's **terrain** breakdown, as ski areas will skew percentages in order to seem more diverse than they really are.

Colorado's top five après spots

- **39° Lounge** Aspen hipsters celebrate a great day on the slopes at the urbane and playful 39° Lounge. See p.261.
- **Kaltenberg Castle** This massive mock palace in Vail is the place to go if you fancy mixing some Bavarian beer-hall atmosphere into your Colorado ski vacation. See p.240.
- **Kochevar's Saloon** For a bit of the Old West, give this rowdy saloon on Crested Butte's main street a gander. See p.269.
- **Breckenridge Brewery & Pub** Great microbrews at Breckenridge's enduringly popular watering hole. See p.191.
- **Fly Me to the Moon Saloon** Quintessential Western ski-town hangout with a hedonistic vibe and live music most nights. See p.382.

The backcountry

Expert skiers and snowboarders will tell you that the ultimate rush is in the **backcountry**, where you pit yourself against untrammeled nature and can carve fresh tracks to your heart's content. But with the thrills comes risk: fatalities from avalanches and other backcountry hazards has grown exponentially with the huge increase in **backcountry** traffic over the past decade. Thankfully you can sample much of the fun with a fraction of the danger by joining a snowcat trip, where you'll be led in a guided group to virgin snowfields. Companies are dotted all over Colorado and generally are within easy reach of most resorts.

Skis in Aspen

The resorts

Within two or three hours' drive of Denver are Winter Park and the resorts of **Summit County** – Breckenridge, Keystone, Copper Mountain, and Arapahoe Basin. All are in range for day-trips by Denverites, and so are easily the state's most **popular** ski areas. Copper Mountain is marginally the best for beginners, while intermediates are spoilt for choice everywhere except Arapahoe Basin – aka "A-Basin" – which is an out-and-out expert's choice. The most enticing among these is **Breckenridge**, with its pretty Victorian downtown and good après ski.

Colorado's other major resorts are more difficult to get to, but generally come with the rewards of better snow and more interesting towns. This mix has given rise to several competing **destination resorts** – places that have tailored themselves to provide attractive bases for a week or two's vacation. Among these are Vail and Beaver Creek, Aspen, Steamboat Springs, Telluride, and Crested Butte. Runs at all of these are meticulously groomed and high standards of service are maintained throughout – particularly with respect to **ski schools** and facilities. Lodges will come complete with classy rustic fittings and roaring fireplaces; there will be a healthy selection of restaurants; and a wide array of off-slope activities will keep even non-skiers busy.

The quality of nightlife at each is also good, so that together they make Colorado the undoubted **après-ski** capital of North America. If nightlife is a priority, be sure to avoid the newer resort villages – which largely attract families – by heading instead for former Victorian **mining towns** like Aspen, Breckenridge, Telluride, and Crested Butte. Vail is perhaps the only exception to this rule, since it's large enough to drive its own party scene.

Your final decision may well come back to the ski areas themselves. The incredible size of **Vail** and **Aspen** puts these two in a league of their own.

Crested Butte

Aspen

Vail has the edge in terms of accessibility from Denver and size – particularly when you include its sister resort Beaver Creek – yet Aspen is more aesthetically appealing. Somewhat more budget-friendly are **Steamboat Springs**, known for the fluffiest and deepest snow; **Telluride**, with its challenging moguls and amazing scenery; and **Crested Butte**, whose steep backcountry is complemented by first-class beginner areas.

Terrain parks

As recently as the early 1990s, most resorts regarded terrain parks as little more than holding pens, a way to keep upstart snowboarders away from the sedate skiing majority. Nowadays young freestyle skiers are almost as prevalent as riders and most major resorts offer a halfpipe, sometimes two, and at least a handful of kickers and rails, while the best cater to a range of skill levels, from mini terrain gardens for kids to huge huckers and towering Superpipes for the daring. A

few pointers: don't jump before checking out all the landings; don't jump until the person before you has reappeared on the other side; and don't snowplow slowly down the middle of a halfpipe – everyone will silently (or quite vocally) curse you for making them wait.

The top five parks

- **Breckenridge** The Freeway Super Park draws Olympic hopefuls to a colossal halfpipe, a half-dozen big jumps, and a nail-biting rollercoaster of rails.
- **Copper** With a range of beginner and intermediate-sized kickers and jumps, the Catalyst park enables skiers and riders to improve gradually until they're ready for the eighteen-foot quarterpipe and exceptional Superpipe.
- **Buttermilk** Nearly two miles long, this summit-to-base terrain park features thirty rails, a fifteen-foot Superpipe, and the kind of gigantic kicker at its base that makes you hope there's an ambulance standing by.
- **Vail** Dozens of tabletop jumps and rails are spread across Vail's four terrain parks – but the show-stealer is the 400-ft-long Superpipe, with eighteen-foot walls.
- **Winter Park** This modest resort's three terrain parks are among the best in the US for their encouraging vibe and good range of obstacles, easing the natural progression of freeriders of all levels.

surrounded by Arapaho National Forest land. A generous continental breakfast is included, as is use of a living room, sundeck, and fire-heated hot tub.

Lift tickets, lessons, and rentals

Multi-day **tickets** are significantly cheaper in off-peak periods, with discounts if you purchase online in advance. Keystone multi-day tickets are valid at Breckenridge and Arapahoe Basin, with restricted use at the more expensive Vail and Beaver Creek.

The brown huts of the **ski school** (☎1-800/255-3715) and **rental outlets** cluster around the Mountain House and River Run lifts. A full day's lesson costs $80 for all levels and can be had at both locations. **Daycare** is available for children aged two months to twelve years (☎970/496-4181), while kids' ski lessons start aged three, snowboarding aged seven.

Resort **rental packages** from $22 for skis or $34 for boards can be booked in advance at ⓦ www.rentskis.com. Quality independent options in River Run include the friendly Polar Revolution board shop (☎970/496-4657) and the custom boot-fitters of Precision Ski (☎970/468-5584).

Mountain runs

First-timers might want to take a few short runs using the surface lifts at the flat Discovery area by the Mountain House before heading straight up the mountain to a wide, gentle meadow of sheltered green runs around the two Packsaddle lifts. If this is too busy try the small learning area, complete with a short beginner chairlift around the summit of Keystone Mountain. Confident beginners can then tackle the long and gentle Schoolmarm to the base or take the gondola back down.

Keystone is a challenging mountain for **intermediates**. After warming up on any of the half-dozen or so shorter blues located on the front face, assured intermediates are best off escaping the busiest areas by heading over to North Peak and the Outback. The eight or so lengthy blues running down Outback, served by the speedy Outback Express chair, are the quietest. On North Face there might be only a trio of intermediate cruisers shown on the trail map, but many of the neighboring blacks are only slightly tougher, though liberally sprinkled with wide, soft moguls.

Except on powder days the busy front face of Keystone Mountain has little to offer **experts**, who should instead head out to the resort's relatively small but challenging and uncrowded expert area the Outback, a section of mountain with both great glade and mogul runs and two treeless back-bowls. Of these two, the southern bowl is less crowded and has an easier traverse out, but the northern option has a steeper, if shorter, fall line. If searching for the trees, keep in mind that the glades on North Peak are only worth exploring when there's a deep snow base. The higher altitude trees below the Outback bowls are more reliable.

Though running half the length of the mountain's front face, Keystone's **terrain park** and **pipe** are not too intimidating, and perfect for the less experienced. The park becomes busier at night as riders with day jobs head here to play under the floodlights. Ice can be a problem here, particularly when poor conditions result in a base that's almost all artificial snow.

Other winter activities

Other winter activities at Keystone include **snow-tubing** (mid-Dec to March daily 8am–8pm; $20) and **ice-skating** (late Nov to early March daily

10am–10pm; admission $10, skate rental $6) on a large five-acre former beaver pond. **Cross-country skiing** is offered at Keystone Cross-Country Center, two miles east of Keystone on Montezuma Rd (late Nov to mid-April daily 9am–4.30pm; $9; ☎970/496-4386). The center has just a dozen miles of groomed trails in the Snake River Valley, but an extensive 32 miles of backcountry trails in the Arapaho National Forest. Rentals ($18) and lessons ($30 1hr group) are offered as well as tours, including a lovely one under the full moon ($29; includes rentals and light supper). Evenings, horse-drawn **sleigh rides** to Soda Creek Homestead, one of the original ranches in the tree-covered valley, are offered by the resort ($70; reservations ☎1-800/354-4386). Following the trip, guests tour several of the old outbuildings before being served a Western-style dinner while a would-be cowboy strums a guitar.

Summer activities

The Adventure Center at Keystone (☎970/668-0866 or 1-800/545-4FUN) offers a range of **activities** including horseback riding, rafting, fly-fishing, and hikes with pack-llamas, as well as a good range of children's programs. The resort also runs the swank **Keystone Ranch Golf Course** three miles to the south (☎970/496-4250 or 1-800/451-5930), though it's often hard to get a tee time.

Where Keystone really excels is **mountain biking**, with lift-serviced trails at the resort and many more fanning out beyond. The resort's gondola service (mid-June to mid-Sept daily 10am–5pm; day-pass $28), takes you to a maze of entertaining riding, from plenty of beginner-level snaking single-track to loose, gnarly drops on technical runs like Wild Thing. A recent addition is Colorado's largest assemblage of handmade wooden trails and obstacles, pioneered on British Columbia's North Shore. Here wooden boardwalks sway in and out of trees, leaving riders to tackle drops of up to six feet. Even if you're not planning to use the lift or even ride the resort's trails, it's worth picking up the free local **trail map** from the gondola ticket offices, as it covers trails well beyond the confines of the resort, including the excellent technical ones around the village of Montezuma.

Eating, drinking, and nightlife

Keystone tries to keep people in the village at the end of the day, with all sorts of **happenings** scheduled throughout the year: themed après ski parties, torchlight parades and snowshoe races, and holiday festival events like a Mardi Gras Parade and an Oktoberfest, to name but a few. Even outside these goings-on there are plenty of slick, if slightly sterile, **restaurants** in the village and a good range of choices beyond, spanning from a gritty local bar to several fine-dining options in out-of-the-way locations like the top of the gondola summit or out on the golf course.

Alpenglow Stube Keystone Resort ☎970/496-4386. The best dining experience in Summit County: take the free gondola ride to the top of North Peak and feast on New American cuisine with a Bavarian edge in beautiful surroundings. At $70 for a six-course meal, it doesn't come cheap, though. Smart dress required (denim banned). The restaurant closes during the spring and fall, when the gondola doesn't operate. Reservations advised.
The Goat Tavern 22954 Hwy-6 ☎970/513-9344. The local dive bar is the place to go for a wild night at Keystone, with regular special nights including pajama parties and out-of-town bands. Daily until 2am.

🏃 **Keystone Ranch** Keystone Ranch Rd ☎970/496-4386. Outstanding gourmet restaurant in a 1930s ranch house with mountain-lodge decor; it's the one-time winner of the Zagat award for best restaurant in Colorado. The six-course menu ($72) includes seasonal main dishes, which might include roasted rack of Colorado lamb, grilled duck breast, elk, or fresh seafood. Reservations recommended.

Pizza Works Snowdance Plaza ℡970/262-0200. Tiny, down-home pizza joint opposite *The Goat Tavern*, with all sorts of toppings along with calzones and stromboli. Counter service or take-out, served by the slice or the pie.

Ski Tip Lodge 764 Montezuma Rd ℡970/496-4950. Intimate gourmet suppers are served at this restored 1880s stagecoach stop. The innovative four-course menu is rotated daily, and you can retire to a comfortable seat next to the rustic fireplace to finish with an indulgent dessert.

Snake River Saloon 23074 Hwy-6 ℡970/468-2788. A full menu of bar food, steaks, and prime rib is served in this locals' bar, one of the best venues for live rock in the area.

Arapahoe Basin

Small in acreage but not in stature, **Arapahoe Basin** has achieved cult status among die-hard skiers and backcountry riders as a no-nonsense ski area. The highest resort in the country, A-Basin – as it's commonly known – offers stark and steep above-treeline bowl skiing that's often exposed to driving winter storms. However, this harsh weather is counterbalanced by the long season, which typically stretches into June. The difficult terrain, combined with slow lifts and spartan amenities (no lodging or restaurants, although there is a cafeteria and bar), serve to largely keep the crowds away, giving the resort an informal feel that extends to its on-mountain and parking lot après-ski, legendary for its fun and friendliness.

With just five lifts accessing a **single open bowl** that funnels back to the base, there is little need for a trail map. Half the mountain is above treeline, but the ski area does offer a few small runs through the pines. There are also several popular (and dangerous) backcountry descents in the immediate area accessed from US Forest Service gates – suitable for the experienced who have carefully taken local advice.

Just 64 miles west of Denver, A-Basin is the closest Summit County resort to towns in Colorado's Front Range, at least when the winding Hwy-6 over Loveland Pass is open. When it closes in bad weather, A-Basin is the toughest Summit County resort to reach (accessed via Keystone). Parking is free and a frequent bus to Keystone, fifteen minutes away, means that it's easy to split your day between here and Keystone.

Lift tickets, lessons, and rentals

Multi-day A-Basin **lift tickets** are available as part of the Vail resorts package – which includes use of Keystone and Breckenridge as well – but in peak season it makes more sense just to buy an A-Basin ticket separately, for around $20 a day less. Kids' tickets are free with the purchase of a full-price adult ticket.

The ski and snowboard **school** (℡970/496-7007) is small and relatively inexpensive (2hr lessons $42), while the High Adventure program offers excellent

---

Arapahoe Basin

Information ℡970/468-0718 or 1-888/272-7246, ⓦ www.arapahoebasin.com

Ticket prices and operating times $51; late Oct to early June daily 9am–4pm.

Mountain statistics base elevation 10,780ft, summit elevation 13,050ft, vertical drop 3978ft, acreage 490, average snowfall 367in.

Lifts and trails five lifts serve 69 trails: beginner 15 percent, intermediate 45 percent, expert 40 percent.

multi-day clinics for experts, including free-skiing camps, tele-skiing lessons, and an avalanche school, taught by enthusiastic local pros for not much money (around $45/day). The resort offers **daycare** facilities (☎970/468-0718) for one- to three-year-olds. Lessons for kids are from age four for skiing, age nine for snowboarding. The base area **rental** hut offers great telemark rentals ($35), decent and inexpensive ski packages (from $24), but only basic snowboards ($32).

Mountain runs

A-Basin is hard to recommend to **beginners**, although first-timers will find plenty of space to find their feet. Otherwise, green runs are limited, particularly for snowboarders, who will find the runs too flat. **Intermediates** fair slightly better. There may not be a wealth of runs from which to choose but at least the mountain's blues are wonderful rolling roads, and offer confident intermediates the chance to develop skills on steeps, jumps, and moguls. Of the two lifts serving the main intermediate area the faster Lenawee lift is preferable to the slow Norway double. Most of A-Basin's black runs are hugely steep and ungroomed and even the blue runs under Cornice Run will challenge rusty **experts**. The most popular focus is the Pallavicini lift, where you can lap precipitous moguls and skinny glades. Gentler runs are strung along the East Wall traverse, but for instant gratification look for the lowest gate just above East Gully.

There is no artificial terrain at A-Basin, so **freeriders** look to the many natural rolls, rocks, cliffs, and cornices for kicks. When open, explore cliff drops on the East Wall; otherwise, take your pick of lines off the long Cornice Run. The trees below Midway conceal tight bumpy corridors, while the rugged, rocky terrain of Palli is a playground for those who can handle landing on bumpy steeps.

Copper Mountain

From the boldest mogul-bashers to the most nervous five-year-old, virtually every type of skier and rider will find fantastic terrain at **Copper Mountain**. The ski area spreads across a wonderful cascading mountain to offer skiing on a par with Vail, yet it remains hugely underrated, with none of its neighbor's fame, glitz, or cost. A key part of the resort's beauty is the way in which the terrain divides so readily between easier and harder skiing areas, largely keeping beginners, intermediates, and experts out of each other's way. The front face, which neatly spreads over two peaks – Copper and Union – is toughest in the east, while gentler slopes such as those in the beginner-friendly Union Creek area, are to the west. Behind the mogul runs on the front slopes of the resort stretch out steep, lonely back bowls: Copper, Union, and Spaulding.

In contrast to the exciting and varied ski terrain, Copper's two **resort villages** – the main **Village at Copper** and the adjacent and more accommodation-focused **East Village** – are a bit boring. Certainly there's no faulting the quality of the dining, entertainment, or accommodation, but there's little variety and almost no sign of local life once the lifts have closed. So unless you are on a family holiday taking advantage of the extensive kids and teen programs and the good-value ski-and-stay deals you'd do better to base yourself at Frisco, just six miles away and linked to Copper by the county's free bus system. Day visitors can choose between the free Alpine and Corn parking lots, connected to all bases via a frequent free shuttle (6am–11pm) or four pay lots ($10–15) marginally closer to the slopes.

Copper Mountain

Information ☎970/968-2882 or 1-800/458-8386, ⓦwww.coppercolorado.com; snow report ☎970/968-2100 or 1-800/789-7609.

Ticket prices and operating times $75; open Nov to mid-April daily 8.30am–4pm.

Mountain statistics base elevation 9712ft, summit elevation 12,313ft, vertical drop 2601ft, acreage 2450, average snowfall 284in.

Lifts and trails 22 lifts serve 125 trails: beginner 21 percent, intermediate 25 percent, expert 54 percent.

Accommodation

All the **accommodation** at Copper Mountain is in pricey condos or somewhat dated hotel rooms, though all have free access to the top-notch Copper Mountain Racquet & Athletic Club. In winter you're unlikely to find a room for under $80 per night – though check the resort website for deals or contact their central reservations (online or ☎1-888/219-2441). Bookings are allocated based on desired size and quality rather than by choice of building; a fifteen percent fee is charged for specific requests. If you don't find anything suitable this way, or you're looking for a better deal, try an independent **property management company** like Copper Vacations (☎970/968-6840 or 1-800/525-3887, ⓦwww .coppervacations.com) or Carbonate Property Management (☎970/968-6854 or 1-800/526-7737, ⓦwww.coppermtncondos.com).

Lift tickets, lessons, and rentals

During the heart of the season, adult **tickets** don't come cheap, though there are occasional ways to get heavy discounts. The Four Pass ($99), for instance, available from King Soopers grocery stores and Breeze/Max shops (such as the one in Dumont, I-70 exit 234), is good for four people. Later in the year, buying individual tickets from King Soopers rather than the mountain saves a few dollars.

Half-day beginner **ski lessons** start at $75 ($123 including lift ticket and rentals), with an excellent roster of classes including all-mountain free-ride instruction and terrain park schooling. Special programs include weekly telemark lessons (no rentals) and women–only sessions. Copper also has great kids and teens programs offering skiing from age three, snowboarding from seven. Call ☎1-866/763-5955 for ski school reservations and ☎1-800/458-8386 ext 38101 for daycare, offered for children aged six weeks to four years.

The three resort-owned **rental shops** (one at each base lodge) have good rates on beginner ski and snowboard packages ($25 and $37/day, respectively) but are fairly expensive for anything else. There's a high-performance ski store in the village, 9600 FT, though it has only a limited snowboard inventory; for boards visit Gravitee, in the *Tucker Mountain Lodge* building (☎970/968-0171).

Mountain runs

First-timers should avoid the green runs directly above the Village, as they are often icy and crowded thoroughfares. Instead start out on the quieter and gentler western slopes at Union Creek in territory rarely visited by advanced skiers. Once confident of your basic skills, try Roundabout, accessed from the top of the American Flyer lift. Novice snowboarders should avoid the flat Woodwinds Traverse from Timberline Express to the Village, as it's trying even for experienced riders.

On crowded weekends **intermediates** should avoid the center of the mountain and warm up on Roundabout. At other times ride American Eagle from the Village and follow any of the half-dozen blue trails snaking down. Next head up the Excelerator lift to try Andy's Encore, a long vertical cruiser laced with flatter sections and drops. On the opposite, western boundary, the blues under the Timberline Express are fun for mellow glades, small natural jumps, and stashes of deeper snow. When ready to step up to blacks, head higher up the mountain from here to the Far West and Retreat trails near Union Meadows; the slightly bumped pistes here are generally peaceful and relatively short.

Experts who've already purchased a pass and don't need to rent gear should consider parking close to the isolated Alpine double-chair on Copper's eastern boundary; this is the most direct route to the forested bumps and cascading powder pockets on the steepest slopes of the front face. Otherwise, start at East Village and ride up Super Bee to Resolution Bowl, a bald crest that shoots behind the front face into tight, cluttered glades and bump runs. Its more southerly aspect can result in patchy conditions, so you might want to head straight for Copper's four alpine bowls instead. The chutes and cornices of Spaulding are tempting, but getting back out involves a long descent to the bottom of Resolution. As for glades, the finest are Sail Away and 17 Glades, both short but with plenty of hidden powder. The snow on the front face is more reliable than in the Copper Bowl, but when conditions are good, head here first to snag a ride on the first-come, first-served free snowcat that follows the boundary out to the chutes and glades of relatively untouched Tucker Bowl.

Copper's **parks** and **superpipe** are well maintained, and Loverly, the main park, caters to all abilities with three distinct tabletop and rail lines to follow. Further down the mountain, in full view of the Village plaza, the Hollywood jump is heavily used, often for Copper's frequent contests. For more laid-back options, try exploring the woods under American Flyer or the minipark and gentle rollers on Roundabout. If you really know what you're doing, try your luck among the cliffs and gullies of Copper Bowl, or hike out along Union Peak to hit the Onion Roll, a giant natural kicker.

Other winter activities

Copper Mountain has a **cross-country** center near the Union Creek base area (☎970/968-2318 ext 6342), from where machine-set tracks and skating lanes wind on enjoyable undulating terrain through the rolling wooded valleys of Arapaho National Forest. You can book rentals ($15/day), lessons ($30/hr), and overnight hut trips ($156/night) through the center. Located slopeside in East Village, Copper's long **tubing** lanes have their own tow (Sun–Thurs 11am–7pm, Fri & Sat 11am–8pm; $14 adults, $8 kids) while Westlake – the artificial lake at the center of the Village at Copper – surrounded by village shops and buildings, is an enticing spot for nighttime **ice-skating** ($4 entry, $6 rental). The **Copper Athletic Club** ($10; ☎970/968-2826) offers indoor pursuits like swimming, tennis, and racquetball, along with fitness machines, massage therapy, and spa services.

Eating and drinking

The resort village has all the usual coffeeshops, sports bars, and places for a pint and a filling bite to **eat**. For fine dining or any real nightlife, however, you'll have to head to Frisco or Breckenridge.

Creekside Pizza Snowbridge Square ☎970/968-2033. Cozy spot tucked away across the creek, offering good-value Italian food, sandwiches, and salads. Weekend après includes $1 slices and $2 microbrews.

Double Diamond East Village ☎970/968-2880. Reasonably priced family-run place dishing up a variety of steaks, sandwiches, pizzas, and mouth-watering burgers in comfy surroundings. Best known for its $7 Friday buffets.

Endo's Village Plaza ☎970/968-3070. Convivial sports bar – the closest thing around to a local hangout – where you can chow down on huge portions of bar food, sandwiches, and salads against a backdrop of arcade games, pool, and big-screen TVs. Open until midnight.

JJ's Rocky Mountain Tavern East Village ☎970/968-2318. Western-themed grill at the base of the slopes that's good for hearty lunches and après shows catering to an older crowd.

The Blue Moose Village Plaza ☎970/968-9666. Slopeside New York-style pizza joint with an outdoor deck that's ideal for a beer or margarita after a day on the mountain. Also offers a local delivery service.

Pravda Village Plaza ☎970/968-2222. Soviet-era Russian-themed place that's really the only late-night option in town, with regular DJs and over 30 different vodkas. A bit hit and miss; expect anything from an evening of mellow lounging to bar-top dancing. Daily 8pm–2am.

Breckenridge

One of the most well-rounded ski-towns in Colorado, **BRECKENRIDGE** couples a well-developed resort and its huge, varied ski area with a pleasant Victorian mining town that knows how to party, and all at prices that are less shocking than Vail or Aspen. Established in 1859, the same year gold was discovered here, Breckenridge managed to avoid becoming a ghost town like many other mining settlements in the area, thanks partly to its role in **silver** as well as gold mining – the former said to be sparked by a barber's comment about the presence of silver dust in a customer's hair. Today, the brightly painted gingerbread houses, shops, and cafés that line the main street as you roll into town are the twee core of a huge **skiing operation** – one of the busiest in the state – which caused the city limits to expand continually over the last decade. Much of Breck's success lies in the resort's great ability to cater to beginner and intermediate skiers, with the presence of a quaint base for families to perambulate in the evening, helping to establish the resort with those looking for a winter holiday experience that rivals the Alps. Things aren't always sedate, though: on a Saturday night this young and vital town can get rowdy, when bars pack out with visitors and seasonal employees from every ski resort in the county. **Summer** is also busy, when bikes are rolled out onto local paths and trails and golfers take advantage of good-value packages at off-season ski lodges.

Arrival, information, and getting around

Several shuttle services link Denver International Airport with Breckenridge (dropping passengers off at a series of stops along Main Street), though transferring from the Greyhound to the county's free bus service is a cheaper but more complicated process – see p.166 for details. The **Welcome Center** is on the north side of town at 309 N Main (daily 9am–5pm; ☎970/453-6018, ⓦwww .gobreck.com), and there's another helpful visitor information center at 137 S Main St (same hours; ☎970/453-5579). Both dispense the useful and free *Breckenridge Magazine* as well as brochures for a self-guided walking tour of the Victorian downtown. While Breckenridge itself is easy to explore on foot, to get to the ski slopes you should use the free local **bus service**, operated during the ski season. The town is also connected to the rest of Summit County via free shuttles from Breckenridge Station to Frisco's transit center.

Accommodation

Aside from a few downtown B&Bs, **accommodation** in Breckenridge usually means a slopeside condo, which costs from around $140 per night in

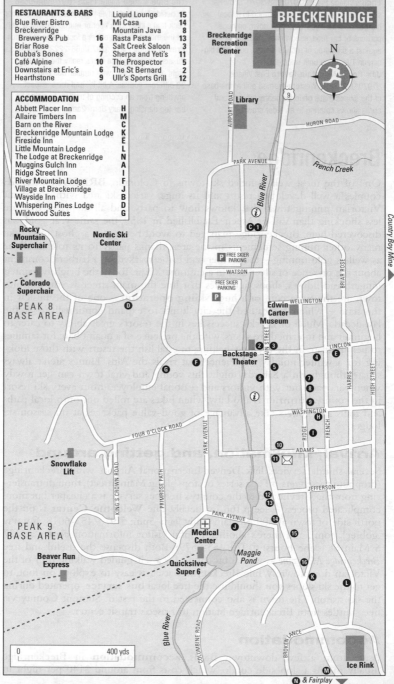

RESTAURANTS & BARS

Blue River Bistro	1
Breckenridge Brewery & Pub	16
Briar Rose	4
Bubba's Bones	7
Café Alpine	10
Downstairs at Eric's	6
Hearthstone	9
Liquid Lounge	15
Mi Casa	14
Mountain Java	8
Rasta Pasta	13
Salt Creek Saloon	3
Sherpa and Yeti's	11
The Prospector	5
The St Bernard	2
Ullr's Sports Grill	12

ACCOMMODATION

Abbett Placer Inn	H
Allaire Timbers Inn	M
Barn on the River	C
Breckenridge Mountain Lodge	K
Fireside Inn	E
Little Mountain Lodge	L
The Lodge at Breckenridge	N
Muggins Gulch Inn	A
Ridge Street Inn	I
River Mountain Lodge	F
Village at Breckenridge	J
Wayside Inn	B
Whispering Pines Lodge	D
Wildwood Suites	G

BRECKENRIDGE

N

Golf course, Frisco, **A** & **B**

Breckenridge Recreation Center

Library

HURON ROAD

AIRPORT ROAD

PARK AVENUE

French Creek

Blue River

C 1

FREE SKIER PARKING

WATSON

FREE SKIER PARKING

BRIAR ROSE

WELLINGTON

Edwin Carter Museum

2 **3**

MAIN STREET

LINCLON

4

E

5

Backstage Theater

G **F**

6

7

HARRIS

8

9

H

WASHINGTON

RIDGE

I

FRENCH

HIGH STREET

FOUR O'CLOCK ROAD

PARK AVENUE

10

ADAMS

11 ✉

PRIMROSE PATH

KING'S CROWN ROAD

JEFFERSON

12

13

PARK AVENUE

14

15

Snowflake Lift

Medical Center ✚

J

Maggie Pond

16

K

L

PEAK 9 BASE AREA

Beaver Run Express

Quicksilver Super 6

COLUMBINE ROAD

Blue River

BROKEN LANCE

Ice Rink

M

N & Fairplay

Rocky Mountain Superchair

Nordic Ski Center

Colorado Superchair

PEAK 8 BASE AREA

D

9

HURON ROAD

Country Boy Mine

0 ————————— 400 yds

winter, though prices for these and all other lodging drop by around a third in summer. To find inexpensive motels you'll have to drive twenty minutes north to Frisco or Dillon. The Breckenridge Resort Chamber (Mon–Fri 8am–5pm; ☎970/453-6018 or 1-888/796-2825) and Breckenridge Central Reservations(☎1-877/791-3968, ⓦwww.breckvacations.com) handle **bookings** for local B&Bs, hotels, and condos, and can advise on prices and package deals for skiers. Breckenridge Accommodations, Inc (☎970/453-9140 or 1-800/872-8789, ⓦwww.breckaccommodations.com) is a longstanding local agency with plenty of condos on their books while Peak Property (☎970/453-1724 or 1-800/458-7998, ⓦwww.peakproperty.com) is a good source of privately owned condos and homes, most on the outskirts of town. A smaller company with great personal service is Kokopelli Ski Holidays (☎970/453-2575 or 1-866/754-5656, ⓦwww.ski-kokopelli.com), who run a number of luxury catered chalets and can organize condos and townhouses too.

Abbett Placer Inn 205 S French St ☎970/453-6489 or 1-888/794-7750 ⓦwww.abbettplacerbnb.com. Simply decorated and relatively inexpensive B&B with a convenient downtown location and facilities which include a garden solarium and hot tub. ⑤

Allaire Timbers Inn 9511 S Main St ☎970/453-7530, ⓦwww.allairetimbers.com. On the southern edge of town, this high-end B&B, in a big log home with great views, has rooms filled with rough-hewn wooden furnishings, and there's a hot tub available for guests. ⑦

🐾 **Barn on the River** 303 N Main St ☎970/453-2975 or 1-800/795-2975, ⓦwww.breckenridge-inn.com. Elegant nineteenth-century home and barn done up in period furniture and antiques and an outdoor hot tub. ⑧

Breckenridge Mountain Lodge 600 S Ridge St ☎970/453-2000 or 1-888/200-0616 ⓦwww.breckmountainlodge.com. Rustic and picturesque motel close to the slopes and town. The 80 rooms are decorated Western-style and facilities include hot tubs, a games room, a summer-only pool, and a ski-rental shop. Continental breakfast included. ⑤

Fireside Inn 114 N French St ☎970/453-6456, ⓦwww.firesideinn.com. Homey little B&B with four floral, antique-filled bedrooms (all with private bath) and several extremely cramped dorm rooms ($26–38) which all share access to a TV lounge and kitchenette. The friendly hosts also provide a computer for free Internet access, plus afternoon tea and cakes. ⑥

Little Mountain Lodge 98 Sunbeam Drive ☎970/453-1969 or 1-800/468-7707, ⓦwww.littlemountainlodge.com. Stylish and luxurious ten-room B&B in a spacious log home. Each room is minimally decorated, and all share an airy and elegant lounge, basement games room with pool table, and secluded outdoor tub. Gourmet breakfast and evening snacks included. ⑥

The Lodge at Breckenridge 112 Overlook Drive ☎970/453-9300 or 1-800/736-1607, ⓦwww.thelodgeatbreck.com. Luxurious spa resort two miles east of town on a cliff overlooking Breckenridge, beside Boreas Pass Rd. Rooms are spacious, simple, and stylish, decorated along several themes – Western, Southwestern, and European. Most have fantastic views including the Ten-Mile Range, Hoosier Pass, and Mount Baldy. Guests have access to a superb health club offering various spa treatments and with indoor pool, several hot tubs, sauna, a weight room, and racquetball courts. ⑦

Muggins Gulch Inn 4023 Tiger Rd ☎970/453-7414 or 1-800/275-8304, ⓦwww.mugginsgulch.com. Attractive post-and-beam lodge located partway between Frisco and Breckenridge, with three roomy suites. Delicious breakfasts and afternoon snacks are included. ⑥

Ridge Street Inn 212 N Ridge St ☎970/453-4680. Comfortable, luxurious B&B in the heart of the historic downtown area, decorated with floral excess. The friendly owner makes great hearty breakfasts. ⑥

River Mountain Lodge 100 S Park Ave ☎970/453-4711 or 1-800/325-2342. Slopeside condo complex with over a hundred units ranging from studios to two-bedroom apartments, all with full kitchens, terraces, and washer/dryers. Housekeeping and a complimentary continental breakfast are included in the rates, and facilities include a pool, steam room, sauna, hot tubs, weight room, and ski-rental shop. ⑦

Village at Breckenridge 535 S Park Ave ☎970/453-2000 or 1-800/800-7829. Large thirteen-building complex at the base of Peak 9 with a whole gamut of lodging options, from basic hotel rooms to three-bedroom apartments, within walking distance of town. Facilities include pools, a dozen hot tubs, and an ice-skating rink. Good-value ski packages are often available. ⑦

Wayside Inn 165 Tiger Rd ☎970/453-5540 or 1-800/927-7669, ⓦwww.breckenridgewaysideinn.com. Some of Breckenridge's most competitively priced lodging is a 5min drive from downtown on the road to Frisco. A gigantic fireplace dominates the welcoming lounge, while rooms, though far more standard motel fare, have log-hewn beds, adding a nice rustic touch. Guests share the outdoor tub, surrounded by meadows. Rates include coffee and a muffin for breakfast. ⑤

Whispering Pines Lodge ☎970/453-2575 or 1-866/754-5656, ⓦ www.ski-kokopelli.com. Friendly, small-scale, luxurious catered lodges with comfortable open-plan lounges, spacious Southwestern-style rustic bedrooms, and a dining area decorated with Colorado furniture and Native American rugs. The food here is gourmet-quality, as well. ⑧

Wildwood Suites 120 Sawmill Rd ☎970/453-0232 or 1-800/866-0300, ⓦ www.wildwoodsuites .com. Relatively small condo complex nestled in woods next to a mountain stream two blocks from Main St. The one- and two-bedroom condos are in a ski-in location and have access to large outdoor hot tubs, sauna, massage service, and ski-rental shop. Continental breakfast included. ⑤

The Town and around

Set at the base of a glorious bowl of mountains, Breckenridge's snug Victorian downtown spreads over a compact twelve square blocks. The old multicolored gingerbread buildings along Main Street, the town's core, have been well preserved and are now occupied by restaurants and gift shops, which draw large numbers, particularly in the summer. The town's local history museum, the **Edwin Carter Museum**, on the corner of Wellington and Ridge (Mon–Fri 1.30–3pm; $3), is good for its insight into the local characters that shaped the town's beginnings. But the bulk of the exhibits are given over to Edwin Carter, a naturalist from New York who in the late nineteenth century built a phenomenal collection of area flora and fauna, while campaigning for the protection of the local environment as it was progressively attacked by open-cast mining methods. To complete the picture of what Breckenridge's early days were like, head two miles northeast to the **Country Boy Mine**, 542 French Gulch Rd (phone for hours; $15; ☎970/453-4405, ⓦ www.countryboymine.com), where the mine tours include drilling and dynamite demonstrations.

△ Breckenridge

Summer activities

Though winter is by far the busiest time in Breckenridge, the town is fast becoming a popular destination in summer too, with visitors taking advantage of the cheaper accommodation and plentiful opportunities to hike, bike, fish, and play golf. A popular local **hike** for those looking to get some serious exercise is the ascent of Bald Mountain (13,684ft), southeast of Breckenridge, a three- to four-hour round-trip from a trailhead off Boreas Pass Road. Another good choice is the Gold Hill Trail south of town, which leads hikers up to the crest of the Tenmile Range, overlooking a tundra of craggy, bald peaks and peaceful valleys. The visitor information center (see p.183) can also provide printed hiking guides for many routes in the Arapaho National Forest.

Also supplied by the visitor center is the excellent and free *Summit County Mountain Bike Guide*, an invaluable resource for **cyclists** exploring the area. Racer's Edge, 114 N Main St (℡970/453-0995), and Carvers, at no. 203 (℡970/453-0132, ⊛www.carverskishop.com), both rent good front-suspension bikes for around $35 per day. As at Keystone, Breckenridge Resort runs chairlift rides to the top of the mountains (adult day pass $22), which, as well as offering stunning views, provide access to great hiking and mountain-biking trails. Breckenridge Resort also offers **toboggan rides** down the dry SuperSlide (summer daily 9am–5pm; $10), mini golf ($7), and a giant maze ($6).

If you'd like to explore the surrounding mountain range on **horseback**, Breckenridge Stables (℡970/453-4438) offer two-hour trail rides from $35. For fishermen, the Blue River runs through Breckenridge and is a favorite **fly-fishing** spot; Mountain Anglers, 31 S Main St (℡970/453-4665), can provide the requisite licenses and equipment and also organize guided trips. Once voted by *Golf Digest* the top public course in Colorado, **Breckenridge Golf Club** on Tiger Run Rd (℡970/453-9104) has greens fees of around $100.

If after all that you still need to let off steam or have a good soak, head to the impressive Breckenridge Recreation Center, 0880 Airport Rd (Mon–Fri 6am–10pm, Sat 7am–10pm, Sun 8am–10pm; day pass $12; ℡970/453-1734), where facilities include a climbing wall and pool.

Winter activities

For those skiing the mountain slopes around town and those who've just finished a day there, there are plenty of other good **winter diversions**, from ice-skating and snowmobiling to dog-sledding and evening sleigh rides. The visitor centers are the best first stop for advice and bookings.

The best place to go **ice-skating** in Breckenridge is at the Stephen C. West Arena, 0189 Boreas Pass Rd (daily 10am–10pm, though hours can vary; $8 admission, $6 rental; ℡970/547-9974), a new covered outdoor rink at the south end of town. For a cozier experience skate at **Maggie Pond**, 535 S Park Ave (daily 10am–10pm; $7 admission, $7 rentals; ℡970/453-2000), a small pond at the base of Peak 9.

Last but not least, dinner **sleigh rides**, incorporating a stop for gourmet food at an out-of-the-way cabin, have become a popular splurge in recent years; one company offering these are Nordic Sleigh Rides ($74; ℡970/453-2005, ⊛www.nordicsleighrides.com).

Cross-country skiing

Breckenridge is well equipped for **cross-country** skiers. The largest network of groomed trails is maintained by Breckenridge Nordic Center, 1200 Ski Hill Rd (daily 9am–4pm; passes $14, rentals from $14, lessons available;

☎970/453-6855, ⓦwww.breckenridgenordic.com), which grooms around 20 miles of track below Peak 8. The trail pass is interchangeable with that of the Frisco Nordic Center, while multi-day passes are also good at the Gold Run Nordic Center (☎970/547-7889), which maintains 9 miles of groomed trails on the town's golf course.

There are also some good **backcountry** Nordic skiing opportunities, particularly south of town near the Hoosier Pass, where snow conditions are usually excellent. Several trails from the top of the pass are a good place to start on explorative forays. There are more cross-country skiing opportunities south of Breckenridge at Fairplay and to the west at Copper Mountain. Call the Dillon Forest Service rangers on ☎970/468-5400 for more info, or stop in at Mountain Outfitters, 112 S Ridge St (☎970/453-2201), for backcountry rentals and route suggestions.

Breckenridge Ski Area

Breckenridge is one of the busiest **ski resorts** in the US, but more for the sum of its parts than for any single feature. The place is not without its problems, though, crowding – by North American, not European standards – being one of them. The resort's convenience, on the side of an attractive town, makes it a popular holiday destination and, as it's within easy range of Denver and Colorado Springs, encourages substantial weekend crowds. The actual ski area itself, while particularly well suited to beginners and intermediates (despite what resort statistics might suggest), is of limited interest to experts not interested in the excellent terrain park, consistently rated among the world's best. Otherwise many slopes are disappointingly flat, and the more challenging upper slopes are often bleak, icy, and beset by a biting wind.

With a long, horizontal strip spanning four peaks of the Tenmile Range, Breckenridge's layout is a bit odd: each peak, despite occupying the same ridge, is distinct from the next, separated by deep gullies, which makes getting from one to the next tricky. The resort has two main base areas: **Peak 9**, accessed by the consistently overcrowded Quicksilver lift from the town's southern edge, and **Peak 8**, a free shuttle bus ride from town.

Aside from a handful of steep bumps and forested chutes in the back, **Peak 9** is best for fast cruising territory on wide blue runs. Peak 9 lifts also serve **Peak 10**, a largely advanced mountain, streaked by groomed blacks, testing bumps, and steep, windswept glades. **Peak 8** lifts access all the resort's above-treeline expert bowls, the celebrated terrain park, and acres of easy meadows. A long traverse from the top of Peak 8's Rocky Mountain Super Chair leads to **Peak 7**, where gentle glades and long blue cruisers await.

Breckenridge Ski Area

Information ☎970/453-5000, ⓦwww.breckenridge.com; snow report ☎970/453-6118.

Ticket prices and operating times $75; open mid-Nov to late April daily 8.30am–4pm.

Mountain statistics base elevation 9600ft, summit elevation 12,998ft, vertical drop 3398ft, acreage 2208, average snowfall 300in.

Lifts and trails 27 lifts serve 146 trails: beginner 15 percent, intermediate 33 percent, expert 52 percent.

Arrival

Skiers **driving** in from I-70 and Frisco should take the North Park turnoff on their way into town rather than risk getting stuck in the traffic endemic to Main Street. Tiger and F-lots are the closest expensive pay lots to the Village at the base of Peak 9, and the lot at the base of Peak 8 fills early. Buses stop at the free Miners and Tailings lots, located off Watson Ave.

In lieu of a car, "Free Ride" shuttle buses (℡970/547-3140) run through town from 6.30am to midnight, serving the Peak 8 and Beaver Run (Peak 9) base areas, outlying condos, and all stops in between. Each of the nine routes operates every twenty to thirty minutes.

Lift tickets, lessons, and rentals

There are few **ticket** deals to be had unless you buy them prior to or very early in the season. Breckenridge multi-day tickets are valid at Keystone and Arapahoe Basin, with restricted use at Vail and Beaver Creek. These can be purchased online (at least fourteen days in advance) for savings of $8 to $20.

Ski school (℡1-888/576-2754) meets at both the Village and Beaver Run areas at the bottom of Peak 9 and at the base of Peak 8. Full-day lessons for beginners (from $85) start in the morning, with half-day options (from $75) in the afternoon. Add $11 to include a lift ticket in the package. Intermediate and advanced half-day lessons (from $55) are available every morning, but are only offered in the afternoons as well if interest is sufficient. Adaptive programs (including rentals) are run through the excellent Breckenridge Outdoor Education Center (℡970/453-6422, ⓦwww.boec.org), while daycare is available for children over six weeks old at the Breckenridge Children's Center (℡970/453-3258).

There are plenty of outfitters in Breckenridge, though relatively few at the actual base of the lifts. **Rates** start at around $20–30 per day for basic ski gear, doubling for top-notch demo gear. Among those offering rentals are Lone Star Sports, at the corner of Four O'Clock Rd and Park Ave (℡970/453-2003), a longstanding local ski store specializing in personalized fitting services, custom ski tuning, and overnight repair services. Carvers Ski and Snowboard Shop, 203 N Main St (℡970/453-0132, ⓦwww.carverskishop.com), usually has good-quality equipment and some of the best rates in town. For good tuning and quality demos, try Mountain Wave Snowboards, 600 South Park Ave (℡970/453-8305) or the respected A Racer's Edge ski shop, 114 N Main (℡970/453-0995 or 1-800/451-5363). Low prices on basic equipment and clothing, along with goggle and glove rentals are available at Colorado Ski and Snowboard Rental, 110 Ski Hill Rd (℡970/453-1477 or 1-800/248-1477).

Mountain runs

Sow-moving surface lifts and flat **beginner** trails are found at the base of Peaks 8 and 9. Peak 8 has the better views, but tree-lined Peak 9 is more sheltered, closer to town, and also has a novice snowboarder slope with minipark. All beginners should avoid the long, busy cat-tracks between peaks, particularly on weekends. Note, too, that on-mountain crowding at Breckenridge can be intimidating for first-timers.

Intermediates have the run of the mountain, though they should stay off Peak 10 until confident enough to handle icy steeps. The rolling blues off Peak 9 have the advantage of being a little longer than those on Peak 8, while Peak 7 generally has emptier slopes and good pockets of glades. When conditions are good the short blacks on the front face of Peak 8 are manageable for confident intermediates, as are the blacks in the back bowl off Chair 6.

Though often icy, the groomed blacks and moguls of Peak 10 are usually the choice of **expert** skiers, with the trails high on the back of Peak 8 nearly as popular. Bump runs in the upper gullies between the peaks are more challenging, but need a fairly deep base of snow, as do the stumpy glades off Peak 10 known as The Burn. Only on calm powder days is it worth exploring the open bowls of Peaks 7 and 8, and even then you need to be prepared to hike up to Imperial Bowl or out toward the Peak 7 summit for the best conditions.

Breckenridge excels in the realm of **pipes** and **parks**. The six-acre Freeway terrain park – with its plentiful and well-designed rails, jumps, and a half-pipe – is on Peak 8, which also boasts a particularly awe-inspiring park that's frequently used in major contests. Less daunting is the minipark tucked away under C lift on Peak 9.

Eating

Breckenridge has a good variety of places to **eat** – and, though few are particularly cheap, prices have a fair way to go before they begin to reach those at Vail or Aspen. Most of the town's nightlife venues offer decent bar food, so check those listings, too.

Blue River Bistro 305 N Main St ☎970/453-6974. Elegant but cheerful bistro with a cosmopolitan menu – featuring a particularly extensive selection of pastas (entrees average $16) – and an extraordinary 75 martinis. Occasional live jazz; open until 2am.

Briar Rose 109 E Lincoln St ☎970/453-9948. Upscale restaurant in a modern building made atmospheric by addition of old relics, in particular a wonderfully atmospheric Victorian-era saloon bar. The specialty is wild game like elk and venison though there's a dependable range of posh steak and seafood dishes on the menu too.

Bubba's Bones 110 S Ridge St ☎970/547-9942. Authentic Southern-style barbecue – hickory-smoked and with a range of homemade sauces – at reasonable prices; entrees cost around $11.

🎿 **Café Alpine** 106 E Adams Ave ☎970/453-8218. Though pricey, this bastion of American fine dining, inside an old Victorian house, is pleasantly informal, and dishes off the constantly changing menu delectable. Inventive use of ingredients – like the pistachio-goat cheese-stuffed sole with roasted red pepper risotto or the brie plate with fig balsamic syrup – results in dishes that are often as colorful as they are tasty.

The extensive wine list has something for every occasion.

Hearthstone 130 S Ridge St ☎970/453-1148. Fine upmarket dining in a restored Victorian building. Serving so-called "Rocky Mountain cuisine," the menu includes rack of elk, trout, wild mushrooms, and some delicious slow-roasted prime rib.

Mi Casa 600 S Park Ave ☎970/453-2071. The best Mexican food in Summit County, including fine *chili rellenos*. Most entrees, like the tangy fajitas, are around $10, and the daily happy hour (3–6pm) is also good value; the margaritas are excellent. Open for lunch and dinner.

Mountain Java 118 S Ridge St ☎970/453-1874. Cozy book-lined coffeehouse serving healthy lunches, low-fat muffins, and gourmet breads along with steaming espresso drinks.

Rasta Pasta 411 S Main St ☎970/453-7467. Large helpings of relatively cheap pasta with a Caribbean twist, set to a reggae soundtrack.

The Prospector 130 S Main St ☎970/453-6858. Tasty, traditional home-cooked breakfasts (including a spicy and excellent *huevos rancheros*) and lunches that focus on traditional American favorites like roasts or meatloaf. Prices are among the lowest in town.

Nightlife and the performing arts

With a plentiful assortment of bars and several late-night music venues, Breckenridge offers the best choice of **nightlife** in Summit County. For those less libation-inclined, the Backstage Theatre, by Maggie Pond at 121 S Ridge St (July–Sept; tickets around $20; ☎970/453-0199, ⓦwww.backstagetheatre.org), puts on nightly performances in summer. For art-house films, visit the Speakeasy Theatre, in the Colorado Mountain College at 103 S Harris St (Wed–Sun;

Ullr Fest

Horned helmets are *de rigeur* at the **Ullr Fest** (pronounced "oo-ler"), a Breckenridge festival in honor of the Norse god of snow. Usually beginning the third week of January, festivities kick off on a Monday with the annual International Snow Sculpture Championships and events in the Ullympics, such as Broom Ball and volleyball with snowshoes, and run into the weekend when there's a parade and fireworks. There are a variety of different events and activities daily, including freestyle ski competitions in ski ballet, mogul skiing, and aerial jumping, plus concerts and the opportunity for kids to go ice-skating with their favorite cartoon characters.

admission \$7.50; ℗970/453-3624). For **listings** of what's on, check out local papers such as the *Summit County Journal* and the *Summit Daily News* (ⓦwww .summitdaily.com).

Breckenridge Brewery & Pub 600 S Main St ℗970/453-1550. This huge brewpub was one of the first in Colorado and is now a landmark at the southern edge of town. The Avalanche Ale is a superb amber and the pub-brewed root beer worth a try as well. The pub's also a dependable option for good bar food – burgers, sandwiches, and salads – from around \$7.
Downstairs at Eric's 111 S Main St ℗970/453-1401. Lively basement sports bar, with a good range of microbrews – 120 beers, though not all microbrew, are on offer – and a massive menu of filling bar food for the outdoorsy types that gather here.
Liquid Lounge 520 S Main St ℗970/453-2782. Funky and urbane bar, where ambient dance music spins on the decks while people lounge in the booths or play pool.

Salt Creek Saloon 110 E Lincoln St ℗970/453-4949. Appropriately, this popular line-dancing venue above the *Salt Creek* restaurant – where men in cowboy hats come to strut their stuff – has the feel of a barn and the spirit of the West.
Sherpa and Yeti's 320 S Main St ℗970/547-9299, ⓦwww.sherpaandyetis.com. Often hectic basement bar that's stage to most live bands visiting Breckenridge.
The St Bernard 103 S Main St ℗970/453-2572. Bustling, low-key drinking den, hidden away in the back of the smart *St Bernard* restaurant, and so easily overlooked.
Ullr's Sports Grill 401 S Main St ℗970/453-6060. Small, neighborhood-style sports bar in the center of town with regular promotions and cheap drinks on Tuesdays.

Travel details

Buses

(All buses are Greyhound unless stated otherwise.)
Frisco to: Denver (4 daily; 1hr 35min); Glenwood Springs (2 daily; 1hr 50min); Grand Junction (2 daily; 3hr 35min); Vail (12 daily; 35min; Vail Resorts Express and Greyhound).

The Northern Mountains

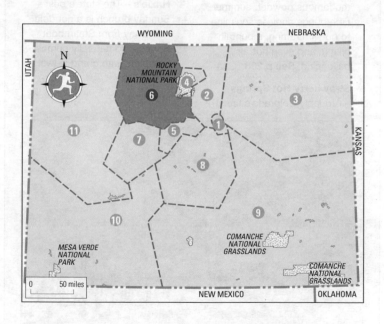

CHAPTER 6

Highlights

✳ **Winter Park** – There's truth in advertising at Winter Park, which has justly dubbed itself "Mountain Bike Capital USA". See p.199

✳ **North Park Moose** – Track down and watch some of the large population of moose that thrive in remote North Park. See p.208

✳ **Steamboat Springs** – During winter, go steep-and-deep in the famous powder; summertime brings endless sunshine to go with rafting, mountain biking, and even hot-air ballooning. See p.208

✳ **Strawberry Hot Springs** – Arguably Colorado's finest

hot springs resort is hidden away in the woods and has a good variety of large land-scaped pools to choose from. See p.214

✳ **The Flat Tops Wilderness** – Real get-away-from-it-all hiking; a highlight is the Devil's Causeway, where a trail barely four feet wide drops away 1500 feet on either side. See p.217

✳ **Hazie's** – The state's best Sunday brunch is a gondola ride away from Steamboat Springs, so naturally comes complete with grand views. See p.221

△ Middle Park

6

The Northern Mountains

Though not that far from Denver and major Northern Front Range towns such as Fort Collins, Colorado's **NORTHERN MOUNTAINS** have remained curiously isolated. Partly this is because there's so much spectacular country in between and certainly nothing that tops the splendor of Rocky Mountain National Park. But the area's low visitor numbers don't do credit to the fantastic opportunities that abound: secluded trails wind alongside high-altitude rivers and lakes in vast National Forests where peace and quiet is paired with beautiful mountain terrain and easy wildlife-spotting. This region is not just a quieter version of areas to the south, though – there's also a subtle shift in mood, as the cowboy towns hereabouts show few signs of self-conscious Old West makeovers and hunting and ranching are the dominant topics of barroom conversation.

The area's main artery, Hwy-40, leaves I-70 in the Clear Creek Valley to climb over Berthoud Pass before dropping down into **Winter Park** and its popular ski resort, at the head of the Fraser Valley. The lower valley, sometimes called **Middle Park**, is sparsely populated, with unexciting **Granby** – Amtrak's last port-of-call in northern Colorado – its main town. From here Hwy-40 follows a series of rivers on its way northwest to **Steamboat Springs**, passing through the tiny mineral spa resort town of Hot Sulphur Springs, the small highway town of **Kremmling** – one of the state's most popular hunting and fishing bases – and vast tracts of untrammeled forest and mountain scenery. Spreading out to the north of Middle Park as far as the Wyoming border is the vast **North Park** valley, where wildlife, particularly moose, flourish, and few people live.

West of North Park and beyond the Continental Divide, when it seems that the towns and the hills can only get smaller and more remote, **Steamboat Springs** appears. This fine old cowboy town has a ski resort which stacks up to the likes of Vail and Aspen and has grown up just enough to become one of North America's premier winter sports destinations. To its southwest loom the aptly-named **Flat Tops**, where dramatic table-top peaks and plateaus offer pristine wilderness hiking.

Winter Park and Fraser

The former railroad center of **WINTER PARK**, 67 miles northwest of Denver, is little more than a sprawling agglomeration of condominiums, outfitters, and shopping malls, there to service the eponymous **ski resort** two miles to the south. Five miles north of Winter Park, the even more utilitarian **FRASER** is home to most of the locals. In the absence of any attractions or sights in either town, visitors generally get straight down to business, skiing in winter and hiking and biking in summer. Winter Park is well known for both of the latter, while a recent cash infusion has helped bring its ski resort up to scratch, making it a good low-key competitor to the Summit County ski areas. The place also has bestowed upon itself the title of "Mountain Bike Capital USA," which is not too far from the truth.

Arrival, orientation, and information

Due to the treacherous and often painfully slow road over the Berthoud Pass, you'll rarely make Winter Park from Denver in less than two hours; take I-70 to Hwy-40 and get off at exit 232. **Rail** service to Fraser/Winter Park is provided by Amtrak's *California Zephyr* and, every Saturday and Sunday during ski season, the Winter Park Ski Train (reservations required; $49; 2hr; ☎303/296-4754,

Ⓦwww.skitrain.com); both leave from Denver's Union Station. Home James Transportation Services runs **shuttle vans** ($42 one-way; ☎970/726-4730 or 1-800/359-7503, Ⓦwww.homejamestransportation.com) from Denver International Airport.

It's easy to **orientate** yourself in Winter Park and Fraser, since virtually everything – lodging, dining, and shopping – is situated along Hwy-40 and is visible from the road. The swank **visitor center** is no exception, at the junction of 40 and Vasquez Rd (daily 8am–5pm; ☎970/726-4118 or 1-800/903-7275, Ⓦwww.winterpark-info.com); they're very helpful and can provide useful free summer trail maps. An additional resource is the county website, Ⓦwww.grand-county.com, which also covers Middle Park.

In winter, an excellent network of free **local shuttle buses** – connecting Fraser, Winter Park, and most local accommodations with the resort – renders cars unnecessary. The buses run every ten to fifteen minutes, using bus stops marked by blue circle signs. Free buses also take passengers from restaurants and bars to the doorstep of their accommodation on Friday and Saturday nights until 2am.

Accommodation

Though a few ski resort options exist, much of Winter Park's **accommodation** is either a shuttle bus ride away from the slopes around Winter Park Resort or in motels or modern lodges in town. Many of these are unusual in that during winter they offer packages that include breakfast and dinner. Also dotted around the valley are a selection of upscale B&Bs. Winter Park Central Reservations (☎970/726-1564 or 1-800/979-0332, Ⓦwww.skiwinterpark.com) can arrange lodging in every available style and also offers a variety of flexible packages with activities such as biking, golfing, and, of course, skiing. For a condo try Winter Park Adventures (☎970/726-5701 or 1-800/797-2750, Ⓦwww.winterparkadventures.com), which can organize units from $60/night for two night minimum stays. In summer there are almost limitless opportunities for backcountry **camping** in the surrounding National Forest; a popular place to head is along Moffat Road in the direction of Rollins Pass (see p.200). The USFS also runs several campgrounds in the area, including *Idlewild* ($12), south of the resort along Hwy-40.

Beaver Village Lodge 79303 Hwy-40, Winter Park ☎970/726-5741 or 1-800/666-0281, Ⓦwww.beavervillage.com. Popular with tour groups, this large A-frame ski lodge, on the resort side of Winter Park, has small, basic rooms sleeping one to six. Buffet breakfast and dinner, served in a school-style dining room, are included, and there's a bar, Jacuzzi and sauna, pool table, arcade games, laundry, and ski shop. Snowmobiling and sleigh rides are also available. Good multi-day packages and kids' rates. ❷–❹

Devil's Thumb Ranch CR-83 ☎970/726-8231, Ⓦwww.devilsthumbranch.com. Down-valley from Winter Park, a rustic lodge and private cabins oozing Rockies charm on the slopes of the Continental Divide, with accommodations ranging from simple rooms with shared baths up to four-bedroom cabins. Rates include use of sauna and Jacuzzi, continental breakfast, and cheese and wine tasting. Their restaurant is renowned for its

fine dining, and there's extensive cross-country skiing from the door. ❹

Engelmann Pines 1035 Cranmer Ave, Fraser ☎970/726-4632 or 1-800/992-9512. Friendly B&B three miles outside Winter Park, furnished with European heirloom furniture. Facilities include a guests' kitchen and living room. All bathrooms have hot tubs. Open May–Oct. ❹

Gasthaus Eichler 78786 Hwy-40, Winter Park ☎970/726-5133 or 1-800/543-3899. German alpine chalet-style house with fifteen stylishly minimalist but comfortable hotel rooms with down comforters and whirlpool baths. The room rate (halved from late April to Nov) includes a delicious breakfast and gourmet dinner as well as shuttle to the ski area. ❼

Iron Horse Resort 257 Winter Park Drive, Winter Park Resort ☎970/726-8851 or 1-800/621-8190, Ⓦwww.ironhorse-resort.com. Old-school condo hotel with worn-in furnishings and a maze of

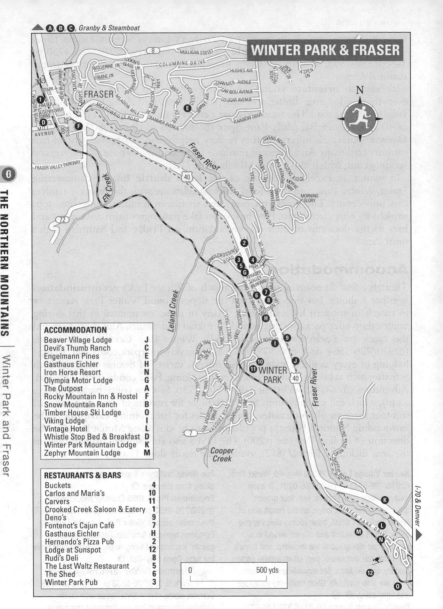

WINTER PARK & FRASER

THE NORTHERN MOUNTAINS | Winter Park and Fraser

❹

ACCOMMODATION

Beaver Village Lodge	J
Devil's Thumb Ranch	C
Engelmann Pines	E
Gasthaus Eichler	H
Iron Horse Resort	N
Olympia Motor Lodge	G
The Outpost	A
Rocky Mountain Inn & Hostel	F
Snow Mountain Ranch	B
Timber House Ski Lodge	O
Viking Lodge	I
Vintage Hotel	L
Whistle Stop Bed & Breakfast	D
Winter Park Mountain Lodge	K
Zephyr Mountain Lodge	M

RESTAURANTS & BARS

Buckets	4
Carlos and Maria's	10
Carvers	11
Crooked Creek Saloon & Eatery	1
Deno's	9
Fontenot's Cajun Café	7
Gasthaus Eichler	H
Hernando's Pizza Pub	2
Lodge at Sunspot	12
Rudi's Deli	8
The Last Waltz Restaurant	5
The Shed	6
Winter Park Pub	3

0   500 yds

198

corridors that's accessible from the slopes. Units range from studios to three premium suites with full kitchens and sun decks. The indoor/outdoor pool, hot tubs, and weight room are a bit basic, but continental breakfast and après-ski are included and kids eat free in the dining room, making it economical for families and groups. **❺**

Olympia Motor Lodge 78572 Hwy-40, Winter Park ☎970-726-8843 or 1-800-548-1992. Standard though comfortable downtown motel with queen beds and some kitchenette units. **❹**
The Outpost 687 CR-517 ☎970-726-5346 or 1-800-430-4538, ⊛www.outpost-colorado.com. Relaxed country ranch tucked away in the pastures

just north of Fraser, secluded yet not too far from town. The lobby is large and comfy, the dining area has an open fireplace, and there's an upstairs lounge with microwave, snacks, video library, and resident spaniels. Choose from antique-furnished rooms in the main house or in the quieter adults-only annex next to the atrium hot tub. ⑤

🏃 **Rocky Mountain Inn & Hostel** 15 CR-72, Fraser ☎970-726-8256 or 1-866/467-8351, ⓦwww.therockymountaininn.com. Plush, immaculately clean, and well-run hostel with large kitchen (the place is located opposite a supermarket), TV room, and deck with grill. Choose between dorms ($25–30) or private rooms (⑥), with a continental breakfast included in rates for the latter. Free Internet and WiFi.

Snow Mountain Ranch 1344 CR-53 ☎970/887-2152 or 303/443-4743, ⓦwww.ymcarockies.org. Simple cabins, vacation homes, and lodge accommodations dotted around 5100 forested acres, the location of the Nordic Center (see p.200), seven miles north of Fraser along Hwy-40. Extensive facilities include a sports center with indoor pool, basketball, roller-skating, climbing wall, outdoor ice rink, restaurants, and library. Good group rates. ④

Timber House Ski Lodge 196 Timber House Cabin Rd, off Winter Park Drive, Winter Park Resort ☎970/726-5477 or 1-800/843-3502, ⓦwww.timberhouseskilodge.com. Traditional alpine-style ski lodge, built in the 1940s in the woods above the Winter Park base area, with access to the slopes. Wood carvings adorn the rustic common areas that focus on huge fireplaces. All rooms are unique and range from six-person dorms ($58) to modern doubles with private bath; the older section of the lodge is cozier, while attic rooms offer the most privacy. Amenities include a sauna and a

huge wooden-barrel hot tub. Gigantic breakfasts, dinner, and afternoon tea all included. ④

Viking Lodge 78966 Hwy-40, Winter Park ☎970/726-8885 or 1-800/421-4013, ⓦwww.skiwp.com. Clean and well-maintained downtown motel, usually the cheapest in town. Coffee and a continental breakfast are included, and extras include a game room, whirlpool, and sauna. ③

Vintage Hotel 100 Winter Park Drive, Winter Park Resort ☎970/726-8801, ⓦwww.vintagehotel.com. Condo-hotel with faded elegance a short shuttle ride from the ski area, where accommodations range from small hotel rooms to three-bedroom condos with full kitchens. Facilities include a game room, lounge, hot tubs, a sauna, and a courtesy shuttle to town. ④

Whistle Stop Bed & Breakfast 178 Fraser Ave, Fraser ☎970/726-8767 or 1-888/829-2632, ⓦwww.winterparkbandb.com. Small, modern B&B on a residential street by the Amtrak station in Fraser. The least expensive in the area, it's run by attentive hosts who prepare huge breakfasts, bake an endless supply of cookies, and can offer advice on just about everything. ④

Winter Park Mountain Lodge 81699 Hwy-40, Winter Park ☎970/726-4211 or 1-800/726-3340, ⓦwww.winterparkhotel.com. Modern chain hotel with indoor pool, hot tubs, sauna, and laundry. ⑤

Zephyr Mountain Lodge The Village at Winter Park, Winter Park Resort ☎970/726-8400 or 1-877/754-8400, ⓦwww.zephyrmountainlodge.com. This mammoth slopeside development is the keystone of a recent new wave of development at Winter Park. Offered are one-, two-, and three-bedroom condos, all sporting luxury rustic-chic decor and priced to match, at least by local standards. ⑧

Summer activities

Winter Park has worked hard to attract **mountain bikers**, and cycling is now the main summertime activity in the valley. The resort has built some 45 miles of terrific trails – arguably the best run by any Colorado ski resort – which can be accessed via the Zephyr Express chairlift; tickets (adult day-pass $22) can be purchased as a package with a front-suspension bike rental for $55. The real local gem, however, is the 600 miles of marked, mapped, and maintained trails all around Winter Park and the Fraser Valley. These include the five-mile paved Fraser River Trail between the two towns, an easy ride good for families. More adventurous riders should definitely try the delightful rolling single-track of the Tipperary Creek Trail, west of Fraser. For the best views, the **Moffat Road** (see box p.200) makes a good ride; the terrain is easy and however far you manage to go, it's all downhill back into town. A free trail map is available at the many local bike stores or from the visitor center. Bike **rentals** are available from Winter Park Sports Shop, 78336 Hwy-40 (☎970/726-5554 or 1-800/222-7547), which has a good selection and knowledgeable staff.

The Moffat Road

For an appreciation of Winter Park's setting and history, take a twelve-mile drive east of town to the Rollins Pass via the rough and rutted **Moffat Road** (also known as the Corona Pass Road), generally navigable with regular 2WD vehicles from June until early November. The railroad once came this way – when the route was the valley's lifeline and the main reason for its existence as a timber camp for Denver – before the construction of the Moffat Tunnel below made this section of line superfluous. The views over Indian Peaks Wilderness to the north are astonishing, and from the summit of the pass 4WD vehicles can head further east to Rollinsville and the Peak-to-Peak Highway (see p.86). For detailed information about remaining railroad sections and a history of the road's construction, pick up *The Moffat Road* leaflet ($1) from the visitor center in Winter Park.

The bowl of mountains surrounding the Winter Park and Fraser Valley is also a tempting prospect for multi-day **hiking** trips, particularly along the Continental Divide trail, which loops around the southern and eastern sides of the valley. The visitor information center can provide free **trail maps**, while a good place for information and gear is Flanagan's Ski Rental and Black Dog Mountaineering, 78902 Hwy-40 (℡970/726-4412), which has a good stock of camping equipment.

Other popular summertime activities include the fast and fun mile-and-a-half-long **alpine slide** ($10), a climbing wall, and a maze. Also in the valley is the **Pole Creek Golf Course**, eleven miles northwest of Fraser on Hwy-40 in the town of Tabernash (℡970/726-8847 or 1-800/511-5076); it's one of the best in the state.

Winter activities

The majority of winter visitors come here to ski or board at Winter Park Resort, but the rest of the valley can be explored in a variety of ways, including **snowmobile** trips up to the Continental Divide, **sleigh rides**, and **dog-sledding**, all three of which are offered by Grand Adventures (℡970/726-9247 or 1-800/726-9247, @www.grandadventures.com). You can also **snowmobile** the Continental Divide with Trailblazers in Fraser ($55/hr, $180/day; ℡970/726-8452 or 1-800/669-0134, @trailblazersnowmobile.com) or around a 25-mile course just north of town with Mountain Madness ($40/hr; ℡970/726-4529 or 1-800-547-3101). The 40-strong team at Dog Sled Rides of Winter Park, Kings Crossing Rd ($275 for two adults for 90min; ℡970/726-8326, @www.dogsledrides.com/winterpark), is best for mushing through the forest.

A popular evening activity is **tubing** at Tubing Hill in Fraser, half a mile behind the Safeway store (Tues–Thurs 2pm–9pm, Fri & Sat 10am–10pm, Sun 10am–9pm; $14/hr; ℡970/726-5954), where you get towed to the top of an icy run to slide down on an oversized inner-tube. Alternatively, you can **ice-skate** at the outdoor Fraser Ice Rink, 601 Zerex Ave (free, no skate rental available; ℡970/726-8882), where bonfires are lit at night.

Cross-country skiers consider the 150-odd miles of cross-country trails in the area, which include plenty of good backcountry options, one of the best in the state. Down the valley from the downhill area is the great cross-country center of Devil's Thumb Ranch, 3530 CO-83, Tabernash ($15, lessons and equipment available; ℡970/726-8231 or 1-800/933-4339, @www.devilsthumbranch.com), where nearly 78 miles of groomed trails fan out into the forest from a central meadow. To get there, drive west from Winter Park to Fraser and turn right onto

CO-83. Another option is the 62 miles of trails at the Snow Mountain Ranch YMCA Nordic Center (passes $12, or package with lessons, rentals, and pass $32; ☎970/887-2152 ext 4173, ⊛www.ymcarockies.org).

Winter Park Resort

Winter Park Resort, one of the oldest continuously operating ski resorts in the US, first opened its lifts in 1944 as a municipal facility – a winter park for Denver, 67 miles away. It was developed as a family-oriented mountain, creating an image it's never quite shaken, though today it's also well known for its expert terrain. Over time regional competition has grown drastically, yet Winter Park has had continued success by being relatively good value and offering plenty of terrain for every type of skier and boarder. This includes skiers with disabilities: Winter Park is home to the **National Sports Center for the Disabled** (☎970/726-1540, ⊛www.nscd.org), the continent's largest such center, which provides low-cost lessons and special adaptive equipment for 2500 people a year, and trains serious competitors for its disabled ski team.

The ski area divides into five interconnected parts: two base areas sit below eponymous mountains, while a less accessible bowl, cirque, and ridge lie tucked out of sight behind these. The resort's main base area is below its namesake, **Winter Park Mountain**, the convenient home for much of the resort's beginner and easier intermediate terrain as well as the halfpipe and terrain parks. Overshadowing it is the larger and more rugged **Mary Jane Mountain**, whose steep long runs – up to 4.5 miles – are sprinkled with steep, narrow, bumpy ridges harboring some of the best mogul runs in Colorado. Mary Jane is also the gateway to reaching the fluffy snows of the high-alpine **Parsenn Bowl**, which rises to 12,060ft, making it a magnet for deep powder. Only via lifts into the Parsenn Bowl can you reach the adjacent **Vasquez Cirque**, whose undeveloped, ungroomed off-piste challenges include cornices and rock outcrops.

Leaving this cirque, you arrive at the third major peak, the uncrowded **Vasquez Ridge**, a gateway to more backcountry and several quiet maintained runs. Winter Park also has three good, imaginatively designed **terrain parks**, features of which are incorporated into the Spring Slash course, when on the last day of skiing in Winter Park skiers don shorts and bathing suits and follow a bizarre course down the mountain to plunge into a sixty-foot pond of icewater.

Parking at the resort is easy, with plenty of free spaces a short shuttle ride from the base, and pay lots offered close to Winter Park.

Lessons and rentals

Winter Park's ski school is excellent, with a huge range of levels and clinics to choose from. Half-day group **lessons** start at $39, with full-day specialty

Winter Park Resort

Information ☎970/726-5514, reservations ☎1-800/453-2525; snow report ☎303/572-7669, ⊛www.winterparkresort.com.

Ticket prices and operating times $63; open mid-Nov to mid-April Mon–Fri 9am–4pm, Sat & Sun 8.30am–4pm.

Mountain statistics Base elevation 9000ft, summit elevation 12,060ft, vertical drop 3060ft, acreage 2762, average snowfall 349in.

Lifts and trails 24 lifts serve 134 trails: beginner 9 percent, intermediate 34 percent, expert 57 percent.

clinics (moguls are a favorite) from $79. Multi-day camps are offered for bump skiers, telemarkers, and women. Kids Adventure Junction, the all-inclusive kids' ski center, serves those aged three to seventeen, while **day care** facilities (☎1-800/420-8093) provide for younger kids – from two months old – or those unwilling to hit the slopes.

There's no shortage of places to **rent** ski and snowboard gear in Winter Park. The resort's rental facilities (☎1-800/979-0328) are located in West Portal, close to the main base area, and at Mary Jane. Basic packages (starting at around $23) include decent equipment, though for performance gear, outlets in town have the edge. Ski Depot Sports, which has four small branches in the area in addition to their downtown store (☎970/726-8055 or 1-800/525-6484, ⓦwww .skidepot.com), has excellent up-to-date ski packages, a more limited selection of snowboards, good boot-fitting and tuning services, and some of the best prices in town. Alternatives include Christy Sports, in Cooper Creek Square, 78930 Hwy-40, (☎970/726-8873, ⓦwww.christysports.com), with ski and snowboard packages from $15 and $22 per day respectively.

Mountain runs

The ski school boasts an enclosed 200-acre **beginner** zone – Discovery Park – where flat open spaces, short tree-lined runs, and gently winding cat tracks beckon. Confident beginners should progress to the ridge between Winter Park Mountain and Mary Jane, where you'll find long green cruisers underneath the High Lonesome Express and to the base of Vasquez Ridge. Unless comfortable in heavy traffic, avoid the busy Cranmer Cutoff back from this area to the base of Winter Park and stick to the slow cat tracks further down the mountain.

There are easy **intermediate** blue runs off every peak and ridge except the Vasquez Cirque. The classic on Winter Park is Cranmer, a wide, rolling cruiser popular with advanced carvers as well as intermediates. For less busy blues, head to the Pioneer lift on Vasquez Ridge, where a few short blacks are suitable for more-talented intermediates. On Mary Jane stay under the Sunnyside lift and dip into easy glades on a gentle pitch through Wildwood and Bellmar bowls. Elsewhere on Mary Jane, as well as on the front face of Winter Park mountain, there are either steeper blues or bump runs that have been groomed on one side. In the exposed Parsenn Bowl, short, gentle powder fields and easy glades are an ideal introduction to off-piste riding.

Winter Park's two biggest **expert** playgrounds are on Mary Jane and in Vasquez Cirque. The latter is exceptional but hard to access, with each run ending in a long green to the base, requiring three different lifts to get back to the summit. If you do decide to session Vasquez try the drops off the exposed cliffs and couloirs of Alphabet and Shadow Chutes or hike to the cornices that span from the double black diamond South Headwall to Jellyroll, a slightly mellower pitch that leads into the trees. For great tree runs, try Backside Parsenn on the opposite side of the valley.

Many experts prefer to focus on the convenient runs of Mary Jane; Riflesight Notch under the Summit Express is littered with hidden cliffs and tempting rocks, and the gladed Pine Cliffs and Sluicebox provide excellent freeriding options. Under the Sunnyside lift try Awe, Baldy's, and Jeff's Chute, all short but sweet double diamonds with a cliff band running through their center.

Winter Park is gradually improving its **freestyle** terrain, but the number and size of jumps are limited and pretty snow-dependant. The halfpipe is excellent, however, and kept lively by tunes blasted from an adjacent yurt. Terrain parks are usually built just above the Snoasis lodge and so easily sessioned using either the

Outrigger or Eskimo Express chairs. For natural hits search the trees on Mary Jane for pinball-type gullies and fallen logs.

Eating and drinking

Winter Park isn't a **dining** standout by any means, but overall the range is sufficient. There's little in the resort village, so most restaurants and bars (several of which do good food, as well) are in town, in plazas and strip malls right beside Hwy-40. Fraser is the best place for groceries.

Laid-back and limited to a few spots, **nightlife** in Winter Park is mostly driven by the locals, so expect to recognize faces after a couple of nights. Drinking kicks off at Winter Park Resort, but peters out early, leaving places along the main drag in Winter Park and Fraser the best option for a late night out. An alternative to spending evenings in bars is to head to the small Silver Screen Cinema (☎970/726-5390) next to *Buckets* (see below).

Unless stated otherwise, all places below are in Winter Park.

Buckets 78415 Hwy-40 ☎970/726-3026. Odd combination of basement laundromat, arcade, and bar that's become a popular hangout for locals. Live music on Monday nights and karaoke on weekends.

Carlos and Maria's Copper Creek Square ☎970/726-9674. Reliably good, inexpensive Mexican restaurant with low-cost margaritas during the daily happy hour, 3.30–6pm.

Carvers 93 Copper Creek Way ☎970/726-8202. Sun-filled bakery with historic prints and ancient skis on the walls, serving a large variety of reasonably priced big breakfasts and some good sandwiches for lunch. A good place to stock up on picnic items.

Crooked Creek Saloon & Eatery 401 Zerex Ave, Fraser ☎970/726-5727. Occasionally wild dining and nightlife venue, serving Mexican and American food and plenty of beer. Regular live music.

Deno's 78911 Hwy-40 ☎970/726-5332. Sports bar serving unexpectedly good food – including pasta ($11), steaks, and spicy Cajun seafood – plus a hundred or so varieties of beer.

Fontenot's Cajun Café Park Plaza, on Hwy-40 ☎970/726-4021. Squeezed into a strip mall, this is a good option to escape the usual ski town menus, Cajun-style: choose from items like gumbo, jambalaya, and crawfish.

Gasthaus Eichler 78786 Hwy-40 ☎970/726-5133. Austrian and German specialties (around $20) like schnitzel, *sauerbraten*, or bratwurst with sauerkraut are served with a gourmet twist in this quaint upscale alpine ski lodge. Reservations recommended.

Hernando's Pizza Pub 78199 Hwy-40 ☎970/726-5409. A comfortable, roomy spot with exceptionally good pizza (try the garlic pie base) and an invitation to decorate a dollar and add it to the 5000-plus already on the walls.

The Last Waltz Restaurant 78336 Hwy-40 ☎970/726-4877. This place opens at 7am to serve satisfying egg-combination breakfasts (the eggs Benedict is great). The lunchtime and dinner menus are more varied, but always include good Mexican food and some superb home-baked desserts.

Lodge at Sunspot Winter Park Resort ☎970/726-1446. Gondola cars are attached to the Zephyr Express chairlift to shuttle foodies to the top of Winter Park Mountain for views over the Continental Divide and a four-course gourmet dinner. Offerings include fresh trout, local lamb, and various wild game options – expect to pay at least $40 per person. Reservations advised. Open for dinner Thurs–Sat.

Rudi's Deli Park Plaza, on Hwy-40 ☎970/726-8955. Huge, tasty deli sandwiches, with chips, coleslaw, or pasta salad, plus homemade breads, soups, chili, and loads of veggie options on the "Herbivore Board." Take out or eat in their small fast food-style space. Half sandwiches from $3.50, whole from $5.

The Shed 78672 Hwy-40 ☎970/726-9912. Pricey but filling Southwestern-Mexican fare is served up at this popular joint, with creative options including chicken baklava, tortilla cashew salmon, Cajun chimichangas, and mango fajitas ($25) – but it's better known as a margarita-drinking and pool-playing hangout, with a well-priced happy hour.

Winter Park Pub 78260 Hwy-40 ☎970/726-4929. Sports bar run by a diehard Green Bay Packers fan; widely referred to as simply "the Pub," and the place to be for free pizza during Monday Night Football.

Middle Park and North Park

North of Winter Park spreads an intermontane basin known as **MIDDLE PARK**, part of a chain of basins that spans north–south across Colorado to include **NORTH PARK** on the Wyoming border, South Park, and the San Luis Valley in the far south. All are surprisingly flat and broad, although they are hemmed in by mountains – some almost 13,000ft high.

Both prime ranching areas, neither Middle or North Park are particularly riveting for visitors, but as corridors through which you must pass en route to Steamboat Springs from either Winter Park or Fort Collins respectively, they are unavoidable. To soak in a bit of their slow pace you might want to break your journey here or even stay the night, as accommodation and food prices around these parts are low.

The two major corridors through Middle and North Park are Hwy-40, which connects Winter Park to Steamboat Springs – linking the modest towns of **Granby**, **Hot Sulphur Springs**, and **Kremmling** in the process – and Hwy-14, which you would drive if you were coming from Fort Collins through the Cache la Poudre Canyon, and which passes through the amiable ragtag town of **Walden**.

These two highways join up at the eastern edge of the region where they combine to climb through forest, crossing back and forth over the Continental Divide at four separate points before arriving at the 9426ft crest of **Rabbit Ears Pass**. From here it's downhill nearly all the way to Steamboat Springs – a journey which demands a fair degree of driver vigilance during winter, as well as appropriate tires or chains.

Granby and around

Sitting high, dry, and windy at the junction of highways 40 and 34, just fourteen miles south of Rocky Mountain National Park, the town of **GRANBY** is notable only as the location of Colorado's most northerly **Amtrak** station. It might just come in handy as a last-ditch choice for accommodation and services within reach of the National Park, though Grand Lake makes a much finer base. During winter, Granby motels also take some of the spillover of weekend ski crowds heading to Winter Park.

Should you end up in Granby for any length of time, try investigating the **Windy Gap Wildlife Viewing Area**, two miles west of town on Hwy-40. This small dammed lake is home to a variety of animals and waterbirds, and a series of interpretive signs helps in identifying the various species of raptor, shorebird, and waterfowl, while coin-operated binoculars can help you pick them out. A wheelchair-accessible trail runs along the north side of the dam and with a little luck and a sharp eye, you might see otters or even beaver ducking amongst the flotsam and jetsam near the banks, or the white-tailed deer who regularly come down for a drink at dusk.

If you pass through Granby in winter you might consider spending a day at its local **ski resort**, **Sol Vista Basin**, two miles south of town (mid-Dec to March; adult day-pass $46; ☎1-888/850-4615, ⓦwww.solvista.com). Describing itself as a "ski area for those fuelled by hot cocoa not adrenaline," Sol Vista won't suit the accomplished skier, but families and beginners may appreciate the lack of crowds, gentle slopes, and clearly demarcated terrain. Its 406 acres spill off a summit elevation of 9202ft, and the resort averages a relatively paltry 220 inches of snow each year. Accommodation is offered in a condo complex, where well-priced lessons and rentals can also be organized. In summer the resort offers **golf**.

Indian Peaks Wilderness

Appearing on maps almost as an adjunct to Rocky Mountain National Park, the **Indian Peaks Wilderness**, encompassing nearly 75,000 acres of mountainous terrain below the RMNP's southern edge, hosts thousands of hikers and climbers yearly. The main attraction is a fine collection of 13,000ft-plus, tundra-covered peaks, and a network of trails and backcountry campsites allowing access to them. Camping permits are required from June until September 15 ($5), and these, along with trail maps and information on hiking conditions, are available at the USFS office in Granby and in Nederland (see p.87). *Colorado's Indian Peaks – Classic Hikes and Climbs*, by Gerry Roach (Fulcrum; 1998), is the comprehensive guide to the area.

Practicalities

The **USFS office**, just southeast of town at 9 Ten Mile Drive (May–Sept Mon–Sat 8am–4.30pm; ☎970/887-4100), has information and backcountry camping permits ($5) for the Indian Peaks Wilderness area just to the north (see box above). If you need to stay, there are several inexpensive **motels** in Granby, the tidiest of which are the *Blue Spruce* (☎970/887-3300; ❹) and *Littletree Inn* (☎970/887-2551; ❸). For a bite to **eat**, check the family-friendly menu at *Remington's*, 52 4th St (☎970/887-3632), which does reasonable Mexican entrees along with all the usual beef and chicken selections, or *Mad Munchies* across the road at 420 E Agate Ave, where you can get good sandwiches and subs made to order.

Hot Sulphur Springs

Perched on Hwy-40 between Granby and Kremmling, **HOT SULPHUR SPRINGS**, with a population of just 480, exudes an altogether more genteel air than its neighbors. The eponymous town springs – allegedly loaded with such health-giving goodies as sodium, chloride, magnesium, potassium, calcium, and fluoride – are now enclosed in a peaceful spa resort, which, together with a decent town museum, comprise fair reasons for a day-visit or even an overnight stay.

The **Grand County Museum**, 110 Byers Ave (June–Aug Wed–Sat 11am–4pm; rest of year variable hours; $4; ☎970/725-3939), features a meticulous collection of buildings salvaged from elsewhere in the region. The main building is a 1924 schoolhouse that contains Native American artifacts, clothing, and firearms from pioneer times, as well as an exhibit on the emergence of winter sports in Colorado.

Hard alongside a busy railway line, the **Hot Sulphur Springs Resort and Spa**, 5617 CO-20 (☎970/725-3306, ⓦwww.hotsulphursprings.com; ❻), has 24 pools and private baths, offers luxurious body wraps and massage, and makes no apologies for its policy of "No smoking, drugs, alcohol, or pets!" Accommodation is in bright motel-style rooms, none of which has a TV, or a single 1840s cabin (❽); **day-use** of the spa facilities is also available (daily 8am–10pm; $16.50; towel rental $1). Other places to **stay** include the clean and cheerful *Canyon Motel*, 221 Byers Ave (☎970/725-3395; ❷), and the very similar *Ute Trail Motel*, 120 E Hwy-40 (☎970/725-0123; ❸). The *County Seat Grill*, 517 Byers, is about the only place to **eat**, with a menu of steaks, burgers, and decent pizzas.

Kremmling

The tiny town of **KREMMLING**, at the junction of highways 40 and 9, is best known for its **excellent fishing**; the Blue River, Colorado River, Muddy

Creek, Williams Fork River, Williams Fork Reservoir, and Green Mountain Reservoir all are nearby. If you're not prepared to just wade in and take your chances with rod and reel, you can have a blue-ribbon fishing experience with Elk Trout ($375/day for two people; ☎970/724-3343), plying their private trout waters with a guide on the Colorado and Blue rivers. If you'd rather get on the Colorado River than in it, the highly regarded Mad Adventures **rafting** company, at the east end of town (☎970/726-5290 or 1-800/451-4844), does half ($44) and full-day ($64) Class II trips. In autumn, Kremmling switches gear slightly, hosting a steady flow of **hunters** heading into the bountiful Arapaho and White River National Forests south of town, in search of a trophy elk, moose, and even black bear.

The tourist **information** office, a tiny log cabin in the "town square" (Mon–Fri 9am–5pm, Sat 10am–5pm, Sun 9am–noon; ☎970/724-3472 or 1-877/573-6654, ⓦwww.kremmlingchamber.com), can help with fishing and hunting advice. For licenses and equipment, stop by the Fishin' Hole at 310 Park Ave, right on Hwy-40 (Mon–Sat 8am–7pm, Sun 8am–5pm). The most venerable **place to stay** is undoubtedly the *Eastin Hotel*, 105 2nd St (☎970/724-3261 or 1-800/546-0815, ⓦwww.hoteleastin.com; ❸), a 1906 boarding house that has operated as a hotel since 1913. For a **meal**, *Big Shooter Coffee*, 204 Park, is an amiable coffeehouse serving up fresh muffins, cinnamon rolls, and ice cream, while the *Quarter Circle Saloon* is the *de rigueur* saloon–restaurant, with burgers, steaks, and Mexican dishes.

Walden and around

WALDEN, 61 miles north of Kremmling via highways 40 and 14, bills itself the "Moose Viewing Capital of Colorado," but what brings most visitors into town in the fall is the opportunity to shoot, not just see, these large mellow beasts. If this doesn't pull your trigger, or you're in town outside the hunting season, you

△ Pioneer Museum, Walden

can explore this friendly but dog-eared town gathered around a single main street and also strike out to nearby sand dunes and wildlife areas.

The only real attraction is the **Pioneer Museum** (mid-June to mid-Sept Sun–Tue 10am–5pm, Thurs & Sat 10am–4pm; donation; ☎970/723-4711), located behind the fine Neoclassical Jackson County Court House, Walden's largest building and only real architectural statement; it's just up the road from the visitor center. Manned by charming local volunteers, the museum spreads over three floors of an old ranch home and tells the story of North Park, which was extremely popular with wildlife and attendant Native American hunters long before trappers and then ranchers and miners moved in. Museum relics therefore include old hunting and ranching tools – with an extensive display of different barbed-wire types – and a selection of disparate oddities like an Edison phonograph, a horse-drawn buggy, and a showroom-condition 1936 Dodge.

The North Sand Hills

Most of Walden's real draws are well beyond town limits, and include the **North Sand Hills**, an area of dunes formed in the same way as the Great Sand Dunes National Park (see p.325). But the North Sand Hills are far more loosely protected by the Bureau of Land Management, so that few areas are out of reach of local rednecks who zip enthusiastically around the dunes on ATVs. Activity is at its most frantic on weekends – particularly Memorial Day, Labor Day, and 4th of July weekends – but outside these times the area is quiet and a wander around on foot well worth the effort. You can also **camp** here for free, though the only facilities are toilets; bring plenty of water and mosquito repellent. The park is 16 miles northeast of Walden and reached via Hwy-125 to Cowdrey and then by following a signed turnoff a mile north. Here CR-6E leads east to North Sand Hills Road, which splits after three miles to lead to the two areas of dunes. The southern area is the more extensive and wanderable of the two – and, though hard work, the trudge up and around the low-slug dunescape reveals some interesting glimpses at the unusually hardy vegetation that manages to survive in the nutrient-poor sands, providing a curious and picturesque contrast to the rest of the fertile valley.

State Forest State Park and the Arapaho National Wildlife Refuge

A more organized Walden-area attraction is the **State Forest State Park** (day pass $5) beside the small town of Gould, 22 miles east of town along Hwy-14. In addition to the usual camping, hiking, and fishing possibilities, there is also a great chance to see **moose**. Several areas of the park have been earmarked as ideal viewing spots, from where it is usually pretty easy to spot the large beasts. For directions, permits, and information drop in at the State Forest State Park Visitor Center, two miles east of Gould at 56750 Hwy-14 (☎970/723-8366 or ⦿www.parks.state.co.us). While you're here don't miss having a look at the **Wire Sculpture Moose**, the work of a Poudre Canyon family who used their welding skills to construct an uncannily realistic specimen, with measurements based on a prize local moose.

Another great place to view wildlife, particularly wildfowl during their migration season, is the 24,000-acre **Arapaho National Wildlife Refuge**, which begins just a mile south of Walden. Information kiosks alongside Hwy-125 (Mon–Fri 7am–4.30pm) will point you in the right direction, which varies according to the season. The best time to visit is during peak migration season in late May when as many as 5000 ducks descend on the wetlands, and in April when Canadian geese begin nesting.

Colorado moose

Until the late 1970s the only **moose** you'd see in Colorado would be stragglers wandering south of the Wyoming border – but concerted efforts over the last thirty years by biologists and wildlife conservationists have changed this. Today a healthy population of over 600 has been nurtured from the 36 initially relocated animals, and a drive on a minor North Park road will often bring you face to face with a thousand-pound moose munching their favorite willow. Part of what's made their reintroduction so successful is the pristine nature of much of the area, which allows an abundance of other species – elk, raptors, beaver, big-horn sheep – to also thrive, and more than half the county's lands are protected to keep things this way.

The best place to start **tracking** moose is with a leaflet issued by the Colorado Division of Wildlife – available at the Walden and the State Forest visitor centers – outlining their favorite haunts. Try getting to these around dawn and dusk, the best times to spot moose, and look hard for movement among the willows and brush fringing streams and ponds. Moose particularly enjoy aquatic plants and are excellent swimmers, with dives of up to eighteen feet recorded. Once spotted, keep your distance from them: though moose rarely pay much attention to humans, when they feel threatened they can become pretty single-minded in their desire to remove you.

Practicalities

The North Park Chamber of Commerce, 416 4th St (Mon–Fri 9am–4.30pm; ☏970/723-4600,) is easily found next to Walden's library (with free Internet), but its hours are unreliable and the amount of printed **information** a little thin. There's better local info, particularly about finding good places to watch wildlife in North Park, at the State Forest State Park Visitor Center (see p.207). The center can also give you information on its four **campgrounds**, rental cabins, and yurts (reservations ☏303/470-1144 or 1-800/678-2267) as well as outlining backcountry camping regulations.

The pick of the town's handful of inexpensive **motels** is the clean and tidy *North Park Inn and Suites*, 625 Main St (☏970/723-4271; ➌), where most of its wood-clad motel units have kitchenettes and all have free WiFi. For rustic luxury try the *Walden Antlers Inn*, 460 Main (☏970/723-8690, ⓦwww .waldenantlersinn.com; ➎), which shares the same address and log-and-rock building with the town's best **dining** option, the *River Rock Café*, (☏970/723-4670). The restaurant's furnishings are also of the rustic dark wood variety, but prices are reasonable and its menu of standards – salad bar, burgers, sandwiches – dependably delicious. Look out for well-priced specials like the $6 meatloaf and excellent selection of homemade pies.

Steamboat Springs and around

The frequently stolen highway sign at the southeastern edge of **STEAMBOAT SPRINGS** simply reads "Welcome to Ski-Town USA." As a piece of self-aggrandizement it would perhaps be better suited to one of Colorado's snootier resorts, but Steamboat actually earned the title for producing more **winter Olympians** than any other ski area in the country – 63 at last count.

The indigenous Ute people were the first to make use of the **mineral sulphur springs** in this part of the Yampa Valley at least eight hundred years ago, and groups of them would stay by the Yampa River for much of the summer. The "Steamboat" tag came much later, courtesy of French trappers, whose imaginations were sparked by the chugging sound made by one particular spring, which remains the official "Steamboat Spring" today. As **miners** in search of silver and copper arrived in increasing numbers throughout the late 1800s, a town site grew and the name stuck.

By 1900, the small-time gold prospectors had given up and given way to "proper" mining companies, which extracted huge deposits of **coal** from the

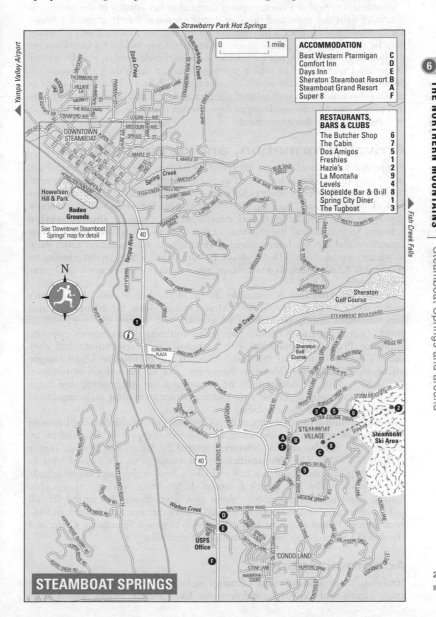

▲ Strawberry Park Hot Springs

▲ Yampa Valley Airport

STEAMBOAT SPRINGS

ACCOMMODATION

Best Western Ptarmigan	C
Comfort Inn	D
Days Inn	E
Sheraton Steamboat Resort	B
Steamboat Grand Resort	A
Super 8	F

RESTAURANTS, BARS & CLUBS

The Butcher Shop	6
The Cabin	7
Dos Amigos	5
Freshies	1
Hazie's	2
La Montaña	9
Levels	4
Slopeside Bar & Grill	8
Spring City Diner	1
The Tugboat	3

▶ Fish Creek Falls

low-lying hills to the south, and **beef cattle** ranches. Both industries pushed for the Denver & Rio Grande **railroad** to extend its line north into Steamboat; its arrival in 1908 spelt boom times for them, and by 1913 more cattle were being transported from Steamboat than from any other single point in the US. The town remained largely a ranchers' domain until the next cultural shift occurred – the opening of the first ski-lifts on nearby **Mount Werner** in 1964.

Steamboat's appeal as a winter-sports destination lies equally in the consistent dumps of light dry snow and the fact that the town still feels as much a home for its residents as it does a playground for its visitors. This lack of pretension may be only slightly apparent in the stylized cowboy-pioneer architecture of the buildings downtown, but events like a summer rodeo series, and the winter "Cowboy Downhill" – in which cowboys race on skis down the mountain before saddling a horse on which to cross the finish line – leave little doubt as to the town's historical and cultural allegiance. And if the locals feel at all hurt that movie stars take up residence in Aspen rather than here, they do a good job of concealing their disappointment.

Arrival, information, and getting around

Yampa Valley Regional Airport (℡970/276-3669) is 22 miles from Steamboat, and during the ski season is serviced by regular **flights** from Denver and several other major US cities; at other times of the year there's just one United Express from Denver. Alpine Taxi (℡970/879-2800 or 1-800/343-7433; Ⓦwww .alpinetaxi.com) handles local **taxi** runs as well as a regular **shuttle service** between Steamboat and the regional airport ($30 one-way) and also between Steamboat and Denver International (twice daily in summer, four times daily in winter; approx 3.5hr; $75 one-way). Be sure to call a few days in advance to ensure you'll have a seat on a shuttle, or you may find yourself stuck in Denver for the night.

Tourist **information** is available at the Chamber Resort Association's visitor center at 1255 Lincoln Ave (Mon–Fri 8am–5pm, Sat 10am–3pm, also Sun 9am–6pm during peak times in summer and winter; ℡970/879-0880, Ⓦwww.steamboatchamber.com), two miles southeast of downtown opposite Sundance Plaza. Staff can help with accommodation reservations and they also sell tickets for most of the town's concerts and events. The USFS **ranger office**, 925 Weiss Drive (Mon–Fri 8am–5pm, also Sat 9am–noon in summer; ℡970/879-1870), is another mile or so east and has information and maps for hiking and camping in the area, and for winter recreation including cross-country ski trails and snowmobiling.

Getting around without a car can be a chore because of the distance between the mountain resort and downtown, but most of the pain is alleviated by an efficient and free **local bus system**, operated by Steamboat Springs Transit (℡970/879-3717). The **five routes** are color-coded, so it's a good idea to collect a schedule on board any bus and take a look at the map inside. Schedules vary seasonally, but there's frequent daily service year-round (roughly 6.30am–2am) for the greater Steamboat area, from downtown to the ski hill and neighboring "condo land." From mid-November until mid-April, Steamboat Springs Transit also runs a shuttle service between Steamboat, Craig, and Hayden ($3.50 one-way, call for schedule information).

Accommodation

Steamboat's **accommodation** offerings include five-star resort hotels, mid-range chains and ski area condos, some basic motor lodges, and a little traditional B&B hospitality for good measure. A more remote alternative is to stay in one of the many ranches in the surrounding area. Prices are highest during winter, and you'll need to reserve well in advance during the peak ski season. On summer weekends, many of the cheaper places are taken over completely by large groups attending various events, so don't count on just showing up and finding a room even then. As Steamboat has no hostel, the best accommodation options for those on a tight budget are the downtown motor lodges on Lincoln Avenue.

If you're here to **ski** then you might find yourself in either **Steamboat Village**, the development on and immediately around the Steamboat ski area, or the aptly nicknamed "**condo land**," a mini-district of homes and condo buildings on the south side of Walton Creek Road. There's plenty to do around Steamboat Village, which has its own clutch of bars, restaurants, equipment- and bike-hire places, and of course the ski resort itself, and it's quite possible to stay, eat, and relax there without ever feeling the need to visit downtown. By contrast there's nothing to do and nowhere to go out in "condo land," so while you might be sleeping there, you'll certainly be looking to the mountain or downtown when it comes time to go out and play. Steamboat Central Reservations (☎970/879-0740 or 1-877/783-2628, ⓦ www.steamboat.com) can arrange ski packages and all accommodation, including condo rental. With last-minute lift-and-lodging deals for around $80–100 per person per night they are well worth considering for stays of a week or more. Steamboat Resorts (☎970/879-800 or 1-800/509-9578, ⓦ www.steamboatresorts.com) is the largest property management company in town and your best resource for choosing condos. Most properties provide outdoor tubs, ski shuttles, and laundry services.

There is one **campground** in Steamboat and three State Park campgrounds within thirty miles of town; the latter incur a day-use charge of $5 per day in addition to a camping fee. At a pinch, the *Dry Lake Campground* (eight sites; $10) is the closest USFS campground, six miles from Steamboat, but it has no drinking water; to get there drive northeast on CO-36, then east on CO-38. A better option, particularly if you want to go for a soak in the hot springs, is *Strawberry Hot Springs* (see p.214), which has a few tent sites ($40 for two) on its wooded grounds.

Hotels and motels

Alpiner Lodge 424 Lincoln Ave ☎970/879-1430. This motor lodge boasts nothing fancier than a central, downtown location. Rooms are clean, and not bad value even in ski season, when you can probably negotiate a rate if you book and pay for several days well in advance. ⑤

Best Western Ptarmigan Inn 2304 Apres Ski Way ☎970/879-1730 or 1-800/538-7519, ⓦ www.steamboat-lodging.com. This is where you'll find the cheapest hotel rooms on the mountain – although juxtaposed with the *Sheraton* and *Steamboat Grand*, that's not really saying much. Ski-in, ski-out from this property, whose rooms have tiny bathrooms but a few handy extras like a bar/fridge, coffeemaker, and, in some, Internet access. ⑦

The BunkHouse Lodge 3155 S Lincoln Ave ☎970/871-9121. Wood-beamed motel located

between Hwy-40 and the Yampa River on the edge of town. Some of the standard – though spotless and newly furnished – motel rooms have river views, and all have mini-fridges and access to an outdoor hot tub and a spacious lounge, where the gratis continental breakfast is served. A free shuttle operates from the lodge's door to the ski area. ③

The Home Ranch 54880 CR-129, Clark ☎970/879-1780, ⓦ www.homeranch.com. Genuine ranch elegance seventeen miles north of Steamboat in the Elk River Valley. Along with a four-star restaurant, indoor equestrian center, and 12 miles of cross-country trails are six handsome cabins and as many snug lodge rooms, some with vaulted ceilings, all beautifully appointed. Cabins ⑨, lodge rooms ⑧

Hotel Bristol 917 Lincoln Ave ☎970/879-3083 or 1-800/851-0872, ⓦ www .steamboathotelbristol.com. This agreeably relaxed and homey old red-brick hotel has tiny rooms, but is as central as you get in downtown Steamboat. A decent free breakfast – a step up from a basic continental – is a nice bonus, as is complimentary Internet access. Weekend rates increase by a third. ⑤

Inn at Steamboat 3070 Columbine Drive ☎970/879-2600 or 1-800/872-2601, ⓦwww .inn-at-steamboat.com. This inexpensive hotel, amid the sea of condos four blocks from the ski area, has the friendly if slightly worn air of a much-used ski lodge. The bright but rather cramped pine-furnished rooms, however, are in tip-top shape, some with arresting mountain views from their balconies. Extras include a heated outdoor pool, sauna, laundry, pool table, generous continental breakfasts, complimentary hot drinks, and evening socials. ③

Mariposa Bed & Breakfast 855 Grand St ☎970/879-1467 or 1-800/578-1467, ⓦwww .mariposabandb.homestead.com. Southwestern-style downtown home with only three rather pokey guest bedrooms, one of which sports an impressive handmade log bed; all have private bathrooms. The breakfast buffet includes fresh smoothies, home-baked goods, and huevos with green chili. ④

Nite's Rest Motel 601 Lincoln Ave ☎970/879-1212. Although it doesn't look too promising from the outside, the *Nite's Rest* has clean, basic rooms to go with its central location. ⑤

Nordic Lodge 1036 Lincoln Ave ☎970/879-0531 or 1-800/364-0331, ⓦwww.rockymountaininn .com/nordiclodge.html. Your basic 1960s motor lodge, but the simple rooms are fastidiously clean, and there's an outdoor pool and hot tub. Best of the rooms are those with their own fridge and microwave. ④

Rabbit Ears Motel 201 Lincoln Ave ☎970/879-1150 or 1-800/828-7702, ⓦwww.rabbitearsmotel .com. The motel's large pair of pink neon rabbit's ears marks the eastern edge of downtown Steam-boat. It's a friendly, comfortable place to stay, with useful features in rooms which include microwave, coffeemaker, and fridge, and the rates include a simple continental breakfast. There are 65 rooms of varying sizes, and some can accommodate four people – ideal for a cozy ski vacation. ⑥

Steamboat Bed & Breakfast 442 Pine St ☎970/879-5724 or 1-877/335-4321, ⓦwww .steamboatb-b.com. Bright and airy Victorian B&B two blocks from Lincoln Ave. The interior feels like a very well-kept home, with antiques tastefully strewn around the seven simple rooms and the cheery dining room where the chatty innkeepers serve hearty cooked breakfasts. Other highlights include a conservatory, outdoor deck, and hot

tub. Rates are often negotiable for stays of three or more nights; advance bookings for winter are essential. ⑦

🏃 **Steamboat Grand** 2300 Mt Werner Circle, ☎970/871-5050 or 1-877/269-2628, ⓦwww.steamboatgrand.com. The resort's mammoth flagship condo-hotel, within walking distance of the slopes. Rooms range from a standard king-bed studio to a five-bedroom pent-house, and there are amenities to match, including restaurants, bars, and a large fitness center with outdoor pools and hot tubs, sauna, and steam room; *The Cabin* restaurant is one of Steamboat's most elegant fine-dining choices (see p.221 for review). ⑧

🏃 **Strawberry Hot Springs** ☎970/879-0342, ⓦwww.strawberryhotsprings.com. Basic but idyllic accommodation is provided on the rambling wooded grounds around the hot springs. The cabins and covered wagons are just a step up from camping – linens are not provided, showering is done in the bathhouse, and bare futons, a gas fireplace, charcoal grill, and gas lamp comprise the amenities. Luxury comes in the form of a converted caboose, complete with bedding, bathroom, and solar lights. Prices may seem a little steep, but all include unlimited use of hot springs during your stay. In winter you'll need a 4WD with winter tires for the last leg of the seven-mile journey from Steamboat Springs. ②

Western Lodge 1122 Lincoln Ave ☎970/879-1050 or 1-800/622-9200, ⓦwww.western-lodge .com. Tired motor lodge with a bleak parking lot, though most rooms have been renovated fairly recently and the larger ones have two queen beds and a fridge and microwave. ⑤

Campgrounds

Pearl Lake State Park twenty-six miles north via CO-129 ☎970/879-3922. Along with 36 tent sites ($14) there are also a couple of very comfortable six-person yurts (④) available for rent at Pearl Lake; each has a double futon and four single bunk beds, with electricity and screened windows. No showers.

Stagecoach State Park seventeen miles south via State Hwy-131, then CO-14 ☎970/736-2436. Good fishing in Stagecoach Reservoir and Morrison Creek is a plus; showers available. 92 sites; $7–18.

Steamboat Campground two miles west of downtown on Hwy-40 ☎970/879-0273. This well-appointed campground has summer-only shaded tent sites on their own little island in the Yampa River, and a handful of no-frills cabins which are available year-round. The laundry and shower block is immaculate, and there is even a communal outdoor hot tub. Tent sites $27, cabins $65. **Steamboat Lake State Park** twenty-seven miles north via CO-129 ⊕ 970/879-3922. The camper services building at Dutch Hill Marina has laundry and shower facilities, and fishing (rainbow and cutthroat trout), swimming, and boat hire are available. There's a visitor center here, too (Sun–Thurs 8am–7pm, Fri & Sat 8am–10pm). 188 sites; ones with electrical hookups $16, tent sites $12.

Downtown Steamboat

The ten blocks of Lincoln Avenue that comprise **downtown Steamboat** is where you'll find most of the town's restaurants and bars, as well as clothing and outdoor gear shops. As Steamboat's "old town," it's pleasantly redolent of its **ranching history**, with a touch of the Old West in the storefronts, not to mention an impressive rodeo arena just across the river (see box p.214). Of course, between the ski resort and the summer recreation opportunities, you may not be spending much time hanging about Lincoln Avenue. But there's no doubting that one of the real niceties of visiting a ski town with over one hundred years of history is that it's not just a bunch of hotels thrown up in front of a ski lift. Really the only two things you might consider doing in town are a (smelly) **walking tour** of the various **sulphur springs** – or better still a soak in one of them – and a visit to the local history **museum**.

Hot springs

To examine the **springs**, you need nothing besides your two legs and the visitor center's free walking-tour map You can otherwise indulge yourself a little at the **Steamboat Springs Health and Recreation Center**, 135 Lincoln Ave (Mon–Fri 5.30am–10pm, Sat & Sun 8am–9pm; $7.50; ⊕ 970/879-1828), which offers hot mineral pools, an outdoor lap-pool and waterslide, and workout

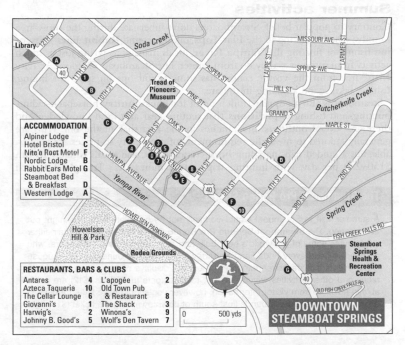

ACCOMMODATION

Alpiner Lodge	**F**
Hotel Bristol	**C**
Nite'o Rest Motel	**F**
Nordic Lodge	**B**
Rabbit Ears Motel	**G**
Steamboat Bed & Breakfast	**D**
Western Lodge	**A**

RESTAURANTS, BARS & CLUBS

Antares	4	L'apogée	2
Azteca Taqueria	10	Old Town Pub	
The Cellar Lounge	6	& Restaurant	8
Giovanni's	1	The Shack	3
Harwig's		Winona's	9
Johnny B. Good's	5	Wolf's Den Tavern	7

0   500 yds

DOWNTOWN STEAMBOAT SPRINGS

facilities. Better still are the secluded 105°F **Strawberry Park Hot Springs** seven miles north of town (Sun–Thurs 10am–10.30pm, Fri & Sat 10am– midnight; $10; ☎970/879-0342, ⓦwww.strawberryhotsprings.com); in winter these are only accessible by 4WD. Here you can slip into a hot pool in a forest setting; the effect is best when it's snowing, making this one of Steamboat's true aprés-ski traditions. If you don't have a car, the springs are accessible by shuttle using Sweet Pea Tours ($25/person including admission; ☎970/879-5820).

Tread of Pioneers Museum

With its collection reflecting the past century of local life, Steamboat's **Tread of Pioneers Museum**, 800 Oak St (summer daily 11am–5pm winter Tues–Sat 11am–5pm; $5; ☎970/879-2214), is most worthy of attention for its **ski exhibit**. The display pays homage to an impressively large group of local skiing and snowboarding stars, as well as Steamboat's father-figure of skiing, Norwegian Carl Howelsen, and it's fun to see for yourself the evolution of skis, boots, and poles. Some of the old metal ski-boots would not look out of place in a film of a lunar landing, while most of the ancient wooden poles prove not all designs have changed so greatly.

A small firearms collection and the display of Ute artifacts upstairs are all staples of these sorts of museums, while two more distinctive items are a lovely square parlor-style grand piano, c.1868, which you can actually play, and an extraordinary piece of 1939 film footage of the spectacular fire which destroyed Steamboat's *Cabin Hotel*, killing two people. Built in 1909, the *Cabin* was the hub of social activity in Steamboat; watching the place burn from the perspective of the photographer – who presumably had just climbed out a window to safety – is an eerie experience.

Summer activities

Contrary to popular belief, Steamboaters don't hibernate during the snow-free months; whether hiking in the **Flat Tops**, biking around **Rabbit Ears Pass**, or just fishing or floating the **Yampa River**, locals manage to wring just as much activity from summer as they do from winter. The Steamboat "Outdoor Activity Map," free from the visitor center, has some useful tips on spots for hiking, fishing, biking, and kayaking in the area.

Steamboat is also a popular launch point for **backcountry** horseback-riding, hunting, and fishing **expeditions** that require gear and local knowledge, and there are several outfitters and ranches in the area that fit the bill. Trips are generally tailored to meet the requirements of each party so prices are negotiable, but a guided trip including horses, equipment, and meals is likely to run $150–220 per day, with hunting trips much more. Del's Triangle 3 Ranch

The Steamboat Pro Rodeo Series

A summer visit to Steamboat would certainly not be complete without a night out at the rodeo. The **Steamboat Springs Pro Rodeo Series** is no amateur affair either – it features some of the world's best bull- and bronco-riders and calf-ropers, who go head-to-head every Friday and Saturday night from mid-June until late August. Other events include barrel-riding, and there are displays of trick-riding along with races and other activities which kids get to participate in. Tickets ($12) are available in advance from visitor information; however you should have little trouble just showing up at the rodeo grounds (just south of downtown) to get a ticket ($13) right before the 7.30pm start.

(☎970/879-3495, ⓦwww.steamboathorses.com), roughly twenty miles north of Steamboat near the town of Clark, offers two-hour horseback rides right up to five-day hunting camps in the Mt Zirkel Wilderness; High Meadows Ranch, 24 miles south (☎970/736-8416 or 1-800/457-4453, ⓦwww.hmranch.com), has self-contained log chalets with kitchen, bathroom, and wood-stove, and offers a similar range of horseback trips.

Fishing and rafting

Fly-fishing for brown and rainbow trout in the Yampa River is popular almost year-round, and Bucking Rainbow Outfitters, upstairs at 402 Lincoln Ave (☎970/879-8747 or 1-888/810-8747), has fishing gear to buy or rent, licenses, and guided trips on their private waters. Another leisurely river activity is **tubing** – cruising the rapids on an old tire inner tube; Buggywhip's (☎970/879-8033 or 1-800/759-0343) rents tubes for $10. On any summer day you'll also see people in kayaks and rafts, although the Yampa is by no means the most challenging white-water **rafting** experience to be had. Buggywhip's and Bucking Rainbow both offer a range of summer rafting opportunities on the Yampa or Colorado rivers (both Class II), Elk or Eagle rivers (both Class III), and Cross Mountain Canyon (July–Aug only; Class IV). Trips start at $43 for the Yampa, $59 for a half-day on the Colorado, and $115 for the hair-raising Cross Mountain. For **kayak** rental and instruction, contact Mountain Sports Kayak School (☎970/879-8794); a basic class costs $25 for an hour, while a half-day's river instruction runs about $100.

Biking

A well-maintained **bike** path runs the length of downtown Steamboat, much of it alongside the river. The most popular mountain bike trails within easy reach of Steamboat are those on Howelson Hill and at Steamboat Resort. The Howelson Hill trails are easily found, simply by riding up the fire road to climber's right of the ski hill. This climbs for a couple of miles before the first of half a dozen marked loops appear on the left. The best option is to cycle to the end of the trail to a grand lookout over the town and resort, before heading back down the hill via each of the loops, which becomes a long and thrilling descent.

Even better and far longer are the trails at Steamboat Resort, with the additional attraction that you can take the gondola (daily late June to early Sept; weekends only early June and late Sept; $25). Beginner and intermediate riders will find plenty to amuse themselves, though the quality of the expert-level lift-accessible trails on the lower mountain does not really compare to the likes of Winter Park or Keystone. However, if you make the effort to climb the dirt road to the top of Storm Peak, you'll be amply rewarded by a descent on the delightful **Pete's Wicked Trail**, which snakes across high alpine meadows and is certainly among Colorado's best.

Perhaps the best half-day loop from town is to ride the **Spring Creek Trail**, which can be done as a twelve-mile loop from town by cycling out along CO-36 and then climbing up CO-38 to the trail head near the *Dry Lake Campground*. From here it is a glorious roller-coaster ride back into town on a trail that twists and turns through a valley of pines and aspens and is suitable for fairly inexperienced riders, but still enjoyable for experts.

Another great out-of-town option is to ride out to the **Mad Creek** trail-head, six miles north along CO-129, from where you have a fairly technical climb on a rocky trail alongside the western edge of the Mt Zirkel Wilderness. Steamboat Trading Company, 1850 Ski Time Square Drive (☎970/879-0083),

△ Flat Top Mountain

and Ski Haus, at Hwy-40 and Pine Grove Rd (☎970/879-0385), both **rent bikes** for around $30 per day. If you have some ambitious biking in mind, it's a good idea to stop in at the USFS office (see p.210) to collect some trail maps and fine-tune your plans.

Hiking

Of the **hiking** opportunities near town, **Fish Creek Falls** is the most popular trail and definitely worth doing. The trailhead is four miles up Fish Creek Falls Road from behind the post office; the parking area ($5) is just below a wheelchair-accessible quarter-mile trail. A second trail from here switchbacks across Fish Creek for three strenuous miles to the falls themselves – where your reward is in the form of several pools ideal for a fresh mountain dip – and another two miles on to Long Lake. More secluded hiking is to be had in the **Mt Zirkel Wilderness** north of town (trail map available with backcountry campsite info from the USFS office), although the whole area has been littered with downed timber since a huge storm and "blowdown" in October of 1997; the subsequent regeneration of the area is still in its rather unattractive infancy. The very best hiking in the area, though, is in the nearby **Flat Tops** (see box opposite).

Winter activities

With an average annual snowfall of over 27 feet, the majority of winter visitors come to **ski** or **board Steamboat Resort's** powdery slopes. Besides offering great conditions for skiers and boarders of all abilities, Steamboat has in recent years become generally considered one of the country's best all-round winter-sports spots. **Howelson Hill** provides for ski jumpers, while surrounding back-country areas have become something of a haven for telemark enthusiasts, with locals increasingly embracing the technical demands of the deep knee-bend turn. If you are inexperienced in the backcountry, you might be tempted by guided ski tours. Other popular local options include snowshoeing, snowmobiling and even a local winter driving school. The best first stop for most backcountry activities is the **USFS office** (see p.210), which provides lots of free maps and advice.

The 235,000 acres of the **Flat Tops** comprise the second-largest wilderness area in Colorado, their distinctive tabletop headlands dominated by the broad grasslands of the White River Plateau. Even from a distance, this chunky, squared-off mountain range looks like an upturned box, punctuated by a handful of daunting 13,000–14,000ft peaks. The fact that the area is home to the largest **elk herd** in Colorado has hunters dewy with anticipation each September, but otherwise the animals are left alone and the Flat Tops retain an air of remoteness beloved by hiking enthusiasts.

Although billed as a Colorado Scenic Byway, unsealed CO-8, which makes its winding way across the Flat Tops, is not really worth driving just for driving's sake; it does, however, provide access to many of the 39 **trailheads** that lead in to the heart of these mountains. The towns of Yampa and Meeker mark the east and west gateways respectively, and each has a USFS office which supplies free detailed trail maps that include informative narratives of many hikes along with the hard facts on distance, elevation, and level of difficulty. There are no "must-do" hikes in an area whose selling point is the chance to experience a little lonesomeness, but the destination which you're likely to hear the most about is the **Devil's Causeway**. This is a section of the plateau divide which separates the Bear River and Williams Fork drainages; a steep three-mile hike takes you to a point at 11,800ft where the plateau narrows to a heart-thumping four feet wide, with a sheer drop of 1500 feet into the valley on either side. The trail that leads to the causeway begins beside Stillwater Reservoir, about fifteen miles from Yampa along Forest Road 900 (take Forest Road 7 west from Yampa for six miles and then drive a further nine miles on Forest Road 900). This same trailhead also allows access to trails to **Trappers Lake**, a popular fishing and recreation spot (five miles one-way; also accessible by car via Trappers Lake Rd) and **Flat Top Mountain**, which commands a panoramic view of up to one hundred miles from its elevation of 12,354ft (four miles one-way). There are also a number of trails which provide access to secluded streams and lakes which support populations of various types of trout; best of these are the Marvine and East Marvine trails, located 35 miles east of Meeker via the scenic byway.

To collect **information** and **maps** in Yampa, visit the USFS office at 300 Roselawn Ave (Mon–Sat 8am–5.30pm; ☎970/638–4516); for details on access to the Flat Tops from the town of Meeker, see p.404. Thirteen USFS **campgrounds** ($12–15) are scattered throughout the Flat Tops too; most are open from mid-May until mid-November, although the area is crawling with hunters from late September so few hikers are inclined to stay out overnight during the fall. Check with a USFS office for a map of campgrounds and for information on amenities and current conditions.

In and around town

Locally, the tamest form of skiing is found on the *Sheraton's* golf course, just off Mt Werner Road, which in winter becomes the Steamboat Ski Touring Center (trail pass $12, gear rental $11, lesson packages from $30; ☎970/879-8180), a **cross-country** skiing facility with 19 miles of trails below the resort. Another good option on the fringes of town is the easy **snowshoe** trek up to Fish Creek Falls (see p.216). If you'd rather skate than hike, head to the **Howelsen Ice Arena**, beside the rodeo grounds at 234 Howelsen Parkway ($5, skate rental $3; ☎970/879-0341). Public skating hours are limited to a couple of sessions daily, so phone ahead.

Besides the usual sleigh rides, horseback riding, snowmobile trips, and snowshoe tours arranged by companies like Steamboat Lake Outfitters (☎970/879-4404 or 1-800/342-1889, ⓦwww.steamboatoutfitters.com), and ice-climbing, dogsledding, balloon trips, and glider flights arranged through the visitor center, Steamboat boasts a unique off-slope activity in the form of the **Bridgestone**

Winter Driving School (from $145; ☎970/879-6104, ⓦwww.winterdrive .com). Here you can throw a car into a 360° turn on ice at the only center of its kind in the US. Cut entirely out of snow, the ten-corner track is used to train Colorado police, truckers, and those who'd rather get into a skid than learn to get out of one.

Out of town

Locals who have tired of options around town often just drive up to **Rabbit Ears Pass**, southeast of town, and explore the carefully segregated USFS trails on **tele-skis**, **snowshoes**, or **snowmobiles**. Rocky Mountain Ventures (☎970/870-8440, ⓦwww.verticalgrip.com) guides backcountry skiing and riding, snowshoeing, and ice-climbing (with instruction) in this area. Twelve miles northeast of town, Buffalo Pass is another oft-used spot for all these activities, as is Steamboat Lake State Park (trail fee $5 per vehicle; ☎970/879-3922). **Rental gear** for cross-country touring and snowshoeing can be hired at Straightline, 8th St and Lincoln Ave (☎970/879-7568). This retailer, as well as most others, have brochures at the visitor center that give a discount of twenty percent on rental prices.

Full-scale guided backcountry adventures are offered by Steamboat Powder Cats, 1724 Mt Werner Circle (☎970/871-4260 or 1-800/288-0543, ⓦwww .steamboatpowdercats.com), who will take you **cat-skiing** in the Buffalo Pass area on 10,000 acres of aspen-, spruce-, and fir-strewn slopes. With plenty of terrain to explore and a catered lunch stop at an attractive cabin in the woods, this is backcountry skiing at its least threatening, and strong riders should opt for the more challenging Level III expeditions to Soda Mountain. Use of powder skis and boards is included in the price (around $300). Full-moon descents ($150) and nonskiing scenic tours ($125) in the twelve-person Bombardier cats are also offered. All of these activities should be reserved well in advance.

Steamboat Ski Resort

Steamboat Ski Resort is famous for its prodigious falls of light dry snow, or "champagne powder," as it's called and even trademarked hereabouts. Such brochure-fodder is usually easy to dismiss, but the truth is Steamboat deserves attention as one of the top all-around winter sports destinations in the region. The dry quality of the snow is vital, but the glorious groves of aspen across its five peaks make for a scenic setting, and the ski area's size means there's little repetition and crowding is rarely a problem.

Concrete condos and a handful of restaurants around the base of the ski area make up **Steamboat Village**. Gondola Square, its center, is encircled by ticket offices and ski shops and naturally is where the gondola begins to swing up lower Christie Peak to Thunderhead Peak. **Christie Peak**, home to a meadow of beginner lifts and trails and the terrain park and pipe, has its own lifts, so those skiing only here can avoid the gondola crowds.

Above the top of the gondola – working from left to right on the trail map – are the steep, tree-filled bowls of **Mount Werner**, the wide-open runs and evergreens of **Storm Peak**, and the aspen glades and long cruisers on **Sunshine Peak**. Out of sight of the base area on the back of the mountain is **Morningside Park**, a small area of pine glades and powder. A fair amount of crossing from lift to lift is required to navigate from peak to peak, though very little traversing is necessary on your way up the mountain. Coming down is a different story, particularly to skier's right of the mountain; BC Ski Way and Right-O-Way are both flat and, come late afternoon, busy, making them a real pain for novice snowboarders and those intimidated by crowds.

Steamboat Ski Resort

Information ☎970/879-6111 or 1-877/237-2628, ⊛www.steamboat.com; snow report ☎970/879-7300.

Ticket prices and operating times $76; lower mountain only $51; open late Nov to early April 8.30am–3.30pm.

Mountain Statistics Base elevation 6900ft, summit elevation 10,568ft, vertical drop 3668ft, acreage 2965, average snowfall 334in.

Lifts and trails 25 lifts serve 164 trails: beginner 13 percent, intermediate 56 percent, expert 31 percent.

6

If you are driving up to Steamboat Ski Resort for the day, you'll find two pay **parking lots** close to the slopes off Gondola Square, as well as a free shuttle-served lot closer to Hwy-40 on Mount Werner Road.

Lift tickets, lessons, and rentals

There are few **lift pass** deals at Steamboat, but the resort can be economical for families on a long stay, as kids ski and rent gear for free when their parents ski or rent for five days or more. At $29 for a full day ($77 with lift ticket), **lessons** for beginners are inexpensive, especially for those with their own gear. Half-day lessons for intermediates and above start at $57. The ski school (☎1-800/299-5017) also offers more expensive bump clinics, women's seminars, pipe sessions, and the opportunity to get first tracks an hour before the upper lifts open. Private adaptive skiing clinics cost $75 for three hours, with equipment available but not included. **Daycare** facilities are on hand for kids aged between six months and six years at the Kids'Vacation Center (☎970/871-5375 or 1-800/299-5017).

Among the best value around for **rentals** is Ski Haus, 1450 S Lincoln Ave (☎970/879-0385), located midway between the town and the mountain. They have good prices on a wide variety of ski rentals, from basic shaped ($20–37/day) to telemark ($29/day) and cross-country ($12/day) packages, as well as inexpensive Burton board rentals ($29/day). Otherwise try Christy Sports, (☎970/879-9011), or Powdertools (☎970/879-1645), both by the gondola base.

Mountain runs

The base of the mountain is dedicated to **beginners** and is served by five magic carpets and three short chairlifts. Treeless, wide, and gentle, the slopes are ideal, but by being surrounded by buildings, crisscrossed with lift towers and other skiers bombing back to base, it's not the most attractive or quiet place to learn. An alternative is to take the Christie lift to access the more interesting green runs that wind their way back through the trees to base. Novice snowboarders in particular may find the wide easy blues off the Sunshine lift the best and quietest place to start linking turns with a bit more momentum.

For a quick mountain heads-up, intermediate and expert skiers can turn up for one of the **free tours** that leave from the top of the gondola daily at 10.30am. After that, **intermediates** should find it easy to explore the ribbons of blues rolling off every lift. Keep an eye on the trail markings, though, as it's easy to stray onto the blacks. All the intermediate runs on Sunshine Peak – usually the quietest slopes – are wide, fast, and generally bathed in Colorado sunshine. Straddling the resort boundary, Tomahawk, a wide roller-coaster cruiser, is perhaps the most varied run, including a couple of mellow aspen glades.

On powder days, Buddy's Run off Storm Peak is at its best, giving a taste of intermediate-level backcountry-style bowl riding, while **experts** should head straight for the Priest Creek lift-line and the adjacent tree runs, Shadows and Closet, where the snow really piles up for skiers and boarders with steely nerves and sturdy helmets. But there are black bump runs and glades scattered across the mountain, with short, steep runs off almost every lift, and the steep chutes of the Christmas Tree Bowl are often in great shape. If you've got plenty of energy you can take the Morningside Park lift and hike up to the metal weather tower for access to the best powder and cliff drops on the mountain.

Back down by the base area Steamboat's **Mavericks Superpipe** is named for the notorious California wave, and for good reason. the expertly groomed pipe is always over 500 feet long. Conveniently it has its own lift, Bashor, which also serves the large **terrain park**, where a whopping sound system booms.

Howelsen Hill

Carl Howelsen, a one-time Barnum & Bailey circus star, arrived from Norway in 1913 and introduced ski-jumping to the ranching folk of Steamboat, who inexplicably took to the eccentric sport by quickly enrolling their kids in ski-jumping lessons. **Howelsen Hill** (day tickets $15; ℡970/879-8499), located directly opposite downtown Steamboat on the other side of the Yampa River, is now one of the oldest continuously operating ski area in Colorado, and Howelsen himself – the "Flying Norseman" – is rightly revered as the state's father of skiing. Steamboat's Winter Sports Club, formed by Howelsen in 1915, was the first official ski club west of the Mississippi. Today, the US Ski Jumping Team trains on the five jumping ramps here, while others enjoy the 70 acres of skiable terrain serviced by two surface tows and one chairlift rising from the edge of town. Snowboarders can make use of a small terrain park and half-pipe, and the hill is lit for **night skiing** (Mon & Fri 4–6pm, Tues–Thurs 5–8pm; $5). Weekly alpine races and public ski jumping nights are held for the experienced as well; it's great fun to participate, or even just to watch.

Eating

Steamboat's **restaurants** include a broad range of cuisines and menu prices, with plenty of cowboy staples like steaks and Mexican food, but also fine French and Italian places and a couple of excellent traditional diners, too. The lion's share are downtown, though satisfying meals are still easy to come by if staying near the slopes.

Antares 57 8th St ℡970/879-9939. Expensive but low-key bistro with a warm and opulent feel that would not be out of place in New York City. The "New World Cuisine" menu includes items like honey shrimp ($17), tournedos of beef "LeBrun" ($26), and sesame-crusted ahi tuna salad ($16). Two huge bonuses are a carefully stocked wine-cellar and some fabulously indulgent desserts – go for a choco-late cappuccino mousse torte or a Meyer's Rum creme brulee ($6). Also has a comfy bar and live jazz on Friday and Saturday nights. Daily 6pm until late.
Azteca Taqueria 402 Lincoln Ave ℡970/870-9980. For great, inexpensive Mexican food on the go, you can't do better than this. With just a couple of tables inside and three more out front on a

sunny deck, locals cheerfully line up at the counter to order burritos, enchiladas, or daily specials like the $6 pork green chili. The enormous $6 breakfast burrito will easily set you up for a day's hiking or skiing. Daily 9am–8pm.
The Butcher Shop Ski Time Square Drive ℡970/879-2484. Family-owned since 1971 and with a genuinely rustic Western atmosphere, this carnivores' delight would probably be better known were it not tucked away from the rest of the on-mountain action. Entrees, including prime cut of beef, rack of lamb, or sauteed elk loin, are priced between $18–30 and are each served up with fresh bread, baked potato, and all the salad you can eat (salad bar on its own is $11).

The Cabin 2300 Mt Werner Circle ⊤970/871-5500. Simple elegance defines the interior of this restaurant inside the *Steamboat Grand Resort*. The former personal chef to John Denver oversees proceedings, and has created a menu which tackles the Rocky Mountains theme – lots of beef and lamb – with considerable panache. The rack of lamb or filet mignon are both excellent choices, but there are good seafood options such as sea bass and salmon as well, and the chilled king prawns come with a spicy cocktail sauce that's at least two parts vodka. Daily for dinner; expensive, with entrees generally around the $30 mark.

Café Diva Torian Plum Plaza, Mountain Village ⊤970/871-0508. Despite the unpromising exterior, this place does fine, intimate slopeside dining, using only the freshest ingredients for their off-beat starters (such as the trout dip served with raisin nut toast), excellent salads, and classic entrees, including elk tenderloin, filet mignon, and Alaskan halibut. The presentation is impeccable as well, making this an expensive but worthwhile splurge.

Creekside Café and Grill 131 11th St ⊤970/879-4925. Quiet breakfast and lunch option, tucked away from the main strip and mostly patronized by locals. Full, fresh breakfast menu includes multiple eggs Benedict and pancake and waffle variations with plenty of fresh fruit. Lunch is based around sandwiches and salads; dinner features inventive pastas. Live local music on Friday nights. Tues–Sun 7am–2pm, dinner served Wed–Sat 5–9.30pm.

Dos Amigos 1910 Mt Werner Rd ⊤970/879-4270. Mexican restaurant which pulls a good après-ski crowd every afternoon. Standard dishes like enchiladas and fajitas are $10–13, a New York strip $15 (dinner only). Après-ski munchies include free chips and salsa and half-price appetizers 4.30–6pm, and if there's nowhere special you have to have to be for a while, try a "Chickarita," a sort of rocket-fuel margarita created by a former barman ("Chiok"), which tastes really pleasant – just before it lands on you like a ton of bricks. Daily: summer from 3.30pm, winter from 2.30pm, until late.

🏃 Freshies 595 S Lincoln Ave ⊤970/879-8099. Isolated between town and the mountain, this diner is mainly visited by locals, who enthuse about the fresh home-cooking and great value. Big combination grills and omelettes ($5–8) make for a great breakfast, while lunch and dinner entrees include burgers, steaks, and pastas; try a grilled chicken salad ($7) for lunch, and herb-crusted salmon ($14) for dinner. Daily 7am–10pm.

Giovanni's 127 11th St ⊤970/879-4141. Best of the more expensive Italian restaurants in town, with an extensive wine list, excellent fresh pasta entrees ($13–18), and plenty of seafood dishes ($18–28) with a Southern Italian bent. Daily for dinner.

Harwig's 911 Lincoln Ave ⊤970/879-1919. Serviced by the same kitchen as *L'apogée* (see below), *Harwig's* is a sort of diet version, with more casual ambience where people nibble samplers of pâté and cheese or stuffed mushrooms ($6–8) at the bar over a glass of red. Among some light and appealing dishes are the warm duck salad, Tuscan fish chowder, and an excellent Thai green chicken curry. Entrees $13–22. Daily 5pm–midnight.

🏃 Hazie's gondola summit, Mount Werner ⊤970/879-6111. While there's undoubtedly a certain romance to dining here on a winter's night with a view of the Yampa Valley, the must-do at *Hazie's* is the summer-only all-you-can-eat Sunday brunch (mid-June until Labor Day 10am–1.30pm; $30). It's a phenomenal spread that includes hot breakfast favorites, all manner of pastries and desserts, fresh prawns, smoked salmon, and sea bass. The price includes the gondola ride up, and on a sunny Sunday you could virtually make a full day of it, walking (slowly) back down the mountain after eating. Keep an eye open too when you're skiing for occasional two-for-one lunchtime entrees; another bargain is the soup-of-the-day plus a basket of fresh bread for $6. Dinner in summer Fri & Sat only, winter Tues–Sat, reservations essential.

The Home Ranch 54880 RCR-129, Clark ⊤970/879-1780. Eighteen miles up the road from Steamboat in the beautiful Elk River Valley, this is one of only two prestigious Relais & Chateaux-recognized restaurants in Colorado. If you can afford the $70 price tag on whatever the gourmet chef has rustled up that day for the five-course dinner, you can probably afford to stay here too (see p.211). More affordable is the buffet lunch ($30), which, in winter, includes use of the property's cross-country trails (20km).

Johnny B. Good's 738 Lincoln Ave ⊤970/870-8400. Friendly Fifties-style diner, often packed with families as it's pretty solid all-round for a standard American breakfast, lunch, or dinner. Best value are the daily specials like a burger, fries, and a shake for $6. Daily 7am–9pm.

L'apogée 911 Lincoln Ave ⊤970/879-1919. Steamboat's upscale French entry, complete with low lighting, attentive staff, and silly prices; a meal takes 2–3hr to get through, so it's for a special occasion only. Escargot, oysters, foie gras, or an exotic charcuterie selection are first up, followed by entrees such as scallopini of milk-fed veal flamed with cognac and cream. Entrees $24–40. Daily for dinner only.

La Montaña 2500 Village Drive ☎970/879-5800. A big hit with moneyed visitors, the chef at *La Montaña* is undoubtedly a very good exponent of Southwestern and Mexican cuisine, but locals will tell you that the prices are a bit much for what actually is pretty straightforward fare (entrees average $22). Dinner only, 5–10pm; closed Mon or Tues except in winter.

Old Town Pub & Restaurant 600 Lincoln Ave ☎970/879-2101. The fine pub menu here features great steaks, fish, and pastas, though prices are a bit high, into the $16–24 range. There are some cheaper pub standards like sandwiches, and the place is agreeably bustling most nights. During Tuesday's "burger night," a large burger with fries can be had for just $4. Daily for lunch and dinner.

The Shack 740 Lincoln Ave ☎970/879-9975. Fiercely popular downtown greasy spoon, where huge breakfasts are doled out in murky surroundings. Ideal for breakfast (Bloody Marys on the menu) when massive egg scrambles, meaty choices, and fluffy pecan or blueberry pancakes are among the offerings. Lunches include a range of burgers and sandwiches, among them a good rib-eye teriyaki steak sandwich for $11. Mon–Fri 6am–2pm, Sat & Sun 6.30am–2pm.

Winona's 617 Lincoln Ave ☎970/879-2483. It's worth reserving a table here for the excellent breakfasts – variations of "eggs Benny," pancakes, waffles, and muffins. Otherwise you can grab something fresh on the run from the in-house bakery: the $2 cinnamon rolls are top-notch. Open daily from 7am for breakfast and lunch.

Drinking and nightlife

As it's something of a family destination, Steamboat isn't really known for its **nightlife**. Further complicating matters, the town's two concentrations of bars – downtown and at the resort – are a good fifteen-minute drive apart. The handful of **bars** there are, however, are well patronized, with local DJs and/or bands scheduled on weekends and closing time generally around 1am. **Movies** are screened at the Chief Plaza Theatre, 813 Lincoln Ave (☎970/879-0181). The free local daily, *Steamboat Today*, available from newsstands all over town, is an excellent source of what's on.

Levels1860 Ski Times Square ☎970/870-9090. Across from the base of the gondola, Steamboat's premier club, though fairly modest, does spread across three "levels." This is where big-name bands and DJs perform, or you can just play pool at one of the many tables. Cover charge ranges from $5–20.

Slopeside Grill slopeside on the Torian Plum Plaza ☎970/879-2916. Family-friendly eatery serving wood-fired pizzas ($8–11), pastas, burgers, and ribs, and its daily happy hour is one of the best in town; $6 for pizzas, $2 for a pint of microbrew (peak season 10pm–midnight, rest of year 7 or 8–11pm), served from a giant outdoor bar made of ice that draws the crowds for après.

The Tugboat Grill and Pub 1860 Mt Werner Rd ☎970/879-7070. The pub food here is not at all bad, with soups and nachos to steak dinners on the menu, but it's really a drinking, dancing, and hollering kind of place – at least when it's busy in winter. Being right on the mountain, the *Tugboat* tends to get the well-heeled crowd that's staying nearest the slopes, so it can get overrun with smoochy vacation couples. The band line-up is fairly reliable, with lots of funky R&B, blues-rock, and reggae; there's usually a cover charge ($5–12), although you're unlikely to be made to pay before 9pm.

Wolf's Den Tavern 703 Lincoln Ave ☎970/871-0008. Dive bar for Steamboat's young and restless where local live bands play. Cover charge varies from $2–10, but often waived before 9pm.

Listings

Banks Community First Bank, 555 Lincoln Ave, and Wells Fargo, at the corner of Lincoln Ave and 3rd St, both have currency exchange and 24hr ATMs.
Bookshops Off the Beaten Path, 56 7th St ☎970/879-6830.
Car rental Avis ☎970/276-4377

Internet access Bud Werner Memorial Library, 1289 Lincoln Ave (Mon–Thurs 9am–8pm, Fri 9am–6pm, Sat 9am–5pm, Sun noon–5pm; free; ☎970/879-0240).
Laundry Spring Creek Laundromat is downtown at 235 Lincoln Ave (daily 9am–9pm;

☎ 970/879-5587); Cheryl's Laundromat is at 1815 Central Park Plaza (daily 24hr; ☎ 970/879-0440). **Medical center** Routt Memorial, 1024 Central Park Drive (☎ 970/879-1322). **Pharmacy** Lyons Corner Drug, 840 Lincoln Ave ☎ 970/879-1114.

Police 840 Yampa St ☎ 970/879-1144. **Post office** 200 Lincoln Ave, and in the Sundance Plaza by Safeway. **Road conditions** ☎ 303/639-1111 or 1-877/315-7623. **Taxi** Alpine Taxi ☎ 970/879-8294.

Travel details

Flights

(All services are United Airlines.)
Hayden (Steamboat Springs) to: Denver (6 daily; 50min).

Trains

(All services are Amtrak.)
Winter Park to: Denver (1 daily; 2hr 30min); Glenwood Springs (1 daily; 3hr 45min); Granby (1 daily; 30min); Grand Junction (1 daily; 6hr).
Granby to: Denver (1 daily; 3hr); Glenwood Springs (1 daily; 3hr 15min); Grand Junction (1 daily 7hr 30min); Winter Park (1daily; 30min).

The Sawatch and Elk Mountains

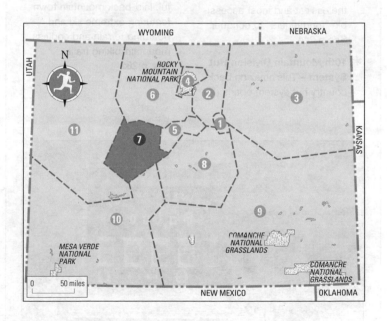

CHAPTER 7

Highlights

✳ **Vail** – Lose yourself in endless Back Bowls of great skiing and riding. See p.229

✳ **Leadville** – Magnificent views and a storied history make this former mining boomtown well worth a night's stay. See p.240

✳ **Mount Elbert** – Bag the state's highest peak, one of the easiest and most accessible "fourteeners" to conquer. See p.244

✳ **10th Mountain Division Hut System** – This amazing backcountry hut system opens up hundreds of miles of cross-country skiing and mountain-biking trails. See p.245

✳ **Maroon Bells** – Head out early for some relatively secluded hiking among a pair of the state's most undeniably attractive 14,000ft peaks. See p.258

✳ **Crested Butte** – A youthful, laid-back mountain town featuring extreme ski and boarding terrain and endless mountain-biking trails. See p.262

△ Silver Dollar Saloon, Leadville

The Sawatch and Elk Mountains

T
he cluster of incredible ski areas at the heart of the rugged **SAWATCH AND ELK MOUNTAINS** are largely responsible for Colorado's reputation as a formidable winter resort destination and have helped shape the state's image in general. The most famous are around **Vail** and **Aspen**, which, along with **Leadville** and **Crested Butte**, are also the most significant towns tucked within these two mountain ranges. All four have radically different personalities and though reasonably close on the map, high mountain passes and indirect roads make journeys between them, particularly in winter, lengthy affairs. Unsurprisingly the region's major resorts are big business and come with the attendant monetary excesses of any large vacation industry, but even if these aren't to your taste or in your budget, it's still worth taking the time to explore this stunning area, which is characterized by seemingly boundless high, picturesque mountains, alpine tundra, thick dark forests, and immense peaks. All this offers exceptional terrain for outdoor recreation, particularly hiking and biking, fishing in summer and backcountry skiing and snowshoeing in winter. And outside the main resorts and particularly in summer it's easy to be part of the action without blowing all your money.

As throughout the Rocky Mountains, the original impetus to turf out the native Ute Indians came from the region's underground wealth. The mining boom ended abruptly with the 1893 silver crash, but not before the major towns were decorated with grand Victorian mansions and opera houses. The economy then limped along until its focus began to switch from the rich seams of precious ore buried deep within the mountainsides to the precious winter snows above them. Initially, the area served as a training ground for the ski-based troops of the **10th Mountain Division**, who honed their winter skills here prior to heading off to fight in World War II. But the mountain division's influence on the area would be much more far-reaching, and although veterans didn't invent ski resorts in Colorado, they were vital in creating the industry. The prevailing continental weather patterns – that drop wet snow on the Californian Sierras, but bless the Rockies with dry, fluffy powder – naturally played a major part as well.

The most famous ski area in the region sprang up alongside the purpose-built resort town of **Vail**, a thirty-minute journey – in good road conditions – on

227

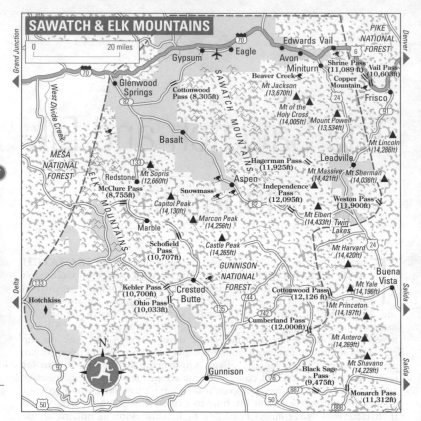

I-70 west of Summit County via Vail Pass. With hundreds of acres of open-bowl skiing and many miles of intermediate trails, this is the largest ski area in the US, even before the manicured acres of its snooty but steep and wild nearby sister resort **Beaver Creek** are taken into account.

There's also skiing in the evocative old mining town of **Leadville**, but on a far more modest scale, making it only a small part of its lure. By Central Colorado standards the town is still off the beaten track, which has helped preserve a sense of its gritty mining past that's best enjoyed in summer before heading off onto nearby mountain-biking and hiking trails – which include spectacular routes up adjacent mountains such as **Mt Elbert**, Colorado's largest.

Squeezed between the Sawatch and Elk ranges, **Aspen** also has its share of glorious mountain terrain and perhaps also is most attractive in summer. But it's the winters here that have made the town one of America's most famous ski resorts. Yet its location – disconnected from I-70, and so two hours further from Denver than Vail – makes it a bit remote, so that the four distinct ski areas are seldom crowded. This encourages the rich and famous who touch down in private jets to visit one of America's premier VIP playgrounds; the result is an elitist town that thrives on high prices.

Things are far more down-to-earth in **Crested Butte**, although this delightful nineteenth-century mining town also has good skiing on its doorstep. In summer it's almost as busy for its excellent hiking and phenomenal mountain-biking routes that twist among rolling wildflower meadows and groves of aspen.

Vail and around

Compared to most other Colorado ski towns, **VAIL**, 120 miles west of Denver on I-70, is a new creation: only a handful of farmers lived here before the resort was opened in 1952. Built as a relatively unimaginative collection of Tyrolean-style chalets and concrete-block condos, at least the town is a compact and pedestrian-friendly place, albeit pockmarked by pricey fashion boutiques and high-priced, often painfully pretentious restaurants. Vail Resorts, which operates the ski area at Vail, also owns its exclusive sidekick, **Beaver Creek**, eleven miles farther west on I-70. This gated resort, full of Alpine-castle-style resort hotels, is even more exclusive than Vail, but both skiers and snowboarders visiting the area will enjoy the fact that tickets between the two are interchangeable, creating a formidable winter sport offer. Between the two large resorts lie a couple of modest little towns: Miniturn, a small railroad town next to the Eagle River, is dotted with galleries and antique shops, and Avon is a sprawling, non descript service town. Neither are of too much consequence to visitors, though you might find them useful as a source of less-expensive accommodation or food.

Arrival, information, and getting around

From Denver International Airport, several companies offer **shuttles** to Vail and Beaver Creek, including Colorado Mountain Express ($68 one-way; 3hr;

△ Cycle race, Vail

RESTAURANTS, BARS & CLUBS

8150	19	Halfmoon Saloon	5
Beano's Cabin	7	Hubcap Brewery	24
The Blue Moose	1	Kaltenberg Castle	23
Blu's	6	La Cantina	11
Bully Ranch	9	Pazzo's	C
Campo Di Fiori	C	The Red Lion	4
Chili Willy's	4	The Saloon Across the Street	21
Cleaver's Deli	16	Seasons at the Green Restaurant	18
The Club	13	Sweet Basil	12
Club Chelsea	8	The Tap Room	17
Covered Bridge Coffee	10	Turntable Restaurant	22
DJ's Classic Diner	3	Vendetta's	14
Garfinkel's	2		

ACCOMMODATION

		JAIL SKI AREA	
Beaver Creek West	L	Lifthouse Condos	A
Best Western	G	Manor Vail Resort	E
Vailglo Lodge	G	Minturn Inn	Q
Chateau at Vail	B	Park Meadows Lodge	J
Christie Lodge	M	Ritz-Carlton	N
Comfort Inn	K	Roost Lodge	F
Eagle River Hotel	O	Sandstone Creek Club	I
Hyatt Regency	O	Simba Run	H
Beaver Creek	P	Sonnenalp Resort	C
		Tivoli Lodge	D

See inset map for more detail

Gore Creek

GOLDEN PEAK

Vail

VAIL VILLAGE

LIONSHEAD VILLAGE

Eagle Bahn Gondola

CASCADE VILLAGE

N FRONTAGE RD

West Vail

N

Eagle River

Minturn

70

6

VAIL

Transportation Center

Colorado Ski Museum

SPRADDLE CREEK ROAD

S FRONTAGE ROAD

VAIL VALLEY DRIVE

CHALET DRIVE

MILL CREEK CIRCLE

BRIDGE STREET

VAIL ROAD

E MEADOW DRIVE

N FRONTAGE ROAD

S FRONTAGE ROAD

Vail Medical Center

W MEADOW DRIVE

Library

VANS HEAD DRIVE

W LIONS HEAD CIRCLE

Gore Creek

Eagle Bahn Gondola

N

0   500 yds

VAIL/BEAVER CREEK

BEAVER CREEK

Beaver Creek

Gore Creek

Avon

BACHELOR GULCH

ARROWHEAD

0   1 mile

70

℡970/926-9800 or 1-800/525-6363, ⓦwww.cmex.com). More convenient but generally more expensive are flights to **Eagle County Regional Airport** (℡970/524-9490), 35 miles west of Vail. Ground transportation from the regional airport to either resort is just $3 on the public bus (nine daily; 1hr), while a taxi (Vail Valley Taxi; ℡1-877/829-8294) costs a staggering $125.

Greyhound buses plying I-70 between Denver (from $25 single) and Grand Junction stop at the **Vail Transportation Center**, 31 S Frontage Rd (℡970/479-2178), on top of the Vail Village parking garage. The best resource for Eagle County bus schedules, the Transportation Center is also home to one of Vail's two **visitor centers** (℡970/479-1394, ⓦwww .visitvailvalley.com), where you can book accommodation, pick up local newspapers, or surf the Web for free; the other center (℡970/479-1385) is next to the Lionshead garage. Beaver Creek's Information Center (℡970/845-9090) is located at the western entrance to the town plaza. For information on local National Forest lands, contact the **White River National Forest Holy Cross Ranger Station** (℡970/827-5715), near the I-70 junction with US-24 to Miniturn.

Vail spreads for eight miles along the narrow valley floor, with successive nuclei from east to west at Vail Village, Lionshead, Cascade Village, and West Vail. The entire complex is pedestrianized with no charge for the central parking lots in summer — in winter none are free — and is served by free shuttle buses to the lifts. **Vail Buses** (6am–2am; ℡970/477-3456) also run regular free shuttles year-round between different areas of town; schedules are printed in the *Vail Valley* magazine. Bus service between and around Avon and Beaver Creek is also complimentary and the two areas are linked to Vail by an extensive network of resort and county shuttles ($2–3 each way). The Eagle Valley transport system, **ECO** (6am–2am; $2; ℡970/328-3520), serves all outlying areas including Miniturn, Leadville, Edwards, and the Eagle County Airport.

Accommodation

In winter finding an affordable **place to stay** can be a problem, as the valley is filled with grand lodges and luxury hotels. Because the town is new, friendly little B&Bs are all but absent as well (though small, nearby Miniturn has a couple). Vail Village, the center of the resort, is the most expensive place to stay, while by Vail standards at least, the **condos** in Avon, beside I-70 near Beaver Creek, are relatively inexpensive. Accommodations in Beaver Creek itself are, however, designed for those who don't need to ask about cost. Your best bet is to contact the **Vail Valley Tourism & Convention Bureau** (℡970/476-1000 or 1-866/362-8245, ⓦwww.vailalways.com) who will reserve rooms, organize transportation and ski packages, and have a website dedicated to cut-price last-minute bookings (ⓦwww.vailonsale.com). You could also try **Vail and Beaver Creek Reservations** (℡970/496-4500 or 1-888/830-7669, ⓦwww.vail.com) who can sometimes come up with good deals, particularly early and late in the season or last-minute.

At least in **summer** prices halve, so that Vail offers accommodations starting as low as $60 a night, and in addition you can camp at the USFS *Gore Creek Campground* ($8–12), six miles east of Vail on I-70, from June to August on a first-come, first-served basis. There are more $12 sites in the reservable USFS *Hale Memorial Campground* (℡1-888/444-6777, ⓦwww.reserveusa.com), fifteen miles south of Miniturn on US-24.

THE SAWATCH AND ELK MOUNTAINS | Vail and around

Vail

Best Western Vailglo Lodge 701 W Lionshead Circle ☏970/476-5506 or 1-800/528-1234. Pleasant chain lodgings a handy two-minute walk from the Lionshead gondola. Rates include a continental breakfast and access to the pool, sauna, and guest laundry. ⑥

Chateau at Vail 13 Vail Rd ☏970/476-5631 or 1-800/451-9840. Central upscale chain motel, with functional rooms, an outdoor pool and hot tub, and its own bar. ⑥

Lifthouse Condos 555 E Lionshead Circle, Lionshead ☏970/476-2340 or 1-800/654-0635, ⓦwww.lifthousevail.com. Mid-range studios where rooms can sleep four in a pinch and come with a kitchenette, free WiFi, and access to a hot tub and exercise room. Online discounts often available. ⑥

Manor Vail Resort 595 E Vail Valley Drive ☏970/476-5651 or 1-800/950-VAIL. Revamped 1960s condo complex at the base of Golden Peak. All units have kitchens, fireplaces, and balconies or patios and access to an outdoor pool, hot tub, and sauna. ⑦

Park Meadows Lodge 1472 Matterhorn Circle ☏970/476-5598 or 1-888/245-8086, ⓦwww.parkmeadowslodge.com. Small studio suites and one- or two-bedroom condos, all with kitchens or kitchenettes, between Cascade Village and West Vail, on the bus route. Laundry, outdoor tub, and rec room on site. Ask for discounts. ⑤

Ritz-Carlton 1030 Daybreak Ridge, Bachelor Gulch ☏970/748-6200, ⓦwww.ritzcarlton.com. Exclusive giant slopeside hotel whose architecture exaggerates features of the great American National Park lodges, but which sports top-notch amenities – including an incredible spa – and elegantly rustic rooms. ⑨

Roost Lodge 1783 N Frontage Rd, West Vail ☏970/476-5451 or 1-800/873-3065, ⓦwww.roostlodge.com. Generally Vail's cheapest accommodation option, this A-frame lodge offers drab motel-standard rooms on the less attractive north side of the interstate in West Vail. Rates include coffee and pastries for breakfast and a free hourly shuttle to town and ski areas. Facilities include an outdoor pool and hot tub. ⑤

Sandstone Creek Club 1020 Vail View Drive ☏970/476-4405 or 1-800/421-1098, ⓦwww.sandstonecreekclub.com. On the north side of the interstate, an ugly condo hotel sporting a dated country club look. Appearance and inconvenience aside, the rates are great by local standards and amenities decent – including indoor and outdoor pool, spa, games room, library, and shuttle services. ⑤

Simba Run 1100 Fall Line Drive ☏970/476-0344 or 1-800/321-1489. Less-expensive condo complex in West Vail. All the spacious units are privately owned and so vary in decor. A private shuttle runs into town during the winter. The complex is served by a large indoor pool, an exercise room, a hot tub, and a steam room. ⑥

🏃 **Sonnenalp Resort** 20 Vail Rd Village ☏970/476-5656 or 1-800/654-8312, ⓦwww.sonnenalp.com. Luxury hotel straight out of a snowy European Christmas card bang in the center of Vail's pedestrian area. Accommodations are split between three equally delightful but distinct buildings: the Bavaria Haus, the Austria Haus, and the Swiss Chalet, decorated in the corresponding styles. The hotel offers a splendid fitness facility with pools and hot tubs, and rates include superb breakfasts. The best deals are packages that can include the likes of skiing, golf, and spa treatments from $150 per person per day – but during the winter peak season you won't get a room here for under $500 per night. ⑨

Tivoli Lodge 386 Hanson Ranch Rd ☏970/476-5615 or 1-800/451-4756, ⓦwww.tivolilodge.com. One of Vail's more inexpensive options, with traditional alpine architecture in a handy location at the foot of Golden Peak. Spacious rooms are bland but comfortable; amenities include an outdoor pool, hot tub, and a sauna. A large continental breakfast is served in the dark and cozy lounge bar. ⑥

Miniturn

Eagle River Hotel 145 N Main St ☏970/827-5761 or 1-800/344-1750. B&B decked out in tasteful Santa Fe-style in the small town of Miniturn, seven miles south of Vail on US-24. ⑦

🏃 **Minturn Inn** 442 Main St ☏970/827-9647 or 1-800/646-8876, ⓦwww.minturninn.com. Friendly B&B in a handsome 1915 hewn-log home and chic new timber-frame lodge on the banks of the Eagle River, both tastefully decorated with handcrafted furniture and simple linens. Rooms have been decorated along local themes, including angling and Nordic skiing; some have their own fireplaces and Jacuzzi tubs. Surprisingly reasonable rates include a full breakfast and après snacks and a sauna. ⑥

Avon and Beaver Creek

Beaver Creek West 0360 Benchmark Rd, Avon ☏970/949-4840 or 1-800/222-4840, ⓦwww.beavercreekwest.com. Bland but clean, comfy, and affordable one- to four-bedroom condos in Avon on the bus route next to Nottingham Park. With three hot tubs and a sauna by the heated outdoor pool. Hotel rooms ④, condos ⑤

Christie Lodge 47 E Beaver Creek Blvd, Avon
ⓣ970/949-7700 or 1-800/551-4326. Dreary-
looking condo with small basic suites, but with
kitchenettes and fireplaces at prices that are cheap
by Vail standards. Handy for skiing Beaver Creek.
Use of a pool, hot tubs, sauna, athletic club, and
laundry are included. ❺
Comfort Inn 161 W Beaver Creek Blvd, Avon
ⓣ970/949-5511 or 1-800/423-4374, ⓦwww
.comfortinn.com. Bright, clean, and inexpensive

chain hotel close to the freeway but a bit far away
from any restaurants. Rates include continental
breakfast, and there's an outdoor pool and tub. ❻
Hyatt Regency Beaver Creek 136 Thomas Place,
Beaver Creek ⓣ970/949-1234 or 1-800/233-1234.
The hub of Beaver Creek Village has almost three
hundred spacious and luxuriously furnished rooms.
Amenities include fitness center with classes, full-
service spa, pool, hot tubs, restaurants, a concierge,
and ski and parking valets. ❽

Vail Resort

Vail's vast mountain divides into three broad areas. The largest is the **Front Face**
– of which only the bottom third is visible from the village – with its beginner
areas, long cruisers, tree shots, upper mountain cliff-drops, and lower-mountain
terrain parks; the ungroomed **Back Bowls** lie behind this area providing open
bowl skiing in powder, of which most is manageable by confident intermediates. Opposite the Back Bowls and facing north is **Blue Sky Basin**, a wilder
portion whose forested slopes suffer less under the sun. The entire gigantic area
is accessed from three main points strung out along the base of the front face. To
the east, the low rise of aspen-covered **Golden Peak** is also permanent home
of the terrain parks and superpipe; from the center of town lifts head up from
Vail Village; while Vail's speedy gondola departs from **Lionshead**.

The size of the area is such that the resort's free three-hour intermediate-level
mountain tours prove useful for orientation purposes. These depart daily at
9.15am from Golden Peak, Lionshead, and Vail Village base areas; while Blue
Sky Basin tours meet at Hawk's Nest Deck at 10am. If you'd rather explore on
your own, it makes little difference where you start your day, as Vail's many lifts
and traverses make it fairly easy to crisscross the upper mountain. But be sure
to factor in distances if arranging a meeting place: Two Elk Lodge is at least
thirty minutes' skiing from Wildwood, while getting to Blue Sky Basin and
back – best done from Teacup or China Bowls – can take the better part of an
afternoon. At the end of the day, the easiest route home is under the gondola
to Lionshead.

Despite the cost, most drivers use Vail's convenient Village or Lionshead **parking garages** ($16 for 6–24hr, free 5pm–3am and if staying under 1hr) on South
Frontage Rd right off I-70 exit 176. On the weekend, it pays to turn up late;
once the structures are full, free parking is permitted on South Frontage Road.
For Beaver Creek, take I-70 exit 167 for Avon and follow Avon Road one mile
south through town to the gated reception center. Regular shuttles stop at the

Vail Resort

Information ⓣ970/476-5601 or 1-800/427-3535, ⓦwww.vail.com; snow report
ⓣ970/476-4888.

Ticket prices and operating times $81 peak; open mid-Nov to third week in April
daily 9am–3.30pm.

Mountain statistics Base elevation 8120ft, summit elevation 11,570ft, vertical drop
3450ft, acreage 5289, average snowfall 346in.

Lifts and trails 33 lifts serve 193 trails: beginner 18 percent, intermediate 29 percent,
expert 53 percent.

free East Lot and from the West Lot below Bachelor Gulch. Covered pay lots are located at each end of the town plaza.

Lift tickets, lessons, and rentals

Day **tickets** for Vail and Beaver Creek are among the most expensive in the nation, though they drop significantly early and late in the season. Online purchasing can also save you substantial amounts, particularly on multi-day tickets (valid at all Vail Resorts).

Vail has an excellent **ski school** (at Golden Peak and Lionshead bases; 8am–4.30pm; ☎970/476-3239), with more than 850 highly qualified instructors, but fees are steep, topping the $50 mark for a day's tuition and lift ticket. For groups of five or six, it's often cheaper to hire a private instructor than sign up for group classes. Vail's adaptive program (☎970/479-3264) is particularly good value for disabled skiers with their own equipment, as a five-day ticket is only $99; equipment rental is extra and only available to those taking a lesson. There are children's centers at both Lionshead and Golden Peak, as well as on-mountain kids' zones and evening programs at the Adventure Ridge activity center, located at the top of the gondola. The Small World Play School (☎970/479-3285; reservations required), provides **nursery facilities** for kids aged two months to six years.

If you need to pick up **rental gear**, you'll do best at Lionshead, but before you do it's well worth nipping up to the visitor center first in search of coupons – these can reduce the total rental cost by up to twenty percent at many outlets. Kenny's Double Diamond, 520 E Lionshead Circle (☎970/476-5500), is a respected name throughout the skiing world, a traditional skier's domain with an excellent boot-fitting service and knowledgeable staff. Vail Snowboard Supply (☎970/479-4434) and basement-dwellers One Track Mind (☎970/476-1397), both in Lionshead, are good options for snowboards; you can book in advance at ⓦ www.rentskis.com to save a few bucks on the $30 deals.

Mountain runs

It's possible to locate a green trail off of every lift on the front face. **First-timers** can start right in town, on Gopher Hill at the bottom of Golden Peak, or head up Lionshead gondola to enjoy the views and sheltered **beginner** terrain next to Eagle's Nest. Both areas have slow beginner lifts. A good next step are the wide, tree-lined slopes below Two Elk Lodge, at the top of the mountain, which are fairly quiet and steep enough for both snowboarders and skiers to build confidence. Avoid the tedious and busy catwalk back to town by taking the Northwoods lift to Mid-Vail or riding down on Riva Bahn.

Intermediates will find great cruising runs all over the Front Face and can try a few bumps, hit an easy glade, or attempt a short black in the fantastically

---

The Colorado Ski Museum

For a look at the development of skiing in Colorado investigate the excellent **Colorado Ski Museum and Hall of Fame**, 231 S Frontage Rd (Tues–Sun 10am–5pm; $1; ☎970/476-1876, ⓦ www.skimuseum.net). Exhibits, videos, and wonderful old photos chart the evolution of the sport here – from Finnish-style snowglide shoes used as early transportation to today's high-tech recreational skiing and snowboarding. The museum also has early gear from the famed 10th Mountain Division, some of whose veterans have been included in the Hall of Fame for their role in developing the local ski industry.

varied terrain of the bowl above Mid-Vail. As varied but quieter is the Game Creek Bowl on the western end of the Front Face Ridge. Its circular orientation means you can usually find excellent snow conditions somewhere, though you may need to traverse to access them. After a recent storm, head to the powder fields in one of the Back Bowls, which can look intimidating but are technically well within range for confident intermediates. China Bowl is a good place to start and **experts** will have a field day bowl-hopping when conditions are right. Otherwise the main expert playgrounds are the tight evergreens above Vail Village and over in Blue Sky Basin with its cliff bands, hair-raising cornices, and straightforward glades. For bumps try the double diamonds on the far eastern boundary of the Front Face.

Once a focal point of the **snowboard** scene in the US, and still the home of a number of pros, the superpipe, tabletops, and hits on Golden Peak are consistently well maintained but better for experienced riders than beginners. For serious cliff-drops with tight landings in the trees look around the Northwoods lift.

Beaver Creek

Newer and snootier than Vail, **Beaver Creek** was developed by Vail Associates in 1980, when a successful lettuce-growing valley was transformed into a gated resort of luxury lodges and condos, connected by outdoor escalators and heated pavements. Despite the luxury of the village below and the impeccable grooming of many of its runs, the forested slopes of Beaver Creek seem wilder than those of its corporate cousins. This is partly because Beaver Creek is spared the crowds of Summit County or Vail, but it's also down to the terrain. Instead of Vail's bleak Back Bowls there are a fine array of narrow runs and some glades spread across the mountain, which help to hide many of the other skiers.

The distribution of the terrain across the mountain is also rather odd. Prime beginner runs are found on the flat summit of imposing **Beaver Creek Mountain**, the largest of three steep-sided peaks rising sharply from the narrow valley floor. **Beaver Creek West** is predominantly an intermediate and beginner hill, and the wide open dish of McCoy Park cross-country center atop the mountain provides spectacular views of the Gore Range. Between the two, the smallest of the three, rocky and forbidding **Grouse Mountain**, is effectively expert-only territory. Here and elsewhere steep pitches cause dense shadows across the lower slopes, which often create icy conditions – one of the ski area's main drawbacks.

Those not staying at the resort are best off **parking** (free) in Avon by the gated entrance to the Beaver Creek road and taking a free shuttle up to the slopes.

Beaver Creek

Information ☎970/845-9090 or 1-800/404-3535, ⊛www.beavercreek.com; snow report ☎1-800/404-3535.

Ticket prices and operating times $81; open late Nov to mid-April daily 9am–3.30pm.

Mountain statistics base elevation 7400ft (Arrowhead), summit elevation 11,440ft (Beaver Creek), vertical drop 4040ft (main mountain – 3340ft), acreage 1625, average snowfall 310in.

Lifts and trails 16 lifts serve 146 trails: beginner 34 percent, intermediate 39 percent, expert 27 percent.

Lift tickets, lessons, and rentals

Beaver Creek operates on a shared **ticket** with Vail, and the packages, prices, and quality of Beaver Creek's **ski school** (adults ☎970/845-5300, kids ☎970/845-5464, adaptive ☎970/845-5465) are similar to Vail's, but beginners benefit from their own indoor meeting place, where they can chat to instructors and watch instructional videos before heading onto the snow. The resort runs a number of **telemark** programs (☎970/845-5313), including beginner lessons twice a week. Equipment is available to rent from the Nordic Demo Center at the bottom of Strawberry Park lift. **Day care** at the resort is provided by Small World Playschool (☎970/845-5325), for kids aged two months to six years, otherwise kids can start ski tuition aged three, snowboarding aged seven.

To test the latest skis, stop in at the Alpine Demo Center on-mountain at the Spruce Saddle Lodge. The Other Side (☎970/845-8969) has been a focal point for the local snowboard scene for years. Reasonable quality but pricey ($35–45) rental packages are available in the village plaza from Beaver Creek Sports (☎970/845-5400) and affiliated snowboard specialists One Track Mind (☎970/845-5420); book online at ⓦ www.rentskis.com for a discount. Ski rentals are about $5 cheaper at Christy Sport's Avon store, 182 Avon Rd (☎970/949-0241), than in the Beaver Creek Lodge branch.

Mountain runs

First-timers can learn right by the village at the base of the front face, where surface lifts and slow chairs serve bunny slopes, but should head up to the better conditions at the top of the mountain as soon as their skills allow. Here gently rolling wide-open meadows are dotted with trees and accompanied by views across the Gore Range. Snowboarders should then quickly be able to get to grips with the gentler blues like Latigo and Gold Dust below. On Beaver Creek West the trails and tree-lined catwalks around Bachelor Gulch are also quiet and excellent for building confidence – this base area is connected with the main by shuttles as well as the lift system.

Beaver Creek West, around the Strawberry Park and Elkhorn lifts, offers a good area of long, rolling, tree-studded runs for **intermediates** to warm up in the morning sun. After this it's worth heading over to the Larkspur lift where there's a good choice of fast routes and gladed trails, with some of the easiest black trails on the mountain.

Of all the steep and difficult runs offered to **experts** at Beaver Creek, the most challenging – and terrifying – are around the Birds of Prey lift. These include the groomed Golden Eagle, along with bump runs Peregrine and Goshawk. Beside these are a similar group of shorter runs on Grouse Mountain, where the steep Royal Elk Glades offer tremendous backcountry-like conditions on powder days. Backcountry gates, right off the summit of Cinch Express, access powder fields and gullies off Beaver Creek's so-called Bald Spot. Both here, and off either side of the Grouse Mountain summit, riders taking their chances outside the boundary are conveniently funnelled back into the ski area. But never ski alone, and take advice from the ski patrol before you venture out.

Even though local **riders** hit up Beaver Creek's steep glades and backcountry whenever the snow cooperates, the resort's terrain parks and features are well designed. Once the snow has built up enough, the Centennial park features a well-maintained superpipe and a good variety of hits and rails. There's also a baby park in the kids' learning area and a slightly bigger minipark off the Birds of Prey summit.

Other winter activities

Snowshoe tours, dog sledding, winter fly-fishing, ice-skating, and more can be organized through the Vail Activities Desk (℡970/476-9090), in the Lionshead gondola building, or through the Beaver Creek resort concierge (℡970/845-9090), in the town plaza. Multi-activity tour operators include Nova Guides (℡719/486-2656 or 1-888/949-6682, ⓦwww.novaguides.com), known for their non-skiing snowcat and snowmobile tours (from $80 per hour).

At the top of the gondola is Vail's **Adventure Ridge** (Tues–Sat from 2.30pm–9pm; gondola ride free; ℡970/476-9090), an **activity center** that comes into its own when the other lifts have closed and it's bathed in rosy light. More usual activities like tubing ($22), ice-skating ($8 rentals, free with own skates), kid's snowmobiling ($22), and snowshoeing ($10) are offered alongside novelties like ski-biking ($62) which is most exciting after dark, when you can zip down the empty slopes using only a headlamp to light the way. Other local activity centers include the Black Family ice rink (℡970/845-9090) in Beaver Creek and the indoor Dobson Ice Arena (℡970/479-2271).

Vail and Beaver Creek operate a couple of **cross-country ski centers**, the largest and most magical of which is Beaver Creek's McCoy Park (℡970/845-5313), with 32km of trails located at the top of the Strawberry Park lift. Call ahead to reserve nature treks or gourmet picnic tours, book lesson packages (from $55), or to register for the monthly Snowshoe Adventure Series fun runs ($20) or the annual Snowshoe Shuffle, the largest such race in the US. The Vail Nordic Center (daily 9am–5pm; ℡970/476-8366) is located by the golf course in East Vail, offering 15km of track, a restaurant, ice rink, and skate rentals, as well as evening sleigh rides. There's no fee to use the track and rentals are reasonably priced (from $17 for skis, $14 for snowshoes). Backcountry ski and snowshoe tours, including monthly moonlight trips ($25), are regularly scheduled.

For **backcountry skiing and riding** forays into the surrounding White River National Forest, contact Paragon Guides (℡970/926-5299 or 1-877/926-5299, ⓦwww.paragonguides.com), who take expert skiers into the backcountry and lead multi-day touring trips using the 10th Mountain Division huts. Or you can access untouched terrain off Ptarmigan Pass with Vail Snowcat Skiing (information ℡970-845-5080, reservations ℡970-926-1839, ⓦwww.vailsnowcat.com); rates are around $350 including lunch, and are suitable for advanced intermediates. Snowcat riding is also available nearby at little Ski Cooper (see p.244).

Summer activities

As the regular host of the Mountain Bike World Cup, it's no surprise that Vail boasts several great **mountain-biking** trails. The most obvious place to head is the 100 miles of trails in the ski area, serviced by two of its lifts (mid-June to Aug daily 10am–4.30pm; $29) and marked on free maps available from the lift ticket offices. The trails on offer are best for strong intermediate and expert riders who can handle the challenges of the 1994 World Cup Course and rough sections of single track twisting their way through the Magic Forest and Old Nine Line – the hardest trail on the hill. Other trails are rather dull fire-roads, with the exception of the cross-country course at the base of the hill which can comfortably be ridden without using a lift. Best of the local stores offering rentals (front-suspension for $35/day) is Vail Bicycle Services, 450 E Lionshead Circle (℡970/476-1233). Local **road bikers** like to head on the Canyon Trail cycle-path over Vail Pass, an eight-mile climb on the way to Frisco another eleven miles from the top of the pass.

It's possible to **hike** around Vail's ski area but the bald runs and ski-infrastructure spoil the outdoor experience. Better to head to **Beaver Creek**, where it's easier to leave the resort trappings behind. A good six-mile round-trip heads out-and-back to Beaver Lake, taking around three or four hours. There are many more hiking trails outside the ski areas; a particularly convenient network from Vail is the North Trail system, a twelve-mile multiple-use trail network on the valley's north side. One easily accessible trailhead to this network lies beside a parking lot off Red Sandstone Road on the edge of town. The difficult Notch Mountain Trail, which climbs just short of 3000ft in under five miles, also begins in Vail and heads to the Mount of the Holy Cross, a peak made famous in the black-and-white photos of William Henry Jackson. The local visitor's center in Vail can give further details of these and other local hikes, as can the Vail Nature Center, 1778 Vail Valley Drive (℡970/479-2291). The best source of information for longer trips, however, is the USFS ranger office near Miniturn (see p.231).

If you're in the Vail valley in May, consider donning a wetsuit to go **white-water rafting** in the Eagle River, running the fun Class IV Dowd Chutes before moving on to more sedate Class II and III water further downstream. Trips with a company like Lakota River Guides (℡970/476-RAFT or 1-800/274-0636, ⓦwww.lakotariver.com) usually run for half a day and cost around $80. Lakota also does several extreme trips that few other commercial companies offer, including the Gore Canyon in August and September, generally considered one of the ultimate commercially raftable challenges in the state. Tours begin with a 500ft rappel before crossing the river on a harness system to get to the put-in; the river itself is full of Class V rapids that require a pretty gung-ho attitude. With this exception, though, after May local waters are a little too low for good rafting, but become ideal for learning how to **kayak**. Alpine Quest Sports, 40690 Hwy-6 in Avon (℡970/949-3350, ⓦwww.alpinekayak.com), offers a two-day beginner course for $165, including all rental gear.

Golfing holidays are a big summer money-maker for Vail, and golfers can select from nine courses in the valley, ranging from the pricey Beaver Creek Resort Golf Club (℡970/845-5775) to the fun and more affordable Eagle-Vail Golf Course (℡970/949-5267), the public course between Vail and Avon.

Also in Avon is the **Avon Recreation Center**, 325 Benchmark Rd (Mon–Thurs 6am–10pm, Fri 6am–9pm, Sat & Sun 8am–9pm; ℡970/748-4060), a complex with a pool, waterslide, sauna, Jacuzzi, and gym.

Eating

Eating out in Vail is generally expensive, and in Beaver Creek – where reservations are required at most restaurants – even more so. But at least the food is generally of a very high standard. It's also worth heading out to the few restaurants in cute Miniturn – though geared primarily to visitors, these are less expensive and there's some good inexpensive Mexican food to be had; for laid-back spots frequented by the local workforce head to Avon or Edwards.

On-mountain dining at both resorts is expensive. If you're on the Front Face at Vail it doesn't take long to nip down for an inexpensive slice or burrito in the village, but if you're going to fork out for lunch, skip busy *Eagle's Nest* and *Mid-Vail*. Choose *Wildwood* instead, which serves filling and tasty barbecue sandwiches and soups for around $10. The glorified cafeteria of timber-framed *Two Elk* boasts the best location, overlooking Vail's Back Bowls and the Gore Range. For a cheaper option try the *Blue Moon* at the top of the gondola, a standard grill, but a fine place for a Backbowls Brew and an appetizer.

Vail

Blu's 193 E Gore Creek Drive ☎970/476-3113. Relaxed restaurant with some of Vail's most modest prices (entrees from around $10); serves American breakfasts, soups, salads, and pizzas for lunches and dinners, plus great desserts.

Campo Di Fiori 100 E Meadow Drive, Vail Village ☎970/476-8994. Airy, upscale Italian, serving moderately priced, tasty pastas ($14–18) without the stuffiness found in many of Vail's upper-end restaurants.

Cleaver's Deli 297 Hanson Ranch Rd, Vail Village ☎970/ 476-1755. Quick pit stop in the village for cheap stuffed bagels, breakfast pastries, and good deals on half-sandwiches and subs (under $5).

Covered Bridge Coffee 227 Bridge St ☎970/479-2883. Good place to start the day with a coffee, pastries, bagels, and to nip into for a lunchtime deli sandwich.

DJ's Classic Diner 616 W Lionshead Circle ☎970/476-2336. A breath of fresh air in the otherwise fairly buttoned-up dining scene comes in the form of this reasonably priced 24hr diner (during ski season, shorter hours outside). Pick up all the usual American favorites, omelettes, or burritos, or enjoy the Vail touch – dessert crepes and a wine list.

La Cantina Vail Transportation Center, Vail Village ☎970/476-7661. Vail's bargain dining spot is little more than a few tables crammed into a corner of the parking garage lobby. But you won't worry about that while you're chowing down on the free chips and fresh salsas, huge burritos and tacos ($3–$5), and washing it all down with the potent margaritas before stumbling up the stairs to catch the bus home.

Pazzo's 122 East Meadows Drive, Vail Village ☎970/476-9026. Pizza by the slice and good hearty portions of lasagna ($10) make *Pazzo's* a ski-bum favorite; it's warm and busy on even the coldest, quietest night.

Seasons at the Green Restaurant Vail Golf Course, 1778 Vail Valley Drive ☎970/476-8057. The gourmet food at one of Vail's top restaurants is only half of the attraction – the

horse-drawn sleighs to and from the restaurant, around Vail Golf Course, make up the other half. The experience costs around $65 and reservations are required.

Sweet Basil 193 E Gore Creek Drive ☎970/476-0125. Snug, expensive bistro overlooking Gore Creek and serving imaginative dishes – like the apple and jicama salad or the portobello mushroom and goat's cheese tarts – as well as having a good line in seafood pastas. Entrees start around $24.

Vendetta's 291 Bridge St ☎970/476-5070. Elegant restaurant with views of Vail Mountain (you can dine outside on a deck in summer) serving fine Italian lunch specials and pasta dinners; entrees start from $15.

Beaver Creek

Beano's Cabin near Minturn, but trips depart from *Beaver Creek Resort* ☎970/949-9090. It's unlikely that lettuce farmer Frank Bienkowski ever expected his secluded cabin to become the poshest place to dine in the valley – but that's just what happened. In winter diners are towed here by snowcat-drawn sleigh to a six-course gourmet meal ($90), in summer on horseback or by horse-drawn wagon, for the one-hour trip. The food is superb and there are plenty of entrees to choose from. Open mid-Dec to Sept.

The Blue Moose Beaver Creek Plaza ☎970/845-8666. Decent pizza, calzones, and subs at reasonable prices. 11am–midnight.

Minturn

Chili Willy's 101 Main St ☎970/827-5887. This casual, inexpensive place is a good place to dig into great Tex-Mex – particularly the fajitas – and knock back a couple of killer margaritas.

The Saloon Across the Street 146 N Main St ☎970/827-5954. Atmospheric restaurant serving classic Mexican entrees ($10) complemented by steak, quail, and fish.

Turntable Restaurant 160 Main St ☎970/827-4164. Another inexpensive option, the *Turntable* is decorated with railroad memorabilia and serves filling breakfasts, burgers, tacos, and burritos (from $6). Open 5.30am–10.30pm.

Nightlife, performing arts, and film

By the modest standards of American ski resorts, Vail's winter **nightlife** is among the best in the country, with the action centered on Bridge Street in Vail Village. Local DJs spin nightly, but bigger shows are scheduled over the weekend. A few major bands are brought to town each season to entertain the holiday crowds, with shows in the Dobson Ice Arena.

Vail has two small **movie** theaters, each with two screens: the Cascade Village, next to *Vail Cascade Hotel*, and the Crossroads Cinema, in the Vail Village

Crossroads Mall (information for both ☎970/476-5661). In Beaver Creek, the plush Vilar Center for the Arts, 68 Avondale Ln (☎970/845-8497 or 1-888/920-2787, ⓦwww.vilarcenter.org), runs an eclectic program of performances and films. In July and August, free Tuesday-night **concerts** are held at 6.30pm at the Gerald Ford Amphitheater, 530 S Frontage Rd (☎970/476-2918). The music varies drastically between the likes of jazz, soul, and rock. Classical performances, part of the Vail Valley Music Festival (☎970/827-5700), can be heard on weekends during the same months. The local *Vail Daily* (ⓦwww.vaildaily.com) is good for **listings**.

8150 143 East Meadow Drive, Vail Village ☎970/479-0607. Live music club with a sprung dance floor and an open-minded attitude to almost-daily performances, ranging from hip-hop crews to flamboyant tribute bands, with funk, rock, and reggae in between.

Bully Ranch 20 Vail Rd, Vail Village ☎970/476-5656. Busy spot in the Sonnenalp that's the best place for a civilized après-ski tipple: renowned for its mudslides (vodka, coffee, Irish cream, and ice cream). Tasty, if expensive, appetizers soften the alcohol punch.

The Club 304 Bridge St, Vail Village ☎970/479-0556. Dingy basement bar with acoustic singalongs or loud rock, at its best as the slopes close.

Club Chelsea 100 E Meadow Drive, Vail Village ☎970/477-2280. Laid-back lounge bar which tends to attract a much older crowd sipping martinis to background piano music or blues.

Garfinkel's 536 E Lionshead Circle, Lionshead ☎970/476-3789. Large upbeat sports bar beside the gondola. Packs out as the lifts close, but otherwise mostly the haunt of a young seasonal workforce shooting pool.

Halfmoon Saloon 2161 North Frontage Rd, West Vail ☎970/476-4314. Odd but successful combination of diner and live music venue, with regular funk and blues, acoustic nights, comedy showcases, and a weekly free taco bar.

Hubcap Brewery 143 E Meadow Drive, Vail Village ☎970/476-5757. Dependably bustling brewpub, with regular live music and good ales. The solid and inexpensive menu is based largely around steaks and burgers.

🏃 **Kaltenberg Castle** Lionshead Plaza, Lionshead ☎970/479-1050. The former Lionshead gondola building is now a massive mock-palace where entertainers wear lederhosen and giant vats brew Bavarian beer. All good fun if you're in a jolly frame of mind.

The Red Lion 304 Bridge St, Vail Village ☎970/476-7676. A Vail institution, this venerable pub gets crammed during après with an older crowd being amused by musicians and entertainers.

The Tap Room 333 Bridge St, Vail Village ☎970/479-0500. The *Tap Room* pulls in the young and stylish for après drinks and snacks, while the equally chic *Sanctuary* club and lounge upstairs stays open late.

Vendetta's 291 Bridge St, Vail ☎970/476-5070. Loud music rules upstairs at *Vendetta's*, which, as well as being an upscale Italian restaurant (see opposite), doubles as the village's late-night hangout, attracting passers-by who come for pizza by the slice ($3) in the front room or head upstairs for beer by the pitcher. Pizza served until 2am, deliveries until midnight.

Listings

Bookshops Verbatim Booksellers, 450 Lionshead Circle ☎970/476-3032.
Internet Vail Library, 292 W Meadow Drive ☎970/479-2184.
Medical Vail Valley Medical Center, 181 W Meadow Drive ☎970/476-2451.

Pharmacy Vail Valley Medical Center (see opposite) or City Market, 2109 N Frontage Rd, West Vail ☎970/476-1621.
Police ☎970/479-2200.
Road and weather conditions ☎970/479-2226.
Taxi Vail 24hr Taxi ☎970/476-8294, High Mountain Taxi ☎970/524-5555.

Leadville

Sitting at an elevation of over ten thousand feet, the wonderfully atmospheric old mining town of **LEADVILLE** has magnificent views across the base of the wide, flat Arkansas Valley to broad-shouldered, ice-laden mountains. Approaching the town, located 38 miles south of Vail on US-24, your first impression is likely to be of giant slag heaps and disused mining sheds. Don't let this put you off: Leadville is rich in character and romance, abounding with tales of gunfights, miners dying of exposure, and graveyards being excavated to get at seams.

The town boomed in the 1880s due to the area's phenomenally high concentrations of precious ores: not only gold and silver, but also molybdenum, manganese, and zinc. It was then the largest smelting center in the country, boasting around 15,000 residents served by four churches, 120 saloons, and 188 gambling houses. Over the last century the town has shrunk to an eighth of its former size, and while most of its historic businesses have disappeared, a large network of old mining trails around town remain. This network offers splendid opportunities for mountain biking and, in winter, exploration on cross-country skis or snowmobiles. These trails are the setting for Leadville's outrageously hard endurance bike and foot races – both a hundred miles long – held in late August. Leadville is also best placed for ascents of Colorado's two tallest peaks: **mounts Elbert** (14,433ft) and **Massive** (14,421ft), which are both relatively easy to bag, and so are busy with hikers throughout the summer.

Arrival and information

Leadville is not served by any form of public transportation, so the best option for those without a car is Dee Hive Tours & Transportation (℡719/486-2339), who charge $70 for their **shuttle service** from Denver – but stipulate a four-person minimum. Leadville's helpful **visitor center**, 809 Harrison Ave (June–Sept daily 10am–5pm; ℡719/486-3900 or 1-800/939-3901, ⓦwww.leadvilleusa.com), is at the north end of downtown. For detailed information on the local National Forest areas contact the USFS Leadville Ranger Station, 2015 Poplar St (Mon–Fri 8am–5pm; ℡719/486-0749), on the northern edge of town.

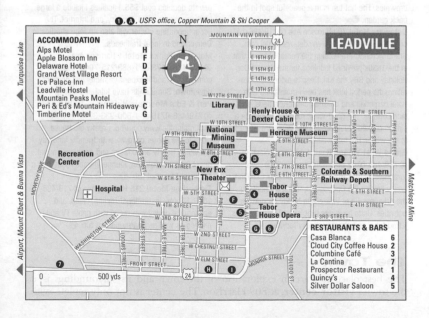

7

THE SAWATCH AND ELK MOUNTAINS | Leadville

Accommodation

Although there is a good selection of **accommodation** in Leadville – including several cozy B&Bs, some budget motels, a hostel, and an atmospheric Victorian hotel – in summer, most choose to **camp** in the area. The large Turquoise Lake reservoir, five miles west of town, harbors six USFS campgrounds ($12–14), which collectively provide almost 300 sites. Head first for the quiet nature of the tent-only *Bellevue* campground directly on the lake's southeastern shore. Around six miles further south, beside Halfmoon Creek, are the popular USFS *Halfmoon* and *Elbert Creek* campgrounds, well-placed for bagging mounts Elbert and Massive; these fill quickly on a first-come, first-served basis. If you're looking for tent or RV sites in town, try the *Leadville RV Corral*, 135 W 2nd St (☎719/486-3111, ⓦwww.mountainrvpark.com; $20), which has showers. Although Leadville's own ski industry is modest, the town is close to several I-70 corridor resorts and it offers a cheap way of skiing locally. Inexpensive ski-vacation packages are also offered by Leadville Ski Country (☎719/486-3836 or 1-800/500-5323, ⓦwww.leadville.com/skicountry), who use a variety of local accommodations to offer three days' skiing, accommodation, and rentals for around $200.

Alps Motel 207 Elm St ☎719/486-1223 or 1-800/818-2577. Great-value, clean motel on the southern edge of town. Some units have fridges and microwaves, all have phones and cable TV. ❸

Apple Blossom Inn 120 W 4th St ☎719/486-2141 or 1-800/982-9279, ⓦtheappleblossominn.com. Centrally located and stylish B&B in wonderful old Victorian property – most rooms are regal affairs, paneled in dark wood, some with stained glass. Top floor apartment sleeps up to nine but is good value even for four. The breakfasts are first-rate, as are the afternoon brownies. The hot tub is in a peaceful spot in the back garden. ❺

Delaware Hotel 700 Harrison Ave ☎719/486-1418 or 1-800/748-2004, ⓦwww.delawarehotel.com. Grand Victorian-era hotel in the center of town, that in the 1880s provided lodgings for the likes of Doc Holliday and Billy the Kid. Despite extensive restoration, the period look has been maintained with floral carpeting and polished oak, brass beds, and lace curtains. The good-value room-rates include a simple cooked breakfast. Ski packages are offered in the winter. Hot tub available. ❹

Grand West Village Resort 99 Grand West Rd ☎719/486-0702 or 1-800/691-3999, ⓦwww.grandwest.com. Modest condo complex between Leadville and Ski Cooper, in a forest overlooking the Arkansas River Valley, and handy for outdoor activities. Units have gas fireplaces, TVs with VCRs, jetted tubs, and shared laundry facilities. ❻

Ice Palace Inn 813 Spruce St ☎719/486-8272 or 1-800/754-2840, ⓦwww.icepalaceinn.com. B&B located on Capitol Hill a few short blocks west of town where the town's Ice Palace once stood – and built from lumber retrieved from it. Rooms are richly decorated with lots of old curios, and the friendly hosts offer good advice on local hikes and cook gourmet breakfasts. Hot tub. ❻

Leadville Hostel 500 E 7th St ☎719/486-9334, ⓦwww.leadvillehostel.com. Friendly, clean, and sociable hostel, where dorm beds run $19–28 depending on room and season and private doubles cost $55. Facilities include a large kitchen, games room, laundry, and Internet. The accommodating owner will also arrange shuttles to Denver and to local trailheads.

Mountain Peaks Motel 1 Harrison Ave ☎719/486-3178 or 1-888/215-7040. Clean, comfortable, and inexpensive motel just north of downtown. Some units have kitchenettes. ❷

Peri & Ed's Mountain Hideaway 201 W 8th St ☎719/486-0716 or 1-800-933-3715, ⓦwww.mountainhideaway.com/bb. Creaky old house close to the center of town, with friendly landlady (providing hearty breakfasts) and good communal guest facilities: kitchen, lounge, games room, and a scenic outdoor hot tub. ❸

Timberline Motel 216 Harrison Ave ☎719/486-1876. Slightly institutional-feeling, clean, and economical downtown motel with cable TV and phones as well as communal hot tub. ❸

The Town

The best place to start an exploration of the town and its surroundings is at the town's **visitor center**, at 809 Harrison. The center is not only replete with activity-specific recreation maps, but also screens (on demand) a short film on the town's local history, a simple affair but featuring evocative oral histories. You can also pick up the magazine-format *Leadville Walking Tour*, which gives the salient details for most of the older buildings along the town's main street.

In light of the insight the film offers, visiting Leadville's rambling **National Mining Hall of Fame and Museum**, 120 W 9th St (May–Oct daily 9am–5pm, Nov–April Mon–Sat 10am–4pm; $6; ℡719/486-1229, Ⓦwww .mininghalloffame.org), is a patchy experience. It's best to skip the museum's mining industry propaganda films (global warming isn't all bad and landscapes can look better after mining) in favor of the lurid globs of precious minerals, reconstructed mine-passages, and atmospheric old photos of weatherbeaten prospectors. The museum's hall of fame is dedicated to mining's kingpins – mostly graying white gentlemen – and also is of little interest.

For a more illuminating romp through the town's grim early history, head for the **Heritage Museum**, further down the road at 102 E 9th St (mid-May to Nov daily 10am–6pm; $3.50; ℡719/486-1878). Glass cases hold snippets on local fraternal organizations, quack doctors, music-hall stars, and the like, while a host of smoky photographs portray the lawless boomtown that in two years grew from a mining camp of 200 people into Colorado's second-largest city. Some old gear of the 10th Mountain Division is on display as well. The museum also has a large foam reconstruction of Leadville's **Ice Palace**, which had been a fanciful attempt by the town to pull in visitors and create jobs. The ice structure – which featured ice walls eight feet thick and 50 feet high surrounding a ballroom, skating rink, restaurant, and even a peep show – took three months to build, went ten times over budget, and, despite attracting gawkers in the thousands, was a struggle to maintain. Eventually all investors pulled out, leaving it to melt.

Also worth a look are two of the town's earliest remaining houses, **Healy House** and **Dexter Cabin** (June–Aug 10am–5pm; $4; ℡719/486-0487), up behind the Heritage Museum. The former is a grandiose Greek-revival clap-board house, the latter a modest rough-hewn cabin mostly used as a gambling den. While you can poke around the Dexter Cabin on your own, you'll be

Horace Tabor and Baby Doe

Of all Leadville's extraordinary tales, the story of **Horace Tabor** is perhaps the most compelling – a classic account of rags-to-riches and back again. Having given up on his own luck to find gold in Colorado, Tabor became a storekeeper in Leadville, supplying goods to prospectors in exchange for a share in potential profits. He hit the jackpot when two prospectors developed a silver mine that produced $20 million inside a year. Tabor collected a one-third share and left his wife to marry local blue-eyed waitress "Baby Doe" McCourt in *the* wedding of 1883 in Washington, DC, which was attended by President Chester Arthur. For a long time Tabor lived a lifestyle that involved trading mines by day and sleeping in silk nightshirts with diamond buttons by night. But by the time of his death in 1899, he was financially ruined thanks to both investment errors and the 1893 silver crash. On his death, **Baby Doe** returned to Leadville to his only remaining mine, hoping for a turn of fortune in the industry, only to become a recluse during her 36 years of residence in the mine's simple cabin; she eventually died there, emaciated and frostbitten. The wooden outhouses of the **Matchless Mine** still stand, two miles out on 7th St (May–Sept 9am–4.15pm, Oct–April call for hours; $4; ℡719/486-4918), and in the crude wooden shack where she died, guides recount the story of Baby Doe's bizarre life in fascinating detail.

given a tour of the Healy House which was, for a time, a boarding house, and has now been furnished to represent that purpose and era. One exhibit is a sheet signed by local bigwigs and subsequently embroidered to represent a kind of Victorian *Who's Who* for the town – amongst the names is the now legendary Horace Tabor (see box, p.243).

Also downtown, don't miss the **Tabor Opera House**, 308 Harrison Ave (May–Sept daily 10am–5pm; $4; ☎719/486-8409, ⊛www.taboroperahouse .net), the contruction of which was funded by Tabor and built from scratch in under 100 days in 1879. You're free to wander onto the stage and around the eerie, dusty old dressing rooms while recorded oral histories tell tales of the grand theater's golden days. They give no details, sadly, of the time in 1882 when Oscar Wilde, garbed in black-velvet knee britches and diamonds, addressed a host of dozing miners on the "Practical Application of the Aesthetic Theory to Exterior and Interior House Decoration with Observations on Dress and Personal Ornament." For a closer look into the Tabor story, visit the **Tabor House**, 116 E 5th St (May–Sept daily 10am–4pm; $4; ☎719/486-2092), which has been reconstructed to look as at did in 1877, when Horace resided here with his first wife, Augusta.

Outdoor activities

The obvious attractions for fit **hikers** are the ascents of **Mount Massive** and **Mount Elbert**, most popularly started from the Colorado Trail trailheads beside Halfmoon Creek around seven miles southwest of town. Both are strenuous hikes, although the trail up each is relatively straightforward, with no real scrambling or full-body climbing involved. The average time for the return trip to the top of either peak from Halfmoon Creek is around six hours – and, due to frequent afternoon lightning storms, it's worth planning to have the hike completed by around midday. A good level hike, ideal for acclimatization, goes around the northern and eastern perimeters of Turquoise Lake. From around the lake there are great views over the water of the Mount Massive Wilderness, with the eponymous mountain at its center.

Mountain bikers also use the lakeside trail, the most technically challenging riding in the area. If combined with a road climb northeast from the lake, this can be made into a good twenty-mile loop descending on a fast dirt road beside the St Kevin Gulch after reaching fine views over town. A section of this route is used for the **Leadville 100**, the town's August hundred-mile mountain-bike race. Another high-energy route, detailed in a free guide from the visitor's center, is the Mineral Belt Tour – which guides you around an excellent twelve-and-a-half-mile loop, half of which is through the old Leadville mining district, while the other half snakes through aspen groves, conifer forests, and wildflower meadows. Bill's Sport Shop, 225 Harrison Ave (☎719/486-0739), **rents** out basic mountain bikes for $30 per day.

In **winter** there's no end of excellent **cross-country skiing** in the area, from quick jaunts on the groomed Mineral Belt Tour to the huge sprawling network of backcountry trails connecting the 10th Mountain Division Hut System (see box opposite). The most popular areas to ski are, however, north of town off US-24 before it crests the Continental Divide to drop into Miniturn. Here the Tennessee Pass Trail System, around thirteen miles from Leadville, offers a network of ski trails tailored to the needs of novice to intermediate skiers.

There are further cross-country opportunities on more regularly groomed trails at the local ski resort **Ski Cooper** (☎719/486-2277, ⊛www.skicooper .com), which lies just eight miles north of Leadville along US-24. Of course,

The 10th Mountain Division and its Hut System

Established during World War II, the **10th Mountain Division** was envisioned as an elite corps of crack troops for missions against the Nazis in the snow-covered regions of mountainous Europe. America's only winter warfare unit, the Mountain Division not only made several indispensable contributions to the war, but later, as veterans returned, became a major force in the development of skiing as a major recreation pursuit.

The 14,000 mountain troops were originally stationed at Camp Hale (dubbed Camp Hell) near Vail, which became the hub for exercises in which soldiers would strike out into the backcountry with ninety pounds of gear in their rucksacks, skiing on seven-and-a-half-foot-long hickory boards at altitudes of over 13,000ft. Conditions were extraordinarily tough although great pains were taken to make life easier. The first snowmobiles, motorized toboggans, and snowcats were all developed as a result of these endeavors. The division's most significant entry into the history books came on the night of February 18, 1945, near Florence, Italy. Having climbed the 2000ft escarpment of Riva Ridge in the dark, the division ambushed the German forces in foggy conditions, taking first the ridge, and on the next day Mount Belvedere. Both actions were later hailed as turning points in the war. During the fighting nearly a thousand 10th Mountain men were killed and more than 4000 were wounded; a memorial to the dead stands at the summit of Tennessee Pass, on the Continental Divide south of Camp Hale.

On their return, many 10th Division soldiers seemed naturally attracted to stay near snow and on skis: over 2000 became ski instructors, and it is claimed that 62 present-day American ski resorts were either founded or originally run by veterans. In Colorado, these included the development of both Aspen and Vail.

The development of the **10th Mountain Division Hut System**, 1280 Ute Ave, Aspen (℡970/925-5775, Ⓦwww.huts.org), was also the brainchild of a former 10th Division soldier. The system enables access to hundreds of miles of scenic backcountry mountain trails that sprawl over 34 square miles of national forest between Leadville, Aspen, and Vail. Well-marked and well-used trails connect the seventeen huts and a maze of side routes enable the creation of any number of different multi-day routes to ski, hike, or bike. While these routes are suitable for less-experienced skiers, skiing hut-to-hut requires a high level of fitness and winter wilderness skills; flawless map, route-finding, and compass skills are essential.

Each of the huts is furnished with basic necessities like wood, a stove, electric lights, and cookware; mattresses up the comfort level of the sleeping quarters, most of which sleep around sixteen people. Among the nicest are the Shrine Mountain Inn and the Fowler/Hilliard hut. To reserve a place in a hut ($25–40 per person per night) call the 10th Mountain Division Hut System, who can also reserve places for the even more remote Alfred A. Braun Hut System, which encompasses six huts between Aspen and Crested Butte. Reservations should be made well in advance for winter and are taken from June 1st for the following season. Paragon Guides (℡970/926-5299 or 1-877/926-529, Ⓦwww.paragonguides.com) run fully supported three- to six-day mountain biking or Nordic skiing trips between the huts; prices start at $990 for three days' skiing and $1660 for five days' biking.

more people come to the small down-to-earth resort to downhill ski or snowboard – attracted by the unpretentious atmosphere, uncrowded slopes, and inexpensive lift tickets. It's one of Colorado's smaller ski areas with only four lifts and 26 runs, spread over 400 acres (thirty percent beginner, forty percent intermediate, thirty percent expert), but there's a good variety of terrain, from gladed tree skiing and challenging moguls to groomed open slopes. For those with the skill and the cash there's the opportunity for some adventurous snowcat-accessible skiing on Chicago Ridge, where 1800 acres of untracked powder by the Continental Divide beckons – though at a steep $250 per day. Otherwise a day of skiing at the resort costs $36.

Eating and drinking

Leadville has a gratifying choice of inexpensive places to **eat** and **drink**. The southern end of town has long been a Hispanic stronghold and still provides a number of good Mexican food cantinas. Nightlife is best on the weekends and focuses on simple pleasures: pool and heavy drinking.

Casa Blanca 188 E 2nd St ☎719/486-9969. Great margaritas and decent Southwestern renditions of Mexican favorites.

Cloud City Coffee House 711 Harrison Ave ☎719/486-1317. Relaxed café where bagels, buns, and good espressos are served in a grand old hotel lobby. Opens at 7am.

Columbine Café 612 Harrison Ave ☎719/486-3599. Inexpensive and imaginative fresh food including Creole dishes and lots of vegetarian options, served in simple diner surroundings. Opens early (5.30am weekdays, 7am weekends) to deliver hearty breakfasts; stays open for lunch, too.

La Cantina one mile south on US-24 ☎719/486-9021. Spartan restaurant where great inexpensive Mexican and Southwestern food is served to diners in worn booths; good homemade tamales or tortillas smothered in a spicy green chili sauce and served with a great homemade salsa.

Prospector Restaurant 2798 Hwy-9 ☎719/486-0455. Upscale joint three miles north of town serving homemade soups, aged steaks, and Cajun food. Leadville's best smarter choice.

Quincy's 416 Harrison Ave ☎719/486-9765. Friendly pub with reasonable steaks, filet mignon for only $7, prime rib at $9, and a good line in cocktails.

Silver Dollar Saloon 315 Harrison Ave ☎719/486-9914. Old wood panelled gin-joint, patronized by Oscar Wilde after his performance at the Opera House, is today a welcoming place, thick with Irish memorabilia.

Aspen and around

Luxury travel magazines might have you believe that a tollgate outside **ASPEN** admits only film stars and the super-rich. This elite ski resort is indeed the part-time residence for the likes of Donald Trump, Jack Nicholson, Michael Douglas, and – until his death in 2005 – Hunter S. Thompson, but in summer the well-preserved Victorian town is one of the state's most attractive and can be an affordable and very appealing place for anyone to come – unless you're on an absolute shoestring budget. The valleys which spread out in all directions from almost the center of town make Aspen a great base for hiking and biking, not least in the famously picturesque **Maroon Bells** or the more remote **Crystal River Valley**. Visiting in winter requires serious cash, though you can save money by skiing in early spring or staying in the railroad town of **Basalt**, sixteen miles west, or in the Glenwood Springs area and commuting in, as much of the local workforce does.

From inauspicious beginnings in 1879, this pristine mountain-locked town developed slowly, thanks to its remote location, to become one of the world's top silver producers. By the time the silver market crashed fourteen years later, it had acquired tasteful residential palaces, grand hotels, and an opera house. Miners were quick to leave, though, and within a year of the crash only a quarter of the populace remained. In the 1930s, with the population slumped below seven hundred, it was ironically enough the anti-poverty WPA program that gave the community the cash to build its first crude ski lift. Entrepreneurs seized the opportunity presented by the varied terrain and plentiful snow, along with the know-how of former 10th Mountain Division soldiers stationed at nearby Camp Hale, and the first chairlift was dedicated on **Aspen Mountain** (formerly called Ajax) in 1947. Skiing has since spread to three more mountains – **Aspen Highlands**, **Snowmass**, and **Buttermilk** – and the social jet set arrived in force during the 1960s. Today each of those mountains has emerged with a distinct reputation and between them have every angle covered from near-perfect beginner areas to fiercely challenging backcountry-style terrain.

In recent years Aspen has been attempting to shake off its over-exclusive image, becoming the permanent host of the **Winter X Games**, and opening all its mountains to snowboarders (the sport was previously banned on the town's eponymous peak). The wealthy elite certainly still come, but so does a whole new set of regulars, and a flourishing, permanent community also manages to exist in a parallel world to the expensive visitors' version, a vital counterbalance to the decadent consumerism of its more ostentatious clientele.

Arrival, information, and getting around

In winter, Independence Pass on Hwy-82, which provides the quickest access to Aspen, is closed, and the detour through Glenwood Springs adds an extra seventy miles to the trip from Denver. Many instead choose to fly into **Sardy Field** (T970/920-5384, Wwww.aspenairport.com), the small airport four miles north of town on Hwy-82; if you fly into Denver, connecting flights bought in advance only cost another $80 or so. Or you can take a **shuttle** (make sure to book in advance) from Denver International Airport; shuttle companies include Colorado Mountain Express (T970/926-9800 or 1-800/525-6363, Wwww.cmex.com), who charge a whopping $108 each way. Another option is to fly into Eagle County Airport near Vail, an 80-minute drive away. Several **car rental** agencies have counters at the Aspen airport, including Dollar (T970/920-2008) and Alamo-National (T970/920-2603).

The town's most helpful source of information is the **visitor center** at 425 Rio Grande Place (Mon–Fri 9am–5pm; T970/925-9000 or 1-800/262-7736,

△ Independence Pass

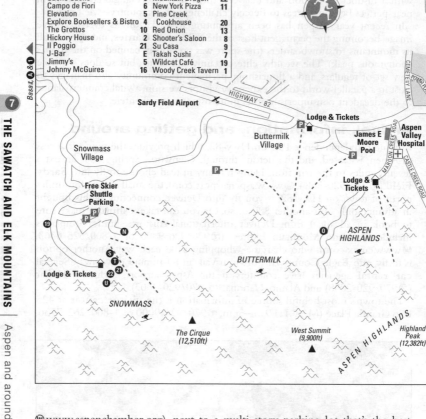

RESTAURANTS, BARS & CLUBS			
39° Lounge	R	Little Annie's	12
Belly Up	17	Main Street	
The Big Wrap	18	Bakery Cafe	3
Boogie's Diner	14	Mezzaluna	15
Cache Cache	6	Mountain Dragon	22
Campo de Fiori	6	New York Pizza	11
Elevation	5	Pine Creek	
Explore Booksellers & Bistro	4	Cookhouse	20
The Grottos	10	Red Onion	13
Hickory House	2	Shooter's Saloon	8
Il Poggio	21	Su Casa	9
J-Bar	E	Takah Sushi	7
Jimmy's	5	Wildcat Café	19
Johnny McGuires	16	Woody Creek Tavern	1

Sardy Field Airport

HIGHWAY - 82

Lodge & Tickets

Buttermilk
Village

James E
Moore
Pool

Aspen
Valley
Hospital

Snowmass
Village

Lodge &
Tickets

Free Skier
Shuttle
Parking

ASPEN
HIGHLANDS

BUTTERMILK

Lodge & Tickets

SNOWMASS

The Cirque
(12,510ft)

West Summit
(9,900ft)

Highland
Peak
(12,382ft)

ASPEN HIGHLANDS

Ⓦ www.aspenchamber.org), next to a multi-story parking lot that's the best place to leave your car while you explore town. The free *Aspen Daily News* ("If you don't want it printed, don't let it happen") is an excellent source of local gossip, news, and food and drink offers. For information on local forests and the three wilderness areas around Aspen – the Hunter Fryingpan, Maroon Bells, and Collegiate Peaks – contact the White River National Forest's Aspen Ranger Station, 806 W Hallam St (Mon–Fri 8am–4.30pm; ☏970/925-3445).

Once in Aspen, the Roaring Fork Transit Agency (☏970/925-8484, Ⓦwww .rfta.com) runs free **public buses** between the four ski mountains and also serves the airport and outlying areas. Conveniently, the winter bus service to the resort area of Snowmass, twelve miles northwest of Aspen, continues to operate until 2.30am ($2). Aspen's bus terminal is the Rubey Park Transit Center in the center of town on Durant Avenue. A **taxi service** is provided by High Mountain Taxi (☏970/925-8294).

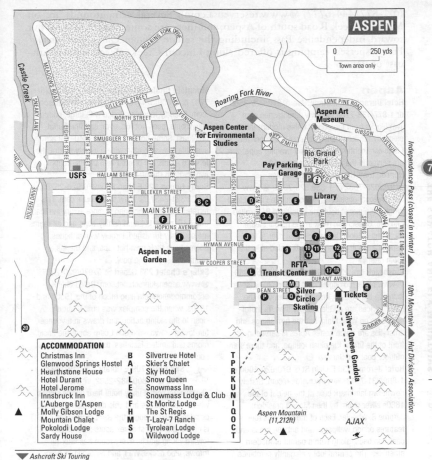

0   250 yds

Town area only

Independence Pass (closed in winter) ▶   10th Mountain ▶   Hut Division Association

Roaring Fork River

LONE PINE ROAD

Aspen Art Museum

GIBSON AVENUE

ROARING FORK DRIVE

MEADOWS ROAD

GILLESPIE STREET

Castle Creek

SNEAKY LANE

NORTH STREET

LAKE AVENUE

Aspen Center for Environmental Studies

PUPPY SMITH

Rio Grand Park

SMUGGLER STREET

EIGHTH STREET

SEVENTH STREET

FOURTH STREET

THIRD STREET

SECOND STREET

FIRST STREET

GARMISCH STREET

Pay Parking Garage

RIO GRANDE PLACE

P **i**

ORIGINAL STREET

WEST END STREET

FRANCIS STREET

HALLAM STREET

USFS

SIXTH STREET

FIFTH STREET

BLEEKER STREET

ASPEN STREET

MONARCH STREET

E

Library

MILL STREET

HUNTER STREET

SPRING STREET

HAGING ROAD

MAIN STREET

2

F

B C

D

3 4

5

HOPKINS AVENUE

G

H

6

7

8

GALENA STREET

I

HYMAN AVENUE

J

9

10 11

12

14

15

16

13

Aspen Ice Garden

W COOPER STREET

K

17 18

L

RFTA Transit Center

DURANT AVENUE

R

DEAN STREET

M

Silver Circle Skating

Tickets

RACE ALLEY

20

P

O

N Q

SUMMER AVENUE

Silver Queen Gondola

Aspen Mountain (11,212ft)

▲

AJAX

ACCOMMODATION

Christmas Inn	B	Silvertree Hotel	T
Glenwood Springs Hostel	A	Skier's Chalet	P
Hearthstone House	J	Sky Hotel	R
Hotel Durant	L	Snow Queen	K
Hotel Jerome	E	Snowmass Inn	U
Innsbruck Inn	G	Snowmass Lodge & Club	N
L'Auberge D'Aspen	F	St Moritz Lodge	I
Molly Gibson Lodge	H	The St Regis	O
Mountain Chalet	M	T-Lazy-7 Ranch	Q
Pokolodi Lodge	S	Tyrolean Lodge	C
Sardy House	D	Wildwood Lodge	T

▲

▼ *Ashcroft Ski Touring*

Accommodation

Though **accommodation** costs in Aspen are high, at least the range of possibilities is wide, spanning from hostel beds and 1960s condo suites to glamorous hotels and restored Victorian B&Bs in Aspen itself, or a slopeside lodge or condo over in Snowmass. Snowmass tends to be a shade cheaper, though in summer it's dead and in winter you're likely to spend a good deal of your time on shuttles heading to the bulk of the area's restaurants and nightlife in Aspen. Most options can be booked through **Aspen and Snowmass Lodging Reservations** (⊕970/925-9000 or 1-888/649-9582, ⓦwww.stayaspensnowmass.com). Another useful contact is McCartney Property Management (⊕1-877/369-8354, ⓦwww.mc-cartneyprop.com), who have a multitude of condos and private homes on their books; you can reserve online. Prices in the entire area at least halve during the **summer**, when **camping** is also a good cheap option; there are nine USFS campgrounds around Aspen, of which only a handful of sites are reservable

(☎1-877/444-6777, ⊛www.reserveusa.com). Several campgrounds are on Maroon Creek Road south of Aspen, and there are some smaller options out toward Independence Pass, including the serene *Lincoln Gulch Campground*. Free dispersed camping is offered along Lincoln Creek, eleven miles south-east of town.

Aspen

Hotel Durant 122 E Durant Ave ☎970/925-8500 or 1-877/438-7268, ⊛www.durantaspen.com. Two blocks from the gondola, this modern inn is elegantly furnished and has a great outdoor tub. Large continental breakfast and evening appetizers are served in the communal lounge. ❻

Hearthstone House 134 E Hyman Ave ☎970/925-7632 or 1-888/925-7632, ⊛www .hearthstonehouse.com. An homage to Frank Lloyd Wright, minimalist boutique hotel, and B&B rolled into one. Guests can relax in the herbal steam room and outdoor Jacuzzi or head over to the Aspen Club and Spa – access is included in the room rate. ❼

Innsbruck Inn 233 W Main St ☎970/925-2980, ⊛www.preferredlodging.com. Dated alpine-style lodge on the outside, eclectically sunny on the inside; prices are a little steeper than its motel neighbors on West Main, but the furnishings and amenities are much better. Après is served in front of the fire in the plush lounge, and there's an outdoor pool and Jacuzzi. ❽

Hotel Jerome 330 E Main St ☎970/920-1000 or 1-800/331-7213, ⊛www.hjerome.com. Stately downtown landmark built at the height of the 1880s silver boom by then Macy's president Jerome B. Wheeler. Each of the spacious rooms features period wallpaper and antique brass and cast-iron beds, along with a gamut of modern amenities. The central lobby elegantly combines Victorian splendor and Rocky Mountain chic and, along with the hotel's bar, *J-Bar*, is worth a look even if you're not staying. ❾

🏃 **L'Auberge D'Aspen** 435 W Main St ☎970/925-8297, ⊛www.preferredlodging .co.Idyllic little cabins – superbly outfitted with kitchens, fireplaces, hot tub, stereos, and VCRs – in a great location close to downtown. ❼

Molly Gibson Lodge 101 W Main St ☎970/925-3434 or 1-800/356-6559, ⊛www.mollygibson .com. Elegant small inn with fifty rooms and some suites only three blocks from downtown. The nine styles of lodging run from plain rooms with court-yard views to suites with four-person hot tubs and lounge. Some units have wood-burning fireplaces and kitchens. Lodge facilities include a courtesy airport van, après-ski bar, two pools, and two hot tubs. Rates include continental breakfast. ❼

Mountain Chalet 333 E Durant Ave ☎970/925-7797 or 1-800/321-7813, ⊛www.mtchaletaspen .com. Friendly mountain lodge with large, comfort-able rooms, pool, hot tub, gym, and fine buffet breakfast. Some dorm-style beds ($40–60) are available in winter, otherwise a variety of straight-forward rooms are offered with prices dropping by two-thirds in the off-season. ❼

Sardy House 128 E Main St ☎970/920-2525 or 1-800/321-3457, ⊛www.sardyhouse.com. This turreted red-brick Victorian is more luxury inn than true B&B: decor is Laura Ashley-style and all rooms are opulently furnished, largely with antiques. Rooms have their own hot tubs, and there's a sauna and swimming pool. ❽

Skier's Chalet 233 Gilbert St ☎970/920-2037, ⊛www.aspenskierschalet.com. Dated chalet accommodation retaining much of the 1950s and 1960s, when the complex was built – but it's close to the skiing action and draws in a younger, fun-loving crowd, who don't care about the basic rooms and limited facilities, though there is a pool. ❻

🏃 **Sky Hotel** 709 E Durant Ave ☎970/925-6760 or 1-800/882-2582, ⊛www .theskyhotel.com. Funky hotel hard on the slopes where the inventive and chic decor has a playful, decidedly 1970s, edge; the *39° Lounge* (see p.261) is one of the hippest après spots around. Geared toward young adults, every room has faux-fur throws, iPod docks, WiFi, and Nintendo in every room. Also has an outdoor pool, hot tub, and fitness room. Prices are steep, though, and even the basic rooms sometimes top $500 per night, though the price includes an evening wine reception. ❽

Snow Queen 124 E Cooper St ☎970/925-8455, ⊛www.snowqueenlodge.com. The oldest Victorian lodge in town is showing its age with rather faded furnishings, especially in the separate loft apart-ments – though by Aspen standards the prices are low. ❺

🏃 **St Moritz Lodge** 334 W Hyman Ave ☎970/925-3220 or 1-800/817-2069, ⊛www.stmoritzlodge.com. Aspen's unofficial youth hostel is in a European-style lodge five blocks from downtown. Its motel-style private rooms and dorms are some of the best bargains in town (weekly and monthly rentals are available) and consequently hard to get. Facilities include a small heated pool,

△ Sky Hotel, Aspen

steam room, kitchen, and a comfortable common room. Dorm beds $26–48. Continental breakfast included in winter rates. **⑥**

The St Regis 315 E Dean St ☎970/920-3300 or 1-888/454-9005, ⓦ www.stregisaspen.com. Aspen's most opulent lodging, a grand red-brick fortress with enclosed courtyards, endless corridors, fiery sculptures, and dark restaurants and drinking dens. Unfortunately, prices are surreal as well. **⑨**

T-Lazy-7 Ranch 3129 Maroon Creek Rd ☎970/925-4614, ⓦ www.tlazy7.com. Western-style decor in one of its most appropriate locations, a variety of small and large cabins in old ranch outhouses, three miles from Aspen Highlands en route to the Maroon Bells. Accommodations are rustic with no phones or TVs, and house up to ten people, with use of an outdoor heated pool and whirlpool. Activities offered by the ranch include horseback riding in summer, snowmobile and sleigh tours in winter. **⑤**

Tyrolean Lodge 200 W Main St ☎970/925-4595, 1-888/220-3809, ⓦ www.tyroleanlodge.com. This dated building, decorated with old skiing parapher-nalia, is great value for big groups, as each room has a kitchenette, two queens, and one twin bed. The top-floor rooms are the most spacious, though fitting five can be tight; some have fireplaces. No complimentary breakfast or hot tub. **❸–❺**

Snowmass

Pokolodi Lodge 25 Daly Lane ☎970/923-4310 or 1-800/666-4556, ⓦ www.pokolodi.com. Modest motel-style rooms beside the Snowmass Village Mall; among them snug quarters for four people to share. Facilities include a pool and hot tub, laundry facilities. A continental breakfast is included in rates as is pickup in a courtesy airport bus. **⑤**

Silvertree Hotel 100 Elbert Lane Snowmass Village ☎970/923-3520 or 1-800/525-9402, ⓦ www.silvertreeproperties.com. Large, full-service hotel right on the slopes with little in the way of visual charms but heavy on creature comforts. The health club includes outdoor pools and tubs, sauna, and steam rooms and there's a ski shop onsite. **⑦**

Snowmass Inn 67 Daly Lane ☎970/923-4202 or 1-800/635-3758, ⓦ www.snowmassinn.com. Both sparklingly well-kept hotel rooms and incredibly cramped condo units are offered in this chalet-style building. Guests have use of a hot tub, swimming pool, and sauna. In winter the minimum stay is five nights. **⑤**

Snowmass Lodge & Club 239 Snowmass Club Circle ☎970/923-5600 or 1-800/525-0710 ⓦ www.snowmassclub.com. Country-club-style resort at the base of Snowmass's ski slopes, whose accommodations are split between hotel rooms and one- to three-bedroom condos. A slopeside ski concierge and a courtesy shuttle to

Aspen are available; facilities include a splendid fitness center – with hot tubs, steam rooms, indoor tennis, squash and racquetball courts, and ski rentals. The minimum stay is usually two nights. Good-value golf and ski packages are sometimes offered. ⑥

Wildwood Lodge 40 Elbert Lane ☎970/923-3520 or 1-800/525-9402, ⓦwww.silvertreeproperties .com. The smaller, plainer brother of the *Silvertree Hotel* shares many of its facilities – including the health club – but is more economically priced. Breakfast is included in room rates. ⑥

The Town

There's not that much to do in Aspen itself, though strolling around the town's leafy pedestrianized streets or browsing in the chi-chi stores and galleries is a pleasant way to spend a couple of hours. Beyond that, you should call in at the excellent **Wheeler/Stallard Museum**, 620 W Bleeker St (Tues–Sat 1–5pm; $6; ☎970-925-3254), located in the 1888 Queen Anne-style former home of Jerome Wheeler, generally considered the town's founding father. The museum charts local history brilliantly by using a staggering array of sources, from artifacts and archived photos to literary references and video presentations.

Wheeler's up-and-down fortunes eventually led to bankruptcy, but before that he built Aspen's two most magnificent Victorian buildings. At the center of town, the solid and commanding **Wheeler Opera House**, beside the pedestrian mall at 320 E Hyman Ave (☎970/920-5770, ⓦwww.wheeleroperahouse .com), attracted the nation's top performers in its heyday and is still in use for various performances. Two blocks to the north, the rather plain and stocky (at least on the outside) **Hotel Jerome** is an equally famous landmark. Step inside to marvel at the lobby's distinctive fusion of contemporary Rocky Mountain chic with traditional Victorian decor, and then take a look at the photos beside the adjacent *J-Bar*, which show the place before its 1985 restoration.

Just north of downtown, on the northern side of the Roaring Fork River, is the **Aspen Art Museum**, 590 N Mill St (Tues–Sat 10am–6pm, Sun noon–6pm; $5, free Fri; ☎970/925-8050, ⓦwww.aspenartmuseum.org). In the absence of a permanent collection this museum can be a bit hit-and-miss, though usually its visiting exhibitions are good. Still, the many commercial galleries sprinkled about town often have bigger names on display – a testament to the bank accounts of local citizenry. Another more spectacular cultural installation is the **Benedict Music Tent**, the permanent main venue for the summertime Aspen Music Festival (see box, p.257); its many billowing canvas curves and sturdy lattice frame combine for an impressively space-age look.

Lastly, a good aperitif for more adventurous sorties into the wilds is a visit to the **Aspen Center for Environmental Studies**, 100 Puppy Smith St (Dec–April Mon–Fri 9am–5pm; May–Nov Mon–Sat 9am–5pm; $2; ☎970/925-5756, ⓦwww.aspennature.org). The center is beside the small Hallam Lake Wildlife Sanctuary, a first-rate reserve in which to watch wildfowl, and summer and winter offer a wide range of guided hikes and ski and snowshoe tours (bring your own gear) led by naturalists.

Winter activities

Most people come to Aspen to **ski** or **snowboard**, with four excellent resorts on distinctively different mountains to choose from. Those who have somehow managed to tire of the massive 5188 combined acres of ski area can head into the **backcountry** – access to which is possible from resort lifts or on tours – or **cross-country ski** on the valley's extensive network. Other popular winter activities include **ice-skating**, **sleigh** and **sled** rides, and **snowmobiling**.

Aspen Mountain, the first peak to be developed into a ski area, consists of predominantly expert terrain, while **Aspen Highlands** offers a backcountry-style playground. **Buttermilk** is a great beginner mountain, and the large, family-friendly **Snowmass** is covered in perfectly groomed cruising runs. The four mountains are connected by Hwy-82, with Aspen Mountain rising just out of downtown and Snowmass the last in the chain, nine miles away. All are included on the same ticket and, though most visitors zero in on one mountain per day, efficient free shuttles between them make transfers painless.

If you've still got energy after the slopes have closed – or are just looking for a relaxing day off – the prettiest spot to **ice-skate** in town is at Silver Circle Skating, across from the Ruby Park Transit Center at 433 E Durant Ave (admission $6.50, skate rental $2.50; ☏970/925-6364), while the Aspen Ice Garden, 233 W Hyman Ave (call for hours; $4; ☏970/920-5141), is a larger year-round indoor rink. **Dog sled rides** are offered by Krabloonik, 4250 Divide Rd, Snowmass ($225 for a half-day; ☏970/923-4342, ⓦwww.krabloonik.com). To be pulled up the Maroon Creek Valley by horses on a **sleigh** or take part in a **snowmobile tour** (from $160), contact the *T-Lazy-7 Ranch*, 3129 Maroon Creek Rd (☏970/925-4614).

Lift tickets, lessons, and rentals

Lift tickets are expensive, though you can book multi-day passes a week in advance to save up to ten percent. In April prices are slashed by around a third, with last-minute lift-and-lodging packages starting at under $100 per person – a huge discount on regular season prices.

The Aspen **ski school** (☏970/923-1227) has an excellent reputation but is also expensive – none of the prices quoted here include lift tickets or rentals, with the exception of the all-inclusive beginners' package ($129). An all-day kid's lesson (ages 7–12) costs $82, the adult equivalent $119. Challenge Aspen offers lessons for skiers with disabilities, starting at $80; lift tickets are half-price and adaptive equipment rental is around $20 (☏970/923-0578, ⓦwww.challengeaspen.com). **Day care** is provided by Snowcubs (☏970/923-0563 or 1-877/282-7736) for kids aged eight weeks to three years. Reservations are required, preferably a month in advance.

Pro Mountain Sports and D&E Ski and Snowboard (☏970/920-2337) are the well-stocked Aspen Skiing Company **rental** chains. Rates run $20–40 with discounts on multi-day rentals or if booked online a week in advance. In town, Hamilton Sports, 520 E Durant Ave (☏970/925-1200), has high-end ski demos and is rated for its ski-tuning skills.

Aspen Mountain

Overlooking town, the mogul-packed monster of **Aspen Mountain** is for experienced skiers only and consists of three ridges (International, Bell, and Gentleman's) between which trails and glades zip down gullies. First thing in the morning, consider taking lift 1A in preference to lining up with the crowds at the Silver Queen gondola. Later in the day, the best skiing and snow are near the summit, though you may find it worth skiing to the base to make use of the speedy Silver Queen gondola to the summit, rather than get caught in slower-moving lift lines further up. The best of the **intermediate** runs are just below the summit and under Ruthie's lift. On a powder day, **experts** should hit the short blacks off the back of the summit for a warm-up. The moguls here tend to be wider and softer than the bumpy, hard wall of double diamonds that make up the lower front face. If conditions are prime, head straight for Trainors, Rayburns, or Bingo Glades, gated areas open only

Information ☎970/925-1220 or 1-800/525-6200, ⓦwww.aspensnowmass.com; snow report ☎1-888/277-3676.

Ticket prices and operating times $78; late Nov to mid-April 9am–4pm.

Mountain statistics base elevation 7945ft, summit elevation 11,212ft, vertical drop 3267ft, acreage 673, average snowfall 300in.

Lifts and trails 8 lifts serve 76 trails: intermediate 48 percent, expert 52 percent.

as snow permits. Aspen Mountain's **freestyle park** is reasonable but only open in spring.

Aspen Highlands

With a ridgetop setting on Loge Peak, **Aspen Highlands** offers splendid scenery as a backdrop for some of Colorado's best adventure skiing and riding. Known primarily for its expert terrain, Aspen Highlands is the least crowded of the four resorts and most enjoyable for those who like moguls or are looking for a backcountry-like experience in gladed terrain or in the bleak, double-black diamond Highland Bowl. There is, however, terrain for all levels, draped on the mountain in a rather odd layout: on the area's front peak, black trails are at the bottom and the sides, greens in the middle, and blues at the top.

Though pleasant, the **beginner** trails are best avoided by the nervous, as the learning area sits in the trees atop a steep rise, invisible from the base area, and is served by a chairlift only accessible via a track that cuts across the black runs on the lower face. **Intermediates** are well served by two high-speed lifts that access mostly straight runs like Gunbarrel, along with a couple of longer, cruising runs. Intermediates looking for good snow are likely to find it early in the day on the Upper Robinsons – usually one of the last on the mountain to see much traffic. Snowboarders should stick to blue runs; one superb top-to-bottom tour cobbles together Broadway and Hayden Meadows with Prospector Gulch before hooking onto Jerome via Golden Barrel. For your first bumps, try Grandprix.

Extremely steep runs with the occasional powder stash are accessible to experts only in the Steeplechase and adjacent gladed Temerity areas, but the most tantalizing **expert** terrain lies behind on Highland Peak. Here the huge Highland offers steep powder faces, rocks, and chutes. Most of the bowl is above timberline but there are glades on the lower flanks. Be prepared to hike, though: it's a good hour to the summit, though you can drop in earlier along the ridge or catch a free ride on the snowcat (11am–1pm) which runs from the top of the Loge Peak lift to the first gate. Aspen Highlands has also become well known for its **Freestyle Fridays**, when local talent get to show off their aerial trickery in front of hordes of onlookers.

Aspen Highlands

Information same as Aspen Mountain.

Ticket prices and operating times $78; open mid-Dec to March 9am–4pm.

Mountain statistics base elevation 8040ft, summit elevation 11,675ft, vertical drop 3635ft, acreage 970, average snowfall 300in.

Lifts and trails 5 lifts serve 130 trails: beginner 18 percent, intermediate 30 percent, expert 52 percent.

THE SAWATCH AND ELK MOUNTAINS | Aspen and around

7

Buttermilk Mountain

At 420 acres, Buttermilk is the smallest of the four mountains and has one of the worst snowfall records in Colorado (100 inches less than its neighbors). Yet it's also one of the best places in the country to learn to ski, with its long, rolling runs at just the right pitch to encourage progression and build confidence. **First-timers** start on flats right by the base lodge, then progress to tree-lined trails at the top of the mountain under West Buttermilk lift. The long, rolling, wide-open, blissfully uncrowded cruising runs here also attract **snowboarders** in droves, and Buttermilk is the center of Aspen's annual December **Boardfest**, during which skiers are banned from the mountain. The epicenter of this festival is Buttermilk's exceptional **rail park**. Though there are some harder runs, experts and advanced intermediates with no interest in rail parks can happily ignore Buttermilk.

Snowmass

Larger than the other three Aspen areas combined, Snowmass boasts the longest lift-served vertical drop in the States. Spreading over a series of four distinct ridges, it's also the most well-rounded of the four mountains, with an extensive network of exquisitely groomed intermediate trails its particular forte. Despite statistics that claim only seven percent of its runs are green, **first-timers** will have no problem finding space on the flat lower slopes, and many mid-mountain blues are easily within the grasp of more confident **beginners**. Snowmass's sheltered, empty trails through the aspen trees on Two Creeks offer a good warm-up for lower **intermediates**. Elk Camp runs are slightly wilder with short, steeper sections, littered with bumps and rollers for high-speed launching. Gentle glades and long gullies are located on Big Burn; advanced intermediates looking for something steeper should try the groomed blacks and mogul runs off Sam's Knob. At midday, one previously closed run is opened for fresh corduroy carving – called the "Noon Groom" – details of which are posted on the daily grooming reports. Higher up off the ridgeline, the Cirque and Hanging Valley Wall offer **experts** rocky, technical descents, though don't attempt the latter toward the end of the day – the traverse out from the top of High Alpine lift is time-consuming. The **Trenchtown** park at Snowmass has some of Aspen's best built jumps along with a handful of sizeable rails. Snowmass's **halfpipe** is also well-proportioned, though it's only cut a couple of times a week and so is often rough. There's also a very basic beginner park.

Cross-country and backcountry skiing

Aspen's "Fifth Mountain" is easily its best value, since the 65km of **cross-country** ski trails groomed by the Aspen/Snowmass Nordic Council (Ⓦ www.aspennordic.com) is one of the most extensive free cross-country trail networks in the US. It can be accessed from both the Aspen Cross-Country Center, 308 S Mill St (Ⓣ 970/544-9246), and the Snowmass Club Cross-Country Center, 239 Snowmass Club Circle (Ⓣ 970/923-3148), both of which offer equipment and lessons (rentals around $15, lessons $30, tours from $50). Should you tire of these trails you can also explore the 22 miles of groomed trails maintained by Ashcroft Ski Touring Unlimited (passes from $10, rentals $20, lessons $45, tours $65; Ⓣ 970/925-1971), centered on the old ghost town of Ashcroft eleven miles west up Castle Creek Road.

Aspen Skiing Corp is happy for skiers to use its lifts to access the **backcountry**, and the exit gates off Highlands and Snowmass are consequently well used. The resort also offers a hand-holding experience by way of its pricey ($250–300) snowcat trips on the back of Aspen Mountain. Those in search of true backcountry adventure should contact Aspen Expeditions (Ⓣ 970/925-7625, Ⓦ www.aspenexpeditions.com) or Aspen Alpine Guides (Ⓣ 970/925-6618, Ⓦ www.aspenalpine.com), both of which run ski mountaineering trips and hut-to-hut tours among the surrounding mountains. Some of these head to 10th Mountain Division Huts (see p.245), trips which can easily be organized independently by experienced backcountry skiers. Overall the best source of local **gear** and **info** is Ute Mountaineer, 308 S Mill St (Ⓣ 970/925-2849, Ⓦ www.utemountaineer.com), which rents all sorts of backcountry skis and snowshoes.

Summer activities

Though far more **summer visitors** go to Aspen for its festivals and boutique shopping, the town's mountain setting also makes it a good hub for hikers and mountain bikers who want to explore trails in the spectacular Sawatch and Elk Ranges. To this end, the free *Ute Scout Hiking and Biking Guide*, available free from the visitor center, is an excellent resource. Many activities, particularly hiking and biking, can be done straight out of town, although some of the best trails are a short drive south near the ghost town of Ashcroft and around the picture-perfect Maroon Bells (see p.258), as well as an hour's drive west in the Crystal River Valley (see p.259).

One of the best short local **hikes** is the Ute Trail, which begins from the southeastern corner of town along Ute Avenue and zigzags steeply upwards to quickly give you great views. The Ute Trail is done by most as an hour-long out-and-back trail, though the path does carry on to hook up with the network serviced by the nearby Silver Queen gondola, 601 Dean St (early June to early Sept daily 10am–4pm; $20/day, $35/week; Ⓣ 970/925-1220), which climbs to the summit of Aspen Mountain. You can also join a free guided nature walk from the gondola's summit, which leaves on the hour from 11am to 3pm.

Even more so than hiking, **cycling** seems to be the main summer pursuit, with the Rio Grande Trail the most convenient and popular ride. The trail cuts through town on its easy but busy four-mile length beside the Rio Grande along an old railroad grade. For more challenging riding, head up Smuggler

Mountain. Going right to the top on the well-graded track is quite a slog, with more than 2500ft of climbing, so most cyclists go only as far as the lookout – about a quarter of the way up – for the fine views over Aspen and the Roaring Fork Valley. Continuing upwards leads to a fork in the path; the left trail heads down to a section of fun single-track which winds down to Hunter Creek and then back to the northern side of town (the right trail continues to the summit of Smuggler). The Hub, 315 E Hyman Ave (☎970/925-7970), has a wide choice of rental bikes, while Timberline, 516 E Durant Ave (☎970/925-3586, ⓦwww .timberlinebike.com), has some of the cheapest rentals, and organizes tours.

The Roaring Fork River, surging out of the Sawatch Range, is excellent for **kayaking** and **rafting** during a short season that's typically over by July. Beware, though, as sections of Class V rapids here are dangerous and every summer sees fatalities. Blazing Adventures, Snowmass Village ($50/half-day; ☎970/923-4544 or 1-800/282-7238, ⓦwww.blazingadventures.com) is a good guide choice. The Roaring Fork and its tributaries also offer splendid **fly-fishing**, although many coming to the area to fish head straight to **Basalt**, eighteen miles north-west of Aspen. Here a long stretch of clear public water surrounded by reddish bluffs, forests, and mountains is, thanks to regular insect hatches, the idyllic location of one of the state's premier fly-fishing spots. For gear and information on local access, check in with the Aspen Outfitting Company, 315 E Dean Ave (☎970/925-3406), or Aspen Sports, 303 E Durant St (☎970/925 6332).

Given the wealth in the area, both **hot-air ballooning** and **golf** have become popular sports – though many visitors are likely to be put off by the expense of either. For $250 the Aspen Unicorn Balloon Company (☎1-800/755-0935, ⓦwww.unicornballoon.com), offers a three-hour flight concluding with a champagne toast. The Aspen Golf Course (☎970/925-2145) is a relatively inexpensive eighteen-hole public course just outside town with greens fees from around $65 – visiting golfers are likely to enjoy the long flights of balls at altitude here.

Aspen's summer festivals

Ever since 1949, when Chicago industrialist Walter Paepcke celebrated the 200th birthday of German writer Goethe by bringing together a mix of musicians, philosophers, and scientists to celebrate here, summer festivals have been an important part of life in Aspen. The flagship event is the nine-week-long **Aspen Music Festival** (☎970/925-9042, ⓦwww.aspenmusicfestival.com), held between late June and late August, when orchestras and operas feature well-known international performers as well as promising students who come to learn from musical masters. Shows are more or less nightly. The main venues are the Wheeler Opera House, the Harris Concert Hall, at the north end of 4th St, and the Benedict Music Tent (see p.252 for the first and last of these). While concerts are the cornerstone of the event, it's well worth attending a workshop or rehearsal as well. Also in the summer are the **Theatre in the Park** (☎970/925-9313, ⓦwww.theatreaspen.org), a two-month series of contemporary plays, and the five-day **Aspen Filmfest** (☎970/925-6882, ⓦwww .aspenfilm.org).

Another major festival is the six-week-long **Dance Aspen Festival** (ⓦwww .aspenballet.com), which starts in late June and usually has reliably good contemporary shows; ticket prices start at $16. During the summer a free daily guide to what's on is available from Aspen's visitor centers. **Tickets** to all events can be purchased at the aforementioned Wheeler Opera House (☎970/920-5570, ⓦwww .wheeleroperahouse.com), whose program of concerts, plays, and dance performances runs year-round.

The surrounding valleys

Four major valleys converge in Aspen, of which **Castle Creek** and **Maroon Creek** stand out as the most interesting. Here you can hike and camp at hot springs, visit the preserved ghost town of Ashcroft, and see one of Colorado's most celebrated views – the famously picturesque Maroon Bells in the midst of the Elk Mountains. The third and fourth valleys are **Crystal River**, where you can visit a marble quarry and a 130-year-old mill power station, and **Roaring Fork**, through which runs Hwy-82 to Leadville. The latter is well worth the drive, at least as far as Independence Pass, to take in its desolate summit and high-alpine scenery.

Castle Creek Valley

The **Castle Creek Valley** follows a course almost due south of Aspen on the route you follow if you're heading to Crested Butte, 37 miles away by mountain bike or Jeep on rough tracks. More modest adventures are on hand en route, though, including a day-hike to the natural **hot springs** of Conundrum Creek. The trailhead is five miles south of Aspen down Castle Creek Road, which begins just west of town. From here an easy creek-side trail leads south down a narrow valley for nine miles. Allow at least five hours to make the return trip and have time for a soak. Free camping is allowed at designated backcountry sites, making the out-and-back hike a good overnight adventure.

A much easier and more accessible valley attraction is **Ashcroft** (mid-June to Aug; $3, guided tours Mon, Wed & Fri 10am; ☎970/925-3721), eleven miles south of Aspen. Once the largest town in the area, with a population of over 2500, its mines attracted investment from Horace Tabor, who once stood the whole town drinks when Baby Doe came to visit (see box, p.243). Today only nine rough-hewn wooden clapboard buildings remain, scattered across a meadow in this dreamy alpine valley. Almost all are boarded up, so it's hard to imagine the two bustling main streets that once housed three hotels and a newspaper office. That said, an Aspen Historical Society information booth and various placards help paint a picture of what this ghost town was once like.

Maroon Creek Valley

Despite the presence of many equally good options, the **Maroon Creek Valley** is the most popular hiking destination around Aspen, particularly for the glacial landscape around the twin purple-gray peaks of the soaring **Maroon Bells**, above the dark-blue Maroon Lake. The Bells are reached via the eleven-mile-long Maroon Creek Road, closed between 8.30am and 5pm to all except overnight campers with permits, disabled travelers, bikers, in-line skaters, and RFTA buses, which leave from the Aspen Highlands Ski Area (mid-June to Sept every 20min 9am–4.30pm; $6 round-trip).

From the end of the road, visitors are funnelled down a single trail to Maroon Lake. From here, it's best to head on a rough track up to **Crater Lake** – an out-and-back trail (3.6 miles round-trip) that takes a couple of hours and gives you some of best possible views of the Bells. A more ambitious prospect is the route up **Buckskin Pass**, a 9.6-mile round-trip which rewards at its end with an awesome vista of the Elk Mountains. The West Maroon Trail, which also begins from Crater Lake, heads over West Maroon Pass and down to Schofield Park, not far from downtown Crested Butte. This 11-mile hike includes a 3000ft ascent and takes approximately eight hours, but is easy enough for inexperienced-yet-fit hikers. You can arrange a taxi pickup from Schofield Park (Town Taxi ☎970/349-5543) or do the 14-mile hike into town along the East Maroon Pass via Gothic. For maps and directions contact the Aspen Forest Service office (see p.248).

Crystal River

Relatively few people visit the out-of-the-way **Crystal River Valley**, but along it are a couple of low-key and unusual mining towns. The larger settlement is **REDSTONE**, a former coal town mostly built by a philanthropist owner, including the lavish, Tudor-style *Redstone Inn*, originally built to house workers. But the real reason to head up the Crystal River Valley is to explore the area around **MARBLE**, famous for quarrying the eponymous material. The town began as a hub for the nearby Yule Marble Quarry, its population at one point exceeding 1500 and linked to the outside world by train. Today, you'll need your own vehicle to get here and visit the ruined old marble mill and scatter of houses that still makes up the town. From

△ Maroon Creek Valley

beside the old mill, a road climbs up four miles beside Yule Creek to the 10,000-square-foot still-working quarry area, from where the rock for the Tomb of the Unknown Soldier and the Lincoln Memorial in Washington, DC, came.

The other road out of Marble continues east past the small Beaver Lake before becoming rough enough to warrant a 4WD vehicle for the journey to the hamlet of Crystal. The track can be the first section of a superb twelve-mile hiking or mountain-biking loop (3–4hr) with great views of the Elk Range. The secluded route begins on CO-314 and follows the idyllic Crystal River closely to **CRYSTAL**, at the center of a large aspen grove. Just before arriving here you'll see the much-photographed **Sheep Mountain Mill**, a restored 1882 vintage powerhouse precariously perched on a rocky outcrop.

Eating

As expected, many of Aspen's classy **cafés** and **restaurants** are decidedly upscale; reservations are essential and entrees often top $25. But many also offer a bar menu featuring only slightly modified versions of entrees at a substantially lower price and usually available to walk-ins. Good budget places also exist and many of them are local bars serving reasonably priced food. The town's famous *Popcorn Wagon*, 305 S Mill St, serves crepes, gyros, and hot drinks for under $5, while Clark's Market, 300 Puppy Smith St, is the downtown **grocery**.

Aspen's **ski area** restaurants are a cut above – even the cafeteria-style lodge eateries are run by respected chefs. Oysters and sushi are served on the outdoor deck at *Gwyn's* on Aspen Mountain, goat cheese pizza in the warming hut at the top of Big Burn, and Mongolian barbecue at Buttermilk; meanwhile, *Cloud Nine* in Aspen Highlands (see below) is the top-rated resort restaurant.

The Big Wrap 520 E Durant Ave ☎970/544-1700. Small café with inventive wraps ($7) summing up various cuisines, from the American mashed potatoes with grilled steak and roasted veggies to the Mexican fajita burritos. Good line in healthy smoothies, too ($4).

Boogie's Diner 534 E Cooper Ave ☎970/925-6610. Worth stepping into for the 1950s diner-style experience alone, the restaurant is lined with vinyl and chrome and serves terrific meatloaf and mashed potatoes ($8.50) and killer shakes ($5), along with a few tofu-rich veggie options.

Cache Cache 205 S Mill St ☎970/925-3835. Elegant restaurant decorated in pastel hues serving items like rotisserie chicken with kalamata olives and capers, an outstanding *osso buco*, and duck salad with candied walnuts ($12). The lively bar serves up smaller, cheaper helpings of excellent food as well.

Campo de Fiori 205 S Mill St ☎970/920-7717. Cramped and noisy bistro with great Italian foods – there's a particularly good selection of antipasti and unusual pastas, like the *malfatti* dumplings, at moderate to expensive prices – complementing the wide range of fine Italian wines.

Cloud Nine Aspen Highlands ☎1-800/525-6200 ext 4715. Early evacuation gear makes up the decor at this former ski patrol cabin at the top of the Cloud Nine lift, now a gourmet bistro that offers Aspen's best on-mountain dining. Lunches are served daily, though after feasting on gruyere-stuffed pheasant sausage with cheese spatzle you might be tempted to call it a day. Instead you can enjoy the ambiance by just having a glass of wine or a quick schnapps on the deck, or by making a dinner reservation, which includes a snowcat trip up and down the mountain.

Explore Booksellers and Bistro 221 E Main St ☎970/925-5336. Great bookstore with high-quality and creative vegetarian food, good espresso and pastries, and a shady roof terrace.

Hickory House 730 W Main St ☎970/925-2313. Rib house that turns out the best sit-down breakfasts in town, from buttery waffles to meaty, southern-style platters. The place packs out for big-screen Monday Night Football when wings are 25¢ and domestic beers $1.

Il Poggio 73 Elbert Ln, Snowmass ☎970/923-4292. Bustling, warm Italian joint that's the pick of the bunch in the unexciting Snowmass dining scene, with good pasta and pizza and decent fresh antipasti, at only medium-expensive prices.

Johnny McGuires 730 E Cooper Ave ☎970/920-9255. Neighborhood sub shop that serves huge,

healthy sandwiches (around $7), accompanied by the deli's much-loved pickles.

Little Annie's 517 E Hyman Ave ☎970/925-1098. Lively, popular, and unpretentious saloon-style restaurant decorated in huge quantities of international golfing memorabilia. Hard to beat for good ol' down-home cookery: potato pancakes, hearty stews, and excellent burgers for lunch; huge trout, barbecued chicken, beef, or ribs for dinner – platters are around $15.

Main Street Bakery Cafe 201 E Main St ☎970/925-6446. Casual café busy in the mornings serving massive, fresh fruit-packed breakfasts and fine baked goods. Hot sandwiches, soups, and salads are served at lunch, while the dinner menu changes nightly. Opens 7am.

Mezzaluna 624 E Cooper Ave ☎970/925-5882. Noisy and hip Italian eatery where the walls are covered in original modern art and the menu dotted with pastas ($14–18) and pricier "big plate" entrees like ahi tuna and lamb shank. A little expensive – save the wood-fired pizza ($5) during après and the cheaper bar menu – but voted among Aspen's top three restaurants by readers of *Gourmet* magazine.

Mountain Dragon 67 Elbert Ln, Snowmass Village Mall ☎970/923-3576. Not the most inventive Asian restaurant in the world, but worth visiting for the après ski drink specials and free appetizers, served 4–6pm daily.

New York Pizza Hyman Ave Mall ☎970/920-3088. Snowboard stickers line the narrow stairs leading up to Aspen's best no-frills dining option, a hectic New York-style pizza parlor. Gigantic pies come smothered in all manner of toppings and are available to go or by the slice (around $3). Also offered are well-priced subs and salads. Open 11am–2.30am.

Pine Creek Cookhouse 11399 Castle Creek Rd, Ashcroft ☎970/925-1044. Ski in or ride a horse-drawn sleigh 1.5 miles from the ghost town of Ashcroft to a gourmet lunch or dinner. Dinner entrees include Rocky Mountain trout, Cornish game hen, quail, and lamb. Dinner prices vary with the menu but usually cost around $70, including the sleigh ride. The price is lower for skiers.

Su Casa 315 E Hyman Ave ☎970/920-1488. Authentic, moderately expensive Mexican food, with a number of excellent *carnitas* (fried pork) dishes, but also a big range of good veggie options like the spinach and mushroom enchiladas. Good margaritas served in an enjoyable courtyard.

Takah Sushi 420 E Hyman Ave ☎970/925-8588. Phenomenally good sushi and pan-Asian cuisine, in a buzzing, cheerful atmosphere. Highly recommended yet quite expensive, sushi running around

$6 a piece; pan-Asian dishes include pad Thai ($18) and Chilean sea bass ($25). Reservations suggested.
Wildcat Café 16 Kearns Rd No. 3, Snowmass ☎970/923-5990. Leave the high-class resort scene behind at this no-frills Snowmass diner. From breakfast to dinner all the standard American and Mexican options are inexpensive and reliably satisfying enough to make regulars of the locals.

Nightlife

Going out in Aspen, the American capital of **après-ski**, is fun year-round and need not be expensive. The scene is dynamic, with a distinctly urban flavor, and people here eat and drink later than at other Colorado resorts, with bands and DJs kicking off well after 10pm. Bars frequently change hands, but those listed below are dependable favorites. Note that nightlife, which in Aspen generally means serious drinking, is not just restricted to bars – many restaurants have bar areas that stay open just as long.

Quiet nights can be spent at the three-screen **Stage 3 Theater**, 625 E Main St (☎970/925-2050), or catching an art-house film or show at the Wheeler Opera House (☎970/920-5770). In summer, several top-notch festivals (see box, p.257) add a bit of verve to the otherwise laid-back scene. Pick up a copy of the free *Aspen Daily News* from street-corner dispensers for detailed listings.

39° Lounge 709 E Durant Ave ☎970/925-6760. *The* place to be when the lifts close, this chic club and bar with its Seventies aesthetic would be equally at home in Manhattan or Berlin. But amid the geometric curves, low lights, flickering fires, and leather sofas, ski boots tap to DJ-spun ambient beats.

Belly Up 450 S Galena St ☎970/920-6905. Cavernous basement venue that hosts everything from big-name bands to calendar-girl contests and has an almost cinema-sized screen for sports events. Not a bad place for a drink on busy nights, otherwise you tend to rattle around in the space.

Elevation 304 E Hopkins Ave ☎970/544-5166. Stylish, warm restaurant that doubles as the town's late-night DJ bar. Has that big-city atmosphere down pat.

J-Bar in the *Hotel Jerome*, 330 E Main St ☎970/920-1000. The historic *Hotel Jerome*'s grand bar is a good place to soak in the hotel's atmosphere and rub elbows with well-heeled guests.

Jimmy's 205 S Mill St ☎970/925-6020. Reliably buzzing bar with a sociable deck and a superb selection of tequilas. There's also a restaurant that serves top steaks and traditional American comfort food like the excellent meatloaf ($10). Sit at the bar if you'd like your entree to be under $10.

Red Onion Cooper St Mall ☎970/925-9043. Aspen's oldest bar is a popular après-ski spot, generally raucous and with a lethal line in Jell-O shots. In summer it's fairly busy with street-side tables in the Mall allowing for entertaining people-watching. Also serves big portions of standard American pub fare (great burgers) and some Mexican food – it's one of the few places in town to get a filling dinner for under $10. Food until 10pm, bar until 2am.

Shooter's Saloon 220 S Galena St ☎970/925-4567. Rowdy and raucous Country & Western bar

Gay Aspen

Though Colorado was once one of the least **gay-friendly** states – for a long time boycotted by the gay community for its discriminatory laws – Aspen has always been, outside of Denver, the state's exception. Along with some of the oldest anti-discrimination laws in US, the town has developed a small gay scene. Even so, the town has no real gay hangouts or bars – except during **Gay Ski Week** (🌐www.gayskiweek.com) in late January when it seems hard to find a straight bar. For local information contact the Aspen Gay and Lesbian Community Information Hotline (☎970/925-9249).

with pool tables, dance floor, and frequent Eighties nights.
Woody Creek Tavern Upper Never Rd, Woody Creek ☎970/923-4585. Unpretentious local bar where ranch hands and rock stars shoot pool, guzzle fresh lime-juice margaritas, and eat good Tex-Mex. The bar is in tiny Woody Creek, seven miles north of Aspen along Hwy-82.

Listings

Bookshops Explore Booksellers & Bistro, 221 E Main St ☎970/925-5336.
Internet Pitkin County Library, 120 N Mill St ☎970/925-4025.
Medical Aspen Valley Hospital, 0401 Castle Creek Rd ☎970/925-1120.
Pharmacy Carl's Pharmacy, 306 E Main St ☎970/925-3273.
Police Pitkin County Courthouse, 506 E Main St ☎970/920-5400.

Post office 235 Puppy Smith St, Aspen, or 1106 Kearns Rd, Snowmass.
Recreation centers Aspen Recreation Center, 895 Maroon Creek Rd (Mon–Fri 6am–8.45pm, Sat 7am–8.45pm, Sun 8am–8.45pm; ☎970/920-5145; $15). State-of-the-art center incorporates a swimming pool, climbing wall, ice rink, and fitness facilities.
Taxi High Mountain Taxi ☎1-800/528-8294.

Crested Butte

The painfully pretty Victorian mining village of **CRESTED BUTTE** began as a thriving gold camp in the early 1880s, but became far more important for the rich seams of coal discovered here a few years later. While coal deposits began to run out in the late 1950s, the town was saved by development of the 11,875-foot Mount Crested Butte into a world-class ski resort a few years later. Now a mountain-bikers' paradise as well, this picturesque former mining town can justifiably claim to be among the best year-round destinations in Colorado, fostering a laid-back lifestyle that perennially attracts some of the state's most soulful ski bums.

Unlike other resort towns that have given in to commercialization, downtown Crested Butte is resplendent with gaily painted clapboard homes and local businesses, and zoning laws ensure that condos and chalets are confined to the resort area, **Mount Crested Butte**, tucked behind the foothills three miles up the road. The peaceful, nature-first vibe that permeates the town is threatened though by a possible mining resurgence: Mt Emmons – the 12,392ft mountain that watches over town – is home to the world's largest molybdenum deposit, the estimated value of which lies at around $7 billion. For almost thirty years locals have fought a plucky battle against a large mining conglomerate, which remains ongoing even though the BLM has sold the land to the conglomerate for $5 an acre, ignoring all local protests. Thankfully, at least market conditions have put things on hold for now. More imminent are developments further up the valley: in 2004, new owners bought the resort and embarked on a multi-year, $200-million capital improvement project, the announcement of which alone almost doubled local housing prices.

Arrival and information

A five-hour drive southwest from Denver along mostly minor highways, Crested Butte is not an easy place to get to, even though Colorado's high desert weather patterns mean that the roads are almost always open – including Hwy-50 over Monarch Pass. Most skiers fly in: regular daily **flights** from Denver, and at least one per week from Atlanta, Dallas, and Houston, touch down at

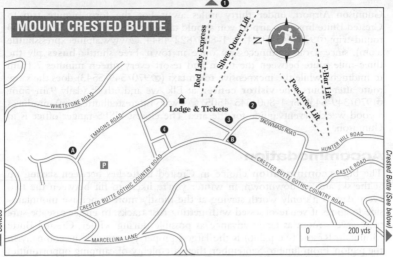

ACCOMMODATION

The Claim Jumper B&B	**I**
Crested Butte Club	**F**
Crested Butte International Hostel	**C**
Cristiana Guesthaus	**E**
Elk Mountain Lodge	**D**
The Great Escape	**G**
The Inn at Crested Butte	**H**
Old Town Inn	**J**
Pioneer Cabins	**K**
Club Med	**B**
The Nordic Inn	**A**

RESTAURANTS & BARS

Avalanche	**4**
Bacchanale	**8**
The Brick Oven Pizza	**11**
Donita's Cantina	**19**
The Eldo	**21**
Firehouse Grill	**2**
Idle Spur	**18**
Kochevar's Saloon	**7**
The Last Steep	**16**
Last Tracks Dinner	**1**
Lil's Land and Sea	**6**
Lobar	**12**
Marchitelli's Gourmet Noodle	**22**
The Paradise	**13**
Pitas in Paradise	**20**
Powerhouse	**15**
Princess Wine Bar and Coffee House	**10**
The Rafters	**3**
Soupçon	**5**
Teocali Tamali	**14**
Timberline	**9**
Wooden Nickel	**17**

Gunnison Airport, under thirty miles away. For the forty-minute trip to Crested Butte from the airport you should take the Alpine Express Shuttle ($53 round-trip; ☎970/641-5074 or 1-800/822-4844, ⊛www.alpineexpressshuttle .com), since a car is unnecessary once in town. Free shuttle **buses** ply the three-mile route between the town and resort every fifteen minutes 7.15am to midnight, while the inexpensive town taxi (☎970/349-5543) does the same route after hours. The **visitor center**, at Elk Ave and 6th St (daily 9am–5pm; ☎970/349-6438 or 1-800/545-4505, ⊛www.visitcrestedbutte.com), produces a good weekly events guide for the area. The closest USFS ranger office is in Gunnison.

Accommodation

The big **accommodation** choice in Crested Butte lies between staying up at the ski area or downtown; in winter you're likely to flit between the two every day, so it's only worth staying at the mostly more expensive mountain-side lodgings if you're obsessed with getting first tracks. In either case, be sure to reserve a room as far in advance as possible during winter; Crested Butte Mountain Resort (see p.266) is the largest property management company in the region. From June to September, there are plenty of camping opportunities in the surrounding National Forest, including the primitive USFS *Lake Irwin Campground* (☎1-877/444-6777, ⊛www.reserveusa.com; $12), ten miles west of Crested Butte on CR-2 and FR-826.

Downtown

🏃 **The Claim Jumper B&B** 704 Whiterock Ave ☎970/349-6471. Six variously themed rooms amid a jumble of Americana and other odds and ends makes this historic log home one of the most enjoyable B&Bs in Colorado. Big breakfasts, a hot tub, sauna, and friendly owners are also vital ingredients. ❺

Crested Butte Club 521 Second St ☎970/349-6655 or 1-800/815-2582, ⊛www.crestedbutteclub .com. Dignified hotel in an 1886 bar and brothel, sporting eight elegant antique-filled rooms. The facilities are a bit tatty but include steam baths, pool and hot tub, and fitness machines. Good continental breakfast included. ❻

🏃 **Crested Butte International Hostel** 615 Teocalli Ave ☎970/349-0588 or 1-888/389-0588, ⊛www.crestedbuttehostel.com. Large, friendly, ultraplush hostel (swipe-card access rooms), where dorm beds cost $22–35 depending on season (private rooms $55–87). Communal facilities are great: the large, comfortable lounge adjoins the dining area and well-equipped kitchen. A large public laundry is on site as well. Free WiFi. Office hours daily 7.30am–noon, 3–9pm.

Cristiana Guesthaus 621 Maroon Ave ☎970/349-5326 or 1-800/824-7899. European ski lodge-style B&B in the center of Crested Butte. All rooms are en suite, and a hearty continental breakfast is served daily. Sauna, outdoor hot tub, and fabulous mountain views round out the package. ❺

Elk Mountain Lodge 129 Gothic Ave ☎970/349-7533 or 1-800/374-6521, ⊛www .elkmountainlodge.net. Renovated 1919 miners' hotel with a homey, worn-in feel and reputedly a resident ghost. The grand piano, indoor hot tub, and library (free Internet) add to the appeal, but it's the friendliness of the staff that really makes the place. Continental breakfast is served in the enclosed verandah. ❻

The Great Escape 329 Whiterock Ave ☎970/349-1131, ⊛www.thegreatescapebnb.com. Intimate, four-room B&B on a downtown residential street with overwhelmingly Southwestern decor. The ski shuttle stops on the doorstep and there's a hot tub. ❹

The Inn at Crested Butte 510 Whiterock Ave ☎970/349-1225 or 1-800/949-4828. Relaxed seventeen-room ranch-style inn with Scandinavian-style rooms and a homey communal lounge, containing games, kids' toys, and musical instruments. The outdoor hot tub has wonderful views, and an large continental breakfast is included in the reasonable rates. ❸

Old Town Inn Hwy-35 and Belleview Ave ☎970/349-6184. Standard motel rooms beside the main highway at the southern edge of town. ❺

Out of town

Pioneer Cabins Cement Creek Rd ☎970/349-5517, ⊛www.thepioneer.net. A cluster of 1920s cabins, ten minutes' drive southeast of town in the

Gunnison National Forest, sleep four to six each and come with wood stoves or open fireplaces, sheets, fully equipped kitchens, and a heavy dose of wilderness. Communal phone and TVs on request. **4**

Mount Crested Butte

Club Med 500 Gothic Rd ⊕970/349-8700, Ⓦwww.clubmed.com. Crested Butte's most exclusive hotel – and America's only all-inclusive ski resort hotel – is right beside the chairlifts. All rooms are outfitted luxuriously, including whirlpool baths; communal facilities include indoor and outdoor hot tubs, a pool, sauna, and gym. **9**

The Nordic Inn 14 Treasury Rd ⊕970/349-5542 or 1-800/542-7669, Ⓦwww.nordicinncb.com. This surreal fusion of Scandinavia and 1950s motel is just five minutes' walk from the lifts. Continental breakfast is included, as is the chance to lounge around the fireplace in the cozy lobby or in the outdoor hot tub with its valley views. Some rooms have kitchenettes. **4**

Downtown

Pretty as it is, it won't take you long to take in Crested Butte's tiny **downtown**. Colorfully painted and lined by the original and eye-catching work of two local artists – who've used chrome bumpers to make a series of striking and unusual sculptures – the six short blocks of **Elk Avenue**, the town's main drag, is lined with a pleasing array of cafés, Wild West saloons, and outdoors outfitters. Keep an eye out for some of the two-story buildings with doors on the second floor, there to allow easy access during deep winter snowdrifts; one is in the alley behind Company Store at Elk Ave and 3rd St. To get a quick introduction to the town's history, head over to the **Crested Butte Mountain Heritage Museum**, 331 Elk Avenue (summer and winter noon–8pm, spring and fall call for hours; free; ⊕970/349-1880), housed in an 1883 restored blacksmith shop, hardware store, and gas station. Portraits of early Butte residents – many of Croatian and Slovenian descent – line the back wall, revealing the hardscrabble character of many who kept the town going in its mining days. The back room ($3) includes exhibits on daily life during the mining era and the evolution of skiing, as well as the **Mountain Bike Hall of Fame**, where a selection of old-school parts bring tears of nostalgia to older bikers.

Winter activities

Located at 9375 feet and averaging some 240 inches of snow a year, Crested Butte has a long **winter activity** season, often stretching from November to April. The main draw is obviously the ski resort north of town (see below), though cross-country skiers, snowshoers, and snowmobilers are well-provided-for after, too. The visitor center is particularly helpful and provides a map of trailheads in the Gunnison National Forest that are open for winter sports.

Cross-country skiers should check in at the Crested Butte Nordic Center, 2nd St and Whiterock Ave (⊕970/349-1707, Ⓦwww.cbnordic.org), which maintains 50km of trails and offers cross-country ski rentals from $18 and snowshoes at $12 per day. Trail passes are $14, though the town-owned trails through town and up to Mount Crested Butte are free. The staff can also provide advice on the extensive backcountry opportunities in the area, including an overnight hike up to the Forest Queen Hut in the ghost town of Gothic. The hut sleeps eight and has a fully equipped kitchen with firewood and drinking water, though food and bedding must be brought ($16/person per night). The Nordic Center is also home to a small free **ice rink** (call for hours; skate rental $6/hr).

Easy guided **snowshoe** tours are offered at the resort (⊕970/349-2211) while Crested Butte Mountain Guides (⊕970/349-5430, Ⓦwww .crestedbutteguides.com) can take you on serious **backcountry** adventures on skis or snowboards, either for the day ($125/person) or overnight ($240/person) from a hut or yurt base. Other possible activities include **horseback riding** (from $40/hr) at Fantasy Ranch Horseback Adventures (℡970/349-5425, Ⓦwww.fantasyranchoutfitters.com); **dogsledding** with the Cosmic Cruisers (℡970/641-0529); or **snowmobiling** with a company like CB Snowmobiles (℡970/209-0109), who offer rentals suitable for both first-timers and experienced riders ($95/$165 for a half/full day's rental).

Crested Butte Mountain Resort

In skiing and snowboarding circles, **Crested Butte Mountain** is best known for extreme terrain, its lifts serving terrifyingly steep bowls and faces that would be out of bounds at many other resorts. It's no surprise, then, that the resort hosts both the US extreme skiing and snowboarding championships. But below the steep upper reaches the lower slopes quickly fan out in a wide web of flat easy blues and greens, keeping the slopes accessible to all – though note that what is defined as intermediate terrain here tends either to be a bit too hard or far too easy. With the ungroomed terrain and greens out of the equation, Crested Butte is pretty small, and a week's vacation for an intermediate is pushing it, particularly for snowboarders, who have to contend with several unavoidable flat spots around the mountain. However, beginners are well served by the selection of greens and the large number of easy blues on which to progress, as well as benefiting from the lack of crowds that come with the resort's relatively isolated location. This may be set to change, though, given the ambitious development program underway: most of the base area is being expanded, revamped, rebuilt, and enlarged, and the opening up of a new area on an adjacent mountain is in the pipeline.

If you've driven up to Crested Butte for a day of skiing, you're as well to leave your vehicle at the **free parking lots** by the visitor center and catch a shuttle up to the slopes. Alternatively you will have to pay $8 for a spot that's further from the slopes than the shuttle bus stop.

Lift tickets, lessons, and rentals

Savings of up to ten percent can be had by booking multi-day **lift tickets** online in advance, which is also the place to look for well-priced last-minute lift-and-lodging packages.

The **ski school** (℡970/349-2252 or 1-800/444-9236) offers beginner's lesson-and-lift packages from $99, but those with some experience can do a group workshop. These are pricey, at $80–90 for 2.5 hours instruction, but at least guarantee a group size maximum of four people. Specialty workshops – including bumps, powder, telemark, and racing – are the same price. The

---

Crested Butte Mountain Resort

Information ℡970/349-2333 or 1-800/544-8448, Ⓦwww.skicb.com; snow report ℡1-888/442-8883.

Ticket prices and operating times $73, open daily late Nov to early April 9am–4pm.

Mountain statistics base elevation 9375ft, summit elevation 12,162ft, vertical drop 2775ft (lift-serviced) or 3062ft (with inbounds hike), acreage 1058, average snowfall 240in.

Lifts and trails 15 lifts serve 106 trails: beginner 23 percent, intermediate 57 percent, expert 20 percent.

Adaptive Sports Center of Crested Butte (☎970/349-2296 or 1-866/349-2296, ⓦwww.adaptivesports.org) has offered tuition and equipment rental since 1987; they also organize other activities including cross-country and backcountry skiing, snowshoeing, ice-skating, dogsledding, and snowmobiling. **Day care** is provided at Kid's World (☎970/349-2258 or 1-800/600-7349) for kids aged six months to seven years; ski lessons can be taken aged three and snowboarding from eight.

The **rental shop** in the Gothic Center is adequate and has, besides the usual gear, telemark and cross-country skis, snowshoes, and helmets. Packages vary between $25–35 per day, with discounts available for booking online. For a wider selection of snowboards, head straight to local snowboard specialists Colorado Boarder, in the slopeside Mountain Mall (☎970/349-9828); close by is Flatiron Sports (☎970/349-6656, ⓦwww.flatironsports.net), the skier's equivalent.

Mountain runs

First-timers get to grips with the basics conveniently close to the base area, with the next logical step heading up the Red Lady Express to the long greens on the lower half of the mountain. However, faster traffic returning from above and a series of flat spots annoying to snowboarders makes the trail here less than ideal. A much better bet is to head over to the Painter Boy and Gold Link lifts, where the blues are so quiet and evenly pitched that they offer ideal learning conditions, particularly for boarders.

With a good chunk of the **intermediate** terrain effectively within the grasp of beginners, it's surprising that much of what's left is extremely taxing. The Paradise Bowl is the prime intermediate area, with a small selection of well-groomed but steep and often icy cruising runs to the base of the Paradise lift. The area of the mountain below – accessed by the East River lift – is less steep, but also less groomed, resulting in challenging bump runs and a couple of small gladed areas.

Most of the **expert** runs are supremely taxing and don't open consistently until January, though in poor years quite a chunk of the ski area stays out of bounds altogether. All but a handful of black runs are deemed double-black diamonds, with some of the difficulties compounded by access which is generally via awkward surface lifts. The easiest area to reach is off the Silver Queen lift, where a wide expanse of treeless bowl and couloir riding gives way to aspen glades. The High lift T-bar places you on top of the infamous Headwall: here, stay low for short, sharp tree runs, or hike up further around the bowl for cliff bands and more powder. Below this area (and accessed by the North Face lift) are a series of slightly easier bowls that tend to hold powder better than Headwall.

With so much interesting and challenging natural terrain, man-made **terrain parks** aren't a high priority at Crested Butte. That said, local involvement means the pipe here is pretty decent, with several good-sized jibs and some quite fearsome jumps in the Canaan Terrain Park.

Summer activities

Once the snow melts and the summer season begins, the Nordic ski trails that dot the valley emerge as scenic **hiking** and **mountain-bike** routes, crisscrossing through the valley's wildflower-covered meadows. This assortment of blossoms – including purple and white columbine, orange scarlet gilia, yellow mule's ear sunflowers, blue lupine, pink wild rose, and violet flax – are celebrated during July's **Wildflower Festival** (☎970/349-2571, ⓦwww.crestedbuttewildflowerfestival .com), when a program of photography, painting, and herbal medicine workshops

Biking the Butte

In summer, **mountain bikers** all but outnumber cars around town, especially during July's **Fat Tire Week** (ⓦwww.ftbw.com), a festival that according to local legend evolved from a race over the rocky 21-mile Pearl Pass to Aspen on newspaper bicycles in the 1970s. Though claims that Crested Butte is the birthplace of mountain biking are disputed by Californians from Marin, no one argues that this is premier mountain-bike country. While the visitor's center can help out with a basic map for the main trails, it's usually best to get a route map and information from a local **bikeshop** before heading out. The Alpineer, 419 6th St (ⓣ970/349-5210), is a good source of info and equipment, as is the Colorado Boarder Bike Shop, 32 Crested Mountain Ln (ⓣ970/349-9828). The latter is at the base of the lifts in the mountain resort, where a good network of trails (lift-serviced; $18) has been built. Both shops rent front- suspension bikes for around $35/day. No mountain-bike holiday in the area is complete, though, without tackling these three **classic trails**:

Trail 401 Without a doubt one of the most incredible rides in Colorado. The trails starts as a seven-mile grind north from Gothic to Schofield Pass on FS-317. From the pass, it's single-track all the way back, starting with a short, sharp section climbing to fantastic views over surrounding peaks before leading into some of the best smooth and fast single-track possible. The trail swings down countless hairpins as it follows the side of the East River Valley back to Gothic. The best part is above the intersection with the dirt road to Schofield, though if you've still got the energy it's better to continue on Trail 401 back to the start than retrace your bike tracks along the road. The loop is around fifteen miles long and typically takes 3–4 hours.

Dyke Trail Heading southwest from Lake Irwin through stands of aspen, this beautiful single-track trail is part of a fourteen-mile loop that uses the Kebler Pass Road, a former railroad bed, to link the trail's two ends. Expect to spend around three hours riding the loop, which starts from Lake Irwin, twelve miles west of Crested Butte along Kebler Pass Road.

Deadman's Gulch Trail A superb longer loop that encompasses a great variety of trails and terrain including some long climbs, fast descents, and a series of famed rolling switchbacks to finish off with. Typically this twenty-mile ride takes around five hours. To reach the start, head seven miles south of Crested Butte on Hwy-135, then a further seven miles along the unsurfaced Cement Creek Road (aka CR-740).

are offered. While mountain biking is the big story around these parts, hikers are also spoilt for choice, with many of the best areas used by both (see box above). To wander around the area's best-preserved **ghost town**, head eight miles north of Crested Butte, passing through the resort area to **Gothic**. The visitor center (see p.264) or the adjacent Alpineer outdoors store have plenty more advice on nearby trails. The best **kayaking**, **rafting**, and **fishing** in the area is found south near Gunnison.

Eating and drinking

Crested Butte boasts a surprising number of gourmet **restaurants**, happily charging less than their equivalents in the more glitzy resort towns. Good, inexpensive food is also easy to find – even around the ski lifts, a filling lunch can be had for around $6. The early après-ski center is *Rafters,* right by the lifts, but by early evening most visitors have found their way downtown to the restaurants or rowdy **local bars**, all of which are within a couple of blocks of each another on Elk Avenue. For other entertainment try the Majestic Theater, at Majestic Plaza (ⓣ970/349-7570), which schedules a mix of blockbusters and art-house **films** on its three screens, while the Crested Butte Center for the

Arts, 606 Sixth St (☎970/349-7487), shows special-interest movies and stages plays, readings, and concerts. Check listings in the *Crested Butte Weekly* (free) or *Crested Butte Daily News* (50¢).

Downtown

Bacchanale 208 Elk Ave ☎970/349-5257. Intimate restaurant with a varied Northern Italian menu including good veal and cannelloni along with a range of specialty desserts. Dinner only; entrees start at around $14. A $2 tapas menu is offered 5–6pm & 8–9pm, and food is served at the bar until 11pm.

The Brick Oven Pizza 229 Elk Ave ☎970/349-5044. Popular downtown hangout with a sunny deck for reliable pizzas and subs. Free delivery.

Donita's Cantina 332 Elk Ave ☎970/349-6674. Excellent Mexican restaurant famed for its tasty homemade salsa. The large, inexpensive portions of chile rellenos, fajitas, or the more unusual spinach enchilada are all well worth trying. Lots of veggie options.

The Eldo 215 Elk Ave ☎970/349-6125. Rustic upstairs brewpub in a long, narrow building that could be straight from the set of a Western. Hosts the sort of up-and-coming roots/rock/funk/bluegrass fusion bands that mountain folk love to twirl to on the frantic dance floor.

Idle Spur 226 Elk Ave ☎970/349-5026. Definitive Colorado microbrewery: a rowdy, cavernous hall with rough-hewn beams, a roaring fire in winter, and the usual hearty American bar food – burgers, salads, and pastas. On Thursday, Friday, and Saturday nights there's live music in back room.

Kochevar's Saloon 127 Elk Ave ☎970/349-6745. Legend has it Butch Cassidy left his gun here as he nipped out the back to avoid capture and, given its Old West saloon feel, you can believe it. The sociable, buzzing neighborhood bar has pool tables, foosball, free popcorn, and regular live bands.

The Last Steep 208 Elk Ave ☎970/349-7007. Friendly restaurant with a tiny bar and a series of simple rooms where well-priced innovative salads, hot sandwiches, and Cajun-cum-Caribbean specials have produced a loyal local following. The Friday night fish-fry buffet is particularly popular.

Lil's Land and Sea 321 Elk Ave ☎970/349-5457. Surf 'n' turf specialist where ingredients come from both coasts to produce fresh and inventive – though pricey – dishes. Try the *ciopinno* seafood stew, or elk medallions with Alaskan king crab legs. Reservations recommended.

Lobar 303 Elk Ave ☎970/349-0480. Part lounge, part sushi bar, *Lobar* adds a hipster element to Crested Butte's traditionally downscale bar scene and so is the place to sink back into a black microsuede sectional sofa, sip a high-end martini – like the Chaitini (rum, green tea, and white chocolate liqueur, $9) – nibble good sushi ($7–15), and take in the occasional live music, running the gamut from jazz to acoustic to hip-hop.

Marchitelli's Gourmet Noodle 411 Third St ☎970/349-7401. Italian, not Asian, with the rich scent of hearty pasta sauces tantalizing those waiting for a table. Great food at good prices, with a spaghetti, salad, and bread early-dinner special for four at $20, served nightly from 5pm.

Pitas in Paradise 214 Elk Ave ☎970/349-0897. Mint-green cabin serving kebabs and lots of veggie options like falafel at a low price. Fresh and simple, with a dining room to match.

Powerhouse 130 Elk Ave ☎970/349-5494. The Mexican food is comparable to the cheaper *Donita's*, though the setting here – a fondly restored 1880s generating station with a huge wooden bar and 65 varieties of Tequila on offer – gives the *Powerhouse* a slight edge.

Princess Wine Bar and Coffee House 218 Elk Ave ☎970/349-0210. Relaxed hangout for ample breakfasts, lounging over a coffee, or grazing on tapas while sipping wine and enjoying live acoustic music.

Soupçon 127 Elk Ave ☎970/349-5448. Housed in a rustic log cabin from the early 1900s, this restaurant does gourmet French cuisine that changes daily but often includes escargot, shrimp, oysters, lamb, and homemade soups. The wine list is extensive and entrees start at around $22. Reservations essential.

Teocali Tamali 311 1/2 Elk Ave ☎970/349-2005. There are a few reasonable Mexican restaurants in town, but this bright little spot is fast and fresh. Their $5 burritos were voted "Best Gut Bomb" in town, and have fillings like pesto and mahi mahi.

Timberline 201 Elk Ave ☎970/349-9831. Upscale Western fine dining with an eclectic twist. Sit in leather booths or on bar stools with cowhide backs and indulge in the likes of Asian steamed mussels, caribou medallions, and Louisiana gumbo. Music on weekends. Entrees $18–28.

Wooden Nickel 222 Elk Ave ☎970/349-6350. The oldest bar and restaurant in town is unsurprisingly cluttered with antiques and curios. Only open for dinner, the menu includes filling favorites that range from potato skins to steak or lobster. After dinner, it becomes a busy drinking hole until final call around 1.45am.

Mount Crested Butte

Avalanche 15 Eammons Rd ☏970/349-7195. Lines go out the door during lunchtime at this well-worn base area grill. Simple, filling food is also served at breakfast and in the evenings, while the bar is propped up at all hours by skiers on leave from the slopes slurping a hot buttered rum ($4).

Firehouse Grill 11 Snowmass Rd ☏970/349-4666. Casual family-friendly sports bar beside the slopes, owned and operated by local firefighters – hence the fire theme. Fun and good for the usual bar and grilled food.

Last Tracks Dinner Mount Crested Butte ☏970/349-2211. Unusual gourmet dining experience that starts with a ride up the Red Lady Express lift and a ski (or snowshoe) to the outdoor

Ice Bar, which is literally sculpted from blocks of ice. Here, a Pomotini ($13) – a deep red martini made using fresh pomegranate juice – is the perfect aperitif before you nip into the wooden cabin for a five-course meal ($69); entrees might include salmon with a ginger demi-glacé or medallions of beef tenderloin in shiitake mushroom sauce. The most memorable part, however, comes after dinner, as you don headlamps to be guided down the mountain.

The Rafters Gothic Building ☏970/349-2298. Big bar at the base of the lifts with a large deck that packs out during happy "hour" (3–6pm), when a wheel's spun on the half-hour to determine drinks specials. Many make the most of the reasonable bar food (burgers, chili, salads, and sandwiches) and stay for the live bands that follow.

Travel details

Buses

(All buses are Greyhound unless otherwise stated.)
Vail from: Denver (4 daily; 2hr 10min); Frisco (4 daily; 30min); Glenwood Springs (4 daily; 1hr 35min; TNM&O and Greyhound); Grand Junction (4 daily; 3hr 40min; TNM&O and Greyhound).

Flights

(All services are United Airlines unless otherwise stated.)
Aspen to: Denver (11 daily; 45 min).
Crested Butte (Gunnison) to: Denver (4 daily; 1hr).
Eagle (Vail) to: Denver (7 daily; 50min).
Grand Junction to: Denver (10 daily; 1hr 10min; United Airlines and Great Lakes Airlines).

The Pikes Peak Region

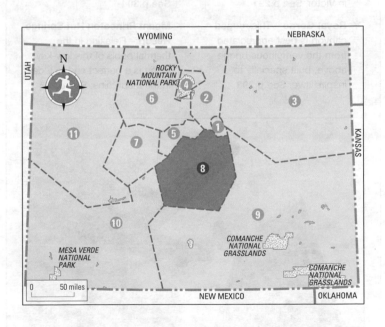

CHAPTER 8

Highlights

✳ **Pikes Peak** – Pikes Peak is an impressive and formidable mountain, and the views a bountiful reward for all those who make the trip. See p.290

✳ **Cripple Creek and Victor** – The former is a Victorian gold-rush town that's been transformed into a gambling center, while mining continues in Victor. See p.291

✳ **Royal Gorge** – This rugged canyon is best appreciated from the vertiginous bridge above, built specially to inspire awe. See p.298

✳ **The Monarch Crest Trail** – Thrill to fantastic high-alpine scenery on this trail, one of the best hikes or rides Colorado has to offer. See p.302

✳ **Rafting** – The state's most popular rafting river – the Arkansas – is unmissable in spring, when snowmelt turns into thundering rapids. See p.304

✳ **Mount Princeton Hot Springs Resort** – Relaxing in the thermal pools of this low-key resort is a perfect end to a day in the mountains. See p.305

△ US Airforce Academy, Colorado Springs

8

The Pikes Peak Region

Any American with a sense of history understands the powerful symbolism of **PIKES PEAK**, the mountain that for some time stood as the most significant landmark in the opening up of the West. Gold prospectors would famously cross the country on long, tiring, and dangerous trails with "Pikes Peak or Bust" daubed on their wagons. Almost as remarkable is the annual migration here every summer, when, as Colorado's most popular summer destination, the Pikes Peak region draws around six million vacationers. Tourism has a long pedigree here and kitsch leftovers from the 1950s and 1960s still litter the area, residual in the many mom-and-pop motels, knick-knack shops, and cheerfully innocent small-time attractions that somehow still form part of the region's economy. This is becoming increasingly driven by the development of gambling in the refurbished nearby former gold mining town of **Cripple Creek**.

To those with a limited interest in highly commercial tourism many of the region's main attractions represent a lesson in how appallingly the tourist industry can spoil something, and it's as well to appreciate this before arriving with expectations of finding nature in its rawest form. The natural attractions here are genuinely world-class – from the eerie sandstone formations at **Garden of the Gods** to the hulking and awe-inspiring **Pikes Peak** and the giddying ravine of the **Royal Gorge**, home to the foaming Arkansas River – but in each case commercialism and road building right into the heart of the attraction tends to make them into roadside gimmicks. That the experiences of standing atop the mountain or staring into the gorge still hold much in the way of wonder attests to their magnificence. Clearly, too, their accessibility is a boon to many who would otherwise not get to such remarkable places. And for the more mobile, even the most hardened nature-seeker will find areas of unquestionable beauty throughout the region. This is particularly true of the **Arkansas Valley**, home to some of the state's best hiking and biking trails and a long stretch of churning and eddying whitewater whose tributaries harbor exceptional rafting, kayaking, and fishing. It's certainly worth spending a couple of days here if you can, but at the same time these areas are also well within range for a day trip from the region's gateway city of **Colorado Springs**, which sports the widest selection of amenities.

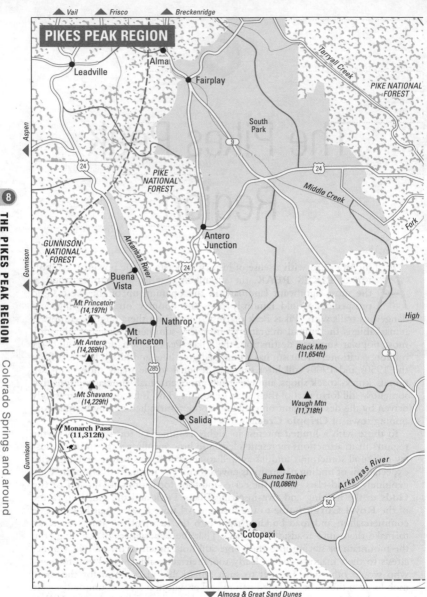

▲ Vail   ▲ Frisco   ▲ Breckenridge

PIKES PEAK REGION

◄ Aspen

Leadville

Alma

Fairplay

PIKE NATIONAL FOREST

Tarryall Creek

South Park

PIKE NATIONAL FOREST

24

9

24

Middle Creek

Fork

◄ Gunnison

GUNNISON NATIONAL FOREST

Antero Junction

Arkansas River

24

Buena Vista

Mt Princeton *(14,197ft)*

Nathrop

High

Mt Princeton

Mt Antero *(14,269ft)*

Black Mtn *(11,654ft)*

9

285

Mt Shavano *(14,229ft)*

Waugh Mtn *(11,718ft)*

◄ Gunnison

Monarch Pass *(11,312ft)*

Salida

Arkansas River

Burned Timber *(10,086ft)*

50

Cotopaxi

▼ Almosa & Great Sand Dunes

Colorado Springs and around

Little more than an hour's drive south of Denver on I-25, where the plains meet the foothills of magnificent Pikes Peak, lies Colorado's second-largest city, **Colorado Springs**. Like Denver, the city has been expanding fiercely across

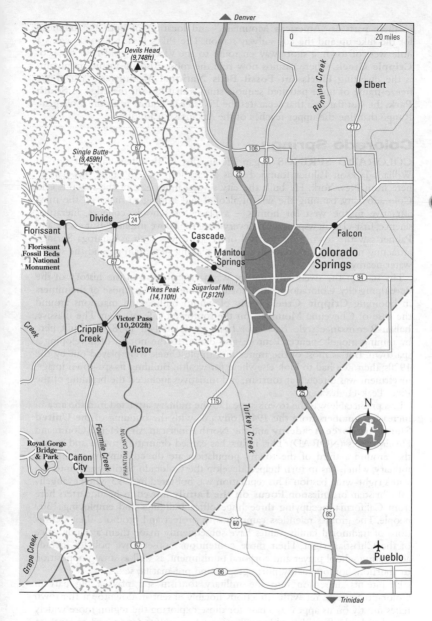

Denver

Devils Head
(9,748ft)

Running Creek

Elbert

Single Butte
(9,459ft)

106

83

25

Divide

24

Cascade

Falcon

Florissant

67

Manitou
Springs

Colorado
Springs

Florissant
Fossil Beds
National
Monument

94

Pikes Peak
(14,110ft)

Sugarloaf Mtn
(7,612ft)

Victor Pass
(10,202ft)

Cripple
Creek

Victor

Creek

Turkey Creek

115

25

N

Royal Gorge
Bridge
& Park

Cañon
City

Fourmile Creek

PHANTOM CANYON

85

Grape Creek

60

Pueblo

67

96

Trinidad

0   20 miles

the plains in recent decades, but the great sprawls of cookie-cutter houses and
malls hold little for most visitors to the area. Almost everything worth seeing
is clustered below the foothills of the mountains. The original downtown area
– **Old Colorado City** – is here, as is cutesy **Manitou Springs**, the attendant geological wonder, **Garden of the Gods**, and a glut of fabricated tourist
attractions. Manitou Springs also rests at the foot of **Pikes Peak**, marketed

in these parts as "America's Mountain," and location of both the trailhead for the hike up and the cog railway station. The Pikes Peak toll road begins a little west of town, a short way en route to the Victorian gold-rush town of **Cripple Creek**, where casinos now rule the roost. Also up in the mountains is the diverting **Florissant Fossil Beds National Monument**, a geologic freeze-frame of huge petrified sequoia stumps that lies on the edge of **South Park**, the vast flat area that separates the Pikes Peak Range from the Collegiate Range that line the upper reaches of the Arkansas Headwaters.

Colorado Springs

COLORADO SPRINGS began life in the 1870s when railroad tycoon William Jackson Palmer founded it as a vacation spot to entice his fiancée here from New York. He built the city several miles east of the raucous Old Colorado City, banning the sale of alcohol and hoping to make it "the most attractive in the west for homes – a place for schools, colleges, literature, science, first-class newspapers, and everything the above implies." But essentially, Palmer saw the town grow to rival other spa towns such as Saratoga Springs, attracting numerous tuberculosis sufferers seeking mountain air and the spring water nearby.

The start of the twentieth century was a crucial time in the history of the developing city. Colorado Springs' fortunes were bound to those of the miners in booming **Cripple Creek**, many of whom built grand mansions around the base of Cheyenne Mountain on the southwest side of town. The massive, Italian-Renaissance style *Broadmoor Hotel*, completed in 1918, was built here by mining mogul Spencer Penrose, also drawn to the notion of developing a spa town. But as most of the mines in Cripple Creek were played out by the 1920s, the town had to look elsewhere for wealth. Building its spa-town image, investment was directed at tourism, and initiatives included the building of the Pikes Peak Highway.

Less predictable was the town's appeal to the military, attracted into the area in increasing numbers from the 1940s onwards with the building of the **United States Air Force Academy** and the North American Air Defense Command Headquarters (NORAD). This influx has caused dramatic growth and meant that around a third of the town's population are directly involved with the military, which has in turn helped develop the Colorado Springs area into the state's right-wing bastion. This reputation was bolstered in 1993 when evangelical Christian organization **Focus on the Family** moved its headquarters here from California, occupying three huge office buildings and employing 1300 people. The group's relentless campaigns to protect and promote their definitions of traditional family values have subsequently made them a major voice of the Christian right. Their more contentious conservative policies include advocating school prayer and corporal punishment, as well as strong opposition to abortion, homosexuality, pornography, and pre-marital sex.

Despite its digression into the military, tourism still plays a big part in Colorado Springs. Yet with attractions notably absent in downtown the town relies mostly on its appeal as a base for those exploring the region more widely – and indeed offers the widest selection of accommodation and restaurants. Aside from attractions with a certain powerful niche appeal, like the **Air Force Academy** or the **Olympic Training Center**, the only place you might want to browse and linger is in the made-over historic suburb of **Old Colorado City** four miles to the west of downtown. Adjacent to this area is **Cheyenne Mountain**, where you'll find much of the best local hiking and biking.

Arrival, information, and getting around

A number of inexpensive **flights** link Denver's DIA to Colorado Springs airport (℡719/550-1972, @www.flycos.com). You could also book the Colorado Springs Shuttle (℡719/578-5232 or 1-877/587-3456, @www.coloradoshuttle.com) which runs a service between the two airports ($47). Taxis from the Colorado Springs airport to downtown cost around $20.

The downtown **bus terminal**, where the Greyhound and TNM&O buses stop, is at 120 S Weber St (℡719/635-1505). Slightly less convenient but far more frequent are the services of the Front Range Express (FREX; ℡719/636-3739 or 1-877/425-3739, @www.frontrangeexpress.com), which began with commuters in mind (all buses have free WiFi) and makes runs up and down I-25 to central Denver. To get to downtown Colorado Springs, get off at the I-25/Tejon Park N Ride stop and hop on a free shuttle bus to downtown.

The bus station is also the hub for local **public transportation** run by Colorado Springs Transit (℡719/385-7417, @www.springsgov.com). Bus #1 is a useful service for visitors, with frequent departures to Manitou Springs and the Garden of the Gods (until 6.15pm; $1.25).

Colorado Springs' **visitor center**, 104 Cascade St (daily: June–Aug 8.30am–6pm; Sept–May 8.30am–6pm; ℡719/635-7506 or 1-877/745-3773, @www.experiencecoloradosprings.com), produces a useful *Official Visitors Guide* and an up-to-date events guide. These can also be picked up at the visitor information booth at the airport near baggage carousel #2. The Pike National Forest Ranger Service, 601 S Weber St (Mon–Fri 8.30am–4pm; ℡719/636-1602), can provide information about the nearby National Forest areas, including Pikes Peak.

Accommodation

Apart from the slew of chain lodging off I-25 at the north end of town, most of the **accommodation** is concentrated either downtown or around Old Colorado City four miles west on Colorado Avenue heading towards Manitou Springs. A large number of posh B&Bs have also set up shop in both areas, but most exclusive of all is the famous *Broadmoor* resort, outside most people's budgets. In all cases rooms in Colorado Springs regularly get scarce in the summer months. **Camping** options are pretty limited in the immediate environs, although a handful of busy commercial campgrounds, like the *Garden of the Gods Campground*, line Colorado Avenue to the west of town. The nearest USFS camping options are near Rampart Reservoir (see p.283) or along the Gold Camp Road (see p.284).

Downtown

Antlers 4 S Cascade Ave ℡719/955-5600 or 1-800/445-8667, @www.antlers.com. Classy modern high-rise on the site of the historic hotel built by the town's founding father William Jackson Palmer. A plush marble lobby sets the establishment's tone, and both the spacious rooms and the well-equipped fitness center on the building's west side have superb views of Pikes Peak. ❼

Hearthstone Inn 506 N Cascade Ave ℡719/473-4413 or 1-800/521-1885, @www.hearthstoneinn.com. Fine B&B in downtown Colorado Springs, with antique-furnished rooms spread across two properties – one a former sanatorium. Fantastic hearty breakfasts served daily. ❺

Holden House B&B 1102 W Pikes Peak Ave ℡719/471-3980, @www.holdenhouse.com.

Another nice B&B, where rooms have a busy floral Victorian-style decor, containing local mining memorabilia, family heirlooms, and various other antiques. A few rooms have fireplaces and large marble tubs. ❻

J's Motel 820 N Nevada Ave ℡719/633-5513. One of a number of motels along Nevada Ave, just east of downtown. There's nothing fancy about the cheap, plain rooms but *J's* does have a pool and a handy location. ❸

Old Colorado City

Amarillo Motel 2801 W Colorado Ave ℡719/635-8539 or 1-800/216-8539. The large rooms are a bit run-down, but still clean enough. The good-value motel also has some units with kitchenettes. ❷

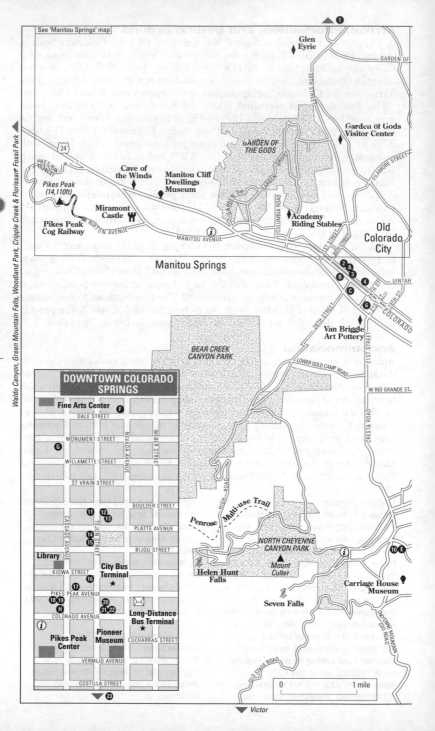

Waldo Canyon, Green Mountain Falls, Woodland Park, Cripple Creek & Florissant Fossil Park

DOWNTOWN COLORADO SPRINGS

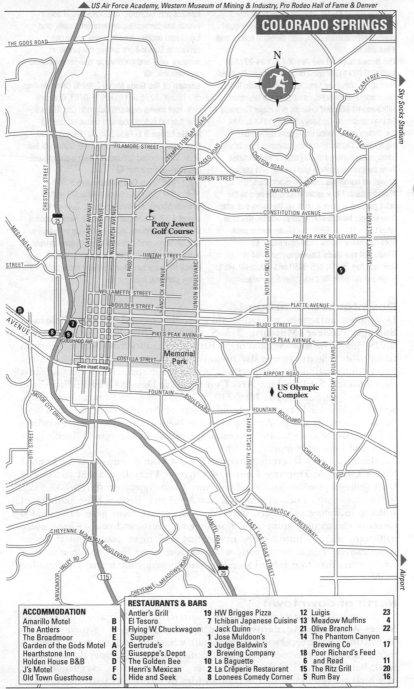

COLORADO SPRINGS

Patty Jewett
Golf Course

Memorial
Park

US Olympic
Complex

See inset map

▶ Sky Socks Stadium

▶ Airport

8

THE PIKES PEAK REGION

279

Apache Court Motel 3401 W Pikes Peak Ave
☎719/471-9440. Small motel in a relatively quiet
location off the main road, with pleasant rooms and
a hot tub. ❸

The Broadmoor 1 Lake Ave ☎719/634-7711 or
1-800/634-7711, ⊛www.broadmoor.com. Perched
high up on Cheyenne Mountain, this gigantic Italian
Renaissance-style hotel, complete with Georgian
ballroom and frescoed ceilings, is a major Colorado
Springs landmark. Originally built in 1918 to rival
the *Antlers*, it has since undergone numerous
expansions. The thirty-building complex now houses
some seven hundred stately rooms, and includes
three swimming pools, a golf course, and stables,
as well as numerous restaurants and bars. It's
always pleasant to wander around the lake in the
hotel gardens or have a drink on the patio, but after
6pm visitors have to don a jacket and tie. Summer
rates begin at over $300, but cheap winter pack-
ages can make rooms more affordable. ❾

Garden of the Gods Campground 3704 W
Colorado Ave ☎719/475-9450 or 1-800/248-9451.
Huge and sociable RV park (sites $23) targeting

families and over-50s; organizes lots of social
events like barbecues, watermelon feasts, and
ice-cream socials. A pool, a spa, and a bus
service to Manitou are among the extras. In
summer, neat and good-value four-person cabins
are available. ❷

Garden of the Gods Motel 2922 W Colorado Ave
☎719/636-5271 or 1-800/637-0703. Ordinary,
well-kept rooms near Old Colorado City. There's
also a small indoor pool and sauna on site. ❶

Maple Lodge 9 El Paso Blvd ☎719/685-9230.
Neat rooms and a heated pool near Garden of the
Gods. The wooded grounds contain a playground
and mini-golf course. ❸

Old Town Guesthouse 115 S 26th
☎719/632-9194 or 1-888/375-4210,
⊛www.bbonline.com/co/oldtown. Built on the
site of a jail, the elegant, rustically themed rooms
here have dataports, VCRs (hundreds of videos to
choose from), and classical CDs. All have private
bathrooms, most hot tubs. Hors d'oeuvres at
check-in and a turn-down service are among the
many personal touches. ❺

Downtown and around

Downtown attractions are rather thin on the ground but the **Colorado
Springs Pioneer Museum**, 215 S Tejon St (Tues–Sat 10am–5pm; free
☎719/385-5990, ⊛www.cspm.org), charts local history from Native American
times to its military present-day basis. Part of the building houses a restored
courtroom, location for a number of *Perry Mason* episodes. More worthwhile is
the **Colorado Springs Fine Arts Center**, 30 W Dale St (Tues–Fri 9am–5pm,
Sat 10am–5pm, Sun 1–5pm; $6; ☎719/634-5581, ⊛www.csfineartscenter.org),
whose architectural style is a playful fusion of Art Deco and Southwestern
Native American design. Art displays span Native American to postmodern,
and some of the more famous pieces include works by Georgia O'Keeffe, Peter
Hurd, and Edward Hopper.

A short bus ride (#1; every 30min; $1.25) east from downtown is the **United
States Olympic Training Center**, 1 Olympic Plaza, Boulder St and Union
Blvd (June–Sept Mon–Sat 9am–5pm, Sun 10am–5pm; free; ☎719/632-5551,
⊛www.usoc.org). Located on a former Air Force base, a huge number of
athletes, including swimmers, wrestlers, and cyclists, train here. Free guided
tours of the training complex – mostly gyms, courts, and pools – leave every
half-hour, after an introductory movie that will make you proud to be an
American. It's best to arrive early, when you are more likely to see athletes at
work, rather than tour around an empty and consequently uninspiring training
facility.

North of downtown

Surprisingly, the most popular man-made attraction in Colorado is the **United
States Air Force Academy**, located fifteen miles north of town on I-25
(daily 9am–5pm; free; ⊛www.usafa.af.mil), where beyond observing cadets in
formation there's precious little to see. A small museum outlines the academy's
work-hard/play-hard philosophy and its commitment to excellence, both
of which are reinforced by the center's film of interviews with cadets about

their experiences and attitudes. More entertaining is the noon formation (12.30pm), where over four thousand cadets assemble and march to lunch, and observing practice take-offs from the Thunderbird Airmanship Overlook. From the best vantage point you can also investigate the extraordinarily stark-looking, but refreshingly multi-denominational, cadet chapel that towers over the parade ground.

Near the Academy's north entrance, the low-key **Western Museum of Mining and Industry**, 125 Gleneagle Drive (June–Sept Mon–Sat 9am–4pm, Sun noon–4pm; $6; ☎719-488-0880, ⓦwww.wmmi.org), displays a vast amount of mining equipment from the Cripple Creek area, including working steam-powered engines and a sluice box where you can pan for gold. More of Western culture is explored south (I-25 exit 147) at the **Pro Rodeo Hall of Fame**, 101 Pro Rodeo Drive (June–Sept daily 9am–5pm, Oct–May Wed–Sun 9am–5pm; $6; ☎719/528-4761, ⓦprorodeo.org/hof). Videos and displays explain the sport's various disciplines and how it developed out of the needs of early ranch work. The Pikes Peak or Bust Rodeo, held at Penrose Stadium, 1045 W Rio Grande Ave (☎719/635-3547), in early August, is a major stop on the professional rodeo circuit.

South of downtown

South of town, just off CO-115 on the way to Cañon City, located in a high-security nuke-proof set of tunnels on giant shock absorbers deep within Cheyenne Mountain, is the **Cheyenne Mountain Operations Center**, where 1400 workers among a number of groups, particularly **North American Air Defense Command Headquarters** (**NORAD**), use the facility as headquarters for the coordination of a system of satellites, radars and sensors that primarily provide early warning of any missile, air, or space threat to North America. Recently, though, their increasingly sophisticated equipment has also provided early warning of ballistic missile strikes elsewhere: in the early 1990s, during Desert Storm, NORAD's capability to detect heat from missile and booster plumes provided warning to civilians and armed forces in Israel and Saudi Arabia. Its most significant appearance on the world stage dates to 1979, however, when a computer system failure warned US Air Force command posts around the globe that a nuclear attack was taking place, nearly bringing on World War III until the airborne nuclear bomb-loaded planes were hastily recalled from the skies.

Nine miles further south is the **May Natural History Museum of the Tropics**, 710 Rock Creek Canyon Rd (May–Sept 9am–6pm; $4.50). The turnoff is marked by a giant beetle, and inside you'll find a massive and quite engaging collection of insects – the life work of one John May. Rather incongruously, the site also contains the Museum of Space Exploration, located in a musty trailer full of clippings about the US space program and an assemblage of junk that feels like yard-sale pickings.

Old Colorado City and around

Due west of downtown Colorado Springs is **Old Colorado City**. Like many frontier towns, Old Colorado City was a rough place, harboring gambling, drinking, and prostitution, by all accounts serving the hypocritical needs of the Victorian gentry of Colorado Springs as much as the desires of miners. Ironically once spurned (at least officially) by decent society, today the core of the old town is now a chic neighborhood. The wooden storefronts and redbrick buildings on its main street have been restored to a gussied-up version of their former selves, but now house mostly boutiques and

△ Garden of the Gods

restaurants. Off the main drag things are suddenly much quieter in the pleasantly leafy neighborhoods where quaint and brightly colored Victorian gingerbread-style buildings abound.

The most rewarding sight hereabouts is the incredible **Garden of the Gods** (daily 5am–11pm; free), on the northern side of Old Colorado City along 30th St. Made from former dunes and sea beds, this gnarled and warped red-sandstone park was lifted up at the same time as the nearby mountains (around 65 million years ago), but has since been eroded into finely balanced overhangs, jagged pinnacles, and massive pedestals. The **visitor center**, at the park's eastern border (daily: summer 8am–9pm; winter 9am–6pm; ☎719/634-6666, ⓦwww .gardenofgods.com), has details of hiking and mountain biking trails. Skip the movie ($2) and instead relax with a drink from the center's snack bar, which has great views over the park.

Further north on 30th Street, around two miles north of Colorado City, **Glen Eyrie** (daily 1pm; $5; ☎719/272-7700 or 1-800-944-4536, ⓦwww.gleneyrie .org), is the former mansion of Colorado Springs' founder, William Jackson

Outdoor activities and outfitters

Though few come to the area specifically for outdoor recreation, the **hiking** and **biking** trails laced through the mountain parks and National Forest lands around Colorado Springs are well worth hitting up. Some of the most spectacular and convenient are in **North Cheyenne Canyon Park** (see p.284). One of the easiest hikes here is the satisfying 3.5 mile round-trip Mount Culter Trail, which climbs 500ft with views of the distant Seven Falls. Further up the valley, another small information booth sits at the base of the trail to **Helen Hunt Falls**. From the road it's a five-mile round-trip to the scenic mountain waterfall, plunging into the narrow North Cheyenne Canyon. In addition to these short and popular trails, there are also several good longer ones, including the excellent single-track Mt Buckhorn Trail, a two-hour ride or a good four-hour hike through woodland with views over Colorado Springs. The trail begins from the Upper Gold Camp Road as the unmarked Buckhorn Cutoff (just before crossing North Cheyenne Creek), which zigzags its way up to the top of Mt Buckhorn for good views over Cheyenne Canyon. From here It's a sandy single-track descent to Captain Jack's – a parking lot on the High Drive Road. By crossing High Drive you can get onto the Penrose Multi-use which heads north then east before descending down a (sometimes slippery) luge-like single-track to the Lower Gold Camp Road, which you can climb back to the start.

Another great trail for both hikers and bikers, with great views of Pikes Peak, is a seven-mile loop that takes in the lush **Waldo Canyon**. Beginning from an easily missed parking lot ten miles northwest of Colorado Springs along Hwy-24, the popular trail takes around three hours to hike and about two hours to mountain bike – though the steep, loose nature of some of the single-track demands some skill and experience. The loop starts steeply, soon working its way clear of the highway and up into beautiful wooded terrain, with some of the area's best views of Pikes Peak and Cheyenne Mountain. The trail begins to descend, then heads to an intersection where mountain bikers usually turn left to complete a clockwise loop, returning back to this point.

Woodland Park, eighteen miles northwest of Colorado Springs along Hwy-24, is a gateway to recreational opportunities in the Pike National Forest. In particular, the **Rampart Reservoir** is a good spot to explore as it offers some excellent hiking, mountain biking, and fishing (rainbow trout), along with great views of Pikes Peak. To get to Rampart Reservoir from Woodland Park, take the turnoff at the southern end of town, beside the *McDonald's* and Team Telecycle bike shop (☎719/687-6165; front suspension bikes from $30/day) onto Baldwin Street. This soon becomes Rampart Range Road, with Rampart Reservoir signposted four miles further on. The Rainbow Gulch trailhead is three miles beyond this sign, and the path here follows a crystal stream leading to the shores of the placid reservoir, encircled by twelve miles of undulating single track. This makes for a superb three-hour mountain bike ride (five-hour hike) with no real climbing, but enough challenging sections to keep experts awake.

Colorado Springs' best **outfitters** include Mountain Chalet, 226 N Tejon St (☎719/633-0732), and Blick's Sporting Goods, at no. 119 (☎719/636-3348), which contains the Pikes Peak Angler, good for advice on local fishing and gear. For **bike rentals** try Bicycle Village, 5660 N Academy Blvd (☎719/265-9346, ⓦwww .bicyclevillage.com), who rent out front-suspension bikes for $30/day.

Palmer. The 67-room, Tudor-style castle reveals his affection for European finery, including roof tiles off an old English church and a fireplace hand-carved by Benedictine monks in the Middle Ages. Today the mansion is in the hands of a ministry, the Navigators, who allow the public to drive through the grounds, arrange regular tours, and serve up cream teas (Mon–Sat 2.30pm; $11; ⊺719/634-0808); reservations are required.

Cheyenne Mountain and around

South of Old Colorado City is **Cheyenne Mountain**. Its large, gently sloping base holds the grand *Broadmoor Hotel* (see p.276) and leafy suburban districts, close to the superb North Cheyenne Canyon Mountain Park. Several small attractions have clustered around the *Broadmoor*, including the **Carriage House Museum** (Tue–Sun 10am–noon & 1–5pm; free; ⊺719/632-7711), opposite the hotel's main building on Lake Circle. The museum houses over thirty vehicles from the collection of Spencer Penrose, the main force behind the building of the Pikes Peak Highway. Most notable among them are a Concord Stage Coach, a Conestoga Freight Wagon, the "Yellow Devil" (Penrose's race car), and Mrs Penrose's 1928 V8 Cadillac. About a mile south of the *Broadmoor*, the **Cheyenne Mountain Zoo** (June–Aug 9am–6pm; Sept–May 9am–5pm; last admission always 4pm; $12; ⊺719/633-9925, ⊚www.cmzoo.org) provides a mountain setting for around 500 animals.

Further west on Cheyenne Mountain is **Seven Falls** (mid-May to Aug 8.30am–10.30pm, Sept to mid-May 9am–4.15pm; day $9, night $11; ⊺719/632-0765, ⊚www.sevenfalls.com), an attraction focusing on a nearly 200-foot-long waterfall cascading down the steep-sided South Cheyenne Canyon. Without a doubt a spectacular spot, particularly during the spring snowmelt, it's unfortunate that the adulteration of the waterfall by additional piped-in music, colored lights, elevators, and Native American dances only lessens their natural beauty.

The falls are better kept at a distance and viewed from **North Cheyenne Canyon Park** (daily: June–Sept 5am–11pm; Oct–May 5am–9pm; free), just north of Seven Falls. The park is based around a steep-sided and densely vegetated canyon, entered into beside the park's information center (daily 9am–5pm; ⊺719/578-6146), which organizes free events like children's wildlife programs and introductory climbing sessions and provides a free map of canyon hikes. From here, the road climbs up the canyon, past trailheads for the Mount Culter Trail and, as it rises to a switchback, the beginning of the hike to Helen Hunt Falls (see box, p.283). Beyond the trailhead the road climbs up to a large dusty parking lot and the junction of three dirt roads. From here, two are open to motor vehicles – High Drive and the Lower Gold Camp Road – and both are scenic drives leading to the western edge of Colorado Springs, passing **Bear Creek Regional Park**, where two miles of easy nature trails have been set out. The third dirt road, the Gold Camp Road, follows the course of an old railroad track to Victor, a 36-mile tour that takes two-and-a-half hours to navigate (road conditions ⊺719/385-5940). The start of the trail is closed off to motor vehicles, but you can join it partway along from the Old Cripple Creek Stagecoach Road. Though not signposted, the start of this route to Cripple Creek is found fairly easily by taking the Old Stagecoach Road, the continuation of Cheyenne Mountain Boulevard, from Penrose Boulevard, about a mile south of the *Broadmoor Hotel*. The craggy mountain scenery in the shadow of Pikes Peak along this route was felt by Theodore Roosevelt to "bankrupt the English language." The road passes a couple of Forest Service **campgrounds** as well.

Eating and drinking

Though there's a cosmopolitan range to choose from, Colorado Springs has a fairly small number of **restaurants**. Most are downtown, though a few worthwhile options operate out of Old Colorado City. The city's downtown **bars** and **brewpubs** are often good sources for cheap, filling, quality food. If nothing catches your eye, nearby Manitou Springs (see p.289) extends the local dining opportunities.

Downtown

Antlers Grille in the *Antlers* hotel, 4 S Cascade Ave. The excellent-value breakfast buffet ($11) and Sunday brunch offer up plenty of choices, and the dark-wood restaurant opens for upscale dinners too, serving Rocky Mountain favorites like elk, buffalo, and trout. On Fridays, wild game is offered at half-price.

El Tesoro 10 N Sierra Madre St ☎ 719/471-0106. This former brothel now doubles as an art gallery and restaurant serving excellent northern Mexican and New Mexican food; the menu features creative departures like mango quesadillas or spinach and mushroom burritos sauteed in white wine ($13). Killer margaritas too. Closed Sun.

Giuseppe's Depot 10 S Sierra Madre St ☎ 719/635-3111. Views over the railroad yards can make for interesting scenery while eating great pizzas, subs ($6), steaks ($16), seafood, or the superb lasagna.

HW Brigges Pizza 333 N Tejon St ☎ 719/471-9984. Student-friendly sports bar serving good-value slabs of pizza pie. Various sports paraphernalia dangle throughout the cavernous restaurant, which turns into a bustling bar later on. Wednesday night is an affordable all-you-can-eat pizza night.

Ichiban Japanese Cuisine 333 N Tejon St ☎ 719/636-3304. Decent-value, carefully prepared sushi for lunch and dinner in a spacious redbrick restaurant. Prices are cut by thirty percent from 5–8pm.

Jose Muldoon's 222 N Tejon St ☎ 719/636-2311. The combination of bar and a restaurant here makes *Muldoon's* a reliable choice for ordering a margarita to wash down Mexican food (entrees around $8) on an outdoor patio. The restaurant holds the record for world's largest margarita (4756.5 gallons); more notable perhaps is the fact that the huge vat was emptied inside four days. Open for lunch and dinner.

Judge Baldwin's in the *Antlers* hotel, 4 S Cascade Ave. The first brewpub in town serves up a good range of beers and excellent inexpensive bar food, like burgers, quesadillas, soups, and salads (all around $6). Open for lunch and dinner.

La Crêperie Restaurant 204 N Tejon St ☎ 719/632-0984. Stylish and small, this popular restaurant does a variety of delicious savory crepes

($9) and other French fare; filet mignon and veal cutlets ($20) also make an appearance on the slightly pretentious menu. Unsurprisingly, sweet crepes ($3) are available for dessert.

🏃 **Luigis** 947 S Tejon St ☎ 719/632-0700. A longstanding family-run institution located nine blocks south of downtown. The superb home-made Italian food makes it a deservedly popular local stop-off; pastas ($9) are offered in a wide range of sauces.

Olive Branch 23 S Tejon St ☎ 719/475-1199. Best known for its huge breakfast menu, featuring numerous types of omelettes ($5). The good vegetarian food served for lunch and dinner has a large selection of salads.

The Phantom Canyon Brewing Co. 2 E Pikes Peak Ave ☎ 719/635-2800. A great place for microbrews, authentic pub food, and even some refined seafood options. Lunch entrees are around $7, dinners $11. Popular evening haunt too, with a number of pool tables.

🏃 **Poor Richard's Feed and Read** 824 1/2 N Tejon St ☎ 719/632-7721. Popular with the college crowd for healthy vegetarian fare and a full range of sandwiches ($6) and pizzas eaten among numerous piles of books. Open until 10pm.

Old Colorado City

Flying W Chuckwagon Supper 3300 Chuckwagon Rd, north past the Garden of the Gods ☎ 719/598-4000, ⊛ www.flyingw.com. A fun and vast outdoor picnic with accompanying wrangler and Western music show. Baked beans, beef, and fresh biscuits are doled out to up to 1400 guests seated at long picnic tables. Arrive early (from 4.30pm) to view the reconstructed Old West town – including a jail, smithy, and various knick-knack shops. Dinner ($19.50 or $26) is served mid-May to August daily 7.15pm, and Sept daily 6.45pm. Outside the summer season (Oct–Dec & March to mid-May Fri & Sat 5 & 8pm) you can dine in the indoor "Winter Steak House," again with entertainment provided.

🏃 **Gertrude's** 2625 W Colorado ☎ 719/471-0887. Upscale restaurant that takes pride in its broad and eclectic menu, including plenty of vegetarian options amongst the sandwiches, salads, soups, pasta, and grilled meats offered.

Lunch ranges around the $10 mark, double that at dinner, which is particularly good for the excellent grill items, which change bi-weekly but usually include several great seafood creations, like the tiger shrimp, ahi, salmon, and mussel stew ($19). Open for breakfast, lunch, and dinner. Closed Mon evening.

Henri's Mexican 2427 W Colorado Ave ℡719/634-9031. Family-owned favorite that pulls in the crowds for home-style cooking like stuffed sopapilla and shrimp chili rellenos ($9). Both their

mole sauce and potent margaritas are superb. Live music on Fri & Sat.

🏃 **La Baguette** 2417 W Colorado ℡719/577-4818. Exposed brick and tall windows offer the backdrop for great people-watching at this French café as locals nip in for breakfast – from 7am – or to pick up a fantastic blueberry croissant. Some of the light lunches (salads, pasta, soups; most entrees under $8) have achieved local cult status, especially the rich and tangy onion soup, served with wonderful fresh bread.

Nightlife and entertainment

Weekend nights downtown are best spent bar- and club-hopping along Tejon Street. The most popular venue for more sedate events is the sleek **Pikes Peak Center**, 190 S Cascade Ave (℡719/520-7469, Ⓦwww.pikespeakcenter.org), which hosts regular symphonies, as well as touring theater and dance performances in the summer. For detailed entertainment listings, check out Friday's "Scene" in the *Gazette Telegraph,* or the free weekly events guide *Go!*, available in stands all over town.

The Golden Bee in the *Broadmoor Hotel*, 1 Lake Ave. This "authentic" British pub was shipped in pieces and rebuilt here and now serves supposed English favorites like kidney pies along with yards of ale while a ragtime piano player encourages a party atmosphere.

Hide and Seek 512 W Colorado ℡719/634-9303. A massive gay bar, complete with country, sports, and dancing-themed areas, that's been open since the 1970s. There's also an onsite restaurant.

Jack Quinn 21 S Tejon St ℡719/385-0766. Cheerful and popular downtown Irish pub with local bands on weekend nights.

Loonees Comedy Corner 1305 N Academy Blvd ℡719/591-0707. Stand-up comedy club east of downtown; mostly local hopefuls but occasionally a nationally known act stops by.

🏃 **Meadow Muffins** 2432 W Colorado Ave ℡719/633-0583. This boisterous and friendly Old Colorado City bar is one of area's best, festooned with trinkets and local memorabilia. There are quite a few pool tables and weekend nights (no cover) see live music, late opening (until 2am), and a heaving dance floor. If the munchies strike, try the quirky Jiffy burger, topped with peanut butter and bacon.

The Ritz Grill 15 S Tejon St ℡719/635-8484. By day an Art Deco-style grill serving American favorites, by night a packed bar attracting a mix of age groups, with live pop music on weekends.

Rum Bay 20 N Tejon St ℡719/634-3522. A vague Caribbean theme is played out in this large downtown bar and club, where the youngish crowd is intent on drinking and shaking on the tiny dance floor. Small cover charge.

Listings

Car rental Most of the major names in car rental can be found in town or at the airport. Enterprise, 803 W Colorado Ave (℡719/636-3900), will deliver cars, while Advantage, 2540 S Academy Blvd (℡719/392-0225) has three branches in town; this one offers free shuttle from the airport.

Golf The municipal and reasonably central Patty Jewett, 900 E Española St (℡719/585-6950) has 27 holes and a $33 greens fee. A more interesting course, with elevation changes, numerous bunkers, trees, creeks, and lakes, is the eighteen-hole Pine Creek, 9850 Divot Trail (℡719/594-9999), where a round costs from $47.

Horseback riding Academy Riding Stables, 4 El Paso Blvd (℡719/633-5667 or 1-800/700-0410, Ⓦwww.arsriding.com), organize one- to two-hour jaunts to the Garden of the Gods (from $33).

Internet The downtown Penrose Public Library, at the corner of Kiowa and Cascade, has free access.

Laundry King's Cleaners, 1536 S Nevada St, is just south of downtown.

Medical Walgreen's operates a 24hr pharmacy at 2727 Palmer Park (℡719/473-9090). Memorial Hospital, 1400 E Boulder St (℡719/444-2273), is east of downtown.

Police ☎719/444-7000; call ☎911 for emergencies.

Post office The main post office is at 201 E Pikes Peak Ave (zip 80903).

Spectator sports Superb atmosphere, cheap tickets, and good seats make the minor league baseball team the Sky Sox (April–Sept; from $6;

☎719/597-1449, ⓦwww.skysox.com), well worth watching. The college football team, the Air Force Academy Falcons (☎719/472-1895 or 1-800/666-8723, ⓦwww.airforcesports.com), are very popular; games (tix around $40) are played on Sat Aug–Nov.

Taxis Yellow Cab ☎719/634-5000.

Manitou Springs

Despite being an incorporated city in its own right, the limits of **Manitou Springs** blend so seamlessly with Old Colorado City that it feels more like another historic suburb of Colorado Springs, ten miles to the east. Long before these towns existed, though, Native American tribes – Arapaho, Cheyenne, Kiowa, and particularly the Ute – considered the mineral springs here sacred, stopping off during annual migrations to buffalo hunting grounds. As early as the 1820s, whites began reporting on the water's health benefits, and within fifty years Colorado Springs founder William Jackson Palmer, along with Dr William Bell, an English physician convinced of the springs' miracle cures, had turned the once tranquil valley into a European-style spa town. Within a few years, bottled concoctions of the spring water, like the optimistically named Manitou Ginger Champagne, were being shipped across the country; as the spa's profile grew, notables like presidents Roosevelt and Grant, P.T Barnum, and Thomas Edison all came for a dip. While few make the pilgrimage today solely to soak, Manitou continues to attract visitors with a motley assortment of attractions and its location near Pikes Peak. The busy center has managed to retain some of its historical feel, but due to a preponderance of gift shops and tacky attractions, the place ultimately comes across as a tourist trap.

Information

The chamber of commerce (☎719/685-5089 or 1-800/642-2567, ⓦwww .manitousprings.org), along with the Pikes Peak Country Attractions

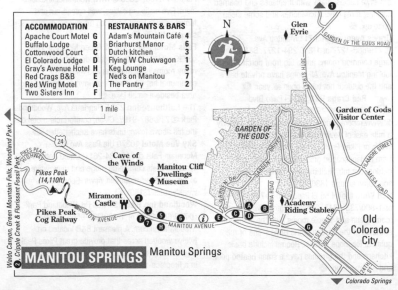

ACCOMMODATION		RESTAURANTS & BARS	
Apache Court Motel	G	Adam's Mountain Café	4
Buffalo Lodge	B	Briarhurst Manor	6
Cottonwood Court	C	Dutch kitchen	3
El Colorado Lodge	D	Flying W Chukwagon	1
Gray's Avenue Hotel	H	Keg Lounge	5
Red Crags B&B	E	Ned's on Manitou	7
Red Wing Motel	A	The Pantry	2
Two Sisters Inn	F		

MANITOU SPRINGS Manitou Springs

Association (⊛www.pikes-peak.com), run a **visitor information center** on the eastern end of town at 354 Manitou Ave (daily 9am–5pm). For tours, a **town trolley** (May–Sept Fri–Sun 8am–7pm; free; ☎719/385-743), complete with historic commentary, runs up and down Manitou Avenue from 30th Street to the Cog Railway.

Accommodation

Dozens of mom-and-pop **motels** line busy Manitou Avenue (called Colorado Ave further east) on its way into town from Old Colorado City. A few **B&Bs** have also clustered around the side streets near Manitou's historic core, offering more luxurious rooms. To avoid the humdrum of town in favor of a peaceful mountain setting, consider heading west of Manitou Springs along Hwy-24, either six miles to the town of Green Mountain Falls or fifteen to Woodland Park.

Manitou Springs

Buffalo Lodge 2 El Paso Blvd ☎719/634-2851 or 1-800/235-7416, ⊛www.buffalolodge.com. The creekside location helps with the rustic charm of a number of different accommodation options that range from badly worn motel rooms to fancy renovated lodgings. Heated pool and hot tubs available and continental breakfast included. ❹

Cottonwood Court 120 Manitou Ave ☎719/685-1312 or 1-888/227-8047, ⊛www.cottonwoodcourt.com. Small and neat motel rooms, most of which are set back from the busy road. All units include microwave and fridge, cable TV, and phones. Rates also include use of the small swimming pool and a continental breakfast. ❸

El Colorado Lodge 23 Manitou Ave ☎719/685-5485 or 1-800/782-2246. Economical Southwestern-style cabins, many with fireplaces and beamed ceilings; most have kitchenettes and some sleep up to six. ❸

Gray's Avenue Hotel 711 Manitou Ave ☎719/685-1277 or 1-800/294-1277. B&B with large common rooms and a big front porch overlooking Manitou Ave. Four have private baths and the outdoor hot tub is open all year. ❹

🏃 **Red Crags B&B** 302 El Paso Blvd ☎719/685-1920 or 1-800/721-2248, ⊛www.redcrags.com. Beautifully located property a mile east of downtown Manitou Springs, with views of Pikes Peak and the Garden of the Gods from its landscaped grounds, duck pond, and outdoor hot tub. Built by town founder Dr Bell sometime around 1880. ❺

Red Wing Motel 56 El Paso Blvd ☎719/685-9547 or 1-800/733-9547, ✉redwingmotel@pikes-peak .com. Clean and simple rooms near the southern entrance of the Garden of the Gods – one of the quietest locations in town. Rooms include basic kitchens and the grounds have a small heated pool and a playground. ❸

Two Sisters Inn 10 Otoe Place ☎719/685-9684 or 1-800/274-7466, ⊛www.twosisinn.com. Originally a late-1800s boarding house for teachers, this inn retains a fine Victorian feel, particularly in its four cozy floral rooms, with antique vanities and en-suite clawfoot tubs. Breakfast, eaten with silverware, is a decidedly gourmet affair. ❺

Green Mountain Falls and Woodland Park

Campground at Woodland Park 900 North Hwy-67, Woodland Park ☎719/687-9684 or 1-800/410-0377. Relatively small campground off Hwy-67 a couple of miles northeast of Woodland Park, with both RV ($25, full hookup) and tent ($20) sites dotted among pine trees. Facilities include laundry, hot tub, swimming pool, and mini-golf.

Elwell's Cabins 2220 Lee Circle Drive, Woodland Park ☎719/687-9838 ⊛www.woodlandparkcabins .com. Five rustic log cabins, well spread-out and furnished with hand-hewn log furniture and antiques, sleep up to four. ❸

Falls Motel 6990 Lake St, Green Mountain Falls ☎719/684-9745. Small roadside motel where many rooms have kitchens and there's a communal hot tub. There's an inviting shady picnic area beside a small lake. ❸

The Lofthouse Inn 222 E Henrietta Ave, Woodland Park ☎719/687-9187. Clean, comfortable motel on the hill above town; units have kitchenettes. ❹

Sky Vue Motel 10370 Ute Pass Ave, Green Mountain Falls ☎719/684-2611. Dated hotel with spacious units containing fridge and microwave along with clear mountain views. Good-value weekly rates ($150). ❸

Woodland Inn B&B 159 Trull Rd, Woodland Park ☎719/687-8209 or 1-800/226-9565, ⊛www .woodlandinn.com. A pleasant B&B located on twelve wooded acres that provide great Pikes Peak views; rooms are spacious and breakfast is served in a fireplace-warmed dining room. ❸

The Town

Sandwiched in a circular redbrick building between trinket shops, the **Shoshone Spring** is the most obvious spring in the center of town, where you can step up and drink the water. For a greater variety of waters, head east along the main road to the small **Soda Springs Park**, where the Cheyenne, Soda, and Navajo springs can be sampled. Despite the decidedly "medicinal" taste of the waters, a walking tour around the rest of the springs is worth the effort to appreciate the town's unusual origins. The Chamber of Commerce (see opposite) can provide a self-guided tour leaflet.

Besides the springs, the only real sight in town is **Miramont Castle**, 9 Capital Hill Ave (June–Aug daily 10am–5pm; Sept–May Tues–Sun 10am–4pm; $4; ℡719/685-1011, ⊛www.miramontcastle.org). The extravagant former residence of a French priest who came looking for a cure for his tuberculosis, the structure is a medley of six architectural styles, with Swiss chalet, San Francisco Victorian, and medieval castle included in the mix. Most of the furnishings are period pieces and various rooms contain odd collections (like dolls) which make a visit enjoyable.

Outlying attractions

Several **attractions** have accumulated around Manitou Springs, including entirely missable ones like the improbably located North Pole and Santa's Workshop. Of them all, the most high-profile is the **Cave of the Winds**, just north of town beside US-24 (daily: May–Sept 9am–9pm, Oct–April 10am–5pm; ℡719/685-5444, ⊛www.caveofthewinds.com), a series of labyrinthine underground caverns that walks the fine line between dramatic natural beauty and crass tourist trap. The tacky 45-minute Discovery Tour ($16) should be avoided in favor of the atmospheric Lantern Tour ($20), which takes you around pretty much the same route, but with only the guidance of hand-held light. The huge limestone walls of the canyon below the caves are used for nightly laser shows (9pm; $10), predictably over-hyped and cheesy, yet still impressive thanks to the beauty of the natural backdrop.

A short way further east along US-24, the **Manitou Cliff Dwellings Museum** (June–Sept 9am–6pm; Oct–May 10am–4pm; $10; ℡719/685-5242, ⊛www.cliffdwellingsmuseum.com) centers around a number of cliff dwellings hauled here in the early 1920s from Montezuma, around 300 miles southwest. Similar to those used by the Ancestral Puebloans around Mesa Verde, the structures, allegedly under threat of souvenir hunters, were moved here in a painstaking process whereby each stone was carefully marked according to its position prior to disassembly and then repositioned exactly to replicate the 600-year-old originals. Sadly, no reference is made to this background in the museum itself. In fact, there's very little illuminating information in the museum at all, though the much larger gift shop has plenty to say (and sell). In front of the dwellings, a rather fuzzy cultural link is made with regular frantic dances by plains Indians; a European cultural equivalent might be Scottish country dancing displays outside a medieval French chateau.

Eating and drinking

Gathered around Manitou's historic area are a surprising number of good **restaurants**, serving up a wide range of food. The **bar** scene, however, is tiny and rarely exciting.

Adam's Mountain Café 110 Cañon Ave ℡719/685-1430. A grandma's-parlor-style café serving mainly Southwestern nouvelle cuisine. Breakfasts include egg burritos as well as excellent muffins and juices, while the lunch menu features mainly sandwiches and pasta ($6–10).

Dinner caters to a wider range of tastes, including Thai-style vegetables and a few good pasta dishes (around $10). Closed Sun & Mon evenings.

Briarhurst Manor 404 Manitou Ave ☎719/685-1864. Former house of the town's founder, Dr William Bell, now a decidedly high-end and romantic place to eat – summer evenings see string quartets play on the patio. The fine gourmet food uses mostly organic ingredients and also features local items like Colorado lamb and Rocky Mountain trout. The Wednesday night buffet ($18) is good value. Open Mon–Sat, smart-casual dress required.

Dutch kitchen 1025 Manitou Ave ☎719/685-9962. Small family-owned restaurant that makes a good lunch stop for its popular range of sandwiches and splendid fruit pies. Closed Fri.

Keg Lounge 730 Manitou Ave ☎719/685-9531. Refreshingly down-to-earth but slightly dingy wood-clad drinking-hole with decent bar food: chicken, seafood, and rib dishes from around $10. Food until 10pm, bar open until 2am.

Ned's on Manitou 729 Manitou Ave ☎719/685-9102. Bohemian bakery that makes for a good place to start the day with slabs of French toast ($6) or numerous baked goods. Good for sandwiches at lunch, too. Open from 7.30am.

The Pantry Green Mountain Falls ☎719/684-9018. Classic American cuisine dished out in a peaceful setting beside the village's small lake; has built up a superb reputation in Manitou Springs for filling home-cooked meals. Open for breakfast, lunch, and dinner.

Pikes Peak

Though there are thirty taller mountains in Colorado, **Pikes Peak**, just west of Colorado Springs, is the state's most famous. For years the symbolic gateway to Colorado's goldfields, the mountain is part of American folklore, enshrined in the slogan "Pikes Peak or Bust," which was daubed on many a covered wagon that headed west. Today, though, it's better known as the summit that inspired Katherine Lee Bates to write a poem entitled "America the Beautiful" – set to music, it quickly became the United State's unofficial second anthem. The 14,110ft peak is named for Zebulon Pike, who crossed its path during an expedition in 1806. After failing an attempt to climb it, he wrote that "no human being could have ascended to its summit." Fourteen years later, Dr Edwin James bagged the peak, and by the end of the century trails had been built to carry rich tourists like Ms Bates to the top. Zebulon, though, must have really rolled in his grave when in 1929, Texan Bill Williams took twenty days and 170 changes of trousers to scale the mountain, while pushing a peanut with his nose. Nowadays, around a quarter of a million people head up each summer via a curvy road, a long hike, or a quaint railway. Whichever route you choose, set off as early as you can, since afternoons tend to be cloudier and often frequented by thunderstorms.

By car or bike

The most obvious way up is the **Pikes Peak Highway** (May–Sept 7am–7pm, Oct–April 9am–3pm; $10/person up to $35/car; ☎719/385-7325 or 1-800/318-9505, ⓦwww.pikespeakcolorado.com), which begins near the town of Cascade, three miles west of Manitou Springs. Though only nineteen miles long (twelve of which are unpaved), the twisting and turning 1916 toll-road takes around two hours to drive. Drivers in the **Pikes Peak Auto Hill Climb** (ⓦwww.ppihc.com), an annual Fourth of July race held since the 1920s, do it in much less time – the record run took just over ten minutes. Naturally there are superb views from many places, although the peak, dominated by a big parking lot, is a bit of a disappointment. Staying at the *Black Bear Inn*, 5250 Pikes Peak Hwy (☎719/684-1051 or 1-877/732-5232, ⓦwww.blackbearinnpikespeak .com; ⑤), partway along the road to the peak, allows plenty of time to enjoy views. Rooms have private baths and there are a few cabins here, too. The road can only be used by **cyclists** traveling in groups with companies like

Challenge Unlimited, 204 S 24th St (℡719/633-6399 or 1-800/798-5954, ⓦwww.bikithikit.com), who rent bikes and provide shuttles to the top, allowing you to freewheel back down – tours start at $98.

By rail

The **Pikes Peak Cog Railway** (mid-May to Nov; $29; reservations advised; ℡719/685-5401, ⓦwww.cograilway.com) was the first mechanical form of transport to ascend the peak, built by mattress magnate Zalmon G. Simmons after he found his mule ride up overly jarring. Opened in 1891, the red carriages of this thrilling railway grind their way up an average of 847ft per mile on a 90-minute journey to the summit; from 11,500ft onwards they cross a barren expanse of tundra, scarred by giant scree flows. From the bleak and windswept top, it's possible to see Denver seventy miles north, and the seemingly endless prairie to the east, while to the west mile upon mile of giant snowcapped peaks rise into the distance. The train leaves from 515 Ruxton Ave in Manitou Springs; round-trips take three hours fifteen minutes, including a 40-minute stop on the chilly summit.

On foot

Though there are trails up from elsewhere (including near Cripple Creek), the **Barr Trail** is the most popular hiking route up Pikes Peak. The thirteen-mile path begins near the Cog Railway terminus, and the steepest part of the entire trail comes first, leveling out as it ascends to the *Barr Camp Cabins* (reservations ℡719/630-3934), seven miles from the trailhead and a mile-and-a-half below the treeline. Here you can camp ($10) or take a bed in a dorm ($15); spaghetti dinners ($7) are served at 6pm, breakfasts also available ($5). Above the camp the alpine tundra takes over, harboring numerous delicate plants, flowers, and bighorn sheep. As the air gets thinner the last few miles of switchbacks make the rocky slopes a hard climb. Typically hikers manage the trail in fourteen hours: nine hours up and five down. Fit and acclimatized mountain bikers – who can ride the trail but not the highway (unless part of an organized group) – can cut that time in half, while the record round-trip for a trail runner is a little over three hours.

Cripple Creek and Victor

Once the richest goldfield in the Rockies, **CRIPPLE CREEK** produced twice as much gold as California's famed mother lode and more, in fact, than any other single geological deposit in the world. The much-chronicled gold camp, fifty miles south of Colorado Springs via US 24, nestles in a grim volcanic bowl on the west flank of Pikes Peak. The gold rush here began in 1891, when cowhand Bob Womack discovered gold on poor cattle-raising land. Though at first no one believed Crazy Bob's tale, he eventually sold his share for $500 (the El Paso mine ultimately proved to be worth around $5 million) and spent most of it on whiskey. Others were more fortunate and Winfield Scott Stratton became the most famous of the Cripple Creek prospectors. Formerly a carpenter making hand-carved fireplaces, he took a second look at his claims after a few years of fruitless searching and a leave of absence (due to promises to his wife), finding a rich vein that would become the Independence Mine. He didn't work it for long and with the proceeds of the sale built a hospital and gave bicycles to the poor. He died a wealthy and much-loved philanthropist. By 1900, sixty thousand people lived in a town boasting eight newspapers, hundreds of saloons, splendid hotels, elegant homes,

△ Cripple Creek

and even a stock exchange. In 1915 the price of gold plunged, and within five years most of the mines were played out. All but a handful had shut by the 1960s, with the economy becoming increasingly desperate. But since 1991, when gambling was legalized in Cripple Creek, the new gold mines in town are its **casinos**. Most of the Victorian buildings have been converted into these, a sprucing-up that has markedly changed their character. What these structures used to be like before gambling set in can be seen seven miles south of Cripple Creek at **VICTOR**, whose gloriously run-down state preserves a more acute sense of history.

Downtown Cripple Creek and around

The casino-lined main street (**Bennett St**) of this 650-inhabitant-strong town backs onto a forbidding rocky plateau, pockmarked by scars and mine dumps. It has always been the main business area in town and, at its eastern end, the **Cripple Creek District Museum** (late May to mid-Oct daily 10am–5pm; rest of year weekends only noon–4pm; $5 or $7 including the Old Homestead Museum – see below) is the best place to gain an appreciation of the frontier town's raucous history. A model of local gold mines made with multiple sheets of glass with mine workings inked on gives an idea of the complexity and density of mining operations here. The museum is in the old railroad station, where, in the camp's heyday, a train passed through every six minutes. Some of these were ferrying workers out to various mines on a route that the **Narrow Gauge Railroad** (June to mid-Oct daily every 20min 10am–5pm; $9.50; ☏719/689-2640), boarded at the depot beside the museum, still trundles. It's a scenic four-mile tour past several abandoned mines, including the site of Bob Womack's original strike.

A block south of Bennett Street runs **Myers Street**, once one of the West's most notorious red-light districts. Its history is remembered in fun tours of the **Old Homestead Museum**, at no. 353 (daily 11am–5pm; $4; ☎719/689-3090), a former high-class brothel filled with many original furnishings. In the opposite direction, heading west from Bennett Street, is an unpaved road leading out of town to the small, conical Mount Pisgah, surrounded by city cemeteries. At the beginning of the nineteenth century the local murder rate averaged eight per month, making some headstones particularly interesting reading. One tombstone was simply inscribed "He called Bill Smith a liar"– but has since been stolen from the cemetery.

One of the last mines to close in the area was the **Mollie Kathleen Gold Mine** (May–Oct daily 9am–5pm; $15), one mile north on Hwy-67, which now gives tours led by ex-miners to gold veins a thousand feet underground. The informative tours take around 40 minutes and include a free sample of gold ore. A few mines do still work the area, and although around $9 billion (at today's prices) has already been extracted, eighty percent of the area's ore is still thought to be underground; many speculate about a rich mother lode deep in Pikes Peak itself.

Victor

There are far fewer attractions in nearby **Victor**, where the streets are literally paved with gold – no one could be bothered with the low-grade ore at the time, so it was used for road surfacing – though the metaphor is rendered worthless by the scrappy town's collection of decaying buildings. But at least the formerly grand buildings have preserved a certain ramshackle authenticity that's been lost in Cripple Creek. One of the few well-preserved buildings is the stately 1899 **Victor Hotel**, where you might pop into the lobby for a quick look at the grand Victorian proportions and to ask the staff if you can have a ride in the aged Otis birdcage elevator. Just downhill is the modest **Lowell Thomas Museum** (June–Sept daily 10am–4pm; free), dedicated to a local boy turned journalist and adventurer. Among the commemorative articles, photos, and memorabilia, a few artifacts from Victor's past have crept into the collection too. But Victor's finest attraction is the **American Eagles Scenic Overlook**, a couple of miles east on a dirt road above town accessed from Diamond Ave, the road running a block above the main street (Victor Ave): a handful of old mine buildings are open for exploration, with interpretive boards provided, but far more memorable are the stunning views west over the surrounding valleys and mountain ranges beyond.

The Shelf Road

From Cripple Creek and Victor, three roads head south to Cañon City and the Arkansas River Valley, around twenty miles away as the crow flies. The most interesting of these is the narrow, winding **Shelf Road**, a dirt road set in precipitous terrain that passes down Helena Canyon, home to bighorn sheep, and close to areas well known for superb **rock climbing** in the **Shelf Road Recreation Area**, eight miles out of Cripple Creek. In cooperation with the Bureau of Land Management of Cañon City, more than four hundred climbing routes have been established across a network of steep cliffs and walls that's so extensive climbers are unlikely to ever feel crowded. Thoughtfully placed expansion bolts open up all manner of technical pitches, bulges, cracks, and slabs. The BLM have a couple of **campgrounds** available in the area, including the *Bank* campsite ($4) near Red Canyon, where most of the good climbing is. Generally flat and with only light traffic, the Shelf Road also makes for good, reasonably easy out-and-back **cycle** rides.

Cripple Creek's **chamber of commerce**, located between the district museum and the scenic railway at 337 E Bennett St (℡719/689-2169 or 1-800/526-8777, ⓦwww.cripple-creek.co.us), provides a self-guided auto-tour leaflet of the area.

The grand 1896 *Imperial Hotel*, 123 N 3rd St (℡719/689-7777 or 1-800/235-2922, ⓦwww.imperialcasinohotel.com; ❹), is the last of Cripple Creek's gold rush **hotels**, and it shows in the numerous antique features, including claw-foot bathtubs and steam-heat radiators. Most patrons, though, seem more interested in the large onsite casino. Another hotel with casino, the *Gold Rush Hotel*, 442 E Bennet Ave (℡719/689-2646 or 1-800/235 8239, ❺), is also very central. If you're looking for amenities like a pool and a hot tub, you'll have to head a short way out of town to the *Gold King Mountain Inn*, 601 Galena St (℡719/689-2600 or 1-800/445-3607, ⓦwww.goldkingmountaininncripplecreek.com; ❺). Of the town's half-dozen B&Bs, the most central is the chintzy *Cherub House*, 415 Main St (℡719/689-0526; ❹), which has rooms with either private or shared baths as well as a hot tub. *Cripple Creek Gold Campground* (℡719/689-2342), seven miles out of town on Hwy-67 to Divide, has pretty **campsites** for both RVs and tents (sites from $15); they also offer short horseback-riding trips in the local Pike National Forest.

The casinos along the main street provide the only **restaurants** in town, and often some cheap deals, including the *Gold Rush Hotel's* 49¢ breakfast.

In **Victor**, the town pride is the Victorian *Victor Hotel,* on 4th St and Victor Ave (℡719/689-3553 or 1-800/713-3553; ❹), whose straightforward modern rooms are above a grand lobby, formerly used as a bank and now providing what little tourist **information** is needed. A few doors down, the *Two Mile Deli* is an inexpensive choice for cheap basic breakfasts and lunches. Opposite, *It's Someplace Else* not only has a classy collection of bras hanging above the bar but also serves pizzas and Mexican food.

Florissant Fossil Beds National Monument

Protecting part of a massive expanse covered by volcanic ash 35 million years ago, **Florissant Fossil Beds National Monument** (daily 9am–5pm; $3; ⓦwww.nps.gov/flfo) is an arid mountain valley littered with fossil-filled rocks and petrified trees. Thirty miles west of Colorado Springs on US-24, the lightly wooded monument contains one of the most perfect records of Eocene natural history found anywhere. This was an era when Colorado was lush with palm trees, redwoods, and willows, while thousands of species of insects thrived around the long-gone Lake Florissant. First discovered by settlers unearthing the skeleton of a mastodon, the area soon became a huge fossil quarry for both scientists and souvenir hunters. And although ninety percent of the unearthed fossils here have been carted away, none of the huge petrified sequoias – despite numerous attempts – could be budged. Various short trails lead between them, such as the shade-free Petrified Forest Loop, along which free hour-long tours regularly go. The half-mile Walk Through Time Loop, behind the visitor center, is also worthwhile, mostly to see the unusual sight of conifers growing from petrified stumps. Another ten miles of hiking trails lead around the area's rolling hills and have become particularly popular with cross-country skiers and snowshoers in winter.

The whole area is still incredibly rich with fossils and it is not hard to find them around the monument. These of course must be left behind, but back on the road to the town of **FLORISSANT**, near the minor road's junction with Hwy-24, the **Florissant Fossil Quarry** (10am–4pm; $7.50) allows you to souvenir-hunt through rocks in an even richer fossil bed. At the main crossroads of the town, the rustic *Fossil Inn* (7am–8pm) offers a good selection of American entrees from $13.

South Park Basin

As Hwy-24 heads west from Florissant town and the Colorado Springs area it drops out of the mountains onto a quilt of rich ranchland pasture that forms the **South Park Basin**. Along with North Park, Middle Park, and the San Luis Valley, South Park is one of four of Colorado's great inter-montane basins, but while the others are known, respectively, for their moose, ranching, and sand dunes, South Park has achieved far greater fame as the setting for the eponymous cartoon series. But in terms of attractions there's really very little here, with only tiny communities dotting the valley.

The largest of these is **FAIRPLAY**, at the northern end of the valley, where it's worth stopping off for a look at the refreshingly uncommercial **South Park City** (mid-May to mid-Oct daily 9am–5pm; $6.50; ☎719/836-2387, ⓦwww.southparkcity.org), a collection of 35 old buildings moved here from abandoned mining towns to form an open-air museum. All the buildings – which include a bank, stagecoach station, general store, and a small onsite brewery – are well preserved or restored, and the 50,000 period artifacts within them give one of the best glimpses into life as it must have been during Colorado's early mining days.

From Fairplay, Hwy-9 climbs toward **Hoosier Pass** (11,541ft) and Breckenridge, 24 miles north, passing the tiny no-nonsense community of **ALMA** along the way. Alma is surrounded by wonderful old mine workings and pristine high-alpine landscapes, some of which can be explored by turning onto CO-8 from Hwy-9 beside the Alma Firehouse. The well-graded dirt road heads west for around six miles before coming to a fork; from here the trails become much rougher, though they're still suitable for 2WD vehicles. One trail heads north to **Windy Ridge**, a stunningly bleak glacial bowl where you can explore several marked trails, while the other leads northeast to the **Bristlecone Pine Scenic Area**, one of several alpine areas in Colorado where stunted, slow-growing trees have contorted themselves into wild, twisted shapes over thousands of years. The most ancient of the specimens are thought to be among the oldest living organisms on earth, approximately 5000 years old – twice the age of California's giant redwoods. Alma is also the trailhead (marked off the highway just south of town) for one of the state's most fabled 4WD routes, over the **Mosquito Pass Road** to Leadville, 21 miles away.

The Arkansas Valley

Cradling one of the state's most impressive rivers and flanked by some of its highest mountains, it's amazing that the **ARKANSAS VALLEY** gets as little attention from vacationers as it does. Aside from the steady stream of whitewater rafters and those transiting en route to the San Juans or the Gunnison region, few people really spend much time here, leaving an area that is not only immensely scenic but also uncrowded and unspoilt, yet highly accessible from both Denver and Colorado Springs.

Apart from the well-advertised rafting and kayaking there is also world-class mountain biking, hiking, and fishing. In winter there's a glut of good places to go snowshoeing, a modest ski resort – **Monarch Ski Area** on the 11,846ft Monarch Pass – and a pleasant, unsung **hot springs** resort in which to recuperate after a day in the outdoors.

The most dramatic stretch of the valley is beside the town of **Cañon City**, where the **Arkansas River** has gouged a foaming route deep along **Royal Gorge**, a sheer-sided canyon. Upstream the valley widens until it pans out into an empty, windswept, and for the most part sparsely populated expanse, though flanked by the **Collegiate Range** in the west and the Pikes Peak mountains to the east. **Salida**, with its red-brick Victorian core, is easily the most attractive town in the valley, with the only real competition coming from the small whitewater rafting center of **Buena Vista**, at the valley's northern end.

Cañon City and the Royal Gorge

Approaching this sprawling mass of motels and prisons, its easy to see how **CAÑON CITY**, nearly fifty miles south of Colorado Springs, has largely been defined by its thirteen penitentiaries. But it's the spectacular nearby **Royal Gorge** to the west from which the city gets its name and its visitors. Most settle for views down into the gorge and the foaming Arkansas River at its base, where the adventurous go whitewater rafting.

The town's present-day form and economy dates back to its 1868 decision to be the site of the state penitentiary (in preference to hosting the state university, which consequently went to Boulder), shaping Cañon City as a stable, though rather dull, administrative place. Since the 1930s, it has also developed as a tourist destination thanks to the building of the Royal Gorge Bridge west of town. But since most of the visitors who head here are either on day-trips from Colorado Springs or on their way to Arkansas rafting trips, the city's small core, a block north of the main drag, has retained

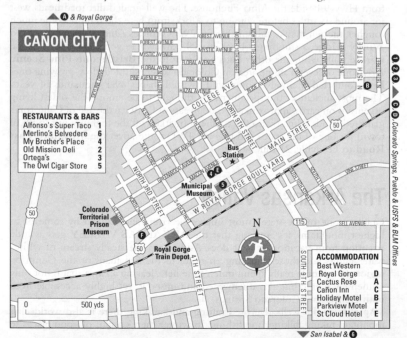

RESTAURANTS & BARS
Alfonso's Super Taco 1
Merlino's Belvedere 6
My Brother's Place 4
Old Mission Deli 2
Ortega's 3
The Owl Cigar Store 5

ACCOMMODATION
Best Western
Royal Gorge D
Cactus Rose A
Cañon Inn C
Holiday Motel B
Parkview Motel F
St Cloud Hotel E

its small-town feel – even though it's sprawled a good way east along Royal Gorge Boulevard (Hwy-50), a road lined with chain restaurants and the aforementioned motels.

Arrival, information, and accommodation

Daily Greyhound/TNM&O **buses** running between Pueblo and Grand Junction stop at the Video House, 731 Main St (☎719/275-0163). For **information**, stop by the chamber of commerce, 403 Royal Gorge Blvd (Mon–Fri 8am–5pm; ☎719/275-2331, ⓦwww.canoncity.com); from June through August they also operate an info booth in the city park. For details on camping or hiking in the local National Forests, check with the **USFS/BLM** office, on the east side of town at 3170 E Main St (Mon–Fri 7.45am–4.30pm; ☎719/269-8500).

There's no shortage of **motels** in and around Cañon City and the Royal Gorge area. Rates can fall as much as half outside the peak season, so be sure to ask around. The majority of **camping** options are located near the Royal Gorge, though free wild camping is also possible in the Wet Mountains portion of the San Isabel National Forest, six miles south of town along Oak Creek Grade Road.

Hotels and motels

Best Western Royal Gorge 1925 Fremont Drive ☎719/275-3377. Reliable chain hotel with a good range of amenities, including a pool, hot tub, playground, and laundry room. ❺

Cactus Rose 44058 W Hwy-50 ☎719/269-7673. Friendly family-run motel near the Royal Gorge, recently renovated with all rooms receiving an Old West makeover. ❹

Cañon Inn 3075 E Hwy-50 ☎719/275-8676 or 1-800/525-7727, ⓦwww.canoninn.com. A relatively high-end motel with 152 large rooms, all with cable TV. There are also several hot tubs and a heated outdoor pool. ❻

Holiday Motel 1502 Main St ☎719/275-3317. Standard inexpensive motel on the main highway, a couple minutes' drive from downtown. Units are worn but clean and come with phones, cable TV, and a/c. ❷

Parkview Motel 231 Royal Gorge Blvd ☎719/275-0624. Located across from the leafy Veterans Memorial Park, this is one of the best-value and most central motels in town. ❷

St Cloud Hotel 631 Main St ☎719/276-2000 or 1-800/405-9666, ⓦwww .stcloudhotel.com. Built in 1883, this centrally located Victorian four-story brick hotel was actually moved from Silvercliffe, 51 miles away, once the silver mines there had been played out. Many of its antique-furnished rooms contain original fittings like claw-foot tubs. ❻

Campgrounds

Cañon City Campground between Hwy-50 and the Royal Gorge's northern tollgate. If you value peace and quiet, the isolated sites of this sprawling free campground are a better bet than local commercial campgrounds – but only if you're fine with the limited facilities (toilets, but no water).

The Town and around

Though most visitors skip Cañon City altogether and head directly west towards the Royal Gorge, there's a handful of attractions in the town's older core worth stopping off for; all three attractions described below are offered on a combined ticket of $9, available at each. Of the three, the unusual **Colorado Territorial Prison Museum**, 1st St and Macon Ave (May–Oct daily 8.30am–6pm; Oct–April Fri, Sat & Sun 10am–5pm; $8; ⓦwww.prisonmuseum.org), beside an obvious working prison, is the most compelling. The museum is located inside the 1871 Colorado Territorial State Penitentiary, which makes up the bulk of Cañon City's west end and still houses some 700 inmates. In the forecourt of the complex, the hulking gas chambers – last used in 1967 – set the tone for the place, which details a rather gruesome 120-year history of incarceration.

This block of the jail was decommissioned in the 1970s when its conditions were deemed too "cruel and unusual" a punishment. Now the cells are used to display a variety of restraining mechanisms as well as an antique electric chair, the last seat for more than 100 people. There are also displays on some of its more notorious inmates, including the locally infamous Alfred Packer, jailed for murder and cannibalism (see p.343). A 45-minute audio guide, included with the price of admission, sheds light on these and various other events and issues in the prison's history.

Much less depressing but no less interesting is the **Dinosaur Depot**, 330 Royal Gorge Blvd (June to mid-Aug daily 9am–5pm; mid-Aug to May Wed–Sat 10am–4pm; $3; ☎719/269 7150 or 1-800/987-6379, ⓦwww.dinosaurdepot.com), marked by the life-sized allosaurus in front of the old train station on Hwy-50. Exhibits relate mainly to the work of local scientists attracted to the area due to the presence of the nearby bone-rich **Garden Park Fossil Area**, five miles north of town along Field Ave (which is the start of the Shelf Rd; see box p.293); the area can be visited on an informative tour (Fri & Sun 10am; $5 includes museum entrance). Back at the Depot, you can view a replica of one of the main trophies found here – "Ms Spike," the world's most complete stegosaurus – while in an adjacent lab you can watch the painstaking removal of rock from around various dinosaur skeletons.

If you're more interested in the area's more recent history, then the mixed bag of local treasures at the **Cañon City Municipal Museum**, 612 Royal Gorge Blvd (May–Aug Mon–Sat 9am–5pm, Sun 1pm–5pm; Sept–April daily 1pm–5pm; $1; ☎719/269-9018), is worth a quick look. These include Ute artifacts, fossils, guns, and the mounted heads of the last of the area's wild buffaloes (shot by poachers in 1897), as well as a log cabin and a stone settler's house from the 1880s.

The Royal Gorge

The **Royal Gorge**, a remarkably narrow and steep-sided thousand-foot chasm eight miles from Cañon City, has become an awkward fusion of natural wonder and unbridled commercialism. That said, the tacky roadside trade en route to the natural wonder – like the mildly diverting Buckskin Joe Frontier Town and Railway, often used as a movie set for Westerns – is easily forgotten once you peer into its vertigo-inducing depths. The Royal Gorge is linked to Hwy-50 around six miles west of Cañon City by a loop of road that passes the north entrance to cross the Royal Gorge Bridge and rejoin the highway. You can visit the gorge from either end, paying at a tollbooth at either side of the bridge. However, if you'd rather not shell out you should come in from the northern entrance (the one nearest Cañon City) and drive to the **free viewing point** just before the tollbooth.

Since its construction – specifically to attract tourists – in 1929, the most popular way of viewing the gorge is from the **Royal Gorge Bridge** (bridge itself daily 7am–dusk, though times of adjacent attractions vary; $21; ☎719/275-7507 or 1-888/333-5597, ⓦwww.royalgorgebridge.com), allegedly the world's highest suspension bridge. You can drive over the gently swaying span (no RVs, buses, or trailers) or just walk on it – the better way to appreciate the dizzying views of the gorge's solid rock walls and the foaming white waters of the Arkansas far below. Entrance to the bridge also allows you to descend to the base of the canyon on the world's steepest incline railway or use an aerial tramway for yet another perspective.

Another way to experience the gorge is to take the **Royal Gorge Route Train** from Cañon City (daily: mid-May to mid-Oct 9am, noon & 3pm;

△ Royal Gorge

mid-Oct to mid-May noon; $33, reservations recommended; ☎303/569-1000 or 1-888/724-5748, ⓦwww.royalgorgeroute.com). Departing from 401 Water St, the 24-mile round-trip takes around two hours, running along a precarious ledge at the base of the narrowest and most rugged portion of the gorge.

The most expensive – but certainly the most exciting and memorable – way to see the gorge is from an inflatable **raft** on the foaming Arkansas River. The run through the canyon includes difficult Class V rapids and is particularly challenging when the river is at full flow in late May and early June, though trips are run until late August. For further information on rafting the Arkansas, see the box on p.304.

Finally, if you are heading in the direction of Cañon City from the Royal Gorge and have a head for mountain driving you should definitely investigate **Skyline Drive**, a giddying roller-coaster road along the spine of a ridge. Built by convicts to provide a thrill for tourists, the one-way highway begins about a mile west of town, climbs up onto the narrow ridge, and follows its undulating course – with incredible views in all directions – before plunging into the western end of town. In total it's a ten-minute detour from Hwy-50.

Eating and drinking

Cañon City's town center contains several inexpensive Mexican **restaurants** as well as a couple of classier joints and friendly neighborhood bars. For the usual array of fast-food joints, head east along Hwy-50.

Alfonso's Super Taco 2801 E Main St 81212 ☎719/276-0186. Mexican takeaway and drive-through with a couple of picnic tables beside Hwy-50. Looks pretty insalubrious but the food is delicious and very fairly priced – most burritos are around the $4 mark.

Merlino's Belvedere 1330 Elm Ave ☎719/275-5558. This moderately expensive restaurant is one of the city's main fine-dining establishments. Italian favorites, as well as salmon, shrimp, and prime rib, are complemented by over-indulgent desserts.

My Brother's Place 625 Main St ☏719/275-9954. Smoky local hangout serving mostly domestic beers to pool players.
Old Mission Deli 1905 Fremont Drive ☏719/275-6780. Good range of budget (entrees $5–7) Mexican food: burritos, chimichangas, chorizo, and superb homemade green chili rellenos.
Ortega's 2301 E Main St ☏719/275-9437. Reliable choice among the many affordable Southwestern-style restaurants in town. The standard Mexican choices are on offer, including great chili rellenos, as well as some Italian and

American dishes. Open for breakfast, lunch, and dinner.

The Owl Cigar Store 626 Main St ☏719/275-9946. Bought with money won playing poker, this Cañon City institution is the place to go for vinyl booths, an old-school jukebox, and inexpensive traditional American diner food like burgers and thick malts. A local watering hole for over a hundred years, its walls are lined with all sorts of artifacts – hunting trophies, photographs, license plates – and there are also a few pool tables.

Salida

Driving through **SALIDA** (pronounced *sa-ly-da*) on Hwy-50 (Rainbow Blvd), you'd be forgiven for thinking that the town is little more than an unappealing strip of chain eateries and budget motels. The highway, though, passes to the south of Salida's Victorian downtown area by a good twelve blocks. This old district of red-brick buildings huddled alongside the Arkansas River is home to a laid-back collection of small local shops, quaint B&Bs, and modest restaurants.

Despite its ready accessibility from both Denver and Colorado Springs, Salida is often overlooked as a tourist destination, most visitors just passing the old railroad town en route to whitewater kayaking, rafting, and fishing trips on the Arkansas in summer (particularly mid-May to late June) and skiing at the Monarch Ski Area. But recently the town has started to lose its undiscovered status, and has come into its own as a base for superb **mountain biking** and **hiking**. And, though it still has a long way to go, Salida's relaxed downtown is a good base to return to after a day in the mountains.

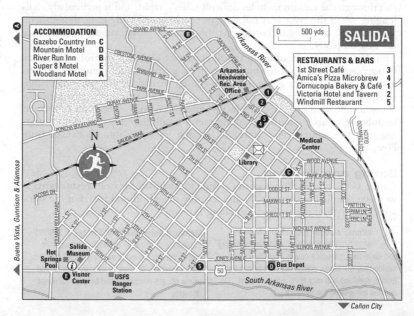

Information

The main source for local visitor **information** is the so-called Heart of the Rockies Chamber of Commerce, 406 W US-50 (Mon–Fri 9am–5pm; ☎719/539-2068 or 1-877/772-5432, ⓦwww.salidachamber.org). It's worth popping in to pick up the free *Chaffe County Guide*, loaded with details for both Salida and Buena Vista, and for the free guide to local mountain biking. A few hundred yards further east, the USFS Ranger Station, 325 W Rainbow Blvd (Mon–Fri 8am–4.30pm; ☎719/539-3591), is the best source of information on hiking and camping in the area. Lastly, the offices of the Arkansas Headwaters Recreation Area, 307 W Sackett St (Mon–Fri 9am–5pm, Sat & Sun 9am–4pm; ☎719/539-7289 ⓦwww.parks.state.co.us), can provide info on recreation and camping throughout the Headwaters Area, which takes in everything surrounding the Arkansas between Buena Vista and Cañon City.

Accommodation

There's a good stock of **accommodation** in and around Salida, including numerous motels lining Hwy-50 on the town's southern side and an impressive array of B&Bs downtown. Generally rates in both will be a little higher in summer than in winter. Campers have several local choices, including a free public-land **campground** three miles south of town along Hwy-50 beside the Arkansas River and the *4 Seasons RV Park* (☎719/539-3084 or 1-888/444-3626), which has full hookups from $25. The Forest Service and Arkansas Headwaters offices in town (see above) can help with many others. Finally, more accommodation is available year-round beside the Monarch Ski Resort to the west (see p.302).

Gazebo Country Inn 507 E 3rd St ☎719/539-7806 or 1-800/565-7806, ⓦwww .gazebocountryinn.com. Once the home of a prominent early twentieth-century merchant, this two-story B&B now offers pleasant, florally decorated guest rooms that look out onto even more flowers in the garden, white picket fences, and the surrounding mountains. There's a hot tub out back and all rooms are en suite. ❺
Mountain Motel 1425 E Rainbow Blvd ☎719/539-4420. This attractive motel, featuring wood-clad cabin-style rooms with kitchens, is one of Salida's best values. ❸
River Run Inn 8495 CO-160 ☎719/539-3818 or 1-800/385-6925, ⓦwww.riverruninn.com. Northwest of Salida, in a picturesque location beside the

Arkansas (good mountain views and trout fishing) this 1882 inn provides B&B accommodation in what was once the county poor farm. Today, you have to pay rather than work for your room and board; choose from a room with or without private bath. ❺
Super 8 Motel 525 W Rainbow Blvd ☎719/539-6689 or 1-800/800-8000. Reliable chain motel located opposite the hot springs pool (see p.302), but with its own hot tub and pool as well. Rates include continental breakfast. ❹
Woodland Motel 903 W 1st St ☎719/539-4980 or 1-800/488-0456. Small motel seven blocks northwest of downtown featuring good-value, spotless rooms – some with kitchens, some with mountain views, and all with access to a hot tub ❸

Outdoor activities

If you're interested in hiking one of the local "fourteeners," try the strenuous ascent of **Mount Shavano** (14,229ft), a four-mile hike from a trailhead fifteen miles west of Salida (take Hwy-50 to CO-250, then take CO-252 to its end). Salida is also close to a couple of major long-distance hiking trails, portions of which can make for good day-trips from town. The five-hundred-mile **Colorado Trail**, which runs between Denver and Durango, travels over the Monarch Pass a half-hour drive west, while the hundred-mile **Rainbow Trail** begins around twenty miles southwest of town, south of the Marshall Pass, and runs east. It passes within about four miles of Salida before following a route along the eastern side of the Sangre de Cristo mountains.

Monarch Ski and Snowboard Area

Though not one of Colorado's most famous, the small, 670-acre **Monarch Ski and Snowboard Area**, 21 miles west of Salida along Hwy-50 (Nov to mid-April; adult day pass $49; ☏719/530-5000 or 1-888/996-7669, ⓦwww.skimonarch.com), has a well-deserved reputation for excellent downhill skiing for all ability levels. The lack of crowds – particularly midweek – and its relatively inexpensive lift tickets have attracted a small but deeply committed group of followers. Located on the Continental Divide, it has reliable light dry-powder snow (around 300 inches each year) and a 1171ft vertical drop served by five lifts. Beginners will find good bunny slopes, while gently meandering trails entertain intermediates. After a storm experts will delight in deep stashes of powder and the drops and log slides hidden in the glades. The 670 acres of terrain breaks down as 14 percent beginner, 42 percent intermediate, and 44 percent expert.

Rentals are available slopeside, but to save time and cash you can get your gear in Salida the night before from the Mt Shavano Ski and Snowboard Shop, 16101 W Hwy-50 (ski packages from $14, snowboards and boots from $19; ☏719/539-3240 or 1-800/678-0341, ⓦwww.mtshavanoskishop.com). Monarch has also become famous for its excellent **snowcat-serviced skiing** ($200/person for the day), which adds nine hundred acres of backcountry terrain packed with deep, untracked powder suitable for well-heeled enthusiasts.

The nearest resort **accommodation** is the musty *Monarch Mountain Lodge* (☏719/539-2581 or 1-800/332-3668, ⓦwww.monarchmountainlodge.com; ⓞ), a hotel three miles from the lifts where rooms have kitchens and access to a pool, hot tub, sauna, and tennis as well as racquetball courts. Adjacent to the hotel are the *Ski Town Condominiums* (☏719/539-7928 1-866/539-7380 www.skitowncondos.com; ⓞ), which sleep four and have kitchens.

A favorite with those worn out by a day spent outdoors is the **Salida Hot Springs Pool**, 410 W Rainbow Blvd (call for hours; $6; ☏719/539-6738, ⓦwww.salidapool.com), where heated water is piped in from five miles away to a large municipal pool and half a dozen hot tubs. The main pool is also used for kayak instruction; call for details.

Biking

The classic mountain biking trail in the area – indeed one of Colorado's best – is the **Monarch Crest Trail**, which begins from the Monarch Ski Area and runs along the Continental Divide for around 25 miles. For a large part, the route follows the Colorado Trail and runs past a string of 13,000ft peaks, supplying absolutely incredible views in all directions. Though the most satisfying variant of the trail is suitable only for experienced bikers, the route can easily be cut short by those running out of energy. The trail is generally rideable from around mid-June to September and is best attempted early in the day, since frequent thunderstorms often make the exposed Continental Divide a bit dicey later on in the afternoon. If you want to **shuttle** up, contact High Country Shuttle ($15; ☏719/539-6089 or 1-800/871-5145, ⓦwww.monarchcrest.com). If renting, stop by Absolute Bikes, downtown by the river at 300 W Sackett St (☏719/539-9295 or 1-888/539-9295, ⓦwww.absolutebikes.com), where an impressive collection of vintage mountain bikes are also on display. Prices start at $30 a day for a front-suspension bike.

Rafting

Though sandwiched between two challenging and exciting stretches of the Arkansas, the stretch of river around Salida itself is rather quiet, best for those in search of more sedate, though still scenic, float trips. The only real noise made on the river occurs during downtown's boisterous **FIBArk** (First in Boating on the Arkansas) **Festival**, held for five days around the third weekend in June. The festival features concerts and various rafting and kayaking events, including the popular Hooligan Race, where crafts are awarded prizes for originality as much as speed, encouraging participants to enter vessels like Viking longboats, beer-keg rafts, and brass beds. Throughout the summer, Canyon Marine, 129 W Rainbow Blvd (Hwy-50; ☎1-800/539-4447, ⊛www.canyonmarine.com), runs relaxed **guided float trips** around Salida from around $43. They also offer wilder, more expensive rides on the roaring portions of the Arkansas north around Buena Vista (see p.304) or east through the Royal Gorge.

Eating and drinking

1st Street Café 137 E 1st St ☎719/539-4759. Friendly, laid-back haunt with a good range of cooked breakfasts and a predictable (though still tasty) selection of American favorites – burgers, sandwiches, and salads – and Mexican food. Prices are moderate.

Amica's Pizza & Microbrew 136 E 2nd St ☎719/539-5219. Hip brewpub with great pizzas and pastas for around $7. Great place to knock back a couple of their exceptional ales too.

Cornucopia Bakery & Café 168 F St ☎719/539-2531. Popular breakfast and lunch spot overlooking Salida's shady riverside park. On offer is a range of soups and salads for

around $7, hot or cold sandwiches, and some tasty baked goods, particularly the scones. Opens at 6.30am in summer, 7am in winter.

Victoria Hotel and Tavern 143 N F St ☎719/539-9003. This spit-and-sawdust place, with beers served in the can, is the most popular downtown nightspot and packs out at weekends, when there's often live music.

Windmill Restaurant 720 E Rainbow Blvd ☎719/539-3594. On the main highway, the inexpensive menu here includes fajitas, taco salads, steak, and seafood. The food is good and filling, and there's a wonderful and extensive collection of old advertising memorabilia strewn about.

Listings

Banks Pueblo Bank & Trust has an ATM on 200 F St.

Golf Salida Golf Club (☎719/539-1060) runs a pretty nine-hole course near downtown with inexpensive greens fees ($16).

Laundry There's a self-service laundromat at 14th and E St (6am–10pm).

Medical Center The Heart of the Rockies Medical Center, 448 E 1st St (☎719/539-6661), provides 24hr emergency care.

Post Office The most central is at 310 D St.

Showers Salida Hot Springs Pool, 410 W Rainbow Blvd (opens 9am; ☎719/539-6738), charges $2.

Buena Vista

BUENA VISTA, a small ragtag town 26 miles north of Salida, fully lives up to its name, with amazing views indeed. The **Collegiate Peaks**, a cluster of towering 14,000ft mountains, loom to the west, and the town sits alongside the rushing Arkansas River, arguably America's busiest stretch of whitewater. The river is the town's lifeblood, and all the action in town centers around the **Buena Vista River Park**, where rafters and kayakers put in and fishermen cast. Other than the river, the town has no sights to speak of, though a few nearby **hot springs** resorts attract those who are weary of body from their adventures on the trails and the water.

Arrival and information

Buena Vista is an easy 115-mile drive east from Denver on Hwy-285 (no public transportation). The highway arrives on the southern edge of town, but a couple of minutes north along Hwy-24 soon brings you to the downtown area. Housed in a small chapel in a park beside busy Hwy-24 as it cuts through town is the friendly **visitor center** (daily 9am–4pm; ☎719/395-6612, ⓦwww .nowthisiscolorado.com). If you're looking for in-depth info on the Arkansas Headwaters Recreation Area, you'll have to head to their office in Salida (see p.301). To clean up and dry off after a day on the river, visit the **laundry** at 10 Linderman Ave (7am–10pm) and the 24hr coin-operated **showers** near Buena Vista River Park.

Accommodation

In the summer (particularly weekends), **accommodation** in Buena Vista fills up fast with rafters. Outside the rafting season, though, things quiet down and prices generally drop by at least a third, making this an affordable though slightly inconvenient base for skiing in Vail or Monarch. If **camping**, the surrounding National Forest land has plenty of sites. These include some handy options due west of town along CO-306 (W Main St) like *Cottonwood Lake* ($14; year-round first-come, first-served). There's a further cluster south of town near the *Mount Princeton Hot Springs Resort* (see opposite), including three small USFS campgrounds near Chalk Creek: *Mt Princeton*, *Chalk Creek*, and *Cascade* (same contact info as above; all $12; open mid-May to mid-Sept). All three take both tents and RVs, but should be booked in advance as they fill up fast.

Rafting the Arkansas

Replete with chunky waves, foaming whirlpools, and swirling eddies, the wild rapids on the Arkansas attract **whitewater kayakers** and **rafters** in their thousands. Thankfully the season is a long one – ranging from late May to late September – meaning the river only gets congested on summer weekends. The favorite stretches are between Buena Vista and Cañon City, with the most exciting sections at either end. The **Royal Gorge** portion has far and away the river's most spectacular scenery, but before you get to the thrilling Class IV and V sections at the bottom of this huge canyon there's a long stretch of Class III waters to negotiate. For a more sustained Class IV experience, you're better off doing the **Numbers**, a quick succession of Class IV and V rapids that at high water leave little room for error. Those who don't find this thrilling enough should try the daring run down **Pine Creek**, where hard Class V rapids put off the majority of commercial operators.

If you want to run the Royal Gorge section near Cañon City, top **operators** include Echo Canyon River Expeditions, 45000 Hwy-50 W, Cañon City (☎1-800/755-3246, ⓦwww.echocanyonrafting.com), and Arkansas River Tours, in Cotopaxi near the start of the section (☎719/942-4362 or 1-800/321-4352, ⓦwww.arkansasrivertours .com). Two experienced operators offering rafting trips in the Buena Vista area are Four Corners Rafting, based in Nathrop to the south (☎719/395-4137 or 1-800/332-7238, ⓦwww.fourcornersrafting.com), and Wilderness Aware Rafting, located at the southern end of Buena Vista on Hwy-285 (☎719/395-2112 or 1-800/462-7238, ⓦwww.inaraft.com). With all of the above, expect to pay around $70–90 for a full day's rafting, including a picnic lunch.

Next to rafting, **kayaking** is the most popular way to navigate local rivers. The skills needed to tackle the most interesting parts of the Arkansas can be learnt at the Rocky Mountain Outdoor Center, 10281 Hwy-50, in Howard between Salida and Cañon City (☎719/539-2420 or 1-800/255-5784, ⓦwww.rmoc.com).

Best Western Vista Inn 733 Hwy-24 N ☎719/395-8009 or 1-800/809-3495, ⓦwww .vtinet.com/vistainn. Large, modern motel with comfortable and well-equipped rooms – with fridges and microwaves – and three outdoor hot tubs with views of the mountains that put the vista into the *Vista Inn*. The B&B deal includes an extensive continental breakfast. ❺

Cottonwood Hot Springs Inn 18999 CO-306 ☎719/395-6434. This hot springs resort, five miles west of Buena Vista on CO-306, offers a buffet of lodging options that include cabins, motel rooms, dorm beds (some in tepees), and a couple of unattractive tent sites. Though lodging seems a little overpriced at first – for a slightly shabby beatnik place – free entry to the laid-back hot spring pools by the creek make the deals pretty reasonable. ❹

Mount Princeton Hot Springs Resort 15870 CO-162, Nathrop ☎719/395-2447 or 1-888/395-7799, ⓦwww.mtprinceton.com. A modern lodge with spacious rooms thirteen miles from Buena Vista (eight miles south on Hwy-285 to Nathrop, then five miles west along CO-162), this is the latest, and most modest, of a string of hotels that have been here since the 1920s, taking advantage of the resident hot springs. ❺

Silver Wheel Motel 520 Hwy-24 S ☎719/395-2955. Basic and clean motel rooms, the cost of which are slashed by around half in winter. ❸

🏃 Trout City Inn near the junction of highways 24 and 285 ☎719/395-8433. Unusual B&B with four guestrooms in a couple of old narrow-gauge railroad cars eight miles east of Buena Vista on the 9346ft Trout Pass. Each carriage is decorated with elegant Victoriana, to provide for a memorable stay. ❻

Vista Court Cabins 1004 W Main St ☎719/395-6557. Cheerful, good-value cabins a short way west of downtown. Some even more inexpensive lodge rooms are also available, with substantial winter discounts offered on both. ❹

Fly-fishing

Though most people's attention is focused on the whitewater of the Arkansas, the river and many of its tributaries also harbor world-class **fly-fishing** – particularly for brown trout, although rainbow, cutthroat, and brook are also abundant in many offshoot streams. In spring and fall, anglers can expect to catch brown and rainbow averaging around a foot. Cottonwood Lake, ten miles west of Buena Vista on Hwy-306 (which begins as Main St), is particularly legendary for big rainbows. Note that many good stretches of the Arkansas are private property, so get advice on where to fish from local outfitters like Ark Anglers, 545 N Hwy-24 (☎719/539-4223, ⓦwww.arkanglers.com), who also run a variety of fishing trips, including a half-day for $140.

Hiking and biking

The obvious targets for serious hikers visiting Buena Vista are the **Collegiate Peaks**, Colorado's greatest concentration of 14,000ft peaks just west of town. Comprising mounts Oxford (14,153ft), Harvard (14,420ft), Columbia (14,075ft), Yale (14,196ft), and Princeton (14,197ft), they were all named for the Ivy League schools whose mountaineering teams were the first to summit the peaks in the early twentieth century. A long and challenging ascent requiring no special equipment is the 8.5-mile trail to the summit of **Mount Harvard**. The upper portion follows the Colorado Trail and is best begun from the Collegiate Peaks Wilderness Area just west of town along CO-306. You can also strike out on an easy eight-mile out-and-back hike to **Kroenke Lake** from here. Another good short hike in the Collegiate Peaks, with a 100-year-old prospector's cabin as its terminus, begins from the Denny Creek Trailhead, two miles west of Buena Vista, again along CO-306. The moderately steep trail climbs four miles to scenic Brown's Pass on the Continental Divide, then descends half a mile to Brown's Cabin, a collection of old cabin ruins near a defunct gold mine.

Further west, towards the barren Independence Pass on a road leading to the Taylor Park Reservoir and eventually Gunnison, is a trail to **Ptarmigan Lake** – actually a couple of lakes nestled among damp meadows just above the timberline and surrounded by bleak high-alpine scenery. The rocky trail also makes a good round-trip ride for experienced mountain bikers, taking around two hours from the trailhead beside CO-306, about ten miles west of Buena Vista.

Before heading out, drop in at the visitor center (see p.304) for the free guide to ten of the area's most popular hikes. If in need of **equipment** or **rentals**, stop at the Trailhead, 707 Hwy-24 N (☎719/395-8001), where mountain bikes go for $30/day or $90/week.

Eating and drinking

Antero Grill Hwy-285, sixteen miles south of Buena Vista ☎719/530-0301. Expensive restaurant serving "Modern American cowboy cuisine" – basically ranch favorites fused with gourmet ingredients that makes for the finest dining for miles around. Appetizers include rock shrimp quesadillas while entrees like braised rabbit or vegetable torte with beef tenderloin tips and roasted sweetcorn mashed potatoes are sure to fill you up. Great dry-aged steaks are also available. The cowboy decor includes a predictable but atmospheric collection of paintings and lassos.
Blue Parrot 304 E Main St ☎304/342-2583. Friendly bar that's a good place to unwind after a day on the river.

Casa Del Sol 303 Hwy-24 ☎719/395-8810. Superb, moderately priced Mexican restaurant serving not just the usual Tex-Mex, but also a range of dishes from different parts of Mexico, from seafood quesadillas to *pollo en mole*.
Coyote Cantina 12985 Hwy-285 ☎719/395-3755. Good, filling, and inexpensive Mexican food in a busy bar at the junction of highways 24 and 285 to Denver, two miles south of Buena Vista.
Evergreen Café 418 N Hwy-24 ☎719/395-8984. A good stop for the extensive breakfast menu (opens 6.30am) and simple burger or sandwich lunches.

Travel details

Flights

Colorado Springs to: Denver (18 daily; 40min).

Buses

(All buses are TNM&O unless otherwise stated.)

Colorado Springs to: Denver (30 daily; 1hr 40min; TNM&O and FREX); Durango (1 daily; 17hr 25min); Grand Junction (3 daily; 8hr) Pueblo (8 daily; 50min); Trinidad (2 daily; 2hr 20min); Vail (2 daily; 5hr 20min; Greyhound).

Southeast Colorado

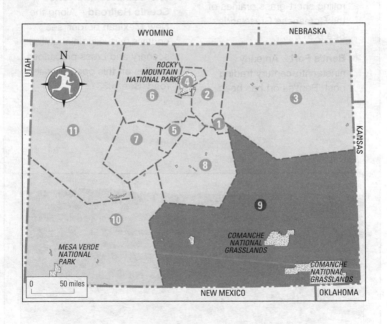

WYOMING

NEBRASKA

UTAH

N

ROCKY
MOUNTAIN
NATIONAL PARK

4

6

2

3

11

7

5

1

8

KANSAS

9

10

COMANCHE
NATIONAL
GRASSLANDS

MESA VERDE
NATIONAL
PARK

COMANCHE
NATIONAL
GRASSLANDS

0   50 miles

NEW MEXICO

OKLAHOMA

CHAPTER 9

Highlights

* **Bishop Castle** – This bizarre
spectacle is the ongoing life's
work of one determined man,
and is not to be missed.
See p.312

* **Picket Wire Canyon** – Over
one thousand dinosaur footprints speckle this desolate
canyon, tucked away in the
rolling short-grass prairies of
the Comanche Grasslands.
See p.317

* **Bent's Fort** – An early
nineteenth-century trading
post, Bent's Fort has been
reconstructed to look as it did
when wagons still rolled along
the Santa Fe Trail. See p.318

* **Great Sand Dunes National
Monument** – Hike and slide
on towering, out-of-place
dunes abutting the Sangre de
Cristo Mountains. See p.325

* **The Cumbres and Toltec
Scenic Railroad** – Along the
New Mexican border, see
endless, virtually uninhabited
scenery and cross precarious
trestles on this open-air railroad. See p.331

△ Dinosaur footprints, Picket Wire canyon

9

Southeast Colorado

P art plains and part mountains, and tangibly Hispanic, most visitors don't really know what to make of **SOUTHEAST COLORADO**, and so leave it well alone. But it's precisely these distinctive features – the sharp, jagged profile of the **Sangre de Cristos**, the surrounding flatlands, and the deep-rooted Hispanic culture – that sets the area apart and makes it a worth a second look.

Traveling in from the north, gritty **Pueblo** is the region's inauspicious gateway town, and best quickly driven through – save perhaps during its late-August State Fair – en route to the **Wet Mountains** or the south. The road to the latter is forced almost to Colorado's southern border by the almost impassable granite Sangre de Cristo Mountains, which run as an unbroken chain for 75 miles, joining the Arkansas Headwaters in the north to the **Spanish Peaks** in the south. A modest and pretty range of mountains, the Spanish Peaks are well off the beaten track and have begun to foster small artist communities, whose main life-line is the run-down and uneventful **Trinidad**, near the New Mexican border.

It's here on the southern fringes of Colorado that its Hispanic culture becomes most evident. Until the end of the Mexican–American War in 1848, when south-central Colorado was finally ceded to the US, most of this area was in Hispanic hands and all the early settlements Spanish or Mexican. Southern Colorado became a vital link between the US and Mexico, with traders busily plying the **Santa Fe Trail** – a route you may likely follow if you enter the state from the southeast. Meanwhile ranchers pioneered the vast, pancake-flat **San Luis Valley**. Sandwiched between the Sangre de Cristos and the San Juan Mountains, this valley feels like a hunk of plains that have been dropped into the mountains, though made scenically spectacular by the surrounding ring of often snow-covered peaks. Although few visitors venture here, the **Great Sand Dunes National Park** is one of Colorado's most striking natural wonders.

The Southern Front Range

In contrast to the mountains that rise dramatically from the plains to the north, the **Southern Front Range**, south of Colorado Springs, sees a much more gradual transition. Here wide-open sagebrush plains – such as those around dull, post-industrial **Pueblo** – turn only very gradually into the rolling **Wet Mountains** to the west and then only slightly more abruptly into the **Sangre de Cristo Range**, around the tiny settlements of **Westcliffe** and **Silver Cliff**.

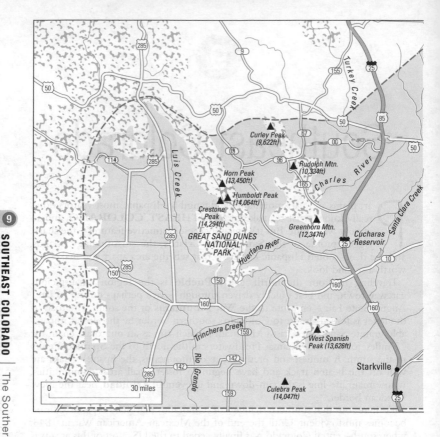

Perhaps this is why the area has never really caught the imagination of visitors: few people venture here, despite some good trails and the presence of the exceptional personal feat of **Bishop Castle**.

Pueblo

Starting life as a trading post and gold-mining supply center, **PUEBLO** quickly grew into Colorado's second-largest city after it was chosen by the Colorado Fuel and Iron Company to be the site of a huge steel mill in the 1870s. For more than one hundred years, coal transported up from Trinidad helped keep the mill's smokestacks fuming, but by the 1980s the mill had all but shut down, leaving an unappealing townscape and an economic void. Still shrinking, Pueblo is now the state's third-largest city, and if there's any cause for optimism it's in the fact that Pueblo has bounced back from being down and out before. During the Christmas celebrations of 1854, the fledgling community decided to invite local Ute into town to celebrate; the natives quickly butchered all but a handful of the drunken revelers. And in 1921, the Arkansas River overflowed, submerging and destroying most of downtown, and claiming scores of lives in the process. Given more enticing opportunities elsewhere in the region, few visitors make it to Pueblo, except during the State Fair at the end of summer, when beds are hard to come by.

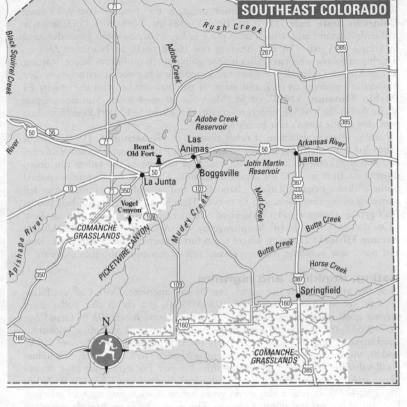

Rush Creek

Adobe Creek

Black Squirrel Creek

River

Adobe Creek Reservoir

Las Animas

Bent's Old Fort

Arkansas River

Lamar

La Junta

Boggsville

John Martin Reservoir

Mud Creek

Vogel Canyon

COMANCHE GRASSLANDS

Apishapa River

PICKETWIRE CANYON

Muddy Creek

Butte Creek

Butte Creek

Horse Creek

Springfield

N

COMANCHE GRASSLANDS

Arrival, information, and accommodation

Buses from both Denver and Grand Junction arrive at the Greyhound and TNM&O bus depot near I-25 exit 101 at 703 US-50 W (☎719/544-6295). The chamber of commerce is on the city's principal downtown street, North Santa Fe Ave, at no. 302 (Mon–Fri 8am–5pm; ☎719/542-1704 or 1-800/233-3446, ⓦ www.pueblochamber.org).

A large number of **hotels** and **motels** have settled a couple of miles north of the city center, around the aforementioned exit 101. There's little lodging downtown, and little available anywhere during the State Fair. One of the cheapest and most basic deals is the *Al-Re-Ho Motel*, 2424 N Freeway (☎719/542-5135; ①), while the nearby *Days Inn*, 4201 N Elizabeth St (☎719/543-8031; ④), with its Southwestern-style rooms and pool, is quite a bit smarter. Downtown, the *Travelers Motel*, 1012 N Santa Fe Ave (☎719/543-5451; ②), is a dreary though inexpensive and central option. The odd-inn-out of the town's bland accommodation selection is the lovely and laid-back ⚘ *Abriendo Inn*, 300 W Abriendo Ave (☎719/544-2703, ⓦ www.abriendoinn.com; ⑤). Its reputation as one of the finest B&Bs in the state is well earned; the house has plenty of stained glass and antique furniture, and some rooms – all en suite – have four-poster beds and hot tubs.

Without a doubt the city's premier event is the roughly two-week-long **Colorado State Fair** ($5–7; ☎719/561-8484 or 1-800/876-4567, ⓦwww .coloradostatefair.com), which takes place in large purpose-built grounds found by taking I-25 exit 97A and heading one block north to Northern Avenue, which you follow west two miles before going north on Prairie Street. Starting in late August, Colorado's biggest fair combines a big rodeo with lots of live music, from country to rock and more. If the fair's not on, visit the nearby **El Pueblo Museum**, 324 W 1st St (Mon–Sat 10am–4.30pm, Sun noon–3pm; $2.50; ☎719/583-0453), which re-creates the adobe 1842 Fort Pueblo trading post, one of the town's first buildings.

Pueblo's premier attraction at other times is the **Rosemount**, 419 W 14th St (Tues–Sat 10am–4pm; $6; ⓦwww.rosemount.org), an opulent 37-room Victorian mansion that contrasts sharply with much of the rest of the rather run-down downtown. Built in 1893 for local banker John Thatcher, the antique-furnished home includes original Tiffany chandeliers and an elaborate thirteen-foot-tall stained-glass window, dedicated to two of Thatcher's children who died young. An Egyptian mummy and a number of other strange souvenirs are also on show.

On the western side of downtown by the Arkansas River is the **Union Avenue Historic District**, where the refurbishment of numerous old railway and warehouse buildings has seen several restaurants and boutiques move in.

Eating, drinking, and nightlife

Near the strip of hotels and motels out by the interstate, *Don's Café*, on Elizabeth St just south of CO-50 (☎719/543-5814), is a cheap blue-collar diner serving good **meals** throughout the day. Downtown, *Rita's*, 302 N Grand Ave (☎719/542-4820), serves a good range of Mexican food, including enormous combination platters for only $6. A more upmarket option is *Rendezvous*, 218 W 2nd St, which offers a pretty eclectic menu – Mexican to Continental – including good-value lunches from $7; Fridays feature live jazz. For a more jumping atmosphere and regular **live music** head to the *Irish Brewpub and Grill*, 108 W 3rd St (☎719/542-9974), which also serves good bar food, including unusual offerings like buffalo burgers and alligator sausages. The most reliable **nightclub** in town is *Peppers*, 4109 Club Manor Drive, just west of the intersection of I-25 and Hwy-50 (☎719/542-8629). Here, occasional live bands are augmented by a steady diet of Sixties, Seventies, and Eighties pop, along with the occasional techno night.

The Wet Mountains

South from Pueblo, I-25 zips through 48 miles of dry, uneventful desert landscape to Walsenburg. But a worthwhile detour – the odd **Bishop Castle** – lies in the craggy **Wet Mountains**, 25 miles west of Pueblo on Hwy-96. Further west, separating the eastern and western halves of the San Isabel National Forest, is the Wet Mountain Valley, a 35-mile-wide belt of rolling hills that makes for ideal ranching country. At the valley's center, the small communities of **Westcliffe** and **Silver Cliff** are bordered to the west by the virtually impassable Sangre de Cristo Range, home to numerous trails and climbing routes.

Bishop Castle

Touted as the world's largest one-man construction project, **Bishop Castle** (dawn–dusk; by donation; ☎719/485-3040, ⓦwww.bishopcastle.org), 34 miles west of Pueblo on Hwy-78, is a tribute to determination and eccentricity. The massive pseudo-medieval castle, a ramshackle affair rising up as high as 160 feet, is the work of Jim Bishop, a former Pueblo steelworker who's been building the thing stone-by-stone for over thirty years. Over one thousand tons of hand-gathered local rocks have gone into the structure, which contains an entertaining mix of dungeon-like rooms, stained-glass windows, flimsy iron spiral staircases, and numerous stone turrets, spires, and flying buttresses – enter at your own risk. Bishop's still toiling away on his surreal masterpiece, and you'll probably spot him working on something or another if you visit. Interestingly, he had no intention of building the castle when he first bought this land – he was only building a small stone cottage, but in response to frequent comments by visitors that it looked like a castle, he decided to go ahead and make it one. Since then, the structure has hosted over seventy weddings and gets more visitors than anything else in the Wet Mountains, all the while remaining free, dedicated to the "hardworking poor people of the world."

Westcliffe and Silver Cliff

Twenty-nine miles west of Bishop Castle, off the junction of highways 69 and 96, the small ranching towns of **WESTCLIFFE** and **SILVER CLIFF** enjoyed their heydays a century ago. The former began as the local railroad terminus for the line from Cañon City, while the latter, smaller and virtually attached to Westcliffe's eastern fringes, was for a brief spell Colorado's third-largest town after silver was found there in 1877. Both proceeded to near ghost-town status, though in recent years Westcliffe has re-emerged as a bit of a base for exploring the outdoors, and its Main Street is now filled with realtors' offices, Western art galleries, and twee emporiums selling Old West gifts and ice cream. Not all of the town's agricultural basis has been forgotten, though, as is proven by the **Westcliffe Stampede**, a rodeo held in late June. This is overshadowed by the far bigger **Jazz in the Sangres** festival (☏719/783-3785, ⊛www.jazzinthesangres .com), held over the second weekend of August.

Outdoor recreation around Westcliffe

Westcliffe, on the doorstep of the Sangre de Cristo Mountains, is well placed to give access to a range of generally underused **outdoor recreation** possibilities. Since most of the Sangre de Cristos, which include 35 peaks over 13,500ft, are hard climbs – the majority requiring some climbing equipment and expertise – most of the hiking in the area centers either around the easy **Rainbow Trail** or others up to mountain passes from where there are good views of the jagged, imposing range. Originally built for forest firefighters, the Rainbow Trail follows the contours of the range's base. Mountain bikers can also use this trail, since it's outside of the protected Wilderness Area that covers much of the Sangre de Cristos.

A good place to access the Rainbow Trail is from the USFS *Alvarado Campground* – see "Practicalities" p.314. Here you can also pick up a trail to **Venable Lakes**, a six-mile return hike to a pair of pretty alpine lakes above the timberline – favorites with anglers for good-sized brook trout. Before heading out, check in with the USDA Forest Service (see p.314), who sell Michael O'Hanlons' *The Colorado Sangre de Cristo – Complete Trail Guide* (Hungry Gulch Press; $13), the definitive guide to trails in the range. If you're interested in exploring the Wet Mountains, pick up a copy of Nadia N. Brelje's *Southern Front Range Trail Guide* (self-published; $15), which reviews trails within a 50-mile radius of Pueblo; it's sold at Bishop Castle.

Other than wander around gift shops, there's not really much to do in either town except stock up before heading into the mountains. A small **museum**, at 713 Main St (summer Thurs–Sun 1–4pm; free), charts the towns' history via a predictable but diverting collection of relics and old photos housed in a nineteenth-century former fire station. The only other real local attraction is **Mission Wolf** (daily 9am–sunset; free; ☎719/746-2919), a sanctuary for former pet wolves in Blue Spring, 41 miles from Westcliffe along Hwy-69 (for 27 miles) and Gardner Road. Around fifty wolves and wolf-dog hybrids are looked after here in environments that try to simulate their natural habitat.

Practicalities

Westcliffe's **information center** (Mon–Sat 10am–4pm, Sun noon–4pm; ☎719/783-9163 or 1-877/793-3170, ⓦ www.custercountyco.com), is at the junction of Main St and northbound Hwy-69. The **USDA Forest Service**, in Silver Cliff at 5 Hermit Lane (☎719/783-2481), has details on the surrounding San Isabel National Forest.

Of the decent range of **accommodation** in Westcliffe, most inexpensive is the *Antler Motel*, 102 S Main (☎719/783-2426; ❷), a bit scrappy but still clean. A better option is the *Westcliffe Inn*, a mile south along Hwy-69 (☎719/783-9275; ❸), where facilities include a hot tub and most rooms have great mountain views. At the more luxurious end of the scale, the central *Main Street Inn Bed & Breakfast*, no. 501 (☎719/783-4000 or 1-877/783-4006, ⓦ www.mainstreetbnb.com; ❺), offers antique-furnished rooms (with private bath) in a renovated Victorian home.

In Silver Cliff, *Yoder's High Country Inn*, 700 Ohio St (☎719/783-2656; ❸), is a clean family-run motel whose rates include continental breakfast. Campers should head to the San Isabel National Forest to the west. The USFS office (see above) can supply details of all the **campgrounds**, but one that's particularly convenient, located by several trailheads, is the *Alvarado Campground* (mid-May to mid-Sept; $10), which has thirty RV sites and seventeen tent sites. To find it, head south from Westcliffe on Hwy-69 for three miles, then go right on CO-302 for seven more.

There's a more limited range of **places to eat**. For breakfast and lunch, try *Karen's Gourmet Coffee*, 104 Main (daily 7.30am–2pm), a small restaurant with a fine range of food – omelettes for breakfast and daily specials like chicken quesadillas and buffalo burgers with blue cheese ($7) for lunch. Further east along Main, at no. 212, *Shining Mountains* is a lunch-only restaurant serving decent Mexican food, along with wraps, burgers, and sandwiches, on its adobe patio. For dinner, Silver Cliff is the best option, with *Yoders*, 700 Ohio St (closed Sun & Wed afternoons), offering dishes like grilled ham steak ($6) and Polish sausage, and the vegetarian-friendly *Pizza Madness*, 715 Main St, where there's a big outside patio.

The Santa Fe Trail

Easing its way out of the Rockies around Pueblo, the Arkansas River continues the next leg of its 2000-mile journey east to the Missouri–Mississippi river system across Colorado's dusty southeastern plains. Hwy-50 pretty much follows its course all the way to the Kansas border, and for the most part traces the former route of the **Santa Fe Trail** as well. Like the Overland Trail in the north (see p.415), this was another part of one of America's great east-west trails, at a time when the nation was in its infancy and still spreading west. It was particularly after Mexico won its independence from Spain in 1821 that the Santa Fe Trail became a vital link in the chain of continental communication. As trade between the new country and the US began to buzz, so too did this main trading route, which linked St Louis, Missouri, and Santa Fe, in today's New Mexico. Some tangible relics from this era – particularly **Bent's Fort** – make travel in this part of Colorado interesting.

The main towns are tightly-knit rural communities like **La Junta** and **Las Animas**, which both have interesting local history museums. The big attractions, though, are in these towns' vicinity within the **Comanche Grasslands**, where you can find ancient Native American **petroglyphs** and even more prehistoric and impressive chains of **dinosaur tracks** – among the longest in the world, and so well worth leaving Hwy-50 for. Back on the highway, be sure to stop at the many roadside stalls that sell fruit and particularly **melons**. The small town of **Rocky Ford**, ten miles west of La Junta, produces particularly juicy cantaloupes, and, during the August harvest season, hosts the Arkansas Valley Fair, which includes a carnival, horse races, a rodeo, and as much melon as you can eat.

La Junta

Small-town life is alive and well in **LA JUNTA**, whose sleepy, well-kept streets have yet to be invaded by chain stores or malls. Like many plains burgs, La Junta began life as a railroad town, its location at the junction of the main and Denver branch lines of the Santa Fe Railroad. The railway still passes through here, but its importance has ebbed and the place is now largely a market town for local ranchers. For travelers La Junta is partly of interest for a couple of local **museums**, but mostly as a base for trips to the **Comanche Grasslands** and **Bent's Fort**.

Orientation in La Junta could hardly be easier: Hwy-50 skirts the northern side of town, separating it from the railroad tracks and the Arkansas River, while the main street, Colorado Avenue, heads due south from the railway depot.

The Koshare Indian and Otero museums

Drive ten blocks south from Hwy-50 along Colorado Avenue, past pleasant Blaine Park and its shaded picnic areas, and you'll find yourself a block east and in sight of the striking adobe **Koshare Indian Museum**, 115 W 18th St (daily 10am–5pm; $4; ☎719/384-4411, ⓦ www.koshare.org). The Indians in question are actually not Native Americans at all but a La Junta Boy Scout group with an overwhelming focus on Native American craft and lore. The whole concept was masterminded by father-figure James Francis Burshears (1909–87), universally called "Buck," who recruited local youths into his tribe, whose performances and interpretations of traditional tribal dances and music have won national acclaim. The round wing of the building houses a giant wooden kiva, where the troop performs its dances (most summer Saturdays at 8pm, less regularly in winter; $5), built with a gigantic self-supporting roof that comprises 600 logs and weighs almost 40 tons. The rest of the building is devoted to a gift shop and a fine little Native American museum. Its collection, the result of gifts and donations from many tribes, includes various clothes, rugs, tools, and papooses, sporting intricate bead work and embroidery done using porcupine quills. There's even some thousand-year-old Ancestral Puebloan pottery. A bit of local color is added by a display of cheerful Western woodcarving caricatures by Colorado-born Andy Anderson. Look out too for the background information about the Koshare Indians, including the remarkable list of requirements demanded from eleven-year-old recruits.

La Junta's other attraction is the modest **Otero Museum**, seven blocks west of Colorado Ave at Third and Anderson streets (June–Sept Mon–Sat 1–5pm; free; ☎719/384-7500), that's dedicated to local history. The highlight is an 1865 stagecoach, once used along the Santa Fe Trail, but the selection of old buildings here – including a schoolroom, grocery store, and fully furnished adobe home – are all filled with diverting antiques.

Practicalities

The closest Greyhound and TNM&O bus station to La Junta, five miles northwest in Rocky Ford, is served by buses to Pueblo. Amtrak trains stop at the depot bang in the center of town at the junction of Hwy-50 and Colorado Ave. From here the La Junta **Chamber of Commerce**, 110 Santa Fe Ave (Mon–Fri 9am–5pm; ☎719/384-7411), is only one block west. Another useful source of local information is the **USFS Comanche National Grasslands Ranger Station**, 1420 E 3rd St (☎719/384-2181).

The range of **accommodation** in La Junta is pretty limited and comes down to a choice between family-owned motels in town or chain motels along Hwy-50 just west of town. The best of the former is the immaculately kept *Midtown Motel*, 215 E 3rd St (☎719/384-7741; ❷), the only lodging option not alongside busy Hwy-50. Around three miles west of town, the dependable *Super 8*, 27884 Hwy-5 W (☎719/384-4408 or 1-800/800-8000, ⓦwww.super8.com) has an indoor pool and hot tub and includes a basic breakfast.

La Junta doesn't have many places to **eat**, and you may find yourself driving a couple of miles out of town for some of the best choices. For a quick breakfast or burger, step back in time into downtown's social hub, *Lori's Corner Café*, 302 Colorado Ave, a Formica-table joint in the corner of a department store. Later on in the day it's worth driving a couple of miles west along Hwy-50 to *Felicia's*, 27948 Frontage Rd (closed Sun), where zesty Mexican dishes show off southern Colorado's Hispanic heritage. For a far grittier experience go to the *Dry Bean BBQ & Steakhouse*, four miles west of La Junta in Swink. Here you'll find the best barbeque in the area, where beef, pork, and chicken are smoked and slow-cooked to perfection. For those looking for fine dining in La Junta, there is only one address: ⚑ *Café Grandmere*, 408 W 3rd St (☎719/384-2711), where a graduate chef offers superb contemporary regional cuisine; the five-course dinners are by reservation only.

Comanche National Grasslands

Scorching heat, short-grass prairie, and twisting rock canyons await those who explore the **Comanche National Grasslands** in summer. But life has managed to exist here for thousands of years, and it's evidence of this, in the form of Native American **petroglyphs** and an extraordinary number of **dinosaur footprints**, that make it worth the trip. Though at first sight quite bleak, the grasslands are home to almost 300 species of birds – including the rare lesser prairie chicken – along with abundant antelope, deer, fox, badger, coyote, and bobcat. All animals, rattlesnakes included (see p.398), are at their most active and easiest to spot at dawn and dusk.

Like the Pawnee National Grasslands in the north of the state, the Comanche National Grasslands were once victims of poor soil management. Ploughing and overgrazing more or less destroyed the land and forced homesteaders to move on during the Great Depression and droughts of the 1930s. Just as in the Pawnee National Grasslands, the federal government purchased vast tracts of land here, carefully restoring them and passing the management on to the US

Forest Service. Split into two separate sections, the Timpas Unit, south of La Junta, is more interesting and accessible than the Carrizo Unit, near Springfield in Colorado's far southeast corner.

Two canyons – **Vogel** and **Picket Wire** – are of particular interest, and both are reached by following Hwy-109 (the southern extension of San Juan Ave, three blocks west of Colorado Ave) south from La Junta for thirteen miles to a signpost at the end of RD-802. Before you head out, visit the Ranger Station in La Junta (see p.316) for an info sheet, and be sure to pack plenty of water, as there's no drinking water in the canyons.

Vogel Canyon

The modest and accessible **Vogel Canyon**, formed by a small tributary to the Purgatoire River, lies just three miles from the intersection of Hwy-109 and RD-802. Drive a mile west and then two miles south from here on dirt roads and you arrive at the trailhead which has also been developed as a picnic area and is a good place to pitch a tent for free. Four short hiking and mountain biking trails begin here. Recommended is the four-mile loop that first heads south along the Canyon Trail and then west along the Prairie Trail before returning along the Mesa and Overlook trails. A sketch map at the trailhead outlines the route, which is relatively easy to follow thanks to stone markers; allow around two hours to complete the loop on foot. Points of interest include the ruins of the Depression-era Westbrook Homestead, just east of the canyon trail, around a quarter mile from the trailhead; and rock art – estimated to be between 300 and 800 years old – at the base of the Canyon's east wall, another quarter mile further along. Just beyond is a spring surrounded by cotton trees, which enabled homesteading and still attracts wildlife. At the intersection of the Prairie and Mesa trails is the ruin of the Barlow and Sanderson stagecoach stop, which was used from 1872 to 1876.

Picket Wire Canyon

The large and relatively remote **Picket Wire Canyon** is awkward to get to, and, unless you have a bike or horse, taxing to explore. That said, exploring the beautiful and serene canyon brings exceptional dividends in the form of the ruins of a nineteenth-century Spanish mission, an adjacent petroglyph site, and the largest dinosaur track site in North America. All three can be visited on a fairly easy eleven-mile hike, for which you should allow at least four hours.

To get to Picket Wire, drive eight miles west along RD-802 from its junction with Hwy-109, then six miles south on RD-25 to a corral and info board. This is the place to park after wet weather if you're in a 2WD, low-clearance car. Otherwise follow the track west for three miles to the trailhead. From here the trail starts almost immediately to descend, getting ever steeper, until you are on the pancake-flat canyon floor. The dirt road that leads upstream along it is obvious, and a four-mile walk brings you to what is left of the Dolores Mission.

Built sometime between 1871 and 1889, the mission is now little more than an awkward pile of mud bricks, but the graveyard is an evocative spot, and clambering on a track just uphill behind it brings you to rock art that is thought to between 300 and 4500 years old. The dramatic date range comes from the lack of research that's been done into it. A little over a mile beyond the mission is the dinosaur track site. Here the limestone rock gives a glimpse of a prehistoric world, where 33-ton and 20ft high brontosaurus walked in groups, leaving deep parallel prints on a lakeshore, and the mere four-ton allosaurus scavenged and hunted, their sharp claws etching a distinct pattern into the mud. These are just a handful of the 1300 prints discovered in the valley.

Bent's Fort

At the height of trade along the Santa Fe Trail, **Bent's Fort** (June–Aug 8am–5.30pm; Sept–May 9am–4pm; $3; ☎719/383-5010 ⓦwww.nps.gov/beol) was its most important landmark, a busy community where American and Mexican traders, trappers, and natives could meet and exchange goods and information. Today it's eight miles northeast of La Junta via highways 109 and 194, and should be equally important on any visitor itinerary; no one passing through the southeast should miss the opportunity to see this snapshot of the past.

Though the fort at the site today is of 1970s vintage, its layout and construction are true to the original design and it has been furnished to convey its original use, complete with trading rooms, a smithy, and even a billiards room. Visit the site on your own with a self-guided tour leaflet, or better still catch a free 45min guided tour (daily: June–Aug 9.30am, 11am, 1pm & 2.30pm; Sept–May 10.30am & 1pm) given by one of the knowledgeable costumed docents.

The adobe fort was originally built in 1833 by three speculative traders from St Louis: brothers Charles and William Bent and Ceran St Vrain, a descendant of French aristocrats who escaped their homeland during the revolution. The trio had good knowledge of the West and rightly saw an opportunity to make their fortunes with a trading outpost – particularly for the fur trade. Located deep in the heart of Indian territory, it was soon realized that good relations with the natives would be a big part of the enterprise's success. Luckily William Bent was said to "have a way with the Indians" and he not only brokered peace between warring tribes but also married a Cheyenne daughter of a holy man, named Owl Woman, to help secure harmonious relations.

Things went well for over a decade, but during the Mexican–American War (1846–48) the fort suffered a reversal of fortune, briefly serving as a military outpost. While army livestock stripped the surrounding land, cottonwood groves were being decimated and buffalo hunting was in sharp decline. Finally a cholera epidemic halved the local Native American population (claiming Owl Woman and several of her brothers) killing off what was left of the trade. Meanwhile Charles's remarkable regional influence made him Provisional Governor of New Mexico, although he died a year later in an 1847 uprising in which a band of Indians and Mexicans shot and scalped him.

Las Animas

Tumbledown **LAS ANIMAS**, fifteen miles east of Bent's Fort along Hwy-194, began life as a military encampment and then boomed as a railroad town, but today the ranching center is hardly worth a stop save for its local history **museum** and the tiny settlement of **Boggsville**, one of the first in the area. If you just want a place to pull off the highway to fish or camp then **John Martin Reservoir State Park** is worth a look.

Kit Carson Museum

Las Animas' densely packed local history museum, the **Kit Carson Museum** (late May to early Sept daily 1pm–5pm; $2; ☏719/456-0453), sits behind the town's most impressive building, a huge grey-roofed courthouse, and beside the road to Boggsville (Carson Ave). The museum itself spreads over several buildings, including an 1882 county jail, a smithy, schoolhouse, and, most impressively, an 1860 stagecoach station. Once used by the Pony Express, the station was painstakingly dismantled and brought here to be rebuilt. Dignitaries that stopped at it – when it was still in use – included eventual president Ulysses S. Grant and explorer Zebulon Pike, who gave his name to Pikes Peak. In comparison the main building is a dull and lackluster affair. Its loosely organized exhibits are worth a quick browse for a sense of local history, but the history of the building itself is no less interesting. Originally built as a POW camp for German officers captured in Africa during the Second World War – the gentlemen remained unguarded throughout their stay – it later housed Jamaican field workers and then operated as a local poor house. In coming years the museum is due to move to a new location at 6th St and Hwy-50, though a date has yet to be set.

Boggsville

The other vaguely worthwhile local attraction is **Boggsville** (May–Sept 10am–4pm; ☏719/456-1358), two miles south of town on Hwy-101 (Carson Ave). In many senses it represents the next stage in local history after Bent's Fort became redundant. Its founder Thomas Boggs once worked at the fort and met his wife Romalda, stepdaughter of Charles Bent, there. On the basis of Romalda's inherited land grant the pair then clubbed together with other pioneers to form a basic but stylish settlement based on ranching and irrigated crops. The hamlet did very well for itself for a while, attracting a number of Western characters, including Kit Carson – with his wife and seven children – to live here in a highly cosmopolitan community that saw natives live alongside European-Americans and Hispanics. Boggs himself spoke no less than thirteen languages: English, Spanish, and eleven native plains tongues. The arrival of the railroad at the competing rough-and-tumble settlement of Las

△ Bent's Fort

Animas effectively put an end to Boggsville's prosperity, though it continued for a time as a refined offshoot. Some of the settlement's buildings have since been restored and you are free to wander, but since they're mostly empty, it doesn't take long to look around.

John Martin Reservoir State Park

Spurred by the needs of thirsty local agriculture and the need for flood control, the 1940s saw the Arkansas River damned fifteen miles east of Las Animas. The resulting two-mile-long lake now forms the basis of **John Martin Reservoir State Park** (day fee $5; ☎719/336-1690, ⓦ www.parks.state.co.us), a local haven for outdoor pursuits. Surrounded as it is by a rather bleak and treeless shoreline, it will never win any awards for beauty, but activities like picnicking, camping, and warm-water fishing – for catfish, bass, crappie, and walleye – are well catered for. Birders will also enjoy the place for its impressive waterfowl population, with visiting white pelicans in summer and bald and golden eagles in winter.

Practicalities

One of the very few places to **stay** or **eat** in Las Animas is the relatively basic *Best Western Bent's Fort Inn*, on the north side of town at 10950 E Hwy-50 (☎719/456-0011; ❹). If this is where you stay, there's probably not much point in looking beyond its **restaurant** for food, since it's the local favorite for steaks and Mexican dishes. Otherwise, try *La Estancia*, 625 Carson Ave (closed Mon) which is slightly better for south-of-the-border food, including the delicious *carnitas*, hearty portions of marinated pork with sauteed onions.

Trinidad and the Spanish Peaks

Unlike most of the Rockies, the twin **Spanish Peaks** (12,683ft and 13,626ft) are the result of volcanic activity rather than folding and faulting. As a result, they have a more conical shape than mountains in neighboring ranges, and are nearly symmetrical. Like much of the rest of the Southern Front Range, the trails that crisscross the mountains here are relatively undiscovered, meaning there's plenty of good peaceful hiking, biking, and riding to be had.

The northern gateway to the Spanish Peaks is the junction town of **Walsenberg**. From here the most usual route south to **Trinidad** heads south 37 miles on I-25. An alternative route is the scenic **Highway of Legends** (largely Hwy-12). This takes twice as long to drive, but is much more attractive, as it cuts through the southern portion of the San Isabel National Forest and travels past the **Great Dikes**, a series of impressive volcanic rock formations.

Trinidad

Once a bustling railhead for freighting local coal, **TRINIDAD**'s formerly grand brick-paved streets are now lined with boarded-up businesses. The cityscape is overshadowed by the interstate flyover and, strangely enough, the town's industry seems to center around sex-change operations, with over 3500 having been performed here to date.

Originally a major stop along the Santa Fe Trail, Trinidad has always had a mix of US and Mexican cultures, perhaps best displayed at the excellent **Trinidad History Museum**, 300 E Main St (May–Sept Mon–Sat 10am–4pm, Oct–April Mon–Fri 9am–1pm; $5; ☎719/846-7217), which is made up of several buildings. One houses the **Santa Fe Trail Museum**, while the other two properties tell the intriguing tales of two of the town's leading families, one Hispanic, the other Anglo-American, in more prosperous times. The relatively plain adobe Baca House was the former home of a rancher, shipping magnate, and politician, while the opulent Bloom House was the Victorian mansion of a ranching and banking family. Much of the impetus to preserve these residences came from Arthur Ray Mitchell, a local artist famous for illustrating pulp-fiction Westerns. His work is commemorated in the **A.R. Mitchell Memorial Museum of Western Art**, 150 E Main St (April–Sept Mon–Sat 10am–4pm; free; ☎719/846-4224), where an insightful collection of photos charting local life from the 1870s onwards can also be seen.

Practicalities

Greyhound and TNM&O **buses** (☎719/543-2775) stop at JR's Travel Shoppe, 639 W Main St, while Amtrak pulls in at the depot alongside the Purgatoire River on Commercial Street. Information is available at the **Colorado Welcome Center & Trinidad Chamber of Commerce**, 309 Nevada Ave (☎719/846-9285, ⓦwww.trinidadco.com), beside the elevated I-25 (exit 15). The **Trinidad Trolley** (May–Sept 10am–5pm; free) starts its tour of the main shops and attractions from here.

One of the cheapest **accommodation** options in the area is the *Budget Host Derrick Motel*, south of town (I-25 exit 11) at 1031 Santa Fe Drive (☎719/846-3307; ④). Located beside a landmark derrick, the motel has pretty mountain views as well as RV sites ($25). Two B&Bs provide more personal lodging: the *Inn on the Santa Fe Trail*, 402 East Main St (☎719/846-7869; ④), is in a late nineteenth-century residence where all rooms have private baths; the *Stone Mansion Bed and Breakfast*, 212 E 2nd St (☎719/845-1625 or 1-877/264-4279; ④), has smart, spacious bedrooms with private bathrooms and gourmet breakfasts.

There are quite a number of tasty, inexpensive **restaurants** in Trinidad. A good place for breakfast is the *Main Street Bakery*, 121 Main, where fresh pastries and pancakes are served along with simple lunches and dinners (Thurs–Sat nights). Further along Main, the *El Paso Café*, at no. 1101, has some of the best Mexican food in town. At the west end of town (I-25 exit 14A), ♪ *Nano & Nano Monteleone's Pasta House and Deli*, 418 E Main St, is a cheerful and cheap restaurant serving up excellent Mexican and Italian food side by side. There's also a deli here, good for stocking up on picnic items.

Ludlow Massacre Monument

Ten miles north of town (one mile west of I-25 exit 27) a monument commemorates the 1914 **Ludlow Massacre**, a tragic episode in American labor history. Having called a strike to gain more humane working conditions and union recognition, miners and their families were evicted from the overpriced Colorado Fuel & Iron Company housing and forced to live in a huge tented city. After frictions and clashes between the mine guards and miners (mostly poor Italian, Irish, and Greek immigrants) the National Guard was called in. They sided with the mine owners and, as tension escalated, the National Guard torched the 1200-strong tent-city, in which several asphyxiated women and children were later found. Mine leaders mysteriously died in captivity, but National Guard leaders, though deemed responsible for the murders, were never punished. Sadly too, the miners returned to work, despite no concessions having been granted. Eventually, federal legislation would take into account their demands – but too late for most of those involved to benefit.

Along the Highway of Legends

The first opportunity to see some of the **Great Dikes**, a landform scattered throughout the Spanish Peaks area, comes a short way south of La Veta along the Highway of Legends. These narrow rock walls, up to 100 feet high and several miles long, were formed by molten lava being forced into volcanic cracks, cooling there as hard rock. **Cuchara**, eleven miles on, is a pleasant little place and until recently the site of a ski resort, whose operations may be resuscitated in coming years. For now it remains a good base for hiking or snowshoeing.

Though you leave the National Forest a short way beyond Cuchara Pass, Hwy-12 continues to wind its way through rolling green hills, passing several smaller communities with low-key recreation facilities. These include **Monument Lake Park**, 36 miles west of Trinidad, a small park around a lake popular for trout-fishing, horseback riding, hiking, and some mountain biking. There are several USFS campgrounds here, along with the municipally owned *Mountain Lake Resort* (☎719/868-2226 or 1-800/845-8006; ❹; closed in winter), which provides Southwestern-style rooms and cabins along with campsites ($10–18) with RV hookups.

Only eight miles from Trinidad on Hwy-12, the **Cokedale National Historic District** preserves a former coke-producing town (coke is a form of coal fuel) that once worked to feed Pueblo's steel mills. Now it's a ghost town, complete with numerous abandoned homes, huge ovens, and giant black slag-heaps. Leaflets at the parking lot provide more information about the site, which was one of few places locally where workers paid a fair rent for homes and were not forced to shop at factory-owned stores – unlike workers at Colorado Fuel & Iron (see box, p.321). A good way to link a visit to Cokedale with a hike is to follow a five-mile hiking trail up here from **Trinidad Reservoir and State Park** ($5 day pass; ☎719/846-6951), on the edge of Trinidad. Highway 12 also passes by the park, which is popular locally for watersports and fishing. You can camp at the *Carpois Ridge Campground* (☎303/470-1144 or 1-800/678-2267; tents $12, RVs $16) west of the dam.

Walsenberg and La Veta

The northern gateway to the Spanish Peaks, nondescript **WALSENBERG** has little going for it besides its location at the convergence of major roads linking the Front Range with Colorado's southwest. Unless you need to stop at the **Huerfano County Chamber of Commerce**, 400 Main St (☎719/738-1065), which is the best source of information for the region, there's really little reason to linger.

Around sixteen miles southwest of Walsenberg on Hwy-160 is neat little **LA VETA**, kept lively by an enthusiastic artist community. Huddled around a short main street, everything in town, including its handful of accommodation options and restaurants, are within easy walking distance, making it a handy stopover. The town is also a good place to check out local art, on display at The Gallery, in the center of town on W Ryus Ave. The primary sight here is the **Fort Francisco Museum** on Main St (May–Sept daily 9am–5pm; $2; ☎719/742-3676), which was built in 1862 to protect settlers from Comanche attacks. A number of its buildings now serve as an open-air museum, and the local history covered includes material on the Ludlow Massacre (see box, p.321) and the carved and painted *santos* of the Penitente brotherhood – an important force in the church both locally and in the San Luis Valley.

Practicalities

The Fort Francisco Museum can provide **visitor information**, although a better source for those wanting to explore is the **San Isabel National Forest Ranger Station**, 103 E Field St (☎719/742-3681). If staying on, campsites ($15) are available from *Bearadise Cabins & RV Park*, 404 S Oak St (☎719/742-6221 or 1-877/460-6221; ❸), which also has good-value cabins. The Victorian *La Veta Inn*, centrally located at 103 W Ryus (☎719/742-3700 or 1-888/806-4875, ⓦwww.lavetainn.com; ❺), is the town's only hotel, and rooms come with private bath. *Hunter House Bed and Breakfast*, 115 W Grand Ave (☎719/742-5577; ❹), offers rooms with shared bath in a small home.

For a **meal**, the *Mainstreet Diner*, at the south end of the eponymous street, has cheap and filling breakfasts. For a selection of baked goods, try the *Ryus Avenue Bakery*, 129 W Ryus Ave, where sandwiches and light lunches are also served (until 1.30pm). The *La Veta Inn* (see above) is a good choice for a standard range of American dishes, while the nearby *Covered Wagon Steakhouse,* 205 S Main St, serves more basic bar food and steaks.

The San Luis Valley

The largest alpine valley in the world, the uniformly flat **SAN LUIS VALLEY** contrasts dramatically with the rest of the Colorado Rockies. Flanked by the impressively jagged and often snowcapped Sangre de Cristo range to the east and the bulky San Juans to the west, this semi-arid grass and sagebrush plain is dotted with isolated farms and the occasional small town. Both the valley's geography and culture make it more reminiscent of New Mexico's southwest than Colorado's wealthy mountain resorts, and though you're likely to be just passing through, the valley's secluded backcountry, Hispanic culture, and cheap accommodation make it worth a look.

When Europeans first arrived, the valley was home to the Ute, who had taken full advantage of the valley's plentiful bison. They zealously protected this area, thwarting settlement attempts until the 1850s when Mexican colonists from nearby Taos (New Mexico) successfully established the town of **San Luis**. The US took possession of the area at the end of the Mexican–American War in 1859, but even today Spanish is still the first language of over half the valley's population.

On the valley's eastern side, the spectacular **Great Sand Dunes National Monument**, nestled beside the magnificent peaks of the **Sangre de Cristo Mountains**, definitely warrants a detour. There's not much in **Alamosa**, the geographical and social center of the valley, though the nearby wetland bird sanctuaries are a favorite nesting ground for bald eagles and both sandhill and whooping cranes. To the southwest, along the New Mexico border, the antique **Cumbres and Toltec Railroad** passes through nearly pristine land at the southern end of the Rio Grande National Forest. Both here and north on the headwaters of the Rio Grande, around **Monte Vista** and **Del Norte**, large trout populations attract fishermen in the summer. Also on the San Luis Valley's western side, tiny **La Garita** is best known for its superb rock-climbing and good hiking. Here and elsewhere in the **Rio Grande National Forest**, which all but encircles the valley, the numerous backcountry trails are used more by bighorn sheep than people.

The southeastern valley

Traveling in from the east, wide Hwy-160 sweeps from Walsenberg past the Spanish Peaks and over the wooded La Veta Pass into the San Luis Valley. The first settlement you come to here is a tiny town named after the adobe buildings of **Fort Garland** (April–Oct daily 9am–5pm, Nov–March Thurs–Mon 8am–4pm; $3; ☎719/379-3512), beside the road to San Luis. Built in 1858, the fort was used mainly to flex military muscle and police the new US territory (see box below). Now a museum, the most interesting building here – simply adorned with period furnishings – is a reconstruction of the residence of Kit Carson, the West's most notorious Indian fighter. Carson came here in 1866, his final posting before death, and was able to use his close friendship with the Ute chief Ouray to help secure a relative peace in the region. Another notable exhibit sheds light on little-recognized black army regiments from this time, dubbed "buffalo soldiers" by local Indian enemies in recognition of their considerable bravery and fighting skill.

A few miles beyond the town of Fort Garland is the dull little farming town of **Blanca**, the closest stop on Greyhound and TNM&O bus lines to the Great Sand Dunes National Monument. You can camp in town, where shaded sites at the *Mt Blanca RV Park* (☎719-379-3201) go for $12; RVs pay $20.

San Luis

The tourist trail in the San Luis Valley usually continues west from Fort Garland and Blanca to the Great Sand Dunes National Monument, meaning that **SAN LUIS**, sixteen miles south of the fort on Hwy-159, is rarely visited. But if your destination is the Toltec Railroad, this way is slightly more direct; and in any case it's worth dropping into the small town if you are interested in sampling some authentic Colorado-style Hispanic culture – and, of course, the associated good food.

San Luis was founded in 1851, making it the earliest major white settlement in Colorado. The **San Luis Museum**, 401 Church Place (May–Sept daily 10am–4pm, Oct–April Mon–Fri 9am–4pm; $2; ☎719/672-3611), does a good

---

The Bloody Espinozas

For the 25 years that Fort Garland served as a military base, almost its entire time was spent policing southwestern Colorado. The most high-profile case to have attracted the fort's attention involved two Hispanic brothers, known locally as "**The Bloody Espinozas**," who in response to a vision of the Virgin Mary decided it was God's desire that all Anglos be driven from the region. The two bandits headed north from the San Luis Valley, ambushing and murdering travelers on roads near Buena Vista apparently at random. When local soldiers were sent to catch them, they did little but return with the corpses of dead men the Espinozas had ambushed, though they did give chase to an innocent man for fifteen miles until they realized their error. On suspicion that a local rancher was harboring the brothers, a local posse hastily headed over and extracted a young man, who – protesting his innocence (rightfully) – was duly lynched. Local soldiers finally caught up with the Espinozas and killed one in a shootout. The other escaped to live in secret with an uncle in the Sangre de Cristos – until, that is, the Fort Garland military scout Tom Tobin was dispatched to capture them. Tobin did so, and returned to the fort with a sack, which when emptied out at his commander's feet produced two bloody, severed Espinoza heads.

job of introducing the valley's history and includes an impressively detailed and brightly colored collection of small religious wood-carvings known as *santos*. Also inside is a recently reconstructed Penitente chapel of the type that formerly served the local lay brotherhood, once an important part of the local Catholic church, and whose practices included self-flagellation. The church still has strong local ties; in 1995 the late Pope John Paul II visited the **stations of the cross** shrine above town. Beginning near the junction of CO-159 and CO-142, a short trail leads up to an impressive onion-domed church past fourteen life-sized statues by local sculptor Humberto Maestas, depicting the crucifixion of Christ. The view from the top of the mesa is an inspiring one; indeed, the crimson sunsets viewable from here are said to have given the Sangre de Cristo – "Blood of Christ" – Mountains their name.

The plush new *San Luis Inn Motel*, 138 Main St (☎719/672-3399 or 1-877/672-3331; ❸), offers a good standard of motel **accommodation** and has an indoor hot tub. More authentic Southwestern lodging can be had at the *El Convento B&B,* a former convent at 512 Church Place (☎719/672-4223; ❹), where rooms contain handcrafted furniture and fireplaces. A little gallery shares the same building and is a good place to view and buy contemporary San Luis Valley **crafts**, particularly pictorial quilting. The excellent *Emma's Hacienda,* 355 Main St, is a long-running family **restaurant** that serves superb Southwestern fare, including delicious red and green enchiladas ($7).

Great Sand Dunes National Monument

Fifty square miles of shifting sand, the **Great Sand Dunes National Monument** is located in a surprising and picturesque location forty miles north of Fort Garland, huddled against the contrasting Sangre de Cristo Range. Over millions of years, fine glacial sands from the San Juan Mountains have been blown east and deposited at the base of the Sangre de Cristos. Looking for a way through the mountains, prevailing southwest winds have been channeled toward the lower part of the range – near the Music, Medano, and Mosca passes – where they've buffeted against the peaks, dropping their load at the base and forming the dunes.

△ Stations of the Cross, San Luis

Though the tallest sand dunes in the country (some rising to around 700ft), their beige color makes it hard to gauge the scale. One reason why they can grow so high is the relative stability afforded by their unusually high moisture content. Although footprints and other surface marks are quickly blown away, the dampness of the sand only a foot below the surface means that the general shapes remain unchanged for centuries. The dunes also harbor a number of small creatures, including two species of beetle, the giant sand-treader camel cricket, and the small kangaroo rat, whose water-efficient kidneys eliminate its need to drink. Most visitors go little further than the "beach" beside Medano Creek, but the climb up the dunes themselves, though incredibly tiring, is not to be missed, especially for the fun **slide down** on dune boards (available for rent) or torn pieces of cardboard. A walk along the sandy trails, squeezed between the dunes and the mountains, and a night spent out at one of the underused backcountry **campsites** is also worthwhile. But for the best views of the whole monument, head south to **Zapata Falls**.

Exploring the monument

At the monument entrance (daily: May–Sept 9am–5pm, Oct–April 9am– 4.30pm; $4 per vehicle; ℡719/378-2312, ⓦwww.nps.gov/grsa), you'll receive a useful **map**; three miles on, the **visitors' center** can inform you about organized nature walks and various events put on at the *Pinyon Flats* campground. Downhill behind the visitors' center is the **Mosca picnic area**, the main gateway to exploring the monument and conveniently located near some of its largest dunes. You can walk to these via the southern flank of the dunes, from where you can choose any line of ascent up – though first, depending on the season, you may need to ford **Medano Creek**.

Along the eastern boundary of the monument, outside the actual body of dunes, trails head north toward **Mosca Pass**. The shortest is the **Montville nature trail**, east of the visitors' center, that runs half a mile beside Mosca Creek providing fine views of the dunes along the way. To the east of the visitors' center the **Mosca Pass trail** betters these views, higher up along this former toll road once used by trappers and prospectors traveling across the mountains into the valley. The trail climbs through a range of vegetation on a seven-mile round-trip to the top of the pass: pinyon-juniper forest, aspen groves, and spruce-fir forest lead eventually on to lush meadows in the Sangre de Cristo Mountains.

Further north, the single road that passes through the park terminates at the *Pinyon Flats Campground*. Just before this, a turnoff onto a 4WD track known as the **Medano Pass primitive road** leads up to the eponymous pass east through the Sangre de Cristos. You can drive this road for two miles in an ordinary car, but beyond the **Point Of No Return** parking lot you'll need a 4WD vehicle or mountain bike, both of which will need to run on low tire pressure

Park safety

Some **careful preparation** is advised for the harsh dune environment. Temperatures up to 140°F have been recorded in summer, though summer nights can get cold – and winters even see snow. The glare from the bright sands makes sunscreen and sunglasses vital. Long sleeves and long pants also help to protect against the huge numbers of mosquitoes around the creek in summer. To avoid the worst of these conditions and the afternoon winds, it's wise to explore early in the day.

for the numerous sandy sections (free air hoses for reinflating are available at the *Pinyon Flats Campground*). The Medano Pass road heads north alongside Medano Creek, then turns east into the mountains to the pass eleven miles away. After around two and a half miles you will pass ghost trees – ponderosa pines killed by encroaching sands at Castle Creek. About a mile and a half further, the pines have been peeled by Utes, who used their barks for food and medicine.

The trailhead for the **Little Medano Pass trail** is also at the Point Of No Return. This sandy trail roughly parallels the primitive road, rising and dipping through thorny shrubs, cacti, and wild grasses. Eventually, five and a half miles further on, beyond the primitive *Little Medano Campground*, it becomes the **Sand Creek Trail**. It's a further six miles to the *Sand Creek Campground*, the most distant part of the accessible dunescape. Deer, elk, black bears, and mountain lions are regularly spotted from this remote trail, and the primitive *Cold Creek Campground*, a mile from the end, is a particularly beautiful spot, sandwiched between the dunes and a rugged mountain valley.

Practicalities

The most unforgettable way to stay here – and one that will leave sand in your gear for weeks – is to pitch on the dune mass itself. Virtually no one bothers to because of the slog up the dunes, but if you're up for it the visitors' center has the necessary and free **backcountry permits**. A backcountry permit is also needed to use the seven lightly used primitive backcountry sites ($14) in the park. Convenience dictates that most campers stay at the large *Pinyon Flats Campground*, the only site in the park accessible by car and usually crowded with RVs. It's run on a first-come, first-served basis, and is often full in July and August.

Just before the monument entrance, the *Great Sand Dunes Oasis Store* (☎719/378-2222) offers showers, laundry, and arid tent sites ($10) as well as a small number of basic cabins (❸). They also conduct two-hour-long **4WD tours** (June–Aug daily 10am & 2pm; May, Sept & Oct daily 11am; $14) along part of the Medano Pass road. Behind the store, the *Great Sand Dunes Lodge* (☎719/378-2900, ⓦwww.gsdlodge.com; ❺) has a restaurant, indoor pool, and pleasant rooms with dune views.

Zapata Falls

Some of the best views over the dunes are had from outside the park's boundaries, around six miles south along Hwy-150 at **Zapata Falls**. Beside a roadside signpost, a gravel road climbs four miles to the picnic and parking area and trailhead, from where there are excellent views of the dunes, their smooth curves elegantly contrasting with the ridge of jagged peaks behind. The falls are only a half-mile round-trip from here, though the final sections – along the rocky, slippery riverbank and stepping-stones leading to the vigorous torrent – are a bit tricky. Below the parking area several interconnecting trails make for pleasant hiking with occasional grand views of the San Luis Valley and the Sangre de Cristo Mountains. The trails also provide some relatively flat, mellow single-track mountain biking.

The northeastern valley

Heading **northeast** from the dunes, the valley's long, straight, and flat roads cross little more than ranchland. It feels much like driving Colorado's eastern plains and there's very little to stop for save a couple of eccentric attractions and a large collection of spiritual centers in tiny **Crestone**.

As out of place in the valley as the dunes themselves, the **San Luis Valley Alligator Farm**, nineteen miles east of the monument on Hwy-17 (daily: May–Sept 7am–7pm, Oct–April 9am–5pm; $10; ☎719/378-2612, ⓦwww .gatorfarm.com), originally began as a fish farm. The introduction of alligators only came about as an ingenious way of processing waste. The creatures are mostly intriguing as they seem so out of place – both the fish and reptiles survive the valley winters thanks to hot springs at the farm. The location of the **UFO Watchtower**, nine miles north of the alligator farm (May–Sept daily 11am–10pm; free; ☎719/378-2271, ⓦwww.ufowatchtower.com), is best explained by the owners, who built it on a whim in response to the many alleged sightings that have taken place in the valley. They offer ten campsites ($10) and a gift shop for alien souvenirs.

Crestone and around

A turnoff at the hamlet of Moffet, another ten miles along Hwy-17, leads after thirteen miles to the spiritual village of **CRESTONE**. Formerly a mining community, much of tiny Crestone has been subdivided, with lots donated to various faiths in 1978 by a rancher with a vision of international spiritual harmony. In its New Age form Crestone now attracts thousands from around the world to its various spiritual festivals, and a small community of artists and writers has settled here.

The village itself is no more than a collection of houses around a general store, and most of the spiritual lots are a little further out of the center – and for the most part tucked away and largely obscured by woodlands. But if you hunt around, you'll find Buddhist (containing one of the largest *stupas* in the western hemisphere), Carmelite, and Zen centers, together with an Ashram and a few environmental projects.

A rudimentary **information board** on the county road that leads to the town can help with orientation and gives an idea of courses on offer. If you are more interested in hiking here, it's best to stop by the Rio Grande National Forest HQ (☎719/852-5941) near Monte Vista (see p.330). One trip worth asking about is the **South Crestone Creek Trail**, which climbs up to South Crestone Lake on a ten-mile round-trip into bighorn sheep country. More trails leave from out of the *North Crestone Creek Campground* ($9), reached on the Alder Terrace road out of town. On the same road, the *Sangre de Cristo Inn* (☎719/265-4975 or 1-800/929-4975, ⓦwww.sangredecristoinn.com; ❹) has rooms with kitchens and a laundry in the same building. South of town about one and a half miles from the information board, the modern *Rainbow B&B* (☎719/265-4110 or 1-800/530-1992, ⓦrainbowbb.com; ❹) provides rooms with shared bath.

Back on the main north–south road, Hwy-17, Salida is 39 miles north of Moffat and there's not much en route save the **Joyful Journey Hot Springs Spa** (Thurs–Tues 10am–10pm; $12; ☎719/256-4328 or 1-800/673-0656, ⓦwww.joyfuljourneyhotsprings.com), a mile south of the junction with Hwy-285. It's an elegant place to soak, offering a number of different massage styles as well.

Alamosa and around

As the one-time northern terminus of the Denver and Rio Grande railway, many of the utilitarian buildings in **ALAMOSA** were thrown up virtually overnight, having been brought here as portable buildings on flatbed rail cars. Despite the decline of the railroad industry, the town has remained an important trading and supply center and nucleus for the whole San Luis Valley. There's no denying it's a functional town, but the low rents here have also attracted a fair number of artists and craftsmen, and the small Adams State College is a lively influence. For visitors, the town is usually just a stop off on the way across the San Luis Valley or down to the Cumbres and Toltec Railroad that starts from Antonito, on Colorado's border with New Mexico border.

Much of Alamosa centers around the main road, CO-160 (Main St), which crosses the Rio Grande on its way through town. For a brief (30min) tour, start just east of the river, on the opposite bank to the shady cottonwoods of **Cole Park**, following the riverside trail north. Less than a mile along you pass the public **Cattails Golf Course** (☎719/589-9515), where golfers take advantage of the valley's average of 350 days of sun. Cross back over the river at State Avenue, taking it as far as 3rd Street, which heads back to Cole Park, to the visitor information center and the **San Luis Valley History Center** (June–Sept 10am–4pm; ☎719/587-0667). This houses a small, but reasonably diverting, collection of old local photographs and artifacts charting the valley's multicultural history.

If you're in town in the spring or fall (March–May/Sept–Nov), head three miles east out of town on Rt-160 to the **Alamosa National Wildlife Refuge**, 9383 El Rancho Lane (refuge: daily sunrise–sunset; office: Mon–Fri 7.30am–4pm; ☎719/589-4021). The massive wetland area around a meandering stretch of the Rio Grande is popular with migrating and nesting waterfowl. Around 20,000 sandhill and whooping cranes (an endangered species with 8ft wingspan) stop here along their migratory routes, and bald eagles nest here too in the spring.

Practicalities

The TNM&O **bus** line serves Alamosa on its Denver to Albuquerque route, stopping on the west side of town outside SLV Van Lines, 8480 Stockton St (☎719/589-4948). Alamosa's **visitors' center** (Mon–Fri 8am–5pm, Sat 9am–4pm, Sun 10am–3pm; ☎719/589-3681 or 1-800/258-7597, ⓦwww .alamosachamber.com) is beside Cole Park and the Rio Grande, and is the best source of info for the entire San Luis Valley. Alamosa Sporting Goods, 1114 Main St (☎719/589-3006), can advise on hunting and fishing regulations for National Forest areas fringing the valley.

The cheapest local **accommodation** is three miles east of town at the *Alamosa KOA* campground, just north of Hwy-160 on Juniper Lane (☎719/589-9757 or 1-800/562-9157). Tent sites go for $22–25, fully hooked-up RV plots for $23–30. Otherwise there are plenty of **motels** to choose from, including the dependable *Super 8*, on the western edge of downtown at 2505 Main St (☎719/589-6447; ❸), and where extras include an indoor pool and hot tub and a reasonable continental breakfast. Barely more expensive but with far more character is the ⚓ *Cottonwood Inn*, in a leafy Victorian neighborhood at 123 San Juan Ave (☎719/589-3882 or 1-800/955-2623, ⓦwww .cottonwoodinn.com; ❹); many of the antique-furnished rooms here have clawfoot tubs. The inn – also a gallery showcasing local art – offers packages that include the Cumbres and Toltec Scenic Railroad (see p.331), tours of local hot springs, horseback riding, and golf.

Alamosa is the sort of town where you'd expect to find heavy breakfasts, good steaks, and zesty Mexican **food** – and it doesn't disappoint. A good place to start the day, even if it's just with a coffee and large cinnamon roll, is *Bauer's Campus Pancake House,* 435 Poncha Ave (☎719/589-4202; closed Tues), a studenty place that serves breakfast until closing time at 2pm. For Mexican food head a block south of Main to the cheery ✕ *Mrs Rivera's,* 1019 6th St (☎719/589-0277), where the great chile rellenos cost only $6. If it's a lean steak you're after, the only place to consider is ✕ *True Grits Steakhouse,* located a couple blocks east of the Rio Grande at 100 Santa Fe Ave (☎719/589-9954). Equal parts noisy, no-nonsense steakhouse and shrine to John Wayne, the massive steak lunches and dinners are very reasonably priced, starting at $7. For a **drink** try the *St Ives Pub and Eatery,* 719 Main St (☎719/589-0711; closed Sun), where there's a good selection of microbrews and all the usual bar food.

South to Antonito and the Cumbres and Toltec Scenic Railroad

The road south is a dusty affair, as is the town of Antonito, the terminus of the Cumbres and Toltec Scenic Railroad, 28 miles south of Alamosa. On the way, though, there are a few diversions worth a look. Three miles south of La Jara is the USFS Conejos Peak Ranger District Office (☎719/274-8971), a good place to pick up information on fishing and hiking possibilities to the west. A couple of miles further on is the turnoff for the almost entirely Mormon town of **MANASSA**. Here, in the log cabin birthplace of the Manassa Mauler, is the **Jack Dempsey Museum**, 401 Main St (May–Sept Mon–Sat 9am–5pm; ☎719/843-5207). The museum uses clippings and artifacts to celebrate the life of the heavyweight boxing great who went on to win the world title in 1919, after years of prizefighting in mining camp saloons like those in Cripple Creek.

Unappealing and run-down, **ANTONITO** is notable only as the terminus of the **Cumbres and Toltec Scenic Railroad** (see box, opposite), though there's good backcountry fishing and hiking west along the Conejos River Valley. TNM&O buses between Denver and Albuquerque stop at the Texaco in town once a day, and Twin Hearts Express (☎505/751-1201) runs a shuttle service from the *Holiday Inn* in Alamosa, at 333 Santa Fe Ave, to the railroad. Round-trips cost $20. The **visitors' center** (☎719/376-2049) is opposite the railroad depot.

Some of the most pleasant **accommodation** is west of town along the Conejos, where numerous campsites and cabins are located (note that most are shut between October and May). An easy walk from the train depot, the *Narrow Gauge Railroad Inn* (☎719/376-5441 or 1-800/323-9469; ❸) is a reasonable motel with some sites for tents and RVs ($10). The *Dutch Mill Café* does standard diner fare and good Mexican dishes. Heading west five miles on CO-17 (in the direction of Chama), *Cottonwood Meadows* (☎719/376-5660; ❸) is well set up for **fishing**, renting comfortable two-person cabins and running a tack shop.

The western valley

Heading northwest along the Rio Grande, through a rich agricultural area that has **Monte Vista** at its heart, the mountains get closer and good **hiking** and **biking** opportunities abound. This is also the start of great trout **fishing** in the headwaters of the Rio Grande, upstream of **Del Norte**, a former supply center and now a gateway to the superb **climbing** further north at **La Garita**.

Monte Vista

Pretty much the only reason you'll want to pop into the nondescript farming town of **MONTE VISTA**, seventeen miles west of Alamosa on Hwy-160, is

The Cumbres and Toltec Scenic Railroad

The **Cumbres and Toltec Scenic Railroad** (☎719/376-5483 or 1-888/286-2737, ⓦwww.cumbrestoltec.com) was originally conceived as a link for a grand railroad to El Paso and Mexico City before it became part of a narrow-gauge railroad serving mining camps by connecting with Farmington, Durango, and Silverton. A must for railroad buffs, the 64-mile run in open cars is an atmospheric tour through pine and aspen groves cut along the mountainous border between Colorado and New Mexico, the line running as far as Chama, NM. On its unhurried, meandering route, the steam trains ascend the spectacular **Cumbres Pass** and run on high wooden trestles above deep pristine gorges like the one at **Toltec**. In early trials, one trestle above Cascade Creek was the site of a derailment – the last for over a century up to the present.

Since both trains depart daily (May–Oct) from Antonito and Chama, the two trains meet during a stop for lunch at the mountain ghost town of **Osier**. By riding one or both trains and using company buses, four different round-trips are possible. From Antonito: to Osier (departs 10am, returns 4.45pm; $59); to Cumbres, returning by bus (departs 10am, returns 4pm; $72); to Chama, returning by bus (departs 10am, returns 6pm; $72); and to Chama by bus, return by train (departs 9.15am, returns 4.45pm; $72). A similar array of options is also possible from Chama, and in all cases under-11s pay half-price. Whichever trip you make, take plenty of clothing, since the mountain passes and open cars can get cold.

to stop by a couple of **information offices** useful for planning time in the mountains. Material on hunting or viewing wildlife can be had at the Colorado Division of Wildlife office, south of Hwy-160 at 722 S CO-1 (Mon–Fri 8am–5pm; ☎719/587-6900), while west out of town the Rio Grande National Forest HQ, 1803 W Hwy-160 (daily 8am–4.30pm; ☎719/852-5941), has information and maps on the National Forest on both sides of the valley. If looking for a **place to stay**, the most novel option is the 1950s-style ☀ *Best Western Movie Manor*, two miles west of town at 2830 W Rt-160 (☎719/852-5921 or 1-866/363-0915, ⓦwww.bestwestern.com; ⑤). The otherwise bland motel units here all look out onto the big screen of the next door *Star Drive-In Movie Theatre*, and soundtracks for the films – screened April to September – are piped into each room.

Mountain bikers and **hikers** visiting Monte Vista should head for the fifteen-mile loop on single-track trails through dense stands of aspen around **Cat Creek**, thirteen miles south of Monte Vista (along CO-15, then right onto Forest Road 250 for seven miles, and follow signs for Deer Creek on Forest Road 271). The first leg of the trail, which begins at a sign for the Cat Creek Horse Trail, climbs the rutted 4WD Deer Creek Trail (aka Forest Road 271); turn onto the single-track climb up Forest Road 703 for the final ascent to fantastic views of the San Luis Valley from Blowout Pass Overlook. The trail takes around two hours to bike and around five to hike, though longer after rainstorms, when it quickly gets muddy. Kristi Mountain Sports, Villa Mall, Alamosa (☎719/589-9759), rents out front-suspension mountain bikes for $20/day.

La Garita

LA GARITA, twenty miles north of Monte Vista off US-285, has earned a superb reputation in the world of rock-climbing. In nearby **Penitente Canyon**, four hundred mostly bolted climbs on both gigantic boulders and sheer walls span the full range of skill levels. Before heading to the canyon, a former nineteenth-century chapel, built by an offshoot of the Penitente lay brotherhood (see p.325), might be of interest. It now houses the **San Juan Art Center**, a co-operative venture displaying and selling Hispanic folk art (May–Sept Mon–Fri 10am–5pm, Sat 1–5pm).

To find the canyon, go one mile west from the La Garita store (which has info on backcountry camping at free local BLM **campgrounds**), veer left after the pavement ends, and then turn right off the main road which heads south, taking the middle of three roads. Looking like a huge bullet-hole in the volcanic dyke, **La Ventana**, a vast natural arch, has commanding views over the San Luis Valley. It's eight miles further south of Penitente Canyon (three miles on 38A, three miles on 32A, right at the second fork once inside the National Forest, and then two miles to the parking area) and is a short but steep scramble up from the dirt road. Around one hundred **bighorn sheep** live here, so have your camera ready.

Del Norte

A supply center for the Rio Grande headwater area, **DEL NORTE**, fourteen miles west of Monte Vista, can also supply information on local hiking and climbing, as well as gear at Casa de Madera, 680 Grande Ave (℡719/657-2336). Check with the Del Norte Ranger District Office, 13308 W Hwy-160 (℡719/657-3321), for the special catch and tackle restrictions applying to the local so-called "Gold Medal" fishing areas. The **Rio Grande County Museum**, 580 Oak St (June–Aug Tues–Sat 10am–5pm, Sept–May Tues–Sat noon–5pm; $1; ℡719/657-2847), has some ancient petroglyphs among its general information on rock-art sites. Relics relating to the exploration of this area by mountain men are also on display, particularly from the failed expedition in quest of a winter route over the Continental Divide, in which a third of the 33-man expedition died.

A couple of **motels** at the eastern end of US-160 into town have straightforward rooms: *The El Rancho*, 1160 Grande Ave (℡719/657-3332; ❷), and the slightly smarter *Del Norte Motel and Café*, no. 1050 (℡719/657-3581 or 1-800/372-2332; ❸), where breakfast and lunch is also served. *Boogie's Restaurant*, at no. 410 (℡719/657-2905), opens at 6am for big cooked breakfasts and serves down-home cooking later in the day. If you've got a sweet tooth, give the coconut cream pie a try.

Travel details

Buses

(All buses are Greyhound/TNM&O.)

Alamosa to: Denver (1 daily; 4hr 55min); Durango (1 daily; 14hr); Pueblo (1 daily; 1hr 15min); Trinidad (1 daily; 6hr 40min).

Pueblo to: Alamosa (1 daily; 1hr 15min); Denver (8 daily; 2hr 45min); Durango (1 daily; 16hr 25min); Trinidad (2 daily; 1hr 25min).

Rocky Ford (La Junta) from: Pueblo (3 daily; 1hr 5min).

Trinidad to: Alamosa (1 daily; 6hr 40min); Denver (1 daily; 4hr 55min); Durango (1 daily; 19hr 25min); Pueblo (2 daily; 1hr 25min).

Southwest Colorado

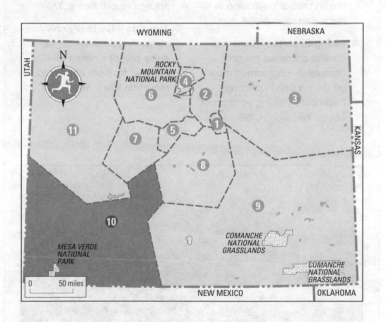

CHAPTER 10

Highlights

* **Wheeler Geologic Area** – It's a long haul out to see this bizarre geological oddity, but that makes the trip all the more rewarding as a result. See p.339

* **Mesa Verde National Park** – Explore the cliffside dwellings of the Ancestral Puebloans, the first major civilization in the region. See p.354

* **Skiing Silverton** – Just one chairlift accesses the only completely ungroomed resort on the continent, offering backcountry skiing at its most accessible. See p.366

* **Ouray** – Coax a jeep along the rough trails that link ghost towns in a region that proclaims itself the "Switzerland of America". See p.369

* **Orvis Hot Springs** – Bathe naked under a starry sky and in the shadow of the mountains at this small, friendly hot springs resort. See p.373

* **Telluride** – Ski terrifyingly steep moguls in winter, or enjoy one of a series of summer festivals in this hip mountain town. See p.374

△ Jeep journey through Southwest Colorado

10

Southwest Colorado

art cracked desert, part craggy mountain, schizophrenic **Southwest Colorado** offers not only variety, but also a blend of peacefulness, scenic beauty, outdoor opportunity, and historical heritage, making the area deeply rewarding to all travelers. The region's centerpiece, the **San Juan Mountains**, could not be any more glorious or alluring. Beginning as rolling hills on all sides before culminating in a crescendo of soaring peaks along the Continental Divide, this jumbled mass of deep-green forest slopes and jagged peaks is the largest, wildest, and least populated range in the state. Colorado doesn't get any more rough or inaccessible: while all the state's other ranges are fairly narrow and so less remote, in the broad San Juans you really can get away from it all. For backcountry purists, this – in particular the large **Weminuche Wilderness** Area – is the place to be.

The less adventurous can explore the mountains along a series of spectacular passes on the two highways that complete a circuit around the range. But this is by no means a quick journey: with homey Victorian towns en route and several tempting side trips along the way – not least to **Mesa Verde National Park** – you'll need at least a week. But to begin to do the region justice, you'll need to spend several more pleasurable days soaking up peaceful alpine landscapes and discovering old ghost towns on foot, using 4WD vehicles, mountain bikes, or even a steam train. Home to several unsung ski areas and world-class ice-climbing, the area is also well worth a trip in winter.

Rising gently from the San Juan Valley, the **Eastern San Juans** are home to sleepy little towns, the **Wolf Creek** ski area, and the tiny spa town of **Pagosa Springs**. These all form worthwhile distractions for travelers on the final leg of an eight-hour drive from Denver to the laid-back regional hub of **Durango**. Home to countless teleworkers and healthy young bohemians – lured into the area by the phenomenal year-round outdoor recreation opportunities – Durango is understandably well equipped for visitors. But its location is also handy, with day trips conveniently done both north of town, where alpine landscapes begin to take shape, and west, where an arid and dusty landscape of rolling hills and shrub-covered mesas begins to assert itself.

After a spell in the mountains, the transformation from alpine scenery to the broad expanses of semi-arid desert in Colorado's southwestern-most corner seems particular dramatic. Certainly the landscape of the **Four Corners region** – where the borders of Colorado, New Mexico, Arizona, and Utah meet – is an integral part of the Southwestern US. This part of Colorado was once home to an ancient Ancestral Puebloan civilization,

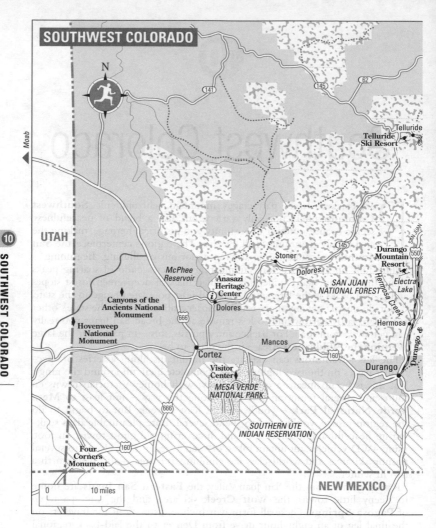

concentrated along what is now the border with New Mexico. It's in these foothills that the highly organized Ancestral Puebloans have left extraordinary thirteenth-century remains – famously including the cliff-dwellings at **Mesa Verde National Park**.

Back in the mountains, the clockwise circuit of the San Juans is completed by heading north from Durango. Here the spectacular **Western San Juans** are bisected by the **San Juan Skyway**. The most spectacular highway in the range, it snakes over a series of stunning high mountain passes to link the atmospheric mining town of **Silverton**, the modestly touristy Victorian resort of **Ouray**, and the turnoff to the picturesque ski-town of **Telluride**.

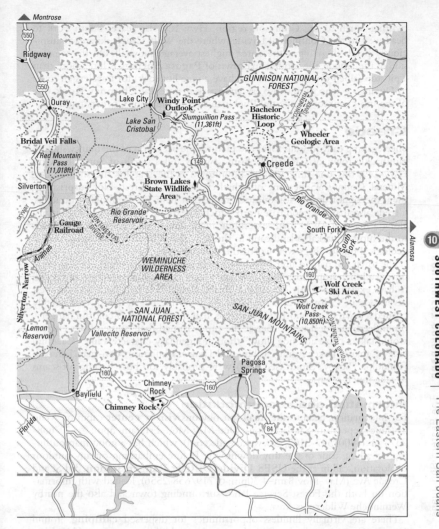

10

SOUTHWEST COLORADO | The Eastern San Juans

337

The Eastern San Juans

In contrast to the western side of the range, where Durango and Telluride typically throb with visitors, the **Eastern San Juan Mountains** form a remote backwater. Here you can drive for hours through incredible mountain landscapes without seeing much on the road save the odd elk or moose. The tiny highway community of **South Fork** is notable only as an eastern gateway for travelers from the San Luis Valley. From here, Hwy-149 cuts north to the sleepy old mining town of **Creede** – the nearest base for forays to the **Wheeler Geologic Area** – and **Lake City**, Colorado's ultimate backwater, before twisting north to the Gunnison region. Hwy-160 also leaves South Fork to head west to the Continental Divide, where the **Wolf Creek** ski area is auspiciously perched, giving it the state's highest average snowfall. On the western side of the Divide, the modest spa town of **Pagosa Springs** is little more than a pit stop (albeit one where you can have a nice hot soak) for travelers en route to Durango – who should also try and work in a stop at **Chimney Rock**, one of the most evocative Ancestral Puebloan sites in the Four Corners region.

Creede

Sheer, gaping canyon walls form the picturesque backdrop of the quirky, slightly ramshackle town of **CREEDE**. Some twenty miles north of South Fork on Hwy-149, this one-time mining boomtown is the seat for the surrounding Mineral County, 95 percent of which is National Forest. Not surprisingly, then, the opportunities for outdoor recreation here are seemingly boundless. Creede also makes a good base from which to explore the area's mining history along a maze of 4WD roads extending in all directions. One such road heads to the most remarkable landscape in the area, the **Wheeler Geologic Area**, a geological oddity that's well worth the difficult trek.

The town was named after Nicolas Creede who, poking around in the ground during a lunch stop above Wagon Wheel Gap in 1889, uncovered ore and is said to have exclaimed "Holy Moses, I've struck it rich!" He had, finding the richest silver lode in Colorado, and the Holy Moses Mine began a rush that quickly created a town of around 10,000 citizens, half miners and half colorful hangers-on. Indeed, the local newspaper at the time claimed that "some of her citizens would take a prize at a hog show," though legendary characters like "Calamity Jane" Canary, "Poker Annie" Tubbs, and Denver's infamous con-man Jefferson Randolph "Soapy" Smith (see p.56) were probably too busy pulling off scams to take much offense.

Information and accommodation

For information, head to the small but obvious **visitor center** cabin on Main St (June–Sept Mon–Sat 8am–5pm; Oct–May Mon–Fri 9am–5pm; ☎719/658-2374 or 1-800/327-2102, ⓦwww.creede.com), which has a good map outlining a walking tour of the tiny downtown. Before embarking on any outdoor exploration, call in at the **USFS Divide District Ranger Station**, 3rd St and Creede Ave (May–Nov 8am–4.30pm; ☎719/658-2556), loaded with information on both the Forest Service lands surrounding town and also the nearby Weminuche Wilderness Area.

There are virtually limitless opportunities for dispersed **camping** around Creede. Campers will also find about a dozen USFS **campgrounds** within twenty miles of town. The most convenient (and most popular, so make reservations) are the *Marshall Park Campground*, seven miles southwest of Creede on Hwy-149, and the *Rio Grande Campground*, another seven miles along the same road (☎719/852-5941, ⓦwww.reserveamerica.com; sites $10). Creede's Victorian main street contains several **B&Bs** and a **hotel**. The cheapest option is the *Snowshoe Lodge* (☎719/658-2315 or 1-866/658-2315; ❸), whose clean motel rooms are on the southeast edge of town. Not much more expensive is the classy *Creede Hotel B&B* (☎719/658-2608; ⓦwww.creedehotel.com; ❹), in the heart of town beside the repertory theatre, and where rates include a good breakfast. Slightly further down the road is *The Old Firehouse No. 1 B&B*, Main St (☎719/658-0212 ⓦwww.theoldfirehouse.com; ❺; May–Oct), with a pleasant communal sitting room decorated with old firefighting memorabilia. Of the twenty ranches and resorts in the area, *Wason Ranch* (☎719/658-2413; ❸), two miles southeast of Creede, has some cabins with kitchenettes as well as some larger riverside cottages that require a minimum two-night stay. *Antlers Lodge*, 26222 Hwy-149 (☎719/658-2423, ⓦwww.antlerslodge.com; ❺), five miles southwest of Creede on the banks of the Rio Grande, is another pleasant option for cabins and motel-style units and is a good place to park your RV ($23).

The Town

Creede's **Main Street**, also known as Creede Avenue, is the obvious focal point of this small town where addresses are considered superfluous. The street takes minutes rather than hours to explore, since the main sights are north of town where mine workings form the backbone of the Bachelor Historic Tour (see below). But in among the low-slung buildings of the main street is Creede's most curious attraction, the **Creede Repertory Theatre** (mid-June to July; matinees from $5, evening shows from $16; ☎719/658-2540 or 1-866/658-2540, ⓦwww.creederep.com), a nationally renowned repertory theater that's been running for over thirty years. The theater's program swings from energetic Broadway musicals to traditional favorites like Shakespeare, and the busiest schedule sees half a dozen different plays performed per week.

North of town, Main Street heads directly to the mouth of the **Willow Creek Canyon**, narrow and pockmarked by multiple old mining operations. A good place to get a feel for the town in its heyday is the **Creede Museum** (June–Aug daily 10am–4pm; $1), housed in the town's former railroad depot behind the city park. Entertaining displays concentrate on biographies of the town's more notorious characters – like Bob Ford, who became a town pariah after ambushing and gunning down the popular outlaw Jesse James – rather than the trainloads of miners who flocked here during the town's boom days. The miners' story is told at the **Creede Underground Mining Museum** (daily: June–Aug 10am–4pm, Sept–May 10am–3pm; $6; ☎719/658-0811), north of town near the start of Willow Creek Canyon. Blasted and dug specifically as a mining museum, the cold underground museum, at a constant 51°F, contains informative displays on drilling, mucking, and blasting, explained from a miner's point of view. Guided tours ($10) are available by reservation.

Bachelor Historic Tour

Further north from the museum along Willow Creek Canyon road is one end of the **Bachelor Historic Tour**, a seventeen-mile loop of dirt roads (4WD not needed) through abandoned mine workings that's become Creede's must-do attraction. The loop has great views of the La Garita Mountains, but the main attraction is the ramshackle wooden structures along the way. If pressed for time, head up Willow Creek Canyon first, since most of the abandoned workings are along here. Otherwise, it's well worth completing the route, which drops you back into the eastern side of town. Before heading out, pick up the excellent illustrated tour booklet ($1) from the visitor center for some useful background to various points along the loop, like a description of **Dead Horse Flats**, where the failing of brakes on teamster wagons regularly sent animals to their death. It also has information about **Bachelor City**, whose 1200 bachelors made the place rough even by Creede standards – strange to imagine, when all that's left now is just a meadow with some scattered rocks and a abandoned cabin.

Wheeler Geologic Area

The result of repeated volcanic ash flows that hardened to be carved by wind and rain into a small 60-acre "town" of spiny spires and dank caverns, the

△ Wheeler Geologic Area

Wheeler Geologic Area is quite a surprise in an area dominated by hanging valleys and smooth high-alpine meadows. Framed by evergreen forests, its dramatic, contorted landscape began life around 40 million years ago, with violent eruptions of lava from volcanoes melting together to form a rise 4000ft thick and over 9000 square miles wide. A million years later another major eruption caused accumulations of ash up to 3000ft deep. Volcanic debris, dust, and pebbles settled into layers on the ground called tuff. Occasional rock fragments (breccia) – sometimes two or three feet in diameter – were also thrown out to nestle in the tuff beds. Under its own weight, the tuff hardened into rock and these breccia lodged in the rock strata were subsequently less susceptible to erosion than the surrounding tuff. Consequently small areas of tuff, protected by pieces of breccia above, survived the wind and water erosion that cleared other material, leaving spindly minarets precariously topped by brecca. Water running from these towers helped not only deepen the gaps between them, but also carved tiny erosion gullies in the form of twisted wrinkles into the rock below.

Whichever means you choose, the **route** to the monument is not an easy one. You can hike, cycle, or four-wheel drive to it, but as hikers have a separate, more direct path, it's around a five-hour round-trip regardless of how you travel. The road, when open (usually late May to Oct), is around fifteen miles long, making for a thirty-mile round trip, though hikers need only cover half that distance to get to the monument. The road and hiking trail begin beside one another eighteen miles south of Creede – take Hwy-149 eleven miles in the direction of South Fork, then follow Pool Table Road (FR-600) seven miles east.

Outdoor activities

Though most drive the Bachelor Historic Tour, it also makes a good three-hour loop on a **mountain bike**, generally done clockwise to get most of the climbing out of the way in the first four miles. The loop begins near the cemetery, marked by a small sign off Hwy-149 on the town's southern perimeter.

Mountain bikes ($18/day) can be **rented** from San Juan Sports, a block west of Main (☏719/658-2359 or 1-888/658-0851). They also rent out backpacking and mountaineering gear, making it a good first stop for **hikers** as well. One of the area's prettiest hikes is up to the high alpine meadow of Phoenix Park, past waterfalls and beaver ponds along the way; the trailhead is at the top of East Willow Canyon, the next valley east of the Bachelor Historic Tour, by the defunct King Solomon Mill.

The Creede area is well known for excellent **fishing**, as it's here that the waters of the Rio Grande start their 1900-mile journey to the Gulf of Mexico. The river snakes past town two miles to the south, but some of the best places to fish are several miles further south on Hwy-149 around the USFS *Marshall Park* and *Rio Grande* campgrounds (see p.338). Another popular fishing spot is the Brown Lakes State Wildlife Area, 25 miles west of Creede along Hwy-149, where large browns and native cut-throat are the main attraction. If you're in the area, it's also worth pausing to see **North Clear Creek Falls**, a little further west along Hwy-149 from the Brown Lakes turnoff and just half a mile from the highway. Here the impressive falls plunge into a deep gorge, and can be viewed from an outlook at the edge. Ramble House, 116 Main St (☏719/658-2482), has a good stock of fishing supplies, sells licenses, and runs lessons and trips, including wade trips from $50 and float trips from $80.

In **winter** the multitude of possibilities for independent exploration of the surrounding area on snowshoes and skis is joined by the chance to go back-country skiing or riding on a **snowcat** trip. Operating nine miles north of Creede, San Juan Snowcat (☏719-658-0430, ⓦwww.sanjuan-snowcat.com) has rates that hover around the $250 mark for a day of exploring the magnificent powder terrain and breathtaking views of the remote eastern San Juans. At 13,250 feet – the highest backcountry snowcat access in North America – you get to explore untracked bowls, chutes, and couloirs, with runs ranging from rolling intermediate glades to extreme faces reaching 55° in pitch.

Eating and drinking

Considering Creede's small size, the selection of **places to eat** isn't too bad. A good place to start the day with a healthy breakfast or a pastry is *Journeys*, 119 N Main (☏719/658-2290), which also does good whole-food lunches. Just southeast of the town center the *Bears' Den*, 905 La Garita Ave (☏719/658-0105), is the town's main diner, patronized by plenty of locals for its good-value homecooked omelettes, burgers, and steaks for breakfast, lunch, and dinner. The *Bears' Den* bar is also a lively place at night, as is the *Tommy Knocker Tavern* on Wall St (☏719/658-0138), a small but popular bar serving Mexican food with regular live music. The pick for fine dining is the *Creede Hotel Dining Room*, back on Main (May–Sept; ☏719/658-2608), a popular pre-theater venue, at which time reservations are advised. Lunches include the usual burgers and sandwiches for $6–10, while the homemade entrees (from $13) served for dinner include tamarind-honey chicken, prime rib, and baked salmon.

Lake City

Fifty miles from both Creede to the southeast and Gunnison to the north, **LAKE CITY** is one of the most remote towns in the Colorado Rockies. Lake San Cristobal, the state's second largest, is only a short way west of town, hemmed in by the huge Slumgullion earthslide (see p.342). Unlike most mining camps, Lake City was never a particularly rowdy place, attracting mostly optimistic pioneers who built a small town full of Greek and Gothic Revival architecture. After the gold rush, the town's population, which peaked at around 5000, steadily dwindled, and by the 1960s it was virtually abandoned. But in the last decade, Lake City has begun to burgeon again, largely with Texans looking for summer homes. It's easy to see why they're attracted, as the peaceful town is a great launch pad from which to explore a network of 4WD tracks and there's also easy access to the **Big Blue** and **Powderhorn Wilderness** areas, both offering secluded backpacking and superb fishing.

A short line of proud Neoclassical buildings have survived intact to form the town's historic core along **Silver Street**. A few of the buildings now house craftsy shops and some restaurants, but the main point of interest is the **Hinsdale County Museum** ($2), south at Silver's junction with 2nd Street. A few exhibits here chart the town's history, but the lion's share of the museum is devoted to the macabre exploits of Alferd Packer (see box opposite).

The most stunning approach into town is from the south over **Slumgullion Pass**. Just north of the pass is the Windy Point outlook, with great views of both Mount Uncompahgre in the distance and the nearby Slumgullion Slide. The mudslide itself came in two distinct thrusts, the first 800 years ago when a huge amount of mud slid five miles down to block the valley, damming the Lake Fork of the Gunnison River and forming Lake San Cristobal. The second, slower and still persisting, slide began around 350 years ago. It's easy to pick out the active portions as they're barren of trees.

Outdoor activities

Many visitors to Lake City are here to go off-road exploring with 4WD jeeps, typically heading along the **Alpine Loop Backcountry Byway**, 65 miles of mostly rough 4WD road that passes old ghost towns and mining centers to link Lake City with both Ouray and Silverton. There are a number of places hiring 4WD vehicles, including the *Gingerbed & Breakfast* (see opposite) who do rentals from around $100 a day.

Hikers will find good trails leading through mixed forest and small alpine meadows to beautiful mountain lakes in virtually any direction. One particularly good trip is the approximately fifteen-mile loop to Thompson, Larson, and Crystal lakes, beginning from the trailhead near the cemetery at the north of town. Despite a couple of steep sections, the trail is generally easy and makes an ideal overnight trip, leaving time for some fishing. Of the many longer and more ambitious hiking options within striking distance of town, the most obvious places to head to are the **Big Blue Wilderness** – which, to the east of town, includes the 14,000ft-plus Uncompahgre, Wetterhorne, and Handies peaks – and the **Powderhorn Wilderness** to the west. Obviously the altitude makes any of the fourteeners harder to bag, but ascending **Handies Peak** is relatively straightforward and the views no less glorious than elsewhere. The trail begins around twenty miles southwest of Lake City off CR-34, a minor road beyond Lake San Cristobal that heads up the north side of Grizzly Gulch. From the top of the peak you can continue down to Sloan Lake to make a loop with CR-34 and avoid retracing your steps. Note that this loop is a full day's work at around ten miles long.

Both wilderness areas are also premium elk habitat and popular for their good trout **fishing**. Just east of town, the fishing in Henson Creek is also good for a short trip, but if you're planning to fish in the area for a while be sure to pick up the guide to local fishing spots ($1), produced by the Chamber of Commerce (see "Practicalities," opposite). Cannibal Outdoors, 355 S Gunnison Ave (☎970/944-2559), can answer fishing questions as well as set you up with gear. For **bike rentals**, contact San Juan Mountain Bikes

Colorado's Cannibal

South of Lake City on Hwy-149, near its junction with CO-30, sits a memorial to five prospectors butchered by the locally infamous **Alferd Packer**. Packer was originally hired as a guide to lead the prospectors from Montrose to the Breckenridge gold strike in February 1874. Against the advice of local Indians, including chief Ouray, who feared the winter weather would spell disaster for the party, they set off, leaving town with only seven days' worth of provisions. Nothing was seen of the party until April, when the relatively healthy Packer turned up alone in Lake City, claiming to have endured near-starvation when his companions left him behind due to an injury. But Packer had little interest in food, being more interested in stiff drinks for which he paid with money from several wallets. Suspicions were naturally aroused and Packer soon changed his story, claiming his companions had developed frostbite and asked him to go ahead without them, taking their personal possessions as some kind of precautionary measure. Nobody believed this story either, and upon further questioning Packer eventually broke down and admitted tearfully that his companions had died one by one, and yes, the remaining survivors had used the bodies when legitimate food supplies ran low. Asked to lead a search party to the remains of the others, he lost his memory on several attempts and the bodies were not found. Packer was jailed anyway in Saguache, in the northern San Luis Valley, from where he escaped before he could be tried. As spring melted the snows around Lake City, local Ute found strips of human flesh, and in June, a **Harper's Weekly** artist stumbled on the skeletons – one had been shot in the back and the others had had their skulls crushed. Ranching under an assumed name in Wyoming, Packer was recaptured nearly a decade later in 1883 and was convicted of murdering and cannibalizing his companions. The conviction was overturned on a technicality; three years later he was re-tried, convicted, and received a 40-year sentence, during which time he became a vegetarian. He was eventually released on health grounds and died in 1907 – he now lies in Littleton cemetery, on the southwestern edge of Denver.

(T970/944-2274) at the north end of town, who rent out front-suspension bikes for $30 a day.

Practicalities

Conveniently, the local chamber of commerce is combined with the USFS and BLM officers to provide a very useful **visitor center**, at Gunnison Ave and 8th St (T970/944-2527 or 1-800/403-5253, W www.lakecity.com).

For its size, Lake City has a surprisingly good range of **accommodation** options. These include two downtown **campgrounds**, one being the *Henson Creek RV Park* at Henson Creek Bridge (T970/944-2394), with basic facilities – showers and laundry – and a pretty creekside location (sites $19), as well as a standard motel, the *Matterhorn Lodge*, on Bluff St (T970/944-2210 or 1-800/779-8028 W www.matterhornmotel.com; ❹). Several local ranches in the area have set themselves up as rustic resorts, including the exclusive *Crystal Lodge*, Rte-149 S (T970-944-2201 or 1-877/465-6343, W www.crystallodge .net; ❻), tucked away in the forest near Lake San Cristobal with several lodging options ranging from simple rooms to luxury cabins. The resort has a gourmet restaurant, a hot tub, several hiking trails, and splendid views of Crystal Peak. The *Gingerbed & Breakfast B&B* (T970/944-2888 or 1-800/421-5509; ❺), in a Victorian home just outside the center of Lake City, offers private baths, hot tub, and cable TV.

There are a fair number of **restaurants** in town, many catering to expensive, gourmet tastes. The *Lake City Bakery*, near the Lake City Market at 922

Wolf Creek Ski Area

Perched on the Continental Divide between South Fork and Pagosa Springs, the **Wolf Creek Ski Area** (☎970/264-5639 or 1-800/754-9653, ⓦwww.wolfcreekski .com) gets more snow than any other resort in Colorado – around 450 inches per year of some of the state's driest and lightest powder, for a season that often starts in early November. The relatively small and wide but squat ski area covers 1600 acres and is served by a mere six lifts that carry skiers and boarders up almost 1500ft to superb views from an elevation of nearly 12,000ft. The ski area has a choice of fifty trails; the terrain divides up as twenty percent beginner, fifty percent intermediate, and thirty percent expert. Though evenly split, it's the **advanced runs** that have made this a local favorite. Extreme skiers and boarders particularly enjoy the Knife Ridge area, a breathtakingly exposed ridge from which you can often launch yourself into chest-deep clouds of fluffy snow through glades, chutes, and bowls. Strong intermediate skiers can try the milder but equally impressive Water Fall area, and even beginners will find good runs here. The resort infrastructure at the base of the lifts is minimal, although rentals are available. The relatively inexpensive tickets (adult day-pass is $45) and reliably minimal lift lines make Wolf Creek a consistently popular – but not too popular – ski area.

Hwy-149 (☎970/944-2613), is a good place to start the day with a varied collection of fresh-baked goods. Later on, the *Blue Iguana*, 808 N Gunnison Ave (☎970/944-1618), is a simple cantina that's a good choice for Mexican food; most of the filling combination plates run around $7. In the heart of old downtown, *Mammy's Kitchen & Whiskey Bar*, 304 Silver St (☎970/944-4142), is a perennial favorite for both its restaurant and bar. The mains, including steak, trout, and roasted duck, are all served with fresh bread and soup. Entrees are $10–15 and the bar stays open until 2am.

Pagosa Springs

Swooping down from the densely wooded Wolf Creek Pass, Hwy-160 arrives in the rolling landscape of the San Juan River Valley, at the center of which nestles the modest town of **Pagosa Springs**. The town owes its location beside the San Juan River to the presence of one of North America's major geothermal springs, and has sprawled out along the main highway to capitalize on its attractiveness to visitors. The hot springs themselves have long been held sacred among Native Americans as a no-man's-land where weapons of feuding tribes, including Ute, Navajo, and Apache, would be laid down and healing mud packs applied. Nearby archeological evidence – a spear point and the foundations of a shelter – also suggest human use of the springs as long as 9000 years ago, making it highly likely that the Ancestral Puebloan people living in nearby **Chimney Rock** also came here. As white settlers moved here in the 1880s, the springs became the focus of attempts at creating a spa town, but the remote location west of Wolf Creek Pass stymied all attempts at creating a large, Manitou Springs-like resort. That's not to say that wallowing in the pools isn't popular – in winter, they're an après ski favorite, while in summer they're the perfect cap to a day spent hiking, biking, or fishing.

Information and accommodation

At the center of town and beside its only stoplight is the **chamber of commerce** (☎970/264-2360 or 1-800/252-2204, ⓦwww.pagosa-springs .com), which publishes the annual *Pagosa Country* magazine, a compendium of local attractions and activities. For more detailed information on National Forest campsites contact the USFS **Pagosa Ranger Station**, at the corner of 2nd and Pagosa streets (℡970/264–2268).

There's a good selection and quantity of **accommodation** downtown, as well as more-isolated options an easy drive away. Rates tend to drop in the winter and **Pagosa Central Reservations** (℡970/731-2215 or 1-800/945-0182, Ⓦ www.pagosaaccommodations.com) is open year-round. The eight area USFS **campgrounds** should keep campers happy – two of the larger, more pleasant options are the non-reservable *Wolf Creek* and *West Fork*, thirteen miles northeast of town along Hwy-160 and FR-684 (sites $10).

Echo Manor Inn 3366 Rte-84 ℡970/264-5646 or 1-800/628-5004, Ⓦ www.echomanorinn.com. Eccentric-looking lodge where the previous owners, inspired by a visit to Disneyland, added towers and gables. The present owners have run with the notion, filling the house with an eclectic array of antiques and collectables. Many of the rooms have great mountain views. Use of a hot tub and shuttle service to both the airport and ski area is included. ❻

Pagosa Lodge 3505 W Hwy-160 ℡970/731-4141 or 1-800/523-7704. Huge resort hotel with around a hundred rooms and extensive leisure facilities – including golf course, tennis courts, and a swimming pool – gathered around a lake, three miles west of town on Hwy-160. ❻

Sky View Motel 1300 Hwy-160 W ℡970/264-5803 or 1-888/633-7047. Small wood-clad motel

units on the western edge of town that are not only usually the cheapest local option but are also regularly offered as part of winter ski packages. RV hookups ($20) are also available. ❸

Spa Motel 317 Hot Springs Blvd ℡970/264-5910 or 1-800/832-5523. Tidy, simple motel rooms in the center of town that come with use of a couple of on-site geothermally heated pools – rather dowdy compared to those at the *Spring Inn*, though (see below). ❹

The Spring Inn ℡970/264-4168 or 1-800/225-0934. Standard motel that happens to have the best hot springs facility in town. Rates for the average rooms are a bit steep, though they include off-hours use of the hot springs. In winter, they offer good packages that include Wolf Creek lift tickets. ❺

Downtown Pagosa

Pagosa's obvious attractions are the steaming **hot springs** at its center. The prettiest collection of pools are at the *Spring Inn* ($15; see above), set in a landscaped area on the banks of the San Juan River. The interconnected pools are a variety of temperatures, the hottest being the painful 112°F "Lobster Pot." Modest competition exists over the road at The Spa at Pagosa Springs (Sun–Thurs 8am–9pm, Fri & Sat 8am–10pm; $8), whose far less attractive baths include an outdoor hot tub and swimming pool and an indoor steam room.

Downtown Pagosa Springs is quickly explored, but for an appreciation of town history it's worth heading to the **San Juan Historical Society Pioneer Museum**, at 1st and Pagosa streets (mid-May to mid–Sept Mon–Fri 9am–5pm; $2; Ⓦ www.sjmuseum.org). Most of the museum's highlights are from the late 1800s, including early domestic items like a horsehide coat along with a fully equipped blacksmith's shop. Those interested in popular Western art should head two miles west of town on Hwy-160 to the **Fred Harman Art Museum** (June–Aug Mon–Sat 10.30am–5pm, Sun noon–4pm; Sept–May Mon–Fri 10.30am–5pm; $4; ℡970/731-5785, Ⓦ www.harmanartmuseum.com), devoted to the cartoonist's work, the most famous of which was his "Red Ryder" cowboy comic strip, estimated to have drawn around 45 million readers during the 1950s.

Outdoor activities

The town's centrally located web of hiking and biking trails around **Reservoir Hill** are worth checking out. One trailhead to the area is located a couple hundred yards southeast of *The Spring Inn*; turn east down San Juan Street, then south after a block to the parking area and trailhead. A variety of hikes and bike ride options on the hill's woodland single-track are detailed here on a signpost, along with estimated times. There are of course plenty of **longer hiking trips**, including a good five-mile round-trip starting from the West Fork trailhead, fourteen miles northeast of town via Hwy-160 and CO-648. The trail to the unmarked **Rainbow Hot Springs** follows the course of the river up the valley, past a couple of free primitive campsites.

As always in the San Juans you don't have to look far to find good **mountain biking** routes. The best advice is doled out at Juan's Mountain Sports, 155 Hot Springs Blvd (℡970/264-4730), who rent mountain bikes for $30 per day. If you are looking for places to **fish**, there are reliable spots in the San Juan River to the north, in the Piedra River about twenty miles west, and at Echo Lake, five miles south of town along US-84. For guided fishing trips in local waters contact Let It Fly (℡970/264-3189).

Eating

The selection of **restaurants** in downtown Pagosa Springs is minimal, while the larger choice alongside Hwy-160 west of town is generally unexciting. Perhaps the best downtown option, open for both lunch and dinner, is the *Elkhorn Café*, 438 Pagosa St (℡970/264-2146), which serves inexpensive American standards (entrees from $5) like meatloaf and pot roast as well as a nice line in fiery Mexican fare. On the eastern edge of town, the *Branding Iron Bar-B-Q*, 4101 Hwy-160 (℡970/264-4268), doles out grilled meat, potatoes, and corn ($8 mains) in a ranch-style setting. Not much further along is *Ole Miners*, 3825 Hwy-160 (℡970/264-5981), where rusty mining artifacts hang on the walls and the food is a classier assortment of mostly seafood, including king crab legs, flounder, and shrimp (entrees from $12).

Chimney Rock

Named for the twin rock spires overlooking a collection of mesa-top ruins, **Chimney Rock** (mid-May to late-Sept daily 9am–4.30pm; $8; ℡970/264-2268, ⓦwww.chimneyrockco.org), seventeen miles west of Pagosa Springs via highways 151 and 160, is the most spectacularly situated Ancestral Puebloan ruin in Southern Colorado. Although only partially excavated, archeologists surmise the site was occupied by around 2000 natives between 925–1125 AD, making this the most distant colony of the huge Ancestral Puebloan settlement at Chaco Canyon in New Mexico, ninety miles away.

The site can only be visited on **guided tours** (daily 9.30am, 10.30am, 1pm & 2pm) that lead past a number of restored ruins. The tours are rather uninformative, as answers to the key questions about why the place was built remain unknown. Most striking is the positioning of several huge *kivas* – circular, stone-lined ceremonial pits or buildings – with the spires of the Chimney Rock, which is thought to be related to astrological events. This would clearly suggest that the entire settlement had ceremonial significance, borne out by its inconvenient location 1000ft above the nearest water source. There's also evidence that this outpost served as a logging center – perhaps offering an explanation for the rapid demise of the settlement, which coincided with the disappearance of all the area's useful timber.

Durango

DURANGO, named after Durango, Mexico, is the largest town in southwestern Colorado and the best hub for exploring both the San Juans and the

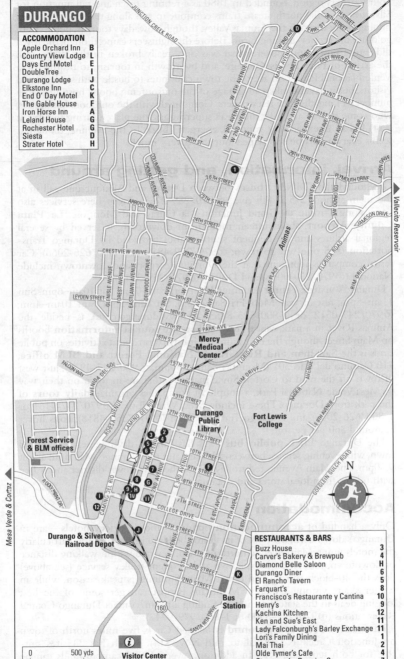

DURANGO

ACCOMMODATION

Apple Orchard Inn	**B**
Country View Lodge	**L**
Days End Motel	**E**
DoubleTree	**I**
Durango Lodge	**J**
Elkstone Inn	**C**
End O' Day Motel	**K**
The Gable House	**F**
Iron Horse Inn	**A**
Leland House	**G**
Rochester Hotel	**G**
Siesta	**D**
Strater Hotel	**H**

RESTAURANTS & BARS

Buzz House	3
Carver's Bakery & Brewpub	4
Diamond Belle Saloon	**H**
Durango Diner	6
El Rancho Tavern	5
Farquart's	8
Francisco's Restaurante y Cantina	10
Henry's	9
Kachina Kitchen	12
Ken and Sue's East	11
Lady Falconburgh's Barley Exchange	11
Lori's Family Dining	1
Mai Thai	2
Olde Tymer's Cafe	4
Steamworks Brewing Co	7

Mercy Medical Center

Durango Public Library

Fort Lewis College

Forest Service & BLM offices

Durango & Silverton Railroad Depot

Bus Station

ⓘ Visitor Center

Mesa Verde & Cortez ◀

▶ Vallecito Reservoir

0   500 yds

N

▼ Airport, Pagosa Springs & Ⓛ

Four Corners region. Founded in 1880 as a refining town and rail junction for Silverton, 45 miles north, steam trains continue to run along the spectacular old mining route through the Animas Valley, though nowadays tourists, not sacks of gold, are the money-making cargo. Before the sightseers came, though, the town slid into a post-boom poverty that was only really broken in the 1950s with the arrival of **Fort Lewis College**, and by growth in tourism to nearby Mesa Verde National Park soon after. The town continues to bustle with students and visitors, but it has also taken advantage of the outsourcing boom, hosting a large number of long-distance teleworkers. Combined with the outdoors enthusiasts, who come to ride and hike the area's superb trails, the place (during the day, at least) has an unexpectedly youthful, energetic buzz. In the evening, though, it seems everyone's a bit too wiped-out to do very much.

Arrival, information, and getting around

Greyhound and TMN&O **buses** between Denver and Albuquerque call in at the main station, 275 E 8th Ave (℡970/259-2755). From here services also head along a route to Grand Junction via Ouray and Montrose. **La Plata County Airport**, about fifteen miles from downtown, is served by several regional airlines and by frequent shuttle buses provided by Durango Transportation ($15 one-way to town; ℡970/259-4818 or 1-800/626-2066). Car rental companies represented at the Durango Airport and downtown include National (℡970/259-0068) and Dollar (℡970/259-3012).

Durango's **visitor center** (summer Mon–Fri 8am–7pm, Sat 10am–6pm, Sun 11am–5pm; rest of year Mon–Fri 8am–6pm, Sat 8am–5pm, Sun 10am–4pm; ℡970/247-0312 or 1-800/525-8855, ⓦwww.durango.com) is beside the Animas River in a park west of town. There are **tourist information** booths on Main Street, though the best source of information about activities on public lands is the **San Juan and Rio Grande National Forest and BLM office**, 710 Camino del Rio 301 (Mon–Fri 8am–4.30pm; ℡970/247-4874), just west of town off the road to Cortez. Since many visitors are in town on their way to Mesa Verde National Park, a couple of companies organize **daily tours** of the park from Durango. These include Mesa Verde Tours (℡970/247-4161 or 1-800/626-2066) and Durango Transportation (℡970/259-4818); costs hover at around $60 per person.

The Durango LIFT **public bus** ($1) has limited daytime service around town, with evening service between N Main and the Durango Mall until about 9.30pm. The Main Avenue red trolley serves the downtown district and is free with tokens from local stores and restaurants.

Accommodation

Only a handful of **accommodation** options – mostly pricey hotels – are in Durango's downtown; the bulk of its visitor beds are in the suburbs, particularly the motels lining Main Avenue north of town. Few are within walking distance of downtown, though an inexpensive and frequent trolley service (see above) does the 40-block run up and down Main. Summer is peak season, while in winter skiers visiting Durango Mountain Resort can get some of the best lodging deals in the state. For help in finding a room, contact Durango Central Reservations (℡970/247-8900 or 1-800/979-9742).

The nearest USFS **campground** is *Junction Creek*, five miles north of town on Junction Creek Rd (April to mid-Nov; $14), which has 34 sites suitable for both tents and RVs. In addition, several USFS campgrounds can be found around the Vallecito Reservoir, twenty miles northeast of town. A good commercial campsite is *Hermosa Meadows*, beside the Animas River eight miles north of town (☎970/247-3055 or 1-800/748-2853), with showers, laundry, and shaded tent sites ($17).

Downtown

DoubleTree 150 Fifth St ☎970/259-6580 or 1-800/222-8733, ⓦwww.doubletree.com. Dependable downtown chain hotel with reasonable rates, large rooms, hot tub, sauna, indoor pool, and restaurant. In winter ski packages are available and a daily shuttle runs to the resort. ❺

Durango Lodge 150 Fifth St ☎970/247-0955. Close to the railroad depot, this is one of the most central motels – hence the slightly higher rates – with unremarkable rooms, a pool, and hot tub. ❺

The Gable House 805 E Fifth Ave ☎970/247-4982, ⓦwww.durangobedandbreakfast.com. On a quiet residential street, an elegant, peaceful, and roomy B&B in a living piece of American Victoriana, complete with fairytale turret and veranda. ❻

Leland House 721 E Second Ave ☎970/385-1920 or 1-800/664-1920. Simple and austere, this sister to the *Rochester* (see below) is a fastidiously renovated 1920s apartment building. All rooms and suites have kitchens or kitchenettes, though breakfast at the *Rochester* is included. ❺

Rochester Hotel 726 E Second Ave ☎970/385-1920 or 1-800/664-1920, ⓦwww.rochesterhotel.com. This very central hotel has swung between having some of the town's grandest lodgings in the 1890s to being its cheapest flophouse. Renovated in the 1990s, it's now a luxurious, period-furnished B&B decorated with cowboy movie memorabilia. Gourmet breakfast included as is use of a hot tub. ❼

Strater Hotel 699 Main Ave ☎970/247-4431 or 1-800/247-4431, ⓦwww.strater.com. Antique-furnished rooms embody the frontier elegance of this longstanding Durango hotel, which at one time housed a brothel. Later, Western writer Louis L'Amour kept a suite where he wrote several novels based in the area. Rates include a great buffet breakfast heaped with fresh fruit, muffins, pasties, pancakes, waffles, eggs, and meat. ❻

The suburbs

Days End Motel 2202 Main Ave (Hwy-550) ☎970/259-3311 or 1-800/242-3297, ⓦwww.daysend.com. Durango's best-value budget option, with indoor hot tub, outdoor heated swimming pool, and laundry. Rooms in the newer block are larger; some have kitchenettes. ❸

End O' Day Motel 350 E Eighth Ave ☎970/247-1722. At the southern edge of town (just a 10min walk from downtown), this small, comfortable motel is one of the cheapest deals around. ❸

△ Strater Hotel

Iron Horse Inn 5800 N Main Ave ☎970/259-1010 or 1-800/748-2990, ⓦwww.ironhorseinndurango .com. Slightly dated but reasonably priced family resort by the narrow gauge rail tracks at the north end of town. All suites have lofts with at least one queen and one double bed; some have kitchens. ❸

Siesta 3475 Main Ave ☎970/247-0741. One of Durango's cheapest motels is way out on its northern fringes. Facilities are minimal, though all rooms have phones and TV, and some have kitchenettes. ❸

Out-ot-town

Apple Orchard Inn 7758 CR-203 ☎970/247-0751 or 1-800/426-0751, ⓦwww.appleorchardinn .com. This collection of simply decorated white wooden cottages near Trimble Hot Springs offer more privacy than the average B&B. The owners are friendly and flexible, planning breakfast menus according to guests' wishes and serving up dinner, too, if required. ❺

Country View Lodge 28295 Hwy-160 E ☎970/247-5701. Large well-maintained hostel with friendly owners, six miles east of Durango beside Hwy-160. On offer are dorm beds ($13), basic private rooms ($30), and camping ($10) in the grassy area behind the hostel, a sociable space sheltered from traffic and beside a mountain stream. Facilities include a large kitchen, lounge, and laundry.

Elkstone Inn 34940 Hwy-550 N ☎970/385-0488, ⓦwww.elkstoneinn.com. Large cedarwood home on the banks of the Animas, with only four guestrooms, but offering massages and a peaceful outdoor hot tub. ❹

Downtown Durango

North–south **Main Avenue** is unsurprisingly the hub of Durango's urban action. Traversing its 40-block-long length is the Main Avenue Trolley (daily 6.45am–6.15pm every 30min; 50¢). Main's northern end is a charmless strip of motels and fast-food joints, but in the Victorian center, things become much more attractive. Here, the street is lined with restaurants, souvenir shops, Southwestern art galleries, and sporting goods stores, almost all of which are housed in century-old Victorian redbrick buildings. At Main's southern end stands the squat depot of the **Durango & Silverton Narrow Gauge Railroad**, the town's main tourist attraction. The train runs up to four round-trips daily between May and October, from 479 Main Ave (all trains leave early morning; $62 round-trip; ☎970/247-2733 or 1-877/872-4607, ⓦwww.durangotrain .com). Using the same route once employed to transport ore from mining districts to the north of town, the steam train shoots out dark plumes of smoke as it chugs through glorious mountain scenery, passing through forests and glades before hugging precarious ledges and crossing exposed trestles high above the roaring Animas River. The round-trip takes around seven hours, including a lunchtime stopover in Silverton. Shorter excursions, running to Cascade Canyon and covering the most scenic areas of the route, run between late November and early May (daily 10am; $45). For all trips, try and **reserve tickets** at least three weeks in advance; if this isn't possible, check early on the day you'd like to travel to try and pick up a cancellation.

Outdoor activities

Lying beside the Animas River, Durango is at the transition of the landscape from lushly wooded steep mountains and rolling meadows to a land of wide, slumbering rivers and slickrock deserts. Opportunities for **outdoor activities** are in as great abundance as scenic variety, and various pursuits draw visitors in about equal measure, including rafting, biking, hiking, fishing, and, in winter, skiing at the terrific Durango Mountain Resort. Whatever your poison during the day, a good place to soothe aches afterward is at **Trimble Hot Springs** (Sun–Thurs 9am–10pm, Fri & Sat 9am–11pm; $11; ☎970/247-0212, ⓦwww .trimblehotsprings.com), six miles north of Durango on Hwy-550. This old-fashioned outdoor spa has been here since 1883, but has been more recently rebuilt to provide an Olympic-size swimming pool along with three natural mineral soaking pools (100°–110°F).

Rafting

Whitewater rafting on the Animas River is second only to the Narrow Gauge Railroad as the local must-do activity – and some trips even combine both. Several companies offer rafting trips in Durango, most of which are easily found in small wooden booths scattered along the downtown portion of Main Ave. The most popular trips are the fairly tame, family-friendly outings on the **Lower Animas**, Class II and III waters south of town. Half-day trips run around $40, while a full day on the water is around $70.

The real gem, though, for those with the courage, money, and time, are the rafting trips further upstream. Dropping steeper and faster than almost any other river in the state, the 28 miles of the **Upper Animas River** south of Silverton provides an excellent venue for one- or two-day whitewater raft and kayak trips. This area boasts continuous Class III water with several Class IV and V sections. Trips include maneuvering around giant boulders scattered throughout No Name rapids, camping at Needleton, and a take-out at Rockwood, below which the canyon narrows too much to make it runnable. From here many companies arrange for rafters to load gear onto the narrow gauge railroad to cover the last thirty miles to Durango by steam, a memorable itinerary that runs around $200 per day per person. Reputable companies offering a full range of local trips include

Biking in Durango

Since hosting the inaugural mountain bike world championships in 1990, Durango has become a world-class center for **off-road biking**. Such is the town's relationship with the sport that numerous stars have either chosen to live or retire here, and it again hosted a round of the Mountain Bike World Cup in 2001. Durango's also famous as the venue for one of the largest bike races in the US, the Memorial Day **Iron Horse Bicycle Classic** – an event in which up to 2000 riders race the narrow gauge railway train 47 miles to Silverton. The event began in 1972 as a friendly wager between two brothers and has since mushroomed into a major three-day festival, including several other bicycle races and events.

For **rentals**, equipment, and advice contact Mountain Bike Specialists, 949 Main Ave (☎970/247-4066), or Pedal the Peaks, 598B Main Ave (☎970/259-6880), who'll both rent out front-suspension machines from $30 per day. You can also rent a bike at Durango Mountain Resort, where several ability-graded trails have been laid out. Classic local trails include:

Telegraph Hill There's no set route around this single-track network on the eastern side of town, but it's challenging and fun enough to have been incorporated into the 2001 World Cup cross-country course. Head up Horse Gulch Rd (the eastern end of Third St) and explore; don't miss riding down the rocky, technical Raider Ridge (on the northwest side of Horse Gulch Rd) with its stunning views over Durango.

Haflin Creek Trail Highly challenging 22-mile loop northeast of town. Experienced riders take around five hours to grind up the long, well-graded climb and the steep, at times death-defying, descent into Haflin Canyon.

Hermosa Creek trail Wonderful, largely downhill 21-mile trail northwest of town. The generally smooth single-track trail cuts through thick, pristine forests and is best done by setting up a shuttle to Durango Mountain Resort. One-way the ride takes around five hours.

Mountain Waters Rafting, at College Drive and Main Ave (☎970/259-4191 or 1-800/585-8243, ⊛www.durangorafting.com), and Mild to Wild Rafting, on Camino del Rio and 11th St (☎970/247-4789 or 1-800/567-6745, ⊛www.mild2wildrafting.com). Several stretches of the Animas are also popular among kayakers, and in late June kayakers from all over the US descend on Durango for the **Animas River Days**, a national-level whitewater competition.

Hiking and fishing

Though Durango hasn't built up the kind of cult status amongst **hikers** as it has mountain bikers, the town still has plenty of fine hiking options. Many favorite biker trails are also great options for hikers; the ultimate challenge is the almost 500-mile **Colorado Trail** (see *Colorado's protected lands* color section) to Denver that starts seven miles northwest of town near the *Junction Creek* campground. For a short, good outing near town try the five-mile round-trip hike on the **Animas Trail Mountain**, with good views of the Animas Valley and river and a likely place to spot elk and deer. The trail starts on the northern fringes of Durango – take 32nd St west, then W 4th Ave north to the end of the road.

For river fishing in the Durango area, the obvious place to head is the **Animas River**, particularly the stretch between Lighter Creek and the Purple Cliffs below town. A quieter place to look for trout in numerous small streams is along the **Hermosa Creek drainage area**, west of and accessed from Durango Mountain Resort. For lake fishing and hooking trout, kokanee salon, northern pike, or walleye, **Vallecito Reservoir**, 25 miles northeast of Durango, has become a popular place – with five marinas renting out fishing boats – though with 22 miles of accessible shoreline it's hardly ever crowded. For fishing licenses and classes call in at Duranglers, 139 E 5th St (☎970/385-4081). For guided trips contact Fly Fishing Durango (☎970/382-0478).

Eating

The turn-of-the-twentieth-century redbrick buildings along Main Avenue house a plethora of **restaurants**, some with their sights set on affluent train passengers, others aimed at young bikers. As usual in Colorado, many of the bars and brewpubs here (see "Nightlife," opposite) also serve good food. The main drag northwest of downtown is where you'll find the familiar fast-food spots, local diners, and large supermarkets.

Buzz House 1019 Main Ave ☎970/385-5831. Popular worn-in coffeehouse with lots of healthy veggie breakfasts, snacks, smoothies, and a large array of coffee drinks. Open Mon–Fri 7am–4pm, Sat 8am–4pm.

Durango Diner 957 Main Ave ☎970/247-9889. Greasy spoon serving the kind of big, filling, traditional breakfasts that no one ever finishes – but the food's filling and cheap and it's a major hangout for locals. Open daily 6am–2pm.

Francisco's Restaurante y Cantina 619 Main Ave ☎970/247-4098. The large Santa Fe-style dining room is a popular choice for the best moderately priced Mexican food in town. Usual Mexican favorites are offered along with more adventurous choices like the "Enchiladas Durango" ($8.50), beef wrapped in blue-corn tortillas smothered in a zesty green chili.

Henry's in the *Strater Hotel*, 699 Main Ave ☎970/247-4431. Ornately decorated with red leather booths and Tiffany lamps, *Henry's* is a Durango institution. The moderately pricey menu is based around good American and classy Italian fare. Entrees vary dramatically in cost from $10 to $25, including veal osso bucco, deep lasagnas, and pepper steak in chutney and cognac, a long-standing house favorite. The varied salad bar is excellent, too.

Kachina Kitchen Centennial Center, 325 S Camino del Rio ☎970/247-3536. Worth the trip to its inconvenient location southwest of town for traditional Southwestern – a mix of Mexican and Native American – fast food at budget prices. Closed Sun.

Ken and Sue's East 636 Main Ave ☎970/385-1810. Upscale Asian fusion place where low-hanging pumpkin-colored lamps

in dark wood booths glow above appetizers like the green salad with apples and gorgonzola and entrees like the pistachio-encrusted grouper with rum sauce on a bed of yams. The original *Ken and Sue's Place*, 937 Main Ave (☏ 970/259-2616) is simpler and more laid-back, but equally popular.
Lori's Family Dining 2653 Main Ave ☏ 970/247-1224. Popular diner on motel row, serving filling breakfasts from around $5, as well as lunches and dinners that include a good salad bar.

Mai Thai 1050 Main Ave ☏ 970/247-8272. Tiny space with five tables, a handful of counter stools, and the most genuine Asian food in town. And at under $10 for a filling meal, the Thai, Indonesian, and Filipino rice dishes, curries, and noodles are a bargain.
Olde Tymer's Cafe 1000 Main Ave ☏ 970/259-2990. Known for the best burgers in town, with specials on Mondays – the huge beef patties are only $3.75 – and Fridays, when tacos are just $1.50.

Nightlife and entertainment

For a university town, Durango's **nightlife** scene is surprisingly quiet, though there are a few dependably sociable venues – including *Lady Falconburgh's*, *Steamworks*, *Carver's*, and *Farquart's* (see below), the latter two of which have live music at weekends – within a few blocks of each other downtown. For a mellower night, head to the *Pelican's Nest*, 656 Main Ave, where there's live jazz nightly, or look into seeing one of the melodramas regularly performed at the *Strater Hotel* (June–Sept; from $15). You might also catch a concert at the Fort Lewis college theater (☏ 970/247-7320) and community concert hall (☏ 970/247-7657), where the San Juan Symphony Orchestra performs (ⓦ www.sanjuansymphony.com). Durango has two **movie theaters**, the old-fashioned Gaslight, 102 Fifth St (☏ 970/247-8133), and Trans-Lux, next door to the bowling alley in Durango Mall (☏ 970/247-9799), east of town on Hwy-160/550; the terrific Durango Film Festival is held in early March (☏ 970/259-2291, ⓦ www.durangofilmfestival.com). If you really want to make a night of it head to the **Sky Ute Casino** (☏ 970/563-3000) in Ignacio, twenty minutes' drive southeast of town. It's no Vegas, but draws crowds all the same.

Carver's Bakery & Brewpub 1022 Main Ave ☏ 970/259-2545. Bakery by morning, brewpub by night, *Carver's* opens at 6.30am for big breakfasts that include excellent granola pancakes. The lunch and dinner menu features tasty, inexpensive Southwestern options like beef or chicken fajitas along with Western dishes like bison, best accompanied by one of four varieties of home-brewed beer.
Diamond Belle Saloon in the *Strater Hotel*, 699 Main Ave ☏ 970/247-4431. Somewhat over-the-top Victorian-style bar where a honky-tonk piano player holds court and pricey cocktails are served.
El Rancho Tavern 975 Main Ave ☏ 970/259-8111. Welcoming brick-walled bar and Durango institution, *The Ranch* is where Jack Dempsey (see p.330) is reputed to have fought his first fight. These days the tavern has pool and football tables in the back, murals on the wall, and free popcorn.
Farquart's 725 Main St ☏ 970/247-5440. Serves what just may be Durango's best pizza, a well-balanced wholewheat crust creation that can be matched with a huge range of toppings. The

linguini and meatballs in marinara sauce is another strong choice, as are the Mexican entrees on offer from around $8. The loud and smoky bar, typically full of students, has a good range of imported and domestic suds.
Lady Falconburgh's Barley Exchange in the Century Mall, 640 Main Ave ☏ 970/382-9664. Popular basement bar – with medieval English drinking-house theme – in the heart of downtown, serving fried snacks and some larger burger and salad-type meals as well. The big draw isn't the food, though, but the extensive beer menu, featuring well over a hundred varieties in bottle and on tap.
Steamworks Brewing Co. 801 E 2nd Ave ☏ 970/259-9200. Peanut shells litter the floor of this huge brewpub, where the giant helpings of good bar food – burgers, pastas, pizzas, salads, and a deliciously messy Cajun Boil – is best eaten on the sunny outdoor patio. The selection of beers can be tried by ordering a sampler, with half a dozen small glasses for $10 – or, if you want a tangy and really potent brew, just get the Steam Engine Lager.

Listings

Bookshop Maria's, 960 Main Ave (Mon–Sat 9am–7pm, Sun 10am–6pm).
Internet Free access at the main public library, 1188 E 2nd Ave ☏970/385-2970 (Mon–Wed 9am–9pm, Thurs–Sat 9am–5.30pm).
Laundry North Main Coin Laundry, 2980 N Main Ave ☏970/247-9915.
Medical Mercy Medical Center, 375 E Park Ave ☏970/247-4311.

Police Durango Police Dept, 990 E 2nd Ave ☏970/247-3232.
Post Office The main post office is at 222 W 8th.
Recreation Center 2700 North Main St (Mon–Fri 6am–10pm, Sat 8am–10pm, Sun 10am–6pm; $3.50; ☏970/375-7300). Has an indoor track and climbing wall, fitness machines, racquetball courts, and indoor pool complex with waterslides and a lap pool.

The Four Corners region

Southwest of Durango the mountains quickly flatten and pine trees are replaced by piñon and juniper on the rolling hills of the **FOUR CORNERS**. Named for the meeting of four state lines in Colorado's southwestern corner, this region certainly has more in common with neighbors Arizona, New Mexico, and Utah than it does with much of the rest of the state, with vestiges of Native American and Hispanic culture not only in the present-day names of the area's towns, but also in the architecture and food.

Workaday **Cortez** is the main town in the Colorado quarter and worth a visit for its surroundings, where areas rich in ancient Native American ruins have been protected as parks and monuments. Doubtless the most interesting is **Mesa Verde National Park**, where Ancestral Puebloan cliff dwellings cling precariously in the high rocky alcoves of the red-rock canyon walls. Further similar structures are dotted around the more remote **Ute Mountain Tribal Park**, where guided tours offer travelers an even more exhilarating sense of discovery. More minor structures are dotted around the **Canyons of the Ancients** and **Hovenweep National Monuments**, and both are worth a look if the parks have whetted your appetite. Be also sure to drop in at the **Anasazi Heritage Center**, an excellent little museum on local prehistoric cultures, and not to miss **Chimney Rock** near Pagosa Springs.

Mesa Verde National Park

MESA VERDE NATIONAL PARK, the only national park in the US devoted exclusively to archeological remains, is set high in the plateaus of southwest Colorado, 37 miles west of Durango along Hwy-160. Between the time of Christ and 1300 AD, Ancestral Puebloan civilization expanded to cover much of the area now known as the Four Corners. Settlements here appear to have been the northern outpost of a civilization that dominated the Southwest

---

Naming the ancestors

Only in the last few years has the term **Ancestral Puebloan** been coined to refer to the ancient peoples traditionally called the **Anasazi**. As a Navajo term that means "ancient enemy," the latter has generally been dropped, as it's considered offensive by some modern Puebloans. The majority, however, have no issue with it, so the renaming probably provides more comment on concerns of political correctness in contemporary culture than ancient squabbles or sensitivities.

for centuries and evolved into the modern-day Pueblo Indians. The earliest dwellings were simple pits, but before vanishing the Ancestral Puebloan people had developed the architectural sophistication needed to build the extraordinary complexes high on the plateaus of Mesa Verde and, more famously, castle-like stone pueblos carved into cliffside niches. It's an astonishing place, so far off the beaten track that its extensive ruins were not fully explored until 1888 – hard to imagine given the well-preserved nature of the archeological sites, as well as the huge numbers of people who visit them today.

The area was named in the seventeenth century, but the ruins weren't noted for another two hundred years. Though photographer William Henry Jackson recorded some lesser sites in 1874, the outside world only really took note of the place after a snowstorm in 1888 when local rancher Richard Wetherill stumbled upon the Cliff Palace. Along with a few others, the Wetherills soon spawned an industry out of finding and selling Ancestral Puebloan artifacts. One particularly good customer was the Swedish count Gustaf Nordenskjöld, who shipped caseloads of ancient pottery to Europe in the 1890s and gave the National Museum of Finland the world's finest collection of Mesa Verde

A History of Mesa Verde

Although archeological finds in the Montezuma Valley around nearby Cortez date back as far as 5500 BC, the **Ancestral Puebloans** who made **Mesa Verde** their home between 500 and 1300 AD appear to be the area's first residents. Their earliest homes were pit-houses dug into cave floors, and it's known that they were skilled potters who led a stable agricultural life. Around 1100 AD, they moved out of the pit-houses to intricate walled villages on the mesa tops, where an extensive system of irrigation ditches and reservoirs was also created. At this time, it's thought that the Mesa Verde population reached its peak of around 2500, meaning it was still only the eighth or ninth largest surface Pueblo community in the Montezuma Valley.

Around a century later, the Mesa Verdeans moved again, this time constructing the spectacular multi-story cliff dwellings for which the park is most famous. Surprisingly, archeologists regard these as an indication that the culture was now in decline, noting that the rather haphazard structures are far less sophisticated than the mesa-top pueblos. The cliffside dwellings, in practice, must have also been less ideal, dangerous for both the elderly and for children, who would have to have been continuously supervised to avoid fatal falls. Moreover, though each complex was near the seep or spring that had originally created the alcove, many would have run dry, making fetching water a constant chore.

Given their shortcomings, it's not known for sure why the cliff dwellings were built in the first place. It's reasonable to suggest that this was for defensive reasons, though there's also no evidence that the Mesa Verdeans were ever attacked. Still, the idea that this was a peaceful group was recently dashed after archeological finds suggested cannibalistic tendencies, and it's thought that the other Pueblo communities in the Montezuma Valley were hostile to those living here. Some also argue that the move occurred to open up more space on the mesa tops for agricultural purposes, as arable land was at such a premium. The biggest mystery of all, though, is why the cliff dwellings were abandoned after only a century. It may have been due to a long drought, though that can't explain the exceptional quantity of artifacts – including jewelry, weapons, and kitchen utensils – left behind. On the other hand, there's no evidence either of a catastrophic or violent end to the civilization. Whatever happened, evidence suggests that the inhabitants of Mesa Verde headed south to join similar people in present-day Arizona and New Mexico, establishing pueblos where their descendants, the modern Pueblo Indians, still live.

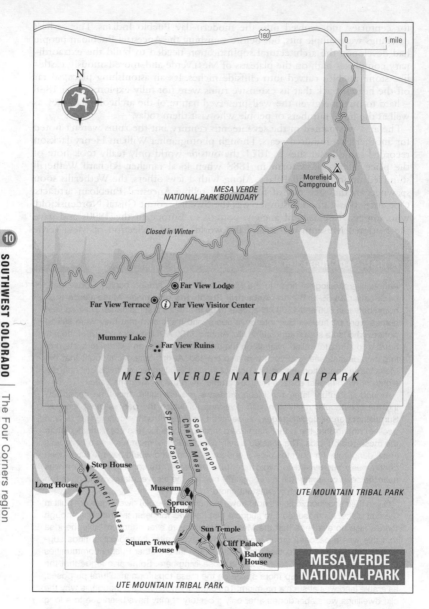

0   1 mile

N

Morefield Campground

MESA VERDE
NATIONAL PARK BOUNDARY

Closed in Winter

◉ **Far View Lodge**

Far View Terrace ◉   ⓘ **Far View Visitor Center**

Mummy Lake   • **Far View Ruins**

M E S A   V E R D E   N A T I O N A L   P A R K

Spruce Canyon

Soda Canyon

Chapin Mesa

◆ **Step House**

Long House ◆

Wetherill Mesa

Museum ◆

Spruce Tree House

Sun Temple

Square Tower House ◆   **Cliff Palace**

Balcony House

UTE MOUNTAIN TRIBAL PARK

UTE MOUNTAIN TRIBAL PARK

**MESA VERDE
NATIONAL PARK**

artifacts. These activities prompted the Antiquities Act of 1906, which prohibited dealing in archeological treasures, and the creation of the National Park proper in the same year.

Mesa Verde's "green table," a plateau densely wooded with juniper and piñon, overlooks distant mountains and arid plains and is cut at its southern edge by sheer canyons dividing the land into narrow fingers. Given these natural barriers there are few hiking opportunities in the park; it's really only the ruins that make it worth a visit. Since the ruins are easily accessible, the park can get crowded in summer, making the best months to come here May, September, and October – when the summer heat also begins to ease off. Since in winter the place is blanketed in snow, only the park's main museum and the Spruce Tree House ruin are open year-round, while what hiking trails there are attract snowshoers and cross-country skiers.

Arrival, information, and tours

Advance **information** on Mesa Verde can be obtained by calling ☎970/529-4455 or visiting ⓦwww.nps.gov/meve. The access road to Mesa Verde climbs south from Hwy-160 a little more than a half-hour drive west of Durango. Once past the **entrance station** ($10 per vehicle, or $5 for motorcyclists, bicyclists, and pedestrians), the road climbs and twists through a barren, burnt-out 23,607-acre area, the result of the virulent Bircher Fire in July 2000 – which was larger than the combined size of all other forest fires the park has seen since records began. Mercifully the areas around the ruins were spared, and by the time you reach the **Far View visitor center**, fifteen miles from the entrance (late April to mid-Oct daily 8am–5pm; ☎970/529-5036), the landscape is back to its green self. Exhibits inside the center cover Navajo, Hopi, and Pueblo crafts and jewelry. Immediately beyond here, the road forks south to the Chapin Mesa area and west to the Wetherill Mesa.

There are free overlooks at most of the ruins, but to tour any of the three major attractions you must buy **tickets** ($2.25 each) at the visitor center. On Chapin Mesa, Cliff Palace is usually open between 9am and 5pm daily from late April until early November, and Balcony House for the same hours between late April and mid-October; at busy times, you can't tour both on the same day (though many couples circumvent regulations by queuing separately for tickets). Tours of Long House over on Wetherill Mesa run between late May and early September and operate 9am–4pm daily.

If you don't want to go it alone, several commercial operators run **tours** of the park. Most leave from Durango (see p.346), though at the park there's the option of joining a bus tour ($37 half-day, $56 full day) from the *Far View Motor Lodge* and *Morefield Campground*; contact either establishment for details (see "Practicalities," p.346).

Chapin Mesa

A couple of miles from the visitor center on the road to Chapin Mesa stands **Far View**, a mesa-top pueblo abandoned early in the thirteenth century, one of the structures that predates the cliff dwellings. Nearby is the artificial **Mummy Lake**. Like so many other constructs in the park, opinion on the lake's origins are divided. Thought for a long time to have been a reservoir, some now believe that this vast depression, capable of holding half a million gallons, might have been an open-air plaza. Four miles onward is the **Chapin Mesa Archeological Museum** (daily: April to mid-Oct 8am–6.30pm; mid-Oct to April 8am–5pm), which holds the park's best displays on the Ancestral Puebloans and also sells tour tickets after the visitor center closes in late fall. A couple of fairly dull two- to three-mile-long nature trails start here, but far more rewarding is the short, steep hike down to **Spruce Tree House**, the only ruin open in winter. It's a neat little village of three-story structures snugly molded into the recesses of a rocky alcove and fronted by open plazas. One *kiva* has been re-roofed to give visitors a feel for the structure in its original state.

Beyond the museum, two one-way six-mile loops known as the **Ruins Road** (April to early Nov daily 8am–dusk) split off to the park's major sites. The **western** loop, the one to skip if pressed for time, first stops at the **Square Tower House**, where an easy stroll leads to views of an eighty-room alcove complex based around the four-story, 26ft-wide Square Tower, the tallest in the park. Further along the road is **Sun Point Overlook**, a great viewpoint from which to appreciate the clustering of twelve distinct cliff dwellings at the other side of Spruce Canyon, including the Cliff Palace, which gives a good appreciation of just how crowded the canyon was in its heyday. In contrast to the cliff sites, the mesa-top **Sun Temple**, next up on the loop, was built to premeditated plans, and though never finished may have been intended to be a major ceremonial center. However, little of its shape and function can be appreciated by walking around its walls, making exploration of the ruin unrewarding.

Cliff Palace

The star of Ruins Road's **eastern loop** is **Cliff Palace**, the largest Ancestral Puebloan cliff dwelling in existence. The incredible location, tucked a hundred feet below an overhanging ledge of pale rock, is made more so when you realize that the 200-plus rooms here once housed a community of around 250 people. Though you can get a great view from the promontory below the parking lot, entering the ruin on a tour is the way to go. Especially on quieter days, walking through empty plazas and past mysterious *kivas* provides a haunting evocation of a lost and little-known world. Fading murals can still be discerned inside some of the structures, while a metal stairway climbs past the original toe- and footholds of the Ancestral Puebloans.

△ Mesa Verde

Balcony House

Beyond the Cliff Palace, the loop briefly passes into a small portion of Ute Mountain Tribal Park (see p.360) before arriving back into Mesa Verde around **Balcony House**, one of the few complexes clearly geared toward defense. Access to the network of rooms here is very difficult, and it's not visible from above. Hourly guided tours involve scrambling up three hair-raising ladders and crawling through a narrow tunnel, teetering all the while above a steep drop into Soda Canyon. Park authorities present it as more "fun" than the other ruins, but unless you share the fearless Ancestral Puebloan attitude to heights, you might prefer to give it a miss.

Wetherill Mesa

Beside a ranger station and snack kiosk at the end of the twisting, twelve-mile drive from the visitor center to **Wetherill Mesa** (late May to early Sept daily 8am–4.30pm; large vehicles like RVs are not allowed on this road) is the terminus of a free **miniature train**, which loops around the tip of the mesa. Time spent waiting for the next train can be occupied by walking down to investigate the **Step House**, where there's a restored pit-house dated to 626 as well as a single alcove pueblo from 1226.

The mini-train stops at various trailheads for hikers wishing to explore minor early mesa-top sites and alcove overlooks, but its principal destination is the **Long House**, the park's second-largest ruin set in a large cave. Hour-long tours descend around sixty steps to reach a central plaza, before scrambling around the 150 rooms and 21 *kivas*. These ruins, though more ramshackle than those at Chapin Mesa, are considered some of the most authentic in the park, since they have been simply stabilized rather than subject to extensive rebuilding programs as at the other main sites early in the twentieth century.

Park practicalities

As most of the park is inaccessible in winter, services such as gas, food, and lodging only operate between late April and mid-October. While most visitors **stay** in nearby towns, there is the *Far View Motor Lodge* (⊕970/529-4421 or 1-800/449-2288; ❺; late April to early Oct), in the park itself near the visitor center. The rooms are rather basic (no phones or TV), though the views from its mesa-top location are fantastic. You can **camp** at the pleasant and large *Morefield Campground* (⊕970/529-4421 or 1-800/449-2288; $19–25 per site; mid-April to mid-Oct), four miles up from the entrance and thus a long way from the ruins. **Food** is available year-round at the *Spruce Tree Terrace* restaurant near the Chapin Mesa museum and also (in season) at the *Far View Motor Lodge*, across from the visitor center, which has a gas station.

Cortez and Montezuma County

Strung out along one lengthy overdeveloped curve of Hwy-160, nothing in **CORTEZ** commands much attention, though the giant Sleeping Ute Mountain to the southwest, visible from all over, makes a dramatic backdrop – by reputedly looking uncannily like a warrior god asleep with his arms folded across his chest. A short drive from town, though, the scrubby mesas and canyonlands of **Montezuma County** offer an amazing array of remote archeological sites, including the spectacular **Ute Mountain Tribal Park** and the **Canyons of the Ancients** and **Hovenweep National Monuments**.

Cortez, therefore, is a great base from which to visit these places, and, to this end, offers a large if similar collection of motels and diners. If you'd rather stay somewhere quieter and less generic try the town of **DOLORES**, ten miles north and near the excellent **Anasazi Heritage Center**, a museum-cum-visitor center, or in the compact and attractive little community of **MANCOS**, sixteen miles east towards Durango on Hwy-160 and eight miles from the foot of the Mesa Verde approach road.

Cortez's **visitor center**, 928 E Main St (daily: May–Sept 8am–6pm; Oct–April 8am–5pm; ⊕970/565-3414 or 1-800/253-1616, ⓦ www.swcolo.org), is on the edge of the city park and, as a Colorado Welcome Center, has information on the entire state.

Accommodation

Accommodation in Cortez centers on a clutch of very similar motels on the main strip, with the range broadened a bit by the presence of a couple big-name chains and a great local B&B. Slightly cheaper lodgings are offered in the nearby towns of **Dolores** and **Mancos**. The best range of local **camping** possibilities are on the banks of the McPhee Reservoir, around ten miles north of town on Hwy-145. If you don't mind camping wild then you'll find plenty of good spots on BLM land in the Canyons of the Ancients National Monument or at the campground at the Hovenweep National Monument 35 miles away.

Aneth Lodge 645 E Main St, Cortez ☎970/565-3453 or 1-877/263-0454. Clean and basic motel with reasonably sized rooms close to the center of town. ❸

Best Western Turquoise Inn & Suites 535 E Main St, Cortez ☎970/565-3778 ⓦwww.cortezbestwestern.com. The smartest option in Cortez itself, with facilities that include a pool. ❺

Budget Host Inn 2040 E Main St, Cortez ☎960/565-3738. Comfortable and well-looked after motel on the way out of town towards Mesa Verde. Facilities include a heated outdoor pool and hot tub; a continental breakfast is included in rates. ❹

Kelly's Place 14663 County Rd G ☎970/565-3125 or 1-800/745-4885, ⓦwww.kellyplace.com. Fine B&B ranch accommodation among the peach orchards of McElmo Canyon, ten miles west of town en route to Hovenweep. All the lodge rooms and cabins are en suite and made very comfortable by the friendly staff, who offer guided hikes of local Ancestral Puebloan ruins, horse rides, and overnight covered wagon trips. ❹

Mesa Verde Motel 191 Railroad Ave, Mancos ☎970/533-7741 or 1-800/825-6372. Comfortable motel with its own restaurant. ❸

Old Mancos Inn 200 W Grand Ave, Mancos ☎970/533-9019. Older inn with some of the cheapest rooms in town. ❸

Rio Grande Southern Hotel 101 S Fifth St, Dolores ☎970/882-7527 or 1-800/258-0434, ⓦwww.riograndesouthernhotel.com. Atmospheric B&B close to the Anasazi Heritage Center in Dolores; rooms are great value, though the cheapest share bathrooms. Closed Dec–Feb. ❸

Eating

Cortez is well geared-up to satisfy the needs of the many visitors that pass through, with several good options for a quick bite, including several Mexican restaurants and eateries.

Dry Dock Restaurant 200 W Main St ☎970/564-9404. Far and away the best restaurant in town, particularly for its great seafood – including fresh oysters – in a pleasant garden setting. Otherwise you'll find steaks, fajitas, and burritos on the menu. Daily 5–10pm.

Earth Song Haven 34 W Main St ☎970/565-9125. Café in a former post office that also serves as a chaotic book and antique store. Great for its all-day breakfasts, coffees, smoothies, and light lunches for around $5. Opens at 7am Mon–Sat, 8am Sun.

Francisca's 125 E Main St ☎970/565-4093. The best place in town for authentic Mexican food at reasonable prices – nothing on the menu is over $10. Consequently it's often packed; if you can't get a table try the similar eatery across the road, which is also great.

Homesteaders 45 E Main St ☎970/565-6253. Old-time Western diner where plates get piled high with a heavy selection of barbecued meals and Mexican fry-ups – most entrees around $8. Closed Sun in winter.

Main Street Brewery 21 E Main St ☎970/564-9112. Slick brewpub with a good range of local ales and even wines, with the usual full menu of bar food. Open until midnight.

Ute Mountain Tribal Park

Abutting Mesa Verde National Park, the **Ute Mountain Indian Reservation** was one of several reservations created when the Victorian-era silver-mining boom pushed the native peoples westward. One part of this reservation, the out-of-the-way **Ute Mountain Tribal Park**, contains a collection of Ancestral Puebloan cliff dwellings that are just as enthralling as Mesa Verde's, but far less accessible or visited. This is probably because the only way to visit them is by joining a Ute-led tour, arranged at the tribe's **visitor center** (April–Oct daily, usually 8am–3pm but hours vary; ☎970/565-3751 or 1-800/847-5485, ⓦwww.utemountainute.com), housed in a former gas station at the intersection of highways 160 and 491. The tour schedule varies according to demand, and although you can theoretically join a tour by turning up at 8.30am, you're much more likely to secure a spot by booking ahead. Both full- (9am–4pm; $42) and half-day (9am–12.30pm; $22) tours are offered; the former is far preferable, because not only does it cover the petroglyphs and potsherd-scattered mounds concealing surface-level pueblos at the base of the cliffs, but it also follows a remote dirt road to several cliff dwellings built at the same time as those at Mesa Verde. These include the eighty-room **Lion House** and the precarious **Eagle's Nest Cliff**, perched in a cavernous natural alcove. It also involves a fair bit of walking and climbing – pack plenty of food and water – and five tall ladders, though only the final two up to Eagle's Nest will bother vertigo sufferers; you can avoid these if you're happy to admire it from below instead. While the tours require you to bring your own (sturdy) vehicle to access the sites, an extra $8 allows up to a dozen visitors to ride in the guide's van, allowing you to both preserve your vehicle and receive a much more detailed commentary. For $12 per vehicle, you can **camp** overnight at a primitive campground close to the main highway.

Four Corners Monument

The only place in the US where four states meet at a single point is at the southeastern end of the Ute Mountain Tribal Park, about 25 miles southwest of Cortez on Hwy-160 and championed by the **Four Corners Monument** (daily: May–Aug 7am–8pm; Sept–April 8am–5pm; $2.50). Here the theoretical corners of Colorado, New Mexico, Arizona, and Utah touch, although the actual land on which the monument stands is part of a Navajo Tribal Park. As little more than the celebration of a series of markings off a bureaucrat's map, the site is understandably bleak and dull. Yet this doesn't deter the steady stream of visitors who ponder the pivotal brass plaque and contort themselves for undignified photos that prove they once simultaneously had a limb in each state. Navajo stalls cash in by selling crafts, trinkets, and fry-bread.

Canyons of the Ancients and Hovenweep National Monuments

The arid lands of the Colorado–Utah border may be scenically desolate, but in archeological terms they are supremely verdant. While the extravagant structures found at Mesa Verde may be absent, the whole area is rich in other Ancestral Puebloan structures. Here the isolated sites that sprout from canyon rims and desert floors are far less spectacular but so abundant that as well as having the highest density of archeological sites in the US, they also contains structures of some consequence, since one distinctive feature here are the tall round towers that are widely believed to have been astronomical observatories. Their remote location and the presence of distant mountains somehow give all the sites a haunting sense of timeless isolation, sharpened by the dearth of visitors. Growing interest in the sites gave rise to the designation of the **Canyons of the Ancients National Monument** (ⓦwww.co.blm.gov/canm) in 2000, and while most of the main structures have probably since been discovered, work remains ongoing and visitors have the chance to join a dig (see p.362).

The first stop on any closer investigation of the area should be the excellent **Anasazi Heritage Center** (daily: March–Oct 9am–5pm; Nov–Feb 9am–4pm; $3; ☎970/882-4811), six miles north of Cortez and three miles west of Dolores.

The center has a magnificent collection of Ancestral Puebloan artifacts, which stems mostly from excavations in an area now drowned by the nearby McPhee Dam – responsible for turning the Dolores River into a broad lake at this point – and includes sandals, blankets, and embroidery, with a reconstructed pit-house helping to give a sense of what life was like. The well-equipped museum also has some hands-on displays, one of which keep kids busy grinding corn. Beside the center is the **Escalante Ruin**, which dates from around 900–1300 AD and which was named for the eighteenth-century Spanish friar who noted the traces of prehistoric Indians here in a 1776 expedition.

The center provides helpful guidance for hiking and biking trips into the nearby National Monument, including updating you on current road conditions for local dirt roads. The most accessible site is off the road from Pleasant View on Hwy-491, fourteen miles northwest of the Heritage Center and Cortez. From here a straight road leads nine miles to the **Lowry Pueblo Ruins** (no fixed hours; free), which is noteworthy as one of the few sites where an Ancestral Puebloan mural remains in place on the walls of a great *kiva*. The mural is removed for preservation in the winter, when damp conditions can make the dirt access road impassable.

The other main sites within the Canyons of the Ancients National Monument are connected by a dusty six-mile trail along **Sand Canyon**, located around fifteen miles west of Cortez along Road G, which leaves Hwy-160 near the airport at the south end of town. Many of the sites here are hard to find, although a few masonry walls – remnants of thirteenth-century single-family dwellings – are easy to spot and explore. The trail is open to mountain bikers as well as hikers.

For the best look at far more extensive remains head further up Road G to the five abandoned villages at **Hovenweep** – which in Ute means "deserted valley" – **National Monument**, 35 miles west of Cortez ($6 per vehicle, or $3 per person). Managed by the NPS, most of this monument is just over the Utah border, while the Colorado portions lie within the Canyons of the Ancients National Monument. The only easy public access is to **Little Ruin Canyon**, which lies just behind the monument's plush **visitor center** (daily: March–Oct 8am–6pm; Nov–Feb 8am–5pm; ☎970/562-4282, ⊛www.nps.gov/hove). A single trail (daily sunrise–sunset) loops around the edge of this shallow cleft and takes about an hour to complete. Along the way is the citadel-like **Stronghold House** and the **Unit-Type House**, where niches in the walls line up with the angle of the sun at the summer and winter solstices. At the head of the canyon, **Hovenweep Castle**, built around 1200AD, is thought to have stood guard over a large pueblo complex gathered on the sandy canyon floor around a perennial spring.

Only **campers** will find somewhere to stay anywhere around Hoveweep, where the 31-site campground ($10; no reservations) stays open year-round.

Joining a dig

It might not be quite like being Indiana Jones for the day, but the chance to join an archeological dig, offered by the **Crow Canyon Archeological Center**, five miles northwest of Cortez at 23390 CO-K, Hwy-491 (☎970/565-8975 or 1-800/422-8975, ⊛www.crowcanyon.org), combines illuminating insight into practical archeology with the excitement of perhaps chancing on some new artifacts. You can join for a day or longer for around $50, and will be helping out with ongoing work at a variety of Ancestral Puebloan sites in the region.

San Juan Skyway

North of Durango, several old Victorian mining towns tucked deep into isolated valleys of the San Juan Mountains are connected by the **San Juan Skyway** (Hwy-550), which passes by some of the most rugged and scenic country in the state and is easily one of Colorado's finest drives. The first stretch north up the Animas River Valley begins tamely, but things heat up as the road passes the ski area of **Durango Mountain Resort** and climbs over Molass Pass – which due to its height and remoteness is said to have the purest air in the US – and into the quaint, slightly ramshackle Victorian town of **Silverton**. From here, the road is known as the **Million Dollar Highway** as it twists and turns its way to **Ouray**, passing abandoned mine workings and rusting machinery along the way. Though this portion of the highway cost a fortune to build – over $1000 dollars a foot at the time – its nickname comes not from the price of its construction but from the gold in the ore-bearing gravel used to make it. Marketers long ago decided that the landscape around Ouray justifies the tag "Little Switzerland," and they're not too far wrong – the valleys in this part of the range are narrow and the peaks high and craggy. So inaccessible is this part of the range that although the year-round resort town of **Telluride** is only around ten miles away as the crow flies, the wall of gunmetal-gray peaks in between forces the road to curve and twist for fifty miles between the two towns. That said, those with courage can nudge a **4WD** vehicle to Telluride via a more direct way on one of the most spectacular off-road routes in an area renowned for its network of tough backroads. Though these routes are also open to **cyclists** and **horseback riders**, the best way to explore this area is on foot. **Hikers** are spoilt for choice in the region, on the doorstep of the **Weminuche Wilderness** and filled with challenging peaks, narrow gorges, forests, and bleak, imposing stretches of high alpine tundra.

Durango Mountain Resort

Formerly called Purgatory, **Durango Mountain Resort** (DMR), 25 miles north of Durango along Hwy-550, has given itself a less daunting name to help build on its solid reputation as a mid-sized, unpretentious, and less expensive alternative to the major Colorado resorts. The small base area recently received a face-lift and new chairlifts and condos are planned, but this modest ski mountain remains decidedly unsophisticated. In the absence of the social cachet or facilities of Telluride, the area overwhelmingly attracts mostly skiers from Texas and the Southwestern states, who enjoy the short lift lines, uncluttered slopes, sunshine – more than any other Colorado resort – and, despite the resort's relatively modest snowfall, generally good snow conditions, with powder days a regularity.

All of DMR is below the tree-line, and while there's little in the way of extreme terrain, most runs are littered with natural bumps and dips producing runs to suit all levels. However, the resort's forte is certainly its high-speed intermediate-level cruising, and even in the absence of a huge amount of acreage or vertical drop, DMR can take a day or two to explore properly. Don't be intimidated by the short, steep rise of the front face as seen from Hwy-550; the fast Purgatory Village Express carries riders over a couple of false summits to a far mellower area of tree-lined greens, rolling, terraced blues, and powdery, bumped-out blacks, a world away from the groomed, steep, racer-style runs visible from the village. There is also an easy way back down to the village: stay to skier's left and ride home on the blues and greens underneath the Twilight lift.

Information ☎970/247-9000 or 1-800/982-6102, ⓦwww.durangomountainresort .com, snow report ☎970/247-9000 ext 1.

Ticket prices and operating times $52, open late Nov to March daily 9am–4pm.

Mountain statistics base elevation 8793ft, summit elevation 10,822ft, vertical drop 2029ft, acreage 1200, average snowfall 260in.

Lifts and trails 11 lifts serve 85 trails: beginner 23 percent, intermediate 51 percent, expert 26 percent.

Accommodation

Despite being primarily a day-use area, there's a fair bit of **accommodation** around DMR, though not much in the way of variety. You might find Durango a handier base, particularly given the competitive off-season rates that can land you a room there for under $30. The two are linked by the Mountain TranSport **ski shuttle** ($5 round-trip; ☎970/247-9000) which runs seven times a day, picking up at motels and hotels en route. Many of Durango's downtown hotels also provide a shuttle service.

Wherever you choose to stay, the best first point of contact for deals and the full selection of local accommodation, including local vacation homes, is **Durango Central Reservations** (☎970/247-8900 or 1-866/294-5187, ⓦwww.durangoreservations.org).

Among DMR's slopeside condo complexes is the giant resort-owned **Purgatory Village Condominium Hotel**, 5 Skier Pl (☎970/385-2100 or 1-800/693-0175, ⓦwww.durangomountainresort.com; ❺) where a wide variety of units – from basic studios with small kitchenettes to larger condos with fuller kitchens – are offered and use of the rooftop hot tubs a definite bonus. Nearby alternatives include the *Inn At Durango Mountain*, 1 Skier Pl (☎970/247-9669 or 1-800/982-6103; ❹), with its range of standard motel units and several independently managed condo complexes a five-minute shuttle ride away. Among these is the family-oriented *Cascade Village* (☎970/259-3500 or 1-800/525-0896; ❽), with a range of lodging options from studios to single-family homes and a restaurant, pool, rental shop, and mountain lodge. The *Hermosa Meadows Camper Park*, 31420 Hwy-550 N #24 (☎970/247-3055 or 1-800/748-2853), is open year-round, with RV spots for $21–30.

Lift tickets, lessons, and rentals

DMR is one of the least expensive resorts in Colorado, and **lift ticket** prices are even better value if you plan ahead. Four- and six-ticket packs are available in the pre-season and in January from local grocery stores (try the City Market in Durango), priced at around $30 per ticket. A useful feature of the Total Adventure ticket is that you can swap a day on the mountain for one of many alternative activities in the program, from soaking in the hot springs to backcountry touring.

Group **lessons** ($35) are scheduled in the morning and afternoon, with specialty clinics held occasionally throughout the season. Including lift ticket and rentals, the $65 "never-ever" packages are good value and guarantee success or free further lessons. Ski lessons are available for kids aged over three, snowboarding from age eight onwards. If you need **day care**, contact Cub Care (☎970/247-9000 ext 5152), who look after kids aged between two months to three years. Based in Purgatory Village, the **Adaptive Sports Association** (☎970/385-2163,

@www.asadurango.org) offers an extensive disabled skier program: lift, lesson, and equipment packages cost $80 and should be booked in advance.

You can get decent **rentals** at the base of the slopes. Purgatory Ski Rentals is the resort's fleet store, while expert skiers should head to Performance Peak for new demos and tuning facilities. Bubba's Boards (packages $28; ☎970/259-7377) is the place to rent snowboards. Choices and prices are slightly better in Durango, where HassleFree Sports – The Boarding Haus, 2615 N Main Ave (7.30am–7pm; ☎970/259-3874), offers ski packages from $13 and step-in beginner board packages from $22.

Mountain runs

Absolute **beginners** will find themselves squeezed into an unexciting meadow area between the highway and Purgatory Village, so will hopefully quickly progress to the more interesting Twilight area, where winding tree-lined greens lie beside flat, easy blues. Confident beginners can then head straight to the summit on Lift 1. From here, cat tracks curve gently back to the base, while the gentle Hermosa Parkway leads to Lift 5.

Almost all the **intermediate** runs at DMR are wide and long, but most feature a series of diversions that prevent them becoming monotonous, including natural bumps and rolls, mellow glades, and mini mogul fields. With most skiers clustering around the front face or in back among the blacks, the terraced blues in between are generally blissfully quiet. Less-experienced intermediates should start on the more gentle runs under Lifts 2 and 3; those with confidence can work up to the thigh-burning intermediate moguls, wide glades, and gentler blacks underneath Lift 8. Particularly fun runs are Boogie and Peace, with their patches of easy trees and the odd mogul field down one side of the trail.

The temptation for **experts** is to head to the far reaches of the resort straight away. A good place to find untracked powder are black-diamond runs like Styx and Lower Hades above the base area. These are among the classic alpine runs found on the steep slopes of the front face, terraced by cat tracks and graced by small aspen groves, the best of which are on **Paul's Park** under the top of Lift 8. The mountain's few cliff drops can be spotted underneath the lower sections of Lifts 3 and 5. Be warned that all three backside lifts close at 3.30pm. Snowboarders in particular do not want to be at the top of Lift 8 at that time, as they'll end up trudging back along the BD&M Expressway ridge – not an expressway by any stretch of the imagination.

DMR's modest **park** and **pipe** are located just below the *Powderhouse* restaurant, where the selection of kickers and rails range from baby on up. Both can be lapped on the creaky, slow Engineer double chair, which runs directly overhead. On busy days, it's often faster to charge around the corner and down to the base area, then head back up the high-speed lift.

Other winter activities

The usual roster of alternative winter activities are offered by the resort: snowmobile trips, dinner sleighrides, a tubing hill (Alpine Snowcoaster; Thurs–Mon 1–8pm; $5 a ride), and snowshoe tours of the San Juan National Forest. More unusual are its **stargazing** sessions ($49), in which a snowcat takes would-be astronomers up the mountain to stare at the heavens through a thirty-inch diameter telescope and keep warm with hot chocolate. All activities can be booked through the Activities Desk (☎970/247-9000) in the ski village.

Groomed **cross-country** trails around DMR are limited: the Nordic Center (☎970/385-2114) opposite the resort has only 10miles of groomed trails (day pass $8.50), but offers lessons, inexpensive rentals, and moonlight tours.

A further 6miles of (free) trails lie out at Vallecito Lake, and are maintained by the Pine River Valley Nordic Ski Club (☎970/247-1573); you'll need to bring your own equipment.

Backcountry Nordic skiers should try to investigate options around Haviland Lake, though plenty exist in the craggy surrounding San Juans for backcountry downhill skiing and boarding. These include spots at Molas and Red Mountain passes, but as avalanche danger is often extremely high, solo missions are not advisable. Stop in at Backcountry Experience, 1205 Camino del Rio (☎970/247-5830) in downtown Durango for advice and equipment. Escorted trips are offered by the **San Juan Skiing Company** (☎970/259-9671 or 1-800/208-1780, ⓦwww.sanjuanski.com), whose **snowcats** operate just behind the resort. Daily rates are $175 but their three-night lodging and skiing packages are much better value.

Eating and drinking
On and around DMR **eating** choices are very limited, with dining trips to Durango – the resort condos run evening trips – or self-catering the norm. The best après spot is *Purgy's*, with its martini bar, outdoor grill, and beer garden. Otherwise the best place to eat is the *Olde Schoolhouse Café & Saloon*, three miles south from the resort at 46778 Hwy-550 (☎970/259-2257), where you can gorge yourself on great pizza and enormous calzones, and wash it all down with locally brewed Ska beer. The main room at the *Olde Schoolhouse* is dominated by the bar, (free) pool table, and cluttered with local memorabilia.

Silverton
Journey's end for the narrow-gauge railroad from Durango (see p.346), **SILVERTON** is one of Colorado's most atmospheric mountain towns, with wide, dirt-paved streets leading off towards the hills on either side of its one main road. The town boomed after the railroad came in 1882, and thanks to the sheer quantity of ore around Silverton – a name said to come from a miner's comment that "there's no gold here, but silver by the ton" – the town fared better than most after the 1893 silver crash. Zinc and copper mining continued until a little more than a decade ago, and while the population has dropped since then, those that remain have so far resisted suggestions that the town's future lies in gambling. They are, however, extremely reliant on the seasonal tourist train, so while the false-fronted stores along "Notorious Blair Street" recall the days when **Wyatt Earp** dealt cards in the Arlington saloon, the town is defined by the restaurants and gift shops that fill up between 11am and 2pm when tourists are deposited in town. From November to March Silverton goes into hibernation, with few visitors and the bulk of businesses closing for the season – although the creation of a new ski area nearby may breathe life into the winter economy here.

Arrival, information, and accommodation
TMN&O buses between Durango and Grand Junction pull into Silverton in front of the *Lunch Box Café*, 1124 Green St. The town's helpful **visitors' center** (daily: 9am–5pm; ☎970/387-5654 or 1-800/752-4494, ⓦwww.silverton.org) is at the southern edge of town at the junction of Greene St and Hwy-550. Although tourism makes Silverton tick, it's pretty quiet here in the evenings, as most visitors are on day-trips via the train. In winter, it's positively dead at most times. There are several USFS **campgrounds** in the area, the most convenient being the free riverside *South Mineral*, around five miles west on Hwy-550 and FR-585.

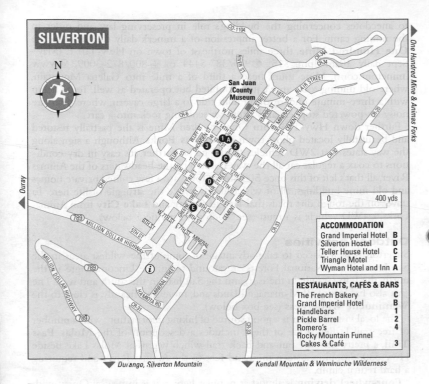

SILVERTON

N

San Juan
County
Museum

One Hundred Mine & Animas Forks

Ouray

0   400 yds

ACCOMMODATION

Grand Imperial Hotel	B
Silverton Hostel	D
Teller House Hotel	C
Triangle Motel	E
Wyman Hotel and Inn	A

RESTAURANTS, CAFÉS & BARS

The French Bakery	C
Grand Imperial Hotel	B
Handlebars	1
Pickle Barrel	2
Romero's	4
Rocky Mountain Funnel Cakes & Café	3

▼ *Durango, Silverton Mountain*   ▼ *Kendall Mountain & Weminuche Wilderness*

Grand Imperial Hotel 1219 Greene St
☏970/387-5527 or 1-800/341-3340. In
the center of town, this grand 1882 hotel has forty
creaky, antique-furnished rooms, each with private
bath, cable TV, and views down the main street or
over the mountains. Rates drop by half between
November and April. **5**

Silverton Hostel 1025 Blair St ☏970/387-0115.
Friendly but thin-walled hostel run by a potter,
whose studio is on the premises. Options include
$13 dorm beds or budget double rooms ($32–42).
Check-in between 8–10am and 4–10pm. Showers
for $3.50.

Teller House Hotel 1250 Greene St ☏970/387-
5423 or 1-800/342-4338. Former miners' boarding
house that now provides Victorian-style guestrooms

in a central location, some with private baths. Non-
smoking. **4**

Triangle Motel 848 Greene St ☏970/387-5780,
ⓦ www.trianglemotel.com. Unappealing but well-
run motel at the south end of town, where rooms
have queen beds and cable TV. Some good-value
two-room suites as well. **3**

Wyman Hotel and Inn 1371 Greene St
☏970/387-5372 or 1-800/609-7845, ⓦ www
.thewyman.com. One of Silverton's finest
establishments features comfortable and elegant
antique-furnished rooms and common areas.
Amenities include gourmet breakfasts, a selection
of six hundred videos, and whirlpool tubs in some
rooms. Non-smoking. **6**

The Town and around

Luckily for those arriving by train and departing a couple of hours later, a
wander around **downtown Silverton**, between colorful false-fronted buildings, is not a time-consuming affair. The bulk of the town's businesses are spread
down the main drag of Greene Street, a block west of Blair Street, where the
steam train arrives. First stop should be the **San Juan County Museum**,
1559 Greene St (daily: June–Aug 9am–5pm; Sept to mid-Oct 10am–3pm;
$3). Housed in the former county jail, the most captivating exhibits relate

Rocky Mountain National Park

National Parks and Monuments

Colorado's National Parks and Monuments are virtually a log book of the state's premium geological features. While the National Parks generally protect entire ecosystems, monuments preserve smaller areas, solitary structures, or archeological sites. The most spectacular of the former is **Rocky Mountain National Park**, a scenic tour de force that holds many of the state's most stunning mountains and valleys. Views from above the tree-line and amid the rocky high-alpine tundra are breathtaking, while easy wildlife-viewing – particularly elk, moose, and deer – is nearly guaranteed further down the mountains.

The scenery in the semi-arid **Sand Dunes National Park** could hardly be more different. The wonderfully incongruous location of these hulking dunes – on the doorstep of the dramatic and virtually impenetrable **Sangre de Cristo Mountains** – is a big part of its appeal; while the scenery over at **Mesa Verde National Park**, in the state's southwest, is unique yet again. Here rolling sagebrush-covered hills harbor a series of complex, well-preserved Native American sites. This insight into a thirteenth-century civilization is not to

Park services

Apart from the natural wonders, what distinguishes all National Parks and Monuments is the high level of **public services** they provide. Roads and trails are well marked and maintained; restrooms are provided at strategic points; and each park has at least one **visitor center**, staffed by rangers on hand to educate visitors and enforce park rules. These visitor centers distribute a range of maps, books, and brochures – many free – and often provide nature walks and educational programs.

Cathedral Rock, Dinosaur National Monument

The Colorado Trail

Colorado's ultimate long-distance backpacking trail, the Colorado Trail runs for 470 miles between Denver and Durango, taking in many of the state's scenic highlights while remaining well off the beaten path along most of its route. The trek is certainly not an easy one, as it follows the Continental Divide for much its way and passes through eight mountain ranges, seven National Forests, six Wilderness Areas, and five river systems. This classic mountain adventure takes at least a month to complete on foot. For books, maps, advice, and information on volunteer opportunities along the trail, contact the Colorado Trail Foundation (Ⓦwww.coloradotrail.org).

be missed, and the mysteries that surround the structures – why were villages built into cliffs? why did the civilization suddenly move on? – create an alluring enigma.

Colorado's most overlooked National Park is undoubtedly **Black Canyon of the Gunnison National Park**, which protects Colorado's mini-Grand Canyon. This deep gorge has depths of up to 2722ft, made more fantastic by the canyon's narrowness all along its length – measuring only 1300ft between the rims at its narrowest point. It takes awhile before the allure of staring into the abyss wears off, and hiking down and back up is an incredible expedition.

Most impressive among them are **Bent's Fort**, a reconstructed adobe trading post; the **Florissant Fossil Beds**, a collection of 35-million-year-old petrified sequoia stumps; the **Colorado National Monument**, with some delicately beautiful desert scenery; and **Dinosaur National Monument**, which got its name from the bewildering number of dinosaur remains found here. The monument is just as impressive, however, for its many scattered petroglyph sites and a glorious canyon.

Wilderness Areas

If it's a wilderness experience you desire, you may find the NPS parks and monuments disappointingly well-developed and, at peak times, overcrowded. Thankfully, if solitude's your goal, there are plenty of excellent protected areas that fall under the umbrella of the Forest Service, in the form of **Wilderness Areas**. The aim here is to preserve the land in its most natural state – commercial activities, motorized vehicles, bicycles, firearms, and pets are prohibited – making it easy to find superb hiking without the strain of overcrowding.

Many of the state's most spectacular Wilderness Areas are at the center of the mountains, particularly in the Sawatch and Elk ranges around Aspen and Crested Butte. The engagingly bleak (and adjacent) **Hunter Frying Pan** and **Collegiate Peaks** wilderness areas are fine examples, as is the rather more popular **Maroon Bells–Snowmass Wilderness**, of which the famed twin red peaks of the Maroon Bells are a part. To the north of these and the I-70 Corridor, at the center of the White River National Forest, lies the **Flat Tops Wilderness**, blessed with a pristine feel, great backpacking trails, and fine wide-open vistas. But perhaps Colorado's wildest, most remote and impressive Wilderness Area of all is the **Weminuche**, which covers a vast and barely penetrable area northwest of Durango. The Weminuche will almost certainly form one of the most memorable legs of any trip along the Colorado Trail (see box).

Picket Wire Canyon

Wildlife

Colorado's wildlife rarely appears on demand but patience and the determination to rise for first light all but guarantee sightings. Keep an eye out, too, when driving around the state – many animals that are generally wary of humans are, oddly enough, more oblivious to cars. What follows is a list of popular Colorado wildlife, and where best to spot them.

- **Bighorn sheep** Sure-footed and limber, bighorns can be seen in Rocky Mountain National Park (see p.142), often in packs at the Bighorn Crossing Zone on Hwy-34.
- **Mountain goats** The rocky tundra above the treeline on Mount Evans (see p.160) is home to a highly visible and extremely tame mountain goat population.
- **Elk** Despite the presence of both the Vail and Aspen ski areas, the 20,000-strong elk population in the White River National Forest (see p.231) always outnumbers the skiers.
- **Moose** These large and mellow beasts are best seen in State Forest State Park, near Walden (see p.207).
- **Wildfowl** Birders should make a beeline for the Arapaho National Wildlife Refuge (see p.207), also near Walden, whose summer population of 8000 ducks doubles in the fall.
- **Bears** The animal most people want to see is one of the hardest to track down – though biking near Durango or hiking up Pikes Peak aren't bad bets (see p.346 & p.290).

National Forests and BLM lands

Wilderness Areas form only a fraction of Colorado's **National Forests**, which means that most of the latter are open to far more liberal use, including by bikes, 4WD vehicles, snowmobiles, and hunters; the right to camp exists nearly everywhere, as well. This sounds as though it could be chaos, but in practice different users rarely get in one another's way. Head to any Forest Service office and the rangers can suggest a number of good spots for any activity you have in mind. The **Roosevelt National Forest** – which is wrapped almost all around Rocky Mountain National Park – is one of the best, both for its many quiet and scenic spots and its accessibility from Boulder and Fort Collins.

Fishing in the Northern Mountains

The state's other large land agency is the **Bureau of Land Management**, which administers gigantic swathes of land – much of it considered relatively worthless desert. BLM lands generally have even fewer restrictions than National Forests, leading to a liberating free-for-all, with most areas open for unrestricted hiking, biking, camping, and motorized vehicles. In some places, like **Fruita**, near Grand Junction, locals have even been allowed (with careful BLM supervision) to carve their own mountain-bike and quad-bike trails.

take a tour with San Juan Backcountry, 1121 Greene St (☎970/387-5565 or 1-800/494-8687, ⓦwww.sanjuanbackcountry.com), who charge $40 per person for two-hour tours. Four-wheeling combined with backcountry camping is also offered for $150 per person per night.

In winter the big draw is the single chairlift up rugged **Silverton Mountain** (☎970/387-5706, ⓦwww.silvertonmountain.com; lift ticket $99). Opened in 2001, this is Colorado's newest and most innovative experts-only ski area. This double-diamond wonderland has no lodge, no liftlines, and no groomed runs – just excellent backcountry skiing in 1600 acres of steeps, glades, and chutes, where fresh tracks in the annual 425 inches of snow are the norm, but with the considerable added bonus of avalanche control and uphill transportation. All skiers and riders explore in groups of six to ten and are accompanied by guides, limiting tickets to forty per day. An avalanche beacon, probe, shovel, and suitable backpack are required (available to rent for $15).

The other skiing opportunities in town remain much flatter, with many good backcountry **cross-county skiing** possibilities (rental equipment available at the *French Bakery*; see below). The town also maintains a free **ice rink**, with skate rental available – oddly enough – at the public library.

Eating and drinking

The selection of places **to eat** in Silverton varies markedly depending on what time of day – and year – you turn up. Summer lunchtimes see the largest choice as many places shutter up when the train leaves town (ie, in the evening) and close completely in winter. **Nightlife** is limited to occasional live music at *Handlebars* (see below), drinking and shooting pool at the spit-and-sawdust *Miners Tavern*, 1069 Greene St, and a mixed bag of theater performances at the **Miners Union Theater**, also at 1069 Greene (July–Sept; ☎970/387-5337).

The French Bakery 1250 Greene St ☎970/387-5976. Part of the *Teller House Hotel*, this bakery serves good omelettes, sandwiches, and soups through to full meals. Its location near the train depot means it's generally packed at lunch. Closed Nov–Feb.

Grand Imperial Hotel 1219 Greene St ☎970/387-5527. Well-known as having the best buffet breakfast, for only $7 and with many cooked options; it's served from 7am and is available to non-guests. You can also pick up sliced burgers and sandwiches here later in the day, or full meals – including pepper-stuffed chipotle steaks ($17) – in the evening.

Handlebars 117 13th St ☎970/387-5395. Atmospheric restaurant and saloon covered in hundreds of antiques and curios, ranging from old wooden skis to musty mooseheads. The menu ranges from regular bar grub to more lavish dinner entrees, including breaded and fried Rocky Mountain oysters from $8. Closed Nov–Feb.

Pickle Barrel 1304 Greene St ☎970/387-5713. Located in an all-wood former general store, the *Pickle Barrel* serves good sandwiches for lunch and more substantial entrees like steak and trout for dinner.

Rocky Mountain Funnel Cakes & Café 1249 Greene St ☎970/387-5450. Jolly little low-priced café that offers the best possible introduction to funnel cakes (big puffy pancakes), with an exhaustive array of options from simple icing sugar to a full Mexican version with beans and guacamole.

Romero's 1151 Greene St ☎970/387-0123. An enjoyable Mexican cantina with tasty, authentic food and fantastic salsa. Prices start from around $8 for entrees.

Ouray

From Silverton, the Million Dollar Highway (Hwy-550) climbs a series of switchbacks past ruins of mines and mills, cresting the aptly named Red Mountain Pass (11,018ft) – where the bare rock beneath the snow really is red – before twisting down into **OURAY**, 23 miles to the north. Beautifully situated in a natural amphitheater-like box canyon 5000ft below surrounding

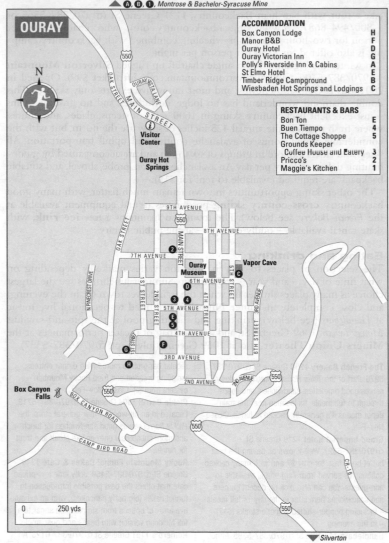

OURAY

N

ACCOMMODATION

Box Canyon Lodge	H
Manor B&B	F
Ouray Hotel	D
Ouray Victorian Inn	G
Polly's Riverside Inn & Cabins	A
St Elmo Hotel	E
Timber Ridge Campground	B
Wiesbaden Hot Springs and Lodgings	C

RESTAURANTS & BARS

Bon Ton	E
Buen Tiempo	4
The Cottage Shoppe	5
Grounds Keeper Coffee House and Eatery	3
Pricco's	2
Maggie's Kitchen	1

Visitor Center

Ouray Hot Springs

Ouray Museum

Vapor Cave

Box Canyon Falls

Box Canyon Road

Camp Bird Road

0   250 yds

▼ *Silverton*

peaks, Ouray began life in the early 1880s as a booming silver town, but was saved after the silver-market crash by the discovery of gold in 1896, allowing the economy here to hum on along.

Unlike its closest neighbors, Ouray has not developed tourism based on either skiing or a railroad. Instead the town has concentrated, since Victorian times, on promoting its hot springs, nowadays along with a furious promotion of **four-wheel driving** on the numerous local rough mountain tracks. Ouray also takes its self-proclaimed status as the Switzerland of America rather seriously, constructing a huge **ice-climbing** wall in a narrow gorge near town every winter.

Arrival, information, and accommodation

Daily TNM&O buses between Durango and Montrose (☎970/249-6873) stop in Ouray (note that there's no official, permanent bus stop). The **visitor center** (daily 8am–6pm; closed Mon & Tues in winter; ☎970/325-4746 or 1-800/228-1876, ⓦwww.ouraycolorado.com), beside the hot springs on the north side of town, publishes the useful *Ouray County Vacation Guide*, which includes a map of 4WD routes in the area. For detailed information on local National Forests, contact the Montrose **Public Lands Office**, 2505 S Townsend (☎970/249-3711).

From the campgrounds and motels on the outskirts to pricey B&Bs downtown, there are quite a few places **to stay** in Ouray. Those establishments that stay open in the winter usually offer not only a substantial discount, but most of the time can also provide half-price lift tickets for Telluride. Of the nearby **campgrounds**, the *Amphitheater Campground* (☎970/249-3711 or 1-800/280-2267), around a mile from its signpost on Hwy-550 at the southern end of town, is one of the most picturesque, perched an almost vertical 700ft above Ouray and offering thirty primitive sites ($14). In town, you can pitch a tent for $16 at *4J+1+1*, 709 Oak St (mid-May to mid-Oct; ☎970/325-4418).

Box Canyon Lodge 45 3rd Ave ☎970/325-4981 or 1-800/327-5080, ⓦwww.boxcanyonouray.com. Mid-range motel in an Alpine-style timber building below Box Canyon Falls Park, where you can bathe in cask-like hot tubs. ❸

Manor B&B 317 2nd St ☎970/325-0207 or 1-800/628-6946, ⓦwww.ouraymanor.com. Renovated three-story 1890 Victorian home, where each room is decorated with an Old West theme – most with private baths and mountain views. There's a hot tub in the gardens and a full breakfast is served daily. ❻

Ouray Hotel 303 6th Ave ☎970/325-0500 or 1-800/216-8779. Grand, central Victorian property with straightforward, comfortable, private-bath hotel rooms, ranging from dark economy rooms to spacious suites. Open May–Oct. ❸

Ouray Victorian Inn 50 3rd Ave ☎970/325-4064 or 1-800/864-8729, ⓦwww.ouraylodging.com. Quality motel rooms that are the lodging of choice for winter ice-climbers – for whom rates are slashed by half (and a free breakfast included) by the friendly manager, who lives to ice-climb. ❻

Polly's Riverside Inn & Cabins 1805 N Main St ☎970/325-4061 or 1-800/432-4170, ⓦwww.ourayriversideinn.com. Large modern property on the northern edge of town near the Ouray Hot Springs, with a wide variety of accommodations – from tiny, basic cabins without running water to pricey and expansive suites. ❸

St Elmo Hotel 426 Main St ☎970/325-4951, ⓦwww.stelmohotel.com. Luxurious B&B on the main drag and home to its own venerable, high-class restaurant. Inside, it's a harmonious combination of polished wood, brass period furnishings, and stained glass, while all rooms are finely decorated and en suite. Outdoor hot tub as well. ❻

Wiesbaden Hot Springs and Lodgings 625 5th St ☎970/325-4347, ⓦwww.wiesbadenhotsprings.com. Small spa hotel with its own private hot springs-fed outdoor pool, a hot tub, and some dingy but atmospheric underground vapor caves. The elegant rooms come in a variety of shapes and sizes; some are suites and some have kitchens. ❻

Downtown and around

As with many former mining towns dotting the San Juans, Ouray's small **downtown** area is lined with grand Victorian structures, built with the spoils of silver and gold mining – an industry detailed in the **Ouray County Historical Society Museum**, 20 6th Ave (May–Oct Mon–Sat 10am–4pm; Nov–April Mon–Fri 1–4pm; $5; ☎970/325-4576, ⓦwww.ouraycountyhistoricalsociety.org). A more interesting choice, however, are the hourly mine tours of the **Bachelor-Syracuse Mine**, 1222 CO-14 (late May to mid-Sept daily 9am–6pm; $12; ☎970/325-4500 or 1-888/227-4585, ⓦwww.bachelorsyracuse.com), located two miles northeast of town via Hwy-550 and CR-14. The tours head 3350ft into a chilly hillside, from which gold, silver, lead, zinc, and copper were once extracted.

△ Ouray

What helps set Ouray apart from the other mining towns, though, are its famed **hot springs**. There are several options in the area, the largest of which is **Ouray Hot Springs** (daily: June–Aug 10am–10pm; Sept–May noon–9pm; $7; ☎970/325-4638), beside the Uncompahgre River at the north end of town. The complex contains a large swimming pool and smaller soaking pool, but has a rather institutional feel. Much more intimate and unique are the facilities offered by the **Wiesbaden Vapor Cave**, on the east side of town at 625 5th St (daily 8am–9.45pm; $10; ☎970/325-4347). Run by a hotel (see p.371), non-guests can pay for use of the vapor cave (a steam room in a roughly hewn underground cave) and pool, as well as for a massage or mud wraps. Another slightly unconventional soaking option is available at the Orvis Hot Springs near Ridgway (see opposite).

Outdoor activities

Traditionally Ouray's major outdoor attraction has been **Box Canyon Falls Park** (daily 8am–8pm; $3), a mile south of town. As in Victorian times, visitors come to walk up a 500ft trail, partly along a swaying wooden parapet, that leads into a dark and narrow box canyon. At the far end, falls thunder 300 feet through a tiny cleft in the mountain, and a clamber up rocks to the lip of the canyon allows visitors to stand high above them on an unstable-looking steel suspension footbridge. With the creation of the **Ouray Ice Park** (free; ⓦwww .ourayicepark.com) in 1995, winters in the canyon also allow visitors to court vertigo. The attraction began with the eccentric idea to set sprinklers on the edges of a narrow crevasse in the canyon, spraying water down the walls and creating sheets of ice a hundred feet tall and half a mile long. Ice-climbers now swarm here to strike their way up the walls, particularly during the **Ouray Ice Festival**, held over the third weekend in January.

With so many trails and mining roads in the area, mountain bikers and hikers are well served. For a mellow ride exploring the Uncompahgre River Valley, head ten miles to Ridgway along CO-17. Largely devoid of traffic, this road parallels Hwy-550 along an old Rio Grande Southern Railroad bed and is so flat that it makes absorbing the surrounding scenery positively relaxing. If you'd like to expend even less energy, San Juan Mountain Outfitters, 2882 CO-23 (☎970/626-5659), run a variety of half- to multi-day **horseback riding** trips.

Four-wheeling

More than anywhere else in the San Juans, the Ouray area is known for its plethora of great **jeeping** roads, running along steep cliffsides and through old mining camps. One of the easier popular local drives is to **Yankee Boy Basin**. The route starts at Camp Bird Road south of Ouray and heads alongside Canyon Creek to Camp Bird Mine, then eastward through flowering meadows. A number of other popular jeep roads head over passes to Telluride. More experienced drivers will enjoy the harder but very scenic **Imogene Pass** to Telluride via the abandoned Tomboy Mine and the remains of a guard station used during some of Telluride's labor-management conflicts. But it's the heart-stopping **Black Bear Pass** that's the most famous local drive. Not only does it include the insanely steep, uneven "staircase" section, it also drops into Telluride on far and away the most memorable route, where suddenly the town appears cradled in the bowl of surrounding mountains far below. Colorado West Tours, 701 Main St (☎970/325-4014 or 1-800/648-5337, ⓦwww.coloradowesttours .com), is one of a number of operators in Ouray that runs 4WD tours (May–Oct); prices begin at $60 for a half-day. They also rent to those with their own vehicle insurance ($135/day, $25/hr). You'll find similar rates at the **Polly's Riverside Inn** (see p.371), who have a fleet of modern jeeps and are one of the few places in town to welcome those who don't have their own insurance.

For **rental equipment**, Ouray Mountain Sports, 722 Main St (☎970/325-4284), is the place to go. In winter they hire out cross-country skis and ice-climbing gear, and in summer they switch over to mountain bikes.

Eating and drinking

Bon Ton in the *St Elmo Hotel*, 426 Main St ☎970/325-4951. Accomplished Northern Italian food served up in the hotel's atmospheric redbrick basement. At $7, the great Sunday brunch is an unmissable deal; otherwise *Bon Ton*'s an expensive choice.

Buen Tiempo 515 Main St ☎970/325-4544. Good range of Southwestern and Mexican food – spinach enchiladas and chili-rubbed prime rib – and a dozen varieties of margarita, served in a lively restaurant where dexterous bartenders have stuck hundreds of dollar bills on the high ceiling.

The Cottage Shoppe 400 Main St. Heavenly homemade ice cream and frozen yogurt, plus a few tasty focaccias sandwiches ($6), good for a light lunch.

Grounds Keeper Coffee House and Eatery 524 Main St ☎970/325-0550. Central café serving espresso drinks and healthy light lunches, including a fine veggie lasagna.

Pricco's 736 Main St ☎970/325-4040. Long-standing moderately priced local favorite with a menu that features steaks, salads, hoagies, and spicy Santa Fe-style chicken, along with some veggie options, too.

Maggie's Kitchen 1700 N Main St ☎970/325-4523. This slice of Americana, in the campground behind the Texaco gas station at north end of town near the hot springs, is good for slap-up diner food, particularly breakfasts – $2 buys a short stack of pancakes, $5 a delicious huevos rancheros. Open May to mid–Oct.

Ridgway

Though only ten miles north of the craggy alpine scenery of Ouray, the red rocks and sparse sagebrush around **RIDGWAY** seem a world apart. The broad ranching valley in which the town sits is almost universally flat, and while the area has attracted the rich and famous – Ralph Lauren has a ranch nearby – it's really best used as a cheap jumping-off point to both Telluride and Ouray. Visitors staying here in winter qualify for half-price lift passes at Telluride, forty miles away, and have the added bonus of being able to soak slope-weary bones at the town's only attraction of note, the friendly and vaguely bohemian **Orvis**

Hot Springs ($12; ☎970/626-5324). Located a couple of miles south of town on Hwy-550, this pretty collection of pools, sauna, and private indoor hot tubs is among the best hot springs facilities in the state thanks to the fantastic views of surrounding mountains and the night sky. The atmosphere is generally chilled-out, although the clothing-optional policy may not be to everyone's taste.

In summer, **campers** can stay at the nearby lakeside **Ridgway State Park** ($4 day-use fee, campsites $12–16), a popular place for trout fishing. In town there's a dependable *Super 8 Motel* (☎970/626-5444 or 1-800/368-5444; ❹) with pool and hot tub, while a good hotel option is the *Chipeta Sun Lodge* (☎970/626-3737 or 1-800/633-5868, ❻www.chipeta.com; ❻), an adobe-style building with good views and rustic, Southwestern-style rooms. Big, creative breakfasts are served here, and a solarium and hot tub inside the third-floor's turret are an added bonus. One of the small number of places to **eat** in town is the *True Grit Café*, 123 N Lena St (☎970/626-5739), where burgers and sandwiches are served amid stacks of John Wayne memorabilia – his movie *True Grit* was filmed around these parts back in the late 1960s.

Telluride

Cradled by the flat base of a bowl of vast steep-sided mountains, **TELLURIDE** lies in one of the most picturesque valleys in the Rockies, one that's reminiscent of the Alps in both natural beauty and dramatic terrain. Beginning as a mining village, settlement in Telluride started to take off from 1875, even though Ute ownership of surrounding lowlands forced prospectors over high mountain passes. In the 1880s, Telluride was briefly home to the young **Butch Cassidy**, who robbed his first bank here in 1889, though the town didn't really develop until the following year, when the Grand Southern Railroad pulled into town. Telluride quickly grew to over 5000 people, but was still considered so far off the beaten track that the train's conductors traditionally yelled "to-hell-you-ride" on arrival into town. By 1930, though, all the mines had closed and the town's population was down to 512. The town seemed destined for oblivion until 1968, when a Californian investor began developing the surrounding slopes and the town's reputation as a great **ski area** was launched – albeit only for the committed, since it remained hard to get to. The building of a local airport changed all that, and these days Telluride rivals Aspen as the prime winter destination for the stars – and one that has become too expensive for many locals to continue to live in. Like Aspen, Telluride also puts on a supremely successful program of summer-season **festivals** that, together with the array of good hiking and biking trails, has turned the town into a strong year-round destination. Thankfully, the town remains a laid-back place, and both the town's Victorian core and overall off-beat but cool vibe have been preserved.

Arrival and information

The **Telluride Airport**, five miles east of town, handles a large amount of traffic, with daily services from Denver and frequent flights from Phoenix, Chicago, Houston, and Newark. The **Telluride Express-Airport Shuttle Service** (☎970/728-6000) meets flights from the airport for the short ride into town.

The **visitor center** is beside the highway into town at 666 W Colorado Ave (daily: summer 9am–7pm; winter 9am–5pm; ☎970/728-3041 or 1-800/525-3455, ❻www.visittelluride.com). **Parking** can be hard to find in town, so use

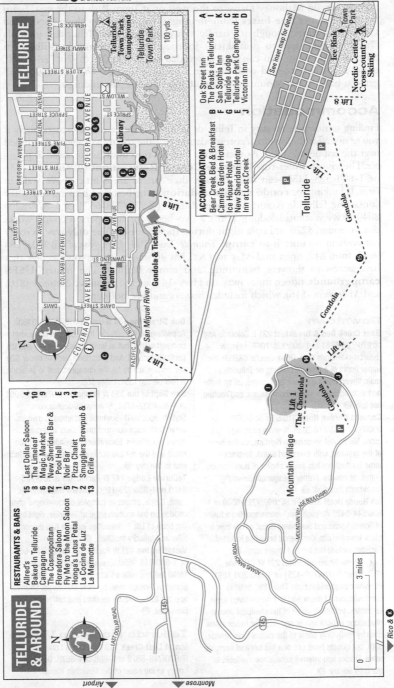

the free lots on Mahoney Drive to the west or at Town Park to the east. From the visitor center **free buses** (7am–midnight) run on a loop along Pacific and Colorado avenues, though it's hardly slower to just walk. Telluride's gondola (7am–midnight; free to non-skiers) journeys to the **Mountain Village** in thirteen minutes, or you can take a free dial-a-ride shuttle (☎970/728-8888), useful if you're burdened with luggage. The Tipsy Taxi (☎970/728-9606) will get you back to the Mountain Village if you stay out past midnight.

Accommodation

Finding somewhere **to stay** in Telluride is nearly always a struggle, particularly if you're not after the condo accommodation that the town has eagerly developed over the last decade or so. As such, your best bet is to book as far ahead as possible. The visitor center-run **Telluride Central Reservations** (☎970/728-4431 or 1-800/525-3455) can help, though their prices are a little above walk-in rates. If looking for **condo accommodation** – the best deal if in a group – try contacting Telluride Resort Accommodations (☎970/728-6621 or 1-877/826-8040, ⊛www.telluridelodging.com); a two-bedroom, four-person condo works out to around $220 and up a night during the ski season. The only way to really cut costs in summer is to **camp**: *Telluride Town Park Campground* (☎970/728-9645; from $12; open mid-May to Oct) has 40 sites near the town center that have access to showers, swimming, and tennis facilities. The nearest **USFS campgrounds**, fifteen miles away on Hwy-145, are the primitive *Sunshine* ($10) and *Matterhorn* ($16), which include showers and RV hookups.

Downtown

Bear Creek Bed & Breakfast 221 E Colorado Ave ☎970/728-6681 or 1-800/338-7064, ⊛www.bearcreektelluride.com. Good, central B&B on the upper floors of a modern building on Telluride's main street, offering a variety of rooms, all en suite and with access to steam room, sauna, and rooftop hot tub. ⑤

Camel's Garden Hotel 310 S Fir St ☎970/728-9300 or 1-888/772-2635, ⊛www.camelsgarden.com. Minimalist modernism right beside the base of the gondola, with oversized baths, fireplaces, large outdoor hot tub, and a choice of hotel rooms, suites, or condos. Rather meager continental breakfasts included. ⑧

Ice House Hotel 310 S Fir St ☎970/728-6300 or 1-800/544-3436. Average hotel rooms sporting a fusion of Scandinavian and Southwest decor, a little over a block from the lifts. Continental breakfast included. Facilities include hot tub and steam room. ⑥

New Sheridan Hotel 231 W Colorado Ave ☎970/728-4351 or 1-800/200-1891, ⊛www.newsheridan.com. This 1895 hotel is filled with period decor and is a much-loved town landmark, yet offers some of the cheapest accommodations in both winter and summer (when rates drop by half). Only some of the rooms have private bath, but guests have use of a hot tub and exercise room. Drinks and Internet access are available in the cozy library. ⑤

Oak Street Inn 134 N Oak St ☎970/728-3383. Appealing on the outside, this hostel is somewhat decrepit within, but at least there's a sauna and it's centrally located. And with dorm beds at under $20 per person, it's by far the cheapest deal in Telluride. A two-person room costs $58.

San Sophia Inn 330 W Pacific St ☎970/728-3001 or 1-800/537-4781, ⊛www.sansophia.com. Stylish, upscale B&B whose enthusiastic owners serve both huge gourmet breakfasts and great après-ski snacks. Each room is wonderfully decorated and the hot tub out back makes for a perfect end to the day. ⑧

Telluride Lodge 747 W Pacific Ave ☎970/728-4400 or 1-888/728-1950, ⊛www.telluridelodge.com. Large, attractive complex of townhome-style condos on the eastern edge of Telluride, right by the base of Lift 7; amenities include two indoor tubs and laundry facilities. ⑦

Victorian Inn 401 W Pacific Ave ☎970/728-6601 or 1-800/611-9893, ⊛www.tellurideinn.com. Motel lodging with a Victorian veneer; it's overpriced yet inexpensive by local standards. Sauna and hot tub available, muffins and coffee for breakfast. ⑥

Telluride Mountain Village

Inn at Lost Creek 119 Lost Creek Lane ☎970/728-5678 or 1-888/601-5678. Boutique luxury in the heart of the Mountain Village.

No room is the same, though all have fireplaces, deluxe kitchenettes with dining tables, TVs, video and CD libraries, and washer/dryers. There are two rooftop hot tubs. Lodging-and lift packages offered online. ⑧

The Peaks at Telluride 136 Country Club Drive ℡970/728-6800 or 1-800/789-2220. Large resort and spa development on the mountain side of town. Ski in and out in winter, play golf just beside it in summer, and avail yourself of over 50 different spa treatments year-round. The excellent facilities include an extensive fitness center with pools and hot tubs, tennis courts, racquetball, and even a climbing wall. ⑧

Dolores Valley

Dunton Hot Springs Dolores ℡970/882-4800, ⓦwww.duntonhotsprings.com. Located just over an hour's drive southwest of Telluride, this nineteenth-century ghost town has been restored into a luxurious rustic retreat, complete with saloon, library, bank, and a bathhouse fed by natural springs. Helitrax (see p.378) offers a pick-up service to guests staying here. ⑨

Downtown and Telluride Mountain Village

Thankfully, despite the influx of chic, Telluride has not lost all of its old-time character: the wide main street, a National Historic District, has low-slung buildings on either side and is still surrounded by gingerbread-style Victorian homes. For a detailed tour of the historic center of Telluride, largely scattered along West Colorado Avenue, it's worth following the walking **tour** printed in *Telluride* magazine, available from the town's visitor center. This guide is no real substitute, however, for joining a **guided** walking tour, run by Historic Tours of Telluride (June–Sept daily 10am; $10; ℡970/728-6639), These begin from Elk's Park, and include a look at some of the town's less obvious historic landmarks. The **San Miguel County Historical Museum**, 317 N First St (Tues–Sat 11am–5pm, Sun 1pm–5pm; $5; ℡970/728-3344, ⓦwww.telluridemuseum.com), is Telluride's modest local museum, which recalls the days when the town had 26 saloons and twelve brothels, and miners sledded down from the mines on their shovels in winter.

The bulk of the ski-related developments at **Telluride Mountain Village** are hidden on the other side of a 2000ft-high mountain ridge. Mountain Village and Telluride proper are connected to one another by a gondola (May to mid-October & mid-Nov to March; free) which heads up one side of the ridge and then down the other – the two are three miles away by road. Though many ski runs descend into Telluride itself, the Mountain Village – a collection of million-dollar homes, all-inclusive resorts and condos, and its own golf course – is really the heart of the ski area.

Winter activities

With a series of awesome black-mogul fields looming over town, it's easy to see what the main local **winter activity** is in Telluride – but the ski area is only one of a number of options. Further skiing opportunities abound, with a **cross-country** center in the valley and many good **backcountry** spots in the mountains; the most exciting terrain is served by the state's only **heli-skiing** operation.

Other activities on offer include dogsledding with Winter Moon Sled Dog Tours (℡970/729-0058); snowmobiling with Telluride Snowmobile Adventures (℡970/728-4475), who take riders to the ghost town of Alta or Dunton Hot Springs; and horseback riding with Telluride Horseback (℡970/728-9611). Sleigh rides, snowbiking, tubing, ballooning, paragliding, ice-climbing, fly-fishing, and trips to Ouray Hot Springs are also available and can be booked through Telluride Visitor Services (℡970/728-4431 or 1-800/525-3455). In town, the Nordic Center (see p.378) rents **ice skates** for use on Town Park's rink, which stays open into the night for skating, hockey, and broomball.

Cross-country skiing and snowshoeing

Cross-country skiers visiting town are well served both around Telluride and in the Mountain Village by the 25miles of free tracks maintained by the **Telluride Nordic Center** (☎970/728-1144), located at the east end of Town Park, who also offer affordable rentals. Intermediate and advanced trails lead from the top of Lift 10 on the mountain to the ghost town of Alta. Otherwise the fairytale Faraway Ranch (☎970/728-9386) runs cross-country and snowshoeing tours and lessons on their groomers and in the Uncompahgre National Forest. But the best deal for **snowshoers** are the free nature walks offered by the local Forest Service; you'll need to rent snowshoes in advance from one of the Telluride Sports stores (see opposite). More adventurous Nordic skiers and snowshoers should try overnight trips to cabins in the **San Juan Hut System**.

Backcountry skiing

The jagged peaks of the San Juans are a magnet for **backcountry** purists, who liken the region's above-treeline slopes to off-piste descents in the Alps. Open bowls sweep off the backside of the ski area, and the resort maintains backcountry access gates – though be sure to get a backcountry update from the ski patrol before you head out.

Further excellent backcountry opportunities lie off Palmyra Peak and in the surrounding San Juans – but be warned that due to steep inclines and fluctuating temperatures, the snowpack here is among the most unstable in the country, and so is effectively open only to those with extensive experience, equipment, and local knowledge. With this in mind, the best option for out-of-towners is a heli-skiing trip with **Helitrax**, 121 W Colorado Ave (☎970/728-8377 or 1-866/435-4754, ⓦwww.helitrax.net). This highly experienced outfit charges relatively low rates by heli-skiing standards; $800 buys you five runs, or about ten to twelve thousand vertical feet of skiing or riding.

△ Ski lift over Telluride

Telluride Ski Area

With an awesome vertical drop of 3552ft and terrain that begins to rival the Alps for scenic beauty, **Telluride Ski Area** is one Colorado's most exciting and dramatic places to ski or ride. As with most other resorts in the state, it gets plenty of light, dry powder to cover its varied slopes, which range from supremely demanding double black diamonds with massive bumps on the **town side** of the mountain, to the mixture of mellower terrain on the **resort side**. Though slightly tamed over the last few years to make more terrain available to intermediate riders, it remains one of Colorado's toughest mountains.

Navigation can be a little awkward, with several lift rides often necessary to work from one end of the resort to the other. The mountain's complexity also extends to the grading of its runs. The usual three categories – green, blue, and black – have been subdivided into single (easier) or double (more advanced) levels of difficulty. This can be useful in finding the right kind of terrain, but note that many of the grades here tend to underrate the difficulty: advanced blues in Telluride could easily rate as blacks at some other resorts.

Lift tickets, lessons, and rentals

Lift tickets are pricey and deals are rare, so lift-and-lodging packages are invariably the best bet for discounts. In high season, classes at Telluride's **ski school** (☏970/728-7507 or 1-800/801-4832) are only available in full-day format, making it a little pricey ($109). Beginner lift, lesson, and rental packages start at $95. Women's weekends and weekend telemark clinics are also available. The Telluride Adaptive Ski Program (TASP; ☏970/728-7537, Ⓦwww.tellurideadaptivesports.org), located in the base of the Mountain Village gondola, offers skiers with **disabilities** equipment rentals, ski buddy and guide services, half-price lift tickets, and full lesson/lift ticket/equipment programs. For day care information and reservations call ☏1-800/801-4832.

Rental gear in Telluride is generally pricey. Telluride Sports is the main outlet, with six locations around town and in the Mountain Village. Snowshoes, cross-country skis, and clothing are also available to rent. Paragon (☏970/728-4525, Ⓦwww.paragontelluride.com) is the local's favorite, with stores at 213 W Colorado Ave, 236 S Oak St, and in the Granita Building in Mountain Village. They also rent snowshoes and Nordic skis. Easy Rider, 200 W Colorado Ave (☏970/728-4734), has board demos as rentals; for more basic packages Slopestyle (☏970/728-9889 or 1-888/7433-321, Ⓦwww.slopestyle.com), at 236 W Colorado Ave and in the *Franz Klammer Lodge* in the Mountain Village, is your best bet.

Mountain runs

Beginners have a huge practice area below Mountain Village, where the wide rolling Meadows are ideal for learning. From here, skiers can progress up Lift

---

Telluride Ski Area

Information ☏970/728-6900 or 1-866/287-5015, Ⓦwww.tellurideskiresort.com, snow report ☏970/728-7425.

Ticket prices and operating times $76, late-Nov to March daily 9am–4pm.

Mountain statistics base elevation 8725ft, summit elevation 12,260ft, vertical drop 3552ft, acreage 1700, average snowfall 309in.

Lifts and trails 16 lifts serve 84 trails: beginner 24 percent, intermediate 38 percent, expert 38 percent.

10 to long, slow cruisers that weave past the gargantuan homes of Telluride's wealthy. Lift 10 is also the easiest way to get to Ute Park, the beginner area in Prospect Bowl. Snowboarders should, however, avoid both Ute Park and the flat and long Lift 10 runs and instead progress from the Meadows to the mellow blues under Lift 4 – avoiding Boomerang and Cake Walk – which flatten halfway down.

Intermediates will find few long cruisers and progression onto the tough blacks difficult, but at least the presence of moguls on even gentler slopes makes it a great place to build bump skills. Start on the easier blues under Lift 4 by the Mountain Village or take Lift 9 to the lower part of See Forever. Named for its panoramic views over the San Juans, See Forever is almost three miles long and easily the best cruiser on the mountain (its upper part is simply a long, flat cat track). Work back to the Palmyra 5 for short powder and mellow mogul runs and then head to the blue rollercoaster dips, bumps, and simple glades of Prospect Bowl under the Prospect 12 chair. On the front face, there's a choice of the exceptionally hard blue Lookout or a winding cat track; unless you want to work on steeps or feel a compulsion to ski the entire mountain, skip both.

Telluride regularly humbles **experts** who've become complacent in their abilities. Many runs, like the incredibly steep Plunge and Spiral Staircase, are dotted with gigantic moguls that challenge even the most advanced skiers and boarders. Thankfully half of many of these runs are split-groomed, with at least one side of the piste flattened to provide an easier way down. Scanning bump runs from the lifts is also helpful; most have tighter moguls down the center and easier lines at their edges. For tree runs try the mellow and widely spaced front face glades. For tighter trees and short bump runs, drop in almost anywhere off the See Forever cat track onto the Mountain Village side, accessible from the Apex 6 or Gold Hill 14. Some of the best freeriding on the mountain is on Gold Hill, where steeps, chutes, cliffs, trees, and lots of powder caches are sure to entertain.

Telluride's Surge Air Garden **terrain park** is well developed, providing both large and small hits and rails, enabling easy progression as your skills develop. Outside the park, the glades on the front face make natural playgrounds and the East and West Drains are both pipe-like gullies.

Summer activities

By June much of the snow on the surrounding mountains has melted, leaving behind flower-covered slopes, high alpine ridges, and trails that draw outdoor enthusiasts of all stripes. Some of the finest **hiking** options are around the 10,500ft ridges in the ski area, accessed via the free gondola. One of the finest excursions away from the resort area is the three-mile round-trip hike to 365ft **Bridal Veil Falls** – the largest in Colorado. To reach the trailhead, follow Colorado Avenue west to where it ends at Pioneer Mill. Other good short hikes include the 1000ft trek up Bear Creek Canyon to a multi-tiered waterfall; follow Pine Street south to the trailhead and the half-mile return trip to Cornet Falls from the north end of Aspen Street; this is also the beginning of the 2.7-mile Jud Wiebe trail, which loops back to town and is a local favorite.

Mountain bikers can also use the gondola for free and there are a variety of trails leading back down either side of the mountain, including some challenging and rocky single-track runs cutting through beautiful stands of aspens on the Mountain Village side. The ultimate local ride is the route over to Moab using the San Juan Hut System. For details of other routes stop by Telluride Sports, 150 W Colorado Ave (☎970/728-4477), where day-rentals run around $30 for a front-suspension bike.

Telluride stands apart from most ski resorts in having an off-season program of worthwhile **festivals** that actually draw crowds from both near and far. Highlights include:

Bluegrass Festival ☎303/823-0848 or 1-800/624-2422, ⓦwww.bluegrass.com. This four-day festival in late June attracts around 10,000 visitors for big-name bluegrass acts. A ticket to the full four days costs around $200, with around another $50 charged for a spot to camp near town.

Jazz Celebration ☎970/728-7009, ⓦwww.telluridejazz.com. Held since the 1970s over the first week of August, this jazz festival has, in the past, featured performances by Herbie Hancock and Etta James.

Chamber Music Festival ☎970/728-8686 ⓦwww.telluridechambermusic.com. Another longstanding August festival begins with an outdoor sunset concert and ends in the elegant surroundings of the Victorian Sheridan Opera House.

Film Festival ☎603/433-9202, ⓦwww.telluridefilmfestival.org. Held over the first weekend in September, past premieres at this quarter-century-old film festival have included **The Crying Game** and **The Piano**. Free films are screened in an outdoor theater. Needless to say, tickets go fast.

The old mining roads around town are also popularly explored with **4WD vehicles**, including the many high-pass routes over to Ouray; see the box on p.373 for more details. Other possibilities include touring the area the old-fashioned way, on **horseback**; Telluride Horseback, 9025 Rte-145 (☎970/728-9611), offers rides from $40 per hour.

Eating

With no fast-food places in town and a plethora of resident hot-shot chefs, Telluride offers many opportunities to **eat** well. At most restaurants haute cuisine and fine wines collide with diners in jeans and fleece unwinding from a day in the mountains – but be warned, food is often pricey and reservations are always recommended.

Allred's Gondola Station, St Sophia ☎970/728-7474. Unbeatable location at the top of the gondola above town, with food to match the views. From gourmet takes on continental classics like the beef *carpaccio* with truffle oil to more tropical creations such as the red snapper with vanilla-poached crab and mango, the menu is sublime; even the dessert section is tough to choose from. If you can't afford dinner, stop in on the gondola ride back to town and sink into the deep leather couches in front of the fire for serious après snacks. Après from 3pm, dinner from 5.30pm.

Baked In Telluride 127 S Fir St ☎970/728-4705. One of the most affordable options in town, where good muffins and pastries are served early, while pizza slices and huge portions of the hearty specials are served throughout the day. The bar is also a lively evening hangout.

Campagna 435 W Pacific Ave ☎970/728-6190. The ambience of a Tuscan home has been recreated in Telluride. Tiny and intimate, the little wooden house has been awarded the highest Zagat rating in the state for its food – traditional, nourishing dishes straight from the Tuscan countryside. From 6pm.

The Cosmopolitan 300 W San Juan ☎970/728-1292. The *Cosmo* is elegant (and expensive) yet relaxed, with a well-stocked wine cellar and friendly sommelier. The chef mixes local ingredients like elk and trout with flavors from around the world to produce upscale bistro dishes like ginger-braised ribs and barbecued salmon.

Floradora Saloon 103 W Colorado Ave ☎970/728-3888. Serving fine food in an Old West saloon atmosphere, this busy restaurant is named after two of the town's most popular Victorian call girls. Food runs from teriyaki-glazed salmon and wild mushroom pasta to standard Mexican and burger favorites. There's a fine salad bar as well. Closed Oct & Nov.

Honga's Lotus Petal 133 S Oak St ⊤970/728-5134. Variety of good Asian dishes with reasonable prices served in stylishly detailed surroundings: deep red and pale green walls, Japanese china, and a quiet tea room with floor seating. The range of food represented spans Japanese, Korean, Thai, and Indonesian to Chinese, with entrees from around $12. Dinner only; reserve a table or wait for a seat in the bar area.

La Cocina de Luz 123 E Colorado Ave ⊤970/728-9355. Some of the best-value meals in Telluride, conscientiously prepared from fresh organic ingredients. Join the line in the tiny space for burritos, tacos, and inventive daily specials. Mon–Sat 9am–9pm.

La Marmotte 150 W San Juan ⊤970/728-6232. Run by a French couple, this cozy two-story converted icehouse resembles a Michelin-starred French country restaurant. Dishes include *filet de boeuf* and *coquilles Saint Jaques*. The epitome of restrained, cultured money in Telluride.

The Limeleaf Swede Finn Hall, 472 W Pacific ⊤970/728-2085. Fresh Thai and Asian-fusion dishes are served in the brightly painted basement restaurant and upstairs bar-cum-lounge. Join the locals between 4 and 6pm for a huge choose-your-own meat 'n' veg stir-fry at happy hour prices ($7 instead of $12).

Magic Market 225 S Pine ⊤970/728-8789. Organic salads, healthy rice and noodle hot dishes, and sandwiches – ideal for a quick and cheap lunch or early dinner.

Drinking and nightlife

Telluride's **nightlife** is often fairly muted, particularly if it's snowing heavily and people are gearing up for an early start on the slopes. But at other times things can get raucous, particularly when a good band passes through town or during the various summer festivals (see box p.381). Some of this cultural momentum, which continues into winter, regularly attracts orchestras, theater, and dance companies. Many events take place in the Sheridan Opera House, 110 N Oak (⊤970/728-6363, ⓦwww.sheridanoperahouse.com), a restored vaudeville theater. The Nugget Theater, 207 W Colorado Ave (⊤970/728-3030), shows indie films as well as blockbusters. See the local *Daily Planet* newspaper for **listings**. If you're simply looking for a place to drink a beer or martini, check out some of the town's restaurants in addition to the selection below. Many have stylish bars and après menus, while the laid-back *Limeleaf* even has a stage, with regular DJ and band nights.

Fly Me to the Moon Saloon 132 E Colorado Ave ⊤970/728-6666. Noisy and boisterous bar with nightly live bands – typically rock, reggae, or R&B – during the ski and festival seasons.

Last Dollar Saloon 100 E Colorado Ave ⊤970/728-4800. Universally called "The Buck," this is Telluride's gritty, smoky, and loud spit-and-sawdust locals' place. Good selection of local beers. Open 11.30am–late.

New Sheridan Bar and Pool Hall 225 W Colorado Ave ⊤970/728-3911. Shoot pool with

the ghost of Butch Cassidy in the Victorian film-set surroundings of the *Sheridan*'s billiard room. The main bar is busy from early afternoon on.

Noir Bar 123 S Oak St ⊤970/728-6682. Dark stylish basement space beneath the *Blue Point Grill*, with a ritzy cocktail menu plus a good chance of a decent DJ and a late-night crowd.

Smugglers Brewpub and Grille at the intersection of San Juan and Pine ⊤970/728-0919. Lively evening hangout with a decent menu of bar food and some good local microbrews.

Listings

Bookshops Bookworks, 191 S Pine ⊤970/728-0700.
Internet Wilkinson Public Library, 100 W Pacific Ave ⊤970/728-4519 (Mon–Thurs 10am–8pm, Fri & Sat 10am–6pm, Sun noon–5pm).

Medical Telluride Medical Center, 500 W Pacific ⊤970/728-3848.
Pharmacy Sunshine Pharmacy, 236 W Colorado Ave ⊤970/728-3601.
Post office 101 E Colorado Ave.

Rec center The Golden Door Spa, at the *Wyndham Peaks Hotel* in the Mountain Village (day-use $50; ☎970/728-2590, ⊛www.goldendoorspa.com), is Telluride's main indoor sports facility. The world-class spa includes steam rooms, saunas and mineral tubs, indoor and outdoor pool and waterslide, and a rock wall and well-equipped gym.

Travel details

Flights

Durango–La Plata from: Colorado Springs (17 daily; 40min); Denver (7 daily; 1hr 20min); Grand Junction (8 daily; 1hr).
Telluride from: Denver (5 daily; 1hr 10min).

Buses

Durango to: Denver (1 daily; 10hr 20min; Greyhound); Grand Junction (1 daily; 4hr 50min; TNM&O); Silverton (1 daily; 1hr 20min; TNM&O).

The Western Slope

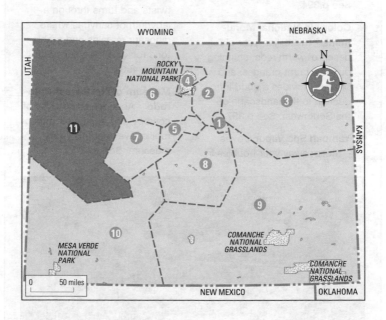

CHAPTER 11

Highlights

* **Black Canyon of the Gunnison** – Colorado's Grand Canyon: not as deep or big, but every bit as dramatic and dizzying. See p.388

* **Fruita** – Thrilling, purpose-built mountain-bike single-track was built here, in western Colorado's arid badlands. See p.394

* **Colorado National Monument** – This billion-year-old desert of warm reds, stunning purples, burnt oranges, and browns provides a good introduction to the landscape of the Southwest. See p.397

* **Yampah Spa Vapor Caves** – Steam away your troubles in this network of natural underground caves. See p.402

* **Rangely's Rock Art** – Hunt for Native American petroglyphs and pictographs lining the roadsides south of town. See p.405

* **Dinosaur National Monument** – The Yampa River elegantly twists and turns through a labyrinth of canyons where dinosaur remains and prehistoric rock art have survived. See p.406

* **Museum of Northwest Colorado** – An astonishing array of cowboy and gunfighter memorabilia awaits at this Craig museum. See p.407

△ Green River, Dinosaur National Monument

The Western Slope

t's a long haul over several mountain passes from Colorado's string of large Front Range cities to the stark and arid **WESTERN SLOPE** of the Colorado Rockies, a region which lies hard on the Utah border and has more culturally and scenically in common with the American Southwest than the rest of the state. Here in the stark and rocky semi–desert, all the main towns and sites of interest cluster tightly around the region's rivers – the area's lifeblood. The epic passage of geologic time in the area – which has thrust dinosaur remains to the surface in several places – has also allowed these rivers to carve dramatic landscapes, particularly several vast and rugged canyons. The **Gunnison River** produced the deep **Black Canyon** on its way to its confluence with the mighty **Colorado River**, which inspired the location and name of the region's largest city, **Grand Junction**. Upstream along the Colorado, the land begins to rise back up into the Elk and Sawatch Mountains at the likeable small spa town of **Glenwood Springs**, beyond which the river (and I-70) pounds its way through **Glenwood Canyon**. North of here, the **northwest** corner of the state remains one of Colorado's least visited regions – so remote that Butch Cassidy and the Wild Bunch used to regularly hole up in these parts. Here the **Yampa River** winds through the region's most scenic stretches within the supremely photogenic **Dinosaur National Monument**, with its rich trove of dino remains and Native American rock art.

The Western Slope is certainly not an obvious vacation destination choice, yet at the same time the area has remarkable natural wonders and wide-open empty spaces. Simple pleasures like camping under the desert skies, piloting a mountain bike along thrilling roller coaster trails, or rafting along the base of deep atmospheric canyons are not quick to lose their luster. The absence of many other visitors can be another great bonus in your appreciation of the area, though be prepared to rough it a little – fancy hotels and gourmet restaurants are hard to come by in this region. That said, the Western Slope has a reputation for delicious wines and scrumptious peaches.

The Gunnison River region

Fed by creeks that cascade from the alpine lakes of the Elk Mountains, the **Gunnison River** begins its 65 mile-long journey to its confluence with the Colorado River at Grand Junction from the **Blue Mesa Reservoir**, the state's largest body of water. Beyond here the river plummets into the spectacular and foreboding **Black Canyon of the Gunnison National Park**, where

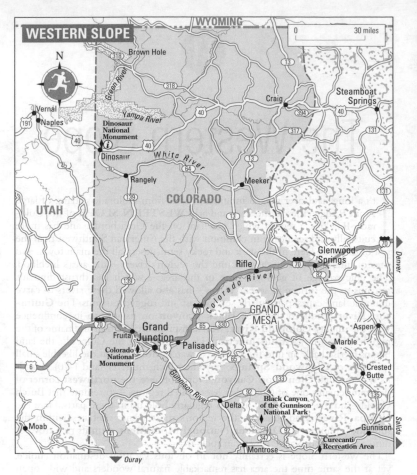

narrow rock walls rise over 2000 feet. The park holds relatively few accessible recreational activities, but there are more in the bleak lands of the **Curecanti Recreation Area** on its eastern fringe and in the **Gunnison Gorge**, just west of the park – a particularly fine stretch to raft thanks to the inspiring scenery (see box, p.390). All the urban bases in the vicinity are dull little crossroads towns: there's the bland workaday burg of **Gunnison**, gateway to Crested Butte, and **Montrose** and **Delta**, both of which lie on roads that connect the San Juan Mountains to Grand Junction and I-70.

Black Canyon of the Gunnison National Park

Splitting a mesa beside the Uncompahgre Valley, the Black Canyon of the Gunnison spans 53 miles between the towns of Delta and Gunnison. The most spectacular portion, a fourteen-mile stretch of canyon fifteen miles from Montrose along highways 50 and 347, became in 1999 the **Black Canyon of the Gunnison National Park** (℡970/641-2337, ⓦwww.nps.gov/blca).

Here the canyon's dark-gray cliffs and jagged spires of Precambrian schist, gneiss, and quartz plunge 2689ft at the highest point to the foaming Gunnison River below. For those who've visited the Grand Canyon, a comparison is inevitable – and while the scale of the Black Canyon is not as impressive, its dimensions certainly are. In several places, the canyon is clearly far deeper than it is wide, and the relative closeness of the two rims makes the visit a more intimate experience.

Formed over two million years by the erosive powers of the mighty Gunnison, the deep gorge was considered a dangerous place by the Ute, whose legends declared you could not return alive from a visit into the canyon. In the 1850s, geologist Wallace R. Hansen challenged the legend and lived to map much of the canyon, writing that "No other canyon in North America combines the depth, narrowness, sheerness, and somber countenance of the Black Canyon." Three years later, John W. Gunnison led a party to the canyon's upper reaches, though the trip was ultimately abandoned short of the gorge floor, leaving a first detailed exploration of its floor to Ferdinand V. Hayden (veteran explorer of Yellowstone) in 1874. But it was not until 1901 that the first recorded trip along its whole length took place, when the Denver and Rio Grande Railroad sent an exploratory party to assess the feasibility of laying track along its base. The party navigated as much of the river as they could on air mattresses, swimming and scrambling where they had to, and eventually covering the 33-mile stretch in nine days. This exploration led to a six-mile diversion tunnel of water for the farms of the nearby plateau, but the railroad was never extended from nearby Cimmaron into the actual Black Canyon itself.

Exploring the park

Most people explore the park along the **south rim**, hopping between hikes of varying lengths – from a few yards to over a mile – that lead to impressive canyon viewpoints. It's easy to get a **backcountry permit** to enter the canyon (from the visitors' center on the south rim or the ranger station on the north rim), but it's such an arduous and dangerous undertaking that few take up the opportunity.

△ Cross-country skiing in Gunnison National Park

Just beyond the **south rim** park entrance ($8 per vehicle; includes detailed map), the East Portal Road heads east to the *East Portal Campground* ($12) in the Curecanti National Recreation Area (see below), while the South Rim Road passes the *South Rim Campground* (102 sites; $18) and travels on to the **visitors' center** on the canyon rim (May–Oct daily 8am–6pm; ☎970/249-1915). The center is a good starting point for the southern rim's only longer hike – the **Rim Rock Trail** – that leads along the canyon rim before looping around along the Uplands Trail, which connects the Oak Flat Trail and heads back to the visitors' center in a two-hour loop. From the visitors' center it's another five miles west to **High Point**, the western terminus of the road that joins a series of overlooks and nature trails beside the precipitous canyon walls. From High Point a trail leads another three-quarters of a mile further west to **Warner Point**, a good place to admire both the northern rim and a portion of the southern rim. The patient wildlife spotter may also see golden eagles, red-tailed hawks, and turkey vultures negotiating the canyon's air-currents below.

The more remote **north rim** (closed in winter) road is reached by a long, unpaved road from the little town of Crawford (near Delta; see p.393) along Hwy-92. While there are a couple of long, secluded hikes here, the views are not nearly as rewarding as those elsewhere.

Curecanti National Recreation Area

Abutting the eastern boundary of the Black Canyon of the Gunnison, the **Curecanti National Recreation Area** offers a range of recreation opportunities around three reservoirs created by dams across the Gunnison River. The recreation area spans from, to the west, the **Morrow Point Reservoir**, which snakes along the upper part of the Gunnison River Gorge, to the sprawling **Blue Mesa Reservoir** in the east. Bleak and windy, most of the land around the reservoirs isn't particularly attractive, though there is great float-fishing for rainbow, mackinaw, brook, and brown trout along with kokanee salmon. Boating and water-skiing also draw people in, as do cross-country skiing, snowmobiling, and ice-fishing in winter.

Two **visitors' centers** beside Hwy-50 serve the recreation area: the Cimarron center (daily 8am–4.30pm) is near the Morrow Point Reservoir, while the Elk Creek center (same hours; ☎970/641-2337) is six miles west of Hwy-50's junction with Hwy-149. **Boat rentals** are available from marinas near each of the

---

Rafting the Gunnison

Rafting or **kayaking** through the Black Canyon of the Gunnison is a severely hard undertaking and one fraught with portages around unrunnable rapids and through large stands of poison ivy on slippery rocks. Needless to say, few bother. But just west of the National Park lies the **Gunnison Gorge Wilderness Area**, effectively the western extension of the Black Canyon National Park, where the river squeezes itself between sheer black-granite cliffs. Most of this stretch is accessible only by raft, and although the rafting itself is generally straightforward (few rapids above Class III), the impressive scenery, remoteness of location, and excellent trout-fishing make the trip – which generally requires an overnight camp – well worthwhile. One of the few commercial outfits that have a license to run this river is the experienced Wilderness Aware Rafting (☎719/395-2112 or 1-800/462-7238, ⊛www.inaraft.com) in Buena Vista (see p.303), who offer both overnight rafting and fishing trips in the gorge from around $350.

visitor centers, though the park service also runs guided boat cruises with good views of the upper canyon; these depart from the Morrow Point Reservoir daily (☎970/641-0402; reservations required).

One of the few local features that the creation of the reservoirs hasn't changed is the **Curecanti Needle** – a 700ft-high granite spire that gives the park its name. This can be seen up close by hiking down the parched and rugged **Curecanti Creek** trail (four miles round trip; 2–3hr), which begins at Pioneer Point Overlook off Hwy-92, six miles from 92's junction with Hwy-50. By contrast, **Neversink** trail (1.5 miles), off Hwy-50 five miles west of Gunnison, is far more verdant, running by the Gunnison River and perfect for bird-watching, including great blue herons.

The recreation area includes eight **campgrounds** with over 300 sites costing around $9 per night. Many are overrun with RVs and are fairly soulless, though the *East Portal Campground* near the Black Canyon National Park has some stunning views from the nearby rim.

Gunnison

The blue-collar ranching and farming town of **GUNNISON** is notable mainly as the turnoff point for Hwy-135, which leads 25 miles north to Crested Butte. Scratch the surface, though, and you'll find that this town is well placed for tapping into the **Gunnison National Forest** to the north, making it a good base for hikers, bikers, and especially anglers. Gunnison can also be used as a cheap base for activities around Crested Butte (though you'll only see worthwhile savings during the ski season).

For a quick appreciation of the town's history, visit the **Gunnison County Pioneer and Historical Society Museum**, on the eastern side of town at 110 S Adams (June–Sept Mon–Sat 9am–5pm; $4). The most memorable item in the museum's collection is a restored narrow-gauge steam train from the Denver and Rio Grande Western Railroad.

Far more exciting are the numerous fishing areas around Gunnison. Just west of town, the **Gunnison River**, as it runs to the Blue Mesa Reservoir, is a particularly productive stretch of water. East of Gunnison, the **Taylor River**, one of the main tributaries of the Gunnison, is also highly regarded for its excellent trout fishing. The Taylor River runs to Gunnison from the quiet **Taylor Park Reservoir**, thirty miles away – an idyllic spot for float-fishing, while above the reservoir's extent, the **Roaring Judy State Wildlife Area** is a favorite for committed fly-fishing enthusiasts. Fishing **outfitters** in the area include Gene Taylor's Sporting Goods, 201 W Tomichi (☎970/641-1845), the Three Rivers Resort and Outfitting (☎970/641-1302), eleven miles north along Hwy-135 to Crested Butte, and the Taylor Park Boat House (☎970/641-2900), beside the Taylor Park Reservoir; they also rent out boats.

Hikers and bikers will want to head southwest of town to the **Hartman Rocks**, several piles of red-granite landforms surrounded by sage, pine, and juniper that cling to the sandy soil. The area provides an interconnected network of trails pleasantly unlike the wooded trails in the rest of the region, and conveniently the most interesting ones are within a mile of the parking lot. Here, the bulk of the igneous ring dykes – where lava-injected magma has cooled and hardened below the earth's surface before being heaved up above it in a series of uplifts – are located. The rocks are reached by traveling west along Hwy-50 for one-and-a-half miles before turning south on CO-38 (aka Gold Basin Road) for four miles.

Practicalities

No regional buses serve Gunnison so those without their own vehicle nearly always arrive at **Gunnison County Airport** (℡970/641-2304). The airport is at its busiest during ski season, when Alpine Express (℡970/641-5074 or 1-800/822-4844) offers a shuttle service to Crested Butte for $40. For town **information**, contact the chamber of commerce, 500 E Tomichi (℡970/641-1501 or 1-800/323-2453); for details of opportunities on forest lands contact the Gunnison National Forest, Taylor and Cebolla Ranger Districts, 216 N Colorado (Mon–Fri 7.30am–4pm; ℡970/641-0471).

The strip of standard **motels** along Hwy-50 (Tomichi Ave) through town includes the basic *ABC Motel*, 212 E Tomichi Ave (℡970/641-2400 or 1-800/341-8000; ❶), and the slightly plusher *Hylander Inn*, 412 W Tomichi Ave (℡970/641-1061; ❹). The *Mary Lawrence Inn*, 601 N Taylor St (℡970/641-3343; ❻), is a small and comfortable B&B on one of the town's leafy side-streets. There are over thirty USFS **campgrounds** within an hour's drive; the forest service office can provide a full list. If the office is closed, head in the direction of the Taylor Park Reservoir, where campgrounds are dotted along the road.

When it comes to **eating** out, the *Sidewalk Café*, 113 W Tomichi Ave (℡970/641-4130), is good for cheap breakfasts, while the similarly inexpensive *Sundae Shoppe Restaurant* (℡970/641-5051) takes care of dinner, with offerings of chicken-fried steak and chimichangas followed by wonderful dessert sundaes. The ranch-style *Cattlemen Inn*, 301 W Tomichi Ave (℡970/641-1061), is the town's answer to fine dining, with an assortment of steaks, chicken, and seafood entrees starting at around $10. Of the handful of **bars**, *The Trough*, 37550 W Hwy-50 (℡970/641-3724), is the best bet, with comedy shows on Thursdays and live bands on Friday and Saturday nights.

Montrose

A hub for ranchers and hunters, parched and sprawling **MONTROSE** is the largest settlement between Grand Junction and Durango. Besides using the town as a stopover en route to the Black Canyon, the only other reason for stopping here is to visit the **Ute Indian Museum**, 17253 Chipeta Drive (daily: mid-May to Sept 9am–6pm; Oct to mid-May 10am–5pm; $3). This small museum sits on land once farmed by the last great Ute chief, **Ouray** (1833–1880), who's best known for negotiating a fragile peace with the federal government in 1873. As part of the peace, he helped broker Ute withdrawal from eastern Colorado into the San Juan Mountains, though after his death this agreement was broken, pushing the Ute further west into semi-arid areas around Montrose and present-day Utah. The small museum does a good job of describing Ute culture, thought to have had the longest continuous history among all the various tribes who at one time inhabited Colorado. Top exhibits include presentations on the bear dance and a display of the ceremonial garb worn by Ouray during treaty talks in Washington, DC. The most interesting exhibits of the **Montrose County Historical Museum** on W Main Street (Memorial Day–Sept Mon–Sat 9am–5pm; $2; ℡970/249-2085) also relate to Ute presence in the area, with a great collection of arrowheads and some superb historical photos, including snaps of Ouray and his wife Chipeta.

Practicalities

TNM&O **buses** from Grand Junction and Durango stop at the bus depot at 132 N 1st St. There's also a small **airport** (℡970/249-8455), which sees the most use in winter when some ski traffic for Telluride touches down here. Shuttles from Telluride are offered by Telluride Transit ($30 per person;

11

970/249-6993). Local information is doled out at the **Montrose Visitor Information Center**, 1519 E Main St (Mon–Fri 9am–5pm; ☎970/249-5000 or 1-800/923-5515), though the **Montrose Public Lands Office**, 2505 S Townsend Ave (☎970/240-5300), is a better choice if looking for outdoor information.

The bulk of Montrose's **motels** line Hwy-50 (aka Main St) on the eastern side of town, including the *Black Canyon Motel*, 1605 E Main St (☎970/249-3495 or 1-800/453-4911; ❸), a standard, modest motel, and the slightly more luxurious *Best Western Red Arrow Inn*, 1702 E Main St (☎970/249-9641 or 1-800/468-9323; ❹). **Campers** intent on staying near town should head east to the *Hangin' Tree RV Park*, 17250 Hwy-50 (☎970/249-9966), where there are laundry facilities and full hookups.

All the usual chain **restaurants** are found on the highways out of Montrose, though pickings in town itself are slim. The *Daily Bread*, at 1st and Cascade streets, is a good early morning stop-off, while decent Mexican and Southwestern-style food can be had at the *Whole Enchilada*, 44 S Grand St (☎970/249-1881), where most entrees cost around $10.

Delta

Strung along Hwy-50 thirty miles south of Grand Junction, **DELTA** bills itself as the "City of Murals," after the vast gaudy paintings on several downtown stores. Delta offers a handy place to stop for supplies before heading out to the northern rim of the Black Canyon and the Curecanti Recreation Area along the slow but hugely scenic Hwy-92. Even if you don't intend to visit the park itself, there are several good places along this road to stop and peer into the canyon.

As seen at the Ute Indian Museum in Montrose, this region still holds some of the last vestiges of contemporary Ute culture in the state, best experienced at the annual **American Indian Pow-Wow & Cultural Festival** (☎1-800/874-1741, ⓦwww.counciltreepowwow.org) held over the fourth weekend in September. The main museum in Delta is a living-history museum, with costumed custodians who cheerfully perform displays of early pioneering activities at **Fort Uncompahgre** ($3.50; ☎970/874-8349), a reconstructed 1852 French fur-trading fort in the Riverside Confluence Park, just north of Delta. The town's **visitor center**, at 3rd and Main streets (Mon–Fri 9am–5pm; ☎970/874-8616), can supply more information on the pow-wow.

The Colorado River Valley

Driving the 75-mile stretch of I-70 that parallels the **Colorado River** between Grand Junction and Glenwood Springs, you can trace the state's transition from full-blown desert through fertile valleys to serious mountain terrain. The small towns along the route are all dismal little service centers and nothing worth pulling off the highway for, so whichever direction you are traveling both Grand Junction and Glenwood Springs become welcome sights, in part for the interesting landscapes that surround both. Head almost any direction out of **Grand Junction** and you'll find extraordinary desert landscapes – the towering red-rock canyons and cliffs of the **Colorado National Monument** rise just south of town. Further west the adjacent territory, around the tiny town of **Fruita**, is premier mountain bike country, with dozens of trails beckoning all those passing through on their way to Moab, Utah, America's most famous mountain bike destination – the two are linked by the epic 140-mile-long Kokopelli Trail.

East of Grand Junction, on the other side of the wide, lazy Colorado River, the skyline is dominated by the huge, verdant tabletop mountain of **Grand Mesa**, a thickly forested area with dozens of peaceful lakes, quiet trails, idyllic campsites, and, in winter, good skiing – both Nordic and downhill – and snowmobiling. **Glenwood Springs** has its own impressive canyon and modest ski resort, but better yet its location on the threshold of the Sawatch and Elk Mountains also makes it an inexpensive base to explore the area around Aspen, particularly the Crystal Valley.

Grand Junction, Palisade, and Fruita

Given its parochial nature, it's hard to believe that **GRAND JUNCTION** is the largest city between Denver, 246 miles east on I-70, and Salt Lake City, Utah, 287 miles west. One of many towns that sprang to life with the arrival of the railroads in the 1880s, it now makes its living primarily through the oil and gas industries and as a buoyant farming center, based on the fruits of the orchards and vineyards around **PALISADE**. Not surprisingly, dusty, sprawling, and generally unattractive Grand Junction is often neglected as a destination, even though its immediate environs abound with outdoor opportunities.

Particularly splendid is the network of hiking and biking trails, many cutting through rugged and spectacular desert country. Especially enticing for hikers is the remarkable scenery of the **Colorado National Monument**, while mountain bikers will relish the prospect of smooth, rolling single-track around **FRUITA**. Both activities are possible year-round, and are in fact generally more pleasant in the winter months.

Arrival and information

Amtrak's daily *California Zephyr* stops at the intersection of 2nd Street and Pitkin Avenue, while Greyhound **buses** pull in at 230 S 5th St. The helpful **visitor center**, 740 Horizon Drive (daily 8.30am–5pm; ☎970/244-1480 or 1-800/962-2547), is beside I-70 three miles from downtown. Additionally, the town runs an info booth in the Amtrak station. Conveniently, the local **USFS** office is located by the visitor center at 2777 Crossroad Blvd (Mon–Fri 8am–5pm; ☎970/242-8211).

Accommodation

An absolute glut of chain **motels** line I-70 three miles north of town, but if you want to actually see anything of the downtown area, you're better off staying in one of the budget motels there.

Best Western Horizon Inn 754 Horizon Drive ☎970/245-1410. Reliable, good-value chain hotel with amenities that include a pool, spa, and free continental breakfast. ❸

Daniel's Motel 333 North Ave ☎970/243-1084. Basic and clean motel rooms, with rates that are hard to beat and a location convenient to downtown. ❷

H-Motel 333 highways 6 and 50, Fruita ☎970/858-7198. Fruita's only lodging option, a cheap but clean motel with cable TV and phones. ❷

Los Altos 375 Hill View Drive ☎970/256-0964 or 1-888/774-0982. Friendly B&B in a picturesque location southwest of town at the foot of the

Colorado National Monument. Communal areas on the third floor make the most of views and there's a large outdoor deck, too. Breakfast includes tasty home-baked goods. ❻

Hotel Melrose 337 Colorado Ave ☎970/242-9636 or 1-800/430-4555. Sociable downtown hostel in a Victorian-era hotel that's still furnished with antiques. Both private rooms ($30; some with private bath) and dorm beds ($12) are on offer, and facilities include a kitchen, lounge, and outdoor BBQ area.

Value Lodge 104 White Ave ☎970/242-0651. Another affordable motel close to downtown, with cable TV, phones, and swimming pool. ❷

GRAND JUNCTION

RESTAURANTS & BARS	
Blue Moon Bar & Grill	4
Dolce Vita	2
Main Street Bagels	6
Main Street Café	7
Rockslide Brew Pub	5
The Rose	1
The Winery	3

ACCOMMODATION	
Best Western	A
Horizon Inn	C
Daniel's Motel	B
H-Motel	F
Hotel Melrose	E
Los Altos	D
Value Lodge	D

MUSIC LANE

N

MUSIC LANE

1ST STREET

NORTHRIDGE DRIVE

PATTERSON ROAD   PATTERSON ROAD

CENTER AVENUE

St Mary's Hospital

7TH STREET

4TH ST.

LITTLE BOOKCLIFF DRIVE

WELLINGTON AVENUE   WELLINGTON AVENUE

RIDGEWOOD AVENUE

LILAC LANE

HILLCREST AVENUE

CEDAR AVENUE

WALNUT AVENUE

9TH STREET

12TH STREET

WALNUT AVENUE

ELLA STREET

WALNUT AVENUE

5TH STREET

PINYON AV.

8TH STREET

9TH STREET

10TH STREET

11TH STREET

PINYON   AVENUE

13TH STREET

WEST MESA AVENUE

ORCHARD AVENUE

MESA CRESCENT

HALL AVENUE

HALL AVENUE

Western Colorado Center for the Arts

HALL AVENUE

MESA AVENUE

M E S A

MESA AVENUE

14TH STREET

INDEPENDENT AVENUE

MOTOR STREET

HALL AVENUE

SHERWOOD DRIVE

Sherwood Park

MESA AVENUE

TEXAS AVENUE

ELM AVENUE

TEXAS AVENUE

S T A T E

KENNEDY AVENUE

1ST STREET

BENGAL DR.

KENNEDY AVE.

FRANKLIN AVENUE

GLENWOOD AVENUE

BUNTING AVENUE

CANTEL AVENUE

KENNEDY AVENUE

BUNTING AVENUE

GLENWOOD AVENUE

C O L L E G E

Fruita & B

Lilac Park

NORTH AVENUE   NORTH AVENUE

C

2ND STREET

BELFORD AVENUE

Lincoln Park

TELLER AVENUE

5TH STREET

6TH STREET

7TH STREET

8TH STREET

9TH STREET

10TH STREET

11TH STREET

12TH STREET

HILL AVENUE

GUNNISON AVENUE

CHIPETA AVENUE

PEACH STREET

OURAY AVENUE

OURAY AVENUE

13TH STREET

14TH STREET

GRAND AVENUE

i

2ND STREET

GRAND AVENUE

E & Colorado National Monument

D

WHITE AVENUE

RICE STREET

ROOD AVENUE

1ST STREET

2

Dinosaur Valley Museum

4TH STREET

3

5TH STREET

4

MAIN STREET

8TH STREET

9TH STREET

10TH STREET

11TH STREET

12TH STREET

13TH STREET

14TH STREET

5

6

Train Station

LAWRENCE AVE.

CHIPUTA AVE.

COLORADO AVENUE

F   Bus Station

UTE AVENUE

UTE AVE.

FAIRVIEW AVENUE

2ND STREET

3RD STREET

Museum of Western Colorado

6TH STREET

PITKIN AVENUE

6

6

bus 70

bus 70

HALE AVENUE

SOUTH AVENUE

D ROAD

RIVERSIDE PARK DRIVE

50

7TH STREET

7

0   500 yds

1

The Town and around

After driving through the unsightly mass of light industry and commercial forecourts that make up Grand Junction's outskirts, the leafy **downtown** comes as a pleasant surprise. Here, Main Street is lined with an affable mix of turn-of-the-nineteenth-century buildings and a number of creative bronze busts and other sculptures. Though the Dinosaur National Monument lies 90 miles north on Hwy-139, Grand Junction is a better place to learn about these prehistoric reptiles, as it's home to both the Devil's Canyon Science and Learning Center (see below) and the extensive and enjoyable **Dinosaur Valley Museum**, 362 Main St (summer daily 9am–5pm; rest of year Tues–Sat 10am–4.30pm; $4.50). The museum's collection includes reconstructed dinos, replica eggs, and casts of footprints and giant bones excavated locally.

Two blocks south along the main drag stands the **Museum of Western Colorado**, 248 S 4th St (Tues–Sat 10am–4pm; $2), a small but diverting museum that does a good job of summing up the history of the area with artifacts including well-preserved Ute baskets, bows, and arrows. The **Western Colorado Center for the Arts**, 1803 N 7th St (Tues–Sat 9am–4pm; $2; ✆970/243-7337), is another good place to get a handle on the region, with its permanent collection of impressive Navajo rugs and rotating collections of other Native American and Western art. If you have kids in tow, you should also make time for the diverting **Devil's Canyon Science and Learning Center**, in nearby Fruita at 550 Jurassic Court (daily 9am–5pm; $5.50). Interactive displays here include an earthquake simulator, a mock dinosaur quarry, and some amazingly lifelike robotic dinos.

For a more adult attraction, you can tour wineries around the small and rather nondescript town of **Palisade**, twelve miles west of Grand Junction; it's the epicenter of Colorado's underrated wine industry. The town appears to be particularly well placed for fruit cultivation – not only do many of the succulent Colorado peaches hail from Palisade, but the hot days here allow grapes to build up sugar while cool nights are said to add a distinctive crispness to local wines. Though the area's wine-growing tradition spans over a hundred years, the ripping out of vines during Prohibition largely put the industry into hibernation, until the last couple of decades when interest has resurfaced. Around half a dozen **vineyards** feature relaxed places to enjoy the wines, including Plum Creek Cellars, 3708 G Rd (daily 10am–5pm; ✆970/464-7586), who've been producing wine since 1984, and the Carlson Vineyards, 462 35 Rd (daily 11am–6pm; ✆970/464-5554), who like to give their wines jolly names like Tyrannosaurus Red or Prairie Dog Blush. Harvest time, in mid-September, is a particularly good time to visit, since the month sees the **Colorado Mountain Winefest**, where area wineries band together to provide live music and appetizers free of charge (✆1-800/704-3667, ⦿www.coloradowine.com).

Outdoor activities

Though the Colorado National Monument is the obvious area draw, there are many worthwhile trails around Grand Junction. Paralleling the town on the north side, the rippled, purple-gray **Bookcliffs**, whose subtle changes of color throughout the day are a delight, are a good venue for **hiking**. The area is managed by the BLM as a reserve to protect wild horses, but is open to use by hikers, horseback riders, mountain bikers, and campers. The cliffs themselves also attract rock-climbers. In Grand Junction, Summit Canyon Mountaineering, 549 Main St (✆970/243-2847), can supply you with relevant information and gear.

Lauded by the mountain biking press as the next Moab, Fruita, thirteen miles northwest of Grand Junction, is an off-road paradise. Indeed, Fruita is connected to the mythical Moab by the 128-mile-long **Kokopelli Trail**, a stupendous off-road adventure. Obviously, though, most bikers concentrate on shorter loops, including the smooth, rolling single-track at the base of the Fruita end of the Bookcliffs, or the more rugged trails that roller-coaster south of town, overlooking the broad Colorado River and the parched landscapes in neighboring Utah. For more information, head to Over the Edge Sports, 202 E Aspen Ave (☎970/858-7220), a block east of the roundabout at Fruita's center. Their knowledge of current local conditions is indispensable, and a map of local trails can be picked up for $1; front-suspension bikes are rented for $28 per day. You can also rent bikes and pick up route details at several shops in Grand Junction, including Bicycle Outfitters, 248 Ute Ave (☎970/245-2699).

Eating and drinking

Grand Junction has no shortage of dreary and familiar fast-food joints in most of its suburbs, but thankfully its tiny and carefully looked-after downtown mall has several good **eating** options that you can browse on foot before deciding between. Most **drinking** and nightlife venues are far more widely spread out, but at least there's a good downtown brewpub.

Blue Moon Bar & Grill 120 N 7th St ☎970/242-1506. Busy bar with a decent range of bar food, sandwiches – including a tasty calamari steak sandwich in pitta bread ($7) – and salads ($7) for lunch, with steaks and pizza in the evening. Often live music here at weekends.

Dolce Vita 336 Main St ☎970/242-8482. Good, moderately expensive Northern Italian food with unusual dishes like polenta with wine-marinated portobello mushrooms or an angel-hair pasta tossed with chicken, capers, and artichoke hearts.

Main Street Bagels 559 Main St ☎970/241-2740. Huge variety of bagels for breakfast or lunch, for take-out or eat-in in the large, laid-back dining area.

Rockslide Brew Pub 401 Main St ☎970/245-2111. Serves up a good variety of beers, but is most popular for its huge portions of food; both the burgers ($7) and Cobb salad ($8) are recommended.

The Rose 2993 North Ave ☎970/245-0606. Cornerstone of the local Country & Western scene. There's live music here almost nightly, making it a reliably fun and popular bar.

Main Street Café 832 S 7th St ☎970/242-7225. A retro 1950s diner with the standard array of good-value meals, from meatloaf to burritos.

The Winery 642 Main St ☎970/242-4100. A fairly expensive but stylish restaurant – exposed brick, stained glass, dark wooden beams – serving reliable steak, prime rib, and shrimp dishes, accompanied by a comprehensive array of local wines.

Colorado National Monument and Rattlesnake Canyon

Millions of years of wind and water erosion have gouged out the brightly colored rock spires, domes, arches, pedestals, and balanced rocks of the **Colorado National Monument**, on cliff-edges overlooking the valley four miles southwest of Grand Junction. This billion-year-old painted desert of warm reds, stunning purples, burnt oranges, and browns is also home to a high arid vegetation of piñon pine, yucca, sagebrush, and Utah juniper.

The Monument ($5 day-pass) has two entrances at either end of the 23-mile **Rim Rock Drive** that passes through it; one at its southern end close to Grand Junction, the other at Fruita. Along with your park pass, you'll receive a leaflet on the Monument, a map, and info on the main points of interest along the way. Even just driving the length of the twisting and curving road is a spectacular experience, and though too busy to enjoy on a bike during weekends, during the week it makes for an invigorating ride. Bikes are banned on all park trails, though, so to explore beyond the road you'll have to strike out on foot. One of the best short hikes is the one-hour **John Otto's Trail**, which affords close-up views of several monoliths. Longer trails get right down to the canyon floor: the six-mile **Monument Canyon Trail** weaves through a series of scenic spots. All trails are depicted on the leaflet you receive on entering, but for more detailed information call in at the **visitors' center** (daily: May–Sept 8am–7pm; rest of year 9am–5pm; ☎970/858-3617, ⊚www.nps.gov/colm), at the north (Fruita) end of the monument. The monument's only **campground**, the basic *Saddlehorn* ($10), is near the visitors' center; campers looking for solitude should take advantage of the fact that you're allowed to pitch a tent anywhere more than a quarter of a mile off the road for free. Rimrock Adventures, in Fruita (☎970/858-9555), offers **horseback riding** trips around the monument and also arrange rafting trips in the area.

Though outside the monument itself, **Rattlesnake Canyon**, which contains some huge and spectacular natural **rock arches**, is most easily reached from the southern end of Rim Rock Drive. Amid bizarrely eroded sandstone canyons, the hardy can strike out, hiking or biking (or even four-wheeling if you have a vehicle with plenty of clearance), to twelve natural rock arches. The largest, Rainbow Bridge, spans around 100 feet and is particularly photogenic late or early in the day, when its shadows lengthen. To get here you need to follow the **Black Ridge Access Road**, which starts eleven miles from the northern (Fruita) entrance to the monument and is signposted at the Glade Park Store. It's a thirteen-mile drive to the trailhead and high-clearance 4WD vehicles are necessary for the last mile and a half; do not attempt this drive in wet conditions as the road gets very slippery and dangerous. From the end of the road, a trail drops down through one arch on the start of a two-mile loop that visits all the main arches in the group. En route, watch your step – the canyon was named Rattlesnake Canyon for a reason (see box below) – though you're highly unlikely to have a problem. The canyon is managed by the BLM, who have an office in Grand Junction at 2815 H Rd (daily Mon–Fri 7.30am–4.30pm; ☎970/244-3000).

Grand Mesa

Rambling over 50 square miles and soaring up to 10,000ft, the thickly forested **Grand Mesa** is the world's largest flat-topped mountain, known for excellent

---

Rattlesnakes

Of all the snakes in the Rockies, the only poisonous one you are likely to meet is the **rattlesnake**. You might not be able to tell a rattler from any other kind of snake; in fact many rattlers don't rattle at all. If in doubt, assume it is one. When it's hot, snakes lurk in shaded areas under bushes, around wood debris, old mining shafts, and piles of rocks. When it's cooler, they sun themselves out in the open, but they won't be expecting you and if disturbed will attack. A bite is initially like a sharp pinprick, but within hours the pain becomes severe, usually accompanied by swelling and acute nausea. Forget any misconceptions you may harbor about sucking the poison out; it doesn't work and even tends to hasten the spread of venom. Since venom travels mainly through the lymph system just under the skin, the best way of inhibiting the diffusion is to wrap the whole limb firmly, but not in a tourniquet, then contact a ranger or doctor as soon as possible. Do all you can to keep calm – a slower pulse rate limits the spread of the venom. Keep in mind that even if a snake does bite you, about fifty percent of the time it's a dry – or non-venomous – strike. Snakes don't want to waste their venom on something too large to eat. However, it's wise to carry a snake-bite kit, available for a couple of dollars from most sports and camping stores.

fishing in a multitude of lakes and its huge network of **hiking** trails. In winter, these trails are turned over to **Nordic skiers** and **snowshoers**, when there's also downhill skiing at **Powderhorn** resort.

The road up onto Grand Mesa, Hwy-65, begins from I-70 twenty miles east of Grand Junction. Around twenty miles from the interstate in the mesa's foothills is **Powderhorn Resort** (☎970/268-5700 or 1-800/241-6997, ⓦwww .powderhorn.com) a small (only 500 acres) but inexpensive (adult day-pass $45) ski resort. Although the terrain breaks down officially as 20 percent beginner, 50 intermediate, and 30 advanced, those seeking black runs will find the half-dozen trails on offer pretty limiting. Only powder days provide expert skiers a good reason to visit – and with 250 inches of snow falling between December and March, the resort certainly gets its share.

From Powderhorn, the twisting Hwy-65 heads south up to the plateau, left here by a period of 600 million years of erosion working on soft rock that surrounded this huge tongue of lava. With over three hundred lakes and reservoirs surrounded by pine and aspen groves, the landscape is remarkably idyllic and tranquil thanks to the absence of any real development. By car, one of the best impressions of the area can be had by following **Lands End Road**, a well-graded eleven-mile dirt track that heads east from Hwy-65 (starting around thirty miles south of I-70). The road leads to a stunning panorama: lakes, plains, sand hills, and smaller mesas separate thick forest on the left from desert on the right, with the snowcrested San Juans far off in the background. The best way to really see the landscape, though, is to **hike**. The finest trail, with startling ridge views, is the ten-mile-long **Crag Crest Trail**, best begun from an eastern trailhead beside FS-121 (east off Hwy-65). This end offers some of the most spectacular views, so even if you don't intend to walk the whole leg, it's worth heading along here for a couple of hours on an out-and-back hike.

Practicalities

The helpful **visitors center**, near the Cobbet Lake junction of FS-121 and Hwy-65 on the southern side of the mesa, can suggest good places to mountain bike and where to head out on cross-country skis or snowshoes in winter. The **Grand Junction Ranger District Office** (☎970/242-8211) can also help with advance planning and can supply details on their dozen pretty USFS **campgrounds** (reservations ☎1-800/280-2267; $6-10; late May to September). Of these, several dot the east side near Alexander Lake, as does a basic café and the *Alexander Lake Lodge* (☎970/856-6240; ⑤), which offers motel-style rooms and cabins. At the bottom of the mesa, five miles north of **Cedaredge**, the hospitable *Llama's B&B* on Hwy-65 (☎970/856-6836; ④) has fantastic breakfasts served on a sundeck, along with the chance to meet resident llamas. In Cedaredge, the *Log Cabin B&B* (☎970/856-7585, ⓦwww.logcabinbedand breakfast.com; ⑤) is in an 1891 log cabin surrounded by two forested acres. Rooms are decorated with antique tools and cowboy artifacts.

Glenwood Springs

Bustling, touristy **GLENWOOD SPRINGS** sits on the western threshold of the Rockies. Just east of town the impressive Glenwood Canyon announces the presence of real mountains, and the town is within easy striking distance of both Aspen (40 miles southeast) and Vail (60 miles east). The town's key attraction has traditionally been the **hot springs** for which its named, which were long used by the Utes as a place of relaxation. Later these drew miners before becoming the target for unscrupulous speculators, who broke treaties and established resort facilities in the 1880s. For some time, Glenwood Springs was every bit as chic as Vail or Aspen are today, though now the town has largely become a service center for nearby resorts, beset by faceless malls, motels, and fast-food outlets along I-70 and Hwy-6 south out of town. The downtown area is still an attractive place, but there's really not much to explore besides the hot springs, which are particularly welcome after a day of skiing at the modest nearby **Sunlight Mountain Resort**. In summer, local activities include biking

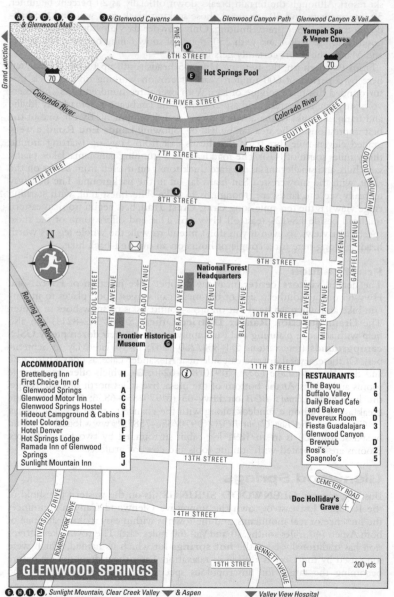

Ⓐ, Ⓑ, Ⓒ, ❶, ❷ ▲   ❸ & Glenwood Caverns ▲   ▲ Glenwood Canyon Path   Glenwood Canyon & Vail ▲
& Glenwood Mall

◀ Grand Junction

PINE ST.

Ⓓ
6TH STREET

Yampah Spa & Vapor Caves

🅷70

Ⓔ Hot Springs Pool

Colorado River

NORTH RIVER STREET

Colorado River

SOUTH RIVER STREET

W 7TH STREET

7TH STREET

Amtrak Station

Ⓕ

LOOKOUT MOUNTAIN

8TH STREET

❹

❺

N

Roaring Fork River

SCHOOL STREET

PITKIN AVENUE

COLORADO AVENUE

GRAND AVENUE

COOPER AVENUE

BLAKE AVENUE

9TH STREET

PALMER AVENUE

MINTER AVENUE

LINCOLN AVENUE

GARFIELD AVENUE

National Forest Headquarters

10TH STREET

Frontier Historical Museum Ⓖ

11TH STREET

ⓘ

ACCOMMODATION
Brettelberg Inn	H
First Choice Inn of Glenwood Springs	A
Glenwood Motor Inn	C
Glenwood Springs Hostel	G
Hideout Campground & Cabins	I
Hotel Colorado	D
Hotel Denver	F
Hot Springs Lodge	E
Ramada Inn of Glenwood Springs	B
Sunlight Mountain Inn	J

RESTAURANTS
The Bayou	1
Buffalo Valley	6
Daily Bread Cafe and Bakery	4
Devereux Room	D
Fiesta Guadalajara	3
Glenwood Canyon Brewpub	D
Rosi's	2
Spagnolo's	5

13TH STREET

CEMETERY ROAD

Doc Holliday's Grave ✝

RIVERSIDE DRIVE

ROARING FORK DRIVE

14TH STREET

BENNETT AVENUE

GLENWOOD SPRINGS

0   200 yds

15TH STREET

❻ Ⓗ, ❶, Ⓙ, Sunlight Mountain, Clear Creek Valley ▼ & Aspen   ▼ Valley View Hospital or skating along the base of **Glenwood Canyon** and exploring the spectacular landscape along the **Crystal River Valley** to the south.

Arrival, information, and getting around

Amtrak **trains** – with daily services from Denver – pull in at the depot at 413 7th St, downtown by the Colorado River. Greyhound **buses**, arriving three times a day from both Denver and Grand Junction, pull in at the *Ramada Inn*, 124 W 6th St. Shuttle services from Denver International Airport include Aspen Limo (☎970/925-1234 or 1-800/222-2112), who charge $60 one-way; they also run shuttles from Aspen's airport for $20.

The **visitor center**, 1102 Grand Ave (open 24hr, staffed Mon–Fri 8.30am–5pm, Sat & Sun 9am–3pm; ☎970/945-6589), stocks the useful *Glenwood Springs Official Guide*, while the USFS **White River National Forest Office** is at 900 Grand Ave (☎970/945-2521). Getting around town is easy enough, as Glenwood Trolley buses (50¢) run every half-hour between W Glenwood Mall and Roaring Forks Marketplace.

Accommodation

Accommodation tends to fill up quickly, so reservations in summer are recommended, especially if you're hoping to stay downtown. In winter, lodging in town is one of Colorado's best deals, with rates often dropping by half. If you're skiing Sunlight, you can get an even better deal with one of their sleep, ski, and soak packages, which include lodging, lift tickets, and passes to hot springs from around $60 per night (call the resort for details of participating accommodations). **Campers** will find plenty of sites in the nearby White River National Forest, including in the Crystal River Valley near Marble (see p.259), though the only sites close to town are at the *Hideout Campground and Cabins* (see p.402).

Glenwood Springs

Hotel Colorado 526 Pine St ☎970/945-6511 or 1-800/544-3998. Modeled after a stately Italian townhouse, this striking sandstone structure is a town landmark. Located near the hot springs, parts of the antique-furnished hotel are a little worn, but charming nonetheless; facilities include a basement health club and a hot tub. ❻

Hotel Denver 402 7th St ☎970/945-6565 or 1-800/826-8820. Plush Art Deco-style turn-of-the-twentieth-century hotel, remodeled in the 1990s to be the most luxurious in town. Close to the hot springs, extras include extensive fitness facilities, fresh cookies at check-in, and a hot muffin delivered with the morning paper. ❺

First Choice Inn of Glenwood Springs 51359 6th St ☎970/945-8551 or 1-800/332-2233. Great-value standard motel at the west end of town, with a striking view of the red mountain faces to the south, a free, good breakfast, and laundry. ❸

Glenwood Motor Inn 141 W 6th St ☎970/945-5438 or 1-800/543-5906. This motel, just a few blocks from the hot springs, is the best deal downtown. Some rooms have refrigerators and microwaves. Facilities include a hot tub and a sauna. ❸

Glenwood Springs Hostel 1021 Grand Ave ☎970/945-8545 or 1-800/946-7835. Somewhat grungy hippie hostel with a spacious dorm (beds $12–14) and cheap private rooms ($26) with shared bath, plus kitchen facilities and a giant record collection. Can also arrange tours and whitewater trips, while in winter significantly discounted tickets to both Aspen and Vail are available. Office closed 10am–4pm.

Hot Springs Lodge 415 E 6th St ☎970/945-6571 or 1-800/537-7946. Adjacent to the hot springs, where soaking is both convenient and discounted. The 107 rooms are fairly standard motel rooms, decorated in a Southwestern style with either a patio or balcony. Extras include guest laundry, outdoor hot tub, and a shuttle to the train station. ❹

Ramada Inn of Glenwood Springs 124 W 6th St ☎970/945-2500 or 1-800/332-1472. The largest chain hotel in town, two blocks from the hot springs, is reasonably priced. Facilities include a fitness center and pool. ❸

Out of town

Brettelberg Inn 11101 CO-117 ☎970/945-7421 or 1-800/634-0481. Fairly basic old condo lodge, with great slopeside location at Sunlight Mountain. On offer are functional studio and one-bedroom units (sleeping up to six) with full kitchens, VCRs, and fireplaces. Facilities include an outdoor hot tub. The nearby base lodge can provide meals in the winter, but in the summer the nearest food's in town. ③

Hideout Campground & Cabins 1293 CO-117 ☎970/945-5621 or 1-800/987-0779. Huddled in the woods off the road to Sunlight Mountain, the *Hideout* has a number of modern cabins, ranging

from studios to three-bedroom units (sleeping up to twelve). Some have fireplaces; all have access to the guest laundry. There's also space for both tents ($18) and RVs ($19). ③

Sunlight Mountain Inn 10252 CO-117 ☎970/945-5225 or 1-800/733-4757. B&B in a traditional-style ski lodge near the base of Sunlight's slopes. Simple rooms are rustically outfitted with pine-board walls, and the onsite restaurant serves great full breakfasts (included in the rates). ⑥

The Town

Of the few historic sights in Glenwood Springs, the most celebrated is the grave of **Dr John R. "Doc" Holliday**, who lies buried on a bluff overlooking the town in the picturesque **Linwood Cemetery**. Holliday, a dentist better known as a gambler and gunslinger, came to the springs for a cure to his chronic tuberculosis but died months later in November 1887, aged 35. In the paupers' section of the cemetery lies the grave of Harvey Logan, aka the bank robber "Kid Curry," a member of Butch Cassidy's notorious gang (see p.408). A good place to brush up on local outlaw history is the **Frontier Historical Museum**, 1001 Colorado Ave (daily: June–Aug 11am–4pm; rest of year 1–4pm; $3), which also focuses on the indigenous Ute as well as the area's pioneer history. Displays include pioneer-era clothing, a bed used by Horace Tabor and his mistress Baby Doe (see p.243), and some illuminating old maps and photos of town.

Heading north from downtown and crossing the Eagle River, the town's main attraction, **Glenwood Hot Springs Pool**, 410 N River St (daily: summer 7.30am–10pm; rest of year 9am–10pm; $12; ☎970/945-6571, Ⓦwww .hotspringspool.com), is heralded by its sulfurous smell. Billed as the "world's largest outdoor mineral hot springs pool," the complex has a rather institutional feel, though the large square pools are made more interesting by the presence of a water slide and special seats into which water is jetted. Next door, you can de-stress in the natural subterranean steam baths of the **Yampah Spa Vapor Caves**,

△ Glenwood Hot Springs

709 E 6th St (daily 9am–9pm; $12; ☎970/945-0667, ⓦwww.yampahspa
.com), where cool marble benches are set deep in a series of hot and humid
ancient caves. Massages ($30) and other treatments are offered as well.

Also on the north side of town are the **Glenwood Fairy Caves**, 508 Pine
St (open daily June–Nov, call for tour times; $10; ☎970/945-4228, ⓦwww
.glenwoodcaverns.com), an old Victorian-era attraction that's recently reopened.
The caverns extend for two miles, with some chambers reaching a height of 50
feet. There are two sightseeing options: the regular two-hour Tram/Cave Tour
($18), including views over Glenwood Canyon from an overlook high above,
and the more adventurous four-hour, dimly lit Wild Tour ($50; no kids). The
caves are connected to town by shuttles leaving from outside the *Hotel Colorado*
– call for times.

Outdoor activities

During the snowy months, the family-oriented **Sunlight Mountain Resort**
(☎970/945-7491 or 1-800/445-7931, ⓦwww.sunlightmtn.com), ten miles
south of Glenwood Springs via Hwy-82 and CO-117, offers some of the
least-expensive skiing in the region (**lift tickets** $45). It's also a forgiving
place to learn the sport before heading to Aspen. The resort divides into
about sixty trails covering 460 acres, stretching up to 2010ft above the simple
base area. Terrain breaks down as 20 percent beginner, 55 intermediate, and
25 advanced; beginners will find ideal practice areas around the Enchanted
Forest. More difficult runs branch off from the top of the 10,000ft **Compass
Mountain**, including some mogul fields and Sunlight Extreme, which has
one of the steepest sections of any US resort. There's also a decent snowboard
park east of the base lodge. For **cross-country** enthusiasts, the resort grooms
twenty miles of unusually wide tracks, the venue for the annual 10km Coal
Dust Classic, one of the state's oldest amateur cross-country races. Shuttle
buses from Glenwood Springs ($1.25; ☎970/945-7491) run from W Glen-
wood Mall.

In summer, consider heading up the twenty-mile-long cycling trail along the
narrow **Glenwood Canyon**, east of town and sandwiched between precipitous
2000ft-high walls. Long impassible, today you'll share the canyon with both the
railroad and the four-lane I-70 highway. Thankfully the latter has been largely
shielded from the cycle path through a combination of tunnels and stilts. The
path starts in town from the east end of 6th Street, and along it are several
trailheads for hikes into narrow canyons, of which the 1.2-mile uphill hike to
Hanging Lake, where waterfalls feed an idyllic deep-blue lake, is the most
popular. The trailhead for this hike is ten miles from Glenwood Springs along
the cycle path. You can **rent** a bike at Canyon Bikes, in the *Hotel Colorado* at
319 6th St (☎970 945-8904), who can provide a shuttle service ($10) so you
can follow the path downhill back to Glenwood Springs.

Eating and drinking

Despite a good range of inexpensive **dining** options, Glenwood Springs is
rarely an exciting place for a night out – though there are a couple of modest
neighborhood bars along Grand Avenue. In summer, you can catch free
Wednesday night (6.30pm) jazz concerts in Two Rivers Park.

The Bayou 52103 Hwy-6 ☎970/945-1047.
Though the menu's claim that the moderately
priced food here is "so good you'll slap yo' mama"
is slightly overblown, the spicy Cajun dishes
– including a fine gumbo and blackened chicken

– are worth the short drive out. Summer weekends
see live music on the patio.
Buffalo Valley Restaurant 3637 Hwy-82
☎970/945-5297. Locally popular saloon-like joint
a mile and a half south of downtown, with good,

moderately expensive Western fare like buffalo steaks and barbecue chicken. Also has a large dance floor with live music, often Country & Western, on weekends.

Daily Bread Cafe and Bakery 729 Grand Ave ☎970/945-6253. Popular downtown spot for breakfast, dishing out delicious fresh-baked goods and egg dishes. Lunches are equally worthwhile, with a good range of chunky sandwiches, soups, and massive salads.

Devereux Room in the *Hotel Colorado*, 319 6th St ☎970/945-6511. Though rather formal, lunch mains – burgers, soups, and salads – can be had for around $7. Prices more than double for dinner, when various Southwestern-influenced gourmet dishes are rolled out.

Fiesta Guadalajara 503 Pine St ☎970/947-1670. Decent family-run Mexican place near the hot springs, with a huge variety of filling options, including more than two dozen combination plates, all priced around $10.

Glenwood Canyon Brewpub in the *Hotel Denver*, 402 7th St ☎970/945-1276. Small, friendly brewpub with pool tables and a number of tasty local hand-crafted microbrews, including a good pale ale named Vapor Cave.

Rosi's 141 W 6th St ☎970/928-9186. Diner-type restaurant in the *Glenwood Motor Inn*; best for a cheap cooked breakfast.

Spagnolo's 812 Grand Ave ☎970/945-8440. Affordable bistro with large helpings of standard Italian fare. The thin-crust pizzas are excellent.

The northwest

Colorado's remote **northwest** is a barren expanse where few towns or places of interest interrupt the rolling hills and many tiny canyons that stretch out in every direction. Almost everything of note lies on the banks of one or other of the region's two great rivers, the White and the Yampa. The small town of **Meeker** lies beside the White River, nestling at the base of a fertile valley and within easy reach of the **Flat Tops Wilderness** to the east. The Flat Tops is the main reason the town is visited in the fall, when thousands of hunters arrive to go after elk, deer, and even mountain lion. Heading west through barren lands – which are overwhelming managed by the BLM – you arrive in the compact little oil town of **Rangely**, worth a stop chiefly for the many examples of **rock art** that dot the badlands south of town. But many of the region's most impressive examples of rock art are an hour's drive to the north, in the beautiful and paleontologically exciting **Dinosaur National Monument**, sitting squarely on the confluence of the Green and Yampa rivers. Heading west from here along the Yampa the landscape becomes less striking, yet more impressively barren and sparsely populated, so the sight of the plain little ranching town of **Craig** is a welcome one, even though there is not much to do here. But, with Steamboat Springs only 42 miles to the west, Craig annually serves as its budget winter base.

Meeker

The proud and quiet community of **MEEKER** feels far more remote than its mere 40-mile distance from the I-70 corridor suggests, and it's attractions are such that the vast majority of the few people who come here are either hunters who book up all the accommodation throughout the fall **hunting season** or those on their way to the lightly visited White River National Forest. Sadly, the town gets its name for the **Meeker Massacre** that occurred here in 1879, which saw Indian agent Nathan C. Meeker and ten other government employees fall foul of a Ute war party. By all accounts, Meeker seemed to have done his best to provoke the Ute: he tried not only to force the nomadic nation to become sedentary farmers, but also insisted on plowing up some of their premier pastures. The final straw came with Meeker's building of an irrigation ditch across a Ute horse-racing track, leading to the attack. The government responded by forcing the removal of the Ute from the northwestern portion of Colorado – banishing them to a reservation south of Vernal, Utah – although to this day most of the confiscated land remains uninhabited.

For a quick look at Meeker's history, check out the **White River Museum**, 565 Park St (mid-April to Nov Mon–Fri 9am–5pm; Dec to mid-April 11am–3pm; free), which displays the carriage used by President Theodore Roosevelt when he came hunting here. East of town is the start of the largely unpaved, but wide and well-graded, **Flat Tops Trail Scenic Byway**, on an 80-mile route east to Yampa. It's a picturesque road through the largely pristine **White River National Forest**, which occupies a broad mesatop formed by molten lava and carved into shape by glaciers on gently rolling hills, now dotted with small lakes and smothered in stands of fir, spruce, and aspen. The road also accesses the **Flat Tops Wilderness Area**.

Practicalities

Meeker's **chamber of commerce** is at W Market and 7th streets (⊕970/878-4492), though for more in-depth advice on the surrounding forests contact the **White River National Forest Ranger Station**, 361 7th St (⊕970/878-4039). There's little in the way of accommodation here, and the *Meeker Hotel*, 560 Main St (⊕970/878-5255; ❸), a handsome redbrick Victorian hotel, is the obvious place to stay. Its modest rooms have recently been renovated (some have private bath), and the lobby sums up the town, with a large mural of the Meeker Massacre and over a dozen stuffed big-game trophy heads. **Campers** will find the convenient, but basic *Rimrock Campground* (⊕970/878-4434; sites $12) beside the road just south of town, at the junction of highways 64 and 13. If heading to the White River National Forest, you'd be better off camping in one of eight pleasant National Forest campgrounds (mid-June to Oct). Twenty miles east of Meeker along CO-8 are the plush cabins of *Sleepy Cat Lodge and Restaurant* (⊕970/878-4413; ❸), whose good **restaurant**, serving mainly heavy beef and chicken entrees (from around $12), is the most popular place to eat in the area. In Meeker itself, *The Bakery*, 265 6th St (⊕970/878-5500), has particularly great fresh breads and pastries.

Rangely

The many gently bobbing derricks around **RANGELY** announce the presence of an oil town that's defined and surrounded by America's sixth-largest oilfield. The town actually began in 1880 as a Ute trading post before quickly becoming a sheep- and cattle-ranching center, and it wasn't until 1900 that a local rancher noticed vague signs of black gold on the White River. By 1903 the first wells had been dug and by the 1940s big business had moved in and the oil really began to flow – by the end of World War II 56 wells were in operation. Oil money has helped finance several civic projects in town, including a pleasant park – Elk Park – and a good recreation center, both three blocks south of Main Street on Stanolind Street. Other than that, the town's amenities are severely limited, without even a major supermarket.

On the eastern edge of town you might explore the **Rangely Outdoor Museum** (April–Oct Fri–Sun 10am–4pm; free ⊕970/675-2612), which gives a good feel for Rangely and includes a fairly diverting collection of local rocks and minerals and an informative exhibit explaining drilling techniques and technology. More worthwhile is the tour of Rangely-area **rock art**, much of which is located and easily accessible along Pintado Canyon south of town along Hwy-139. The mix of petroglyphs and pictographs here is the work of both the Fremont Culture (650–1150) and the Utes (1200–1880), depicting deer, buffalo, and sheep along with many symbolic abstract forms, including a large Kokopelli.

Practicalities

A useful little map and guide for a driving tour of the rock art sites can be picked up from the Rangely **chamber of commerce**, 209 E Main St (daily 9am–5pm ☎970/675-5290, ⓦwww.rangely.com). The chamber also has a list of local **accommodation**, which doesn't stretch beyond a few motels on Main Street and a campground. The basic *4-Queens*, 260 E Main St (☎970/675-5035, ❸), is clean and comfortable enough and includes rec center passes in its rates, but if you have a tent or RV you might be happier under the shade of the cottonwood trees at the quiet east end of town at the *Rangely Camper Park*, 940 E Rangely Ave (☎970/675-8211; $12). There aren't any showers here, but you can use the ones at the rec center for $3. Rangley has an abysmal selection of **restaurants**, but at least the American staples at *Magalino's Family Restaurant*, 124 W Main, are decent and reasonably priced.

Dinosaur National Monument and around

Straddling the Colorado–Utah border, **Dinosaur National Monument** was originally created to preserve a rock stratum in Utah – seven miles north of Jensen on Hwy-149 – which has over the years provided brontosaurus skeletons and other astonishing remains to museums around the world. Eventually park boundaries were extended upstream along the remarkably picturesque Yampa and Green River canyons to include a swathe of surrounding rugged badlands, in which a maze of gorges harbor many examples of Native American rock art. Much of this was threatened by plans to dam the Yampa but, for now at least, its continued existence seems assured.

Dinosaur Quarry

Though it was commonly known among paleontologists that northwestern Colorado once teemed with a miscellany of dinosaurs, it wasn't until Earl Douglas's 1909 discovery of eight brontosaurus tailbones that the rush to excavate really started. Nearby finds included complete skeletons, and although many have been removed, a remarkable number still remain at the monument. To see them you need to head to **Dinosaur Quarry**, 41 miles east of park HQ on the Utah side, along Hwy-40 via Jenson. Here a small **visitor center** (daily: May–Oct 8am–4.30pm; Nov–April 8am–7pm) gives you an introduction to prehistoric life before you head up to the excavation site – a shuttle is provided in the summer. Here a tilted layer of sandstone has been painstakingly exposed to display an incredible three-dimensional jigsaw of fossilized dinosaur bones, left in situ for imaginative visitors to piece together.

The Colorado side

The **Colorado side** of the monument is primarily of interest for its remarkable views over the surrounding badlands – though if you have time to explore you'll also be rewarded with a series of Native American rock art sites. The gateway to this part of the monument is the park HQ and **visitors' center** (June–Aug daily 8am–4.30pm; Sept–May Mon–Fri 8am–4.30pm; ☎970/374-3000), one mile east of the town of Dinosaur on Hwy-40. From here a 31-mile road leads into the monument, with its spectacular terminus at **Harpers Corner**, where a ten-minute hike brings you to a dramatic rocky outcrop and a phenomenal view of the goosenecks of the Green and Yampa rivers, approaching their confluence at imposing **Steamboat Rock**. Equally amazing views of this landform are offered from the *Echo Lake Campground* and picnic area, reached along the smooth dirt road of Echo Park. The road descends deep into a canyon before arriving at a campsite which was used by Native Americans since time immemorial. Evidence of their presence can be found at various marked sites along the road, the most significant of which is beside a small creek near the base of the canyon – around two miles from the Yampa River – where there's a vehicle pull-out. A two-hour **hike** begins just above here and offers perhaps the most imposing views of Steamboat Rock. To find the unmarked trail, walk around 50 yards south from the vehicle pull-out and use vague tracks to scramble up east out of the canyon. Once on the canyon rim the tracks become more defined and it's easy to follow them to various viewpoints before retracing your steps.

Browns Park

Upstream of Dinosaur National Monument on adjacent lands along the Green River lies an even more desolate and remote area stretch of badlands, protected as **Browns Park National Wildlife Refuge** (daily 7.30am–dusk; ☎970/365-3613, ⊛brownspark.fws.gov). This area was once so remote that local outlaws – including the notorious Butch Cassidy and the Sundance Kid (see box, p.408) – hid out here between heists in the 1890s and early 1900s. The area remains extremely remote even today; it's around a 90-mile drive from the refuge to the nearest towns of Craig or Dinosaur via Hwy-40 and CO-318. This distance ensures only a smattering of visitors bother with the trip, preserving it as a pristine area for deer, elk, pronghorn antelope, moose, beavers, and over 200 species of birds. The route to Browns Park is unclear in places, so it's best to call in advance for accurate **directions**.

Monument practicalities

The nearest settlement to the Colorado section of the National Monument is the tiny, fly-blown town of **DINOSAUR**, where the **Colorado Welcome Center**, beside Hwy-40 at 101 Stegosaurus Way (May–Oct 8am–6pm; ☎970/374-2205), is a great source of information on local unmarked rock art sites. The town includes a couple of reasonable budget **motels**, including the *Hi-Vu*, 122 E Brontosaurus Blvd (☎970/374-2267), and the *Terrace*, at no. 312 (☎970/374-2241). There's nowhere to really **eat** or buy groceries, although the *Bedrock Depot*, beside Hwy-40 at 214 Brontosaurus Blvd, has tasty homemade ice cream and makes deli sandwiches to order.

Craig and around

Unusually for Colorado, the economic base of the gritty coal-town **CRAIG** – a supplier of electricity to three states – is firmly industrial. Most of the few visiting outsiders are hunters, who come to stalk game in the surrounding landscape of small mountain ranges and rocky desert basins. If that's why you're here, a first stop should be Craig Sports, 124 W Victory Way (☎970/824-4044), where you can procure a hunting license and supplies.

Otherwise the list of local attractions is short, with the **Museum of Northwest Colorado** (Mon–Sat 8.30am–5pm; free) the only exceptional one among them. Tucked away at 590 Yampa Ave, it houses some quirky oddities such as a record-weight mountain lion, stuffed and displayed together with the photo taken at the scene of its demise, but is largely renowned for its extraordinary

Without a doubt the two most engaging characters to roam northern Colorado and southern Wyoming, **Butch Cassidy** and the **Sundance Kid** remain legends not only of the Old West but of a romantic outlaw existence in which breaking the law became an expression of personal freedom. Thanks in large part to being mythologized in the classic 1969 Hollywood film **Butch Cassidy and the Sundance Kid** (which starred Paul Newman and Robert Redford), these two former thieves and cattle rustlers continue to cast a long shadow across the Rockies.

Butch Cassidy was born **George LeRoy Parker** in the Mormon town of Beaver, Utah, on April 6, 1866. Taught the fine art of cattle-rustling by local ranch-hand Mike Cassidy, George borrowed his mentor's last name, then picked up the handle "Butch" while working as a butcher in Rock Springs, Wyoming. He pulled his first bank job in Telluride, Colorado, in 1889, and soon found himself in the company of a like-minded group of villains known collectively as the **Wild Bunch**. Among their number was one **Harry Longabaugh** – the Sundance Kid – who picked up his nickname following a jail stint in Sundance, Wyoming. The Wild Bunch were eclectic in their criminal pursuits, and the gang's resume included horse-rustling as well as robbing trains, banks, and mine payrolls. Between them they gave away a fortune in gold to friends, supporters, and even strangers in need, establishing their reputation as latter-day Robin Hoods.

The image of a dashing, philanthropic band of outlaws did not sit well with authorities, who mustered teams of lawmen to go after them. The gang took to laying low through the winter months at **Brown's Hole** (now a renamed wildife refuge; see p.407), a broad river valley in remote northwest Colorado. Brown's Hole attracted a gathering of cowboys, fur-trappers, outlaws, and Indians, a self-made community with its own rules which made the perfect retreat for Butch and his cohorts. They were also known to visit (and raise hell in) the southern Wyoming towns of Baggs, Rock Springs, and Green River. Their saloon excesses were tolerated, though, because at the end of a spree they would meticulously account for every broken chair and bullet-hole, making generous restitution in gold. The gang, however, was eventually undone by their own vanity and love of a good time. During a visit to Fort Worth, Texas, five of them posed for a photograph in smart suits and derby hats, looking so dapper that the photographer proudly placed the photo in his shop window, where it was seen by a detective from the famous Pinkerton's agency.

Wearying of life on the run, Butch and Sundance sailed for **South America** in 1902 with **Etta Place**, the beautiful teacher with whom Sundance had fallen in love. They were soon cutting a dash in Argentina, Bolivia, and Peru, running a successful ranch and trying their hand at gold-mining, while robbing the occasional bank or train as well. The Hollywood version was true enough to this point, but Butch Cassidy did not die in a hail of bullets at the hands of Bolivian soldiers in 1909 as depicted in the film – although it seems that the Sundance Kid did.

Positive identification of the two men killed during the **shoot-out** was complicated by the damage done by hundreds of bullets and a lack of reliable witnesses. A number of Butch's friends in Rock Springs puzzled greatly over how he could have died in 1909 and still have shown up to go out drinking with them in 1920. A local mechanic even claimed to have repaired Butch's car in 1921, while the last say belongs to Josie Morris, an old girlfriend from Butch's Brown's Hole days; she insisted that he came to see her on his return from South America, and claimed furthermore that Butch died an old man in Johnny, Nevada, sometime during the 1940s.

collection of antique guns, saddles, spurs, and cowboy gear. This collection of **cowboy and gunfighter memorabilia** includes a 1900s saddle custom-made for Buffalo Bill Cody, and an ivory-handled "Peacemaker" gun, allegedly used in an 1890s double killing in Wyoming.

Practicalities

Information is available at the chamber of commerce on 360 E Victory Way (☎970/824-5689 or 1-800/864-4405, ⓦwww.colorado-go-west.com). Good budget **accommodation** can be had at the basic *Craig Motel*, 894 Yampa Ave (☎970/824-4491; ❷), usually the cheapest place in town; all rooms have phones and cable TV. For a little more money, you get a lot more facilities at the *Holiday Inn*, 300 Hwy-13 (☎970/824-4000; ❹), a notch above most motels in town and with a good little fitness facility that includes an indoor pool, a hot tub, and an exercise room. Craig has an impressive quantity of mediocre fast-food joints and family **restaurants**, the best of which is the casual *Golden Cavvy Restaurant and Lounge*, 538 Yampa Ave (☎970/824-6038), serving a selection of soups, salads, sandwiches, steaks, and plenty of deep-fried goodies. If you like Mexican, you're better off heading to the modest *La Plaza Restaurant*, 994 Yampa Ave (☎970/824-7345), for excellent burritos.

Travel details

Trains

(All services are Amtrak.)
Grand Junction to: Denver (1 daily; 8hr); Glenwood Springs (1 daily; 2hr).

Buses

Grand Junction to: Denver (4 daily; 4hr 20min to 5hr 20min; Greyhound); Durango (1 daily; 4hr 50min; TNM&O); Silverton (1 daily; 3hr; TNM&O).

Flights

(All services are United Airlines unless otherwise stated.)
Gunnison to: Denver (4 daily; 1hr)
Grand Junction to: Denver (10 daily; 1hr 10min; United and Great Lakes); Durango (8 daily; 1hr).

Contexts

Contexts

A brief history of Colorado

As much as anywhere in the US, Colorado is shrouded in the mythology of the American West, with fabled characters from dime novels – including tough mountain men, hardworking cowboys, savage Indians, grizzled miners, and conniving, fleet-footed outlaws – all contributing to the romanticized image of the state as a place for the free-spirited.

Native civilizations

The earliest traces of **human presence** in Colorado suggest some parts of the state were inhabited as early as 8000 BC, by a primitive society made up of the descendants of those who had migrated from Siberia to Alaska across the Bering Strait around 12,000 BC. Evidence of these nomadic cultures have been pieced together from various archeological finds, including piles of bones from slaughtered mammoths and primitive quartzite quarries north of the state line in Wyoming. Additionally, records of ancient societies are supplemented by **petroglyphs** (rock etchings) and **pictographs** (rock paintings), scattered in pockets of former settlement throughout Colorado – though most are estimated to be no older than about 2000 BC.

But the first real civilization to grace Colorado moved into the southern foothills of the Rocky Mountains around 500 AD. Known as the **Basketmaker Culture**, this people were part of a society located in today's southwestern states, where their descendants, the Pueblo tribes, still live. These **Ancestral Puebloans** occupied the southwest corner of Colorado in a society of increasing sophistication. This culminated in the building of the remarkable stone cities in the **Mesa Verde** area (see p.354), which include some spectacular cliffside dwellings, serviced by advanced water-storage and irrigation systems. After around eight hundred years of habitation in the region, the Ancestral Puebloans seem to have moved away quite suddenly. Quite why this happened is one of the most enduring questions in American archeology; one possibility posits a period of drought in the fourteenth century that made farming in the area impossible.

Much less is known about the early history of the rest of the state. By the time of the first European contact, the profusion of native tribes here were broadly divided into two main groups: those of **Shoshonean** and those of **Algonquin** linguistic stock. The former, particularly the **Ute**, peopled the western slopes of the Rockies and most of the mountainous terrain. Algonquins – tribes including the **Apache**, **Comanche**, **Kiowa**, **Cheyenne**, **Arapaho**, **Crow**, **Blackfoot**, and **Sioux** – tended to roam mainly on eastern plains. The number of people living in the mountains themselves was, however, tiny by today's standards.

With so much space to roam, it's not surprising that relations between tribes were only occasionally punctuated by friction. The harmonious balance seems to have been upset by the **first contact with Europeans**, which occurred south of the Rockies, between the Pueblo tribes and the Spanish. In a revolt against the Spanish colonizers in New Mexico in 1680, the Pueblo, along with the Navajo and Apache, who clubbed together to drive the Spanish out, suddenly found themselves in possession of a large number of **horses**. Within fifty years virtually every Rocky Mountain tribe had traded or stolen enough horses to build up a decent herd. Contact with Europeans also led to the spread of **firearms**. These leaked into the many tribes in the northern Rockies during the **Seven Years War** (1756–63), during which both French and British colonial powers courted the support of different tribes. But it was through the trade with trappers that the major influx of guns into Native American cultures came, when animal pelts could be swapped for guns, which were to become a major influence on Native American ways.

Access to horses and guns increased the level of contact between tribes in the region, heralding a **golden age** at the end of the eighteenth century for many of them. Those with the greatest herds of horses found hunting easy and were generally able to expand their territory; creating a fearsome culture based on warring and living as roving hunters, following the buffalo on the plains. The mountain-based Ute, too, expanded their spheres of operation throughout the mountains and even occasionally into the eastern plains, frequently fighting with the Cheyenne, Arapaho, Comanche, and Kiowa who occupied this territory.

European exploration

The first whites to lay eyes on what later became Colorado were probably the Spanish. Though accounts are a little unclear, it seems that in 1541 **Francisco Vasquez de Coronado** approached the mountains from the south before crossing the southeastern corner of Colorado, in search of the fabled Seven Gold Cities of Cíbola. Discouraged by the absence of these from further exploration, de Coronado turned back to the southwest, where his party raped and pillaged with abandon.

The early eighteenth-century Old World powers divvied up the territory between them, despite their having little or no knowledge of the lands or natives that inhabited them. The **Spanish** had the most significant foothold close to the region; the **French** also made major claims on the territory, though by 1762 had ceded all land west of the Mississippi to the Spanish. In a spate of political wrangling that followed the wilting of British power on the continent after the **War of Independence** (1775–76), the bulk of the Rockies reverted again to French ownership as part of territory attached to Louisiana. Nevertheless, the Spanish maintained a small toehold in the area, in fact sending the first expedition that deliberately set out to explore a portion of the region. The 1775–76 **Domínguez–Escalante** expedition visited portions of both Colorado and Utah, providing the first written accounts of the area, in a search for a useful overland route to connect the Spanish Missions in New Mexico with those in California.

French interest, on the other hand, was minimal. The only French influx came in the form of a small number of mountain men – possibly less than 100 – who, having ventured in to trap beaver, mostly found homes among the indigenous people and never left the region. While the French also contributed names to some features in the northern half of the territory – like the **Cache la Poudre Canyon** – French possession was short-lived. Napoleon, fearing that guarding the territory would spread his armies too thinly, decided to sell the vast and – popularly considered – fairly useless wilderness to President Thomas Jefferson for $15 million as part of the 1803 **Louisiana Purchase**.

American exploration

Keen to prove the worth of the new territory, and no doubt curious as to what he'd just bought, Jefferson quickly dispatched explorative parties to the west. The most famous and successful such expedition was that of **Lewis and Clark**, who set off on what was to be a two-year, 8000-mile trip across the northern part of the US in 1804, their remit being to detail everything they saw.

In 1806 Jefferson dispatched **Zebulon Pike** and sixteen other soldiers to survey the southern end of the range. By all accounts Pike ran a much more bumbling and incompetent expedition, however he did have a crack at bagging what would be later called **Pikes Peak**, though failing and declaring it unscaleable. From here he headed southwest into the San Luis Valley, where he was content to hole up for a while – until his arrest by the Spanish, on whose territory he had apparently unwittingly wandered. He was imprisoned in Santa Fe and the diplomatic horse-trading that followed to secure his release led to an informal agreement that the Arkansas River through Colorado be the boundary between the Spanish and American territories.

Both of these expeditions sparked cautious excitement about what riches the West had in store for courageous explorers. Back East, newspaper ads were placed to recruit trappers to supply local markets with beaver pelts; famous **mountain men**, like Jim Bridger, Jim Baker, Tom "Broken Hand" Fitzpatrick, and "Uncle Dick" Wootton being part of this first wave of recruitment. Mountain men crucially helped open up the West by fostering generally good relations with the Native Americans. Each group found the other a useful trading partner – guns being exchanged for pelts; but many mountain men also went further, marrying, or at least fathering children by, Native American women. One such mountain man was **Kit Carson**, who actually married two natives, and later became crucial, both in his role as guide for Lieutenant John C. Fremont in his exploration of the Yellowstone area, and later as a mediator between the US government and native tribes, including the Ute. This era was also infamous for its **Mountain Men Rendezvous**, when trappers and traders all gathered together in places like Browns Park or Bent's Fort in a welcome opportunity to leave the quiet mountains and return to the plains, not only to trade but also to raise hell, in an orgy of drinking, fighting, and gambling. Native Americans would also attend the Rendezvous, evidence of the friendly relations between the two groups.

Territorial divisions and westward migrations

While the first handful of Americans were cautiously settling in Colorado, global political wrangling resulted in the US getting a much firmer grip on the region. The Spanish influence and interest in North and Central America was beginning to wane in the early nineteenth century, so that in 1821 an independent Mexican state was born. Early Mexican relations with the US were very good, sparking off an era of intense trading between them; the Santa Fe Trail emerged as an important route across southern Colorado. But the fledgling Mexican state was too weak to hold onto its land claims both in Texas and in Colorado, and after a period of violence and warring, its boundaries were redrawn to more-or-less their present position in the **1848 Treaty of Guadalupe Hidalgo**. Obviously, this left behind significant Hispanic communities in southern Colorado, surrounded by mountain ranges that continued to be known as the San Juan and Sangre de Cristo mountains. At around the same time (1846), political maneuvering between the US and Britain resulted in all land south of the 49th Parallel becoming US territory. The lines were now drawn for the development of the region by the US.

The first great incursion by whites into the West was in the form of **wagon trains** heading for the verdant valleys of Oregon and the gold camps of California. Between 1840 and 1868, around 300,000 pioneers passed through northeastern Colorado on the **Overland Trail**, or just north of it on the **Oregon Trail**, a route along the North Platte River in southern Wyoming and then over the gentle South Pass west. Conditions along the dusty trail – in places as much as three miles wide – were harsh, and many travelers were woefully unprepared for the trials of the trip, including bad weather, wild animals, diseases, and stampedes. With their oxen tiring, many West-bound emigres had to discard possessions by the side of the trail. In the words of one traveler: "The road, from morning to night, is crowded like … Broadway … piles of bacon and hard bread thrown by the side of the road … trunks, clothes … boots … spades, picks, guns."

The side of the trail was littered not only with possessions, but with graves, too. An estimated one in seventeen emigrants died along the way, with on average ten graves for every mile of trail. Women had a particularly bad lot, an estimated one in five of them being pregnant, with many dying during childbirth, and nearly all having small children in their care. In turn, the children were particularly susceptible to disease and accidents, like falling out of the wagons or becoming lost and crushed among livestock. Not surprisingly perhaps, emigrants were not overly impressed by the territory through which they passed; one wrote, "This is a country that may captivate mad poets, but I swear I see nothing but big rocks … high mountains and wild sage. It is a miserable country."

Early settlement and the fate of the natives

The arrival of huge numbers of pioneers, even though they weren't actually settling in the region, marked the start of an important **change in relations** between whites and Native Americans. Whereas relations with the explorers had been reasonably friendly, by the 1850s the sheer number of travelers passing through the region began to cause difficulties. Not only did transient herds of cattle wear out grazing lands, but local buffalo stocks suffered a double setback as settlers killed thousands for meat. Objections were occasionally voiced in the form of raids on passing wagon trains, which met with severe reprisals from the US Army, who moved in to establish trading posts to protect the route.

Since few in the wagon trains considered making Colorado their home, frictions with native peoples for a while subsided, but in the late 1850s and early 1860s the activities of prospectors sparked several **gold rushes** in the region – drawing miners deep into Native American territory. Americans arrived in madding droves, digging anywhere that seemed promising – the rather bemused natives looking on with surprise, curiosity, and tacit acceptance. Of the first major strikes, the most famous was the 1858 find in Denver, which sparked the fabled "**Pikes Peak or Bust**" gold rush, which prospectors would proudly scrawl on the side of their westward-bound wagons. The finds in Denver actually proved to be tiny, but by the following year gold had been found around the Clear Creek Valley, a short ways to the west, and the towns of Central City, Idaho Springs, and Georgetown sprung up as a result.

The gold camps in the mountains provided the first good reason for settlement there, and so heralded the start of the modern-day Rockies. The mountains underwent their most dramatic changes: hillsides were ripped open in search of precious ores while in other places tourism – increasingly becoming the fashionable pursuit of the wealthy – prompted the emergence of spa towns.

It also marked the beginning of the end for the traditional lives of the Native Americans. Not only were the sheer numbers of new arrivals offensive to local populations, but the settlers' complete ignorance of local culture and disrespect for Native American practices caused frictions and triggered a more aggressive role on the part of the natives.

Relations that had traditionally been surprisingly peaceful began to sour, and the US government took the stance that the presence of the Native Americans was an obstacle to industrious development. Two decades of **conflict** followed, making for one of the most pitiful chapters in American history, during which Native Americans were moved from coexistence to segregation to marginalization. The milestones in this process were scores of **treaties** initially guaranteeing exclusive native rights to areas, only to be subsequently broken and reshaped at legendary speed and whenever new economic opportunities, like seams of ore or good grazing lands, presented themselves for exploitation. The Ute, for example, having been granted a huge area of the San Juans in an 1860 treaty, found their rights rescinded a mere five years later after gold strikes in the mountains, leaving them with poor parched lands along the Colorado–Utah border.

The loss of rights and territory angered many tribes, who countered with guerilla strikes on various forts and occasionally at homesteaders as well, events upon which the American government took a hard stance, particularly once its own instability during the **Civil War** (1861–65) had ended. In Colorado the major events in the process of subjugating the Native Americans were carnage, such as the 1864 Sand Creek Massacre – see p.123. Perhaps the only moment of martial glory for the Natives in the so-called **Indian Wars** was the 1876 battle at **Little Bighorn** in Montana, in which General George Custer was routed by a combined force of Sioux, Cheyenne, and Arapaho warriors. But the wars were only part of the campaign against native tribes and were accompanied by a more insidious core policy to exterminate the buffalo and starve the natives off the land. In total, more than four million buffalo were shot on the plains, their meat generally left to rot.

Economic and political development

At around the same time as the Native Americans were being pushed out of the mountains, another great obstacle to the area's development – its distance from the east and west coasts – was being overcome with the advent of the **railroad age**. Thanks to huge investment after the end of civil war, the late 1860s saw the transcontinental railroad push its tracks west through the region. The eastern and western ends of the railway were finally joined in Utah's Promontory Mountains on May 10, 1869; an event marked in a momentous ceremony during which four symbolic spikes – two of them gold – were driven into the ground.

The coming of the railroad encouraged **ranchers**, who – with the buffalo gone – would not only have access to endless free grazing, but also to the all-important eastern markets. Vast herds came into the region, often owned by absentee businessmen and kept by huge teams of cowboys. The dominance of the plains by the large ranchers and their manner of riding roughshod over the interests of homesteaders precipitated a number of cattle wars across the region. Soon railroad spurs fed into the mountainous parts of the region, prompting miners to pour in and ore to flow out. The export of logs was also possible and pretty soon the region had built up a formidable economy based on the extractive industries, which helped earn Colorado **statehood** in 1876.

Yet dependence on agriculture and the extractive industries provided only a fickle economic base. The brutal **winter of 1887–88** – which included a single blizzard that dumped enough snow to bury cattle completely – saw around 400,000 cattle perish and both smallholders and wealthy ranchers go bankrupt. Similarly, mining in the mountains provided, at best, a precarious basis for livelihoods. The early Colorado gold mines were quickly played out, and silver mining soon became the main source of income thanks to the discovery of rich lodes around Leadville and Aspen. Both swarmed with miners until the dramatic **silver crash** of 1893, when overnight the US moved off the silver standard, making almost all mines worthless. Thankfully, the lull in the Colorado economy was to be a short one, and in the 1890s major finds at Cripple Creek, near Colorado Springs, sparked the **last great gold rush** in the country. Although the area was rich in the mineral, few miners actually made much money from gold itself. Interest in mining the ore was generated by the artificially strong position of stock in mines, owing to the US use of the gold standard. Since the economy could only expand as fast as gold was mined, even loss-making mines were good for the national economy, with the result that the 700 working mines around Cripple Creek were represented by some 12,000 mining corporations selling stock. And while all the glamour was focused on the mines of Cripple Creek, the region also developed an extraordinarily strong coal mining industry, while in southern Colorado Pueblo grew to become a major steel town.

But the mining industry was **fraught with tensions** in the early twentieth century. Workers in large mines were often severely exploited, forced to live in company housing and paid in coupons to shop at company stores. Morale was poor, and as mines became less profitable, the actions of mine owners often made pay and conditions even worse. Tensions escalated into clashes at many mines. Perhaps the worst conflict of all occurred when the National Guard was called in to keep the peace in Cripple Creek, Telluride, and Trinidad during the Ludlow Massacre of 1914 (see p.321).

America's playground

The **Great Depression** of the 1930s hit Colorado hard, particularly since the state had yet to develop beyond its dependence on the extractive industries. But the same era yielded a new direction for the region that would grow to become the mainstay of its present-day economy: **tourism**. The old Victorian properties, formerly bars, brothels, gambling dens, and hardware stores during the mining era, have now been renovated to host art galleries, outdoor shops, and bakeries.

The transformation of the region was mirrored in the life of the celebrated frontiersman **Buffalo Bill** (see p.83), who in his lifetime made the journey from Pony Express rider and scout to become the organizer of a world-famous Wild West Show. Similarly Colorado began to sell its natural attributes to the leisure industry in the twentieth century. Tourism began tentatively in spa towns like Colorado Springs and Glenwood Springs, which had been attracting the elite since the 1890s, but with the dawn of the motorcar age in the 1920s, the Rocky Mountains began to lure large numbers of ordinary vacationers. Initially, interest was largely centered on the natural wonders of the remarkable **National Parks**. Yellowstone National Park, created in 1872, was the best known, but tourists also explored the spate of other national parks that had recently been created in the region, namely Mesa Verde (1906) and Rocky Mountain (1915). Numbers of visitors particularly boomed after World War II, when gasoline rationing ended and tourists withdrew money from bulging savings accounts to mass in the Rockies in record numbers. Several towns in the region were quick off the mark to court this new economic opportunity: Colorado Springs, for example, built an auto route up Pikes Peak and the Royal Gorge Bridge, both specially designed to give motorists splendid views.

The post-Depression era also saw the first **ski resorts** evolve, mainly first as entertainment for locals. Curiously, it was World War II that acted as a catalyst for the development of Colorado's resorts. As the chosen location of a large training camp for the **10th Mountain Division** (see box, p.245), the Sawatch and Elk Mountains of Colorado would see veterans return from fighting to become a major postwar impetus behind the development of resorts like Vail and Aspen. These resorts especially took off in the late 1960s, and by the 1970s began to overtake summer recreations as the main tourist activity. With so much swank new infrastructure in place, ski resorts have subsequently concentrated on developing off-season tourism, based on conferences, golfers, hikers, and, more recently, mountain bikers.

Present-day society

The rise in enthusiasm for outdoor activities was mirrored by an increasingly active **environmental movement**, which steadily gained momentum throughout the second half of the twentieth century. Encouraged by successful protests – including voting down an initiative to attract the 1976 Olympic games to Colorado on the basis of ecological concerns – the state became known for a brand of hippie-activism centered in university towns like Boulder, even though much of the state is part of a Republican heartland.

The greatest changes over the last decade or so though have been economical. As a knock-on effect of the closeness of so many splendid recreation opportunities, most major towns in Colorado have experienced rapid growth, thanks in part to the footloose **high-tech industries**. Not only did towns like Durango become fashionable among teleworkers in the 1990s, but Denver, too, embarked on an orgy of expansion, doubling its population in that decade alone. By 2000 Colorado's population had reached 4,301,261: an increase of over 1 million in just ten years. Such is the rate of economic development across much of the state that today a major debate is how to halt or control its growth – particularly in old mountain towns, where deluxe second homes are pricing locals out of the market. Urban centers like Denver, Boulder, and Colorado Springs are experiencing similar issues as expensive homes encroach on the adjacent mountains, forcing new roads and consequently encouraging more traffic everywhere.

Just as in national politics, where pundits look to Colorado to see the earliest hints of national trends, the state will also pioneer approaches to solving the twin riddles of maintaining the natural heritage and quality of life while encouraging economic growth that are common to much of the American West. Its success in balancing preservation with exploit will no doubt create a powerful blueprint, not only for neighboring states but also for the many other world regions which struggle with these issues at the start of the twenty-first century.

The natural environment

Rubbing shoulders with nature in its purest forms is doubtless one of the real thrills of traveling in Colorado, and the state's diverse ecosystems – which include plains, deserts, alpine meadows, forests, and high alpine tundra – in its many protected areas certainly provide ample opportunity to appreciate a wide array of plants and animals in a natural setting. The layout of these landscapes and ecological zones across the state is clear and simple – with the state separating into three well-defined north–south-running thirds: plains cover the eastern third of the state; the mountains the middle; the semi-arid desert plateaus the west. Each of these landscapes has its own distinct history and delights, while the kinds of flora and fauna found in each is based largely on altitude. The following overview can only give a brief outline of Colorado's sophisticated geological and natural history; but if this whets your appetite, be sure to investigate some of the books listed on p.425.

Geology and terrain

Simple as the geographical distribution of Colorado's natural environments may be, the story of their geological creation is complex and spans vast timescales. Effectively defining the state, not only topographically but also in terms of its weather patterns, the **Rocky Mountains** are its pivotal geological feature. Like mountain ranges the world over these peaks were produced by the effects of plate tectonics. In this process the approximately 60-mile-thick plates of rock that make up the earth's crust – and are squeezed together like lilies on a pond – constantly shift upon its molten core. Their movement, which averages around an inch per year, involves abrasion and collision with one another – at its most tangible as earthquakes and volcanoes – causing the more gradual formation of mountain ranges via a crumpling process that spans millions of years. The weakness in the North American plate, that extends some two thousand miles from central New Mexico all the way up to northeastern British Columbia in Canada, put part of this band of mountains into Colorado and also effectively divided North America along the **Continental Divide**, from which the pattern of trans-continental water flow is dictated. Rivers on the west of the divide drain into the Pacific Ocean, those on the east into the Atlantic or Arctic oceans.

Colorado's Rockies essentially began life around 300 million years ago when a period of unusually intense plate tectonic movement began raising long blocks of crust to form the ancestral Rocky Mountains. The weathering of these peaks then produced landscapes similar to today's Appalachians: with the vertical red sandstone rocks at Red Rocks Amphitheatre (see p.84) and Garden of the Gods (see p.282) some of the last visible remnants of this era. During much of the time in which Colorado's ancestral Rockies were being eroded they were covered by a shallow inland sea which deposited marine shales containing shellfish and many other sea creatures. Then as these seas retreated west they turned the state into a coastal plain where river deposition and wind-sculpted sand dunes laid the foundations for the sandstone strata that today define the Western Slope and neighboring Utah.

Replacing this relatively dry climate, a more humid **Jurassic** era climate created a marshy landscape where the attendant lush vegetation provided a perfect habitat for **dinosaurs**. These beasts walked Colorado in great numbers, as evidenced by the region's superb fossil records, which were deposited prior to the thick layers of coal left during the following **Cretaceous** period. It was at the very end of this era that today's Rocky Mountains began to be formed. During a second intense period of tectonic uplifts known as the **Larimide Orogeny**, a string of hills was produced which varied from jagged, incised peaks to flat-topped crags. As these grew, rivers began to carve many of the state's signature deep canyons, while mineral-rich solutions percolated up through cracks and fissures to produce valuable mineral veins in the igneous rock that would later underpin several mining booms, not least the late-nineteenth-century gold and silver rushes. Volcanic activity also formed part of this process of folding, faulting, and mountain-building, and was particularly vibrant in Southern Colorado: exposed walls of igneous rock – called dikes – provide particularly striking evidence around the Spanish Peaks (see p.320).

This era continued, albeit at a lesser rate, until the late **Tertiary Period** – up until around 5 million years ago – with movement in the latter half of the era producing the Colorado Plateau, which pushed up much of the region, turning 9000ft mountains into "fourteeners" (peaks 14,000ft or higher), and so making Colorado the highest state in the US.

Finally Colorado's Rockies have more recently been shaped by heavy **glaciation**, particularly during the **Pleistocene** era (1.8 million to 10,000 years ago), when a sizeable portion of the earth was covered in ice. This process ground down mountains, smoothed out valleys, and also left series of mountain lakes when the glaciers receded. Glacial activity continues to affect the landscape of the area's higher mountain ranges.

Colorado's ecosystems

Each of Colorado's distinct landscapes has produced distinct **ecosystems** and attendant communities of plants and animals. In reality the boundaries between them are blurred by local conditions, yet ecologists can broadly divide each of these according to the dominant species in evidence. These divisions produce zones that closely follow differences in altitude, with similar flora and fauna being found at similar elevations all around the state.

The plains and Western Slope are the realm of the **Lower Sonoran Zone**, which is typified by the presence of sagebrush, scrub oak, prairie dogs, and pronghorn antelope on the ground, while red-tailed hawks and golden eagles are among the birds that swoop above. With gradual gains in elevation, this gives way to the **Upper Sonoran Zone**, where piñon pines, junipers, lupines, and Indian paintbrush flourish to provide a habitat for mule deer, coyotes, and piñon jays.

The **Transition Zone** begins at elevations of around 6000 ft. Aspens in particular thrive in these areas, and are among the first species to repopulate areas in the wake of wildfires and avalanches. Lodgepole and ponderosa pines and blue spruce are the other dominant trees at this altitude, and mixed with both are wild geraniums and the distinctive white and lavender state flower, the columbine. Animals thriving here include black bears, beavers, porcupines, elk, mule deer, Albert's squirrels, and many bird species including Steller's jays.

Above the Transition Zone but below the treeline – that is, between about 9000 and 11,500 feet – lies the **Canadian Zone**, where thick, dark forests of

Engleman spruce and subalpine and Douglas firs shelter more solitary animal species like lynx and wolverine. Where the trees begin to thin and temperatures begin quickly to cool comes the **Hudsonian Zone**, where grouse-like ptarmigans, marmots, and pikas eke out a living. These species also venture into the tundra and talus rocks of the lofty **Alpine Zone**, which generally exists above the treeline at around 11,500ft. The edge of this zone is often starkly demarked by the wind-twisted spruce trees known as *Krummholz*, above which the only vegetation to be found are slow-growing plants such as mosses, lichens, and a variety of delicate wildflowers, which can all survive on the thinnest soil and air and with a minimal supply of water. Because they grow so slowly – the tiniest wildflower may take many years to reach maturity – any damage done to these plants impacts dramatically on the alpine ecosytem, so hikers have a special duty of care while exploring these areas. The various species of **wildflower** you might come across are too numerous to detail here; among their number are the columbine, alpine sunflower, elephanthead, alpine buttercup, and alpine phlox. There are several excellent books on Colorado's wildflowers that include color photos to help with identification (see "Books," p.425). Despite the spartan conditions the Alpine zone is also the favored environment of mountain goats and bighorn sheep.

The only remaining ecosystem of real consequence in Colorado is the relatively footloose **Riparian Forest**, which can occur in all the above zones save the Alpine. The cottonwoods, alders, box elders, and willows which make up this forest typically cluster around water sources and so provide attractive homes for beavers, muskrats, skunks, foxes, and raccoons.

Wildlife

Colorado boasts a line-up of **animals** that includes some of the most fascinating and alluring mammals on the continent, among which are the black bear, the moose, and the mountain lion. Inevitably, there's a mix of excitement and frustration that goes with spotting animals, because they don't show up on demand; in fact, the more intelligent and secretive of them make a point of avoiding human contact altogether. You can, however, reliably expect to see certain animals, and even to have quite close encounters with some of them, particularly if you are prepared to get up around dawn when they are at their most active.

Large mammals

One of the larger of the animals you're most likely to encounter is the **elk** (also called "wapiti," an appropriately descriptive Native American word meaning "white rump"); the larger bulls weigh up to 900 pounds, and sport huge antlers which alone can weigh as much as 50 pounds. The most dramatic time to observe elk is during the fall rut, which generally begins in September and may go on into early November. The bulls strut and display their necks and antlers to the cows, but the most extraordinary part of their display is an unearthly call to a potential mate called "bugling" – a bizarre ear-piercing squeal. Gatherings of elk are a common sight at many locations in the Rockies, in all sorts of landscapes: low forests, alpine tundra, and so on.

Another beautifully antlered creature is the **mule deer**. Roughly one-third the size of an elk – and only a quarter of the weight – the mule deer is further distinguished by the much lighter, almost tan coloring of its coat, an overly generous set of mule-like ears, and a short, black-tipped tail attached to its cream-colored rump. The male's antlers are quite delicate too, flowing with balance and symmetry. You may encounter mule deer almost anywhere below the treeline, including forested areas bisected by hiking trails. A little smaller and heftier than the mule deer is the **pronghorn antelope**, which typically occupies grassy flatlands and can often be spotted grazing by roadsides and on ranch properties. Pronghorns have a greyish hide and short horns that jut inwards.

The title of Rocky Mountain mascot goes to the extraordinary Rocky Mountain **bighorn sheep** – there is no more indelible image than a lone bighorn perched on a rocky ledge, lord of all he surveys. Both rams and ewes grow horns, although the two are easily distinguished as the ram has the classic "C"-shaped horns, while the ewe's grow as almost vertical spikes, up to eight inches long. Rams put on an extraordinary display during the rutting season, roughly mid-November through December, when they square off and crack horns with a sickening impact to assert their authority and establish mating rights. Bighorns are the archetypal high-country dwellers, great at negotiating rocky ledges and dealing with cool temperatures, and mostly stick to the alpine reaches.

The largest member of the deer family is the **moose**. With the largest bulls reaching seven feet at the shoulder and weighing 1000 pounds, their bulbous heads topped by a broad spread of antlers, and with a pendulous dewlap slung beneath the chin, this marvelous animal, once encountered, is not easily forgotten. Their long gangly legs are built for wading, and moose generally browse the wetland grasses and aquatic plants found along rivers and in riparian meadows. Even bigger than these behemoths are woolly **bison**, weighing up to a ton and found in a few National Parks and specially maintained Bison Ranges.

Predators: bears and mountain lions

Many visitors to the Rockies hope most of all to see – from a safe distance – potentially dangerous predators such as the black bear and mountain lion. **Black bears** are commonly seen in forested areas throughout the state, but are most usually spotted at roadsides, campgrounds, or even exploring the scavenging opportunities in mountain towns themselves. Far more secretive, much harder to spot, and generally more dangerous to humans is the **mountain lion**. Also referred to as a puma or cougar, this sleek, handsome animal has perhaps the most accurate Latin name of all – *felis concolor*, or the one-colored cat. Mountain lion sightings have increased throughout Colorado in recent years, and while some would suggest that this is evidence of expanding populations, it's more likely that their habitat is shrinking under pressure from suburban development, bringing them into closer proximity with humans. Certainly these cats are often spotted in the many mountain parks that surround the Denver area, particularly in Jefferson County and around Boulder.

If you do end up too close to either species, remember the special rules of engagement that go with encountering them (see box, p.424).

Coyotes and various rodents

Affectionately known to some Native American peoples as the "singing trickster," the **coyote** (*canis latrans*) is a highly adaptable and opportunistic predator fairly common in Colorado. Coyotes hunt small prey such as rodents and rabbits, but also scavenge the carcasses of bigger animals such as elk, deer, and even

CONTEXTS | The natural environment

bison when the opportunity arises. Sometimes confused with wolves from afar, coyotes are much smaller (weighing around 30 pounds, in comparison with 120 pounds for a gray wolf), and unlike wolves they'll often appear by roadsides and in populated areas where a free meal might present itself.

One of the sorrier tales of human impact on wildlife is that of the **beaver**, nature's most energetic engineer, whose pelt was at one time so desired for hat-making that the animal was very nearly wiped from the face of the earth. The largest rodent in North America, the beaver is entrusted with designing and building wetland habitat for countless plants and animals. Its dam-building creates ponds and marshy meadows which in turn support wetland grasses and trees such as willow and cottonwood, as well as waterfowl and grazing animals like moose, elk, and deer. Faced with natural predators such as coyotes, bobcats, and foxes, the beaver is battling to make a comeback – the overall balance of many mountain ecosystems depend upon its success.

Among the other interesting animals that you need a fair bit of luck to see are the bobcat, badger, river otter, raccoon, muskrat, weasel, and pine marten. More common are the **pika**, a small but rotund rodent which announces its presence by squeaking loudly as it pops out from its rocky hideaway, and the **yellow-bellied marmot**, which closely resembles a groundhog. Marmots are inveterate sunbathers, and may be seen on exposed, sunny rock outcrops at lower mountain elevations and almost anywhere on the alpine tundra.

Birds and fish

Nearly every manner of **bird** can be found in Colorado, often in wildlife refuges, from bald eagles – relatively rare in the lower 48 – to colorful song-birds and trumpeter swans, the world's largest waterfowl. The "Books" section reviews a number of guides that are handy for birding and identifying the species. As for **fish**, there's no shortage of them in the numerous mountain lakes and rivers, and even if you've no interest in casting for them, you can't fail to miss seeing folks throwing a line in any available stream. Various species of trout are most prevalent, notably rainbow, lake, and cutthroat. There are also pockets of **salmon** left, though the future of this once plentiful fish looks grim.

When animals attack . . . and even when they don't

A small number of animals native to the Rockies have been known occasionally to **attack humans**; bears and mountain lions are the obvious candidates, but others may also react aggressively including elk, moose, and bison. Keep in mind that there isn't an animal alive in the Rockies that can't outrun a human, and if a bear, bison, elk, or moose decided to go after you, it could certainly catch you. The basic **code of conduct** when observing wildlife is to stay at a non-threatening distance – if an animal reacts to your presence, then you're too close. It's actually far more likely that you would pose a threat to an animal than vice versa. Every year thousands of animals are killed on roads in the various National Parks and elsewhere, so it's important to **observe speed limits** and be particularly careful while driving early or late in the day when animals are most active.

Books

I t would be hard to argue for Colorado as a literary hotbed, though to be sure the rugged lands and postcard images have fired the imagination of many. The books below include those most evocative of Colorado, as well as ones that proved most entertaining and useful during the research and writing of this guide. The majority should be easy to find on the Internet or can be ordered by your favorite bookstore. Some of the specialist trail and climbing guides may only be available in the specific region they cover.

History and biography

William Bueler *Roof of the Rockies: A History of Colorado Mountaineering.* A thoroughly readable and engaging history of early mountaineering in Colorado, written by a veteran climber.

John Rolfe Burroughs *Where the Old West Stayed Young.* A homespun history of the deeds and misdeeds of the cattlemen, frontier-folk, and outlaws of northern Colorado, southern Wyoming, and Utah, based largely on first-hand sources and interviews. It's a more compelling read than you might expect, and includes vivid accounts of several cattle wars, as well as episodes from the life and times of Butch Cassidy and the Wild Bunch.

William F. Cody *The Life of Hon. William F. Cody, Known As Buffalo Bill.* Larger-than-life autobiography of one of the great characters of the Wild West.

Clyde A. Milner II, Carol A. O'Connor, and Martha A. Sandweiss (eds) *The Oxford History*

of the American West. As the title suggests, this doesn't just focus on Colorado, but it's nonetheless a fascinating collection of essays, covering topics that range from myths and movies to art and religion.

Duane Smith *Mesa Verde National Park.* An informative and wide-ranging history of Mesa Verde, from its earliest inhabitants to the contemporary problems of running – and ruining – a National Park.

Elliot West *The Saloon on the Rocky Mountain Mining Frontier.* An academic yet readable volume that emphasizes the centrality of the saloon to Western culture.

Richard White *It's Your Misfortune and None of My Own.* Dense, authoritative and all-embracing history of the American West, that debunks the notion of the rugged pioneer by stressing the role of the federal government.

Culture and society

Eleanor Genres, Sandra Dallas, Maxine Benson, and Stanley Cuba (eds) *The Colorado Book.* Fascinating and eclectic collection of snippets about Colorado – from

literary excerpts to travel writing, poems, and songs.

William Henry Jackson and John Fielder *Colorado: 1870–2000.* An extraordinary photographic essay compiled by renowned Colorado lensman John Fielder. Armed with a collection of photographs taken by William Henry Jackson (1843–1942), Fielder revisits the sites depicted in Jackson's photos and composes identical shots to illustrate the change – or lack of it – in each subject in the years since. A superb, if somewhat expensive, coffee-table book.

Travel

Isabella Bird *A Lady's Life in the Rocky Mountains*. An engaging collection of letters written in the 1870s by the intrepid English travel writer. Overall they make for a charming, occasionally humorous portrayal of frontier life.

John Dunning *Denver*. Evocative accounts of the Queen City of the Plains, with a particularly engaging look at the underbelly of life here in the mid-twentieth century.

John Wesley Powell *The Exploration of the Colorado River and its Canyons*. John Wesley Powell and a team of nine men set out to explore the Colorado River in 1869, a scientific expedition that led through the last uncharted territory of the United States. This book details what turned out to be a massive and fearsome adventure, and its best moments compare well with the more harrowing tales of Lewis and Clark.

Glenn Randall *Longs Peak Tales* A series of tall-tales-and-true, including pioneering routes to the summit and several ill-fated climbing expeditions – some comic, some tragic – representing over one hundred years on Longs Peak.

Flora, fauna, and geology

Peter Alden (ed) *National Audubon Society Field Guide to the Rocky Mountain States*. Lavishly illustrated and extremely informative guide to the flora and fauna of the Rockies, covering everything from lichens and wildflowers, spiders and beetles, to feral horses and mule deer. There's also an appendix detailing parks and preserves, images of the constellations you can see at night, and sections on the topography and geology, ecology, and weather patterns of the region. Invaluable.

John Emerick and Cornelia Fliesher Mutel *From Grassland to Glacier: The Natural History of Colorado*. A detailed and readable guide that would be useful to anyone journeying through Colorado and with an interest in its various ecosystems.

Outdoor activities

Caryn Boddie and Peter Boddie *A Hiker's Guide to Colorado*. This picks out 75 great hikes in the state, with full route descriptions and maps.

John Carrey and Cort Conley *The Middle Fork: A Guide*. An indispensable, mile-by-mile guide for rafters. Great details on the history of early exploration.

Deborah Frazier George *Colorado's Hot Springs*. Useful companion guide if you intend to soak your way around the state.

Stephen Hlawaty *Mountain Bike America: Colorado*. If you buy only one book on mountain biking in Colorado, make it this one. The author describes not only 50 of the best rides in the state, but his descriptions, and maps, are consistently reliable.

Brian Litz and Kurt Lankford *Skiing Colorado's Backcountry*. Perhaps the best Colorado backcountry ski guide available, with detailed information on both skiing and boarding – and carrying the seal of approval of the revered Colorado Mountain Club.

Dennis McKinney *Guide to Colorado State Wildlife Areas*. Useful book that points hunters and fishermen in direction of their quarry.

Gerry Roach *Colorado's Fourteeners*. The seminal mountaineering guide to the state, packed with detail and useful color maps.

Scott S. Warren *100 Classic Hikes in Colorado*. Good hiking guide, with options of widely varying difficulty scattered throughout the state. Neatly laid-out and made easier to follow by useful little sketch maps.

Fiction

Jack Kerouac *On the Road*. Cult beatnik meanderings through the US, with an exciting account of time spent in Denver and Central City, Colorado.

William Kittredge (ed) *The Portable Western Reader*. A comprehensive anthology featuring some of the great American writers, with everything from tales of Native Americans to the poems of Walt Whitman, stories of Jack London, and travel writing by Steinbeck and Hemingway. Each tidbit may only serve to whet your appetite for the complete work, but it does cover a lot of ground and is scrupulously edited.

Travel
store

Travel Specials
First-Time Around
the World
First-Time Asia
First-Time Europe
First-Time Latin
America
Travel Online
Travel Health
Travel Survival
Walks in London &
SE England
Women Travel

Maps
Algarve
Amsterdam
Andalucia & Costa
del Sol
Argentina
Athens
Australia
Barcelona
Berlin
Boston
Brittany
Brussels
California
Chicago
Corsica
Costa Rica &
Panama
Crete
Croatia
Cuba
Cyprus
Czech Republic
Dominican Republic
Dubai & UAE
Dublin
Egypt
Florence & Siena
Florida
France
Frankfurt
Germany
Greece
Guatemala & Belize
Hong Kong
Iceland
Ireland
Kenya & Northern
Tanzania
Lisbon
London

Los Angeles
Madrid
Mallorca
Malaysia
Marrakesh
Mexico
Miami & Key West
Morocco
New England
New York City
New Zealand
Northern Spain
Paris
Peru
Portugal
Prague
The Pyrenees
Rome
San Francisco
Sicily
South Africa
South India
Spain & Portugal
Sri Lanka
Tenerife
Thailand
Toronto
Trinidad & Tobago
Tuscany
Venice
Vietnam, Laos &
Cambodia
Washington DC
Yucatán Peninsula

Dictionary Phrasebooks
Croatian
Czech
Dutch
Egyptian Arabic
French
German
Greek
Hindi & Urdu
Italian
Japanese
Latin American
Spanish
Mandarin Chinese
Mexican Spanish
Polish
Portuguese
Russian
Spanish

Swahili
Thai
Turkish
Vietnamese

Computers
Blogging
iPods, iTunes &
music online
The Internet
Macs & OS X
PCs and Windows
Playstation Portable
Website Directory

Film & TV
American
Independent Film
British Cult Comedy
Chick Flicks
Comedy Movies
Cult Movies
Gangster Movies
Horror Movies
Kids' Movies
Sci-Fi Movies
Westerns

Lifestyle
eBay
Ethical Shopping
Babies
Pregnancy & Birth

Music Guides
The Beatles
Bob Dylan
Classical Music
Elvis
Frank Sinatra
Heavy Metal
Hip-Hop
Jazz
Book of Playlists
Opera
Pink Floyd
Punk
Reggae
Rock
The Rolling Stones
Soul and R&B
World Music
(2 vols)

Popular Culture
Books for Teenagers
Children's Books,
0-5
Children's Books,
5-11
Conspiracy Theories
Cult Fiction
The Da Vinci Code
Lord of the Rings
Shakespeare
Superheroes
Unexplained
Phenomena

Sport
Arsenal 11s
Celtic 11s
Chelsea 11s
Liverpool 11s
Man United 11s
Newcastle 11s
Rangers 11s
Tottenham 11s
Poker

Science
Climate Change
The Universe
Weather

Visit us online
www.roughguides.com
Information on over 25,000 destinations around the world

- **Read** Rough Guides' trusted travel info
- **Access** exclusive articles from Rough Guides authors
- **Update** yourself on new books, maps, CDs and other products
- **Enter** our competitions and win travel prizes
- **Share** ideas, journals, photos & travel advice with other users
- **Earn** points every time you contribute to the Rough Guide
  community and get rewards

ROUGH GUIDES

BROADEN YOUR HORIZONS

Small print and Index

A Rough Guide to Rough Guides

Published in 1982, the first Rough Guide – to Greece – was a student scheme that became a publishing phenomenon. Mark Ellingham, a recent graduate in English from Bristol University, had been traveling in Greece the previous summer and couldn't find the right guidebook. With a small group of friends he wrote his own guide, combining a highly contemporary, journalistic style with a thoroughly practical approach to travelers' needs.

The immediate success of the book spawned a series that rapidly covered dozens of destinations. And, in addition to impecunious backpackers, Rough Guides soon acquired a much broader and older readership that relished the guides' wit and inquisitiveness as much as their enthusiastic, critical approach and value-for-money ethos.

These days, Rough Guides include recommendations from shoestring to luxury and cover more than 200 destinations around the globe, including almost every country in the Americas and Europe, more than half of Africa, and most of Asia and Australasia. Our ever-growing team of authors and photographers is spread all over the world, particularly in Europe, the USA, and Australia.

In the early 1990s, Rough Guides branched out of travel, with the publication of Rough Guides to World Music, Classical Music, and the Internet. All three have become benchmark titles in their fields, spearheading the publication of a wide range of books under the Rough Guide name.

Including the travel series, Rough Guides now number more than 350 titles, covering: phrasebooks, waterproof maps, music guides from Opera to Heavy Metal, reference works as diverse as Conspiracy Theories and Shakespeare, and popular culture books from iPods to Poker. Rough Guides also produce a series of more than 120 World Music CDs in partnership with World Music Network.

Visit www.roughguides.com to see our latest publications.

Rough Guide travel images are available for commercial licensing at www.roughguidespictures.com.

Rough Guide credits

Text editor: Hunter Slaton
Layout: Jessica Subramanian
Cartography: Maxine Repath, Jasbir Sandhu
Picture editor: Siobhan Donoghue
Production: Aimee Hampson
Proofreaders: Serena Stephenson, Amanda Jones
Cover design: Chloë Roberts
Photographer: Christian Williams
Editorial: **London** Kate Berens, Claire Saunders, Geoff Howard, Ruth Blackmore, Polly Thomas, Richard Lim, Clifton Wilkinson, Alison Murchie, Karoline Densley, Andy Turner, Keith Drew, Edward Aves, Nikki Birrell, Helen Marsden, Alice Park, Sarah Eno, Joe Staines, Duncan Clark, Peter Buckley, Matthew Milton, Tracy Hopkins, David Paul, Lucy White, Ruth Tidball; **New York** Andrew Rosenberg, Steven Horak, April Isaacs, AnneLise Sorensen, Amy Hegarty, Sean Mahoney, Ella Steim
Design & Pictures: **London** Simon Bracken, Dan May, Diana Jarvis, Mark Thomas, Jj Luck, Harriet Mills; **Delhi** Madhulita Mohapatra, Umesh Aggarwal, Ajay Verma, Ankur Guha, Pradeep Thapliyal, Sachin Tanwar, Anita Singh

Production: Sophie Hewat, Katherine Owers
Cartography: **London** Ed Wright, Katie Lloyd-Jones; **Delhi** Rajesh Chhibber, Jai Prakash Mishra, Ashutosh Bharti, Rajesh Mishra, Animesh Pathak, Karobi Gogoi, Amod Singh, Alakananda Bhattacharya
Online: **New York** Jennifer Gold, Suzanne Welles, Kristin Mingrone; **Delhi** Manik Chauhan, Narender Kumar, Shekhar Jha, Rakesh Kumar, Amit Verma, Amit Kumar, Rahul Kumar
Marketing & Publicity: **London** Richard Trillo, Niki Hanmer, Louise Maher, Jess Carter; **New York** Geoff Colquitt, Megan Kennedy, Katy Ball; **Delhi** Reem Khokhar
Custom publishing and foreign rights: Philippa Hopkins
Manager India: Punita Singh
Series editor: Mark Ellingham
Reference Director: Andrew Lockett
PA to Managing and Publishing Directors: Megan McIntyre
Publishing Director: Martin Dunford

Publishing information

This first edition published January 2007 by
Rough Guides Ltd,
80 Strand, London WC2R 0RL, UK
345 Hudson St, 4th Floor,
New York, NY 10014, USA
14 Local Shopping Centre, Panchsheel Park,
New Delhi 110017, India
Distributed by the Penguin Group
Penguin Books Ltd,
80 Strand, London WC2R 0RL, UK
Penguin Putnam, Inc.
375 Hudson Street, NY 10014, USA
Penguin Group (Australia)
250 Camberwell Road, Camberwell,
Victoria 3124, Australia
Penguin Books Canada Ltd,
10 Alcorn Avenue, Toronto, Ontario,
M4V 1E4, Canada
Penguin Group (New Zealand)
Cnr Rosedale and Airborne Roads
Albany, Auckland, New Zealand
Cover design by Peter Dyer.

The publishers and author have done their best to ensure the accuracy and currency of all the information in **The Rough Guide to Colorado**, however, they can accept no responsibility for any loss, injury, or inconvenience sustained by any traveler as a result of information or advice contained in the guide.

3 5 7 9 8 6 4 2

Help us update

We've gone to a lot of effort to ensure that the first edition of **The Rough Guide to Colorado** is accurate and up to date. However, things change – places get "discovered", opening hours are notoriously fickle, restaurants and rooms raise prices or lower standards. If you feel we've got it wrong or left something out, we'd like to know, and if you can remember the address, the price, the time, the phone number, so much the better.

We'll credit all contributions, and send a copy of the next edition (or any other Rough Guide if you prefer) for the best letters. Everyone who writes to us and isn't already a subscriber will receive a copy of our full-color thrice-yearly newsletter. Please mark letters: **"Rough Guide Colorado Update"** and send to: Rough Guides, 80 Strand, London WC2R 0RL, or Rough Guides, 4th Floor, 345 Hudson St, New York, NY 10014. Or send an email to **mail@roughguides.com**.

Have your questions answered and tell others about your trip at **www.roughguides.atinfopop.com**.

Acknowledgments

The **author** thanks the people of Colorado for being a friendly and energetic bunch, in particular Rob for the countless ways in which he helped (excluding the lengthy poker sessions); Monica and Albert for the stellar Mexican sustenance; and Kath for appreciating trees and not laughing at my skis too much. Thanks also goes to the many others who helped my trips go as smoothly as possible, including Darcy Morse, Heidi

Thomsen, Katelyn Krumperman, Natalie Hatch, Melanie Roberts, and Larry Dale Ursich. At Rough Guides, credit goes to Andrew Rosenberg for giving the book the go-ahead and for careful guidance along the way; and to Hunter Slaton for his stellar work at the editorial desk and generally being a top bloke – your hard graft was appreciated. Finally, thanks to fellow authors Alf Alderson and Cam Wilson for their contributions.

Readers' letters

Thanks to the readers who took the trouble to write in with their comments and suggestions (and apologies if we've inadvertently omitted or misspelt anyone's name):

Alan Fox, Al LePore, Jonathan Flynn, João E. Gata, and John M. Orrell

SMALL PRINT

Photo credits

All photos © Rough Guides Pictures except the following:

Introduction
p.1 Skiing in Vail's backcountry © Jeff Cricco/ Colorado Tourism Office
p.10 Street sign in Downtown Denver © Brian Gadbery/Colorado Tourism Office

Things not to miss
01 Wildflowers © Jeff Cricco/Colorado Tourism Office
05 North American Indian Pow-Wow © Bruce Coleman/Alamy
08 Silverton Mountain backcountry © Tom Stillo/ Colorado Tourism Office
19 Ice-climbing in Ouray © Danito Delimont/ Alamy

Color insert: Skiing and snowboarding
Ski school at Steamboat Springs Resort © Larry Pierce/Colorado Tourism Office
Crested Butte © Tom Stillo
Freestyle skiing in Crested Butte © Tom Stillo

Color insert: Colorado's protected lands
Brown Bear © Stock Connection Distribution/ Alamy

Black and white photos
p.110 Overland Trail Museum © Brian Gadbery/ Colorado Tourism Office
p.113 Greeley cattle © Brian Gadbery/Alamy
p.152 Gift shops in Grand Lake © David Moore/ Alamy
p.186 Breckenridge at night © Bob Winsett/ Corbis
p.229 Cycle race, Vail © Jeff Cricco/Colorado Tourism Office
p.386 Green River, Dinosaur National Monument © Larry Pierce/Colorado Tourism Office
p.389 Cross-country skiing in Gunnison National Park © Tom Stillo/Colorado Tourism Office

Index

Map entries are in color.

INDEX

441

I

Map symbols

maps are listed in the full index using colored text

-----	Chapter division boundary	⚔	Battle site
-.-.-	International border	⌂	Caves
-..-..	State border	⛳	Golf course
=⟨17⟩=	Interstate highway	🏛	Monument
=⟨89⟩=	US highway	♜	Fort
=⟨12⟩=	State highway	♜	Tower
——	Dirt road	▪	Pueblo
··········	4WD road	♀	Museum
——	Railway	★	Bus stop
------	Trail	✈	Airport
------	Gondola/ski lift	♦	General point of interest
------	Hiking trail	ⓘ	Tourist office
)·······(	Tunnel	✉	Post office
	River	◉	Accommodation
≍	Bridge	P	Parking
⌃⌃	Mountain range	⊞	Hospital/clinic
▲	Peak	▬	Building
⇗	Mountain pass	⊹	Church
⚐	Ski area	⬭	Stadium
𐊗	Cross-country skiing	⊞	Cemetery
⚐	Campsite	▨	Park
⌂	Lodge	▨	Forest
⚑	Waterfall	▨	Glacier
∴	Ruin	▨	Indian reservation
🌋	Butte